THE INTERNATIONAL LAW ON FOREIGN

INVESTMENT

Give ... dition of an autho ... has rarely been ... veloped to prote ... and to control ... conduct on their ... examining the effectiveness of bilateral and regio ... also considers the reverse flow of investments from emerg ... industrialising powers such as China and Brazil and explores the retreat from market ... iented economics to regulatory controls. By offering thought-provoking analysis of not only the law, but related developments in economics and political sciences, Sornarajah gives immediacy and relevance to the discipline. This book is required reading for all postgraduate and undergraduate international law students specialising in the law of foreign investments.

M. SORNARAJAH is C.J. Koh Professor at the Faculty of Law of the National University of Singapore and the Tunku Abdul Rahman Professor of International Law at the University of Malaya at Kuala Lumpur.

D1340591

THE INTERNATIONAL LAW ON FOREIGN INVESTMENT

THIRD EDITION

M. Sornarajah

CAMBRIDGE
UNIVERSITY PRESS

CAMBRIDGE UNIVERSITY PRESS
Cambridge, New York, Melbourne, Madrid, Cape Town, Singapore,
São Paulo, Delhi, Dubai, Tokyo

Cambridge University Press
The Edinburgh Building, Cambridge CB2 8RU, UK

Published in the United States of America by Cambridge University Press, New York

www.cambridge.org
Information on this title: www.cambridge.org/9780521763271

© M. Sornarajah 2010

First published 2010

Printed in the United Kingdom at the University Press, Cambridge

A catalogue record for this publication is available from the British Library

ISBN 978-0-521-76327-1 Hardback
ISBN 978-0-521-74765-3 Paperback

1006190312

To Ramanan

Contents

Preface to the third edition

Since the second edition of this book, the international law on foreign investment has witnessed such enormous activity that a new edition is justified within five years. The number of arbitration awards based on investment treaties has increased, resulting in several books written solely on the subject of investment treaty arbitration. New works have appeared on several aspects of the law on foreign investment. This work has held the area of the law together without fragmenting it any further. The carving out of an international law on foreign investment itself may have furthered fragmentation in international law. Yet, the aim was to ensure that the base remained clearly in international law principles. That aim does not appear to have been preserved in many of the later works which sought to carve out further areas as free-standing ones. The original niche of this work remains unaffected. It seeks to establish the foundations of the law clearly in the international law rules on state responsibility and dispute resolution rather than approach it with the central focus on investment treaties and arbitration which seems to have attracted the practitioner more than the scholar.

It also has a focus that is different from that of the other works in the field. It is written from the perspective of development. The claim to neutrality of the works in the field cloaks the fact that they deal with an asymmetrical system of the law created largely to ensure investment protection. The fact that it does not follow this routine does not by itself make it a partial work. As before, the criticisms of this work have been made best by my students who have come from all over the world. I have taught courses based on this book in London, at the Centre for Transnational Legal Studies, in Toronto, at Osgoode Hall Law School, at Dundee at the Centre for Petroleum and Natural Resources Law and at my own home institution, the National University of Singapore, which, through its joint programme with the New York University Law School, attracts a global body of students. All possible criticisms that could be made of its central approach are reflected in the work. No criticism can be more valuable to an academic than those made by young minds coming fresh to the subject. In many ways, the stances that were taken in the first two editions seem to be justified in light of the global economic crisis and the retreat of some of the tenets of free market liberalisation that it is alleged to have brought about.

That the subject will continue to undergo rapid changes is very clear. Even as the preface is written, new developments are taking place. As I sat to write it, the Lisbon Treaty of the European Union came into effect giving the EU competence over investment policy and investment treaties. It is not possible in this edition to speculate what the effects of the Treaty might be. States, particularly in Latin America, are pulling out of investment treaties and the ICSID Convention. The United States and South Africa have announced major reviews of their investment treaties. Some treaties are being made without an investor–state dispute-resolution provision. There is an evident retreat from the perception that investment protection is the only purpose of the investment treaty by the recognition of defences often on the basis of the relevance of the international law generally and of the international law on human rights and the environment in particular. In any event, the newer treaties are beginning to include concerns relating to labour rights, human rights and the environment. The impact of sovereign wealth funds as foreign investors has to be assessed. These changes are captured in this edition, but the manner in which they will take hold is still unclear.

As indicated in the previous editions, this area of the law is in constant change simply because different interests clash and outcomes differ based on constantly changing power balances. As a consequence, it is not an area to be studied by looking at only the language of the treaties and the awards interpreting them (the approach taken in the conventional texts on the subject), but in light of a variety of factors, among them the movement of power balances among states, the dominance and retreat of particular economic theories at given periods and the prevailing viewpoints within the arbitral community. This edition seeks to capture these changing factors which are responsible for the rapid developments that have taken place in the law.

As in the case of the previous editions, I thank those who have travelled the same path with me in the study of this exciting branch of international law. Working with those at the Division on Investment and Enterprise at UNCTAD, particularly with James Chan and Anna Joubin-Brett, has enabled me to keep abreast of the new developments that have taken place, especially in the economic aspects of the field. My academic friends, Peter Muchlinski, Frederico Ortino, Gus van Harten, Kerry Rittich, Karl Sauvant, Wenhua Shan, David Schneiderman, Kenneth Vandevelde, Jiangyu Wang and Jean Ho, have always been good sources of information, criticism and commentary, for which I am grateful. The work was first written at the Lauterpacht Centre for International Law at Cambridge. Its Directors, Sir Eli Lauterpacht and Professor James Crawford, have remained supportive. I thank also my graduate students, Huala Adolf, George Akpan, Lu Haitian and Adefolake Oyewande Adeyeye, who worked with me in aspects of this field.

I thank Finola O'Sullivan, Sinéad Moloney, Richard Woodham, Daniel Dunlavey and Martin Gleeson for the care taken over the production of my book.

The National University of Singapore has facilitated my research in every way I wished for. It has been a pleasure to be an academic at the NUS.

I commend to the readers of this work the excellent website run by Professor Andrew Newcombe of the University of Victoria, Canada, at http://ita.law.uvic.ca, which provides the texts of and other documents concerning investment treaty awards, and the equally excellent website run by Luke Peterson, www.iareporter.com, which reports on developments in the field. Both are free services of immense help to students of this field. Most of the arbitral awards cited in this work are to be found on these websites.

Thanga was there, as always. Ahila has now studied this area of the law. Ramanan and Vaishnavi have careers of their own. The book has grown up with them.

Preface to the second edition

The international law on foreign investment has witnessed an explosive growth since the last edition. The decade had witnessed a proliferation of bilateral and regional investment treaties, and a dramatic rise in litigation under such treaties. The attempt to fashion a multilateral instrument on investment within the World Trade Organization has given the debate on issues in the area a wider focus. This edition seeks to capture such developments.

In the course of the decade, I have had the good fortune of being involved actively in many facets of the operation of this area of the law. During such activity, I have acquired many friends who work in the area. My association with UNCTAD has brought me in contact with Karl Sauvant, Anna Joubin-Brett, Victoria Aranda and James Chan. It has also given me the opportunity to work with Arghyrios Fatouros, Peter Muchlinksi and Kenneth Vandevelde, the academic leaders of this field. They have added much to my understanding of the law. The many hours of arguments with them, in various parts of the world, have added to the pleasure of studying this area of the law.

The first edition was written while I was a visiting fellow at the Lauterpacht Centre for International Law, University of Cambridge. The successive Directors of the Centre, Professor Sir Eli Lauterpacht and Professor James Crawford, have continued to encourage my efforts in this and other areas of international law.

My many students in Singapore and Dundee have always challenged me so that I was taught by them to know and remember that there are other ways in which the law could be looked at. To my critics, my answer would be that I am constantly made aware of their criticisms in the classroom. I have accommodated those criticisms in the text.

I thank Finola O'Sullivan, Alison Powell and Martin Gleeson for the care taken over the production of my book.

My research student, Lu Haitian, prepared the bibliography.

Thanga was there, as always. Ahila, Ramanan and Vaishnavi happily are now old enough to let their father alone.

Preface to the first edition

This book was written while I was on sabbatical leave from the National University of Singapore. I thank the Vice-Chancellor, the Council and Dean of the Faculty of Law for the generous terms on which I was granted the leave.

I spent the sabbatical year as a Visiting Fellow at the Research Centre for International Law of the University of Cambridge. I thank Eli Lauterpacht, the Director of the Centre, for many acts of kindness in making this year a happy and productive one.

I am grateful to Professor James Crawford, Whewell Professor of International Law at Cambridge, who read and commented on an early draft of this work, to Professor Detlev Vagts, Bemis Professor of International Law at Harvard, who enabled me to spend a month of research at the Harvard Law School and to Robin Pirrie, Fellow of Hughes Hall, Cambridge, who was helpful with his advice. I remain responsible for any errors and omissions.

As always, Thanga has been an unfailing source of strength. Ahila, Ramanan and Vaishnavi have given up time that should have been theirs.

Table of cases

Abbreviations

AC	Appeal Cases
AD	Annual Digest of Public International Law Cases
AJIL	American Journal of International Law
All ER	All England Reports
ALR	Australian Law Reports
ASIL Proceedings	American Society of International Law Proceedings
BYIL	British Yearbook of International Law
CLR	Commonwealth Law Reports
CMLR	Common Market Law Review
EHRR	European Human Rights Reports
EJIL	European Journal of International Law
F Supp	Federal Supplement
Hague Recueil	Hague Recueil des Cours
ICLQ	International and Comparative Law Quarterly
ICSID Rev	ICSID Review – Foreign Investment Law Journal
ILJ	International Law Journal
ILM	International Legal Materials
Iran–US CTR	Iran–United States Claims Tribunal Reports
JIA	Journal of International Arbitration
JIL	Journal of International Law
JWTL	Journal of World Trade Law
KB	King's Bench Reports
LJ	Law Journal
LQR	Law Quarterly Review
LR	Law Review
MLR	Modern Law Review
PCIJ	Permanent Court of International Justice
SJ	Solicitors Journal
UNRIAA	United Nations Reports of International Arbitral Awards
WLR	Weekly Law Reports
YCA	Yearbook of Commercial Arbitration

1

Introduction

Few areas of international law excite as much controversy as the law relating to foreign investment.[1] A spate of arbitration awards resulting from investment treaties has added much to the debates in recent times. These have been followed by massive literature analysing the law resulting from the treaties and the arbitration awards. Since the awards often conflict, the confusion has been exacerbated. Though the conflict in the awards is often attributed to the inconsistencies in the language in the treaties each tribunal had to interpret, the more probable explanation is that there are philosophical, economic and political attitudes that underlie the conflict which in turn reflect the underlying causes for the controversies that have existed in the area for a long time.

The law on the area has been steeped in controversy from its inception. Much controversy has resulted from the law on the subject being the focus of conflict between several forces released at the conclusion of the Second World War. The cyclical nature of the ebbs and flows of the controversy is evident. The ending of colonialism released forces of nationalism. Once freed from the shackles of colonialism, the newly independent states agitated not only for the ending of the economic dominance of the former colonial powers within their states but also for a world order which would permit them more scope for the ordering of their own economies and access to world markets. The Cold War between the then super-powers made the law a battleground for ideological conflicts. The non-aligned movement, which arose in response to this rivalry, exerted pressure to ensure that each newly independent state had complete control over its economy. One avenue for the exertion of such pressure by the non-aligned movement was the formulation of new doctrines through the use of the numerical strength of its members in the General Assembly of the United Nations. Several resolutions were enacted asserting the doctrine of permanent sovereignty over natural resources and calling for the establishment of a New International Economic Order, the aim of which was to ensure fairness in trade to developing countries as well as control over the process of foreign investment. The oil crisis in the 1970s illustrated both the power as well as the weakness of the states which possessed natural resources. It brought

---

[1] Compare Harlan J in *United States* v. *Sabbatino*, 374 US 398 (1964), who said, regarding one aspect of this branch of the law: 'There are few if any issues in international law today on which opinion seems to be so divided as the limitation of the state's power to expropriate the alien's property.' The statement seems equally applicable to other areas of the international law on foreign investment.

about industry-wide shifts through collective action organised by the oil-producing states. The producers of other mineral resources were not able to achieve the same success.

The ability of the developing states to exert their collective influence on shaping the law shifted dramatically towards the end of the twentieth century. Sovereign defalcations associated with the lending of petrodollars dried up private lending by banks. Aid had already dried up due to recession in the developed states. The rise of free market economics associated with President Reagan of the United States and Prime Minister Thatcher of the United Kingdom gave a vigorous thrust to moves to liberalise foreign investment regimes. The acceptance of an 'open door' policy by China and the success of the small Asian states like Hong Kong and Singapore, which had developed through liberal attitudes to foreign investment, made other developing states choose a similar path.[2] The dissolution of the Soviet Union led to the emergence of new states committed to free market economics. Developing states began to compete with each other for the foreign investment that was virtually the only capital available to fuel their development. Third World cohesion, which drove the ideas behind the New International Economic Order, was on the verge of collapse, though it had by then evolved competing norms challenging the previously existing ones. The vigorous espousal of free market economics by the International Monetary Fund and the World Bank also led to pressures being exerted on developing countries to liberalise their regimes on foreign investment. Neo-liberal economic theories became prominent. The view that the market will allocate resources fairly came to be adopted in the domestic economic sphere. Liberalisation of assets in the international economy became the favoured policy. In the context of this swing in the pendulum, the developing states entered into bilateral treaties containing rules on investment protection and liberalised the laws on foreign investment entry. They also participated in regional treaties like the North American Free Trade Agreement (NAFTA) and sectoral treaties like the Energy Charter Treaty. The World Trade Organization (WTO) came into existence with the avowed objective of liberalising not only international trade but also aspects of investment which affected such trade. The link between international trade and international investment was said to justify the competence of the WTO in this area. The Singapore Ministerial Conference of the WTO decided to study the possibility of an instrument on investment.[3] New factors had entered the area of the international law on foreign investment. Many of the new instruments of the WTO dealt directly with areas of foreign investment.[4] But, the WTO was unable to bring about a comprehensive instrument on investment.

---

[2] Though initially it was thought that these states achieved prosperity by the adoption of liberalisation measures, this view has since been queried, with many holding the view that astute interventionist measures by the state combined with selective liberalisation measures and regulation of foreign investment were the reason for the growth.

[3] The move to create an instrument on investment within the WTO failed as a result of concerted opposition from developing states.

[4] Intellectual property was covered by the Trade-Related Aspects of Intellectual Property Rights (TRIPS) instrument. The General Agreement on Trade in Services (GATS) deals with the services sector and covers the provision of services through a commercial presence in another country, which is foreign investment in the services sector. The Trade-Related Investment Measures (TRIMS) instrument deals with performance requirements associated with foreign investment. The Singapore and Doha Ministerial Meetings of the WTO agreed to consider an instrument on investment and an instrument on competition which would directly impact foreign investment. But, these efforts failed, signalling disenchantment with the free market model of development.

Economic liberalism was generally triumphant at the end of the last millennium. The impact of its triumph was felt on the international law on foreign investment. The incredible proliferation of bilateral investment treaties was evidence of this triumph. United Nations Commission on Trade and Development (UNCTAD) reports indicate that the 1990s began with some 900 treaties and ended with over 2,900 treaties. The treaties created jurisdiction in arbitral tribunals at the unilateral instance of the foreign investor. After *AAPL* v. *Sri Lanka*,[5] where such unilateral recourse to arbitration on the basis of appropriately worded dispute-settlement provisions in treaties was first upheld, the number of arbitral awards based on standards of treaty protection of foreign investment increased substantially. This in turn led to the articulation by these tribunals of principles which confirmed and extended notions that favoured movement of foreign investment and their treatment in accordance with external standards. It also restricted governmental interference with such investment significantly by considerably expanding the notion of compensable taking to include regulatory takings.[6]

There is evidence of yet another swing taking place at the beginning of the new millennium. Successive economic crises in Asia and Latin America attributed to the sudden withdrawal of foreign funds have led to the re-evaluation of whether the flow of foreign funds and investments is the panacea for development as originally thought. The Organization of Economic Co-operation and Development (OECD) attempted to draft a Multilateral Agreement on Investment (MAI) in 1995 thinking that the time was ripe for such an effort, given the seeming willingness of developing countries to liberalise their economies and enter into bilateral economic treaties. But, during the discussions, the members of the OECD, all developed states, found that they could not agree among themselves on the principles of the rules on foreign investment protection. The attempt also spawned a protest coalition of environmentalists and human rights activists who complained that the draft of the MAI emphasised the protection of investment without adverting to the need to protect the environment and human rights from abuse by multi-national corporations. An important idea had been articulated during this protest that the multinational corporation may be an agent of progress and deserves protection but that it could also be an agent of deleterious conduct, harmful to economic development. In this case, it requires not protection but censure through the withdrawal of such protection and, even, the imposition of liability. As a result, there have been various efforts made to formulate standards of conduct for multinational corporations.

The collective protests against the MAI were a prelude to the protests against globalisation that were to mar the meetings of economic organisations like the WTO, the IMF and the World Bank at Seattle, Prague, Montreal and other capitals of the Western world. These protests have continued. The protests signified the emergence of lobbies within the developed world which required the rethinking of issues relating to foreign investment. The protests signified that the dissent was not the concern solely of developing states but that sections within the developed

---

[5] *Asian Agricultural Products Ltd* v. *Sri Lanka* (1990) 4 *ICSID Reports* 245.
[6] Thus, for example, in *Santa Elena* v. *Costa Rica* (2000) 39 *ILM* 317; (2002) 5 *ICSID Reports* 153, an environmental measure was held to be expropriatory. Later awards, which recognised that such regulatory takings may be non-compensable, cast doubt on these trends.

states were concerned with the fact that the law was being used in a manner that gave protection to the interests of foreign investment to the detriment of the interests of the eradication of poverty, the protection of the environment and the promotion of human rights. New forces that could reshape the law had been released. There were dramatic disclosures of massive corporate frauds resulting in disenchantment with once admired corporations, resulting in stringent corporate disclosure laws. These events have been accentuated by the global economic crisis resulting from the massive unsecured loans given by banks in Europe and North America. There has emerged a disillusionment with neo-liberal policies that had been adopted in the previous decade. The law, particularly the international law on foreign investment, was an instrument of effecting neo-liberal policy, and the issue has to be faced whether some of the changes made in the past need to be changed in light of new circumstances. The instrumental role that the law played may have to go into reversal.

A new phenomenon that has emerged in the area is the role of non-governmental organisations (NGOs) committed to the furtherance of environmental interests and human rights and the eradication of poverty. These NGOs operate within developed states and espouse, to a large extent, what they believe to be the interests of the people of the developing world and the world as a whole. In addition, there are the protest movements against globalisation which also seek to espouse causes that favour developing-world interests, ranging from economic development, the writing-off of Third World debt and foreign investment.[7] It has been suggested that, with the increase in the gap between rich and poor within developed states brought about by globalisation, there is a Third World within developed states ready to protest against excessive reliance on free market ideas.[8]

More dramatic has been the fact that there has been a change in the patterns of foreign investment. Newly industrialising countries such as China, India and Brazil have become exporters of capital. Sovereign wealth funds of many small countries are playing leading roles in acquiring established businesses in developed countries. As a result, developed states in North America and Europe are becoming massive recipients of foreign capital. These changes will result in the assertion of sovereign control of such investments by the developed states and a selective relinquishing of the inflexible rules on investment protection that these states had built up.

This trend is already evident as leading companies of the United States and Europe are taken over by foreign investors from Asia and elsewhere. The rules the developed states crafted to protect the foreign investment of their nationals will soon come to haunt them. As a result, they may be bent on backtracking on these rules and creating, as developing countries did in the past, significant sovereignty-based defences to liability and redrawing the boundaries of investment protection.[9] These sovereignty-based defences are often the

---

[7] This clash of globalisations is discussed in M. Sornarajah, 'The Clash of Globalisations: Its Impact on the International Law on Foreign Investment' (2003) 10 *Canadian Foreign Policy* 1.

[8] Caroline Thomas, 'Where Is the Third World Now', in Caroline Thomas (ed.), *Globalisation and the South* (1997) 1.

[9] This is already evident in the introduction of exceptions relating to regulatory takings, defences based on the environment, the devising of an exceptional regime for taxation, self defined national security exceptions and broad necessity defences which can be found in the US and Canadian model investment treaties. The changes resulting in the recognition of defences to liability justify a new chapter in this edition.

refuge of the developed states in response to the neo-liberal expansions that were made. That this reaction took place over such a short period attests to the responsiveness of the law to the changes that are effected by circumstances as well as by the expansive attempts at the interpretation of instruments in the field by decision-makers in the area, principally, arbitrators.[10]

But, still, there will be considerable restraint in dismantling the existing system. As the power of multinational corporations increases,[11] developed states will continue to espouse their interests not only because of the enormous power that these corporations achieve through lobbying but also because it is in their interests to do so. The expansion of trade and investment increases the economic power of developed states. They have traditionally seen the need to ensure the protection of the multinational corporations responsible for such trade and investment as coincidental with their own interests.

The multinational corporations themselves must be seen as distinct bases of power capable of asserting their interests through the law. Their individual economic resources far exceed those of many sovereign states. Their collective power to manipulate legal outcomes must be conceded. It is a fascinating fact that, through the employment of private techniques of dispute resolution, they are able to create principles of law that are generally favourable to them. That they can bring about such outcomes through pressure on their states is obvious. It is notable that textbooks on international law do not contemplate the legal personality of these corporations when they wield so much power in international relations.[12] The role of these actors in the international legal system is seldom studied due to the dominance in the field of positivist views which stress that states are the only relevant actors in international relations.[13] They provide a convenient cloak for hiding the absence of corporate liability. Positivism also enables law-creation by an entity often held to lack legal personality. By employing low-order sources of international law such as decisions of arbitrators and the writings of 'highly qualified publicists', it is possible to employ vast private resources to ensure that a body of law favourable to multinational corporations is created. This, again, is a phenomenon that international lawyers have been reluctant to explore lest it shakes the hoary foundations on which their discipline is built.

There will be entirely new types of multinational corporations entering the scene. The state-owned oil corporations of China and India are aggressively entering the field and seeking mergers with existing multinational corporations. The investment funds of many rich, smaller states like those in Singapore and Dubai as well as those newly industrialising

---

[10] C. Duggan, D. Wallace, N. Rubins and B. Sabahi, *Investor–State Arbitration* (2008), suggest that the United States, which had opposed the Calvo doctrine that international law has no relevance to foreign investment and only national laws have competence, may now be adopting that doctrine. They observe, at p. 488: 'It is indeed ironic that the United States – long the leading opponent of the Calvo Doctrine – may now be considered its proponent, at least in regard to national treatment and indirect expropriation.'

[11] It has been pointed out that multinational corporations exist in developing states as well. But, they are nowhere near as large as US and European multinational corporations and cannot wield the same degree of influence.

[12] Writers on international relations, however, concede the power of these corporations to affect the course of international relations. Their behaviour, as a consequence, is extensively studied in that field. It is unfortunate that there are no parallel studies in international law. There are, however, efforts being made to grapple with the problem in international law. Jennifer Zerk, *Multinationals and Corporate Social Responsibility* (2006).

[13] C. Cutler, *Private Power and Global Authority: Transnational Global Law in the Political Economy* (2003).

states which have excess capital will enter the scene as actors who will shape the rules of the game. The very states which wanted strong rules in the area may baulk at the prospect of these rules being used in a manner favourable to these new actors.[14]

The rapid changes in this subject area call for an understanding not only of the role of states and multinational corporations but also of the role of NGOs. In addition, since much of the exploitation of natural resources takes place on the land of minorities and tribal and aboriginal groups, the interests of these groups also have to be taken into account in the development of the law. It is an area in which international law is clearly moving away from the old positivist notion that international law is shaped entirely by the activities of states. Even as techniques to protect foreign investment are coming to be explored more fully through the creation of standing for multinational corporations, so, at the same time, by contrast, there is pressure to ensure that the subject reflects the concerns of human rights and environmental interests through the imposition of liability on these corporations. These emphasise, not the protection of the investments of multinational corporations, but their social and corporate responsibility to the host communities in which they operate. These concerns are reflected in the increasing volume of literature that is devoted to the new directions that foreign investment law has taken.[15]

The interplay of various economic, political and historical factors shaped, and continues to shape, the development of the international law on foreign investment. If international law is generated by the eventual resolution of conflicting national, business and social interests, the international law of foreign investment provides an illustration of these processes of intense conflicts and their resolution at work. It is an area in which the interests of the capital-exporting states have clashed with the interests of capital-importing states. The resultant resolution of the conflict, if any resolution is indeed achieved, indicates how international law is made and how open-ended the formulation of its principles are in the face of intense conflicts of views among states as to the law. These conflicts become accentuated when other actors in the field are divided in their views and support the contesting norms that each camp espouses. Positivist studies of the subject which emphasise the rules in treaties and arbitral awards fail to capture the rich policy implications behind the shaping of these rules through a constant clash of interests.

As a result of such clashes, the field provides for the study of international law as an interdisciplinary subject in which ideas in the sphere of economics, political science and related areas have helped to shape the arguments. Yet, for all its richness, the field has

---

[14] An instructive situation is the effort of the Chinese state oil company, Sinopec, seeking to buy into the American oil company, Unocal. The matter created considerable concern and the offer fell through. In the United States, national security and other concerns were cited as reasons for opposing the merger.

[15] There is a concentration in the new literature on foreign investment arbitration. For the literature, see C. McLachlan, L. Shore and M. Weiniger, *International Investment Arbitration: Substantive Principles* (2007); C. Duggan, D. Wallace, N. Rubin and B. Sabahi, *Investor–State Arbitration* (2008). These works are a result of increasing practitioner interest in the area. There is also a second edition of C. Schreuer, *The ICSID Convention: A Commentary* (2nd edn, 2009). A. Newcombe and L. Pradell, *Law and Practice of Investment Treaties* (2009) is an excellent book developing the law on the basis of investment treaties. There are works which deal with the impact of external forces on the law. See, for example, J. Zerk, *Multinational Corporations and Corporate Social Responsibility* (2006); J. Dine, *Companies, International Trade and Human Rights* (2005); D. Kinley, *Human Rights and Corporations* (2009).

seldom been looked at as a whole, until recently.[16] It is necessary to carve out a niche for the subject within international law so that the manner in which the norms of international law are affected by the seemingly irreconcilable interests that operate in this area could be studied more intensively.[17]

Interest in the area also arises from the fact that the trends in this field cannot be explained on the basis of any existing theory of international law. Most theories of international law are rooted in positivism and are aimed at explaining law as an existing, static phenomenon, unaffected by political and other trends. These theories are incapable of being applied to a situation where the existing principles of law, formulated at a time when they were kept in place by hegemonic control and dominance, are under attack. Other theories are idealistic, seeking to achieve objectives based on morality and conscience. These theories are also inadequate to explain a situation in which different value systems of somewhat equal moral validity are in collision. Where existing rules supported by the established group of nations are subject to attack by relatively new members of the international community,[18] they become feeble and, until they are replaced, a situation of chaos or normlessness will exist. The task of decision-makers and scholars will be to examine the conflicts in the norms in the area and ensure that adjustments are made to bring about some acceptable norms so that the situation of normlessness may be ended. This book is a contribution to this process in an area of abundant normative conflicts. The identification of the conflicts in norms will itself facilitate the process of a future settlement of the conflicts and bring about a clearer set of rules on the international law of foreign investment.

---

[16] After the first edition of this book, a spate of new books on this and related areas appeared. R. Dolzer and C. Schreuer, *International Investment Law* (2008) concentrates on rules of investment treaties and arbitration under them. P. Muchlinksi, F. Fortino and C. Schreuer, *Handbook of International Investment Law* (2008), is an edited book which lacks a coherent theme, but collects together chapters on distinct aspects of the law. P. Muchlinksi, *Multinational Corporations Law* (2007), approaches the subject from the perspective of multinational corporations. One result of the profusion of arbitral awards has been a spate of books on the subject, as indicated in the previous footnote. Many of them have been written from the perspective of practitioners in the field, and are often papers presented at conferences, commenting on recent awards. There are older works: R. Pritchard (ed.), *Economic Development, Foreign Investment and the Law* (1996); and D. D. Bradlow and A. Escher (eds.), *Legal Aspects of Foreign Investment* (1999). For even earlier studies, see I. Delupis, *Finance and Protection of Foreign Investment in Developing Countries* (1987); Z. A. Kronfol, *Protection of Foreign Investment* (1972); and G. Schwarzenberger, *Foreign Investment and International Law* (1969). There are now specialist journals: *Foreign Investment Law Journal*, published by the World Bank; and the *Journal of World Investment* (Geneva). For a French study, see P. Laviec, *Protection et Promotion des Investissements: Etude de Droit International Economique* (1985). Specific areas of the law on foreign investment have also attracted book-length studies. See, for example, R. Dolzer and M. Stevens, *Bilateral Investment Treaties* (1996); M. Sornarajah, *The Settlement of Foreign Investment Disputes* (2000); and C. Schreuer, *The ICSID Convention: A Commentary* (2nd edn, 2009). The newer works on investment arbitration have been indicated in the previous footnote.

[17] The creation of new subjects within international law must be addressed with caution, as the charge is made that these are studied without any foundation in the major discipline of international law. This is a legitimate criticism. An unfortunate facet of this area of the law is that many arbitrators who have made awards in the area have no grounding in international law and approach issues from an entirely commercial perspective, without regard to the public law elements in the disputes or to the public international law doctrines that may apply. Specialisation, within international law, helps to enhance the law. Also, often in modern times, the law has to be explained to persons who may not have the inclination to study the whole area of international law. The fact is that the areas of international law are burgeoning so rapidly that they cannot be addressed by a generalist with sufficient depth. There is a need for specialist works, well grounded in basic principles of international law. As indicated in the previous footnote, there are studies on more specialised aspects of this area of international law.

[18] The European origins of international law have been extensively commented on. One view is that new nations are born into the world of existing law and are bound by it. See D. P. O'Connell, 'Independence and State Succession', in W. V. Brian (ed.), *New States in International Law and Diplomacy* (1965). The opposing view is that they may seek revision of existing principles of international law, as they are not bound by these rules. This dispute takes an acute form in many areas of international law. For general descriptions of the disputes, see R. P. Anand, *The Afro-Asian States and International Law* (1978). The attack on Eurocentric international law is more evident in this field, as the conflict is between the erstwhile colonial powers which are now the principal exporters of capital and the newly independent nations which are the recipients of such capital.

The normative conflicts are accentuated by the fact that parties interested in this area of the law have become diverse. NGOs engaged in the promotion of single issues such as the protection of the environment from the hazardous activities of multinational corporations or the protection of human rights from violation by elites of states in association with multi-national corporations have entered the fray. Large law firms see the area as a lucrative field of practice. They may seek to promote rules that cater to their interests in maintaining volatility in the area, ensuring wide bases of liability and a continuation of arbitration as the means of settlement of investment disputes. Arbitrators have agendas in that the field is one that provides scope for the lucrative pursuit of their profession. These interests often collide, increasing the fragility of the law.

1. The definition of foreign investment

Foreign investment involves the transfer of tangible or intangible assets from one country to another for the purpose of their use in that country to generate wealth under the total or partial control of the owner of the assets.[19] There can be no doubt that the transfer of physical property such as equipment, or physical property that is bought or constructed such as plantations or manufacturing plants, constitute foreign direct investment. Such investment may be contrasted with portfolio investment. Portfolio investment is normally represented by a movement of money for the purpose of buying shares in a company formed or functioning in another country. It could also include other security instruments through which capital is raised for ventures. The distinguishing element is that, in portfolio invest-ment, there is a separation between, on the one hand, management and control of the company and, on the other, the share of ownership in it.[20] Investment treaties also define the nature of the foreign investment that is protected through their provisions. As a result, definitions differ according to the purpose for which they are used. It is emphasised that this work is not confined solely to the law created by treaties.[21]

1.1 The distinction between portfolio investment and foreign direct investment

In the case of portfolio investment, it is generally accepted that the investor takes upon himself the risks involved in the making of such investments. He cannot sue the domestic

---

[19] Compare the definition of foreign investment in the *Encyclopaedia of Public International Law* (vol. 8, p. 246), where foreign investment is defined as 'a transfer of funds or materials from one country (called capital-exporting country) to another country (called host country) in return for a direct or indirect participation in the earnings of that enterprise'. The difficulty with this definition is that it is broad enough to include portfolio investment. The IMF, *Balance of Payments Manual* (1980), para. 408, used a narrower definition which excluded portfolio investment. It defined foreign investment as 'investment that is made to acquire a lasting interest in an enterprise operating in an economy other than that of an investor, the investor's purpose being to have an effective choice in the management of the enterprise'. A definition that includes portfolio investment should demonstrate that its inclusion for the purposes of the international law on foreign investment is justified.

[20] Such a distinction is drawn in the texts on economics, and is also a sound basis for distinguishing direct and portfolio investment in the law. Thus, control is stressed in the following definition in E. Graham and P. Krugman, *Foreign Direct Investment in the United States* (1991) p. 7: 'Foreign direct investment is formally defined as ownership of assets by foreign residents for purposes of controlling the use of those assets.'

[21] Because of the extensive practitioner-oriented interest in treaty-based investment arbitration, there is an over-concentration on the law under investment treaties in the literature, despite the fact that contract-based arbitration continues and the roots of the law are also in other sources, such as customary practice on diplomatic responsibility.

stock exchange or the public entity which runs it if he were to suffer loss. Likewise, if he were to suffer loss by buying foreign shares, bonds or other instruments, there would be no basis on which he could seek a remedy.[22] Portfolio investment was not protected by customary international law. Such investment was attended by ordinary commercial risks which the investor ought to have been aware of. But, customary international law protected the physical property of the foreign investor and other assets directly invested through principles of diplomatic protection and state responsibility.

One view maintains that there should be no distinction between portfolio investments and foreign direct investments as to the protection given to either by international law. This view is based on the assumption that there is no distinction between the risks taken by either type of investor, both being voluntarily assumed.[23] But, this view is not accepted generally in international law, where it is clear that foreign direct investment alone is subject to the protection of customary international law. Several reasons are given for this difference in treatment. The foreign investor takes out of his home state resources which could otherwise have been used to advance the economy of the home state.[24] The home state is said to be justified in ensuring that these resources are protected.[25] Portfolio investments, on the other hand, can be made on stock exchanges virtually anywhere in the world. Since the host state cannot know to whom linkages are created through the sale of shares on these stock exchanges, there can be no concrete relationship creating a responsibility. This is not so in the case of foreign direct investment where the foreigner enters the host state with the express consent of the host state. Nevertheless, the trend of the law in the area may be to create responsibility towards those who hold portfolio investments through treaties. This is a trend associated with the liberalisation of the movement of assets. Opinions are found in some publications that portfolio investments are now to be included in foreign direct investments. To a large extent, such opinions are influenced by the fact that treaties defining investments include shares in the definition of foreign investment. But, as will be demonstrated, shares in this context mean the shares of a joint venture company in which the foreigner present in the host state has invested, and is not meant to include shares held by a non-resident and purchased entirely outside the host state. There will be continued uncertainty attached to the question whether portfolio investment is protected in the same manner as foreign direct investment in international law. The better view is that portfolio investment is not protected unless specifically included in the definition of foreign investment in the

---

[22] Unless, as *Fedax* v. *Venezuela* (1998) 37 *ILM* 1378, would have it, an investment treaty could be interpreted as extending to portfolio investments.

[23] I. Brownlie, 'Treatment of Aliens: Assumption of Risk and International Law', in W. Flume, H. J. Hain, G. Kegel and K. R. Simmond (eds.), *International Law and Economic Order: Essays in Honour of F. A. Mann* (1997), p. 309 at p. 311.

[24] This is not much of a reason, as portfolio investment also constitutes resources within the state which could have been used within the state if not committed to a company overseas. But, sums of money that are used in portfolio investments are often small, shares being bought by individuals on stock exchanges.

[25] But, again, the reason breaks down. The home state itself takes a risk in allowing these resources to leave the state. The question is why should it not have to bear the consequences of its own risk if the resources were to be harmed. Obviously, there is no answer to this logical issue, other than the pragmatic one that powerful states have conferred protection on the person and the property of its citizens who work or invest abroad.

relevant treaty.[26] The issue is considered later in this volume when dealing with investment treaties and their extension to cover portfolio investments.

1.2 Definition of foreign investment in investment treaties

The tendency of many treaties in the area of foreign investment, particularly the model
treaties drafted by the United States and other capital-exporting states, has been to broaden
the scope of the definition of foreign investment.[27] The objective behind this is to ensure that
treaty protection could be given to a wide variety of activities associated with foreign direct
investment. This objective has to a large extent been facilitated by the attitudes taken by
arbitral tribunals and writers in the area. It is important for those who negotiate treaties to
understand the purpose behind the making of these extensions.[28]

  Several arbitration awards have been concerned with the issue as to whether the transactions that gave rise to the disputes could be characterised as investments. They are dealt
with in the chapter on investment treaties. All of them contain definitions of foreign investment. But, these definitions apply only in the context of the protection given by the treaties.
The notion of foreign investment may be wider than that contained in the treaty definitions,
though these definitions also seek to capture a complete range of the types of foreign
investments. But, for the moment, it is sufficient to indicate that one technique has been
to identify foreign direct investment as having distinct criteria such as commitment of assets
into a project with the object of profit and permanence and with a view to the risks arising
from legal, political and economic changes. Controversy has centred on whether economic
development is a criterion that marks foreign investment protected by international law.
Certainly, one policy justification for the protection of foreign investment through the
mechanism of international law has been the argument that it promotes economic development. It is interesting to note that, in early arbitrations in the field, a distinction was made
between, on the one hand, foreign investments in developed countries which were subject to
the host state's domestic law and, on the other, investments in developing countries which
were subject to a supranational or international legal system on the basis that the agreements
in the developing countries involved high risk but were made to promote economic development. Indeed, the contracts made in developing countries were designated 'economic
development agreements' so as to reflect this distinction.[29] The controversy has continued
under investment treaties which, their preambles suggest, are made in order to promote
economic development through the flows of foreign investment. This controversy is dealt
with in greater detail in Chapter 5 below.

---

[26] There are treaties, such as the ASEAN Framework Agreement on Investment, which specifically exclude portfolio investments
from the scope of the treaty.
[27] Vandevelde has explained the concerns behind the definition of foreign investment in US bilateral investment treaties. See
K. Vandevelde, *United States Investment Treaties* (1992), p. 261.
[28] Sometimes, a distinction is made between an asset-based definition, which simply lists the types of property which amount to
protected investments, and a corporation-based definition, which lists the assets which are owned by the corporation which
makes the investment. No material difference flows from this distinction.
[29] J. Hyde, 'Economic Development Agreements' (1962) 105 *Hague Recueil* 271.

1.3 The evolution of the meaning of the term 'investment'

It is clear that, from early times, the meaning of investment in international law was confined to foreign direct investment. The evolution of the international law was towards the idea that the responsibility of the state would arise if it did not treat the alien in accordance with a minimum standard of treatment. This standard of treatment was extended to his physical property. Physical presence in the host state and injury suffered at the hands of the host state or its agencies was the basis of the development of the law. The early discussion of the law on state responsibility for injuries to aliens took place in the context of either physical abuse or the violation of the rights of the alien to physical property held by him in the host state. The genesis of the international law on foreign investment was in the obligation created by the law to protect the alien and his physical property and state responsibility arising from the failure to perform that obligation. In terms of customary international law, the obligation was created largely through the practice of the United States which asserted the existence of such an obligation in its relations with its Latin American neighbours. As foreign investments grew, the law was extended to protect the tangible assets of the foreigner from governmental interference by way of the taking of such property. The early cases dealt with the destruction of property or the taking of land belonging to the foreigner. The concept of taking was also narrow, for only tangible assets could be taken by the state. This original feature of an economic asset in the form of physical property protected by a legal right under the law of the host state has always remained the starting-point of the definition of an 'investment' for the purposes of this area of the law. This still remains the paradigm case upon which extensions later came to be made. The failure to have regard to this factor has led to many errors by those who have sought to extend the scope of the protection of the law beyond parameters that were drawn by its essential principles.

Progressively, consistent with this essential feature, the term 'investment' was extended to include intangible assets. Initially, these consisted of contractual rights in pursuance of which the foreign investor took his assets, such as machinery and equipment, into the host state. The rights associated with the holding of property such as leases, mortgages and liens came to be included. There are cases that indicate that loans also fell into this category. There was difficulty in the case of shares in companies. In the *Barcelona Traction Case*,[30] the International Court of Justice held that a shareholder's rights in a company that was the vehicle of the foreign investor could not be protected through the diplomatic intervention of the home state of the shareholder. The much criticised view taken by the Court was that only the state in which the company was incorporated could intercede on behalf of the company and that the shareholders of the company had no independent interests that were protected by international law. It indicated a problem as to the protection of the rights of the share-holder which continues to befuddle international law.[31] The situation becomes more difficult

---

[30] [1970] *ICJ Reports* 1. The position was affirmed in the more recent ICJ decision, *Diallo Case*, ICJ (Judgment, 24 May 2007).

[31] This is particularly seen in the case law under the International Convention on the Settlement of Investment Disputes. In the ICSID Convention, shareholder rights are to be protected only where the host state gives its consent to treat the corporate vehicle for the investment as a foreign corporation for the purpose of ICSID arbitration. Complex litigation has resulted on the issue of corporate nationality. See further on this, M. Sornarajah, *The Settlement of Foreign Investment Disputes* (2000), pp. 194–207.

where the foreign investor operates his investment through a company that is incorporated under the laws of the host state or is a minority shareholder in such a company. The International Convention on the Settlement of Investment Disputes (ICSID) seeks to overcome this through the requirement that the host state specifically agrees to regard the company as a foreign company despite its incorporation as a local company, if, for purposes of dispute settlement, the locally incorporated company was to be regarded as a foreign company.

In response to the *Barcelona Traction Case*, the issue of shareholder protection was addressed directly in bilateral investment treaties by including shares in companies within the meaning of the term 'investment'. The shares that are referred to in such treaties are shares in a company that is to serve as a vehicle for the investment that is contemplated and presumably not portfolio investments.[32] It is unfortunate that this reference to shares has been read by some as meaning that portfolio investment is protected by these investment treaties. Such an interpretation is made without regard to the reason for the inclusion of shares in the definition of investments.

There were further developments which took place in the area since the *Barcelona Traction Case* and the inclusion of shares in corporations established by the foreign investor within the meaning of foreign investment. There are now statements in publications which state that shares are investments that are protected by investment treaties, without having regard to the specific history that led to the inclusion of shares in investment treaties. These statements give the impression that portfolio investments are protected by international investment law the same way foreign direct investments are. This view, which is expansive, does not accord with the context in which the law was developed. Some treaties expressly counter the possibility of such a view being adopted by excluding portfolio investments from the definition of protected investments. The fact that some treaties contain express protection for portfolio investment while giving protection to shares in companies also supports the view taken here.

The next phase of the extension made through treaties was the inclusion of intellectual property rights within the meaning of foreign investment. Widespread copying of inventions made in developed states was the reason for the extension of protection to intellectual property rights. Many of these rights were associated with the making of foreign investments. When a new invention was to be manufactured in the developing state or when new technology was to be transferred by a foreign investor to a local partner within a joint venture, it would be necessary to provide for the protection of the intellectual property rights associated with the venture. When such a need for the recognition of intellectual property rights arose, the treaties extended the meaning of foreign investment to include intangible

---

[32] But, it is evident that, whatever change is made by the treaties, this will not affect the manner of the protection that could be given to companies under the ICSID Convention. This nicely proves the point that the definition of investment in the ICSID Convention remains unaffected by the changes to the meaning of the term 'investment' that are later made through treaties and other means of developing international law. The different approaches to shareholder protection under the ICSID Convention and the bilateral investment treaty show that the meanings of the term 'investment' in the different treaty instruments do not coincide. If this view is correct, then the use of the term 'investment' has a temporal meaning varying from treaty to treaty depending on the period in which it was drafted.

rights associated with intellectual property, thus increasing the scope of the meaning of foreign investment which had hitherto been confined to the physical assets of the foreign investor. Analytically too, the situation was different, for the intellectual property was created by the local law through the recognition of the right by an act of the host state. So, technically, it was property that was created by the host state in the foreigner that was being protected. The types of intellectual property that are to be recognised are often elaborately spelt out in the treaties to include patents and copyright which are rights technically granted to the foreign investor by the host state laws, as well as lesser rights such as know-how. The policy justification for the protection of intellectual property rights through investment treaties is that there will be more technology transferred to developing countries if such intellectual property is protected through investment treaties. When a state interferes with these intellectual property rights, it is interfering with property it had itself created in the foreign investor. The treaty internationalised the rights once they had been created and required them to be protected in accordance with the standards of the treaty. The argument that the state can control the property it had created can no longer apply as a result of the operation of the treaty. This process of the internationalisation of the property that was created under the local law is the basis of the protection of intellectual property which is adopted in the field of both foreign investment and international trade. It is clear that, in the area of international trade, the Agreement on Trade-Related Aspects of Intellectual Property Rights (TRIPS) agreed under the auspices of the World Trade Organization operates on the basis of the same technique.[33] TRIPS, however, does not give a remedy directly to the foreign investor, as investment treaties do. As a result of this internationalisation, any state interference with intellectual property thereafter becomes a breach of treaty which amounts to an expropriation and has to be compensated.[34] Wide interpretations are sometimes given to the concept of the taking of property in treaties. As a result, there is a danger that the compulsory licensing of patents and parallel imports by the state can amount to taking and involve the state in liability for breach of the treaty standards. This danger arises in areas such as pharmaceuticals. The parallel import of an AIDS drug manufactured cheaply in another state stands in danger of being regarded as a violation of treaty standards as a result of this widening of the meaning and scope of the term 'foreign investment' and of the notion of 'taking'.[35]

The protection of intellectual property under bilateral and multilateral investment treaties, the WTO regime and the earlier regimes will mean that there will be an absence of

---

[33] There is burgeoning literature on TRIPS. The rationale behind the instrument has provoked much controversy. See S. Sell, *Private Power, Public Law: Globalisation of Intellectual Property Rights* (2003); C. Arup, *World Trade Organization Knowledge Agreements* (2008).

[34] Modern treaties, however, provide an exception in the situations where compulsory licensing of the technology is permitted under domestic patent law. Such compulsory licensing is not expropriation. There are also treaties which are devoted entirely to the protection of intellectual property. The TRIPS regime on intellectual property is augmented by both the investment treaties and the intellectual property treaties. TRIPS may well serve as the floor, whereas higher levels of protection could be created by bilateral or regional treaties.

[35] The argument would be that such a parallel import interferes with the expectations of profit of the patent holder and therefore amounts to a taking. Under TRIPS, the parallel import of drugs imported for epidemics became an issue which has been resolved. But, the issue remains unresolved under the investment and intellectual property treaties. The question as to what amounts to a taking is discussed in Chapter 10 below.

coordination as to how the law in the area will be developed. The remedies provided and the mechanisms employed are different. The investor may have a unilateral remedy under an investment treaty whereas only a state could invoke the dispute-settlement mechanism of the WTO for violation of the TRIPS standards. The substantive law on protection may also be differently stated. No real claims have yet arisen in which the law has been considered.

Once the idea that the concept of foreign investment need not be confined to tangible assets took hold, there were further inclusions of intangible rights in the list of matters which are to be included in the definition of the term foreign investment in the treaty. One such inclusion is the contractual rights which the foreign investor acquires as a result of its relationship with the state and its agencies. It is generally conceded that a breach of a contract which the state has made with a foreign investor does not by itself give rise to an international remedy.[36] There are obvious reasons for this. There may be good reasons for the breach by the state, for example defective performance by the foreign investor. There is also the possibility of settling the claims that arise through domestic litigation. There is a view that distinguishes between the violation of a contract through a commercial act by the state and a violation through the use of its sovereign powers. On this view, the conclusion is drawn that a violation through the use of sovereign power would amount to a breach of international norms. Even if the distinction can be drawn, the issue as to whether a contractual violation *per se* gives rise to responsibility in the state remains a moot point. There is authority for the view that a contractual violation made through the exercise of sovereign power incurs responsibility in the state.[37] The other view is that there must be an exhaustion of local remedies and a clear denial of justice for such a result to follow. This view accords with the customary law on the subject.

The conflict may be resolved by treaty. The treaty inclusion of contractual rights in the definition of the term 'foreign investment' would mean that, upon the breach of a contract by a state, an international obligation arises on the state that caused the breach of contract. As a result, a right arises in the foreign investor to seek remedies under the treaty. Again, the contract which is ordinarily subject to the laws of the host state becomes effectively internationalised as a result of this technique being adopted in the treaty. This internationalisation enables the foreign investor to have recourse to the remedies that are provided for him in the event of a violation of his rights under the treaty.[38] This results from the inclusion of contractual rights within the definition of foreign investment and not from the so-called umbrella clause,[39] the effect of which is contentious.[40] So, crucial to the strategy of protection is defining foreign investment to include the contractual rights of the foreign investor in the definition of foreign investment.

---

[36] See further Chapter 10 below.

[37] The view is stated and the authorities canvassed in S. Schwebel, *International Arbitration: Three Salient Problems* (1986).

[38] Awards have established that the claims arise not from breach of the contract but from the consequent breach, if any, of the treaty rights of the foreign investor. The manner of the breach may indicate such breach of treaty rights.

[39] An umbrella clause is a catch-all provision which seeks to protect all assurances and commitments made to the foreign investor. Properly speaking, where the contractual rights are already included in the definition of the foreign investment, the umbrella clause must logically refer to extra-contractual interests, the protection of which seems logically difficult as they do not create legal rights or interests of the required specificity.

[40] The effect of the umbrella clause is discussed in Chapter 5 below.

A further extension of foreign investment is to include the administrative rights that the foreign investor acquires in the host state. Why is the extension to include administrative rights so important? In the 1970s, influenced to a large extent by the views of the United Nations Committee on Transnational Corporations that foreign investment could be beneficial to the host economy if the foreign investment is harnessed to the economic development of the host economy, developing states began to enact legislation that was designed to screen foreign investment having regard to the effects such investment would have on the domestic economy. Much of the screening was done through administrative agencies. Such administrative agencies have over time undergone transformation in line with the prevailing and changing philosophies relating to foreign investment in that country. Obviously, when economic liberalism takes hold, there will be a more permissive approach. The dismantling of these screening procedures and the recognition of a right to entry is one of the aims of treaties based on economic liberalism.[41] But, there will be greater control when there are more restrained attitudes to foreign investment, especially if some crisis, such as a financial crisis, results which is attributed to foreign investment. The tide of economic liberalism did not result in the dismantling of screening legislation in many states. They continue to be maintained. In Canada, for example, the Foreign Investment Review Act, introduced in response to the Gray Report which commented on the intrusion of large US multinationals into Canada, has not been dismantled. This was despite the later conclusion of the North American Free Trade Agreement which liberalised the flow of foreign investment and trade in the region including the United States, Canada and Mexico.

The functions of these administrative agencies change from time to time. Their basic functions are to take administrative measures both to facilitate as well as to control foreign investment. Such roles are carried out in almost all states to varying degrees. Even where it is not carried out at the entry stage, there would be various administrative procedures involved such as environmental licences and planning permissions, which the foreign investor has to secure before he can commence his investment project. Such licences are administrative rights which the foreign investor acquires at either the entry or the post-entry stage. The treaties define all these administrative rights as constituting foreign investment. The justification for this is easy to understand.[42] If the government were to withdraw any of these administrative rights, the foreign investor will not be able to operate his foreign investment. His plant and machinery will remain his, and, to that extent, there has been no interference with his physical assets but they will be of no use to him for he cannot operate them without having the necessary administrative licences. Hence, from the point of view of the capital-exporting states, it is only logical that protection be given to these administrative rights which are indispensable to the purpose for which the foreign investor entered the host state. But, the inclusion of these administrative law rights within the definition of investments greatly restricts the right of the state to exercise regulatory control over the foreign

---

[41] NAFTA recognised a right of entry and establishment. The draft Multilateral Agreement on Investment of the OECD also sought to recognise such a right.

[42] Administrative lawyers refer to such rights created through licences as 'new property'. The licences are indispensable to the conduct of the regulated activity.

investment. It also enhances the possibility of interferences with the licences for regulatory reasons being regarded as taking of property. An issue that will arise is whether the withdrawal of a license for violation of the conditions attached to it is a regulatory measure which does not violate treaty or other norms. This issue will be dealt with when considering expropriation.

So far, the discussion has shown that, in defining the foreign investment which is to be given protection, the capital-exporting state adopts the obvious strategy of defining the foreign investment protected by the treaty to include three principal concerns. These are, first, to protect the physical property of the foreign investor; second, to extend protection to the intangible rights which are themselves to be regarded as property and to be protected as such; and, third, to include within foreign investment the administrative rights that are necessary for the operation of the investment project. The latter rights are granted by the state, as are intangible rights relating to most intellectual property. Technically, the state which gives can take back what it gives. But, the treaty has the effect of lifting out of the realm of domestic law the right that is given to the foreign investor and subjecting it to treaty protection so that the right cannot be withdrawn without engaging the responsibility of the state.[43] But, where the right that is given by the domestic law is subject to conditions created in that law, there cannot possibly be treaty violations where the right is withdrawn for violations of the conditions.

There has been a tendency to extend the meaning of investment in treaties. A variety of attempts have been made to test the limits to which the meaning could be extended. Arguments have been made that the costs associated with preparations for the making of the investment should be included in the definition of investment. In *Mihaly* v. *Sri Lanka*,[44] the strategy of litigation was based on the notion that the costs involved in tendering for a project and negotiating it should be considered as investment if the negotiations fail for improper reasons after an expectation as to their success has been created. There have also been efforts to argue that the legitimate expectations of the foreign investor constitute rights which can be protected through expansive interpretations of treaty provisions. If new rights are effectively created by treaties for foreign investors, the meaning of investments for the purpose of those treaties will be correspondingly enlarged. This meaning, however, will not be received into general law. In the *Ceskoslovenska Case* (1997),[45] the ICSID tribunal considered the question whether the failure to repay a loan, which the Slovak government had guaranteed, could be regarded as a foreign investment within the meaning of the ICSID Convention. The tribunal said that there was 'support for a liberal interpretation of the question whether a particular transaction constitutes a foreign investment'. It took the view that the language in the Preamble to the ICSID Convention permits 'an inference that an international transaction which contributes to cooperation designed to promote the economic development of a contracting state may be deemed to be an investment as that term is understood in the Convention'. This purposive view that any activity

---

[43] That treaties can do so is well recognised. In the areas of minority rights, treaties have often done this. Rights in immigration law can also be subjected to treaties.
[44] (2002) 17 *ICSID Rev* 21.   [45] *Československá Obchodní Banka* v. *Slovakia* (1999) 14 *ICSID Rev* 251.

that is considered to promote economic development should be considered an investment is again too expansive to receive acceptance. A loan may benefit economic development but it lacks the other essential criteria of foreign investment such as the entry of personnel into the state and the direct generation of profits as a result.[46] Such expansive views are the product of the dominance of economic liberalism and must be regarded as passing fashions that do not accord with legal prescriptions. Indeed, the schisms which have developed within investment arbitration flow from the divisions between arbitrators who adopt neoliberal views and those who show a fidelity to the principle that undue expansion of the base on which parties submitted to arbitration is not warranted. Financial transactions are commercial transactions and are settled through mechanisms provided by domestic law. It was not in the contemplation of states that the treaties on foreign investment should affect such transactions. It is not within the function of tribunals to read into treaties meanings that extend concepts beyond what sovereign states had intended so as to enlarge their own roles. To do so over-zealously would invite non-compliance and consequent injury to the system that has been built up. The legitimacy of foreign investment arbitration is increasingly questioned as a result of the expansive interpretation of the provisions of investment treaties.

Another case in which an expansive interpretation was taken was *Fedax NV* v. *Venezuela*.[47] In this case, there was an assignment of promissory notes. The respondent state, Venezuela, argued that the assignment did not amount to 'a direct foreign investment involving a long-term transfer of financial resources-capital flow from one country to another'. The claimant had in fact acquired its interest in the promissory notes by way of an endorsement of the notes by a separate company with which Venezuela had made a contract. The tribunal dealt with academic views on the subject and held that they all supported 'a broad approach to the interpretation' of the term 'foreign investment' in the ICSID Convention.

Some academic writers have also formulated wide definitions of the term 'foreign investment'. Thus, Schreuer, after stating that the types of foreign investment have undergone changes, observed that 'the precise legal forms in which these operations are cast are less important than the general economic circumstances under which they are undertaken'.[48] This is again a policy-oriented approach which invites the ICSID tribunal to broaden the meaning of the term 'foreign investment' beyond what the parties may have had in mind. It is clear that an opportunity for making new law by broadening the scope of foreign investment is being created by the *dicta* of the ICSID tribunals and in the academic literature. This enables the broadening of the jurisdiction of the tribunal beyond what may have been intended by the parties to the investment treaty. It is a trend that was a sign of a period in which neo-liberal views on foreign investment supported the broadening of the jurisdiction of the arbitral tribunals as well as substantive provisions of treaties through expansive

---

[46] Loans are traditionally protected through other techniques. Because of the immense bargaining power of the lender, he will be able to secure dispute resolution before the courts of his country and ensure that there is enforcement against the assets of the borrower in his own state. The need for the protection of loans as investments has seldom arisen.

[47] (1998) 37 *ILM* 1378.   [48] C. Schreuer, *The ICSID Convention: A Commentary* (2nd edn, 2009).

interpretations. This is not a sound view as it will provoke obvious reactions from the states. A more cautious approach to treaty interpretation is necessary and is visible in some of the more recent awards.

Foreign investment attracts the greater attention of international law for the simple reason that it involves the movement of persons and property from one state to another and such movements have the potential for conflict between two states. It involves the securing of competitive advantages over local entrepreneurs both within the market as well as from the state authorities. The resulting integration of the foreign investor into the host economy makes his involvement in the internal economic and political affairs of the host state inevitable.[49] Conflict is inherent in such situations. Disputes that arise between parties to international sales and financial transactions are largely settled through domestic courts or through international commercial arbitration. The intervention of the machinery of international law may become necessary for the settlement of disputes arising from foreign investment. Because movement of persons is involved, it is possible to link the protection of foreign investment to the already existing norms on the diplomatic protection of aliens. Historically, this area of the law has been built up as a part of the area of the diplomatic protection of citizens abroad and of state responsibility for injuries to aliens.[50] Since the function of diplomatic missions was the protection of nationals living in the states to which the missions were assigned, the protection of the property of these nationals also became a concern of such missions.[51] The right of diplomatic missions to intercede on behalf of the property rights of their nationals came to be asserted in the diplomatic practice of capital-exporting states. Since this right of protection of the alien can be extended to the protection of foreign investment, it was a logical step to argue that this right could be utilised to protect the investments made by aliens. The roots of international law on foreign investment lie in the effort to extend diplomatic protection to the assets of the alien. The extension of the right was contested from the time it was asserted on the ground that it leads to unwarranted interference in the domestic affairs of the host state. Foreign investment is an essentially intrusive process which takes place entirely within the territory of a host state. To be able to lift that process out of the domestic sphere and subject it to international norms requires a nice balancing of international interests in the protection of the investment and the interests of the host state in regulating the process having its own benefits in mind. That is essentially what the international law on foreign investment is about. The definition of foreign investment must be rooted in this historical sense and not be extended beyond the meaning attributed to it in state practice and the precise words used in the treaties.

---

[49] R. Gilpin, *The Political Economy of International Relations* (1987), p. 33.

[50] For early works on the area, see E. M. Borchard, *The Diplomatic Protection of Citizens Abroad* (1915); F. Dunn, *The Protection of Nationals* (1932); A. V. Freeman, *The International Responsibility of States for Denial of Justice* (1938); C. F. Amerasinghe, *State Responsibility for Injuries to Aliens* (1967); and R. B. Lillich (ed.), *International Law of Responsibility for Injuries to Aliens* (1983). For a recent work on diplomatic protection, see C. F. Amerasinghe, *Diplomatic Protection* (2008). The topic is currently being studied by the International Law Commission.

[51] L. T. Lee, *Consular Law and Practice* (1991), p. 124.

2. The history of the international law on foreign investment

2.1 The colonial period

The history of foreign investment in Europe can be traced to early times. There is no doubt that such investment existed in Asia, the Middle East, Africa and other parts of the world.[52] Early European institutional writings on the treatment of aliens by their host states set the stage for later controversies in the area of foreign investment law. One view was that aliens should be given equal treatment with the nationals. Vitoria suggested that, because trading was an expression of the feeling of community that is inherent in man, the alien trader must be given equality with the national.[53] This view would have justified trade and investment as natural rights. The alternative view required that aliens be treated in accordance with some external standard, which was higher than the national standard.[54] The latter view was motivated by the concern that the standards of treatment provided to nationals in a host state may be low and therefore unacceptable. Both views were premised on the idea that the law should be designed to further the free movement of trade and investments across state boundaries. They were intended to serve the interests of states which had the ability to expand their overseas trade. The espousal of these views, and more famously of the freedom of the seas, by Grotius is seen by some historians as enabling the entry of European powers into Asia and Africa.[55] In the context of modern times, the question whether history is repeating itself or is at an end remains a relevant one. It is possible to argue that there is an effort to attempt to impose standards of investment protection preferred by the more powerful states on other states through the instrumentality of international law. This is a proposition that deserves further exploration.

In the eighteenth and nineteenth centuries, investment was largely made in the context of colonial expansion. Such investment did not need protection as the colonial legal systems were integrated with those of the imperial powers and the imperial system gave sufficient protection for the investments which went into the colonies.[56] In this context, the need for an international law on foreign investment was minimal.[57] Within the imperial system, the protection of investments flowing from the imperial state was ensured by the imperial

---

[52] Each of these systems had laws which governed trade and investment between nations. See C. H. Alexandrowicz, 'The Afro-Asian Nations and the Law of Nations' (1968) 123 *Hague Recueil* 117.

[53] Vitoria, *De Indis*, III, 5. The assumption was that this standard of national treatment was the highest he could expect and that he should not be discriminated against in the host state. The view was stated at the time of Spanish expansion in Latin America. Some writers have noted the duplicity that was inherent in this view. A. Anghie, 'Francisco Vitoria and the Colonial Origins of International Law' (1996) 5 *Social and Legal Studies* 256. Grotius also stated the freedom of trade and investment, but many believe that the sanctimonious efforts to promote such rights as natural rights hid the purpose of promoting Dutch colonial expansion in the Indies.

[54] Vattel was among the first writers to favour an external standard. Vattel, *The Law of Nations* (1758), II, 8, 104.

[55] M. van Ittersum, 'Profit and Principle: Hugo Grotius, Natural Rights Theories and the Rise of Dutch Power in the East Indies' (PhD thesis, Department of History, Harvard University, Cambridge, MA, 2002).

[56] One facet of this protection was to ensure that colonial legal systems were changed in order to accommodate European notions of individual rights of property and freedom of contract. See A. G. Hopkins, 'Property Rights and Empire Building' (1980) 40 *Journal of Economic History* 787, who pointed out that notions of collective ownership of property which were widely prevalent in the colonies were replaced by European notions of individual property.

[57] This explains the reason why the law first grew in the American context, where investment flows from the United States into Latin America had to be secured in a non-colonial context.

parliament and the imperial courts.[58] The power to lobby for such laws would have been enormous as it was the major trading companies which had first established colonial power in the states that were later integrated into the imperial system.[59] Since the imperial system ensured the protection of the flows of capital within the system, there was no need for the growth of a separate system of law for the protection of foreign investments. Where investments were made in areas which remain uncolonised, a blend of diplomacy and force ensured that these states did not interfere with foreign investors too adversely. In states which stood outside the imperial system, enclaves into which the jurisdiction of the state did not extend were established so that trade and investment could be facilitated. The system of 'extra-territoriality' was imposed by treaties resulting from the use of force. In these enclaves, the law that was applied to European traders was the law of their home states.[60]

Power was the final arbiter of foreign investment disputes in this early period. The use of force to settle investment disputes outside the colonial context was a frequent occurrence. The use of overt or covert force to coerce the settlement of disputes continued even after the Second World War and into the post-colonial period. There were spectacular instances of such uses of force.[61] But, doctrine had to be constructed to justify the use of force.[62] Capital-exporting countries, which operated outside the colonial context, were keen to devise some legal justification for pursuing the claims of their nationals and for the use of force if such use became necessary.

It was in the relations between the United States, still a fledgling power, and its Latin American neighbours that the need for the development of an international law relating to foreign investment played a role during the period prior to the Second World War.[63] These developments have dictated the course of the law for a considerable period of time. In the foreign investment relations between the United States and the Latin American states, one sees the clash between the idea that an alien investor should be confined to the remedies available in local law to the citizen and the idea that he must be accorded the treatment according to an external, international standard. It is an interesting aside to note that the United States in its formative years, as an importer of European capital, had experiences similar to those which developing countries presently have, and took stances not dissimilar to those developing countries now take.[64] But, after its emergence as a regional economic

---

[58] Thus, Britain relinquished control over the legislatures of the Empire settled by Anglo-Saxons in 1932 with the Statute of Westminster. The Asian and African colonies had to wait until after the end of the Second World War.

[59] The British and Dutch East India Companies played major roles in the establishment of their respective states' colonial rule.

[60] The system of extraterritoriality caused as much resentment as colonialism. In Asia, such enclaves existed in China, Thailand and Japan. The practice was also prevalent in the Middle East. See L. T. Lee, *Consular Law and Practice* (1991), pp.8–9.

[61] The incident involving *The Rose Mary* [1953] 1 WLR 246 is an example. The overthrowing of the governments of Mossadegh in Iran and Allende in Chile are the more obvious instances in recent history of forcible, though covert, interventions to assist foreign investment.

[62] As, some would argue, was the case with the invasion of Iraq in 2003. One of the first acts of the administration that was set up in Iraq after the invasion was to liberalise the entry of foreign investment, particularly into the oil sector. This sparked off speculation that oil was the reason for the intervention.

[63] A passionate statement of the exploitation of Latin America is contained in E. Galeano, *Open Veins of Latin America: Five Centuries of Pillage of a Continent* (originally published in Mexico in 1971; English translation published by Monthly Review Press, 1973).

[64] A. Chayes, T. Ehrlich and A. F. Lowenfeld, *International Legal Process* (1969), p. 851: 'When the United States was a less developed state, it had experiences with foreign investors not unlike those of today's developing societies.' Now that it is becoming one of the largest importers of capital, it is becoming conscious of the need to assert regulatory controls over foreign investments.

power, it insisted that its Latin American neighbours should treat foreign investors in accordance with international standards. The Latin American states vigorously pursued the debate by insisting, in a series of conventions and in their own laws and constitutions, that the provision of equal treatment to foreign investors satisfied the requirements of international law.[65] In many ways, this tussle between the United States and the Latin American states was to be replayed on a global scale in the post-colonial period. But, the law that was generated in the early period of this confrontation between the United States and the Latin American states had little to do with the taking of alien property to bring about economic reforms. It involved instead cases of attacks by mobs or political vendettas carried out for profit by juntas in power. The takings of foreign property that were involved in these early disputes are qualitatively different from the takings that resulted from economic reforms in later periods both in Latin America and elsewhere. The uniform application of principles to both types of interference with foreign investment is an unfortunate facet of the law which was introduced by early writers who failed to see the distinction between the two types of interference with foreign investment. The capricious grabbing of property for the personal advancement of elite groups is different from the taking of property by a government for the purpose of economic reform. But, early writings failed to emphasise this distinction. This initial failure continues to affect the law, which often fails to make a qualitative distinction between the two types of taking.

The Russian revolution and the spread of communism in Europe led to the taking of foreign property which was justified on the basis of economic philosophy. This initiated a debate among international lawyers as to the standards that should be satisfied to make such interference with foreign property acceptable in terms of international law. Many of the claims which arose as a result of these nationalisations were eventually settled by lump-sum agreements. They reflect a compromise between the two conflicting views as to the appropriateness of the standards that have to be met for valid interference with foreign property. Though important as indicating state practice, the use of lump-sum agreements did not shed any light on the resolution of the question as to the external standard that had to be satisfied for a valid interference with alien property rights.

2.2 The post-colonial period

It was only after the dissolution of empires that the need for a system of protection of foreign investment came to be felt by the erstwhile imperial powers, which now became the exporters of capital to the former colonies and elsewhere. It is convenient to divide the post-war developments into four periods in order to trace the developments which took place. The period immediately following the ending of colonialism witnessed hostility and

---

[65] The inspiration was provided by the writings of Carlos Calvo, an Argentinian foreign minister and jurist. In his *Le Droit International* (vol. 6, 5th edn, 1885), he said: 'Aliens who established themselves in a country are certainly entitled to the same rights of protection as nationals, but they cannot claim any greater measure of protection.' This statement, that aliens are entitled to national treatment only, was adopted in the First International Conference of American States (Washington, DC, 1889) and included in the Convention on the Rights and Duties of States adopted at the Seventh International Conference of American States (Montevideo, 1933).

antagonism towards foreign investment generated by nationalist fervour.[66] Such nationalism was itself a result of the anti-colonial movements which spread throughout the colonised
parts of the world. There was also a need felt on the part of the newly independent states to
recover control over vital sectors of their economies from foreign investors, largely nationals
of the former colonial powers. The result was a wave of nationalisations of foreign property.
These nationalisations resulted in intense debates as to what the international law on foreign
investment protection was, each opposing group of states contending for a different set of
norms in the area. In this period of political nationalism, there was more rhetoric generated
than law. But, in the course of the conflict, there was also an effort to articulate the
conflicting principles through the use of legal terminology. The capital-exporting nations
argued for an external international law standard protecting foreign investment, whereas the
newly independent nations argued for national control over the process of foreign investment, including the ending of foreign investment by nationalisation.

    These feelings of hostility have now been largely assuaged as the rearrangement of
the economies of the newly independent states has been completed. In the second period,
the developing states took a more selective and measured approach to foreign investment.
In the natural resources sector, particularly in the oil industry, dramatic changes took place as
a result of the collective action by the oil-producing nations which ended the dominance of
the industry by the major oil companies. These processes were accompanied by the
articulation of new principles by the capital-importing states. Though nationalism still
remains a threat to foreign investment,[67] it is unlikely that a new wave of nationalism will
sweep across a vast area of the globe as it did during the immediate post-war era. Yet,
individual states or regions may go through the same phenomenon, and the arguments which
were used during the period of nationalism will once more be dusted off and used.[68] If one
looks at the controversial areas of international law as involving a process of argument, then
the arguments used during one period are likely to be used when conditions similar to those
in that earlier period recur. The arguments which were formulated during this period of
nationalism to oppose the more established norms of the capital-exporting states will be used
again in appropriate circumstances. The package of norms which came to be called the 'New
International Economic Order' (NIEO) contained the norms favoured by the newly independent states.

    One major change in this period was the increasing acceptance that nationalisation in
pursuance of economic reform or reorganisation will not be considered unlawful in international law.[69] This change indicates the capacity of movements within international relations

---

[66] Much of it lingered on for some time. See, for example, C. Himavan, *The Foreign Investment Process in Indonesia* (1980), for
     the antagonism that the prolonged colonial struggle left in Indonesia.
[67] On the role of economic nationalism in international society, see J. Mayall, *Nationalism and International Society* (1994),
     pp. 70–110.
[68] As in the case of Iran, for example, where a once-thwarted nationalism took a more virulent form later, leading to the overthrow
     of the Shah and the expulsion of US businesses from the country. In both instances, the nationalisations which resulted gave rise
     to celebrated disputes. The first resulted in the *Anglo-Iranian Oil Company Case* [1952] *ICJ Reports* 93 and the second led to the
     creation of the Iran–US Claims Tribunal which considered the claims of US citizens who had suffered injury during the uprising.
[69] It is difficult to show that nationalisation in pursuance of economic reform was ever considered unlawful in international law. It is
     simply the case that, in earlier times, the law was discussed in the context of takings by states controlled by dictators for the

to displace prevailing norms with those which more readily reflect the trends within the international community.

The second period was a period of rationalisation undertaken by the state. Though, at the international level, the capital-importing states continued to maintain collective stances, requiring changes to the rules relating to the conduct of international economic relations (including foreign investment), they were also busy adjusting their own legal systems. These adjustments reflected more pragmatic approaches to issues of foreign investment. Thus, there was a divergence between the attitude a state may take at the international level through the articulation of the package of norms associated with the New International Economic Order and what it may take at the domestic level. While, at the international level, a state may join other states in taking a stance as to the international law position it supports, its domestic position may be different as it may seek to attract foreign investment as a strategy of economic development. It may also sign bilateral investment treaties that are at variance with its international position. This pragmatic position was adopted in response to the need to maintain the idea of sovereign control over foreign investment at the international level while at the same time being able to attract multinational corporations into the state through the creation of an appropriate climate favourable to foreign investments. This explains the variation that exists between the stances that states have taken at different levels of interaction in this field.[70]

Several factors have led to this inconsistency of attitudes at these different levels. At the domestic level, the debates as to the role of multinational corporations within the host economies of developing states led to the view that even small states could utilise the resources of multinational corporations to encourage economic development. The success of small states like Singapore and Hong Kong demonstrated this. Ideology and economic nationalism gave way to more pragmatic attitudes whereby states which formerly saw the need to assert the sovereignty of the state over foreign investment now sought to use that sovereignty in a more constructive fashion. This explains the apparent inconsistency in the stances of developing countries. While supporting normative changes at the global level that were protective of sovereign control over foreign investment, they were busy making bilateral investment treaties which strengthened the structure of foreign investment protection and foreign investment codes concerning tax and other incentives.[71]

The third period took pragmatism in this area even further. There had been significant shifts in the international economic scene. Communism had receded, and the existence of an ideologically based source of counter-norms that were hostile to notions of property on which foreign-investment protection is based had lost its force. Developing countries

---

benefit of the ruling coterie, and the rule extended to takings in pursuance of economic reforms. However, there are assertions of the legality of takings in pursuance of economic reforms in early literature. See J. Fischer Williams, 'International Law and the Property of Aliens' (1928) 9 *BYIL* 20, who denied the existence of any rule preventing nationalisation in international law. Also, see A. P. Fachiri, 'Expropriation and International Law' (1925) 6 *BYIL* 159, in accord. Both writers discussed the issue in the context of takings inspired by economic reforms.

[70] Sometimes, the wrong conclusions are made from this variance. It is an error to conclude that a state which has altered its domestic law on foreign investment to favour such investments or which has concluded a large number of bilateral investments has thereby given up its desire for sovereign control over foreign investments. Such an error is too often made in the literature on the subject. This point is discussed further in Chapter 3 below.

[71] S. Krasner, *Structural Conflict: Third World Against Global Liberalism* (1985).

progressively introduced more open policies on foreign investment. This was not only because the prevailing economic philosophy favoured the liberalisation of foreign investment regimes, but also because there was competition for the limited amount of foreign investment that could flow into these states.[72] The old distinction between capital-importing and capital-exporting countries also became blurred. Europe and the United States were now among the largest recipients of foreign investments. The free movement of investments within areas in North America and Europe, where liberal regimes of foreign investment flows had now been established through regional treaties, created tension among these states.[73] The inflexible stances to foreign investment that were taken in the past on the basis of ideological predispositions no longer had any force. There was, as a result, a willingness to compromise over what the law required.[74]

To a large extent, in the period after the ending of the Cold War, the events that occurred in the area of foreign investment were also furthered by the rise to dominance of neo-liberal policies promoted, largely by the World Bank and the International Monetary Fund. These required liberalisation of the entry of foreign investment, national treatment after entry, protection against violation of certain guaranteed standards of treatment, and secure means of dispute settlement. These policies needed to be implemented if states were to secure financial assistance from the international financial institutions. States also had to sign bilateral investment treaties providing guarantees for the protection of foreign investment. This neo-liberal package significantly influenced attitudes to investment law. It is possible to detect trends which show that arbitrators sought to interpret the texts of treaties in such a manner as to further neo-liberal prescriptions rather to than give effect to the intention of the parties to the treaty.

Another feature of the law in this third period was that developed states are now experiencing situations that were confined in the past to developing states. The United Kingdom and Canada revised their petroleum contracts by legislation on the ground that they had become disadvantageous to state interests.[75] The United States enacted legislation controlling the inflow of foreign investments which raised national security concerns. Under NAFTA, itself a product of neo-liberal tendencies, the provisions covering investment, which were originally intended to impose obligations of protection on Mexico, the developing country partner, soon became the basis for claims of violations of investment obligations against the United States and Canada. Disputes brought against the latter two states have shown the extent of the adverse use to which treaty principles could be put and

---

[72] Aid had dried up due to recession as well as policies unfavourable to the granting of aid. Banks did not provide loans to states after the petrodollar crisis, leading to a greater awareness of risks in sovereign lending. This left foreign investment as the only available means of external finance for economic development.

[73] The European Union is committed to internal flows of investment within its member states. In North America, Chapter 11 of NAFTA contains investment protection rules which parallel the US model bilateral investment treaty. Clashes will occur when the treaty rules are seen as eroding the sovereignty of the participating states to an unacceptable degree.

[74] There are two clear instances of such compromise positions in recent times. One is the American Law Institute's *Restatement on Foreign Relations Law*, which deviates from the previously accepted official position of the US State Department on the issue of compensation for nationalisation. The other is the World Bank's Guidelines on Foreign Investment (1992), which also depart from the traditional norm of full compensation in favour of the formula of appropriate compensation, but redefine appropriate compensation to mean usually market value compensation.

[75] P. D. Cameron, *Property Rights and Sovereign Rights: The Case of North Sea Oil* (1983).

the types of claims that inventive lawyers could make based on the texts of treaties, thus opening a Pandora's Box of problems for states (and lucrative opportunities for 'lost lawyers').[76] Canada has been concerned with decisions under the provisions of NAFTA which appeared to interfere with its power to regulate the environment.[77] The extent of the litigation brought under the investment provisions of NAFTA have subjected the two developed states to the same experience of having to defend their regulatory policies before foreign tribunals that developing countries had earlier been subjected to.[78] There is considerable opposition to the system within the United States and Canada to this restraint on the regulatory powers of the state.

Developed states have now become the largest recipients of foreign investments. As a result, they may come to question facets of the law that they themselves had helped to fashion as they increasingly become targets of litigation under regional and other treaties. Evidence of this is beginning to appear. The issue as to whether an interference on environmental grounds amounts to a 'taking' of property which has to be compensated has arisen in many cases concerning Canada, the United States and Mexico.[79] The modern treaties of both the United States and Canada contain strong statements permitting regulatory action taken to preserve the environment. Likewise, the issue as to whether a foreign investor should be given the same treatment as a state corporation in a mixed economy under the national treatment provisions of an investment treaty arose in a case involving Canada,[80] but the tribunal sidestepped a decision in the case.

In the 1990s, neo-liberal theory required a market-oriented approach to the problems of the world. Relevant aspects of the theory were the liberalisation of capital markets and the assurance of freedom of movement to multinational corporations. The rapid economic progress made by East Asian states fuelled notions of economic liberalism, and pressure to open up markets was directly applied. This was despite the fact that the East Asian economies progressed without themselves adopting neo-liberal policies, as state control was the dominant policy in all the economies of East Asia.[81] The World Trade Organization (WTO), which is committed to a philosophy of free trade, came into formal existence in 1995. It adopted instruments which affected investments.[82] The OECD embarked on an attempt to draft a Multilateral Agreement on Investment (MAI), though this was discontinued in 1998. But, the endeavour showed that, by the middle of the 1990s, the fervour for economic liberalism had reached a high point. Ideas such as rights of entry and

---

[76] The term 'lost lawyers' is borrowed from A. Kronman, *The Lost Lawyer: Failing Ideals of the Legal Profession* (1993).

[77] *Ethyl* v. *Canada* was based on the claim that an announcement that the production of a chemical additive manufactured by the US company would be banned caused a depreciation in the price of the shares of that company and hence amounted to a taking. Canada asked for a reconsideration of the takings provision in NAFTA after this case.

[78] For the impact of this on constitutionalism, see D. Schneiderman, *Constitutionalising Economic Globalisation: Investment Rules and Democracy's Promise* (2007).

[79] Apart from *Ethyl* v. *Canada*, other recent cases involving environmental issues are *Metalclad* v. *Mexico* (2000) 5 *ICSID Reports* 209; (2001) 40 *ILM* 55, *Methanex* v. *United States* (2003) and *Santa Elena* v. *Costa Rica* (2000) 39 *ILM* 317; (2002) 5 *ICSID Reports* 153. *Methanex* is still being litigated. *Ethyl* v. *Canada* was settled through the payment of a sum by Canada.

[80] *United Parcel Services* v. *Canada*.

[81] See, for example, J. Ohnesorge, 'Developing Development Theory: Law and Development Orthodoxies and the Northeast Asian Experience' (2007) 28 *University of Pennsylvania Journal of International Economic Law* 219.

[82] The extent to which they affect investments is surveyed in Chapter 6 below.

establishment dominated the discussion of investment principles and found their way into some treaties.[83] Treaties were concluded which contained the prior consent of states to the arbitration of any disputes which arise from foreign investments at the unilateral instance of the foreign investor. The ability of the foreign investor to invoke such arbitral procedures gave rise to an increase in the number of arbitration awards involving foreign investments, thus contributing further precedents to the law. This was a period that generally saw the triumph of liberal economic views of foreign investment and an attempt at the transposition of these views into international law.

The fourth period saw the prevailing fervour for economic neo-liberalism rolled back by the economic crises precipitated by the growth of liberalisation that induced not just the flow of funds into developing states in the good times but also a rapid outflow of those funds when things turn bad. The successive economic crises in Russia, Mexico, Asia and Argentina have led to much rethinking of the prescriptions of economic liberalism. The increasing gap between the rich and the poor on a global scale, and the resulting schism in the attitudes to globalisation, have also led to a review of the wisdom of unmitigated capitalism. This rethinking is also reflected in the law. The ability of capital to move around without restriction has been seen as the cause of much of these woes, and capital controls have been seen as a remedy by some states as well as by economists.[84] Coming at a time when the opposition to the MAI led to its withdrawal, the Asian economic crisis also contributed to a rethinking of the premises on which foreign investment law was based. The attitudes that will be adopted to foreign investment will go through cyclical changes. It could well be that the very favourable climate that existed for foreign investment in the last decade of the twentieth century may give way to a lukewarm attitude in the future, particularly if the promises of liberalisation do not materialise. Globalisation, which proved favourable to foreign investment, has also released forces of fundamentalism and ethnic identity which compete against further liberalisation of the economy. In ensuring that these forces are placated, the state may have to rein in the trend towards further liberalisation.

But, the institutions that were created on the basis of economic liberalism may not maintain their original vigour in the years to come. Despite the demonstrations against it, the World Trade Organization remains in place, but with a developing-country group that vociferously demands that attention be given to the problems of economic development. They demand the removal of measures adopted in the TRIPS Agreement that deny access by poorer peoples to medicines. They quarrel with the ideas behind the General Agreement on Trade in Services (GATS) that enable the total liberalisation of trade sectors. The Doha Development Round captures the discontent and the willingness of developing states to resist rules they feel lack fairness. These rules were forced through in times of neo-liberalism, but, with the rejection of neo-liberalism, are coming to be contested. At the Singapore Ministerial Meeting of the WTO, the issue of an investment code was mooted, but

---

[83] The US bilateral investment treaties recognise such rights but they are entered into subject to broad sectoral exceptions. NAFTA also contains provisions on pre-entry rights.

[84] Malaysia and Argentina resorted to capital controls in order to deal with their economic crises. George Soros, at whose door the Asian economic crisis was laid by the Malaysian Prime Minister, himself advocated the need for controls.

at Doha there was a requirement that the issue of investment should be considered in light of the development dimension. At the Cancun Ministerial Meeting, which was concluded in September 2003, the larger developing countries opposed consideration of investment unless there was agreement to expand the discussion to include not only the protection of investment but also the potential liability of multinational corporations for the harm they may cause to the host state. As a result, investment has been removed from the agenda of the WTO. Another episode during the height of the period of economic liberalism was the effort on the part of the OECD to draft the MAI. Though the MAI failed, there will be fresh efforts made to bring about multilateral and regional investment treaties which have the promotion of investments through protection as their aim. But, the effect of the attempt to agree the MAI was to marshal the forces opposed to the impact of economic liberalism and the expression of the principles behind it in the form of binding codes. Those opposed to the MAI argued that there was too great a concentration on the protection of foreign investment, thus favouring multinational corporations, without any concern for issues such as protection of the environment, the development of poorer states and the protection of human rights.

The forces hostile to liberalisation have already left their mark on the law. They will also gather strength in the future. The movement for corporate responsibility will not be confined to the domestic spheres but will seek to create a global system that recognises the liability of multinational corporations. There is an increasing awareness of the need to develop rules relating to the environmental liability of multinational corporations through international law. There will be greater concern with the impact of the activities of multinational corporations on human rights, economic development and the rights of indigenous communities in the host states. These trends will counterbalance the trend towards enhancement of the protection of the investment of multinational corporations and their ability to move capital and profits freely around the world. New interests have been brought into the existing conflict of interests.

These developments have shifted the focus onto new areas that had hitherto not been the focus of international investment law. Developments in the area of human rights gave an impetus to some of these changes. As domestic courts declared that they could exercise jurisdiction over crimes against humanity, there was a growing number of prosecutions brought against multinational corporations before the courts of the home states of the parent companies for the damage they caused to the environment or human rights in host states. In the United States, the Alien Tort Claims Act, an obscure statute enacted in 1876, gave jurisdiction to the US courts over any wrongs against public international law. The statute was the basis on which many actions against torture committed in various countries of the world were brought in the United States. An offshoot of such litigation was allegations of torture done in the course of the exploitation of natural resources or the construction of large projects by multinational corporations. There have been many instances of such litigation in which jurisdiction was assumed. So far, there have been no instances in which damages have been awarded. There are, however, many instances of settlement of the cases through the payment of monetary compensation to the affected claimants by multinational corporations. In addition, other common law jurisdictions are receptive to the idea of litigation concerning torts committed by multinational corporations outside the jurisdiction.

The most important of the changes in the modern period is the rise of the large developing states, Brazil, China and India. They are the homes of large multinational corporations. Brazil has stood outside the investment treaty system and is not a party to the ICSID Convention. It belies the neo-liberal theory that says that, unless states participate in such a system, investment flows will not take place. These three states also have large multinational corporations with the capacity to invest overseas. Already, there is visible evidence of companies from these states taking over large failing companies in the United States and Europe and becoming significant investors in both regions. The states in Europe and North America will increasingly become respondents in claims brought by these companies before arbitral tribunals.[85] It will be interesting to see the response of these erstwhile capital exporters when faced with legal claims based on the laws they themselves had created for the protection of their own investors. Lawyers in these countries will invent new defences to liability, or the states themselves may seek to withdraw from the system that they created. Withdrawal is a technique that the United States has previously used to express displeasure with international systems.[86]

Disparate forces will be at work within the law in this area. The forces of economic liberalism did have a nearly complete sway in the last decade of the twentieth century, but competing forces began to appear as a result of a succession of economic crises and a definite change in the global situation. The NGOs which have sectional interests will be powerful players exerting pressures towards the acceptance of their favoured solutions. Developing states may discover their previous solidarity, in this field at least, as they did in beating back the provisions of the WTO instruments that seemed unfavourable to their interests. Each of these opposing groups will support a different set of norms relating to investment protection. They will also differ on issues such as rights of access, types of treatment of investment and dispute resolution. The impact of the interplay of these forces on the international law on foreign investment is difficult to assess. These forces will always be extant within the international community, with ascendancy of one group of norms at one period and a decline at another. At each stage of this cycle, marks will be left on the law, because law is the instrument through which expression is given to the fundamental tenets of each group of ideas. These marks can never be wholly erased by either set of norms, which makes the study of this area challenging. The law that can be stated lacks clarity. To those who see law not as a set of static rules but as an evolving process, this situation should be taken as a normal phenomenon in the law.

[85] An Indian national has brought an ICSID claim against the UK. *Sanchetti* v. *UK* (for the facts, see the Court of Appeal judgment regarding a stay order, reported at [2008] EWCA Civ 1283). A Chinese national has a pending ICSID claim against Peru. *Tza Yap Shum* v. *Peru*, ICSID Case No. ARB/07/6 (Decision on Jurisdiction and Competence, 19 June 2009). There is a claim pending against Germany: *Vattenfall AB* v. *Germany* (request filed on 30 March 2009). The long lists of NAFTA cases against the United States and Canada are well known and can be found on several websites, including that of the US Trade Representative.
[86] The United States withdrew from systems it did not favour, or refused to participate. It has pursued a unilateralist policy in many fields. It did not subscribe to the International Criminal Court. It kept out of discussions of human rights.

3. An outline of the book

The purpose of Chapter 2 is to identify the factors which work to shape the law on foreign investment. The major events in the historical development of the subject are identified at greater length than explained in this introductory chapter. The nature of the multinational corporation and its counterpart, the state corporation, and the legal problems involved in the manner of their organisation are identified. The sources of international law which have been used to fashion the contending principles are described. It is shown that the sources in the construction of the contending sets of principles are weak sources of international law. What is passed off as custom by the different contending groups can hardly satisfy the stringent standards required by international law for graduating state practice into custom. There is an absence of multilateral treaties which have a direct bearing on the subject of foreign investments. Indeed, the recent unsuccessful efforts of the OECD in bringing about such an instrument demonstrate the difficulties inherent in such an attempt. There are many arbitral awards and opinions of jurists supporting one system of rules, and there is a series of General Assembly resolutions supporting the other. It will help in the understanding of the nature of the area to accept that both contending sets of principles are, at present, based on the weakest sources of a weak system of law. There is little to be achieved through the pretence that one set of norms has displaced the other. Both rely on weak sources of the law. Chapter 2 outlines the nature of the sources that have been used to construct the competing structures of the international law on investment.

Chapter 3 contains a study of the nature of the control that legislation in developing countries seeks to exert over foreign investment. The assertion of control over the process of foreign investment has been an aspect of the strategy of the capital-importing countries in seeking to contest the older norms on foreign investment protection. While contesting these norms at the international level, they also enacted legislation which exerts national control over the entry, establishment and operation of foreign investments. The aim of such legislation is to attract foreign investment into the state while ensuring that the investment is geared to the economic goals of the state and that the potential harmful effects on such goals are eliminated. There are three levels at which host states take stances. These stances may be at variance with each other but they are explicable on grounds other than inconsistency in attitudes. At the domestic level, states are inclined to enact legislation having their domestic goals in mind and in such a manner as to exploit fully the advantages of foreign investment and diminish the possible harmful effects. At the bilateral level, states make treaties, again often having particular objectives in mind. These objectives may be at variance with the stances they take at the multilateral level. At the multilateral level, developing states may have common objectives which they seek to pursue in order that change may be effected to international law at a global level. The charge of inconsistency merely fails to take into account the fact that the objectives at the three levels are induced by different considerations.

Chapter 4 deals with the controls that the home state of a multinational corporation may exercise over the corporation's activities abroad. Flowing from this control, the issue is addressed as to whether the home state has the duty to control abuses committed by the multinational corporations that affect the host state and its citizens. The extent to which home state measures could control the misdeeds of multinational corporations has increasingly attracted attention, particularly in relation to stances made by states and other actors in opposing multilateral agreements on investment.

Chapter 5 traces the development of the customary rules advanced by developed states which constrain the power of the host state and create rules which confer protection for foreign investments. This chapter is important, as it illustrates the system that had been advanced on the basis of an international minimum standard which creates responsibility in the host state. Such a minimum standard, and other standards of treatment, act as constraints on the power of the host state. This chapter bridges the two parts of the book, for it demonstrates how the rudimentary system of investment protection was supported. It thus serves as a prelude to the later chapters discussing liability arising from failure to conform to treatment standards and from expropriation.

Chapter 5 contains an analysis of the trends that can be seen in these bilateral investment treaties. The rapid increase in the number of these treaties has been a phenomenon of the modern law. Many claims are made that they constitute customary international law. Such claims are based on superficial analyses. It is evident that, though the outer shells of these treaties are similar, their contents vary markedly. They strike internal balances between notions of protection and notions of sovereignty in different ways. The chapter contains a study of the content of these treaties and an analysis of their impact on the law.

Chapter 6 contains a survey of the efforts made by international institutions to bring about uniform norms in the area. There have been many guidelines and draft codes generated by these organisations. None of them has been successful. The most recent of them has been the draft Multilateral Agreement on Investment (MAI) prepared by the OECD. The inability to bring about a multilateral code indicates the existence of a division of views among developing states and developed states. The failure of the MAI illustrates that even developed states may disagree on certain aspects of the law on foreign investment. The protests generated by the MAI indicates the extent to which the international law on foreign investment has become embroiled in the politics of globalisation. Yet, in the recent past, there have been successes with regional agreements on investments. They have been able to set up viable dispute-settlement processes which give effect to the rules contained in these agreements. Also, the project to bring about a multilateral agreement has been handed over to the World Trade Organization, where it has met with resistance from developing countries. Yet, it has to be recognised that, in certain areas such as technology and services, there has been progress made in the context of the WTO and there is a possibility that the impact of the WTO on the international law of investment will be greater in the future. Its present and future impact therefore has to be assessed, and this is an additional task this chapter attempts.

The final chapters deal with issues of dispute settlement and liability. Such liability flows from breaches of treaty and other obligations. Chapter 7 deals with breaches of contractual obligations. The proliferation of investment-treaty-based arbitration has diverted attention away from this important area which was the original basis of investment law, in the context of which much theory was formulated. It captures the policy clashes that dominate all areas of investment law. It continues to be important, as many arbitrations are still conducted by both ICSID and non-ICSID tribunals on the basis of contracts alone. The significance of this type of arbitration to the law must not be lost sight of through an over-concentration on treaty-based arbitration. The latter captures the attention of the practitioner but at the cost of history and theory which are rooted in contract-based arbitration. The two interact in many ways.[87] If international law is being fragmented, then there is further fragmentation of the area of international investment law where the tendency is to treat the waxing phenomenon of treaty-based arbitration as a distinct area. This is unsound in the context of the criticism that awards are being made purely on commercial grounds without an understanding of the principles of international law or public law which should be the underlying factors for an appreciation of the problems in the area.

Chapter 8 commences consideration of the settlement of disputes that arise from allegations of treaty violations. It deals with the jurisdictional issues, and the later chapters deal with the substantive law. As the number of arbitrations commenced on the basis of treaty violations increases, states are increasingly contesting the jurisdiction of arbitral tribunals. The tenacity with which states have contested jurisdiction in many cases indicate that they did not expect that the treaty provisions relating to jurisdiction would be used in the manner in which they are being used. As a result, many jurisdictional objections on grounds that may not have been thought of earlier are being used in order to challenge jurisdiction. It is a phenomenon that may also indicate some negative features of treaty-based investment arbitration that are becoming apparent. These trends are analysed in this chapter.

Chapter 9 deals with the breach of treatment standards. The breach of treatment standards has become an important cause of action in recent times, as a result of NAFTA litigation. Developed countries seldom expropriate property. The opportunity to level charges of violations of treatment standards particularly in the context of the use of regulatory powers, remains, however. The NAFTA litigation against Canada and the United States is a novel phenomenon, in that developed states have now become the targets of a law that they themselves helped to create. The use of treatment standards in such litigation opens up new possibilities in the area. There has been a shift in the area, discernible in the more recent awards, to the 'fair and equitable' standard of treatment. There has been creative use of this standard, and new rules are being formulated by tribunals on the basis of this standard. This has raised issues as to the legitimacy of the techniques used by tribunals.

Chapter 10 deals with the issue of taking of property. The central feature of expropriation had earlier been the debate as to the standard of compensation. This has been displaced in modern times by the issue of what amounts to a taking. Again, there have been fluctuations in the fortunes of neo-liberal attempts at expansion, which considered any depreciation in the value of property to be expropriation, to a reaction that has forced the admission of an exception that recognises that the exercise of regulatory powers is not expropriation under treaty. These different trends are explored in Chapter 10.

---

[87] The umbrella clause and the issue of the exclusivity of the arbitration clause in the contract are but two instances.

Chapter 11 deals with the controversial question as to the nature of compensation for the expropriation of foreign property. This again is a theoretical dispute in international law. Its significance may have passed, yet it affected much of the thinking in the development of the law. For this reason, the chapter is kept virtually intact from the previous edition, and the old debate on the subject continues to be relevant. The new developments are taken into account. Inflexible stances have been taken in the past on this issue. There is a general acceptance that compensation must be paid. The ideological position that no compensation needs to be paid has lost support. The quantum of compensation still remains subject to dispute. The Hull standard of 'full' compensation seems to have gained support, particularly in bilateral investment treaties, but the alternative standard of 'appropriate' compensation still retains vigour. There has been an effort to transfer the emphasis onto valuation standards, but these efforts have not diminished the fact that the issue of the standard of compensation has to be settled first.

The final Chapter deals with the growth of defences to liability. As in the case of resistance to jurisdiction, states are reacting to the expansionary views taken by tribunals either by creating defences in the newer treaties they make or by pleading defences either on the basis of the interpretation of the text of the treaty or on the basis of customary international law. This chapter surveys a growing and innovative phenomenon that is a response to the increase in the number of investment arbitrations.

The issue of compensation for expropriation is of historical value as most litigation takes place on the basis of treaties which specify the standard of compensation. Yet, the debate exposes the extent of the divisions that existed on this subject, and provides an interesting clash in international law between the different groups of states. For that reason and because there are still cases being brought on the basis of customary law, the area will continue to be of importance.

The book seeks to identify the major features of an international law on foreign investment. It demonstrates that such a branch of international law is in the process of development and can be isolated for separate study. The fact that many of the areas in it are replete with controversies is not a reason against its separate treatment. The major areas of international law, such as the law on the use of force, are similarly controversial. But, that has not impeded its treatment as a distinct branch of international law. The time is now ripe for the isolation and separate development of this branch of international law. The separate treatment of controversial areas, such as that of foreign investment, will help in the identification of the nature of disputes in this area and lead to the formulation of acceptable solutions. This book is a contribution to the development of this important area of international law.

2

The shaping factors

All law involves a resolution of conflicting interests. But, unlike other areas of law, international law lacks a centralised authority which could resolve conflicts of interest. Whereas in a domestic system there are decision-making authorities which can resolve such conflicts, in international law the absence of such an authority means that conflicts will be protracted. This situation will exist until some adjustment of the conflict is made in the course of time, either through negotiated settlements resulting in treaties, or through practices resulting in custom. The adjustment will embody principles which receive a measure of acceptance by states. All these involve consensual processes. International law embodies a long series of adjustments made in response to conflicts.[1] As the process of adjustment never ends, the law continually remains in a state of flux.

The international law on foreign investment is an example of this process of adjustment. Its lack of clarity in many areas results from the intensity of conflict of divergent interests. Essentially, the conflict relates to the nature of the control that could be exercised over the foreign investment. Host states argue for national control subject to a minimum of external constraints, whereas capital-exporting states argue for greater constraints on national control in the hope of ensuring the protection of foreign investment.[2] Various other actors such as non-governmental organisations (NGOs) with a diversity of interests have come onto the scene, thus adding further to the existing uncertainty. Elucidation of the nature of the conflicts in the different areas of this field of law will help in understanding the issues involved. The historical factors which shaped the law were set out briefly in the introductory chapter, and the changes that have taken place in the framework within which foreign investments are made were also discussed there. This chapter elaborates further the legal context in which foreign investment operates.

---

[1] Part of this sentence is taken from Phillip Jessup, *The Use of International Law* (1959), p. 12. He identified some of the conflicts which have shaped international law. At pp. 17–20, Judge Jessup refers to the conflicts involved in the area of foreign investment, pointing out that there was no 'balanced bargaining power', in this area, but that 'Latin American leadership contributed to the balancing Calvo doctrine which has been slowly making its way toward general acceptance'. An absence of a balance in power has been a constant factor in the area of this law. The collective power of the capital-exporting states, multinational corporations, the global law firms and the academic establishment in international law supports traditional norms of investment protection. They are matched only by developing states, non-governmental organisations and a few academics without sufficient resources to counterbalance the power of those supporting investment protection.

[2] The external controls which developed states seek to impose are manifested in the efforts to create multilateral instruments on investments.

The chapter then goes on to consider the risks to foreign investment. The changes in the international political context in which foreign investment takes place have also increased the risks to foreign investment. In the colonial period, risks to foreign investments were virtually non-existent. But, the ending of colonialism and the consequent emergence of economic nationalism have brought about greater risks to the whole process. The nature of these risks has to be understood, for much of the law in this area is aimed at the reduction of the risks that arise to foreign investment. In the past, it was thought that risks to foreign investment arose only in developing states and socialist states. The experience of disputes under NAFTA belies this belief.[3] It demonstrates that governments of both developed and developing countries take measures which are protective of their own economic interests and take refuge in sovereignty-centred arguments in order to justify them.[4]

It is very evident that, contrary to the assertion of some writers,[5] sovereignty is very much an issue and that the stances taken in recent arbitral disputes by developed states are assertive of rights flowing from sovereignty to the same extent as reflected in the views of developing states. The belief that new rules of global governance have eliminated sovereignty-related principles in this area is not quite correct. No such rule seems to have emerged, and efforts at creating them will witness a reversal. With the global financial crisis taking hold in 2008, states will assume greater regulatory functions which would require assertions of sovereignty. Thus, sovereignty is a concept that sees ebbs and flows according to circumstances. The construction of a theory of sovereignty that will stand firm for all time is a chimerical exercise.

The success of legal solutions in countering the risk of government interference will depend on the extent to which the aim of reduction of risks to foreign investment is achieved. After dealing with the nature of the risks, this chapter discusses the major actors in the foreign investment scene and the legal problems which arise in connection with dealing with each of them. Some of the complexities which arise come about because of the structure of the multinational corporations which make the investments. The nature of state corporations in developing countries, with which multinational corporations have often had to cooperate in making investments in developing countries, adds to the problems. Despite the movement towards privatisation, state corporations still exist and play a dominant role in many industrial sectors of different states. The reversal of privatisation will enhance the role they play in the future. The description of the roles these different entities play in the making of investments is necessary for the understanding of the law in the area. A section of this chapter identifies the problems which the different legal characteristics of these actors create. The role of new actors such as NGOs is also set out. The final part of the chapter deals with the sources of the international law of foreign investment.

---

[3] NAFTA cases, which can involve only the three state parties, Canada, Mexico and the United States, have increased in number in recent times. Many of the cases involve the United States and Canada as respondents.
[4] In the case of the United States, see *Methanex* v. *United States* (2005) 44 *ILM* 1345. The pleadings are available at www.naftaclaims.com.
[5] In the area of international trade, the view that sovereignty is in abeyance is often articulated. See J. H. Jackson, *Sovereignty, the WTO and the Changing Fundamentals of International Law* (2006).

In effect, the chapter is intended to emphasise the major changes that have taken place in the present political economy of foreign investment. The shift in emphasis in the sources of law is a consequence of these changes. A clear identification of these changes is a necessary preliminary to the study of the subject. The first is the freeing of the major part of the world from colonialism and the impact this change had on the legal thinking related to the creation of new structures for foreign investment as well as for the protection of such foreign investment. Unlike in the past, where power alone was the arbiter, it became necessary to construct legal methods for the protection of such investments. The second is the nature of the actors on the scene. The growth of multinational corporations and the emergence of state corporations have been factors with which the law has had to contend. The third factor is the democratisation of the process of law-making within the international community. The Eurocentric nature of international law has been subjected to challenge in the field of international economic relations through an attempt to fashion law by means other than the traditional source of law-making, sometimes with success.[6] The subject also lends itself to the analysis of how neo-liberalism and globalisation have shaped the law, particularly in the period since the writing of the first edition. In this period, there was an evident, though short-lived, triumph of neo-liberalism which emphasised the free movement of capital and investments and consequently stricter standards of investment protection and resolution of investment disputes. These immediately came to be reflected in the law, changing the balance in favour of the views held by capital-exporting countries. There was a profusion of bilateral treaties incorporating high standards of investment protection. There was also an increase in the number of arbitration disputes involving foreign investment. Many of them contained extensions of the law protective of the interests of multinational corporations. However, a multilateral instrument on investment is yet to be agreed. The effort to create competence in the WTO over investment failed. With the increasing disenchantment caused by successive economic crises, there is a restoration of the balance as neo-liberalism comes to be countered by opposing ideas. With the prevailing global economic crisis, widely attributed to neo-liberal ideas, there will be further erosions in the vigour of neo-liberalism. The retreat of neo-liberalism, the shift of economic power to new players like China, India and Brazil and the impact of NGOs promoting interests such as the environment and human rights in the area will bring about changes. The global economic crisis of 2008 will also bring new actors, such as sovereign wealth funds, into the picture. Developed states will be intent on controlling their investments, thereby dismantling norms of liberalisation they had built up in the preceding years. As reverse flows of investments from some erstwhile developing countries to the developed countries take place and as developed countries become the largest recipients of foreign investment, there may not be the same desire for norms of investment protection and promotion the developed countries themselves had built in the past. The aim of this chapter is to survey the nature of these changes as a preliminary to an exploration of the legal norms relating to foreign investment in the succeeding chapters.

[6] Whether the powerless majority can meaningfully make law without the consent of the powerful is a thorny issue. Some would support the democratic, quantitative principle as the best method of law-making.

1. The historical setting

It is necessary to elaborate on some of the historical information provided in the introductory chapter so that the evolution of the law in this area may be better understood. Prior to the Second World War, foreign direct investment did not face any risks except in states which were not under colonial rule. But, many of these latter, nominally independent states were either protectorates, such as the states of the Middle East, or were subject to some form of dominance so that European investments had sufficient protection.[7] Protection of foreign investment in these areas was based on military power. Power ensured that foreign investment, usually flowing from the metropolitan power into its colonies, was adequately protected. Gun-boat diplomacy was sufficient to ensure that both trade and investment were protected.

1.1 State responsibility for injuries to aliens

The system of state responsibility for injuries to aliens and their property was therefore first established in the part of the world where no such colonial relationship existed, but power, nevertheless, played a determining role.[8] The genesis of many of the rules of state responsibility is to be found in the relationship between the United States and Latin America. The early rules on diplomatic protection were devised in the context of injuries suffered by US citizens in Latin American states. The struggle again reflected the binary nature of the norms in this area. The United States sought to externalise the norms that governed aliens and their property. It argued for an international minimum standard in accordance with which the foreigner should be treated. It built into the international minimum standard, norms that were favourable to the foreign investor and were, to a large extent, based on US domestic law standards.[9]

The foreign investor was entitled to compensation according to an external standard, which came to be described in the hallowed formula used by Cordell Hull that compensation should be 'prompt, adequate and effective'.[10] The foreign investor was entitled to dispute resolution before an overseas tribunal, if the remedies provided by the host state proved inadequate. The Latin American states countered this stance by focusing on the fact that

---

[7] Most of these areas were subject to capitulation treaties, which imposed a system of extraterritoriality on them. The system insulated the foreigners living and trading in these areas from the application of the local laws and subjected them instead to the laws of their home states. This system prevailed in China and Thailand and in many areas of the Middle East.

[8] E. M. Borchard, *The Diplomatic Protection of Citizens Abroad* (1915); F. S. Dunn, *The Protection of Foreign Nationals* (1932); C. F. Amerasinghe, *State Responsibility for Injuries to Aliens* (1967); and M. Sornarajah, *The Pursuit of Nationalized Property* (1986).

[9] It is a fact of history that, in every age, a hegemonic power seeks to externalise the key concepts of its own law so as to enable it to maintain its power. In a regional context, the United States had attempted to create such external standards of investment protection in its relations with Latin America. For a powerful Latin American view on US economic control of the region, see E. Galeano, *Open Veins of Latin America: Five Centuries of Pillage of a Continent* (originally published in Mexico in 1971; English translation published by Monthly Review Press, 1973).

[10] Cordell Hull, who was Secretary of State during the Mexican expropriations of 1938, stated this to be the standard in a letter to his Mexican counterpart. The letter stated: '[U]nder every rule of law and equity, no government is entitled to expropriate private property, for whatever purpose, without provision for prompt, adequate and effective payment thereof.' Hackworth, *Digest of International Law*, p. 657. Ever since, the standard has been espoused by the United States and has been referred to as the Hull doctrine of compensation.

the foreign investor entered the host state voluntarily, assuming the risks of the investment there. On this basis, they argued that the foreign investor, like any other person in the state including their own citizens, was entitled only to a national standard of treatment provided to both foreigner and citizen alike by the local laws. Enunciated in the form of the Calvo doctrine, this came to be generally accepted by the Latin American states.[11] Later, both stances were to be internationalised.[12] The European states, once they gave up their colonies, had to structure a system of investment protection, and they found the existing American system a convenient one to adopt.[13] The developing states of Africa and Asia, once independent, espoused the Calvo doctrine. Its universalisation was sought to be accomplished by instruments associated with the New International Economic Order which the developing states sponsored in the General Assembly of the United Nations. At the inter-state level, diplomatic protection and state responsibility became the bases on which investment protection was accomplished. But, there was no guarantee of the success of such a method of protection. For one thing, a state may refuse to espouse a claim because it may consider a foreign investment claim expendable in the pursuit of other foreign policy objectives. There was also no guarantee of success in that it was unclear as to what the international law was, in view of the conflict of norms. There was a general reluctance to take issues of foreign investment law to the International Court of Justice. The uncertainty in the law that may be exposed by a ruling by the Court may be a reason not to force an authoritative pronouncement. The developed states may prefer to maintain at least the mirage that their set of norms constituted international law.[14]

State responsibility in this area, though feasible, remains a solution of last resort. It is for this reason that the devising of remedies that multinational corporations can themselves resort to has played a more important role. This is an instance in which private power has played the dominant role in shaping international norms for quite some time. The use of international law by private corporations flies in the face of traditional theory but has nevertheless gone largely unnoticed. No doubt, the more successful techniques of protection have been created through such private power acting in tandem with state power, but the ideas that have driven the field were nevertheless initiated through largely private means. The area of international foreign investment law effectively belies the old notion that only states are effective arbiters of the content of international law. Private power, in the form of both multinational corporations and, more recently, NGOs, always has a significant role in the shaping of this area of international law.[15] Positivism provided a

---

[11] The doctrine is associated with Carlos Calvo, an eminent Latin American jurist and diplomat.

[12] See, for example, Article 2(2)(c) of the Charter of Economic Rights and Duties of States.

[13] There is a paucity of state practice regarding investment protection. The state responsibility cases involved European states, but the heavy influence of US practice and US writings on the subject in the early twentieth century is evident.

[14] The three cases in which the ICJ has dealt with disputes involving foreign investment are the *Barcelona Traction Case* [1970] *ICJ Reports* 1; the *ELSI Case* [1989] *ICJ Reports* 15; the *Diallo Case*, ICJ (Judgment, 24 May 2007). See further M. Sornarajah, *The Settlement of Investment Disputes* (2000).

[15] There are studies of the role of private actors in international relations. See L. Sklair, *The Transnational Capitalist Class* (2001). For the role of non-governmental organisations, see R. O'Brien, *Contesting Global Governance* (2000). In international relations, the work of Claire Cutler has traced the role of private power in the making of international norms. See C. Cutler, *Private Power and Global Authority* (2003); Susan Sell has detailed the role of the pharmaceutical companies in bringing about TRIPS. S. Sell, *Private Power, Public Law* (2003).

convenient cloak to hide this fact by insisting that only states acted in the international sphere.[16] The accommodation of such private power in the theory of international law is a challenge that awaits the international lawyer. It will probably not be taken up because there is little incentive to remove the cloak and reveal the extent to which international law is an instrument of both private and public power. The manner of the evolution of the law through such power can now be stated. It developed largely in the different sectors in which investments were traditionally made. The oil sector played the dominant role.

1.1.1 The natural resources sector

Foreign investment in natural resources was necessary to ensure the raw materials for production in the Western states. The cycle of trade during the colonial period was to transfer resources from the colonies to the metropolitan states so that they could be converted into manufactured products or used to fuel industries in these states. The early oil companies and companies which operated in the other natural resources sectors used concession agreements to tie up production in large areas of land for considerable periods of time.[17] This picture which formed in the oil industry was reproduced in other mineral industries.[18] The similarity of the pattern around the world was another feature of this process. International business transactions up to modern times have features that are similar, facilitating the formulation of a seemingly uniform law around the world.[19] The role of imitation in this process is strong. Concession agreements often effected transfers of sovereign powers over vast tracts of land to foreign corporations for long periods of time, in return for the payment of royalties calculated on the quantity of oil produced at a fixed rate.[20] The system was kept in place by an elaborate web of power exerted by the home state and a concerted dominance exerted within the international system itself by the dominant powers.[21]

---

[16] It is evident that many of the early doctrines were advocated to enhance the power of the old colonial companies like the Dutch East India Company. The freedom of the high seas attributed to Grotius was, according to historians, not a neutral doctrine, but a doctrine articulated to favour the privateers employed by the Dutch East India Company. The tract on *mare liberum* was originally written by Grotius to justify the sinking of the Portuguese vessel, *Santa Catarina*, off the coast of Malacca, by Dutch privateers.

[17] The evolution and the politics of the oil industry are well described in D. Yergin, *The Prize: The Epic Quest for Oil, Money, and Power* (1991).

[18] Mining was controlled through legislation which ensured that the state had ownership interests in the operation. In Indonesia, mining was regulated by the Mining Law, which made the contract of works in which the government participated the sole method of operation. For Australian law from an investment perspective, see A. Fitzgerald, *Mining Contracts* (2000).

[19] This phenomenon becomes the basis for the arguments relating to a *lex mercatoria*. The wide prevalence of the joint-venture form in foreign investment is an example in modern times. See M. Sornarajah, *The Law of International Joint Ventures* (1992). The existence of a common form facilitates the formation of what is referred to as *lex mercatoria*, the claim to the existence of a universally valid international business law, again created through entirely private processes. Its bases are to be found in the writings of scholars and in arbitral awards rather than in the normal sources of international law such as treaties harmonising the law. The *lex mercatoria* is, in the conception of some writers, the law that applies to foreign investment contracts. During periods of globalisation, contract forms used within industries are imitated and uniform laws grow up in relation to them, facilitating the idea of a transnational law. As arbitral awards come to be made interpreting contractual terms and writings based on them grow, the law becomes concrete.

[20] The *Aminoil* arbitration indicates the classic situation of a petroleum agreement. The concession, which was made in 1948, was to last for sixty years. The royalty was fixed at two shillings and six pence per barrel of oil. These agreements are described in H. Cattan, *The Law of Oil Concessions in the Middle East and North Africa* (1967); A. Z. El Chiati, 'Protection of Investments in the Context of Petroleum Agreements' (1987) 204 *Hague Recueil* 9; Kamal Hossain, *Law and Policy in Petroleum Development* (1979); and A. S. El Kosheri and T. Riad, 'The Law Governing a New Generation of Petroleum Agreements' (1986) *ICSID Rev* 259.

[21] Thus, the Iranian revolution in 1952 which affected the oil interests of the major British and US companies was ended through the collective exercise of power by Britain and the United States. The rule of Mossadegh was ended, and the rule of the monarchy was restored. In the context of what happened two decades later, when the Shah was overthrown and an Islamic form of

Some of these concession agreements have been subjected to legal analysis as they were subjects of international arbitrations. Thus, in *Aminoil* v. *Kuwait*,[22] the concession agreement which was involved was originally entered into between the Sheik of Kuwait, at a time when Kuwait was a protectorate of the United Kingdom, and a US oil company. The royalty which was to be paid was two shillings and six pence for every barrel of oil. The arrangement was to last for sixty years. The terms of the contract were not to be changed without the consent of both parties. Events showed that the agreement was not able to withstand the political and economic changes which took place within the industry. The agreement was renegotiated on two occasions. The price of oil sky-rocketed during the oil crisis of the 1970s. But, the oil company insisted on paying the same sum of two shillings and six pence per barrel that had been originally agreed upon in the concession agreement. The windfall profits were not to due any inherent merit on the part of the company but to external industry trends.[23] As the company was not willing to part with a larger share of these profits, the state intervened and took over production of the oil. In these circumstances, it is inevitable that a state would intervene. The case nicely illustrates that power balances within long-term contracts involved in the area of foreign investment could shift as a result of external circumstances and that, if the contract proves inflexible, it will provoke a conflict that results in government intervention.[24]

Concession agreements were not confined to the petroleum sector but were utilised in other mineral resources sectors as well.[25] The Ashanti goldfields concession concluded in Ghana provides an example of an agreement to prospect for gold that was to last for 100 years from the date of the agreement. The ruby mines in Myanmar (Burma) were subject to similar concessions.[26] Similar agreements existed throughout the developing world. They were executed in the context of unequal bargaining power, the rulers of the states either not having the power to resist the terms that were imposed on them or not having the expertise or desire to bargain for better terms. The people of the state were seldom beneficiaries of these transactions.

These agreements were repugnant from the perspective of democratic notions of sovereignty. Often, they were signed by rulers who did not understand the implications of the contracts they were concluding or they did not care as, being absolute rulers, they could utilise the royalties they received for their own benefit.[27] In some instances, these

government established, it is contestable whether such interventions accomplish a useful purpose. They merely fuel more extreme forms of nationalism. A. W. Ford, *The Anglo-Iranian Oil Dispute* (1954); J. Walden, 'International Petroleum Cartel: Private Power and the Public Interest' (1962) 11 *Journal of Public Law* 64.

[22] *Aminoil* v. *Kuwait* (1982) 21 *ILM* 976. For a discussion of the dispute, see A. Redfern, 'The Arbitration Between the Government of Kuwait and Aminoil' (1984) 55 *BYIL* 65.

[23] Rearrangements in the Venezuelan oil industry in 2006 were justified on the basis of windfall profits. Generally, taxation of windfall profits will not amount to expropriation.

[24] Taxation of windfall profits has now become a feature in the oil industry. When wild upward swings occur in the price of oil, oil-producing states tend to recover the benefits of the profits made by foreign oil companies through windfall taxes. It is unlikely that such taxation would be construed as amounting to expropriation. For further discussion, see Chapter 10 below.

[25] D. Smith and L. Wells, *Negotiating Third World Mineral Agreements* (1975).

[26] For an interesting account of the scheming and exploitation that accompanied these transactions, see R. V. Turrell, 'Conquest and Concession: The Case of the Burma Ruby Mines' (1988) 22 *Modern Asian Studies* 141.

[27] It is an interesting point as to whether international lawyers who promote the norm of democracy would concede that concessions and other foreign investment agreements signed by dictators or unrepresentative governments should be considered invalid. It is possible to argue that the norm of self-determination, now having acquired a near *ius cogens* status, would invalidate concession agreements signed by unrepresentative rulers.

agreements were facilitated by the fact that alien governments were in control of the states in which they were made. Thus, in Namibia, the South African government, during the period of the mandate, ensured that the concessions that were made favoured the interests of their own multinational corporations. The validity of such contractual arrangements made through coercion or with unrepresentative governments is doubtful in modern international law.[28]

The structure of the mineral industries was obliged to undergo change with the independence of the states in which they were sited.[29] In the petroleum sector and, to a lesser extent, in the other mineral resources sectors, rapid change was brought about by collective action initiated by cartels of producer countries. There were dramatic shifts, particularly in the petroleum sector where state oil corporations were created and vested with ownership of the oil resources in the territory of the state. The old oil concessions were cancelled. Thereafter, the concession agreement ceased to be the norm within the oil industry and was replaced by production-sharing agreements under which ownership of the oil remained with the state oil corporation. In this new form of agreement, foreign corporations perform a participatory role, with the state-owned corporation having control of the operations. Such agreements reflect the shift in the power relations that has taken place within the oil industry.[30] The shift was aided by the formulation of international law doctrines such as the doctrine on the permanent sovereignty over natural resources. Scholarly views as to the nature of such doctrines may differ.[31] Some regard them as *ius cogens* principles and others as mere *lex ferenda*. But, this argument has been rendered academic. In many states, the principle, once formulated at the international level, has been incorporated in constitutions and in foreign investment codes.[32] Contracts like the production-sharing agreement in the oil industry operate on the basis of this principle. The doctrine has operated at three distinct levels. After its formulation at the international level, it has been translated into national legislation in the form of constitutional provisions and foreign investment codes. It has also led to the drafting of contracts which ensure that the host state has greater control over the exploitation of mineral resources. The production-sharing agreement in the oil industry provides the best example. It is futile to argue that the doctrine has no legal substance and is an expression of desirable norms when it has been used so consistently. In the mineral resources industry, which it was principally designed to affect, the doctrine of permanent sovereignty over

---

[28] It would be interesting to speculate whether contracts made in post-Saddam Iraq under the foreign investment law promulgated by the American-instituted administration will be considered valid after a new regime takes over. The uranium contracts made in Namibia when that country was under South African control were considered invalid. So, too, contracts made by Pakistan in East Pakistan just before it became Bangladesh were regarded as invalid.

[29] For an excellent consideration of the issues that arise in the Australian mineral sector, see A. Fitzgerald, *Australian Mining Law* (2002).

[30] Indonesia was a pioneer in introducing the new arrangements into the petroleum industry. They were widely copied. See S. Rochmat, *Contractual Arrangements in Oil and Gas Mining Enterprises in Indonesia* (1981).

[31] For a survey of the different views of the doctrine, see generally Nico Schrijver, *Permanent Sovereignty over Natural Resources: Balancing Rights and Duties* (1997); M. S. Rajan, *The Doctrine of Permanent Sovereignty over Natural Resources* (1982).

[32] See, for example, Article 12 of the Philippines Constitution; and the Constitution of Papua New Guinea. In Indonesia, section 10 of the Mining Law requires all mining to be carried out through a contract of works over which the Ministry of Mining exerts supervisory control.

natural resources reflects a change that is now well established. In any event, it merely asserts a truism in international law that the sovereignty of a state includes control over all persons, incidents and substances within a state unless such control has been removed by treaty. The demise of the New International Economic Order is greatly exaggerated. Its philosophy of concentrating sovereign control over foreign investment lives on in constitutional provisions, foreign investment laws and contractual practices adopted in many developing countries. It would appear now that the emphasis on regulation is also being adopted by developed countries.

Though control over the natural resources sector by foreign corporations has been broken, the ownership of technology and capital that these corporations possess still makes them significant players in this sector. Nationalisation may have ended direct control. Indeed, modern legislation reserves the natural resources sector to state corporations or, alternatively, to nationally controlled corporations. Yet, alliances with foreign corporations have become necessary in order for the sector to operate, as these foreign corporations possess the technology and capital necessary for the exploration and exploitation of these resources. The interests that multinational corporations create in order to carry out activities in this area need protection and become a focus of the international law on foreign investment. There was a discernible swing towards the protection of the interests of foreign investors associated with the trend towards liberalisation in the 1990s. But, it could well be that, with the onset of the global economic crisis and the failure of neo-liberal policies, there is a reversal of these trends. The events in Latin America which now sees states seeking to reassert control over their natural resources sector portends such change.[33] As indicated, developed countries are as keen to exercise regulatory control through taxation and other measures.

1.1.2 The plantation sector

In many colonies, plantations were created by European powers. Most of these colonies had operated self-sufficient agricultural economies prior to colonisation. The colonial powers used the land that was previously agricultural for the planting of export crops. Thus, in Sri Lanka, tea, rubber and cocoa which were not native to the island were introduced. Vast tracts of agricultural land were converted to the production of these export crops. The changes were effected through large colonial companies which bought up the land and set up vertically organised industries which were responsible not only for the production of these export crops but also for their subsequent transportation to and sale in European markets. The corporations controlled these markets, the tea sector being the classic example. Companies such as Brooke Bond, Liptons and Twinings exerted global control. Long after colonialism ended and the tea estates were nationalised, control over the markets remained with these corporations. Distribution of these products in the markets of developed states continued to be controlled by these corporations.

---

[33] Privatisation of public energy companies which accompanied the adoption of neo-liberal ends has been brought to an end in Latin America by the new leftist governments. The Argentinian economic crisis of 2001–2 ended liberalisation measures in that country.

1.1.3 The manufacturing sector

Multinational corporations dominate the manufacturing sector. The sector was initially operated through wholly owned corporations established in the home states of colonial powers. They were, however, different from the modern multinational corporation. Due to slow communications, it was possible for managers in far-flung outposts to run the affairs of the corporation by themselves. In the case of the modern multinational corporation, central control over subsidiaries has become a reality due to instant communications. The modern multinational corporation has, as a result, acquired a considerable amount of global power through its integrated networks of production. Different patterns of diversification of production dependent on the sourcing of materials and cheap labour have emerged within the various manufacturing sectors.

It was at one time argued that this network of control over the subsidiaries of multinational corporations, which by the nature of their operations become integrated into the economies of host states, would undermine the sovereignty of these states.[34] Control became a central feature of the conflict between host states and multinational corporations. There is clear evidence of this struggle for control in the foreign investment legislation of many host states.

In their efforts to maintain control over foreign investment, host states have enacted legislation through which the entry of multinational corporations and their subsequent operations are carefully regulated.[35] At the same time, the home states of multinational corporations have argued for a system of open entry and for the liberalisation of the movement of multinational corporations by arguing for and introducing into investment treaties the right of pre-entry national treatment. This right would enable the multinational corporation to establish a business on the same terms as a national of the host state.[36] The tussle between the right to regulate entry and establishment and complete liberalisation of entry and establishment is a characteristic of the conflict between the different sets of norms. Neither set of norms is dominant. Even in instruments in which liberalisation seems to be dominant, there are sectors which remain subject to regulation and excluded from the protection granted by the general norms that may apply to other investments.[37]

With the entry into the picture of sovereign wealth funds and the ongoing global economic crisis, the fervour for liberalisation will naturally diminish. The national security dimension of sovereign wealth funds belonging to foreign states, some of which are perceived as potentially hostile,[38] will assume importance. Entry of these wealth funds will be made through the acquisition of shares in existing companies and through mergers. Existing laws on entry through acquisitions and mergers will be used to control such

---

[34] The early literature on multinational corporations shows a preoccupation with this issue. R. Vernon, *Sovereignty at Bay* (1971). The extent to which this legislation meshes with policy in investment treaties and the extent to which it should be given effect when disputes arise remain thorny points in investment arbitration. Certainly, the investor enters the state knowing of these laws, and has an obligation to abide by them.

[35] See Chapter 3 below.

[36] Good examples are contained in NAFTA and the bilateral investment treaties entered into by the United States.

[37] NAFTA provides the classic example where parties can still close sectors to entry and establishment.

[38] China is the obvious example. There have been bans on the efforts to acquire shares in Unocal (an American energy corporation) and in the mining sector in Australia. Yet, Chinese capital will be heavily courted.

acquisitions and mergers. Such control will be exercised not on purely economic grounds but on perceived dangers to national security, belying the neo-liberal premise that it is only economics that matter in the area of foreign investment.

The interests of host states are generally articulated through the requirement that entry is made into the state through the establishment of a joint venture with a local partner. In sectors in which foreign ownership is restricted to a certain percentage of the market, it is natural that joint ventures reflecting that percentage of participation are formed.[39] Partnership with a local partner ensures that some profits stay at home and that the local partner acquires expertise in business as well as of the technology, and, if a state entity is a partner, local control over the investment is effectively assured. Here, the claims made at the global level for control of the economy have been translated into national law through legislation.

Multinational corporations, in turn, have responded to these measures with strategies that would ensure that they retain control over their subsidiaries. The requirements of joint venture legislation will be defeated by making partnerships with nominees or with local businessmen who will not insist on exercising their right of control.[40] Indigenisation measures are similarly thwarted by the sale of shares to local persons who are favourable to the continuation of foreign control. Sometimes, there is no single winner in this struggle for control.[41] If such arrangements are concluded without legal dispute, then all may be well. If, however, legal disputes arise, the illegality involved in such arrangements may well prejudice the ability of the foreign investor to obtain a legal remedy.

Prevailing weaknesses in the economy, such as corruption, could be exploited to thwart the purposes of the legislation. There are different views as to whether protection will be given to multinational corporations which violate the internal laws of the host state. In *Shott* v. *Iran*,[42] a tribunal held that the shares purchased through a nominee in violation of the law after the foreign quota of shares had been reached cannot be protected. But, there are other awards which indicate that, where there is a climate in a host state that condones certain illegalities, the law should ignore those illegalities.[43] The latter view seems unacceptable, as it condones and thus promotes the violation of the host state's laws. With the rise in normative prohibitions against corruption, it is unlikely that this view would survive scrutiny today. It cannot, for example, be argued that the existence of rampant bribery in a state excuses bribery altogether and that the court or tribunal should disregard it.[44]

---

[39] In *Fraport* v. *Philippines* (ICSID, 2007), a failure to follow the domestic law disentitled the foreign investor to the protection of the investment treaty. Though the decision is subject to annulment procedure, it illustrates the Philippines law which requires minority participation in project ventures by foreign investors.

[40] As *Fraport* v. *Philippines* (ICSID, 2007) demonstrates, such schemes are clearly illegal. If disputes arise from these arrangements, it is unlikely that the foreign investor would succeed. Though, in some systems of arbitration, the local laws cannot be pleaded, it is unlikely that this proposition can withstand an obvious illegality. The rule was fashioned during a time when local laws were not transparent. In modern times, when the laws are transparent, it is to be expected that foreign investors know and conform to them.

[41] T. J. Biersteker, *Multinationals, the State and Control of the Nigerian Economy* (1987).

[42] (1990) 24 *Iran–US CTR* 203 at 218.

[43] *Biloune* v. *Ghana Investment Board* (1993) 95 *ILR* 184.

[44] *Fraport* v. *Philippines* (ICSID, 2007) indicates that arbitral tribunals will refuse relief to foreign investments made otherwise than in accordance with local laws. But, this result depended on the formulation of the protected investment in the investment treaty. An investment made through bribery will also be regarded as a nullity and thus not entitled to relief in the event of a dispute.

1.1.4 The financial sector

The financing of foreign investment was not a major problem in the past. Much of the capital was raised in the home states of the multinational corporations in the form of venture capital. But, in recent times, international banks have come onto the scene and are increasingly financing the making of foreign investments as well as major projects. The roles these financial institutions play, the forms of transactions used by them and the regulation by both the host and the home state of these transactions fall within the field of the international law of foreign investment. Where the nationality of the bank financing the investment is different from that of the foreign investor or the multinational corporation, the interests of the bank can be given protection by its home state. As a result, several home states could have claims based on nationality to exert pressure on the host state which acts to the detriment of the foreign investment.

1.1.5 Intellectual property

There was hardly any law on the cross-border transfer of intellectual property at the formative stages of this branch of the law. The law was fashioned in the context of the protection of tangible assets. It is only in recent times that the protection of the intangible assets of the foreign investor has come to be discussed.[45] With the information-technology and biotechnology industries being largely dependent on intellectual property, the protection of such property has become of crucial importance.

The transfer of technology to the host state is regarded as one of the benefits of foreign investment to the host state. The host state has an interest in ensuring that such a transfer does, in fact, take place. Host states insist on such transfers of technology to local personnel in the hope that local skills in the industry could thereby be developed, with a view to the local manufacture of the product in the future. The requirement that foreign investors operate through joint ventures also makes it more difficult to keep technological processes secret within the joint venture. These policy changes come at a time when foreign investors prefer to risk technology than capital and equipment in the making of the investment.

The tendency in developing countries to disregard the standards of protection for intellectual property recognised in international conventions makes this an area of concern for developed states. The fact that much of industry in new areas, such as biotechnology, computer science and related fields, will depend on the protection of intellectual property has resulted in developed states requiring greater protection for intellectual property. The dilemma in the area is that these rights are created by local law in each state. The problem then was to induce the local law to ensure that such rights are created and protected in accordance with a desired, external standard.

Capital-exporting states have developed a three-pronged strategy to deal with the problem. The first strategy of taking unilateral measures against recalcitrant states is confined to the United States. Under section 301 of the Omnibus Trade Act, trade sanctions may be imposed on states that do not confer adequate standards of protection against violations

---

[45] The effect of taking over of know-how and similar rights was discussed in the *Chorzow Factory Case* [1928] PCIJ Series A No. 17.

of intellectual property rights.[46] The legislation and threats to use it continue despite the fact that multilateral measures have been successfully instituted in the field.

The second strategy is to include intellectual property rights within the definition of foreign investment and thus extend the protection of bilateral treaties dealing with investments into the area of intellectual property. The pattern in all bilateral investment treaties is to extend the definition of foreign investment to include intellectual property rights. There are also bilateral treaties which specifically deal with the protection of intellectual property, which usually contain standards that are more robust than the standards contained in multilateral treaties.[47] But, increasingly, investment treaties now provide for the compulsory licensing of intellectual property, thus establishing a balance between protection and the social needs of the host community.

The third approach has been to include the protection of intellectual property through the World Trade Organization. The TRIPS Agreement seeks for the first time to create external standards as to intellectual property rights created by the domestic laws of each member state. This is based on the assumption that international trade distortions occur when such rights are not protected. A high volume of goods incorporating such rights are transferred in the course of international trade or are manufactured within states for export to other states. Hence, the argument made by the developed states was that the protection of intellectual property rights is the concern of an international trade regime.[48] The distinction between trade and investment became blurred here, because multinational corporations were engaged in both trade and investment through technology. Also, technology was used in the manufacture of goods by foreign investors and it was thought proper that such technology should be protected through the same measures.

Developing countries oppose such comprehensive protection. In their view, the TRIPS agenda was not about free trade but rather about externalising control over domestically created intellectual property rights through the creation of an international regime with dispute-settlement functions. It involved considerable loss of sovereignty over purely internal processes that may have vital economic significance to the state. The industrialised states had already created a sophisticated body of legal principles on intellectual property

---

[46] The legislation enables the surveillance of standards of protection of intellectual property in each state by the United States Trade Representative (USTR). The USTR is required by the 1988 amendment introduced by the Omnibus Trade and Competitiveness Act to investigate allegations made by private parties of violations of such property rights in foreign countries. The USTR may adopt a range of measures including the listing of countries, the specification of time limits within which offending practices are to be eliminated and, finally, trade sanctions if these violations are not rectified. Determinations are made annually as to violations in reports published by the USTR. States which violate standards are listed. Inclusion in the list amounts to a threat of action by way of trade sanctions in the event that the alleged violations are not corrected. The validity of these measures has been challenged, with varying degrees of success, before GATT and WTO panels. In 1998, a WTO panel held that the so-called '301 action' was not inconsistent with the WTO because of the commitment of the United States not to use it in a manner inconsistent with its WTO obligations. The European Union has a similar mechanism but has not been active to the same extent. See M. Bronckers, 'Private Participation in the Enforcement of WTO Law: The New EC Trade Barriers Regulation' (1996) 33 *CMLR* 299.

[47] P. Drahos, 'BITs and BIPs: Bilateralism in Intellectual Property' (2002) 4 *Journal of World Intellectual Property* 792. These treaties, specific to intellectual property, are intended to ratchet up the standard of protection given by investment treaties. Free trade agreements, negotiated bilaterally, also contain provisions on intellectual property protection. See, for example, the United States–Jordan Free Trade Agreement (October 2000).

[48] B. Hoekman and M. Kostecki, *The Political Economy of the World Trading System* (2001), pp. 274–300; J. Wattal, *Intellectual Property Rights in the World Trade Organization: The Way Forward for Developing Countries* (2000); K. Maskus, *Intellectual Property Rights in the Global Economy* (2000); and D. Mathews, *Globalising Intellectual Property Rights* (2003).

rights. They were now being universalised. The TRIPS measures were clearly aimed at developing states and the manner in which they conducted trade and investment.[49] Yet, there was insufficient cohesion among developing countries to resist TRIPS. Many had already been either coerced into enacting appropriate legislation on intellectual property through the threat of unilateral sanctions or had already done so in the belief that such legislation was necessary to attract foreign investment. Besides, there was a free market mood sweeping the world in the mid-1990s which was generally favourable to the adoption of the instrument. There was also the promise of market access if TRIPS was accepted.[50]

The TRIPS Agreement has significance for foreign investment in several ways. Multinational corporations which are required to enter into joint-venture alliances with local partners by developing-country laws may wish to keep the transfer of technology separate by making separate contracts covering this aspect with the locally incorporated joint venturer. The technology that is so transferred needs protection as foreign investment as it is made in connection with such investment. The goods that are manufactured may incorporate technology that needs protection. The processes that are employed in extraction or manufacture by a foreign investor also need protection. For a variety of reasons, the TRIPS instrument will impact foreign investment. Initially, where there is a violation of the standards of the instrument, protection will have to be sought from the local courts under the local laws which would have incorporated the TRIPS standards. There is a duty on member states to provide adequate enforcement procedures and remedies. Where such remedies are not provided, recourse may be had to the home state, which could take the matter to dispute settlement through the WTO processes. This becomes possible largely in situations where the policy of the host state affects intellectual property rights. It is unlikely that situations affecting individual foreign investors could be construed as involving violations of TRIPS. But, it is possible that there is a duty in the laws of states to take up the cause of individual foreign investors, in which case the WTO system could become the avenue for providing remedies to individual investors.[51] The law under the WTO and its processes has assumed significance for an aspect of foreign investment.

There has been a revival of a North–South debate on the issue of technology protection. The Doha Declaration reflects this by incorporating changes that permit compulsory licensing of intellectual property that is needed in times of emergencies caused by epidemics and other situations of social distress. The human rights issues involved in the sale of drugs for AIDS victims in developing countries and the issue of parallel imports of generic drugs brought about a conflict before domestic courts, particularly in South Africa. Other domestic courts have also shown a reluctance to deal with patent protection

---

[49] Susan Sell has detailed the pressures that led to the TRIPS agreement. The large pharmaceutical companies were instrumental in exerting pressure to bring about such protection through the WTO. S. Sell, *Private Power, Public Law: The Globalisation of Intellectual Property Rights* (2003).

[50] The Agreement on Textile and Clothing would not have been concluded if TRIPS had not been accepted. These provided for better market access.

[51] In the United States, it could be argued that there is a duty on the United States Trade Representative to take up the cause of any individual company which suffers harm in international trade.

under the TRIPS regime in situations where societal interests have conflicted with patent protection. In these situations, the foreign investors themselves have sought to withdraw from the dispute rather than court adverse publicity that would result from pursuing litigation.[52] The human rights perspectives to the problem impact on the aspects of patent protection to such an extent that the concerns of the majority in the protection of health and development may overwhelm the interests of the minority in the protection of intellectual property.[53]

2. Conflicting economic theories on foreign investment

Theoretical conflicts have had an impact on shaping legal attitudes to foreign investment. Leaving aside the Marxist theories,[54] the conflict is between two extreme theories, one of which maintains that foreign investment is wholly beneficial to the host state while the other maintains that, unless a state veers away from dependence on foreign investment, it cannot achieve development.[55] There are theories which seek to adopt a middle course between these extreme views. All theories focus attention on the economic development of the host state, particularly the host developing state. Lawyers who favour complete protection for foreign investments rely on theories which emphasise the positive effects of foreign investment on economic development. This view gained impetus during the high point of globalisation when arguments made for the liberal flow of multinational capital had wide acceptance and many legal instruments in the field reflected these views. There was also a formulation of legal principles on the basis that they would promote such beneficial flows of capital. Lawyers holding the opposite point of view argued to the contrary, relying on economic theories which emphasised the deleterious nature of foreign investment on the host economy. They also articulated competing legal principles on the basis of these economic theories. They were not articulated on the basis of any in-depth study of the economic aspects of the problem but were a reaction to what the policy of the law should be, based on assumptions made on superficial understandings of economic views on the subject. The literature on the subject does not reveal any survey made of the economic assumptions on which the law is based. The references to the economic bases of the law are scanty at best and are made as secondary justifications for conclusions already reached. Yet, the conflicting economic theories had a definite impact on the articulation of the legal principles, and it is necessary to have an understanding of these theories.

---

[52] Thus, in the *Novartis Case* (2006), the Chenai High Court in India was not deterred by TRIPS from holding that a generic drug may be produced and marketed. The threat to take the issue to the WTO did not eventuate. In South Africa, litigation regarding the parallel import of AIDS drugs was discontinued.

[53] This is notwithstanding the argument that the patent holder benefits all by the innovation he had made. This argument, which is at the root of the intellectual property system, is increasingly losing force.

[54] In classic Marxist theory, there would be no scope for an international law on foreign investment as there will be no concept of private property which is central to the existence of such law.

[55] The theories are presented in a stark fashion in this section. There are, of course, various nuances in their formulation by different scholars. For the purpose of understanding the effect of the economic theories on the formulation of the law, a stark presentation of the competing theories on foreign investment is preferable. For statements from an economic point of view, see T. J. Biersteker, *Multinationals, the State and the Control of the Nigerian Economy* (1987), pp. 3–51.

2.1 The classical theory on foreign investment

The classical economic theory on foreign investment takes the position that foreign investment is wholly beneficial to the host economy. There are several factors which are relied on to support this view. The fact that foreign capital is brought into the host state ensures that the domestic capital available for use can be diverted to other uses for the public benefit. The foreign investor usually brings with him technology which is not available in the host state, and this leads to the diffusion of technology within the host economy. There is new employment created, whereas, without foreign investment, such opportunities for employment would be lost. The labour that is so employed will acquire new skills associated with the technology introduced by the foreign investor. Skills in the management of large projects will also be transferred to local personnel. Infrastructure facilities will be built either by the foreign investor or by the state, and these facilities will be to the general benefit of the economy. The upgrading of facilities such as transport, health or education for the benefit of the foreign investor will also benefit the host society as a whole. A focus on these beneficial aspects of the foreign investment flows enables the making of the policy-oriented argument that foreign investment must be protected by international law. Such protection will facilitate the flow of foreign investment and lead to the economic development of less developed countries. It provides a strong, seemingly altruistic policy justification for the protection of foreign investment through the principles of international law. The theory does not explain why, despite all these benefits, there is still state interference with foreign investment. Nor does it explain why, after such a long period of foreign investment flows, no economic development has taken place and resource-rich countries remain abysmally poor.

Events in the recent past have given a great boost to the view that foreign investment brings uniform benefits to developing countries. The dominance of free market theories in the United States and Europe ensured that the classical view on foreign investment dominated thinking on the subject. The process of globalisation was regarded as inevitable due to advances in technology. This view promoted the idea that multinational corporations, which were the harbingers of globalisation, should have unlimited movement around the world and that their investments should be protected so that the process of global integration could be advanced. The new mood was enhanced by the dissolution of the communist states and the much vaunted triumph of capitalism.[56] The 1990s were the heyday of economic liberalism, embodying the classical view on foreign investment. Economic liberalism swept the world, and was encouraged by international economic institutions like the World Bank and the International Monetary Fund.[57] The conditions attached to loans granted by such institutions were an effective means of the dispersal of these views. Privatisation, liberalisation and macro-stability were the prescriptions given by these institutions to attract foreign investment which would, it was assumed, contribute to development.

---

[56] F. Fukuyama, *The End of History and the Last Man* (1992).   [57] J. Stiglitz, *Globalization and Its Discontents* (2002).

Practical considerations also led to the dominance of the classical view in the 1990s. The financial crisis brought about by defalcations on sovereign borrowings had led to banks being unable to lend money for development projects. Aid as a development policy was frowned upon by the new leaders of the United States and Europe as it was inconsistent with the notions of economic liberalism. With the dissolution of the Soviet Union, new states came into being. They espoused free market ideologies and began to court foreign investment. The only capital that was available was that provided by multinational corporations. There was strong competition among developing countries and the new states emerging from the collapse of the Soviet Union for the available foreign investment capital. The espousal of the classical theory became necessary in order for states courting the multinational corporations to prove that they were receptive to the need to protect their capital. This accounts for the sudden burgeoning of bilateral investment treaties in the 1990s and the favourable foreign investment laws giving guarantees and incentives to multinational corporations. In the area of international trade, the success of economic liberalism was reflected in the acceptance of the World Trade Organization with its new disciplines relating to intellectual property (TRIPS), services (GATS) and investment (TRIMS). This set the stage for greater involvement by the WTO in investment.

Added to this was the attitudes taken by the World Bank and the International Monetary Fund. They made loans conditional on the acceptance of ideas embedded in economic liberalism. The term 'Washington Consensus' came to epitomise the notion that the two financial institutions acted in concert with the government of the United States in imposing conditions that were based on notions of economic liberalism. There were theories in international law being formulated favouring the instrumental use of international law to favour the interests of the United States and neo-liberalism. In this context, the classical theory on foreign investment which had its base in notions of economic liberalism gained great currency.

Despite all this acceptance of the classical theory, there is no evidence yet that its tenets are based on accurate evidence. Though initial capital inflows may take place through foreign investment, there is evidence that outflows by way of repatriation of profits are greater than the inflow.[58] Some studies indicate that capital outflows associated with foreign investment may be twice as much as the initial inflows.[59] The presumed advantage of the new technology that is brought in by the foreign investor may also be incorrect, as it is usually the case that the technology that is introduced into the host state has become obsolescent in its state of origin. Consumer tastes are created for products of little social utility. A classic example is the introduction of breast-milk substitutes by multinational companies and the creation of a demand through advertising. The claim that management skills are transferred may also be illusory as the senior positions requiring greater skills are

---

[58] J. R. O'Neal and F. H. O'Neal, 'Hegemony, Imperialism and the Profitability of Foreign Investment' (1988) 42 *International Organization* 347.

[59] H. Cunningham, 'Multinationals and Restructuring in Latin America', in C. Dixon, D. Drakakis-Smith and H. Wads (eds.), *Multinational Corporations and the Third World* (1986), p. 46.

seldom within the reach of local personnel. The claim that infrastructure facilities are built to serve the new investment may also be contested, as the health and educational facilities that are created are only accessible to the elite within the host state (as they are the only ones who can afford to use the facilities). The alliance between the elite of the host state and the personnel of multinational corporations has unhealthy effects on the political life of the host state.[60] The absence of regulatory controls over the sudden influx of foreign investment brings about social and economic confusion within the state. Besides, despite the introduction of these policies in countries like Argentina and Indonesia, there seems to have been a worsening of the economic situation. Many African countries have enacted laws that are favourable to foreign investment without seeing any increase in foreign investment in real terms. The foundations of the classical theory have been contested on these various grounds.

Despite the refutable assumptions on which the classical theory of foreign investment is based, it has had a strong hold on the policy underlying the international law on foreign investment. It is maintained by economic power. It is espoused by the international institutions that are controlled by capital-exporting states. Therefore, it finds expression in many international instruments. The preambles to bilateral investment treaties state the belief that the foreign investment flows between the parties will benefit the development of the host parties.[61] They commonly assert that such investment will 'stimulate the flow of capital and technology and economic development of the Contracting Parties'. Since virtually every developing country has made such treaties, this is evidence of a widespread belief in the tenets of the classical theory. Literature produced by the World Bank is clearly based on the classical theory. The Convention on the Settlement of Investment Disputes between States and Nationals of Other States (the ICSID Convention) begins with the statement of the belief that provision for the settlement of disputes arising from foreign investments will increase the flow of foreign investment. Such flows are stated to be beneficial to the economic development of developing countries. The preamble states that the contracting states agreed on the Convention after 'considering the need for international cooperation for economic development and the role of private international investment therein'. The Multilateral Investment Guarantee Agreement, which provides for the insurance of foreign investment against political risks, was promoted on the basis that it would have 'considerable potential to remove barriers to international investment and give new vigour to the development process'.[62] The World Bank's Guidelines on the Treatment of Foreign Direct Investment issued in 1992 encapsulate the philosophy of the classical theory when it recognises:

that a greater flow of foreign direct investment brings substantial benefits to bear on the world economy and on the economies of developing countries in particular, in terms of improving the long term

---

[60] For a review of the literature on the subject and a refutation of the view that foreign investment leads to repressive government, see J. M. Rothger, 'Investment Dependence and Political Conflict' (1990) 27 *Journal of Peace Research* 255.

[61] The basis of such belief has been seriously dented by reports which indicate that there is no evidence at all for such a claim. UNCTAD, *World Investment Report, 2003*, p. 89. An aggregate statistical analysis does not reveal a significant independent impact by bilateral investment treaties in determining investment flows.

[62] I. Shihata, *The MIGA and Foreign Investment* (1988).

efficiency of the host country through greater competition, transfer of capital, technology and managerial skills and enhancement of market access and in terms of the expansion of international trade.

Recent literature emanating from the World Bank and other studies takes the view that there is no hard proof to the claim that these instruments do promote foreign investment.[63]

The classical theory, without doubt, provides the policy basis for the formulation of many documents which relate to the international law on foreign investment. The theory has also influenced the thinking of arbitral tribunals. Thus, for example, in *Amco* v. *Indonesia*, an arbitral tribunal asserted that 'to protect investments is to protect the general interests of development and developing countries'.[64] Long after schisms in investment arbitration had developed and the legitimacy of the system came under scrutiny, experienced arbitrators still seek to justify the rules that have been formulated on the rationale provided by the classical theory. Thus, writing after considerable doubt had come to be expressed regarding investment treaties and the system of investment arbitration under them, Brower and Schill continued to justify the existing system of investment protection on the basis of the classical economic grounds. They stated:[65]

What should, after all, not be forgotten in this debate is that both capital-importing and capital-exporting countries derive benefits from increased flows of foreign investment. Apart from the transfer of technology connected to foreign investment, the creation of employment, additional tax revenue, etc., investment treaties create a legal infrastructure for the functioning of a global market economy by protecting property rights, offering contract protection, establishing nondiscrimination as a prerequisite for competition through national and most-favored-nation treatment, and making effective dispute-settlement mechanisms. Perfect market conditions presupposed, this leads to the efficient allocation of capital, economic growth, and development, and benefits both capital-exporting and capital-importing countries through an increase in overall well-being.

Implicit in these formulations is an enduring belief that all foreign investments should be protected because they are beneficial to the development goals of the host states. Since only developing states need such development, the further assumption is that the instruments are addressed to developing states and the law is created for developing states alone, thus entrenching the division between developed and developing countries within the international law on foreign investment. The experience of litigation under NAFTA demonstrates that the law on the protection of foreign investment is as relevant to the dealings of investments between developed countries like the United States and Canada as they are to investments made in developing countries.

The classical theory also spawned the theory relating to 'economic development agreements'. This theory posited that foreign investment contracts made in developing countries, unlike those made in developed countries, promoted economic development and hence should be treated as akin to treaties and protected through principles of international law. Despite the obvious fact that the idea is offensive to the notion of the equality of states

---

[63] For a discussion, see Chapter 5 below.   [64] *Amco* v. *Indonesia* (1984) 23 *ILM* 351 at 369 (para. 23).

[65] C. N. Brower and S. W. Schill, 'Is Arbitration a Threat or a Boon to the Legitimacy of International Investment Law?' (2009) 9 *Chicago Journal of International Law* 471 at 496.

and was quickly given up, vestiges of it can be seen in modern writings.[66] Though the theory was given up, there remains a strong strand of arbitral awards based on the notion that foreign investment contracts can be internationalised.[67]

The classical theory will continue to maintain its vigour in international law due to the support it receives from powerful sources. These include not only capital-exporting developed states and international financial institutions that are controlled by them but also multinational corporations which are themselves sources of power in international relations. They have the capacity to shape the norms of international law not only by lobbying their states but also by exerting power through private means of law-making. Conservative international lawyers do not concede this, but the subsidiary sources of international law, the writings of publicists and the decisions of tribunals, including arbitral tribunals, are eminently manipulable towards the creation of an international law that applies to foreign investments. The law stated through these low-order sources is passed off as international law.

The uniform belief that foreign investment leads to economic development is difficult to accept. There is evidence that, where a multinational corporation integrates its operations through production in a developing country, beneficial results to the economy of the host state take place. But, this may not be the case where a multinational corporation moves in to exploit scarce resources or labour, or exports what are known as 'dirty industries'.[68] Studies, particularly in terms of law, no longer look at the issue of foreign investment in purely economic terms. Within economics itself, the idea that there is a single explanation of the effects of foreign investment on development or that there is only a single and uniform means of achieving economic development is heavily contested.[69] There are studies which look at the effect foreign investment has on ethnicity within the host state.[70] There are other studies which are concerned with the human rights and environmental impact of foreign investment. It is futile to cite economic theories alone as justifications for the formulation of policies on the international law on foreign investment. Opponents are likely to ask whether, even if the economic theories are sound, the political and other considerations should not be taken into account in devising a global policy on foreign investment.[71] The vigour of the classical theory in shaping law has been considerably dented. The onset of the global economic crisis in 2008, widely attributed to the adoption of neo-liberal policies which required liberalisation and a

---

[66] For an early statement, see J. N. Hyde, 'Economic Development Agreements' (1962) 105 *Hague Recueil* 271; *Revere Copper and Brass Inc.* v. *OPIC* (1978) 56 *ILR* 258 is entirely based on the theory. For a rejection of the theory, see I. Pogany, 'Economic Development Agreements' (1992) 7 *ICSID Rev* 1.

[67] This topic is dealt with in Chapter 7 below.

[68] Dirty industries are highly pollutive industries which cannot be established in the home state because of stringent environmental laws.

[69] Joseph Stiglitz, Danny Rodrik and Ha-Joon Chang are economists whose works deny the basis of the single effect theory of neo-liberalism. See Ha-Joon Chang, *Bad Samaritans: Rich Nation, Poor Policies and the Threat to the Developing World* (2007); and J. Stiglitz, *Making Globalisation Work* (2006). Amartya Sen's works have also been influential. For his recent work, see A. Sen, *The Idea of Justice* (2009).

[70] See, in particular, the work of A. Chua, *World on Fire: How Exporting Free Market Democracy Breeds Ethnic Hatred and Global Instability* (2003).

[71] One of the reasons for the failure of the OECD's effort at bringing about a multilateral agreement on investment was its reliance entirely on economic justifications for the instrument.

reduction of regulatory control over market mechanisms, will accentuate this decline. But, its influence will remain because of its continued espousal by powerful states and institutions.

2.2 The dependency theory

The dependency theory is diametrically opposed to the classical theory, and takes the view that foreign investment will not bring about meaningful economic development.[72] It was a theory popularised by Latin American economists and political philosophers, though work based on it has been done in other parts of the world.[73] The theory focuses on the fact that most investment is made by multinational corporations which have their headquarters in developed states and operate through subsidiaries in developing states. The proposition is that the subsidiary devises its policies in the interests of its parent company and its shareholders in the home state.[74] As a result, multinational corporations come to serve the interests of the developed states in which they have their headquarters. The home states become the central economies of the world, and the states of the developing world become subservient or peripheral economies serving the interests of the home states. Development becomes impossible in the peripheral economies unless they can break out of the situation in which they are tied to the central economies through foreign investment. The resources which flow into the state as a result of foreign investment are seen as benefiting only the elite classes in the developing state, who readily form alliances with foreign capital. This results in human rights violations as conditions favourable to the operations of multinational corporations have to be maintained by legislation or force. Indigenisation measures and efforts to exert control by permitting foreign investment through joint ventures are seen as failures. The foreign investor is able to defeat these attempts at control through his alliance with the elite classes.[75]

This theory comes to the diametrically opposite conclusion to that of the classical theory, in that it holds that foreign investment is uniformly injurious. It holds that, rather than promoting development, foreign investment keeps developing countries in a state of permanent dependency on the central economies of developed states. Unless a developing state can break out of the situation of dependency, economic development becomes impossible in that state. The panacea that is advanced is to reject foreign investment rather than attract it. The theory reflects the long-held animosity to foreign investment in the

---

[72] For a review of these theories, see R. Peet, *Global Capitalism: Theories of Social Development* (1991), pp. 43–51; B. Hettne, *Development Theory and the Three Worlds* (1988); P. Evans, *Dependent Development: The Alliance of Multinational, State and Local Capital in Brazil* (1979); and T. J. Biersteker, *Multinationals, the State and the Control of the Nigerian Economy* (1987). The prominence of the theory resulted from the work of Raul Prebisch, whose work with the Economic Commission for Latin America suggested a link between the decrease in the wealth of the poorer states coinciding with an increase in the wealth of the rich states. There are various strands of the dependency theory.

[73] For Africa, see S. Amin, *Unequal Development: An Essay on the Social Formation of Peripheral Capitalism* (1976); see also S. Amin, *Obsolescent Capitalism: Contemporary Politics and Global Disorder* (2003).

[74] A factor to take into account is that shareholdings are now very diffuse, as shares are traded on exchanges around the world.

[75] See D. Bennet and K. Sharpe, *Transnational Corporations versus the State* (1985); for the view that communist states were able to institute controls over multinationals more effectively than capitalist states, see M. M. Pearson, *Joint Ventures in the People's Republic of China: The Control of Foreign Direct Investment under Socialism* (1991), pp. 14–19.

Latin American states. It is perhaps a natural outcome of the dominance of the United States in the economic life of Latin America.[76]

There was a *volte-face* in the 1990s on this position in Latin America, with many Latin American states now supporting the trend towards liberalisation. This occurred to such an extent that not only have these states participated in the making of bilateral investment treaties but preparations were made to negotiate a Free Trade Agreement of the Americas which would have contained investment provisions. A succession of economic crises, particularly in Argentina in 2001–2, and an increasing shift towards the left in many Latin American states, saw a reversal of these policies. The dependency theory, however, cannot be said to be the major influence in Latin America at present.[77] Yet, the theory did encourage many of the nationalisations that took place on that continent. Its significance is that it provided a rationale for restructuring the economy and for excluding foreign investment. In the life of nations, there is a cyclical pattern in which theories lose and regain favour. The force of the dependency theory within Latin America and outside that continent cannot be entirely written off. The adoption of neo-liberal policies in some Latin American states led to economic crises. The Argentinian economic crisis had dramatic consequence for international investment law as it gave rise to a succession of investment disputes submitted to arbitration. The reaction to this was a dramatic departure from neo-liberal programmes, towards policies which are increasingly hostile to foreign investment, demonstrating that the trends are cyclical, with the failure of one policy leading to the acceptance of the other.

Dependency theorists see economic development not in terms of flow of resources to the host state but as involving the meaningful distribution of wealth to the people of the state. The appeal of the theory in times when globalisation has created increasing disparities in wealth should not be under-estimated. On this view, there cannot be development unless the people as a whole are freed from poverty and exploitation. Development becomes a right of the people rather than of the state. The appeal of the theory to international lawyers attracted by the rights of people over the rights of states is obvious.[78] If a shift does occur towards the recognition of the rights of people, the role of international law in investment protection will require radical rethinking.

The protests against globalisation and its impact on international law are evidence of a rift that is taking place. The writings of some international lawyers tend towards the view that international law should arise from the will of the people rather than the practice of states. The reaching out of peoples effectively began when opposition mounted to the Multilateral Agreement on Investment (MAI) sponsored by the OECD. This opposition grew out of the fact that the MAI provided protection to multinational corporations without addressing the environmental and human rights harms that these corporations cause. These

---

[76] C. Kay, *Development and Underdevelopment in Latin America* (1988).

[77] Brazil, which had stood outside the system and had not participated in investment treaties, saw spectacular economic progress. Fernando Henrique Cardoso, who was President from 1995 to 2003, had, as a professor, written extensively on the dependency theory. But, the policies he adopted were often alleged to be neo-liberal.

[78] A major strand within international law denies the rights of peoples. See J. Crawford (ed.), *The Rights of Peoples* (2001).

protests, effectively interlinked through the new technology of the Internet, then grew into the movement against globalisation. The dependency theory has relevance in that movement in that it symbolises a way in which local interests could be protected against the interests of multinational corporations. Unlike the classical theory, the theory sought to integrate non-economic interests, such as human rights and the environment.

2.3 The middle path

The animosity which is directed at multinational corporations is the basis of theories such as the dependency theory. This animosity has become somewhat dented in recent times. In an age where communism has proved unsuccessful and the superiority of a free market economy to marshal the means of production has gained acceptance for a period, theories which are hostile to private initiative as the means of generating growth are unlikely to make headway. Equally, at a time of the ongoing global economic crisis brought about by an unregulated market, it is unlikely that states would accept a view based entirely on the classical theory on foreign investment. Many states have seen more wisdom in a pragmatic approach to the problem than in ideological stances. The fear that multinationals pose a threat to the sovereignty of developing states has receded with the increasing confidence of the developing states in managing their economies. Multinational corporations have also left behind the role of being instruments of the foreign policy of their home states. On occasions they have even formed alliances with developing countries to the detriment of their home states.[79] Some of the larger multinational corporations are capable of conducting foreign policy for their own benefit.

The reduction of hostility towards multinational corporations was furthered by the studies of the United Nations Commission on Transnational Corporations (UNCTC).[80] While supporting the view that foreign investment through multinational corporations could have harmful results in certain circumstances, these studies showed that, properly harnessed, multinational corporations could be engines that fuel the growth of the developing world.[81] The reports of the UNCTC generated other works on multinational corporations which contributed to the debate on the role of multinational corporations in the 1980s. The debate, no doubt, had an effect on the formulation of legal attitudes to foreign investment in developing countries and fashioned the legal techniques they were to use to control foreign investment. It also had an impact on the forms through which developing countries preferred to receive investments. Attitudes evolved over time. The laws that were shaped by the older attitudes have not entirely been dismantled by those laws which were shaped by the new attitudes. Each period has left its mark on the domestic laws of states.

---

[79] The obvious examples are alliances made by oil companies with oil-producing states which may be adverse to their oil importing home states.

[80] This body, now much truncated, functions within UNCTAD and, in a sign of the times, takes a less robust position than it used to.

[81] The views expressed by the Commission received support from an influential group of American and European scholars. See, for example, Fred Bergsten, *American Multinationals and American Interests* (1978).

The studies of the UNCTC on the role of foreign investment helped to identify the beneficial as well as the harmful effects of foreign investment. The beneficial effects identified were very similar to those already identified by supporters of the classical theory of foreign investment. There was definite support for the view that foreign investments made by multinational corporations benefit the local economy through the flow of capital and technology, the generation of new employment and the creation of new opportunities for export income.

While pointing out the benefits brought by foreign investment, these studies also identified the deleterious effects of foreign investment. For the first time, serious efforts were made to identify the precise types of activity of multinational corporations which could harm the host economy. This enabled the host countries to take regulatory measures to counter harmful practices. They also resulted in efforts to fashion codes of conduct for multinational corporations, thus generating principles which, though not international law, will have an influence in shaping the course of the development of the law for the future. The underlying theme of the draft codes of conduct was that multinational corporations should avoid certain identifiable conduct which was seen as harmful to the economic development of the poorer states.[82]

Some of the harmful effects these studies identified may be briefly stated. The studies pointed out that multinational corporations defeated the tax laws of states by engaging in transfer pricing. This practice involved fixing an artificially high price for an item permitted to be imported at concessionary rates bought from the parent company. Tax credits were later claimed on the basis of this artificial price.[83] There were practices associated with transfers of technology, widely touted as one of the benefits brought by foreign investment, which deprived the host economy of the benefits of the transfer. There were many restrictive clauses introduced into the transfer agreement which prevented the transferee from obtaining the full benefits of the transfer. They were intended to maximise the benefit to the transferor, but their indirect effect was to hurt the host economy.[84] Thus, there were restrictions on the export of the goods manufactured with the technology, grant-back provisions which required that new inventions or adaptations made by the transferee be given over to the transferor, tie-in clauses which required associated products to be purchased only from the transferor, and similar restrictions controlling the use of technology.[85]

Successive financial crises have also dented the force of the classical view and the liberalisation of entry standards to some extent. Both the Mexican and the Asian financial crises were attributed to the sudden withdrawal of foreign investment, particularly portfolio

---

[82] See Chapter 6 below for a description of the code of conduct on multinational corporations. The codes have remained drafts. The schism between the different groupings of states left several matters unresolved.

[83] See further S. Picciotto, *International Business Taxation* (1992), pp. 171–228.

[84] UNCTAD also worked on a code on restrictive business practices which did not progress beyond the draft stage. There is a difference in the strategy of UNCTAD and that of the contemporary discussions on how to grant competence to the WTO over competition.

[85] An effort within UNCTAD to introduce a code of conduct on the transfer of technology proved unsuccessful due to developed-country opposition.

investment. In the context of these events, there has been some re-examination as to the forms of foreign investment that would be beneficial and those which would not be.[86]

The studies also indicated that the nature of the technology which was exported was often obsolete and hazardous. The extent of the harm to the environment caused by the export of such technology was identified in these studies, and there have been dramatic examples of the potential harm to both life and the environment that such obsolete technology could cause. The Bhopal disaster, caused by a gas leak in a plant set up by a multinational corporation, involved colossal damage to life and property. Such instances indicate that multinational corporations often use technology in developing states which they are not permitted to use in their own home states, because it is cheaper to do so and there are no regulations or effective supervision to prevent the use of such harmful technology.[87] The need for the control of such export of hazardous activity has been demonstrated often as a result of environmental and other harm caused by multinational corporations.

The benefits which multinational corporations bring are also thwarted by the global practices they adopt to maximise profits. The restrictive business practices which they are able to adopt on a global scale prevent the host state from maximising the export potential of goods manufactured within its territory. The carving of the world markets into segments in which each subsidiary operates may be beneficial to the multinational corporations but not to the host states, as exports to some areas are thereby prevented. These are problems the host state cannot address by itself. Hence, efforts have been made to construct codes on restrictive business practices. They have not materialised to any significant extent, but efforts to create them also contribute to the growth of an international law on foreign investment. Recent movement has been to include competition as a WTO discipline. This, however, is resisted by many developing states, as they see in it an attempt to prise open their markets rather than an effort to help them reduce the restrictive practices of multinational corporations. The introduction of competition law principles into the WTO regime may also not solve this issue, as the present indications are that these efforts are intended to introduce such laws at the domestic level.[88] When some developing states, like China, introduce competition laws, they may also be intended to keep large foreign companies out of their markets or screen out investments that lack any benefit.[89]

The idea that foreign investment is generally beneficial to development is no longer accepted in academic literature. While there is evidence of its development effects, there is

---

[86] E. Carrasco and R. Thomas, 'Encouraging Relational Investment and Controlling Portfolio Investment in Developing Countries in the Aftermath of the Mexican Financial Crisis' (1996) 34 *Columbia Journal of Transnational Law* 531. Both the Mexican crisis in 1994 and the Asian financial crisis in 1997 raised doubts as to unregulated financial flows, at least in short-term capital markets.

[87] The issue has been raised as to whether a home state has responsibility in international law for permitting multinational corporations to set up in other states with defective technology the use of which would not have been permitted in the home state. M. Sornarajah, 'State Responsibility for Harms Caused by Corporate Nationals Abroad', in C. Scott (ed.), *Torture as Tort* (2000), p. 491.

[88] At the Cancun Ministerial Meeting of the WTO in September 2003, consideration of the package of issues known as the 'Singapore Issues', which included competition, was deferred.

[89] China introduced competition laws in 2008. One of the first uses of them was to prevent a merger between Coca-Cola and a local soft-drinks manufacturer. Here, the competition laws were used as an entry-prevention device.

also evidence that it may limit growth.[90] There must be other conditions, such as human capital, present for foreign investment to have a positive impact on economic development. As a result of these changing viewpoints, it is unlikely that the classical view will continue to be a guiding influence on policy-making relating to foreign investment in developing countries.

Once it is conceded that multinational corporations can both benefit and harm economic development, it is easy to adopt the position that foreign investment should be harnessed to the objective of economic development and must be carefully regulated to achieve this end. The influence of this view, which strikes a middle course, has been significant. There is an indication that many developing countries, which are increasingly enacting regulatory frameworks within which multinational corporations are to function, have taken some leads from this theory.[91] Many developing states have now enacted legislation to set up screening bodies which permit entry to or give incentives to investments which are approved by these bodies. Some have legislation designed to ensure that technology transfers are effected without too many restrictions on their use by the transferee. On the international level, the theory has been the basis on which codes regulating the conduct of multinational corporations are sought to be formulated. The theory, which accepts that multinational corporations can engineer development, if properly harnessed, challenges many propositions relating to international law which have been stated on the basis of the classical theory. Unlike the classical theory, which favours liberalisation and the freedom of movement for multinational corporations on the assumption that this promotes development, the newer theory requires the recognition of the right of regulation of the foreign investment process by the host state. The classical theory mandated absolute rules of investment protection and their uniform application to all investments. The basis of this position has been shaken by the increasing acceptance of the view that foreign investment should be entitled to protection only on a selective basis. Protection depends on the extent of the benefit it brings the host state and the extent to which it has conducted itself as a good corporate citizen in promoting the economic objectives of the host state.[92] There is an obligation to abide by the laws and regulations of the host state which are designed to capture the maximum benefits the foreign investment can bring to the host state's economic development. The *quid pro quo* for profiting from operations in the host state for a multinational corporation is that it should ensure that the laws that seek to enmesh its operations with the economic objectives of the state are obeyed.

A mix of regulation and openness is seen as desirable. The heavy regulatory regimes which existed in the past have given way to new regulatory regimes based on pragmatism. The strategy of rapid industrialisation desired by developing countries requires capital,

---

[90] A. Sumner, 'Foreign Investment in Developing Countries: Have We Reached a Policy "Tipping Point"' (2008) 29 *Third World Quarterly* 239. Interestingly, some of the studies critical of the impact of foreign investment came from the OECD and the World Bank, generally known to promote neo-liberal views on the subject.

[91] This is particularly evident in the legislation of Australia, a resource-producing country conscious of environmental protection.

[92] The idea that an unscrupulous investor is not entitled to protection is coming to be stated in arbitral awards. See *Robert Azinian* v. *Mexico* (1998) 5 *ICSID Reports* 269. This trend has relevance also to the use of the fair and equitable standard, as fairness must take into account the effect of the investment on the host state as well as the measures that the state takes which affect the foreign investor.

which only multinational corporations are able to provide. This reality requires the adoption of new policies that show a willingness to accommodate the interests of multinational corporations. This has included approaches at both the domestic and international level. At the international level, states have made bilateral investment treaties.[93] The thrust of these treaties was to give protection to foreign investment, but more recent treaties are increasingly balancing the interests of the state with that of protection.

At the domestic level, the adoption of legislation based on the middle approach is evident. There is a strong imitative effect in foreign investment legislation. Since there is also competition for the capital of multinational corporations, states want to ensure that their legislation is more open or at least does not lack the features found in the legislation of other states in the region. While incentives to entry are often imitated, there is no desire evinced in such legislation to dismantle existing regulation unless a clearly demonstrable benefit exists. The institution of administrative controls is seen as necessary to enhance the economic objectives of the state in receiving the foreign investment. International law also has to respond to these changes. A uniform view that all investment has to be protected through international minimum standards is no longer a viable notion, as the practice of states indicates that states do not subscribe to the idea that all foreign investment is entitled to such a minimum standard. The externally imposed minimum standard insulates the multinational corporations without creating any corresponding duties. That idea has to be abandoned in view of the competing notions that extend protection only to multinational corporations which act in accordance with the laws and policies of the host states in which they operate. In the alternative, such a minimum standard exists only to the extent that the multinational corporation abides by the regulatory standards mandated by the host state. In that context, it would be invidious for a multinational corporation which causes damage in the host state to seek the protection of the minimum standards of treatment in international law when the state acts to prevent such conduct. International law itself may impose a requirement of conformity with environmental standards upon actors such as multinational corporations. Compliance with internal laws is a precondition to access. It is also a precondition to the protection that is afforded by international law. These prescriptions may evolve, but not without a schism in the law. Already, the evidence of such a schism may be seen in determining when a regulatory interference amounts to an expropriation for which compensation needs to be paid.[94]

Successive economic crises have dented prevailing viewpoints as to the uniformly beneficial effect of foreign investment. With the global crisis of 2008, the appeal of the classical view that foreign investment uniformly promotes economic growth will be further diminished. Many states adopted policies of strengthening their domestic sectors rather than relying on foreign investment.[95] Changes have also taken place as to the nature

---

[93] The practice of China is instructive. On this, see N. Gallagher and W. Shan, *Chinese Investment Treaties: Policy and Practice* (2009).

[94] This issue is discussed in Chapter 9 below.

[95] In Asia, after the Asian economic crisis of 1997–8, attributed to the sudden withdrawal of foreign investment, Thailand adopted a policy of 'Thaksinisation' which effectively meant strengthening the domestic sector. Malaysia instituted, and has kept, currency controls. Similar restrictive controls on investment can be seen in Africa, where Nigeria, Eritrea and the

of the flows of foreign investment. There is a greater South–South flow, which may mean that bargaining will be conducted among relative equals. Generally, the area has become one in which rapid changes can be expected, and these changes will come to be reflected in the law.

3. Actors in the field of foreign investment

In the past, foreign investments were made by individuals or groups of loosely organised associates venturing abroad to make quick profits.[96] It is evident that much of the law on state responsibility for injuries to aliens developed in order to provide protection for such businessmen who operated in foreign countries. Though similar investments could take place in modern times, the larger percentage of investments take place as a result of decisions of multinational corporations to invest abroad. Unlike the old types of foreign investment which were usually of limited duration, the adventurers returning home with their profits once the venture had ended, the new types of investment made by multinational corporations are intended to last for a long period of time. The focus of the law has consequently shifted from the protection of single individuals or groups of individuals to the protection of the process of investment made by multinational corporations.

A related phenomenon is that the areas of trade which the multinational corporations seek to enter are within the sole preserve of state agencies or entities in many developing countries. State control of the industry or economic sector is exercised through the medium of these state agencies. The wave of privatisations has not swept away control by the state in the more important industrial and natural resources sectors. In fact, privatisation has been ended in most states with the failure of neo-liberal policies and resulting economic crises. The foreign corporation entering a state will often have to do so in association with a state entity. The new laws on foreign investment in many developing countries as well as the former socialist states make this mandatory.[97] It is a technique which enables the state to have continuous control over the investment. It ensures that its economic goals are restated by its representatives at meetings of the boards of the joint venture corporations through which the foreign investment is made. This has implications for the law on foreign investment. Any study of the subject will therefore have to take into account the role which multinational corporations and state entities play in foreign investment.[98] There are other actors besides these two important entities. International institutions enter the fray, usually to support one or other of the

---

Central African Republic increased controls on foreign investment. In Latin America, changes were instituted by left-leaning governments. Widespread nationalisations took place in the natural resources sector. Privatisation instituted during the neo-liberal period has been dismantled.

[96] In Scots law, from which the term 'joint venture' is taken, a joint venture originally meant a group of 'adventurers' going together into a business overseas. They went together because the associated risks were greater.

[97] In the Philippines, for example, the Anti-Dummy Act involved in *Fraport* v. *Philippines* (ICSID, 2007), makes it mandatory for industrial projects to be entered into by foreign investors in minority participation with local ventures. Privatisation has been ended in many Latin American states. In Venezuela, oil companies were required to migrate into new alliances with state companies, in accordance with pre-existing laws which had hitherto been ignored.

[98] On the role of multinational corporations and the law, see P. Muchlinski, *Multinational Corporations and the Law* (2nd edn, 2008).

viewpoints that are in conflict in this area. Thus, the World Bank, the International Monetary Fund and the OECD generally support the views of the developed world that there should be liberalisation in foreign investment, whereas the United Nations Commission on Trade and Development (UNCTAD) had the traditional role of supporting the viewpoint of the developing states. Various NGOs also play a role. These have come onto the scene relatively recently as a result of the protests against environmental depletion and human rights abuses attributed to multinational corporations. They are usually engaged in promoting single issues, but these issues have an impact on foreign investment. A fifth possible set of actors is private chambers of commerce which may buttress the views that favour multinational corporations.[99] Newcomers on the scene are the sovereign wealth funds. These are funds owned by developing countries which achieved spectacular economic growth and accumulated large capital reserves. These funds, usually managed by a state-controlled entity, now seek to invest in developed states, which are eager to have them as a result of the economic crisis of 2008 onwards.

There are therefore six principal groups of actors who have an impact on the international law on foreign investment. The roles they play need to be examined.

3.1 The multinational corporation

The multinational corporation is a relatively new phenomenon in international trade and investment. Some writers deny this by pointing to large corporations like the British and Dutch East India Companies, which operated in the past. Apart from their large size, there is little in common between these old corporations and the multinational corporation of modern times. The organisational structure of the multinational corporation and the speed with which it can exercise control over its network of worldwide subsidiaries set the modern multinational corporation apart from the old colonial corporations.

The threat that the multinational corporation poses to the sovereign state was a pre-occupation when multinational corporations first started to invest abroad. Backed by its own immense financial resources, as well as by the power of its home state which stands behind it, the fear was that the multinational corporation may influence the political course of the state in which it seeks to invest. It could scuttle the economies of weak states simply by relocating its operations elsewhere. The negative aspects of multinational corporations have been the focus of the dependency theory which was considered above. There are positive aspects of multinational corporations which are emphasised by other theories. Despite this enormous power both for good and for harm, the multinational corporation has hardly been recognised as an entity capable of bearing rights and duties in positivist international law.[100] Obviously, this position may have to change, given the reality that it is as dominant an actor on the international economic scene as the

---

[99] The International Chamber of Commerce has had a leading role to play. It has attempted drafts of codes on foreign investment and other instruments relating to the subject.

[100] D. Ijalye, *Extension of Corporate Personality in International Law* (1978); I. Seidl-Hohenveldern, *The Corporation in and under International Law* (1987); P. Muchlinski, *Multinational Corporations and the Law* (2nd edn, 2008).

state. Many multinational corporations command financial resources that are greater than many states can muster. Large hegemonic powers act to advance the interests of their multinational corporations.[101] Within the international law on foreign investment, there is clear indication that multinational corporations possess both rights and duties. There is a clear tendency to hold them responsible for certain types of conduct, though at the moment this is done largely through domestic law.[102] Yet, the recognition of the multi-national corporation as a single entity and the recognition of its responsibility for violating international norms is slowly emerging. Though the draft Code on Transnational Corporations, which sought to achieve this, never progressed beyond its status as a draft, the principles it contains may well come to be recognised in the course of time.

Multinational corporations also wield significant power to shape the law on foreign investment to their advantage. Quite apart from wielding influence on their home states to ensure foreign investment protection, they are also able independently to influence the making of legal norms. Their role is an illustration of the fact that private power can be used to formulate norms with claims to be principles of international law. It is possible to argue that investment protection, which was devised through the system of arbitration of invest-ment disputes, had much to do with the impetus given to the idea by multinational corporations and their advisors. These corporations devised the contractual forms on which the elaborate system was built through the argument that foreign investment contracts are akin to international treaties and are hence subject to principles of international law. In this way, foreign investment contracts were put beyond the reach of the domestic laws of host states.[103] The theory was built on the basis of the low-order sources of international law such as general principles of law, the writings of highly qualified publicists and uncontested arbitral awards. These sources can be manipulated. It would not be too far-fetched to argue that they were manipulated in order to secure the protection of foreign investments made by multinational corporations.

Multinational corporations bring about considerable lobbying pressure to ensure that treaties are favourable to foreign investment protection. The classical view on foreign investment would perceive multinational corporations as being incapable of anything but good. On the basis of the theory that wealth creation, which is the principal reason for the existence of the multinational corporation, brings benefits to all, including those in the developing world, the multinational corporation is perceived as incapable of misconduct. At any rate, the policy justifications for the law protecting the foreign investment of the multinational corporations are made on that basis. That may be the motivating philosophy of the United States and other developed states.[104] As a result, there is a clear coincidence

---

[101] The allegations that the Iraqi war (2003) was fought by the United States at the instance of the large oil and construction companies, if true, supports this possibility.

[102] Litigation against multinational corporations for violation of international principles on human rights and the environment are increasingly being brought under the Alien Tort Claims Act in the United States.

[103] For the development of the theory of internationalised contracts, see further M. Sornarajah, *The Settlement of Foreign Investment Disputes* (2000). See also Chapter 10 below.

[104] The course of the law in the United States in particular has been favourable to corporations, and the dominant thinking is that misconduct on the part of multinational corporations is rare. This is so despite spectacular instances of corporate fraud and misconduct in the United States in recent times. Successful prosecutions of such practices have been rare.

between the interests of the multinational corporation and many developed states. But, with the United States itself returning to regulatory structures to help it avoid the worst effects of the economic crisis of 2008, it is unlikely that it could support an international system that did not seek such regulation with any credibility. As a result, it is possible to envisage controls, even if piecemeal and confined to specific areas, appearing in the future. This is evident in the area of human rights, where the conduct of multinational corporations has caused anxiety. A United Nations rapporteur has been tasked with the formulation of policy on how the situation could be addressed. Other areas such as environmental protection and the control of bribery have also been addressed.

Yet, the power of multinational corporations to ensure that their home states maintain stances favourable to the protection of their global investments is very clear. They are able to secure legislation which ensures that errant states are penalised through withdrawal of aid and other facilities.[105] They are also helped by their home states through international agencies which they control; states which are hostile to multinational corporations are denied privileges conferred by these agencies.[106] The International Monetary Fund and the World Bank are examples of such institutions. Voting in these institutions is weighted according to monetary contributions. Developed states, particularly the United States, have greater ability to influence policy in these institutions because of their greater voting power. The International Monetary Fund has instituted measures which would ensure the adoption of a free market philosophy by those states to which it lends. The power of multinational corporations to exert influence globally in the shaping of the international law of foreign investments, quite apart from their economic and organisational strengths, makes them influential actors in this sphere.

In the field of international relations, the role of the multinational corporation in international politics has been more honestly articulated than in the law. The shift of economic power from states to markets and the role played in markets by multinational corporations has been studied by a succession of scholars.[107] The charge that the law purposefully hides the role of the multinational corporations, yet vests rights in them without recognising their responsibility, is one that is difficult to avoid.

3.2 State corporations

State corporations, through which states have entered the sphere of international trade, are a phenomenon of the twentieth century. They were the principal agencies through which communist states engaged in international trade. Outside communist states, welfare states also came to use state corporations in sectors like health, education, transport and communications where the provision of essential services to the public was regarded as more

---

[105] In *Santa Elena v. Costa Rica* (2000) 39 *ILM* 317, (2002) 5 *ICSID Reports* 153, the award discloses the fact that the threat of withdrawal of aid to Costa Rica under the Hickenlooper Amendment played an important role in the dispute reaching arbitration.

[106] J. Stiglitz, *Globalization and Its Discontents* (2002), p. 71.

[107] The writings of Susan Strange initiated these studies. S. Strange, *Retreat of the State: The Diffusion of Power in the World Economy* (1996); C. Cutler (ed.), *Private Authority and International Affairs* (1999).

satisfactorily performed by the state. The state would be motivated not by profit alone but by the need to provide a public service.[108] It was thought that, with the privatisation of the public sector, state entities may go out of vogue in the developed countries. This has not come to pass. With the dismantling of earlier privatisation measures, state corporations have been given new life in many developing states. Though they may function in association with private enterprises, they continue to maintain primacy in many economic sectors involving foreign investment. The functioning of state entities ensures that the sectors in which they operate remain monopolies.

State entities will continue to play an important role in developing countries. In developing countries, the theory behind the operation of state entities is that profitable sectors of the economy should be operated by the state so that the profits will not go into private hands but into the state treasury to benefit the people as a whole. Also, the provision of essential services remains a function of the state. A purported advantage is that the non-profit-making state entity will supply remote consumers whereas a private entity may find such consumers expendable.[109] Laudable though such motives may be, the tendency towards corruption undermines the achievement of such an objective in many states.

State corporations hold monopolies in sectors which multinational corporations seek to enter. The natural resources sector, which has traditionally attracted multinational corporations, is usually controlled by state entities. Since foreign investment codes in most developing countries now permit foreign investment entry only through joint ventures, it becomes inevitable that foreign investment entry into many sectors has to be made in association with these state entities. The advantages of such an entry is that the foreign corporation enters a monopolistic market, and thus is assured a share of the monopoly profits and a ready source of supply of products or resources.

In a joint venture, the motives of multinational corporations and the state entity will often be in conflict. The multinational corporation is driven by the need for immediate profit. The state entity, on the other hand, has long-term economic objectives of development and seeks to pursue these through the joint venture with the multinational corporation. The synergy that is essential for the success of the joint venture will be lacking in such an association and the potential for conflict is great. The disputes which could arise pose many problems for the law of foreign investment. Unlike multinational corporations, the state agency has a claim to greater recognition in international law. There are rules of international law which give it a favoured status and to a degree make it immune from the process of domestic courts. The whole issue of the applicability of sovereign immunity to state entities has been thorny, but is now being resolved by the wide acceptance of the rule that such immunity cannot be claimed by a state entity which engages in commercial activity.[110]

---

[108] The theory was that private companies would not provide services to areas where the provision of services was deemed uneconomical, whereas state corporations would.

[109] The fear that CanadaPost, a monopoly, could be diluted as a result of the entry of foreign courier services through the liberalisation of entry provided by NAFTA featured in the arbitration dispute involved in *UPS* v. *Canada*, UNCITRAL Arbitration Proceedings (NAFTA) (Award on the Merits, 24 May 2007). The tribunal avoided pronouncing on this issue.

[110] The subject is now covered by legislation in most states. Such legislation provides for jurisdiction over essentially commercial acts of the state entity. But, difficult problems of characterisation continue to trouble the courts.

But, many doubts still remain as to the scope of the rule and its future clarification by domestic courts, and national practice will contribute to the formation of rules that may clarify matters. But, for the moment, the case law on the subject has been so complex and replete with inconsistencies that it is difficult to argue that the change in the law has made the situation any better.

Multinational corporations have begun to take a long-term approach to the problem. As a result, they may be more willing to take a conciliatory approach to such conflicts. Their self-interest in maintaining oligopolistic positions in world markets may make it desirable from their point of view to seek an accommodation of their interests rather than to seek conflicts. There is also the problem that the state will be willing to assist its entities by enacting laws that will favour its entities in its dealings with multinational corporations if the need for such a course arises.[111] In these circumstances, the position of the multinational corporation becomes tenuous. In the face of an intransigent state, a multinational corporation has little by way of legal weaponry to use, at least for as long as it wants to preserve good relations within the state.

3.3 International institutions

International institutions do not directly act in the sphere but still have a role to play in bringing about rules that affect foreign investment. They are created for specific purposes, and foreign investment may fall within their ambit. Thus, the World Bank and the International Monetary Fund are financial institutions which oversee development objectives, the flow of funds and other financial matters involving states.[112] The World Bank has played an active role in foreign investment on the basis of the belief that foreign investment flows promote economic development. It expressly subscribes to the classical theory that foreign investment brings such benefits to poorer states that it must be promoted. The promotion largely takes place through legal and other devices that the World Bank has created in order to remove risks to foreign investment in developing countries. These devices are based on the belief that the elimination of political risks to investments that exist in developing states will result in greater flows of foreign investment into these states and lead to their economic development.

The Multilateral Investment Guarantee Agency (MIGA) was created by the World Bank to provide for a scheme of insurance against political risk in developing states. The idea is that the provision of such insurance will facilitate investment flows. Likewise, the International Centre for the Settlement of Investment Disputes (ICSID) was created in the belief that the provision of neutral arbitration facilities for investment disputes between foreign investors and host states will boost investor confidence in the host states which participate in the ICSID Convention. Such increased confidence will result in flows of

---

[111] Third World states are not alone in adopting such a course. In *Settebello Ltd* v. *Banco Totta e Acores* [1985] 1 WLR 1050, Portugal enacted legislation to help a state entity resile from contracts it was not able to fulfil.

[112] For a more detailed statement of the functions of the World Bank, see L. Tshuma, 'The Political Economy of the World Bank's Legal Framework for Development' (1999) 8 *Social and Legal Studies* 89.

investment into these countries. Though these institutions have existed for some years now, it is difficult to assess whether they have helped to increase the flow of investments into the developing world. African states which have participated wholeheartedly, virtually creating compulsory jurisdiction in arbitral tribunals (including ICSID) through investment treaties, have not increased the flow of investment to any significant degree.[113] Studies within the World Bank seem to show that there is no correlation between participation in investment treaties and the flow of investments.[114]

Together with the IMF and US government agencies, the World Bank is credited by commentators with the 'Washington Consensus'. This is a package of policy prescriptions which the three institutions are claimed to promote based on neo-liberal assumptions as to how the global economy is to be organised. In the sphere of foreign investment, this takes the form of support for essentially the tenets of classical economics that foreign investment flows are uniformly beneficial and should therefore be promoted. As noted, there has been a retreat from this position in recent years.

The United Nations Commission on Trade and Development (UNCTAD) was created through the endeavours of developing states. Though its original mandate was to address issues of development from the standpoint of developing countries, it is now a much reduced force due to a lack of sufficient backing. Yet, its studies on investment and its various reports and conferences have had an effect in shaping state and other attitudes to issues relating to foreign investment.[115]

The WTO is another organisation with an increasing interest in the area of foreign investment. It already has an instrument, the Trade-Related Investment Measures (TRIMS), which deals with the prohibition of performance measures adopted in connection with investments. The competence over such measures is acquired on the basis that their employment in investment distorts international trade. TRIMS prohibits the use of certain performance requirements which are considered trade distortive. The General Agreement on Trade in Services (GATS) is more directly involved with foreign investment. It applies also to multinational service providers who establish a commercial presence within the host state and provide services while being present in the host state. It is clear that such providers are indistinguishable from foreign investors. As far as the services sector is concerned, GATS establishes the competence of the WTO over a significant type of foreign investment which will be regulated by a WTO instrument. To the extent that intellectual property amounts to a type of foreign investment, TRIPS (Trade-Related Aspects of Intellectual Property Rights), which contains the WTO regime

---

[113] For the extent of African participation in ICSID arbitration, see A. Asouzu, *International Commercial Arbitration and African States* (2001).

[114] M. Hallward-Driemeier, 'Do Bilateral Investment Treaties Attract FDI? Only a Bit ... And They Can Bite' (World Bank Development Research Group, Working Paper No. 3121, 2003); for the text, see http://econ.worldbank.org/view.php?type=5lid=29143.

[115] UNCTAD publishes the World Investment Report annually. Its 2003 Report deals with many aspects of the international law on foreign investment. It also has a series of studies on aspects of investment treaties, and has published studies on bilateral investment treaties. The now defunct United Nations Commission on Transnational Corporations (UNCTC) was absorbed into UNCTAD, thus giving it competence over studies relating to multinational corporations. It publishes a journal, *Transnational Corporations*. It has completed a series of studies on different aspects of a multilateral agreement on investment. These studies constitute a comprehensive statement of the law in the area.

for intellectual property, also becomes relevant. Existing instruments already provide for wide WTO competence over aspects of foreign investment.

After the OECD efforts at formulating a Multilateral Agreement on Investment failed,[116] there was a move to establish an instrument on foreign investment within the WTO. The Singapore Ministerial Meeting of the WTO required the issue to be studied, and the Doha Ministerial Meeting sought to hasten the process. The Doha Declaration requires the matter to be looked at in the context of the development dimension and the right to regulation of the economy. There has been resistance to such an instrument from developing states. If such an instrument were to result, WTO competence over foreign investment would be established. The process of acceptance of a discipline on investment, however, will involve a tussle in which NGOs are likely to play a leading role. At the Cancun Ministerial Meeting in September 2003, most of the developing countries opposed an investment instrument within the WTO. A decision was deferred on the package of issues known as the 'Singapore Issues', of which investment is one.

The task of the global institutions has been to promote economic liberalisation around the world. In doing so, they have subscribed to economic models which favour business. The policy interests of the dominant states dictate outcomes within these institutions. As a result, they clash with other interest groups which have non-economic concerns such as equity, justice, the promotion of human rights, the protection of the environment and the advancement of the economic development of the poor. These interest groups are largely represented by NGOs.

3.4 Non-governmental organisations

The impact of NGOs is a new phenomenon. The role that they could play on the international scene was dramatically revealed in their ability to coordinate an international campaign against the acceptance of the Multilateral Agreement on Investment.[117] Their mobilising capabilities were repeatedly revealed in protests against the WTO at Seattle and Cancun, at successive World Bank meetings and whenever institutions regarded as being associated with neo-liberal notions met in Western capitals.[118] Since their first rush onto the international scene was in connection with a foreign-investment-related issue – the scuttling of the MAI – they are likely to continue to play a leading role in determining such issues.[119]

The main plank in their protests against the making of investment codes is that they emphasise protection of multinational corporations without at the same time taking into

---

[116] This identifies the role of the OECD as an institutional actor. Besides the failed attempt at the MAI, it has played a role in the field by conducting studies on the subject.

[117] R. O'Brien, *Contesting Global Governance: Multilateral Economic Institutions and Global Governance* (2001).

[118] This is significant, as the protests against neo-liberal capitalism did not take place in developing states but in the capitals of the developed world. One view is that the yawning gap between the rich and the poor had brought the Third World into the developed states, in that the poor in the rich world were acting as surrogates for the poor in the developing states. C. Thomas, 'Developing Inequality: A Global Fault-Line', in S. Lawson (ed.), *The New Agenda in International Relations* (2001), p. 71.

[119] For the role of NGOs in the failure of the MAI, see S. Picciotto and R. Mayne (eds.), *Regulating International Business: Beyond Liberalisation* (1999).

account the environmental degradation and the human rights abuses of which they are capable. The view that is advanced by environmental and human rights groups is that a multilateral code on investments should be a balanced one conferring protection on foreign investment but also attributing responsibility when there are violations of environmental and human rights standards by these corporations.[120]

It is evident that NGOs will have a significant role to play in the future development of the international law on foreign investment.[121] Their role has already helped to shift the law from the protection of multinational corporations to a consideration of their responsibility for misconduct. The construction of such a law on purely economic models without consideration of the social and political dimensions is not possible. NGOs ensure that the social dimension is kept in the forefront of issues. They are also instrumental in developing litigation strategies to test out the possibility of imposing responsibility on parent companies for abuses by their subsidiaries of environmental and human rights in other countries.

3.5 Other actors

There are other actors with an interest in the area. The International Chamber of Commerce has had a long association with the subject. Though a private organisation, consisting of participating chambers of commerce around the world, it was one of the early proponents of an international convention on foreign investment. The Abs–Shawcross Convention it adopted did not achieve acceptance. Its arbitration services have been utilised in settling foreign investment disputes. There are other private bodies which study the area.

3.6 Sovereign wealth funds

Sovereign wealth funds are the latest players on the foreign direct investment scene. Some developing states, flushed with money as a result of flows of profits resulting from globalisation and the adoption of neo-liberal policies, have created funds with their surplus capital for making investments in developed countries. The states which made quick profits were the smaller city states like Dubai and Singapore which thrived during the neo-liberal period by providing the services necessary in an age of globalisation. But, the most dramatic rise was that of China. China's sovereign wealth funds are the cause of some anxiety in the West, given that China is still seen as a potentially hostile state. Some of China's investments in foreign banks and financial institutions went bad as a result of the crisis brought about by sub-prime lending. But, China has also invested heavily through the acquisition of shares in existing companies in developed countries. Since the investments are made in listed commercial entities, so issues arise as to whether these investments are protected by

---

[120] The responsibility of multinational corporations for environmental and human rights violations is dealt with in Chapter 4 below.
[121] The International Institute for Sustainable Development has played a significant role. It has drafted a model investment code which takes account of environmental, human rights and other concerns along with that of protection of investment.

the same international legal regimes that protect private foreign investment. There has been little discussion of this point. *Prima facie*, the investment would appear to be no different from investments made by any private foreign investor.

The one issue that has drawn attention is the effort made by sovereign wealth funds to invest in the natural resources and other vital sectors of the US economy. The US view is that national security issues are raised when such acquisitions are attempted. In two instances, the US government has intervened in the acquisition of shares with national security implications,[122] despite the fact that it has courted China for investment funds. There has been resistance to the acquisition of shares in the mineral resources sector in Australia by Chinese sovereign wealth funds. There is little doubt that the growing financial power of sovereign wealth funds will cause further problems in the area. So far, efforts to resolve this issue have resulted only in guidelines as to the investments these sovereign wealth funds make.[123]

4. Risks in foreign investment

The risks to foreign investment increased after the end of the colonial period. Whereas, in the colonial period, an investor from an imperial state taking assets into the colonies had almost absolute protection, the picture changed dramatically after the independence of the former colonies. Where investment was taken into countries which were not under colonial domination, protection was secured through diplomatic means, which often involved the collective exercise of pressure through the threat of force or economic sanctions by the home states of the investor. Gun-boat diplomacy was reduced as a result of the outlawing of the use of force by the United Nations Charter and the increasing possibility of condemning states which resort to aggression to maintain their positions in world trade and investment.[124]

In the absence of protection through the exercise of military power, there has been an increase in the risks to foreign investment in the modern world. Consequently, there has been a search for legal methods of conferring protection upon foreign investments. The analysis of these legal methods of protection is the main focus of this book. But, an understanding of the nature of the risks to foreign investment is a necessary preliminary to such an inquiry.

The principal risks to foreign investment come from certain uniform and identifiable forces. The presence of these factors will result from either regime change or changes to the existing political and economic policies of the host state. Such changes pose a threat to

---

[122] This involved acquisitions of shares in American ports by Dubai Ports and in Unocal by the Chinese National Oil Company (CNOC), a state enterprise. The result was the Foreign Investment and National Security Act of 2007 which enhanced the Exon–Florio Amendment.

[123] See further P. Rose, 'Sovereigns as Shareholders' (2008) 86 *North Carolina Law Review* 83; B. Reed, 'Sovereign Wealth Funds: The New Barbarians at the Gate? An Analysis of the Legal and Business Implications of their Ascendancy' (2009) 3 *Virginia Law and Business Review* 97.

[124] The attack on Egypt following the nationalisation of the Suez Canal in 1957 was perhaps the last instance when the protection of property was given as a justification for an armed attack.

foreign investment. The right of a state to change its economic policy is recognised in modern international law, though that right may now come to be circumscribed by the increasing number of treaties on international investment and trade to which states are becoming parties. Unless so circumscribed, the right to change economic or other policies is an aspect of the sovereignty of states. The Declaration on Principles of International Law Concerning Friendly Relations and Cooperation Among States recognised this right when it declared that 'each state has the right freely to choose and develop its political, social, economic and cultural systems'.[125] The system of government or the economic policies which a state prefers to follow are matters exclusively for the state.[126] The International Court of Justice asserted this right in the *Nicaragua Case* when it stated:[127]

A prohibited intervention must accordingly be one bearing on matters which each State is permitted, by the principle of State sovereignty, to decide freely. One of these is the choice of a political, economic, social and cultural system, and the formulation of foreign policy. Intervention is wrongful when it uses methods of coercion in regard to such choices, which must remain free ones.

When a state decides to effect changes to its economic policies, there is a potential threat to foreign investment. It is necessary to understand the underlying causes for a state wanting to make such changes before examining whether the right of the state to effect these changes can be restricted in any way.[128] The first is political hostility to foreign investment, which is generated by ideological inclinations against the influx of foreign investment. The second is a nationalistic concern over the domination of the economy by foreign elements which may result in xenophobic hysteria directed at foreign investors. The third relates to changes that take place globally within an industry. Such changes may be to the disadvantage of foreign investors, as they would be required to renegotiate the bargain originally made in light of the changes. The fourth is where an incoming government seeks to rewrite contracts made by the previous regime. The fifth situation is one in which the state finds the fulfilment of the contract onerous in light of changed circumstances. The sixth is a deterioration in the general law-and-order situation in the country which makes the foreign investment a target for attack by groups of dissidents or marauders. The seventh is where a state feels it necessary to intervene in a foreign investment in order to exercise a regulatory power such as the protection of investment or some economic interest. An eighth is where there is internal corruption or where a corrupt government has been replaced by a new government. These and other types of risk situations are obviously not mutually exclusive. They often occur at the same time in one state, and the resultant threat to foreign investment as a result of this combination is great. But, for the purpose of examination, these risk factors are dealt with separately.

---

[125] GA Res. 2625 (XXV) of 1970. Article 1 of the Charter of Economic Rights and Duties of States states that every state has 'the sovereign and inalienable right to choose its economic system'.

[126] There is, however, an effort made to indicate that international law prefers a democratic system within a state and that rules must be devised in such a manner as to further this goal. Some have gone to the extent of articulating a right to intervene militarily in another state in order to promote democracy. G. Fox and B. Roth (eds.), *Democratic Governance and International Law* (2000).

[127] [1986] *ICJ Reports* 186, para. 205.

[128] Risk analysis in foreign investment is an independent discipline. See, for example, T. Brewer (ed.), *Political Risks in International Business* (1985).

4.1 Ideological hostility

Communist ideology is opposed to private capital and private means of production.[129] With the fall of the Soviet Union, the force of communism has been dented. The remaining communist states like China and Vietnam are experimenting with mixed systems that permit the influx of foreign investment even into sectors of the economy that are controlled by state entities provided the foreign investor makes a joint venture with these entities. Yet, socialism, as distinct from communism, is also averse to property rights and remains a potent force in the politics of most nations. Whenever socialistic notions take hold in a state, a threat to foreign investment and to private capital will arise.

In states which are opening their doors to foreign investment, there are still political forces which remain antagonistic to foreign investment either because they are socialist or because they resent the possibility of foreign control of business sectors.[130] Where groups with ideological beliefs opposed to foreign investment come to power, there will be a definite threat to foreign investment. The incoming government will seek the reversal of previous attitudes to foreign investment. It may also want to dismantle the foreign investment which had been allowed into the state by the previous government. It may regard the terms on which entry was permitted as too favourable to the foreign investor and require them to be changed.[131] Regime changes, particularly those ideologically inspired, pose problems for foreign investment.[132] The involvement of multinational corporations in the politics of the host states is largely aimed at forestalling the possibility of unfavourable regime changes.[133] Such involvement itself poses problems, for, if a group which the foreign investors opposed comes into power, there will be additional grounds for the group to interfere with the foreign investment.

4.2 Nationalism

Nationalistic sentiments pose a threat to foreign investments. Particularly at times when the host economy is in decline, prosperous foreign investors who are seen to control the economy and repatriate profits will be easy targets of xenophobic nationalism.[134] They are

---

[129] China's history is instructive. From the communist revolution in 1947 until the declaration of the 'open door' policy in 1978, China adopted the communist view that did not recognise private property and hence foreign investment. After independence in 1948, Indonesia rejected foreign investment, until 1967, when the Suharto regime took power.

[130] In India, a combination of nationalism and socialism brought about a situation unfavourable to foreign investment, but this now co-exists with other more dominant forces which favour foreign investment.

[131] Thus, Venezuela, under Chavez, sought to rewrite petroleum contracts in 2007. This required a 'migration' to forms of contract mandated by existing laws which had been hitherto ignored during the neo-liberal phase. Most oil companies complied, though arbitration has resulted from challenges by some companies to the programme.

[132] A recent instance is the fall of Suharto in Indonesia. The incoming government sought to rescind existing contracts, alleging that they were improperly made. The situation resulted in many disputes, some going to arbitration, for example *Himpurna* v. *Indonesia* (2000) 25 *YCA* 13.

[133] Codes of conduct usually forbid multinational corporations from interfering in the domestic politics of host states. But, such interference is necessary to ensure that the multinational corporation's interests are represented to the host state. The issue concerns the boundary between proper and improper interference.

[134] This is by no means a developing-country phenomenon. The first work that reviled multinational corporations with xenophobic vigour was written in the context of France. J. J. Servan-Schreiber, *The American Challenge* (1969).

ready targets for opportunistic politicians who may see advantage in such a situation to bring about a change of government. It is also easy to deliver the promise of taking over or divesting ownership of established foreign-owned business ventures. It is a popular measure, which would appease nationalistic forces.[135]

Religious fundamentalism is of a like character. The Iranian revolution of 1979 was both nationalist and fundamentalist. It resulted in the taking of US business interests. The Iranian situation illustrates the futility of political manoeuvring to protect foreign investment. In 1952, when the Mossadegh government sought to nationalise foreign-owned assets in Iran, it was overthrown by the joint efforts of the United Kingdom and the United States. The monarchy, which favoured foreign capital, was reinstated. But, several years later, Iranian nationalism took an even more virulent, anti-American stance. Such virulence may not have been present if not for the earlier interference in the efforts of a milder government. The driving out of US business after the installation of the Ayatollah Khomeini resulted in the Iran–US Claims Tribunal set up to determine the claims of US companies which had suffered damage as a result of the Iranian revolution.

SPP v. *Egypt*[136] is an arbitration which illustrates the manner in which nationalistic feeling may engineer foreign investment disputes. The government of President Sadat had relaxed the rules on the admission of foreign investment in Egypt. In response to the government's efforts to promote investment in the tourist trade, Southern Pacific Properties Ltd (SPP) entered into an agreement with the Egyptian Government Tourist Corporation to build a tourist complex near the pyramids. The company had commenced building when an outcry arose about the building of such a project so close to a historic monument. The matter was frequently raised in the Egyptian Parliament, and became a popular issue through which the government could be confronted. After the assassination of President Sadat, the incoming government of President Mubarak found it prudent to halt the building of the complex. SPP had to pull out, even though it had begun construction of the project. The dispute resulted in protracted arbitration that took place before several tribunals, and the arbitration gave rise to litigation concerning the enforcement of awards in several states.

Nationalistic feeling plays a dominant role in the restriction of the flow of foreign investment in developed states, too. The perception of US dominance of Canadian industry has been a thorny issue in the past. Both in France and in Canada, the possibility that cultural values could be swamped if US entertainment companies were to be given a free rein in these states has been a long-held fear. It is one of the reasons advanced for the failure of the Multilateral Agreement on Investment. Likewise, in the United States, Japanese ownership of real estate and foreign encroachment of traditional industries such as the automobile industry have caused concern. Astute politicians find foreign investment a convenient subject to focus attention upon in order to secure votes.

[135] As President Mugabe of Zimbabwe showed, existing politicians can retain power by whipping up a xenophobic frenzy against those who are seen as foreign and as controlling the economy.
[136] (1992) 8 *ICSID Rev* 328.

4.3 Ethnicity as a factor

Alongside nationalistic factors, the role of the ethnic structure of the host state on foreign investment has become a focus of attention.[137] The hypothesis is that, in the developing world, foreign investors make alliances with vigorous minorities that control business and thereby provoke a backlash in the majority community which holds political power due to its numerical superiority, particularly in developing countries which operate on democratic principles.[138] This situation of ethnic nationalism poses a threat to foreign investment. The institutions of the free market and democracy are not effectively mediated in developing states, as they are in the developed world. As a result, the potential for risk to foreign investment in these states is enhanced unless there are effective mechanisms that have been set in place which ensure that the demands of the majority ethnic group to a share in the economic benefits of foreign investment are met. It is also relevant to note that, in the context of nationalism, foreign investors who prosper in periods of market liberalisation are in the same situation of economically dominant ethnic minorities. When forces of nationalism return to power, they become targets.

Market liberalisation promoting foreign investment may accentuate the problems arising from ethnic nationalism as foreign investors make alliances with the economic elite of states, who usually belong to minority groups. Measures like privatisation, taking place in the context of corruption, visibly enhance the wealth of these minority groups and their allies. Such situations contain the seeds of instability.

Some states, like Malaysia and now South Africa, have sought to deal with the problem through constitutional means to ensure that the majority community has the opportunity of sharing the economic cake in proportion to its size. Such solutions have met with a measure of success.[139] When treaties on investment protection are made by such states, the internal laws, which are no doubt discriminatory, are preserved from being subjected to treaty obligations.[140] In states which have not worked out such an accommodation, the instabilities inherent in the situation pose a threat to foreign investment as the dominance of the alliance between foreign investment and the local entrepreneurial minority groups will become a target of political animosity.[141] Nationalisation of foreign investment often becomes an option in such circumstances.[142]

---

[137] This has largely been due to the studies of Amy Chua. See, for example, A. Chua, 'The Paradox of Free Market Democracy: Rethinking Development Policy' (2000) 41 *Harvard International Law Journal* 287; and A. Chua, 'Markets, Democracy and Ethnicity: Toward a New Paradigm for Law and Development' (1998) 108 *Yale Law Journal* 1. The thesis is comprehensively stated in her book, A. Chua, *World on Fire: How Exporting Free Market Democracy Breeds Ethnic Hatred and Global Instability* (2003).

[138] The assumption is that there is a tension between the free market and democracy, as the free market makes a minority rich whereas democracy gives power to the majority. This tension is reconciled in developed societies through various means, including the creation of welfare facilities, the myth of equal access to avenues of success, and tax measures visibly designed to accomplish the redistribution of wealth. Such instruments for mediating the paradox are non-existent in developing countries.

[139] The Black Empowerment Act in South Africa resulted in several measures requiring the transfer of some economic power into the hands of the indigenous black people. This has been challenged as violating investment treaties. *Piero Foresti, Laura de Carli and Others v. South Africa*, ICSID Case No. ARB(AF)/07/01.

[140] It would be difficult to contemplate such states giving national treatment to foreign investors when the laws discriminate between nationals.

[141] The Chinese in Indonesia and the Indians in Fiji provide examples.

[142] A. Chua, 'The Privatisation–Nationalisation Cycle: The Link Between Markets and Ethnicity in Developing Countries' (1995) 95 *Columbia Law Review* 223.

4.4 Changes in industry patterns

Where there are changes in an industry throughout the world, those changes will likely affect ownership patterns within that industry, and this will affect the foreign investor's interests throughout the world. The best illustration of this proposition is afforded by the changes that took place in the oil industry. The oil crisis in the 1970s was provoked by the concerted effort on the part of the oil-producing nations to take control of the oil industries in their states and to fix the price of oil. Previously, the major oil companies of Europe and the United States had controlled the production of oil in these states. The legal instrument through which entry was made into the oil-producing states was the concession agreement. As explained in the previous chapter, the principal feature of the agreement was that there was a transfer of virtual sovereignty over vast tracts of oil-rich land for a substantial period of time, often over half a century, to the foreign company to explore for oil and recover and market it when found. In return, the host county would receive a royalty on the amount of oil produced.[143] The early concession agreements were made in the colonies or in states which were protectorates of the home states of the companies which obtained the concessions. The power of the home states also guaranteed the stability of the concessions. Legal techniques were not the only determinant of the security of the concession regime.[144]

Dramatic changes consequently took place in the industry. With the more representative governments replacing authoritarian regimes that relied on the imperial powers for their continuance, political demands for the cancellation of the concession agreements became strident. On the global level, there were concerted efforts made by the former colonies for the creation of doctrines, which justified the cancellation of the concession agreements.[145] The doctrine of permanent sovereignty over natural resources was proclaimed through a General Assembly resolution and became a means through which this transformation could be effected by law. Military pressure to make the host state abide by the obligations in the concession agreements were no longer feasible as the use of force for such purposes would have attracted the adverse scrutiny of the international community. The concerted efforts made by the oil-producing nations to change the rules of the oil industry and fix the price at which oil would be sold became successful with the formation of the Organization of the Petroleum Exporting Countries (OPEC). The old concession agreements could not withstand these changes. They had to be replaced by other types of agreements. The production-sharing agreement, pioneered by the Indonesian state oil company, Pertamina, became the industry-wide agreement that came to replace the concession agreement, reflecting the changes that had been effected. It passed the risk of oil exploration onto the foreign company and enabled the state oil company to regulate exploitation of the oil.

---

[143] H. Cattan, *The Law of Oil Concessions in the Middle East and North Africa* (1967); A. Z. El Chiati, 'The Protection of Investments in the Context of Petroleum Agreements' (1987) 204 *Hague Recueil* 1.

[144] The point is nicely illustrated by the role of the Anglo-Iranian Oil Company in the politics of Iran. The British and American governments secured the overthrow of the regime that nationalised the company in 1952.

[145] The doctrine of sovereignty over natural resources was the principal doctrine.

Where windfall profits result to the foreign investor, the state is likely to intervene and seek changes to the contract. This will be particularly so where the windfall accrues as a result of external events and is not the result of the skill of the foreign investor.[146] It is interesting to note that the United Kingdom and Canada also restructured existing contracts so that the state could obtain more benefits from the oil produced, when it was realised that the profits accruing to the oil companies were larger than expected.[147] The Venezuelan measures at restructuring the petroleum industry at a time of high profits have also led to disputes, though the majority of the foreign firms complied. Where windfall profits occur, particularly in the extractive industries, governments will see these profits as being made without any inherent merit on the part of the foreign investor. They may be willing to nationalise such industries in order to secure all of the profits, particularly if they feel confident of running the business themselves. Alternatively, they may seek other forms of contract, which ensure that more of the profits stay at home. It must be determined in each case whether the rearrangements sought amount to expropriation which should be compensated. Another issue in these circumstances is whether the increase in taxes amounts to an expropriation. Such issues are discussed in Chapter 9 below.

4.5 Contracts made by previous regimes

Incoming governments may wish to change the contracts made with foreign investors by previous governments. This may take place where there are allegations of corruption in the making of contracts,[148] or where the legitimacy of the previous government is doubted on objective grounds by the incoming government.

There are occasional instances of disputes arising where a new state has been created in the territory in which the contract was to be performed and the new state refuses to accept any succession to the obligations undertaken by the government previously in control of the territory. In these circumstances, as there is no rule of succession of obligations assumed towards individuals, there is no remedy that would be provided in international law.[149] Where a foreign investor makes an investment with an unrepresentative government, the incoming democratic government may claim a right to rescind the contracts made by the previous government by seeking to doubt the legitimacy of both the previous government and the contracts it made.[150] Its credibility to do so may be greater if the terms are visibly

---

[146] The dispute in *Aminoil* v. *Kuwait* (1982) 21 *ILM* 976 provides the classic illustration. The windfall profits were due to the hike in the price of oil brought about by the oil cartel and not due to any inherent superiority in the methods used by the foreign investor.

[147] P. Cameron, *Property Rights and Sovereign Rights: The Case of North Sea Oil* (1983).

[148] A series of arbitration disputes arose involving Indonesia when the government of President Suharto fell. The incoming government alleged that the contracts made during the regime's tenure had been secured by corrupt means. Likewise, the contracts made by the Marcos government in the Philippines and the Abacha government in Nigeria were regarded as suspect by the succeeding governments. Likewise the fall of the Bhutto regime in Pakistan and the Suharto regime in Indonesia were followed by disputes in which bribery was alleged.

[149] *Société des Grands Travaux de Marseille* v. *Bangladesh* (1980) 5 *YCA* 177.

[150] The validity of the contracts made in Namibia under regimes controlled by South Africa has been questioned. See C. M. Pilgrim, 'Some Legal Aspects of Trade in Natural Resources in Namibia' (1990) 61 *BYIL* 248. See, in particular, the discussion of the *Urenco Case* at pp. 266–78. The case (which is unreported) arose from Decree No. 1 of the United Nations Council on Namibia, which banned all trade in the natural resources of Namibia done in pursuance of contracts made during the regime controlled by South Africa.

seen to be disadvantageous to the state. Many international lawyers have claimed that international law has moved towards the recognition of democratic governance. If this is so, then uniform application of the view requires that it be extended to contracts made by foreign investors with unrepresentative governments and that the rule not be confined to providing a justification for military intervention in the affairs of undemocratic states.[151] The issue will arise in situations such as post-Saddam Iraq as to the validity of the oil contracts made by the post-Saddam administration, which was set up by the United States without the agreement of the United Nations. The contracts made by the administration in the Iraqi oil industry will suffer from instability as their validity comes to be questioned.[152]

Contracts made with military regimes will also pose a problem. Quite apart from the opportunity for capricious takings in such military regimes, they are unrepresentative and are determined by the preferences of the junta in power. An incoming democratic regime may declare that it is not bound by contracts made by the military regime. The extent to which democracy and self-determination are normative factors affecting the exercise of power of governments in the conclusion of contracts is yet to be settled.[153] One view is that the foreign investor who made the investment agreement with a totalitarian government consciously took the risk of its validity being contested by a later democratic government and hence need not be protected. Yet, to the extent that an incoming democratic government derives benefits from the investment, there could be a case for the protection of the investment through international law, particularly in circumstances where such investment has been shown to be beneficial to the state.[154] In the extractive industries, the case for the invalidity of such contracts may be greater because an unrepresentative government cannot act on behalf of a people in whom sovereignty over natural resources is vested under international law.[155]

4.6 Onerous contracts

Foreign investment contracts, which become too onerous to perform, are also subject to the risk of government intervention. In these circumstances, states will reduce the loss that could be suffered by the state or the state agency by interfering legislatively with the contract. The facts of *Settebello* v. *Banco Totta Acores*[156] are illustrative. A state-owned shipyard in Portugal had made a contract to build a large oil tanker. There were penalty

---

[151] The rule relating to democratic governance has been discussed largely in the context of the legitimacy of intervention to promote democracy in the target state. As such, it becomes a highly contentious doctrine. Those who favour the existence of such a rule do not address the situation of foreign investment contracts made with totalitarian governments, which may indicate that the norm proposed is not to be uniformly applied but is a covert basis for undermining governments that states do not approve of.

[152] The situation is similar to the uranium contracts made in Namibia when South Africa was in control of that country.

[153] A modern instance is *Yaung Chi Oo Ltd* v. *Myanmar* (2003) 42 *ILM* 540; (2003) 8 *ICSID Reports* 463.

[154] See *Westinghouse* v. *Philippines*, where, in dubious circumstances, a contract made during the Marcos regime was given effect, despite its being rescinded by the incoming Aquino government. The same situation was repeated in *Fraport* v. *Philippines* (ICSID, 2007), when a successor government alleged that bribery took place during the previous regime. The contract-based arbitration is pending. In the ICSID arbitration, the tribunal found that it lacked jurisdiction because a local law had been violated.

[155] This assumes that the doctrine of sovereignty over natural resources forms a rule of international law. Some have argued that it forms an *ius cogens* norm of international law, in which case the argument advanced here has greater force.

[156] [1985] 1 WLR 1050.

provisions in the contract for late performance. The shipyard was unable to meet the time limit set in the contract and was in danger of having to pay a large penalty. The Portuguese government intervened through legislation and altered the penalty provisions in the contract. The other party was unable to obtain a remedy in such a situation either within or outside Portugal.

4.7 Regulation of the economy

The modern state, despite its adherence to an open economy, contains a substantial amount of regulatory mechanisms which control the economy. In the case of developing countries, adherence to the middle path, which has been described above, makes such regulatory control intense. With the onset of the global economic crisis in 2008, and with the retreat of liberalisation, there will be an increase in the regulation of foreign investment, particularly in developed countries. What is described as 'investment protectionism' is an increasing phenomenon which witnesses the imposition of controls over the entry of foreign investment either through existing laws on mergers or national security or through the adoption of new methods of investment control. Such investment control has existed in developing countries and may increase in response to the economic crisis.

The scope for interference with foreign investment, which does not adhere to the policy objectives behind the regulations increases with the adoption of such policies. Regulations are usually implemented through licensing systems, and the sanction is withdrawal of the licence. Without the licence, the foreign investor cannot operate lawfully. The role of regulation and the extent to which it is permissible become important issues in the law. Many recent cases have considered the question as to when a regulation is permissible and when such regulation becomes expropriatory so that it has to be compensated. Regulation in the field of the environment is the most common cause of disputes. The issue whether regulatory interference could amount to expropriation or to violation of the treatment standards in the investment treaties will increasingly arise before arbitral tribunals. Consequently, there would be scope for greater refinement of the circumstances in which an expropriation would be considered as regulatory.[157]

4.8 Human rights and environmental concerns

The burgeoning law on human rights and environmental protection also creates instability in an area of law that was designed solely with the single objective of protecting foreign investment. The creation of competing objectives of protecting human rights and the environment from the abuse of multinational corporations leads to a recognition of the regulatory right of the state to interfere in circumstances where the multinational corporate investor abuses human rights such as labour rights or causes environmental damage. The increasing recognition of such a regulatory right will undermine the aim of investment

---

[157] These issues are discussed in later chapters.

protection and require the recognition that a state has the right to intervene in an investment that poses a danger to the environment or involves an abuse of human rights.

With some poetic justice, the disputes that have highlighted the issues of environmental protection have arisen in the context of investments made in the context of the NAFTA provisions on investment.[158] They have involved allegations of environmental abuse made by one developed state party to the treaty against multinational corporations from the other developed state party. In many of these cases, the issue has been raised of whether a regulatory interference to promote environmental interests could amount to a taking of property. This issue will be considered more fully in Chapter 8 below. For the moment, it is necessary to note that competing concerns of environmental protection and the protection of human rights could trump the interests of investment protection in certain circumstances.[159] This introduces a new element of instability into the international law on foreign investment.

The effort towards the recognition of responsibility in terms of international law for the violation of human rights has gathered momentum in both domestic and international law. No longer does the hoary idea of lack of personality nullify the responsibility of multi-national corporations for abuses of human rights. Within domestic systems, the responsi-bility of multinational corporations under the laws of their home state for involvement in human rights abuses is coming increasingly to be recognised. This is most evident in the United States, where an Act made in 1789 has been revived in order to base litigation against US multinational corporations for wrongs under international law committed abroad.[160] This trend may take hold in other domestic jurisdictions as well.[161]

Equally importantly, there are movements within international law towards the recog-nition of the liability of multinational corporations for environmental and human rights abuses.[162] These movements should have an impact on how investment disputes are decided. Hitherto, the emphasis on investment protection has acted to exclude other factors. This may not be possible in the future as such an approach is inconsistent with trends in international law. Investment treaties are located within international law and have to be interpreted in the context of such law.[163] It would not be fitting that they continue to be interpreted without reference to wider international law and only with regard to commercial interests. Wider societal values must be taken into account. Development,

---

[158] The classic case is *Methanex* v. *United States*, where measures taken against a Canadian company manufacturing an alleged carcinogen was involved. In *S. D. Myers* v. *Canada* (2000) 40 *ILM* 1408; (2002) 121 *ILR* 7, the situation involved the transport of toxic substances.

[159] This is as yet a remote possibility, if the *dictum* in *Santa Elena* v. *Costa Rica* (2000) 39 *ILM* 317; (2002) 5 *ICSID Reports* 153, that even taking for valid environmental reasons has to be compensated, is accepted.

[160] On the Act, see G. Fletcher, *Tort Liability for Human Rights Abuses* (2008).

[161] In the UK, in *Cape* v. *Lubbe* [2000] UKHL 41, litigation in respect of a tort committed abroad was recognised.

[162] O. de Schutter (ed.), *Transnational Corporations and Human Rights* (2006).

[163] See further R. Suda, 'The Effect of Bilateral Investment Treaties on Human Rights Enforcement and Realisation', in O. de Schutter (ed.), *Transnational Corporations and Human Rights* (2006). p. 73. The extent to which international law principles should guide international trade tribunals has been discussed. See J. Pauwelyn, *Conflict of Norms in Public International Law: How WTO Law Relates to Other Rules of International Law* (2003); and J. Harrison, *Human Rights Implications of the WTO Organization* (2007). Some provisions in TRIPS, the agreement on intellectual property, had to be changed to accommodate compulsory licensing and parallel imports in light of the controversy surrounding cheaper anti-AIDS drugs. It is evident that trade or investment principles which emphasise the interests of traders and investors over the public interest will have to yield.

which lies at the root of modern international investment law, is such a value, representing not only economic considerations but also other issues such as human rights and the environment. Unless such values are incorporated in the law, the system will begin to face dissent sufficient to undermine it. Some principles of human rights have *ius cogens* status and will override inconsistent principles of investment protection.

4.9 The law-and-order situation

Instability in the law-and-order situation in a state poses a threat to foreign investment. Where the political situation foments animosity against foreigners and targets their property, difficulties will arise. These usually arise when the government is unable to contain marauding mobs and gangs of criminals or when the government itself foments uprisings against foreigners, as the government in Zimbabwe did in 2002 when it felt itself under political threat.[164] Such situations are usually provided for in terms of international law through rules that engage the responsibility of the state where it fails to give protection to the interests of the foreigner from anticipated attacks on his person or property.

However, the foreign investor could well be the reason for the discontent. The long-running dispute in the Ogoni region in Nigeria provides an example where the people of the region allege that they have to bear the environmental degradation caused by oil exploitation while the profits go to the central government. Similar problems arise in mining and other investments made in the ancestral lands of the aboriginal people.

5. Sources of the international law on foreign investment

Claims relating to the norms of an international law of foreign investment can be accepted as principles of international law only if they are based on an accepted source of public international law. These sources of international law are stated in Article 38(2) of the Statute of the International Court of Justice. It will be useful to indicate the sources on which the principles of an international law on foreign investment are established.

5.1 Treaties

Multilateral treaties are a source of international law, as they evidence an acceptance of a principle of international law by parties to the treaty. There are, however, no relevant treaties among a large number of states which furnish a comprehensive codified law on foreign investment. At the conclusion of the Second World War, there was an effort to create an International Trade Organization, and some of the rules of its charter would have had relevance for foreign investment.[165] But, the effort to create such an organisation was

---

[164] The Mugabe regime, facing opposition, diverted attention by means of a scheme for seizing the property of white farmers and handing the property over to the indigenous people. A claim brought by several farmers on the basis of the Netherlands–Zimbabwe investment treaty has been arbitrated and damages awarded to the farmers.

[165] J. E. S. Fawcett, 'The Havana Charter' (1949) 5 *Yearbook of World Affairs* 320.

unsuccessful, though such an organisation was eventually created in 1995 in the form of the World Trade Organization. The Abs–Shawcross Convention, essentially a private endeavour with the backing of the International Chamber of Commerce, sought to formulate such a code on foreign investment. It was not accepted by states and is therefore of little precedential value.[166] The code sought to state principles which were entirely favourable to capital-exporting countries, but they were unacceptable to developing states. It was sponsored by Germany in the OECD, but efforts to have it adopted were abandoned. The OECD was to attempt a Multilateral Agreement on Investment in the 1990s, but again the attempt met with failure, largely because of dissension within developed states as well as because of the opposition generated by NGOs to a code that took into account only the interests of multinational corporations. The only successful convention in the field is the ICSID Convention. But, this is a procedural convention only, setting up machinery for the settlement of investment disputes through arbitration. Clearly, the technique adopted by the developed states and the World Bank, which was instrumental in bringing about this Convention, was that, if procedural means for protection were created, then recourse to these procedural means of protection through arbitration would enable the building of substantive principles of investment protection. That strategy seems to have met with partial success. But, carried to extremes, states will become wary of this approach and tend to withdraw from the system.[167]

The WTO has been assigned the task of preparing an investment discipline by the Singapore Ministerial Meeting. The Doha Ministerial Meeting reiterated the desire to formulate an instrument on foreign investment. But, the nature of the schisms between states on this issue was already visible at that time. The differences surfaced prior to the Cancun Ministerial Meeting in 2003. The project within the WTO on an investment instrument floundered as a result of a coalition of developing countries, led by India and China, opposing the move. Generally, the efforts at the making of multinational agreements in this field have served only to indicate the nature of the dissension among states as to what the rules on foreign investment at the global level are.

There have been several regional treaties on foreign investment. The strongest provisions are those contained in Chapter 11 of NAFTA. The provisions of this chapter largely track the model bilateral investment treaty of the United States. It creates a framework for the free movement of investments within the NAFTA region. The treaty provides for a strong investor–state dispute-settlement mechanism, giving the investor a unilateral right to invoke arbitration against the host state. There has been much case law generated under NAFTA, and considerable literature has been generated because much of this case law indicates that NAFTA will provide restraints on the exercise of regulatory powers by states. Since the treaty affects developed states, namely, the United States and Canada, anxieties expressed earlier by developing states regarding restraints on sovereignty in investment

---

[166] G. Schwarzenberger, *Foreign Investment and International Law* (1969); Lord Shawcross, 'The Problems of Foreign Investment in International Law' (1961) 102 *Hague Recueil* 334.

[167] The illustration is provided by some Latin American countries such as Bolivia and Ecuador withdrawing from the ICSID Convention.

treaties are now coming to be expressed by US and Canadian commentators. Both states have new model treaties based on their experience as respondents in investment arbitrations. The US model treaty has not pleased conservative commentators.[168] The regression from older norms can be explained by the fact that the United States is now a massive importer of capital and thus has to be concerned with its regulation.

There are other regional treaties. The ASEAN Treaty on the Protection and Promotion of Foreign Investment contained strong provisions, but, since only approved investments were protected by the treaty, there was sufficient room provided for regulatory control over the entry of foreign investment. The later ASEAN framework Agreement on Investments, however, created the concept of an 'ASEAN Investor' and permitted freedom of movement within the ASEAN area to the entity or person who fell within the definition. These earlier ASEAN treaties have now been replaced with a new treaty, the ASEAN Comprehensive Treaty on Investments. Other regional treaties, such as the Mercosur Agreement, create similar regional arrangements with protection granted in varying degrees to the foreign investment of the participating regional states. There is an increasing practice to negotiate free trade agreements. Some of them are bilateral, and some are regional. These agreements contain provisions on investment protection. The most spectacular of them, if it ever comes into being, will be the Free Trade Agreement of the Americas, which would cover the whole of North, Central and South America. It is, however, evident that this project for such a widespread treaty will have to be abandoned. With the economic crisis of 2008 indicating that the fervour for liberalisation has considerably diminished, enthusiasm for such treaties will abate. The notion of uncontrolled national treatment which these treaties contemplate will sit uneasily with the view that the economic crisis of 2008 will lead to increasing control over the economy.

Besides these regional treaties, there are bilateral investment treaties, which at the last count numbered almost 3,000. Relying on this impressive number, some have argued that these treaties create customary international law.[169] Though the repetition of the rule in numerous treaties may create customary international law, regard must also be had to variations in the structure of the treaties in which the rule is embedded. Bilateral investment treaties, though similar in structure, vary as to detail to such an extent that it would be difficult to argue that they are capable of giving rise to customary international law.[170]

The debate whether investment treaties create customary law will linger. As the project to devise a multilateral treaty has floundered, the effort to introduce investment-protection norms through the backdoor of customary international law will increase on those bent on absolute investment protection. The investment treaties, coupled with the interpretation placed on them, will be used in order to construct the belief that a widely accepted body of customary principles has been created on the basis of the treaties and the arbitral awards based on them.

---

[168] S. Schwebel, 'The US 2004 Model Bilateral Investment Treaty: An Exercise in the Regressive Development of International Law', in *Liber Amicorum Robert Briner* (2005).

[169] The genesis of this view is in F. A. Mann, 'British Treaties for the Promotion and Protection of Foreign Investments' (1982) 52 *BYIL* 241.

[170] This point is developed further in Chapter 5 below.

But, such a thesis will not even get off the ground. Not only are the treaties diverse in their formulation, but the arbitral awards that interpret them exhibit such divergence that it is unlikely that common principles can be extracted from them. Much rethinking will need to be done on recapturing the regulatory space that has been sacrificed as a result of the treaties and the encroachments on this space made by arbitral tribunals, which often show a near-fundamentalist zeal for investment protection to the exclusion of other considerations such as economic development, human rights and the environment.

5.2 Custom

A widespread custom is a source of international law, as it expresses an *opinio iuris* within the international community that the principle involved is obligatory. There are few customs in this sense in the field of foreign investment. There is, however, a custom that, when property is taken over by a state, otherwise than in the exercise of its regulatory powers, there must be payment of compensation, though there is still no agreement on the manner in which this compensation is to be calculated.

Developing states have used their numerical strength in the General Assembly to adopt resolutions in the area of foreign investment. The extent to which such resolutions can create international law has been a matter of intense debate. The view has been expressed that the principles contained in General Assembly resolutions constitute 'instant customary international law' in that they are evidence of an *opinio iuris* of the international community formed at a solemnly constituted assembly.[171] However, the proposition was initially formulated in the context of, and was confined to, areas that were not governed by existing legal norms. There is also the view that frequently asserted resolutions of the General Assembly have a law-creating effect.[172] But, developed states would argue that they had already established norms in this area through a consistent assertion of claims based on those norms. Given this fact, General Assembly resolutions will at best have the effect of articulating a different set of norms that apply in this area. The resolutions on permanent sovereignty over natural resources,[173] on the Charter of Economic Rights and Duties of States[174] and on the New International Economic Order are the most prominent resolutions which have been passed in this area. The resolution on permanent sovereignty over natural resources can be regarded as a mere assertion of sovereign control over natural resources within the territory of the state. It merely asserts a self-evident principle and hence would receive general acceptance in modern international law.[175] The need for the assertion of permanent sovereignty over natural resources arose out of the existence of a theory that had been built up in international law that contracts made by multinational corporations with host states in respect of natural resources were binding and had the force of quasi-treaties. There was a need to displace such doctrines through the assertion of competing, rather self-evident principles.

---

[171] B. Cheng, 'United Nations Resolutions on Outer Space: Instant International Customary Law' (1965) 5 *IJIL* 23.
[172] *Nicaragua Case* [1986] *ICJ Reports* 14 at 99–100.   [173] GA Res. 1803 (XVII) of 1962.
[174] GA Res. 3281 (XXIX) of 1974.   [175] The assertion that it is an *ius cogens* principle is, however, contested.

Efforts have been made to dismiss resolutions asserted in connection with the New International Economic Order as 'soft law' or as *lex ferenda*.[176] They are supposed to have only a hortatory significance. But, this area is governed by rules that are built up through arbitral awards and the writings of publicists, in themselves the weakest sources of law. In that context, the relegation of instruments collectively made by states to a status inferior to that of the views of individual arbitrators and writers is merely an expression of a preference for certain views the impact of which on the law cannot be significant.[177]

There are two objections to the relegation of the principles contained in General Assembly resolutions to an inferior status. The first is that, to the extent that the resolutions seek to establish exclusive control over economic activity, including foreign investment, within the territory of a state, they assert a generally established proposition of international law. No state, developed or developing, doubts the proposition that it has total control over all economic activity which takes place within its boundaries. This is a self-evident principle of state sovereignty. The need for developing states to assert such a principle was based on the notion that, though decolonisation ended political dominance, economic dominance by multinational corporations over the former colonial powers continued to persist. The recovery of economic control was achieved through a spate of nationalisations. It was necessary to assert the validity of these nationalisations. The permanent sovereignty resolutions coincided with these takings of the property of foreign investors and the restructuring of the economies of the newly independent states. There was a specific need for these resolutions in the context of what was taking place. Otherwise, the resolutions were stating a rather innocuous principle of state sovereignty with which there can be no quarrel, except that they also affected the laboriously built-up theory that foreign investment contracts had a status in international law akin to treaties. The continuing significance of the resolutions in modern law is that they refute the theory that foreign investment contracts undergo a process of internationalisation that makes them subject to principles of international law or transnational law. The need to attack the resolutions proceeds from the need on the part of multinational corporations to preserve this theory of the internationalisation of the foreign investment contract.[178] It is unlikely that any state in the world would seek to contest the proposition that it has exclusive competence as to the disposal of the natural resources within its territory

Second, dismissal of the norms contained in the resolutions as 'soft law' or as *lex ferenda* must presuppose the existence either of rules that are based on a higher level in the hierarchy of the sources of law or of a field that is not governed by any rules at all. Neither seems to be the case. There are competing rules, such as the notion of an internationalised

---

[176] In *Texaco* v. *Libya* (1977) 53 *ILR* 389, the arbitrator, Professor Dupuy, characterised the permanent sovereignty resolution as *lex ferenda*. I. Seidl-Hohenveldern, 'Hierarchy of Norms Applicable to International Investments', in W. P. Heere (ed.), *International Law and Its Sources: Liber Amicorum Maarten Bos* (1989), p. 147, placed General Assembly resolutions 'at the bottom of the scale of rules dealing with international investments'.

[177] The writer acknowledges that the same criticism could be made of his views. There is no monopoly on prejudice. But, the objection is to writers who dress their opinions up as scientific truths without acknowledging the selectivity of their exercise. But, the views of solitary arbitrators like Dupuy in *Texaco* v. *Libya* (1977) 53 *ILR* 389 can hardly stand against consistent assertion of a self-evident principle by the large majority of states.

[178] This theory is dealt with in Chapter 9 below.

contract referred to above. These rules are formulated in (often uncontested) arbitral awards and in the writings of publicists (which are often not unanimous on the point). The test in this situation should be one of opposability of the different sets of norms. The old norms supported by the capital-exporting states seek to set up an international standard of treatment for foreign investment. These norms depend to a large extent on the opinions of individual arbitrators and publicists. They constitute subsidiary sources of international law. The law created by such low-order sources has little weight when juxtaposed with the view expressed by a large number of states in the General Assembly. At the least, the opinions of these states so expressed must have the effect of neutralising the views stated by mere individuals even in positivist theory. Mere neutralisation of these norms will not be sufficient, as this will create a situation of normlessness. It is therefore necessary to accept the set of norms that is consistent with basic rules of international law. The notion of economic sovereignty, which the General Assembly resolutions seek to support, accords with the principle of state sovereignty. This is the organising principle of the modern international system, though its erosion through progressive rules in the sphere of human rights and the establishment of peace has to be acknowledged. To the extent that the General Assembly resolutions merely assert the principle of sovereignty over territorial incidents, they state the obvious. Except to the extent that the right to control foreign investment has been subjected to treaty control, the state continues to retain the right to control foreign investment. Such a view will not be contested in respect of foreign investment made in a developed state. There is no basis to argue that the situation is somehow different in respect of developing states.[179] The resolutions of the General Assembly merely claim these basic rights for newly independent states. The necessity felt to deal with the situation through treaties that is reflected in current state practice is an acknowledgment of the fact that there has been a failure to create norms favourable to investment protection through weak sources of international law.

The formation of customary principles has been associated with power. The role of power in this area is evident. Powerful states sought to construct rules of investment protection largely aimed at developing states by espousing them in their practice and passing them off as customary principles. They were always resisted. The Latin American states, for example, resisted US claims to an international minimum standard of treatment of aliens and their property. Nevertheless, the norms that were supported by the developed states were maintained on the basis that they were accepted as custom, though that was never the case. The significance of the General Assembly resolutions associated with the New International Economic Order is that they demonstrated that there were a large number, indeed a large majority, of the states of the world which did not subscribe to the norms maintained by the developed world. After that, it was no longer credible to maintain that there was in fact an international law on foreign investment, though the claim continues to be made simply because of the need to conserve the gains made for investment protection by developed states.

---

[179] In the 1960s, a body of literature did in fact make this distinction, which flies in the face of the doctrine of equality of states, another basic, though fictitious, organising principle of the international system.

The role of power was particularly evident in the period of ascendancy of neo-liberalism when efforts were made to bring about multilateral rules on foreign investment by agreement. Direct methods of doing so failed when the OECD efforts at such an agreement collapsed due to a lack of unanimity among the developed states which attempted its negotiation. Thereafter, the shift was to the view that such a system could be brought about through arbitral awards based on a network of investment treaties and through the writings of commentators whose articles were often published in several places in the hope that repetition would make up for their lack of cogency. The need for global standards of governance for uplifting the masses of the underprivileged (an idea reminiscent of the standards of civilisation of a former age) and the rule of law were combined to advance the neo-liberal cause. The notion was that, once the rules contained in investment treaties (which treaties were regarded as identical) are processed through arbitration, they should be accepted as global rules.[180] The strategy has not worked. Writers have pointed out that investment treaties contain widely disparate standards, despite being similar in form. Even treaties of the same state do not contain identical principles and standards. They differ depending on the perceptions and needs of the different times at which they were made.[181] Neither have the interpretations placed on treaty provisions by arbitrators been uniform. Differences between awards have given rise to doubts about the viability of establishing common global rules on investment protection, and have resulted in the questioning of the very legitimacy of the system. These issues are discussed more fully in later chapters.

5.3 General principles of law

General principles of law are recognised as a source of law, but the weight accorded to this source of law is not as great as for the sources discussed above. Positivist legal scholars, who ascribe the rules of international law to the consent of states, treat custom and treaty as the only significant sources of international law. The limited scope of the role of general principles of law as a source of international law is generally accepted by authorities.

Yet, many claims as to the existence of principles of the international law on foreign investment have been based on general principles of law. Thus, much of the support for the payment of full compensation upon expropriation of foreign property is based on arguments relating to notions of unjust enrichment and acquired rights being general principles of law. Similarly, notions of equity are relied on to support similar rules. The principle that compensation must be paid is itself said to be a general principle of law.[182] General principles of law will therefore supply much fodder for arguments in this area of the law.

---

[180] The neo-liberal technique of processing preferred norms through judicial means is the basis of the work of Professor Hirschl. See R. Hirschl, *Towards Juristocracy: The Origins and Consequences of the New Constitutionalism* (2004).

[181] See the survey of Chinese practice in N. Gallagher and W. Shan, *Chinese Investment Treaties: Policy and Practice* (2009).

[182] Thus, in the *Chorzow Factory Case* [1928] PCIJ Series A No. 17, p. 29, the Permanent Court of International Justice said that 'it is a general conception of law that every violation of an engagement involves an obligation to make a reparation'. The statement dealt with the violation of a treaty obligation, but is used indiscriminately to support the payment of compensation in any taking.

These arguments will have to be evaluated carefully. The capacity of general principles to contribute to the law must be acknowledged. But, it must also be remembered that there is a high degree of subjectivity which attends the use of general principles of law. It is often possible to demonstrate that arguments based on general principles are intended to support an *a priori* assumption of the writers using them.

General principles of law have been used widely by arbitral tribunals in extracting principles applicable to investment contracts. There is a systematic pattern in their use by arbitral tribunals and precedents have been built on the basis of past awards recognising general principles. The existence of some general principles, consecrated by long acceptance within arbitral jurisprudence, cannot be denied. Consequently, general principles have acquired a role in the shaping of rules in the area of foreign investment protection. However, tribunals have used general principles in a manner which may not be acceptable to states. They have often selected rules that favour the promotion of investment protection and which are detrimental to the interests of the host state. This result can be explained only on the basis that the present arbitral system is inclined towards investment protection rather than towards the acknowledgment of norms that may favour developing states.[183]

Many examples of the selection of such norms may be given. The most important is the norm relating to the sanctity of contract. This norm denies the right of the state to change a foreign investment contract unilaterally. The notion of sanctity of contract is stated to be a general principle of law. Yet, the principle is taken from nineteenth-century systems of contract law which emphasised freedom of contract and the bargain struck as a result of the exercise of this freedom. The erosion of this doctrine forms the basis of the modern developments in the law of contract.[184] Yet, these developments that undermine the notion of sanctity of contract are ignored, and it is stated as a rule of international law, to the exclusion of the exceptions that undermine it in domestic contract systems.

Another example concerns the question as to whether an agreement between a foreign investor and the host state or a host state entity is akin to the *contrat administratif* of French law. Under the French concept, the administrative contract could be changed unilaterally in the public interest. If the parallel between administrative contracts and foreign investment contracts can be drawn and it can be shown that the notion of administrative contract is not confined to French law but is a general principle of law acceptable to all major legal systems, then the argument becomes possible that international law should accept the general principle that unilateral changes to foreign investment agreements in the public interest are permissible in international law. Though there is overwhelming acceptance of the view that administrative contracts are not peculiar to French law, arbitral jurisprudence has refused to accept this principle, favourable to developing states, as a general principle of law.[185] The acceptability of the law based

---

[183] For an interesting sociological work which considers the neutrality of arbitration and the possibility that arbitrators, particularly in the arbitration of foreign investment disputes, may show obvious prejudices, see Y. Dezalay and G. Bryant, *Dealing in Virtue: International Commercial Arbitration and the Construction of a Transnational Legal Order* (1996).

[184] P. Atiyah, *The Rise and Fall of the Freedom of Contract* (1979).

[185] See Arbitrator Dupuy in *Texaco* v. *Libya* (1977) 53 *ILR* 389. For a further consideration of the issues involved, see M. Sornarajah, *The Settlement of Foreign Investment Disputes* (2000).

on the subjective selection of general principles will be increasingly subjected to scrutiny and rejection. The norms based on general principles of law are, in any event, weak norms. They cannot resist norms proceeding from sources which rely on consensual processes among states.

5.4 Judicial decisions

Judicial decisions are a subsidiary source of international law. Though stated to be a subsidiary source, the decisions of the International Court of Justice and its predecessor have had an immense influence in shaping the principles of international law. There are four significant decisions of these courts in the area of foreign investment. The first, the *Chorzow Factory Case*,[186] a decision of the Permanent Court of International Justice, remains the basis for any discussion of issues of compensation for the taking of foreign property. The second, the *Barcelona Traction Case*,[187] concerned corporate nationality and the diplomatic protection of shareholders of corporations. The third, the *ELSI Case*,[188] concerned issues as to what amounts to a taking and whether liquidation of a foreign corporation by a court could provide the basis of a claim that there was a denial of justice for which responsibility arose in the state. More recently, *Diallo* v. *Congo*[189] dealt with the issue of corporate nationality and essentially confirmed the view taken in the *Barcelona Traction Case* that corporate nationality was determined by the place of incorporation. There are other decisions of the International Court of Justice which have peripheral relevance to the subject.

Arbitral awards made on disputes arising from foreign investment transactions also contribute to the subject, although many of the early awards were made unilaterally and their value is diminished for this reason. Yet, both the awards made by *ad hoc* tribunals as well as those made by institutional tribunals, particularly those made by tribunals constituted under the ICSID Convention, provide evidence of possible norms which could be used for the construction of norms of international law.[190] The emergence of differences of opinion between arbitral tribunals is a problem that has led to the questioning of the system of investment arbitration. This issue is discussed more fully later.

The decisions of the Iran–US Claims Tribunal also contribute principles which have to be taken into account.[191] There is one view that the awards of the Tribunal will have limited value as the Tribunal was set up by two states, and lacked a control mechanism, and there was already provision for the enforcement of the awards in the Algiers Accord (the instrument providing for the creation of the Tribunal). The precedential value of the Tribunal's awards will have to be considered carefully, as the Tribunal was created by treaty and had to apply the treaty's principles to the disputes. The exact terms used in the treaty have significance.

---

[186] [1928] PCIJ Series A No. 17. [187] [1970] *ICJ Reports* 1. [188] [1989] *ICJ Reports* 15. [189] [2008] *ICJ Reports*.
[190] See further M. Sornarajah, *The Settlement of Foreign Investment Disputes* (2000).
[191] The jurisprudence of the Tribunal is well served by the extensive analysis contained in G. Aldrich, *The Jurisprudence of the Iran–United States Claims Tribunal* (1996); and C. Brower, *The Iran–United States Claims Tribunal* (1998).

3

Controls by the host state

The right of a state to control the entry of foreign investment is unlimited, as it is a right that flows from sovereignty. The entry of any foreign investment can be excluded by a state. But, a sovereign entity can surrender its rights even over a purely internal matter by treaty.[1] Some regional and bilateral treaties now provide for the right of entry and establishment of investments to the nationals of contracting states.[2] Where such pre-establishment rights are created by treaty, the denial of a right of entry to any investor from one of the contracting states would amount to a violation of the treaty, unless it can be shown that his investment is not covered by the treaty.[3] Where the treaty permits both the right of entry and national treatment after entry to nationals of the contracting states, the right of control over the investment on the basis that the investment was made by an alien is entirely lost to each of the contracting states. Where such a treaty applies to the foreign investment, the treaty completely extinguishes the right of control the state has over the foreign investment, except where the treaty itself provides exceptions to this situation. It may still be the case that, in circumstances of necessity, the treaty rights of the foreign investor could be suspended.[4] Yet, it has to be concluded that such treaties diminish the right of control which the state has over the foreign investor. The extent to which different standards of treatment have an impact on the power of the host state to exercise control over foreign investment is discussed at the end of this chapter. For the moment it is assumed that, as in customary international law, unaffected by treaty, the host state has an absolute right of control over the entry and establishment and the whole of the process of foreign investment.

Once an alien enters a state, both he and his property are subject to the laws of the host state. This result flows from the fact that the foreign investor has voluntarily subjected himself to the regime of the host state by making entry into it. The unqualified right to exclude the alien prior to entry becomes somewhat modified after entry as the alien then

---

[1] Thus, in the case of entry by refugees, the Refugee Convention will control the rights of the refugee, which may be more certain than the rights of an alien. G. S. Goodwin-Gill, *International Law and the Movement of Persons Between States* (1978).

[2] The clearest example of this is to be found in the North American Free Trade Agreement (NAFTA). US, Canadian, Japanese and South Korean investment treaties provide for pre-entry national treatment, whereas European treaties generally avoid such treatment.

[3] There are wide sectoral and other limitations made to the right of entry. Thus, NAFTA permits sectoral limitations, and the list of excluded sectors attached by each of the participants is long.

[4] As the course of the Argentinian cases shows, this too is problematic.

comes to enjoy a status which is protected by international law.[5] Apart from the treaty protection that may be accorded to aliens, it is difficult to determine the source from which protection for such status is to be drawn.[6] Where conditions are attached to entry, the nature of the status that is protected is varied by the conditions.

The unlimited right of the state to control entry by an alien was stated by the Privy Council in the following terms:[7]

One of the rights possessed by the supreme power in every state is the right to refuse to permit the alien to enter that state, to annex what conditions it pleases to the permission to enter it and to expel or deport from the state, at pleasure, even a friendly alien, especially if it considers his presence in the state opposed to its peace, order and good government, or to its social or material interests.

This statement, transferred to the situation of the foreign investor, would mean that conditions could be attached to the entry of a foreign investor into a host state. Conditions could also be attached to the manner in which he operates his business. The proposition applies equally to a foreign corporation which makes the investment. The draft Code of Conduct on Transnational Corporations states a similar proposition in the following terms:[8]

States have the right to regulate the entry and establishment of transnational corporations including determining the role that such corporations may play in economic and social development and prohibiting or limiting the extent of their presence in specific sectors.

Judge Oda stated a similar proposition in his separate opinion in the *ELSI Case*[9] as regards the establishment of companies in foreign states. He observed:

It is a great privilege to be able to engage in business in a country other than one's own. By being permitted to undertake commercial or manufacturing activities or transactions through businesses incorporated in another country, nationals of a foreign country will obtain further benefits. Yet these local companies, as legal entities of that country, are subject to local laws and regulations; so that foreigners may have to accept a number of restrictions in return for the advantages of doing business through such local companies.

The rule so stated is not a new one. It originates from a rule relating to the power of exclusion of aliens which sovereign states possessed by virtue of their sovereignty. The power of exclusion implies the power to admit conditionally and withdraw the licence to do business where the condition is not satisfied. The rule is universally recognised.[10] The competing

---

[5] J. Brierly, *Law of Nations* (5th edn, 1963), p. 276. Brierly suggests that, after entry, the alien is entitled to 'a certain standard of decent treatment'. Others have referred to the same idea as an international minimum standard. The content of that standard is, however, a matter of dispute.

[6] The suggestion is that the practice of developed states supports the existence of an external standard.

[7] *Attorney-General for Canada* v. *Cain* [1906] AC 542 at 546. See also *Schmidt* v. *Secretary of State for Home Affairs* [1969] 2 Ch 149 at 168, where Lord Denning said: 'At common law, no alien has any right to enter this country except by leave of the Crown; and the Crown can refuse leave without giving any reason.' The common law has been modified by statute.

[8] UNCTC, 'Proposed Text of the Draft Code on Transnational Corporations', E/1988/39/Add.1 (1988).

[9] [1989] *ICJ Reports* 15 at 90.

[10] For the United States, see *Elkin* v. *US*, 142 US 65 (1892); and *Shaffer* v. *Heitner*, 433 US 188 (1977). Ralston observed: 'A nation may by general provisions exclude a certain class of individuals entirely or place limitations upon their admission subject to the duty to inform them of the special conditions of entry when they seek admission.' J. Ralston, *The Law and Procedure of International Tribunals* (1926), p. 270.

trend is based on the idea that there should be no restriction on the flow of foreign investment. This notion can be traced to Vitoria, who spoke of the natural human urge to trade and the need to protect the right of a person to trade wherever he pleases.[11] The United States has made efforts to maintain the notion of free investment flows through its treaty practice. It has a reputation for being a state which has openly admitted foreign investments.[12] Its adherence to such an idea is now to be doubted in view of the Exon–Florio Amendment to the Omnibus Trade and Competitiveness Act of 1988, which enables the President to prevent inflows of investment which threaten national security. There are also sectors of the US economy which are restricted to nationals.[13] As the United States and Europe become massive capital importers, it can be expected that their ideas on foreign investment will change and that it would adopt protectionist stances.[14] The conflict between the liberal idea of free flows of investment with the notion of sovereign rights of control of entry of investment is evident here. Powerful states, which see benefits in maintaining the stance of economic liberalism, have not been able to adhere to such liberal ideas in their own policies.[15] Economic liberalism has remained an ideal, whereas the prerogative power of the sovereign state to exclude aliens or to impose conditions on their entry is an accepted principle of the law. Increasingly, this power of exclusion will come to be exercised by developed states, particularly when foreign sovereign wealth funds seek to acquire shares in vital economic sectors.

On the basis of the rule that conditions could be imposed upon alien entry, the whole process of the foreign investment could be controlled by the host state's laws. The law of the host state could specify the legal vehicle through which the foreign investment should be made, the nature of the capital resources that should be brought from outside the state, the planning and environmental controls that the manufacturing plant should be subject to, the circumstances of the termination of the foreign investment and other like matters. While regulating the entry of foreign investment, a state could also seek to attract foreign investment into its territory by holding out incentives attractive to such investors. Increasingly, such legislation takes the form of a code or a single piece of legislation which states all the pertinent rules relating to the making of a foreign investment in a state. Besides facilitating the promotional purposes behind such codes, the existence of a single code enables the foreign investor to acquaint himself with the laws on foreign investment of a state more easily.

A state is not strictly bound by any unilateral commitments it makes at the time of the entry as to the applicability of future changes it makes to its laws unless there are treaty

---

[11] It has been suggested that these high-sounding altruistic ideas cloaked colonial expansion. See A. Anghie, *Imperialism, Sovereignty and the Making of International Law* (2005).

[12] This US policy dates from early times. The first US Treasury Secretary, Alexander Hamilton, articulated the policy in the following terms: 'Foreign capital, instead of being viewed as a rival, ought to be considered as a most valuable auxiliary, conducing to put in motion a greater quantity of productive labour and a greater portion of useful enterprise than could exist without it.' Quoted in C. D. Wallace (ed.), *Foreign Direct Investment in the 1990s* (1990), p. 1.

[13] The United States reserves these sectors when it makes bilateral investment treaties which grant rights of entry to the nationals of the other contracting state.

[14] This is already evident in the treatment of the attempts by Chinese investors to buy shares in US companies in the oil and other important sectors. The attempt by the Chinese National Oil Company to buy shares in Unocal did not succeed.

[15] S. Neff, *Economic Liberalism and the Law of Nations* (1991).

obligations which require the state to honour commitments made to other states as to the treatment of investments made by their nationals. To the extent that they are unilateral promises, they cannot bind the state or create obligations in favour of any third party.[16] Whether contractual commitments made to the effect that future laws will not affect a specific investment will fetter a state's legislative power to extend the law to that investment is, however, a hotly debated issue. As much as an alien who poses a threat to national security after he enters the country may be deported and the threat he poses thereby removed, so a foreign investment which proves to be adverse to the national interest may be terminated in accordance with the domestic law. The extent to which this right of the state is subject to standards of customary international law remains a matter of conjecture.[17] The aim of investment treaties is to restrict this right by providing for standards of treatment and creating rules against expropriation.

Laws controlling foreign investment are on the increase. Even states which maintain an open policy as regards foreign investment are now beginning to impose restraints on the inward flow of foreign investments. The reason for this lies in the rapid changes that are taking place in the picture of foreign investment flows around the world. The traditional exporters of capital are increasingly becoming recipients of capital. With greater cohesion anticipated in the European common market, there is an increase in the flow of foreign investment into the region in anticipation of these changes. The United States, the major exporter of capital, is now a recipient of massive inflows of foreign investment.[18] Increasing globalisation enables capital to move around the world more rapidly. The scope for such movements undermining the economy of states is great. A succession of economic crises has added to the fear that the rapid withdrawal of capital from states could destabilise their economies. As a result, there is a greater wariness as to foreign investment and an increasing readiness to control them. The picture that emerges is one of ambivalence. On the one hand, there is a desire to attract investment. On the other hand, there is a need to control it.[19] A state seeks to balance these competing functions through its investment laws. Though these are matters which may affect developing countries more, it is likely that the current economic crisis will ensure that developed states also follow similar patterns.[20]

The shifts in the pattern of investment flows have caused concern among these erstwhile exporters of capital who have realised the need for the control of such inflows so as to prevent their national and business interests being threatened. The example of the

---

[16] It must be remembered, however, that, in the context of treaties, a unilateral promise to arbitrate has been held to create an obligation to arbitrate. Other unilateral commitments have been held to create legitimate expectations the violation of which may give rise to damages where the investment is protected by an investment treaty containing a promise of fair and equitable treatment. See further Chapter 9 below.

[17] One may reason that there must be some objective criteria to assess situations of necessity. But, in the absence of any machinery that can judge this, a state is the arbiter of what situations justify breaking obligations on the ground of necessity. The possibility of the breach being litigated is remote.

[18] E. Graham and P. Krugman, *Foreign Direct Investment in the United States* (1991).

[19] This ambivalence is demonstrated in attitudes to investment flows from China. Such investment flows are courted by the United States, as China has capital that could help lift the United States out of the global economic crisis, but, at the same time, the United States is wary that important sectors of its economy could be subjected to Chinese control through the acquisition of shares in companies that operate in these sectors.

[20] Flows of investment into developed countries take different forms such as mergers and acquisitions, which are controlled through different regulatory mechanisms such as securities regulations and antitrust laws.

Exon–Florio Act in the United States has already been referred to.[21] The growth of sovereign wealth funds will lead to fears that their investments have political and other strategic goals that may affect national security interests. Such fears will result in increasing controls over the entry of foreign investment.

There have been moves to widen the scope of national security legislation to include the screening of foreign investment entry into the United States. Existing antitrust and securities law and other regulatory mechanisms may also be used to control investment flows. Within the European Community, a similar result is sought to be achieved through the use of competition laws to ensure that large foreign multinational corporations do not enter and drive out smaller European firms through abuse of their dominant position. Merger controls may be used to achieve the similar result of keeping out large foreign firms from the European markets. Many European countries have stringent reporting requirements for foreign investment. It could well be that competition laws could come to be used for similar purposes in the future in developing countries as well.[22] One problem that could be addressed through competition laws in developing countries occurs where entry is made by foreign multinational companies in association with existing large firms in the host state, thereby reducing or eliminating the possibility of any competition within the market. Often, this has significance not only for the market structure but also for the internal political power balance within the state.[23]

The use of foreign investment laws to scrutinise the entry of foreign investment into host states will be increasingly resorted to for various reasons in both developed and developing states. The satisfaction of nationalist lobbies concerned about increasing control of the economy by foreign states, the perception of some types of investment as being deleterious to the interests of the state, the fear that national companies may not be able to withstand competition from an incoming foreign company which may have superior technology and other resources are reasons for developed states to seek to control the influx of foreign investment. Many developed states have direct legislation on the entry of foreign investment.[24]

In the developing states, there is a similar body of law controlling the influx of foreign investments, though the reasons for such legislation are somewhat different. Socialist states, like China, Vietnam and Cuba, also began to promote the entry of foreign investments in the hope of attracting much needed capital and technology, and have enacted foreign investment codes. The first part of this chapter contains a study of such laws and the objectives behind the legislation enacted by developing states, including the socialist states.

---

[21] F. P. Waite and M. R. Goldberg, 'National Security Review of Foreign Investment in the United States' (1991) 6 *Florida Journal of International Law* 191; D. Baily, G. Harte and R. Sugden, 'US Policy Debate Towards Inward Investment' (1992) 26 *JWTL* 65.

[22] The view taken in using the new Chinese anti-monopoly legislation, enacted in 2008, is illustrative. The first case related to the prevention of a merger by Coca-Cola with the leading Chinese soft-drinks manufacturer on the basis that there was no benefit accruing from such a merger. It will be interesting to see whether the Chinese authorities will seek to apply the legislation extraterritorially to prevent mergers which Chines companies were stopped from making on the basis that these foreign mergers will impact Chinese markets. EU antitrust law has been applied extraterritorially to demonstrate concern over mergers taking place outside the EU.

[23] Thus, in Indonesia, studies show that foreign investment often aligns itself with the dominant Chinese companies within the state. This creates ethno-nationalistic problems and focuses hostility on the minority Chinese community.

[24] D. Flint, *Foreign Investment Law in Australia* (1986). The mechanism described largely continues in effect.

There are seemingly incompatible aims sought to be achieved by such legislation. On the one hand, the legislation evidences a desire to attract foreign investment by offering incentives and guarantees against potential risks such as expropriation. On the other hand, the legislation seeks to regulate both the entry and the operation of the foreign investment in the host state. As a result, the role, if any, which international law plays in the process of foreign investment seems restricted. But, it may come to be argued, with increasing vigour in the future, that even these regulatory measures will have to conform to minimum standards and that the violation of these standards will amount to an actionable wrong in international law.[25] The network of investment treaties will also be exploited to advance such arguments. In this way, international law will continue to retain its significance for the process of foreign investment. The law is best seen as involving a clash of the different interests, with one set of interests prevailing over others depending on the external circumstances.

The techniques and the degree of control adopted in such legislation may differ. But, they all aim to subject the process of foreign investment to the administrative control of the host state. In some legislation, the vehicle through which foreign investment could make an entry is identified. The host state seeks to increase its leverage over the foreign investment by limiting entry through devices over which control could be more easily exercised. Thus, the foreign investment laws may provide that entry may be made only through a joint venture with a local partner and specify the type of shareholding that the foreign party may have.[26] In many instances, the joint venture could be made only with a state entity, thus ensuring that the government policy in a particular industry is given expression at every stage of the venture in which the foreigner participates. The second section of the chapter deals with the legal vehicles which have been devised to ensure that an element of control by the host state or by host state interests is maintained continuously in the working of the foreign investment. Here, again, the strategy of the host country would be to ensure the localisation of the foreign investment process by ensuring that the form that is chosen to implement the foreign investment is amenable to local pressure. It seeks to defeat the possibility of the internationalisation of the foreign investment by increasing contacts with the state. The foreign investor would, in turn, seek to incorporate into this form as many international elements as possible to secure his investment by removing it from the scope of the local control devices.

Despite these efforts at regulating any foreign investment which comes into its territory, a state is never fully able to localise the foreign investment. The nature of the process of foreign investment is such that it will always have international elements. There are three important areas of international law which confer protection on the alien and his property. The first relates to the rules of state responsibility for injuries to aliens.[27] There are strong

---

[25] There is an increasing sign of this development in recent litigation. Thus, in *Amco* v. *Indonesia*, 1 *ICSID Reports* 589, after a long and protracted arbitration of the dispute, the eventual conclusion was that the manner of the withdrawal of the licence given to the foreign investor was without sufficient due process and that damages should be awarded on this basis. In *Ethyl* v. *Canada*, the complaint concerned a ministerial announcement of an environmental measure.

[26] Compare the situation in *Fraport* v. *Philippines* (ICSID, 2007), where the Anti-Dummy Law restricted foreign participation in the venture to 40 per cent.

[27] C. F. Amerasinghe, *State Responsibility for Injuries to Aliens* (1967).

claims that certain minimum safeguards are provided to an alien and that these minimum standards of treatment cannot be violated by the host state. Though, in the past, these minimum standards of treatment were abusively used to provide pretexts for intervention by powerful states and attracted a measure of resentment, in modern times these standards assumed a new form through association with developments in human rights. But, it still remains an issue whether the arguments based on human rights standards have relevance to this field.[28] Many of the claims as to the law in this area related to the extent to which a state owes a duty to protect foreign businessmen and their property from rioters during civil unrest. The extent of the customary law standards that protect the foreign investor and, to that extent, restrict the right of control of the host state are dealt with at the end of this chapter.

The increasing regulatory standards imposed on foreign investment will also result in novel arguments based on state responsibility. These will take the form of seeking a review of the exercise of such regulatory decisions in accordance with certain minimum standards acceptable to international law. It is conceivable that a body of international administrative law dealing with administrative wrongs could be constructed on the basis of new decisions involving such types of wrong. Such a law postulating common standards of procedural protection against the use of the discretionary power of administrative bodies may be discernible in the trade and investment areas. This is visible in the efforts of arbitral tribunals creatively to read into the once dormant standard of fair and equitable treatment notions of protection of legitimate expectations and transparency, and thereby extend the scope of liability.[29] The second area through which international law operates is through rules relating to international trade. Some of the regulations controlling foreign investors, such as the use of local components, may violate principles of free trade. There is an effort to include rules on investment within the competence of the World Trade Organization. The instrument on Trade-Related Investment Measures (TRIMS), for example, seeks to prohibit performance requirements associated with foreign investment.[30] On the other hand, some measures, particularly those on the control of the use of environmentally harmful methods of production, may be justified by movements that have taken place in the sphere of international environmental law.

A third area in which international law restricts the sovereign rights of the host state to impose whatever measure it pleases relates to the bilateral and regional investment treaties which have increased in number in recent times. It is well accepted in international law that sovereignty over a purely domestic matter could be restricted if there is an international treaty dealing with that matter. Bilateral and regional investment treaties, which are relatively recent efforts at investment protection,[31] seek to impose certain agreed standards of

---

[28] The right to property is isolated as the right to be protected. International human rights systems are ambivalent about the unqualified right to property.

[29] This is discussed more fully in Chapter 9 below.

[30] Performance requirements are conditions which require the foreign investor to use local components and labour, to export a percentage of the production or to locate in certain areas of the state. These conditions are prohibited in some bilateral investment treaties. On the basis that they distort trade, there is a move to prohibit them through WTO instruments, the TRIMS being an example of such an instrument. If the project to move the MAI to the WTO succeeds, then performance requirements will probably feature in the new efforts.

[31] They are generally dated from 1957, which was the year of the treaty between Germany and Pakistan.

treatment on the foreign investors of the state parties. The significance of these treaties to the international law on foreign investment is considerable. At least as between the parties to the treaties, they constitute the law on foreign investment. The treaties have a certain and definite content. The impact of these treaties is dealt with in Chapter 5 below.

The system of absolute regulation based on sentiments hostile to foreign investment has now passed. In its place, there has been instituted a system that is favourable to foreign investment. States are now more accommodating to foreign investment because they believe that such investment could be harnessed to aid in their development. A United Nations report described the trends relating to foreign investment legislation in developing countries in the following terms:[32]

In the early 1970s, fortified by their strengthened bargaining position as the centres of economic growth and as recipients of investments by transnational corporations in the developing world, most of these countries introduced rigorous regulatory regimes for foreign investment and technology. The basic objective of such regimes was not to discourage or diminish the flow of foreign resources but to regulate them. These regulations provided, inter alia, for the screening and registration of foreign investment; the prohibition or restriction of foreign participation in specified sectors; the control of take-overs; the restriction of foreign capital to minority holdings in certain sectors; specific regulation of technology agreements; the prohibition of restrictive business practice; and performance require-ments for subsidiaries of transnational corporations, such requirements relating to exports and integration with the domestic economy. However, since the mid-1970s, many of these countries have initiated policies and strategies that depart in certain significant respects from these early regimes. These new policies on the whole portray a more flexible and pragmatic approach aimed at facilitating and speeding up foreign investment inflows.

This may represent an over-optimistic assessment of the picture. Much of the regulatory structures that were put in place earlier still remains, despite the fact that the world has moved through a phase of economic liberalism that favoured the movement of foreign investment without restriction. There was a great move towards privatisation, resulting in the selling of state enterprises in the 1990s, but there was disenchantment with such measures due to political and other factors. Nationalism, ethnicity and other factors required states to retain a control over the flows of investment into their states.[33] Economics alone do not dictate the outcomes in the law on foreign investment. As a result, at no stage did a law that favours an entirely open economy come about in any state. The weak market structures of developing countries require the state to intervene more consistently and use policy prescriptions to achieve economic objectives. In that context, it is unlikely that the laws will undergo any dramatic change.[34]

Successive economic crises in Asia and Latin America have dented the force of neo-liberal views on foreign investment. Privatisation and other liberalisation measures that were

---

[32] UNCTC Third Survey, pp. 56–7.

[33] The role of ethnicity has been widely studied by Amy Chua, who has pointed out the retention of ethnic balances within pluralistic societies has required states to exert control over foreign investment lest such investment upset the balance within these societies by making alliances with economically strong minority groups.

[34] UNCTAD, *World Investment Report, 2003*, pp. 86–8, indicates three types of regulation in developing countries: attracting investment; channelling it to benefit development; and avoiding the harmful effects of investment.

taken during this period have been reversed in many states.[35] In Latin America, there was a leftward shift which reversed many of the changes made earlier.[36] This trend towards reversal of liberal investment policies may be replicated in developed countries as well when the effects of the global economic crisis of 2008 begin to take hold. Administrative control over investment entry may be a feature that becomes common to both developed and developing countries.

In modern times, there is a greater discretion vested in the administrative bodies screening investment entry to permit entry for investments considered desirable on more favourable terms. No state has taken its fervour for foreign investment to the extent of removing all controls on the flow of foreign investment into the host state. Yet, there was heavy competition for investments in the 1990s, which resulted in a competition to ensure that controls were relaxed and greater incentives were given to foreign investment. Even in this period, when conditions were favourable to foreign investment, there was no effort to remove controls over the influx of foreign investment entirely. It could well be that the laws would be more rigorously enforced in response to the economic crisis. A case-by-case, regulatory approach to foreign investments will have fresh implications for the protection of foreign investment that enters a state under such an administrative regime. The foreign investment comes to be made not only on the basis of a contract of investment as in the past but also on the basis of licences granted by the regulatory body. The process of entry ceases to be a private law measure alone and assumes public law features. Those who have addressed the issue in terms of international law have been preoccupied with the contractual aspects of the situation. The introduction of public law features into the process of foreign investment entry has consequences which are yet to be analysed.[37] The response to this new development took several forms. Investment treaties responded to it by including the licence within their definition of foreign investment, for it came to be realised that the mere withdrawal of the licence would nullify the objectives of the foreign investment leaving the property and ownership of it intact. Hence, it was necessary to redefine the taking of property to include the cancellation of a licence. Also, there was a need to introduce into the international law of foreign investment the same concepts that protected administrative licences in domestic law. This is seen in the requirement that due process should be provided before there is a withdrawal of a licence. This requirement began to appear in the provisions on expropriation in investment treaties as well as in case law on the subject.[38] It is important to understand the nature of the public law controls that have been instituted. The change that has been brought about as a result of the institution of these administrative measures will

---

[35] In Thailand, for example, the Asian economic crisis of 1997–8 was attributed to the sudden withdrawal of foreign assets. As a result, policies were changed so as to favour local investment which will not relocate in the face of potential economic crises. The policy of 'Thaksinisation', named after the then Prime Minister Thaksin, placed an emphasis on promoting local industries and business.

[36] In Venezuela, there was a requirement that companies 'migrate' to new structures that reflected greater national control, particularly in the petroleum sector.

[37] P. Cameron, *Property Rights and Sovereign Rights: The Case of North Sea Oil* (1983); T. Daintith, *The Legal Character of Petroleum Licences: A Comparative Study* (1981); G. van Harten, *Investment Treaty Arbitration and Public Law* (2007).

[38] See, for example, *Amco v. Indonesia*, where the tribunal held that violation of the due-process requirement prior to cancellation of the licence was the basis of the award of damages.

affect the claims and arguments that have been made about the rules of the law of foreign investment in the past. The foreign investor who enters the host state is estopped from arguing that he entered only on the basis of the investment contract as he would consciously have followed the legal requirements prescribed by the regulations and accepted the conditions that his investment had been subjected to. In these circumstances, where there has been an administrative interference by the state on the basis that the foreign investor had not complied with the conditions of entry, it would be futile to look upon the situation as a mere breach of the agreement on the basis of which entry was made. Equally, the state cannot capriciously interfere with the investment by cancelling a licence that it had awarded without providing adequate reasons for such a course and without giving an opportunity to the foreign investor to explain why those reasons should not apply. From the point of view of investment protection, the creation of machinery to review the adequacy of these reasons through external arbitral tribunals has been the most effective counter to these developments involving the use of discretionary administrative power over foreign investment.

1. Regulation of entry

Until recently, the control of foreign investment was effected, if at all, through immigration laws. There were no specific rules which controlled the influx of foreign investment. In times of war, there was control over enemy businesses, and restrictions were imposed on trading with the enemy and on the movement of alien businessmen present within the state.[39] But, these measures were seldom continued into peacetime.[40] Since state sovereignty provides the justification for such measures, there is no reason why such measures could not be continued in peacetime.[41]

In recent times, there has been a rapid movement towards the institution of foreign investment laws on a global scale. In developed countries, nationalism and protectionism have been the motives for the restriction of foreign investments.[42] There is no uniform policy that is maintained. The Canadian experience is instructive. The Foreign Investment Review Act was enacted in response to a report which indicated the dominance of US multinational corporations in the Canadian economy.[43] But, the Canada–US Free Trade Agreement nullified the assumptions on which the legislation was based as it liberalised the flow of investments between the two countries. Canada enacted new legislation in view of the treaty, but some limited controls over US investments still remain.[44] The North American Free Trade Agreement (NAFTA) entrenches that process.[45] But, Canada was

---

[39] Even in times of war, an alien owed a duty of allegiance to his host state. *De Jaeger* v. *Attorney-General of Natal* [1907] AC 326.

[40] M. Domke, *Trading with the Enemy in World War II* (1943).

[41] The Trading with the Enemy Act was continued in peacetime by the United States to deal with states perceived as hostile states.

[42] Periodically, politicians emerge who seek popularity on the basis of protectionism. See further, for the United States, P. Choate, *Agents of Influence* (1990).

[43] F. P. Waite and M. R. Goldberg, 'National Security Review of Foreign Investment in the United States' (1991) 3 *Florida Journal of International Law* 191.

[44] J. Raby, 'The Investment Provisions of the Canada–United States Free Trade Agreement: A Canadian Perspective' (1990) 84 *AJIL* 344.

[45] The dismantling of NAFTA featured prominently during the 2008 presidential campaign in the United States.

one of the early states to withdraw from the negotiations for a Multilateral Agreement on Investment sponsored by the OECD on the ground, among others, that open entry for investments would mean that its cultural industries would be swamped by foreign influences.

Nationalistic sentiments play a role in Australia's foreign investment laws as well.[46] In Europe, the domination of the economy by US multinational corporations is a fear that has engineered indirect legal responses.[47] The United States, despite its avowed allegiance to free market notions, does not permit certain types of investments to enter its territory. Its antitrust laws are used to prevent dominant foreign firms from entry into US markets. The United States has adopted legislation designed to keep out foreign investment inconsistent with its national security.[48] The legality of the measures that are adopted raise interesting questions. These measures are not dissimilar in effect to those adopted by developing states. Their legality may be considered along with the legality of the measures taken by developing states.

Many developing states, and more recently the erstwhile communist states of Eastern Europe now moving towards market economies, have constructed more elaborate methods of foreign investment regulation. The prevailing philosophy in the 1980s was that investment brought in by multinational corporations could be beneficial to host states, provided such investment could be properly harnessed to the economic development of the host state. But, in the 1990s, the world was caught up in the vortex of economic liberalism for a variety of reasons. The prevailing philosophy was one of liberalisation and privatisation.[49] The laws instituted in the 1980s came to be changed, though not entirely, in favour of the new philosophy of liberalisation. It is for this reason that there is an apparent inconsistency within these new foreign investment laws. On the one hand, the laws that have been enacted provide guarantees relating to repatriation of profits and against nationalisation of the property of the foreign investor without payment of compensation. They contain many tax and other incentives in order to entice the foreign investor. On the other hand, these legislations also contain devices to screen the influx of foreign investment and to permit entry only to investment that is considered desirable. They also contain many other regulations which seek to maximise the benefits which foreign investment could bring to the economic development of the host state but which appear to be restrictive of the manner in which the foreign investor could operate within the host economy. The techniques that have been used need to be isolated and examined. With successive economic crises, there were further changes to investment laws. There were efforts to dismantle privatisation and restore some of the earlier techniques of control. As a result of these fluctuations in policy, no coherent theme emerges from the investment laws of states. There seems to be a jumble of laws made at different periods reflecting

---

[46] The fear of Japanese dominance is regarded as a reason for the controls that have been instituted. The Australian economy, however, has traditionally been controlled by foreign interests, British and American. See further D. Flint, *Foreign Investment Law in Australia* (1986). More recently, there is a perception of hostility to Chinese investment.

[47] S. Reich, 'Roads to Follow: Regulating Direct Foreign Investment' (1989) 43 *International Organization* 543.

[48] The Exon–Florio Amendment to the Omnibus Trade and Competitiveness Act of 1988.

[49] See D. Coyle, *Governing the World Economy* (2000), for a view favourable to economic liberalism.

different policy preferences to be found in the foreign investment laws of most states. But, some trends do exist, and it is on these trends that attention is focused. First, the nature of the guarantees and incentives are examined, and this is followed by an examination of the types of regulation that control the process of foreign investment. The study is comparative. There is a great deal of similarity in the legislation on foreign investment among developing states, presumably because states imitate the more successful devices used in other states or because they use models suggested by international organisations. Examples are taken from the legislation of the principal states which use the different techniques of foreign investment control.

1.1 Guarantees against expropriation

Legislation on foreign investment usually contains guarantees against the expropriation of the foreign investment without payment of compensation. States with a history of expropriations are especially intent on giving such guarantees so as to remove any fear of expropriation that the investor may have on the basis of this history. Existing and erstwhile communist states are keen to give such guarantees in their legislation to dispel any idea that they still have ideological predispositions towards expropriation. Thus, Article 5 of the Foreign Enterprise Law of China provides the most explicit guarantee possible: it states that, in the event of any expropriation, full compensation will be paid.[50] This guarantee is intended to remove what the foreign investor fears to be the greatest threat to his investment. Such guarantees are usually given by high-risk countries in the hope that risk perceptions arising from past nationalisations will be counteracted by the guarantees.[51] Low-risk states obviously have little need to issue such guarantees. These guarantees, along with bilateral investment agreements which are also entered into in large numbers by the same states, have a signalling function. They indicate to foreign investors that past policies relating to foreign investments have undergone dramatic changes.

The value of these unilateral guarantees is disputed in the literature.[52] There are two opposing views. On the one hand, as a matter of internal constitutional law, it would

---

[50] But, the internal laws of China are inconsistent. In the Joint Venture Law, it is merely stated that foreign investment will be protected 'according to law' (Article 2).

[51] The Eastern bloc states, when converting to an open economy and permitting foreign investment, signalled their change in attitudes to nationalisation and the issue of compensation for nationalisation by guaranteeing against nationalisation and promising to pay compensation in the event of nationalisation. Under socialist theory, no compensation needs to be paid in the event of nationalisation. N. Katzarov, 'The Validity of the Act of Nationalisation in International Law' (1959) 22 *MLR* 639. The new legislation promises the 'actual value of the property' as compensation. See, for example, Article 22 of the Act amending the Enterprise with Foreign Participation Act 1990 of the old Soviet Union. There is stronger language on guarantees in the new Russian legislation on foreign investment. See the introductory note and text in (1992) 31 *ILM* 397. Article 7 guarantees against expropriation and promises 'swift, adequate and efficient' compensation, a paraphrasing of the Hull standard. States like Myanmar (Burma) and Cambodia also include such guarantees because they are new to the idea of attracting foreign investments and have to signal changes of policy.

[52] The leading text on the subject is A. A. Fatouros, *Government Guarantees to Foreign Investors* (1962). Vagts observed that these guarantees 'seldom have significant legal effect although it is conceivable that they could later disable the country from making various arguments to international tribunals in defense of measures taken against foreign investment'. D. Vagts, 'Protecting Foreign Investment: An International Law Perspective', in C. D. Wallace (ed.), *Foreign Direct Investment in the 1990s* (1990), p. 102 at p. 104. But, they have been given effect by arbitral tribunals: *SPP* v. *Egypt*, 3 *ICSID Reports* 101; (1983) 22 *ILM* 752. Also, they may create expectations in the investor which may be protected by the treaty standard of fair and equitable treatment.

appear that a guarantee given by one government cannot be binding on a succeeding government, particularly if there has been a revolutionary change of government.[53] It is the latter type of regime change that poses the greatest threat to foreign investment. Where the incoming regime has ideological stances different from those of the previous regime, it is arguable that there has been such a basic change within the state that the promises made by the previous government cannot be binding on the incoming revolutionary government.[54] On this reasoning, the guarantees that are made in foreign investment codes have no value or meaning at all except as devices to attract foreign investment.

On the other hand, there is the view that guarantees that are held out to foreign investors do have legal implications, despite regime changes. It is suggested that these guarantees have the effect of indicating a willingness on the part of the state to refer disputes that arise from the foreign investments attracted by the guarantee to an international rather than a national tribunal for settlement. This would be especially so if the guarantee against expropriation is coupled with the promise of dispute settlement by an overseas tribunal. On this view, a unilateral guarantee against expropriation, at the least, provides support for transferring any dispute arising from the expropriation of the foreign investment into an international sphere. It is suggested that it will also ensure that the fact that a guarantee was made would be taken into account both in determining the legality of the taking and in determining the quantum of damages.

This issue was raised in *SPP* v. *Egypt*.[55] The claimant had entered into an agreement to build a tourist complex near the Egyptian pyramids in response to an investment campaign embarked upon by government agencies after the announcement of the liberalisation of Egypt's foreign investment laws by the government of President Sadat. The building of the complex so close to historical monuments became a political issue. The new government formed after the assassination of President Sadat cancelled the project. The question was raised as to the liability of the government and its tourist agency, which was a party to the agreement. In finding liability, an arbitral tribunal focused upon the fact that guarantees had been given to the foreign investor in attracting him to the country and that the violation of these guarantees must engage the liability of the state. The tribunal referred to the Egyptian investment legislation which stated: 'Projects may not be nationalised or confiscated. The assets of such projects cannot be seized, blocked, confiscated or sequestrated except by judicial procedure.' The tribunal relied on this and other provisions in the legislation to determine that, as the 'policy of the law is to accord greater security to the investment', there was justification for an international arbitral tribunal to exercise jurisdiction over the dispute. The conclusion in the award is, however, contestable. The guarantee in this

---

[53] I. Delupis, *Finance and Protection of Investments in Developing Countries* (1987), pp. 27–32. For an Australian case involving later legislative changes to contracts contrary to guarantees given, see *Commonwealth Aluminium Corporation* v. *Attorney-General* [1976] Qd 231.

[54] Often explained as changes in the *grundnorm*. According to the theory of Hans Kelsen, all legal systems have a base in a fundamental legal principle which validates all other principles of the legal system. When a revolutionary change takes place, this fundamental or basic norm changes, justifying the making of changes to other legal principles in the system.

[55] (1983) 22 *ILM* 752.

particular award merely referred to the requirement of judicial procedure and not to a review of the taking by an international tribunal. Yet, the fact remains that unilateral guarantees are capable of being used at least as subsidiary arguments for exercising arbitral jurisdiction and awarding damages to the foreign investor where such guarantees have been violated.

However, as a matter of strict law, unilateral guarantees against expropriation without full compensation have no international effect, unless backed up by a treaty commitment and jurisdiction is created in a foreign arbitral tribunal to safeguard this commitment. Though unilateral acts of states do have some binding force, the instances in which such binding force has been ascribed to such unilateral acts have related to matters of international concern and have given rise to expectations as to the conduct of the state making the declaration in other states.[56] This cannot be said of unilateral guarantees against expropriation which are directed to the foreign investor alone. The guarantees are addressed to individuals or entities such as multinational corporations which do not have personality in international law; just as treaties cannot be made with those who lack international personality, no obligations can flow from guarantees given to those who lack international personality. The guarantees obviously operate in the context of national law and not in the context of international law.[57]

But, to the extent that capital-exporting states now actively participate in insurance schemes for their nationals investing abroad and in other activities associated with foreign investment, it may be credibly argued that these guarantees are addressed to the home states of foreign investors as well as to the investor, particularly if the schemes were designed to ensure that the premiums payable for investments in the host state were reduced by the home state as a result of the guarantees.[58] So, too, where there are investment treaties giving protection to the investment, unilateral guarantees may have significance in that their violation may amount to a violation of treaty standards of protection.[59] If this argument is valid, a case can be made for an obligation to the home state of the investor in situations where the guarantee had not been honoured.

---

[56] The *French Nuclear Test Case* [1974] *ICJ Reports* 253 is cited as authority for a large number of wide propositions in this area. In that case, a unilateral statement made on television by a French minister that France would desist from further tests was used as a peg on which the International Court of Justice could hang its withdrawal from an embarrassing situation.

[57] The issue as to whether estoppel operates to prevent the state from arguing its entitlement to change the law is a possibility. Though estoppel applies in inter-state relations (*Eastern Greenland Case* [1933] PCIJ Series A/B No. 5), there is little authority that it applies in relations between a state and a private entity with no international personality. The validity of the legal commitment given to the foreign party is the crucial issue. In *Oil Field of Texas* v. *Iran*, the question of estoppel was raised, but this specific issue was not argued. On estoppel, see further D. W. Bowett, 'Estoppel Before International Tribunals and Its Relation to Acquiescence' (1957) 33 *BYIL* 176. In a different context, see T. Nocker and G. French, 'Estoppel: What's the Government's Word Worth?' (1990) 24 *International Lawyer* 409. In municipal systems, it is doubtful whether estoppel lies against the government when it acts in the public interest. For the common law, see *Brickworks Ltd* v. *Warrigah Shire Council* (1963) 108 CLR 568.

[58] One difficulty in maintaining this argument is that the insurance of foreign investment is an internal act of the home state. It is not one which would normally have international significance.

[59] This situation has to be carefully considered. A commitment, it is argued, may come to be protected by an 'umbrella clause' in the treaty, or it may amount to a violation of a legitimate expectation and hence of the fair and equitable standard of treatment. Both involve contentious issues.

To the extent that expectations were created in the foreign investor by the unilateral guarantee, the guarantee could have an effect on the assessment of compensation where the foreign investor suffers damage as a result of action by the government contrary to the guarantee. It may also be an argument to support the payment of full compensation on the ground that the foreign investor was enticed into the state by the guarantee.[60] As a general proposition and as a matter of domestic constitutional law, however, a guarantee addressed to entities such as multinational corporations which have no personality in international law can have no effect in customary international law other than as a pious declaration of intent.[61] The result will be different if there are specific treatment standards which protect guarantees and assurances given to the foreign investor.[62]

1.2 Guarantees relating to dispute settlement

Unilateral guarantees relating to the settlement of disputes that arise from a foreign investment by a neutral arbitral tribunal abroad can be found in the foreign investment legislation of some states. These guarantees are given in the hope that there would be greater flows of foreign investment if impartial methods of seeking remedies in the event of government intervention are made available to the foreign investor.[63] Where a dispute subsequently arises between the state giving such a guarantee and a foreign investor, the dispute could be submitted to arbitration by a foreign arbitral tribunal in accordance with the provision. The theory on which arbitral tribunals have accepted jurisdiction is that the legislative guarantee contains an offer to arbitrate which the foreign investor converts into an agreement to arbitrate by instituting proceedings before the tribunal. He exercises an option under the law available to him, thereby granting jurisdiction on the usual contractual basis to the arbitral tribunal.[64]

There are, however, internal constitutional difficulties with such guarantees. In constitutional systems that feature a separation of powers, it is a contentious issue as to whether the judicial power of decision over a dispute that arises within the territory of the state could be transferred to a foreign tribunal by the legislature in absolute terms in respect of all future disputes.[65] The fact that the local court system is bypassed altogether

---

[60] The American Law Institute, *Restatement on Foreign Relations Law* (vol. 2, p. 199), which states a general principle of just compensation, thus departing from the traditional US stance of prompt, adequate and effective compensation, argues that full compensation must be paid where the investment was specifically encouraged or authorised by the state.

[61] The domestic parallel to such guarantees is perhaps the letter of comfort. Such letters are ordinarily intended to provide some support for a course of action without creating any binding obligations on those issuing them.

[62] This statement is made having regard to the view that the assurances may have significance where (i) the fair and equitable standard of the treaty is interpreted as protecting the legitimate expectations created by the guarantee or (ii) the umbrella clause in the treaty is interpreted as protecting the assurances. The situations are dealt with in Chapter 9 below.

[63] Examples of this are to be found in the legislation of many African states. The similarity in the forms of such legislation is remarkable. They result either from models or advice provided by international organisations or because of the competition that exists within the region to attract foreign investment.

[64] The reasoning was accepted in *SPP* v. *Egypt*, 3 *ICSID Reports* 101; (1983) 22 *ILM* 752.

[65] The African states providing such guarantees generally operate under models that recognise the separation of powers. In *Loewen* v. *United States* (2003) 42 *ILM* 811, a judgment of the courts of Mississippi awarding exorbitant damages was alleged to be a taking within the provisions of NAFTA. The case starkly raises the question of whether the appeals system of the United States could be bypassed, and the matter of the propriety of a decision of a US court being brought before a NAFTA tribunal. In Canada,

in matters of vital national concern will also cause political concern. So far, these issues have achieved little visibility. If the legislation containing the guarantee is a nullity in national law, it would be difficult to argue that it should nevertheless have effect on the international plane. Nevertheless, treaties are said to operate on a different plane and treaty obligations survive on the international plane even if the national laws conflict with them.

1.3 Tax and non-tax incentives to foreign investors

Many states provide tax holidays and other incentives to foreign investors in order to attract them to invest in their territories. These incentives are usually available only to investors who fall into specific categories such as those who bring in high technology or who locate their regional headquarters in the host state. There is, of course, nothing in international law which prevents the granting of such tax holidays and incentives. Whether such an incentive should be given or not is a matter that lies within the discretion of the state authorities. There is considerable debate as to the usefulness of such incentives in attracting foreign investment.[66]

Tax incentives are a useful way of ensuring that the foreign investor acts in the manner desired by the host government. Thus, for example, tax incentives may be granted where new equipment is purchased to modernise the plant or on condition that some of the shares in the investment are transferred to nationals of the host state. In this way, a state may seek to achieve an objective indirectly whereas a direct requirement may give the impression of hostility to foreign investment.[67]

The granting of incentives to desirable investors but not to other investors raises the issue of discriminatory treatment. There can be no objection to discrimination based entirely on economic factors. There may be violations of national treatment and most-favoured-nation treatment involved as well. But, provided an adequate basis for the differential treatment, such as the need to attract certain types of technology or to direct the foreign investor into certain channels of production, can be shown, there will be no illegality involved in such discrimination.

Such discrimination between foreign investors may be opposed on the ground that it distorts international trade. One purpose of tax incentives and other concessions, apart from attracting desirable investment, is to mask the fact that there are performance requirements imposed upon foreign investors. Such performance requirements may also be opposed on the basis that they cause distortions in international trade. There are economic reasons for opposing tax incentives. They may violate provisions of the TRIMS agreement of the WTO. Assuming the incentives are not associated with performance requirements, tax incentives *per se* are permissible in law.

---

the issue was raised in *United Postal Workers Union* v. *Canada*. The court rejected the view that the NAFTA provision on foreign investment dispute settlement was unconstitutional. Also see D. Schneiderman, *Constitutionalising Economic Globalisation: Investment Rules and Democracy's Promise* (2008).

[66] For a recent discussion, see UNCTAD, *World Investment Report, 2003*, pp. 123–7.

[67] M. Fordham, *Tax Incentive for Investment and Expansion in Singapore* (1992).

1.4 Screening of foreign investment entry

The ideal of freedom of entry for the purposes of trade was advocated by the old institutional writers like Vitoria and Vattel.[68] The ideal of freedom of trade is now articulated through the institution of the World Trade Organization. The liberalisation of flows of foreign investment is also an articulated goal. Many bilateral and regional treaties made in recent times provide for the right of entry and establishment of foreign investment. These treaties extend national treatment to the pre-entry phase as well, but the right is not recognised as an absolute right, as parties to these treaties continue to make wide limitations on entry into certain sectors. They also exempt some of their laws from the scope of investment treaties through the use of appropriate formulae.[69]

The starting-point of the discussion, however, must be the customary international law position that a state, in pursuance of its sovereign rights, has the right to refuse entry to any alien. It is well accepted that a state may institute measures to keep out foreign investment that is considered harmful to its interests. The function of screening entry is accomplished through administrative agencies. These administrative agencies may require that a feasibility study be made of the proposed foreign investment, indicating the potential benefits of the investment to the local economy. Since many of these states permit entry only through joint ventures, and the making of feasibility studies is a sound preliminary exercise even between purely private parties to such joint ventures,[70] the requirement may not seem onerous. But, as in the case of private transactions, disputes could later arise as to the accuracy of the information that was supplied in the course of these preliminary investigations. Unlike in the case of private transactions, the fact that statements made in the feasibility study could amount to misrepresentation may have more severe consequences, at least in the eyes of the public authority that issued the permit to enter. Over-zealous representations as to the benefits of the foreign investment made in order to secure entry can easily be reduced into the legal language of misrepresentation and fraud.[71] In its internal law, such misrepresentations may provide justification for interference with the foreign investment agreement.[72] Whether it will also justify the termination of the foreign investment under international law may be a moot question. But, if there was deliberate fraud on the part of the foreign investor, there will be no wrong done to him if there is a termination of privileges that were illegitimately secured. The determination as to misrepresentation should be preceded by a hearing at which the foreign investor has due process rights. Though the latter proposition is

---

[68] Vitoria asserted loftily the fundamental human right which inheres in all men to trade with people of other lands and thus fulfil the human urge to communicate (*De Indis*, III, 5). The cynic would maintain that this lofty pronouncement was meant to promote the right of powerful states to impose their trade on less powerful states. The stance of promoting the free flow of investment finds expression in an OECD Code of Liberalisation of Capital Movements (1986). This is a non-binding code.

[69] Thus, many investment principles define the foreign investment given protection by the treaty as foreign investment 'made in accordance with the laws and regulations' of the host state.

[70] Preliminary negotiations prior to the formation of a joint venture include exchanges of information relating to each partner's input, the complementarity of the resources that each could supply to the venture and other factors.

[71] See *Azinian* v. *Mexico*, ICSID Case No. ARB(AF)/97/2.

[72] In *Amco* v. *Indonesia* (1988) 27 *ILM* 1281, a failure to comply with capitalisation commitments given by the foreign investor was used to justify the cancellation of the permit. But, the tribunal did not pronounce on the legitimacy of this justification, being more concerned with the manner of the cancellation of the permit. It held that due-process safeguards were not provided, justifying an award of damages to the foreign investor.

based on contestable authority, it is a rule of prudence that a fair hearing should be given to the foreign investor prior to any interference with the foreign investment by state authorities. The protracted dispute in *Amco* v. *Indonesia*[73] illustrates the difficulties that attend commitments made in the course of preliminary contacts with administrative agencies that screen investments.

The primary task of the administrative agency is to ensure that the foreign investor brings tangible benefits to the host state. The agency will have regard to the impact of the foreign investment on the local economy. It has the task of ensuring that local entrepreneurs are not affected by the entry of a powerful foreign company into an industrial sector.[74] Again, the question of discrimination against a foreign national arises, if such measures are taken before or after entry. But, such discrimination must be considered lawful unless there is a treaty commitment to provide national treatment in like circumstances. There are sound economic reasons for excluding foreigners from certain industries. In developing countries, such exclusion is rationalised on the basis that it would be better that basic industries be handled by local entrepreneurs, as otherwise a state could be left stranded by a foreign multinational which relocates. Another reason is that the entry of a foreign business giant may stifle the emergence of an entrepreneurial class within the state or destroy infant industries. Care is therefore taken to ensure that, while high-technology industries which local entrepreneurs cannot handle without help from outside are open to entry to foreign multinationals, low-technology, labour-intensive areas are reserved for nationals. Developed states may also adopt a policy of keeping foreign investors out of certain industries. Industries associated with the production of military equipment are seldom open to foreign interests. This is justified on national security considerations.

There is general acceptance that a state may impose conditions upon the entry of any alien, and such a principle includes conditions imposed upon foreign investors as well.[75] Whatever the position may have been in the past, in times of rapid movements of political and economic refugees, developed states will not be inclined to support a rule that permits unlimited and unconditional access by aliens to their territories.[76] Yet, bilateral and regional investment treaties and WTO instruments such as the GATS will promote the establishment of freedom of entry for foreign investment in the services sector, at least to a limited extent.

---

[73] This flows from the fact that the possibility arises of a denial of justice in the absence of a fair hearing. The extent to which such a hearing should be held for the making of a purely administrative decision is unclear. In *Amco* v. *Indonesia*, 1 *ICSID Reports* 209, the tribunal appeared to be inclined to the view that such a hearing should be given prior to the making of an administrative decision. This is a contentious proposition. Traditionally, a denial of justice should not be found except in the clearest of cases of judicial impropriety. See Judge Tanaka in the *Barcelona Traction Case* [1970] *ICJ Reports* 1.

[74] Many investment codes include a list indicating the sectors in which investment by foreign investors cannot be made. Some sectors are reserved for state corporations. Some are reserved for local business people. Some legislation also identifies areas into which foreign investment may enter only in joint venture with local entrepreneurs. The Mexican legislation provides an example. In Mexico, the petroleum sector is reserved for Pemex, a state monopoly. Other sectors are reserved for local business. When Mexico ratified NAFTA, consistent with its domestic laws, it excluded these sectors from the scope of NAFTA, which provides for both pre-entry and post-entry national treatment. Economic literature that opposes neo-liberal tenets believes in infant-industry protection in developing countries. See Ha Joon Chang, *Bad Samaritans: Rich Nation, Poor Policies and the Threat to the Developing World* (2007).

[75] F. V. Garcia-Amador, L. Sohn and R. R. Baxter, *Recent Codification of the Law of State Responsibility for Injuries to Aliens* (1974), p. 369.

[76] Whether a distinction must be drawn between the entry of business and the entry of persons is questionable, but there is a definite trend, at least in the positions adopted by developed states, to draw such a distinction.

GATS will permit a 'commercial presence' within the territories of those members who have permitted such a presence in those sectors which have been indicated by member states. As yet, the general rule that states have the right to exclude entry remains substantially unaffected. But, once a services provider obtains entry through establishment requirements under GATS, he will be protected by investment treaties if he qualifies as a foreign investor under them.[77]

There is a rule of non-discrimination on racial grounds. Its application is relevant, particularly after entry is made by the foreign investor. Except in the case where discrimination is clearly directed at an ethnic group,[78] there cannot be any international wrong committed by discriminating between investors or types of investment. Where a state fears economic domination by a particular foreign power and limits the entry of the nationals of that power who are of a distinct racial group, the question may arise as to whether this is racial discrimination.[79] The issue is one which will cause anxiety as the potential violation of a cardinal rule, the rule against racial discrimination, is involved, but the better view is that such discrimination does not amount to racial discrimination.[80] A discriminatory provision based on objective factors or a reasonable cause cannot be regarded as violative of the rules against racial discrimination.[81] The situation is akin to nationalisation decrees directed at a specific racial group. The general rule is that such a decree will be unlawful on the ground of racial discrimination.[82] But, if the decree is intended to end the economic dominance of a particular foreign national or ethnic group, there is room for arguing that the rule against racial discrimination is not violated by the decree.

1.5 Requirements of local collaboration

It was a pattern in the states of Eastern Europe, prior to the fall of communism, and in many developing countries to permit foreign investment only in collaboration with a state entity of the host state. This enabled the socialist states which saw the advantages of foreign investment to marry socialist ideology with the admission of foreign investment on the ground that ultimate control over the investment remained with the state. The rationalisation was that state policy was consistently implemented through the presence of the state entity's

---

[77] In *Patrick Mitchell* v. *Congo*, the issue was raised as to whether the provision of legal services was a protected investment. It must be shown that the services provided fall under the provisions of the treaty.

[78] Even this may seem doubtful in the economic sphere. The free movement of persons and goods within regional groupings like the EC depends on nationality and the exclusion of nationals of other states. This discrimination between groups of persons has been held to be lawful.

[79] *Sramek* [1984] *Yearbook of the European Commission on Human Rights* 294; *Land Sale to Aliens Case* (1973) 77 *ILR* 433.

[80] This opinion is based on the analogy of the nationalisation measures after the ending of colonialism. Ordinarily, nationalisation measures which are directed against a definable national group are discriminatory. But, nationalisations directed at nationals of the colonial power were aimed at ending the economic stranglehold that the former colonial power had on the economy of the newly independent states, and were therefore widely held to be lawful. There may be similar connotations in the trade measures of the United States.

[81] Brownlie formulated this proposition in the following terms: 'The fact that the primary criterion involves a reference to race does not make the rule discriminatory in law, provided the reference to race has an objective basis and a reasonable cause.' I. Brownlie, 'The Rights of Peoples in Modern International Law', in J. Crawford (ed.), *The Rights of Peoples* (1988), p. 1 at p. 9. Nevertheless, the formulation in the text causes much anxiety to the present writer for the reason that a rule so formulated can be used to cloak racial discrimination.

[82] *Oppenheimer* v. *Cattermole* [1975] 1 All ER 538.

nominees on the board of the joint venture. This policy persisted in many Eastern European states even after the fall of communism and the advent of free market economics. The model spread to the communist states of Asia, where it still remains the principal method through which foreign investment is made in these countries.[83] There is a widespread preference for collaborative joint ventures as the method for foreign investment entry in many developing market economy states. Ethnicity also has a role to play in the determination of the structures that are preferred. In Malaysia, the preference that is given to *bumiputra*[84] requires that companies are structured in accordance with a prescribed formula as to shareholdings. This mandates that entry is made by foreigners through minority shareholdings in existing companies or newly established ones. Ethnic policies, rather than economic ones, as well as other political considerations, have a role to play in determining the collaborative structures through which entry is made in many states.[85] In developed states, a joint venture structure between local and foreign business is usually not mandatory. Joint ventures may, however, be used for various reasons such as the need to pool resources and technology or the need to diversify the risks of failure involved in the venture.[86]

Foreign investors may themselves prefer joint ventures in developing countries because it diversifies the risk, gives the foreign investor a lower visibility and provides them with a local partner who will often be an effective mediator with the local government. From the point of view of investment protection, the requirement that entry be made through joint ventures accentuates problems. Since the joint venture entity would always be locally incorporated, problems of corporate nationality and shareholder protection will arise. In the context of arbitration, this has posed problems as the question of whether the arbitration is domestic or international arises. Issues of standing before international arbitral tribunals could arise as the host state will consider the joint venture to be its corporate national.[87]

Exceptions to the requirement of entry through local participation are made by some states in circumstances where the multinational corporation is prepared to make a commitment to export the whole or a large percentage of its products, thus earning revenue for the host state and providing employment for its workforce, or where the investor is prepared to locate in areas designated as industrially backward and thus help in the development of those areas. In the former situation, difficulties may arise after entry where export commitments are not kept. In these circumstances, the host state may well terminate the foreign investment, as it will be unwilling to permit sales on the local market which it may have reserved

---

[83] In China, for a long time, joint ventures were the principal method of foreign investment entry. But, now, wholly owned subsidiaries are permitted, subject to certain conditions. The situation is similar in Vietnam, Laos and Cambodia, the remaining Asian socialist states.

[84] Literally, the 'children of the land'. The Malays are not indigenous to the land. There are the *orang asli* of Malaysia, whom the Malays themselves regard as the indigenous people. In South Africa, the Black Empowerment Act requires discrimination in favour of the black people who were discriminated against during the *apartheid* regime.

[85] The literature on foreign investment has assumed economic considerations to be the dominant ones. But, this is not so. In many states, ethnic and political considerations play a more dominant role in determining the policy as to foreign investment.

[86] See further M. Sornarajah, *Law of International Joint Ventures* (1992).

[87] This categorisation is relevant under the ICSID Convention, where arbitration can take place only if the investor is a national of another state. For the case law on this, see C. Schreuer, *The ICSID Convention: A Commentary* (2nd edn, 2009); and M. Sornarajah, *The Settlement of Foreign Investment Disputes* (2000). The categorisation is also relevant for the enforcement of the award because only international awards may be enforced under the New York Convention on the Enforcement of Foreign Arbitral Awards.

for its own industries. Again, the question of discrimination between nationals and foreign investors could arise, and the answer must be that such discrimination is justified as it is based on economic grounds. It may be unlawful if there is a bilateral investment treaty affirming absolute national treatment even at the pre-entry stage between the host state and the home state of the foreign investor mandating national treatment of the foreign investor. In the absence of such a treaty, there is no international law basis for claiming violation of national treatment.[88]

1.6 Capitalisation requirements

States may require that a foreign investor seeking entry should bring in all the capital or a certain percentage of it from overseas. A state's interest in ensuring that capital is brought from outside by the foreign investor is to prevent him raising capital on the local markets. If he were permitted to do so, local savings that could be utilised for home-grown projects of benefit to the state would be absorbed in serving the interests of the foreign investor. The attraction of local investors to invest in shares in a project with a large foreign corporation will divert investment funds that could have gone to finance local entrepreneurs or local projects. There are economic reasons justifying such discriminatory treatment. The obvious one is that an assumed benefit of foreign investment – that it leads to capital flows from outside into the host state – will be nullified if the investor raises his capital on the local markets.

Where a foreign investor agrees to capitalisation requirements and later fails to comply, a right to terminate or otherwise interfere with the foreign investment arises in the host state. This right arises as a matter of the internal law of the host state. The exercise of this right cannot amount to an international wrong provided due process standards have been met. The protracted dispute in *Amco* v. *Indonesia*[89] involved this issue. In that case, one of the conditions on which the foreign investor was permitted to participate in the project in Indonesia for building a tourist complex in a joint venture with an Indonesian partner was that he would bring an agreed sum of capital into the country from abroad to capitalise the venture. Under the law, he would have had to obtain certificates from the Bank of Indonesia to show that such capital had in fact been brought into the country. It was alleged that he had not brought in such capital. Though the foreign investor claimed that he had done so, there was no certification to this effect from the Bank of Indonesia. This was used as one of the grounds for the cancellation of the agreement by the administrative agency. The initial ICSID tribunal found for the foreign investor, but the award was nullified on the ground that the tribunal had not given sufficient consideration to the issue relating to capitalisation.

---

[88] The United States holds out the principle of national treatment for investment as the norm. Thus, President Reagan's Policy Statement on Foreign Investment (9 September 1983) stated: 'The basic tenet for the treatment of investment is the national treatment principle ... Exceptions should be limited to those required to protect national security.' Whether national treatment is permitted in the United States after the Exon–Florio Amendment is itself doubted. J. E. Alvarez, 'Political Protectionism and United States International Investment Obligations in Conflict: The Hazards of Exon–Florio' (1989) 30 *Virginia Journal of International Law* 1.

[89] (1983) 23 *ILM* 354; (1988) 27 *ILM* 1281.

A fresh tribunal later found for the foreign investor on the ground that a proper procedure had not been followed in the cancellation of the foreign investor's privileges to operate in the country as the decision to cancel was not taken according to due process standards. The tribunal ruled that there had been a denial of justice for which responsibility arose. The ruling gives rise to the necessary conclusion that, if minimum standards of procedural safeguards had been given to the foreign investor before a decision had been taken, the cancellation of the privileges would have been justified. The Indonesian position in challenging the initial award has been explained by Reisman in the following terms:[90]

Indonesia apparently felt that it had to challenge the award because if a country establishes a programme to induce foreign investment and grants licences on the basis of that programme, but discrepancies of as much as sixteen per cent of the foreign commitment to invest are internationally determined to be irrelevant such that the host government may not terminate the licence, the country will find itself in the position of being unable to enforce its own law.

This situation clearly has significance for considering whether a regulatory interference could amount to an expropriation. Where the foreign investor fails to conform to conditions that were imposed at the time of entry and the investment is terminated as a sanction for such failure, an argument that the interference amounts to expropriation can scarcely be maintained. Prudence would require that such interference be preceded by procedural safeguards.[91]

1.7 Requirements relating to environmental protection

The host state and its agencies will have regard to the environmental effects of the entry of the foreign investment. There is a belief that multinational corporations often export hazardous technology whose use is not permitted in their home states and that they cut costs in developing countries by not including environmental measures that they would have been forced to take in their home states.[92] The Bhopal disaster in India underlines these general fears.[93]

Environmental impact studies are required to be made prior to permission for the entry of the foreign investment. Permission will be denied if the effects on the environment would be harsh. But, environmental standards in many developing countries are not high.

In developed countries, greater emphasis is placed on the effect of the foreign investor's activity on the environment. An investment project or agreement may be cancelled, even after it has commenced, if it can be shown that the harm to the environment is irreversible or outweighs the benefits of the project. Thus, in the dispute concerning sand-mining on Fraser Island close to the Great Barrier Reef, the Australian government terminated a concession which had been given to two US corporations to mine sand on the island. The sand contained

---

[90] M. Reisman, 'The Breakdown of Control Mechanism in ICSID Arbitration' (1989) 89 *Duke Law Journal* 739 at 774.
[91] It is interesting to consider whether what took place in *Amco* v. *Indonesia* was a regulatory expropriation.
[92] G. Handl and R. E. Lutz, *Transferring Hazardous Technologies and Substances* (1989).
[93] Indian Law Institute, *The Bhopal Litigation* (1989).

zircon and rutile. There was no market for these minerals in Australia. An environmental impact study showed that the adverse effects of such sand-mining on the environment of the Great Barrier Reef were considerable. The Australian government refused to give customs clearance for the export of the minerals, thus in effect terminating the concessions. The US corporations had spent large sums in setting up the project. Though the United States, the home state of the multinational corporation which had the concession, intervened diplomatically to protest the cancellation of the concession, the Australian government stood its ground. It was willing to have the dispute submitted to the International Court of Justice. The High Court of Australia upheld the validity of the conduct of the Australian government.[94] There is general acceptance that a state has a right to cancel agreements or investment projects which cause significant environmental harm.[95] The right flows not only from the sovereignty of the state which permits the state to protect its territory from environmental harm but also from the fact that, in modern international law, a state is a repository of the right to safeguard the environment in the interests of humankind.

But, *Metalclad* v. *Mexico*[96] and *Santa Elena* v. *Costa Rica*[97] may run counter to these views. In the former, a project to construct an underwater waste-disposal system in a Mexican province had been given clearance by the federal government. But, protests occurred at the site because of fears that the construction would interfere with the sub-terranean streams which supplied water to the people in the vicinity. The provincial authorities refused permission for the construction. The tribunal, constituted under NAFTA, held on the facts that there was a taking and that compensation had to be paid. It is unsettled yet as to how arbitral tribunals will deal with regulatory interference on environmental grounds. A trend was developing not to take environmental considerations into account.[98] But, with the holding in *Methanex* v. *United States* reviving the exception as to regulatory taking and the inclusion of the exception as well as specific provisions on the environment in investment treaties, it would now appear that interference justified on environmental grounds could be regarded as regulatory taking.[99]

The progressive evolution of the right to a clean environment as a human right and as a norm incorporating higher values may lead to an inflexible right for the state to interfere in order to protect the environment and to regard this interference as not amounting to a taking which is not compensable. But, the right must be exercised on objective grounds. The fact that an environmentally sensitive area such as the Great Barrier Reef[100] is involved makes the proof of objective circumstances much easier. Sophisticated arguments relating to the protection of intergenerational equities could be utilised to justify the state's conduct in these circumstances.[101] But, there is a definite clash here between the protection of the environment and the protection of foreign investment. Arbitral tribunals, which usually accentuate

---

[94]   *Dillingham-Moore* v. *Murphyores* (1979) 136 CLR 1.   [95]   *International Bank of Washington* v. *OPIC* (1972) 11 *ILM* 1216.
[96]   (2000) 5 *ICSID Reports* 209.   [97]   (2002) 5 *ICSID Reports* 153.
[98]   This statement is made on the basis of *Santa Elena* v. *Costa Rica* (2000) 39 *ILM* 317; (2002) 5 *ICSID Reports* 153.
[99]   See the discussion on expropriation in Chapter 10 below.
[100]   The Great Barrier Reef is regarded as one of the natural wonders of the world, and is listed under the World Heritage Convention.
[101]   E. Brown-Weiss, *In Fairness to Future Generations* (1989).

the interests of foreign investors over those of the environment, are prone to decide in favour of investment protection.[102]

Provided it is based on objective factors, the state's right to exclude investment that could cause harm to its environment is justifiable. But, it is sometimes difficult to determine whether the motive behind the interference is concern for the environment or whether the interference is a protective measure designed to keep foreigners out of the economy.[103] Where it is clear that the measure is induced by purely environmental considerations, it would be difficult to argue that consideration should not be given to this fact. In the cases that have been decided so far, the environmental motive behind the regulation was stated as an afterthought. In *Methanex* v. *United States*,[104] the United States successfully argued that a measure that was intended to protect the health and welfare of citizens was a regulatory taking. The case will have far-reaching implications for environmental interferences by the host state.

An interference with a right to proceed with the investment after permission to enter has been granted is more problematic. If the evidence has come to light only after the investment has been made, the present movements in international law will support the view that nothing should stand in the way of the cancellation of the foreign investment project if the threatened harm outweighs the benefits of the investment. Quite apart from the protection of its national interests, the state's interference with the project will be justified by the burgeoning principles of international environmental law. The state will have the weight of rhetoric as well as principle behind it to support such an interference. Despite the pro-investment stances taken in cases like *Santa Elena* v. *Costa Rica*, environmental regulation is permissible, and such regulation should not be treated as expropriation in circumstances in which the primary motive for the interference was protection of the environment.

1.8 Requirements relating to export targets

The strategy of development adopted by developing states has moved away from manufacturing within the state as a means of reducing imports to a strategy of earning income through the export of goods. The model for such development is provided by the newly industrialising states – Singapore, South Korea, Taiwan and Hong Kong – whose exports led to the spectacular growth of their economies. The shift of emphasis from import substitution to export-led growth has made developing countries turn to investment by multinational corporations in the hope that they would manufacture and export products from their countries and thus earn foreign exchange. To this end, there have been efforts made to induce exports by multinational corporations by the conferment of privileges or through tax and other incentives. The requirement of entry in collaboration with a local partner is often dispensed with if the majority of the production is for export. In some states, export targets are a compulsory condition of entry.

---

[102] *Metalclad* v. *Mexico* (2000) 5 *ICSID Reports* 209; (2001) 40 *ILM* 55; *Santa Elena* v. *Costa Rica* (2000) 39 *ILM* 317; (2002) 5 *ICSID Reports* 153; and *Tecmed* v. *Mexico* (2006) 10 *ICSID Reports* 54 are cases which support this view.
[103] *S. D. Myers* v. *Canada* (2000) 40 *ILM* 1408; (2002) 121 *ILR* 7.   [104] *Methanex* v. *United States* (2005) 44 *ILM* 1345.

The United States has consistently opposed such export quotas on the basis that they amount to performance requirements. Its programme of bilateral investment treaties also seeks to eliminate such requirements. It has sought the elimination of such restrictions on foreign investment in the Uruguay Round of the GATT negotiations. The argument was that the imposition of export requirements was distortive of international trade. The Trade-Related Investment Measures (TRIMS) that came into existence along with the establishment of the World Trade Organization deals with performance requirements but does not affect the imposition of export requirements. US investment treaties, however, contain prohibitions on performance requirements.

It is unlikely that countries intent on a foreign-investment-assisted export policy will agree to dispense with export requirements.[105] The imposition of these requirements will accentuate conflicts between the host state and the foreign investor. Foreign investors will find it difficult to meet the requirements that have been imposed in the present conditions. With recession in the world markets in 2008 and the possibility of protectionist policies against cheap imports from developing countries being implemented by developed countries in response, there will be difficulties in satisfying the export requirements of host states.

In addition, multinational corporations themselves adopt a policy of preventing competition among their subsidiaries by carving out geographical markets and preventing export by their subsidiaries into the territories of each other. As a result, export quota requirements will be more difficult to meet. The failure to do so will bring about more conflicts between foreign investors and host states. Such conflicts will be difficult to resolve. The state will seek to justify interference with or the termination of the foreign investment on the basis of the non-fulfilment of the terms on which entry was granted to the foreign investor or seek to impose some other form of sanction. The foreign investor, on the other hand, will seek the remedies provided for him under the contract and have recourse to arbitration. As most arbitral tribunals now seek to emphasise the contract on the basis of which entry was made rather than the public law conditions imposed on the entry, the state party may feel aggrieved and refuse to abide by the award, thus exacerbating the dispute. Public law controls over investment are a new phenomenon. Arbitral tribunals are prone to a contractual analysis of the process of foreign investment. They have yet to come to grips with the problem of accommodating these controls to a system which prefers to assimilate foreign investment agreements to private contracts.[106]

1.9 Requirements relating to local equity

One uniform pattern emerging from the legislation on foreign investments in developing countries relates to the preference that there should be local equity participation in foreign

---

[105] In policy literature, there is increasing support for developing countries maintaining performance requirements. See Ha-Joon Chang, *Kicking Away the Ladder: Development Strategy in Historical Perspective* (2005), for the argument that these requirements were maintained by developed countries during their period of development.

[106] On the inability of arbitrators to think in terms of public law issues in investment arbitration, see G. van Harten, *Investment Treaty Arbitration and Public Law* (2007).

investments. There was a rapid divestment of shares in existing foreign investment companies so that local shareholding targets could be achieved when indigenisation measures in
states like Nigeria were announced.[107] In Malaysia, too, for reasons of ethnicity, shareholding structures were imposed on company shareholdings. The role of ethnicity in
shaping policies of foreign investment is largely reflected in the types of company structure
that are mandated. Foreign investment has to conform to these structures when it enters a
country, ensuring that its corporate vehicle is designed in accordance with the policies
mandated by the state in hitherto foreign-owned corporations. Often, the legislation would
specify the percentage of the shares that had to be divested, and detail the stages and the
timeframe within which such divestment was to be effected. Malaysia provides a good
example of such laws. It announced its 'New Economic Policy' in 1970, which was to be
implemented within twenty years. Within this period, Malaysia wanted to restructure its
economy to ensure that foreign nationals participated in the economy only as minority
shareholders.[108] There was to be an equitable participation by all ethnic groups in the
economy according to a quota.

It is relevant to note that equity restrictions are not imposed on economic grounds alone
but have political and other motives. Addressing equity requirements through economic
instruments like investment treaties or WTO instruments is bound to fail as the primary
concerns of many states in introducing equity requirements are political rather than economic. The economic considerations may be to create relations based on agreements from
which the foreign investor cannot easily withdraw and thus prevent the disruption that
relocation by the foreign investor would cause. But, political motives are a stronger reason
for such requirements. These requirements seek to ensure that the foreign investment
meshes with the national policy to promote the development of groups within the state
which have traditionally been disadvantaged. The making of foreign investment benefiting
only elite groups will serve only to increase divisions within society. For this reason, the
laws of many states direct foreign investors into alliances based on ethnicity.[109] Such states
are unlikely to accept efforts to dismantle equity requirements based on economic considerations alone.

Strong economic considerations also exist for the insistence that foreign participation in
industry be made only through joint ventures. This enables a more effective transfer of
management and technology to the local joint-venture partner and, consequently, the max-
imisation of one of the assumed benefits of foreign investment. It will also ensure that the
state's policies are better reflected when decisions as to policy are made. This consideration

[107] The indigenisation measures adopted in many African countries also had the aim of ensuring the divestment of shares of foreign companies into local hands. The Nigerian indigenisation measures have been widely studied. F. Beveridge, 'Taking Control of Foreign Investment: A Case Study of Indigenisation in Nigeria' (1991) 40 *ICLQ* 302; N. Tobi, 'Legal Aspects of Foreign Investment and Financing Energy Products in Nigeria' (1991) 14 *Dalhousie Law Journal* 5; O. Osunbor, 'Nigeria's Investment Laws and the State's Control of Multinationals' (1988) 3 *ICSID Rev* 38; and T. J. Biersteker, *Multinationals, the State and the Control of the Nigerian Economy* (1987).

[108] The New Economic Policy in Malaysia was to end after twenty years, but technically is still in operation.

[109] South Africa provides a recent example. The Black Empowerment Act seeks to give economic priorities to the black citizens of South Africa based on the need for positive discrimination after the *apartheid* policy of white supremacist regimes.

applies with greater force in industries which are state monopolies whose industrial policy has been clearly laid down.[110]

It is clear that the requirements relating to local equity in new foreign investment ventures bring obvious economic advantages to the host state. Quite apart from the fact that a smaller proportion of the profits will be repatriated abroad, it ensures that the state has direct or indirect control over the venture. It also ensures that a local entrepreneurial class, which will profit by its association with foreign investors through the acquisition of managerial and business acumen, will emerge. The criticism of these measures is that they give rise to an elite group of local businessmen who form associations with foreign capital and enable governments that are favourable to their business interests to remain in power. Sometimes, it is alleged that this association between foreign capital and the local elite leads to repression and human rights abuses. Indigenisation measures in any state will become less vigorous once the process of indigenisation has been completed and the visible dominance of foreign investment has diminished. Political pressure for such measures will no longer be a pressing concern.

Though measures relating to local equity may have been put in place, the vigour with which they are pursued will depend on several factors such as the sufficiency and willingness of the administrative authorities and the relative bargaining strengths of the state and the foreign party. Where there is a foreign investment project which the state is keen to attract into the country, it will seek to do so, exercising its discretionary powers to overlook the entry requirements. It is the bargaining strength of the foreign investor that will dictate the manner in which the entry requirements are applied to him. Equity requirements are being relaxed in many states in order to achieve other advantages. Increasingly, states permit foreign investors prepared to locate in certain underdeveloped regions of the state or willing to export larger percentages of their manufactured products to set up wholly owned enterprises or to increase their equity ownership considerably. Many states also permit wholly owned enterprises in industries that are new to them and which they prefer to attract.

There have also been efforts to circumvent the requirements relating to local equity participation. The usual method has been to hold shares through a nominee who has the necessary qualifications to satisfy the requirements of local participation. These avenues for circumventing the law are obviously illegal.[111] A foreign national who suffers penal consequences as a result of attempts to circumvent the law has no remedy through any form of diplomatic intervention by his home state. It is also doubtful whether foreign investments made in transgression of the host state's laws are entitled to any protection under international law.[112]

The requirement that entry be made in collaboration with local business has meant that the preferred form of entry was through a joint venture. This is a logical consequence of the

---

[110] There is a pattern that the original requirement of entry through joint ventures is phased out. Chinese investment laws provide an example where the laws start with joint ventures but later provide for wholly owned foreign enterprises. Indonesian law also evolved in this manner. The preference for joint ventures, however, remains, manifested in other ways. Thus, the existence of state monopolies would mean that a sector could be entered only through a joint venture with the state monopoly.

[111] *Fraport* v. *Philippines* (ICSID, 2007).   [112] *Shott* v. *Iran* (1989) 23 *Iran–US CTR* 351.

measures relating to the indigenisation of the economy. The joint venture has become the most important vehicle for foreign investment in recent times across the world, for various reasons. From the point of view of investment in developing countries, entry regulations have been the most important reason for their formation. Both the joint venture in the manufacturing and mineral sectors as well as the production-sharing agreement in the mineral sector were agreements which were structured with the aim of maximising local control of the investment. But, as in all foreign investment contracts of long duration, an internal balance between internationalisation and localisation is struck during the bargaining process that precedes the drafting of the agreement. That balance keeps changing, depending on various factors such as fluctuations in the demand for products, political changes in the country and the health of the global economy as a whole.

1.10 Other requirements

There are several other requirements which can be found in the foreign investment legislation of states. They may be explained as efforts at maximising the benefits of the foreign investment to the local economy. There may be requirements relating to the level of employment of local staff, thus ensuring that the perceived benefits of the transfer of skills to the local labour force and management are made a reality. There may be a requirement for local research relating to products and the adaptation of the products to local conditions. There may be a requirement that the processing of minerals should take place locally so that more activity associated with the mineral industry takes place within the state and more value is thereby added to the product within the state before export. The imposition of such requirements could also be justified as based on the sovereign rights of the state to regulate economic activity that takes place within its territory.

As a result of the policies adopted by developing countries towards foreign investment, some new forms of foreign investment which have the flexibility to give effect to larger economic and social policies have emerged. Some of them are dealt with in Section 2 below.

1.11 Regulation and expropriation

It is abundantly clear that foreign investment has to work within the regulatory framework of the host state. Where admission of a foreign investment is conditional, the failure to meet those conditions justifies interference. Where licences need to be obtained and are made conditional, again the failure to meet those conditions justifies the withdrawal of the licences. In all these instances, there can be no doubt as to the domestic legality of the measures if the procedures mandated by the law have been followed. The issue is whether such interference can amount to an expropriation under international law. The basic assumption would be that it would not amount to an expropriation, as the foreign investor was admitted on the condition that local laws are obeyed. This must be the starting-point of analysis. The result would vary in accordance, not with customary international law which has nothing to say on the point, except perhaps that it insists on due process prior to interference, but on treaty constraints. The extent to which there are such constraints and the difficulty of determining when regulation crosses the line and amounts to expropriation under treaty provisions are discussed in Chapter 8 below.

2. New forms of foreign investment

Unlike earlier forms of contract which favoured the foreign investor, modern forms of foreign investment contract ensure that the contractual balance favours the host state. The early measures of ensuring such change lacked sophistication. The picture has since changed. There is now a greater pragmatism in the manner in which foreign investment is handled, though one must not forget that basic passions such as nationalism and xenophobia are yet dormant and can be aroused by the astute in the pursuit of power. Equally, endemic corruption defeats these aims in many developing states. The prevailing philosophy that foreign investment can be harnessed to serve the economic development of the host state is the basis of some of the regulatory measures that were detailed above. They are based on the recognition that foreign investment is beneficial to the host economy provided there is careful regulation of such investment. In keeping with this philosophy, the preferred forms of foreign investment have also changed. The contractual forms through which foreign investments now enter are more amenable to public control than the earlier forms and are instruments through which state policy on foreign investment could be given expression. To this extent, they are more in the nature of public contracts than ordinary commercial contracts. They are designed to mesh with the regulatory controls that host states seek to exert over foreign investment. The view that these contracts are located in commercial laws is no longer tenable, though dispute settlement relating to such contracts is befuddled by notions that these transactions are no different from commercial transactions.

The principal representative forms of foreign investment are the joint venture and the production-sharing agreement, both of which are briefly described below. They are supported by agreements such as the management agreement (which is based on the separation of ownership and control so that the manager controls a project in return for a fixed sum whereas the profits of the project go to the state), the transfer of technology agreement (where the technology required for the project is supplied by the foreigner) and similar devices through which the state is able to ensure that it controls the project and has a larger share of the profits. These new types of foreign investment contract have been described in the literature.

2.1 The joint venture

The joint venture is a collaborative arrangement between two or more businesses to achieve a particular objective or to participate in another fresh project which may be more successfully pursued as a result of their pooling of resources or technology. The spreading of the risk of failure enables the parties to proceed with the project with more confidence whereas bearing the risk alone would have made any of the parties unwilling to embark on it. Two principal forms of joint venture are recognised. One is the partnership joint venture, which is not very different from a partnership in the common law, except that it is formed with a precise project in mind. The second form is the corporate joint venture, where the parties enter into an agreement to incorporate a company through which they will carry out their business objectives. The constitutional documents of the company will reflect the main points on which there is agreement between the parties.

The joint venture is an American contribution to commerce. Its use in international business is now widespread. In the developed countries, the joint-venture form has been used in many high-technology industries, and in particular in industries such as the aviation industry where the scope for international business cooperation is great. It has become popular for the reasons that the penetration of new markets through local business partners is easier, the risks are diversified and market information is more readily gained through the local partner.

In developing countries, in addition to these reasons, there are the more compelling reasons that foreign investment entry can usually be lawfully made only in collaboration with a local partner. If the industry into which entry is sought is a state monopoly, this will mean that the joint venture will have to be made with a state corporation. This has advantages as well as disadvantages from the foreign investor's point of view. One advantage is that the foreign investor will be able to share in monopoly profits in a captive, monopoly market. Another advantage is that the investor will have a link with the state so that matters such as customs clearances, export permits and other administrative matters connected with entry and later with the functioning of the joint venture will be smoother. The disadvantages are that the state will seek to represent its objectives through the state corporation and ensure that its policies are reflected in the functioning of the joint venture. The constant presence of the directors of the state entity at board meetings of the joint venture corporation will provide the means of securing the adequate airing of the state's policy on the direction the joint venture should take. Since state policies will clash with the profit motives of the foreign investor, the situation is tailor-made for conflict. In any dispute, the state will not hesitate to use its legislative and administrative powers to ensure that the joint venture toes the line that it has drawn. The foreign investor will not be able to assert his will in such circumstances. The nature of the control that the foreign investor may be able to exert varies with the nature of the project. Where there is high technology involved and access to it can be gained only through the foreign partner, the role of the local partner will generally be a passive one. Continued utility to the project, as a supplier of finance and technology and as a means of access to markets abroad, is the key to the control that the foreign investor can exert.

In socialist states, joint venture with the state entity is usually compelled by legislation, particularly in vital sectors of the economy. The situation is similar in sectors of the developing states which have mixed economies. In the mixed economy states, entry can be made in collaboration with private business in the non-public sector of the economy.

Increasingly, however, wholly foreign owned enterprises are coming to be permitted in many sectors.[113]

2.2 The production-sharing agreement

A change to the dominant form of contract has also occurred in the oil industry. Previously, the concession agreement was the prevailing form of contract through which the oil industry functioned in the oil-exporting countries. The concession agreement contemplated a passive role for the host state, which was confined to receiving royalties for the oil that was exported. The concession agreement is no longer used, as oil-producing countries have sought greater control over the industry. The new agreement, which replaced the concession agreement, reflects the fact that there has been a shift of power away from the oil companies to the oil-producing states. The production-sharing agreement is based on the concept that the ownership of oil is always in the state, and that the state alone has the right to its disposal, a reflection of the principle of permanent sovereignty over natural resources. The risk of oil exploration is borne by the foreign corporation, which is given a licence for the exploration of parcels of land or sea where there is a prospect of finding oil. When oil is found, the foreign corporation may extract the oil and is given a certain percentage of it, so that it may recover the expenses of the exploration and secure a reasonable profit. The percentage of the oil given to the foreign corporation progressively diminishes as the expenses are recouped by sale until eventually the whole project is taken over by the state oil corporation.

The state retains ownership of the oil, subject to the right of the foreign corporation to its share of production. There is usually provision for joint management of the project with the state oil company.

Both the joint-venture agreement and the production-sharing agreement are legal techniques which demonstrate that host states are asserting their power over incoming investments. The amount of power that can be asserted will depend on the relative bargaining strengths of the parties. A state which is desperate for investment is not going to be too assertive in case it scares away such investment, whereas a state which is perceived as a safe state from which profits can be made will seek to maximise the benefits from the foreign investment for itself while ensuring that the foreign investor still has adequate incentives to remain and do business in that state.

The joint-venture agreement and the production-sharing agreement illustrate the manner in which the older types of agreement such as the concession agreement have been replaced to ensure that there is greater state control over foreign investment even at the contractual stage which is indispensable to the entry of the foreign investment. Other forms of contract that are used in the area reflect this element of public control as the central fact of foreign

---

[113] In manufacturing sectors, this appears to be the trend, but, in mining sectors, the requirement that there should be state participation still persists. Likewise, some sectors, such as civil aviation, continue to be subject to entry with local participation. Laws requiring local participation have not been dismantled, despite liberalisation.

investment transactions, illustrating the obvious feature of public law controls as central to foreign investment in both developed and developing countries.

3. Constraints on control: customary international law

As a general principle, a state may do whatever it pleases on its territory. The modern assertion of such sovereignty in the economic sphere is effected through the principles of economic self-determination and permanent sovereignty over natural resources. The Seoul Declaration of the International Law Association combined these two principles of economic sovereignty by stating that 'permanent sovereignty over natural resources, economic activities and wealth is a principle of international law'.[114] One could argue that such a principle always existed in international law, and that the articulation of principles relating to economic self-determination became necessary only in the context of the need to dismantle domestic economic structures in the post-colonial era. The notion of permanent sovereignty is not confined in the resolutions to natural resources but extends to all economic activities of a state.[115] This extension need not be considered dramatic or novel.[116] The right of control over the economic affairs of the state is one which European states have claimed and exercised consistently. It is a facet of the state's inherent sovereignty to control all people, incidents and objects that are within its territory. Such a right is not confined to European states. On the principle of equality of states, there is no reason why the same right should not be exercised by other states.

But, state sovereignty is subject to the principles of customary and treaty-based international law. The subjection of state sovereignty to these principles may be explained either on the ground that international law is a system of higher law or on the positivist basis that there has been consent of the state to be bound by treaty and customary principles of international law.[117] Developing countries have not denied the relevance of international law to foreign investment. The most controversial document in the area, the Charter of Economic Rights and Duties of States, acknowledges the fact that the rights it articulates are subject to 'the fulfilment in good faith of international obligations'.[118] The chairman of the drafting committee of the Charter has explained that the Charter 'accepts that international law may act as a factor limiting the freedom of the state'.[119] The problem relates to the content of the international law, which limits the host state's treatment of the alien investor. The content of this body of customary law continues to be relevant, incorporated as it is into modern investment treaties through treatment standards such as the international minimum standard

---

[114] Section 5 of the Seoul Declaration of the International Law Association (1988).

[115] International Law Association, *Report of the Sixty-Fourth Congress* (1990).

[116] H. Neufeld, *The International Protection of Private Creditors from the Treaties of Westphalia to the Congress of Vienna* (1971), p. 55.

[117] Compare M. Shaw, *Title to Territory in Africa* (1986), p. 16, who states: '[C]ompetences associated with the concept of territorial sovereignty may be seen as derived ultimately from the norms of the international legal order itself', with formulations that regard international law as being based on self-limitations of power by states.

[118] Many developing states did not accept Article 2(2)(c) of the Charter of Economic Rights and Duties of States, which expressed the view that matters of nationalisation were for the state to decide.

[119] J. Castenada, 'La Charte des Droits et Devoirs Economiques des Etats' (1970) 16 *Annuaire Francais de Droit International* 31.

and the fair and equitable standard of treatment.[120] As to the content of customary law in the area, there are different claims made by different groups of states.

In the area of foreign investments, there is a claim made by capital-exporting countries as to the existence of a body of customary international law, which, if it exists, will limit the state's sovereignty to impose restrictions on foreign investors. The body of customary law relates to an area referred to in the texts as state responsibility for the treatment of aliens. This law imposes standards upon states as to the treatment of aliens who are present in their territories. Whether this body of law forms part of customary international law is questionable as its universality has been denied by some authors.[121] It is undeniable, however, that treaties on foreign investment could limit the state's sovereignty to treat the foreign investor in violation of the treaty standards which protect him. There are no multilateral treaties containing substantive rules on foreign investment. The existing multilateral treaties have only a limited significance for this area of law. The General Agreement on Tariffs and Trade (GATT) has little relevance to the field. The disciplines attached to the World Trade Organization, especially those on intellectual property (TRIPS), investment (TRIMS) and services (GATS), have considerably greater significance, and are considered in Chapter 6 below. There are multilateral agreements relating to the arbitration of investment disputes and the insurance of foreign investment.[122] The extent to which the rules on state responsibility in international law, if they exist, may impact on the requirements and restrictions imposed by the new foreign investment codes are examined in the first section of Chapter 6. The extent to which regulatory devices may conflict with customary international law and with GATT and other treaty provisions is examined in the second section of Chapter 6. The nature of the treaties and other instruments which may affect a state's treatment of foreign investment are dealt with in Chapters 5 and 6.

3.1 State responsibility for injuries to aliens

The rules relating to state responsibility for injuries to aliens contain the body of international law which seeks to confer a standard of treatment of aliens who enter states for various

---

[120] The US model bilateral investment treaty of 2004 expressly subjects the fair and equitable treatment standard to customary international law to prevent any expansionary interpretation of the standard.

[121] S. Guha-Roy, 'Is the Law of State Responsibility for Injuries to Aliens a Part of Universal International Law?' (1969) 55 *AJIL* 562. More recently, a United Nations report stated:

The traditional concept of State responsibility as a body of international standards for the protection of individual aliens was questioned when it was perceived as either inequitable or inadequate for the purpose of addressing the concerns of an international community which lacked homogeneity as to political, economic and developmental values and goals. While it cannot be asserted that a new doctrine of state responsibility prevails, it is clear that the traditional concept no longer commands universal support.

There were several American lawyers who viewed the law of state responsibility as partial to the interests of the developed states long before Guha-Roy. Thus, Judge Jessup regarded the law on state responsibility as 'an aspect of the history of imperialism or dollar diplomacy'. Lissitzyn regarded it as an example of international law 'developed in response to the requirements of the Western business civilisation'. O. J. Lissitzyn, 'International Law in a Divided World' (1963) 532 *International Conciliation* 58. For more recent views, see UNCTC, 'Outstanding Issues in the Draft Code of Conduct on Transnational Corporations', E/C.10/1985/S/2 (1985), para. 53. P. Trimble, 'International Law and World Order' (1990) 42 *Stanford Law Review* 811 at 835, regards the law on state responsibility and minimum standards of conduct as having only a regional significance in the Latin American context.

[122] The ICSID and the MIGA Conventions, both sponsored by the World Bank, are discussed in Chapter 6 below.

reasons, including for the purpose of doing business.[123] They create liability in the host state for failure to observe the prescribed standards in its treatment of aliens. An alien who leaves his state carries with him the protection of his home state. This rule of diplomatic protection of nationals comes down from early times.[124] It was a less objectionable right than the right to use military force in the protection of nationals, a right which continues to be asserted as a justification for military intervention. The legality of such intervention in modern international law is subject to doubt.[125]

The theory of state responsibility for injuries to aliens rests on the idea that an injury to an alien is an injury to his home state. In effect, it involves a fiction that is used to overcome the deficiency of personality in the alien to take up his own case in an international forum. The fiction involves a stress on the link of nationality between the alien and his home state and the notion of injury caused to that state through the medium of the alien as a result of this link. The law was explained by the Permanent Court of International Justice in the following passage:[126]

[I]n taking up the case of one of its nationals, by resorting to diplomatic action or international judicial proceedings on his behalf, a state is in reality asserting its own right, the right to ensure in the person of its nationals respect for the rules of international law. This right is necessarily limited to intervention on behalf of its own nationals because in the absence of special agreement the bond of nationality between the state and the individual which alone confers upon it the right of diplomatic protection, and it is as part of the function of diplomatic protection that the right to take up a claim and to ensure respect for the rules of international law must be envisaged.

Though the notion that diplomatic protection of aliens and the idea that an injury done to an alien is an injury done to his home state through the medium of the alien have been basic principles of international diplomacy,[127] the scope for abuse of the principle is obvious. Development of these

---

[123] C. F. Amerasinghe, *State Responsibility for Injuries to Aliens* (1967); see also C. Eagleton, *The Responsibility of States in International Law* (1928); F. Dunn, *The Protection of Foreign Nationals* (1932); A. Freeman, *International Responsibility of States for Denial of Justice* (1938); F. G. Dawson and I. L. Head, *International Law, National Tribunals and the Rights of Aliens* (1971); F. V. Garcia-Amador, L. B. Sohn and R. R. Baxter, *Recent Codification of the Law of State Responsibility for Injuries to Aliens* (1974); E. Jimenez de Arechaga, 'International Responsibility', in M. Sorensen (ed.), *Manual of Public International Law* (1968), p. 362; R. B. Lillich (ed.), *International Law of State Responsibility for Injuries to Aliens* (1983); M. Sornarajah, *The Pursuit of Nationalized Property* (1986); and James Crawford, *The International Law Commission's Articles on State Responsibility* (2002).

[124] The rule is usually traced from Vattel, *Les Droit de Gens* (1758).

[125] The threat of such intervention by European powers was the basis of the 'gun-boat diplomacy' practised in early times to bring pressure to bear to obtain advantageous commercial policies for their nationals. In modern times, the protection of citizens continues to be stated as a justification for military intervention. It has been used as a justification for military intervention chiefly by the United States in the cases of its intervention in Puerto Rico, Grenada and Panama. Non-intervention was a principle consistently articulated by Latin American states because of the frequency of interventions in their domestic affairs. See G. Arangio-Ruiz, *The United Nations Declaration on Friendly Relations and the System of Sources of International Law* (1979), p. 118. For a survey of the international law on military intervention, see L. Damrosch and D. Scheffer (eds.), *Law and Force in the New International Order* (1991), pp. 111–84. However, wide notions of intervention and the use of force are now resurfacing in international law. There are claims that force may be used in order to promote democracy, and that anticipatory force could be used in order to prevent possible terrorist attacks. The events after the intervention in Iraq to overthrow the regime there adds to the uncertainty in the law.

[126] *Panevezys–Saldutiskis Railway Case* (1939) PCIJ Series A/B No. 76, p. 16.

[127] The rule of mediate injury to the state is also traced to Vattel, who wrote in 1758 that: 'Whoever ill treats a citizen injures the state which must protect the citizen.' E. de Vattel, *Classics of International Law: The Law of Nations or the Principles of International Law* (C. Fenwick trans., 1916); P. Remec, *The Position of the Individual in International Law According to Grotius and Vattel* (1960). Vattel's view was reformulated in the *Panevezys–Saldutiskis Railway Case* by the Permanent Court

principles is based on unexceptional sources.[128] There is general recognition that there is state responsibility for direct wrongs done to aliens. Yet, there has been considerable tension generated between developed and developing states as to the application of the rules of state responsibility and diplomatic protection in the area of foreign investment. The disagreement has largely been focused on the standard of treatment to be accorded to the alien.

The developed states have maintained that aliens must be treated according to an international minimum standard, which could be a higher standard than that accorded by a host state to its own nationals.[129] This international minimum standard is asserted as a general principle that applies to the treatment of aliens. But, there is a component in this standard that has special relevance to the treatment of foreign investment. The existence of this minimum standard is asserted in investment treaties. Modern arbitral awards have also recognised that there are minimum standards with which the host state must conform in its treatment of foreign investors.[130] The minimum standard is an external standard which enables developed states to introduce standards of treatment that they expect for their foreign investors but which developing states may have difficulty satisfying. The failure to conform to the minimum standard of treatment creates a cause of action against the violating state. Such a violation could be pursued through dispute-settlement mechanisms. Most of the cases in which these standards of liability have been articulated involved injuries to the person of the alien. The most dramatic cases, such as the *Neer Claim* or the *Roberts Claim*, concerned injuries to the person of the alien, and it was in the context of such injuries that the old rules came to be stated. Injury could be caused directly by agents of the state such as soldiers, or indirectly, for example by mobs. In the latter case, responsibility arose in circumstances where there was negligence in protecting the alien or a wilful disregard of the duty to protect the alien. The extension of the idea to the property of the alien was not the focus of these early cases. Such an extension came much later and became the basis for building up a law on the protection of foreign investment. Thus, a powerful technique was created which could be manipulated to secure the interests of developed states and their foreign investors. The technique, developed in customary practice, is now stated in treaties. A particular phenomenon regarding the development of treaties is that the fair and equitable standard of treatment stated in them, which had remained quiescent for over half a century, has now assumed significance as an all-embracing standard. This development is treated in greater detail later on. The discussion here is confined to customary law.

Some developing countries, however, have maintained that an alien is entitled, at most, to the same treatment as the citizens of the host state. The heyday of a joint position being

---

of International Justice. Vattel had said: 'Whoever ill treats the citizen indirectly injures the state, which must protect the citizen. The sovereign of the injured state must avenge the deed and, if possible, force the aggressor to give full satisfaction or punish him, since otherwise the citizen will not obtain the chief end of civil society, which is protection.'

[128] The principles are constructed through: (1) *Mavrommatis Palestine Concession Case* (1929) PCIJ Series A No. 2, p. 12, where the Court stated that a state asserts its own rights when it espouses the cause of its national; (2) *Panevezys–Saldutiskis Railway Case* (1939) PCIJ Series A/B No. 76, where the need for the link of nationality between the state and the national whose right was taken up was stressed; and (3) *Chorzow Factory Case* (1928) PCIJ Series A No. 17, where restitution as the basis of damages for the wrong done to the national through the violation of treaty rights was stated.

[129] For a history of the rule, see E. Borchard, 'The Minimum Standard of Treatment of Aliens' (1940) 38 *Michigan Law Review* 445; A. Roth, *The Minimum Standard of International Law as Applied to Aliens* (1949).

[130] *American Machine Tools* v. *Zaire*, 5 *ICSID Reports* 11.

adopted by developing countries came when the resolutions associated with the New International Economic Order were being debated in the 1970s. The Charter of Economic Rights and Duties of States articulated this position in clear terms.[131] While generally adhering to the standard of national treatment, these states also claim that in exceptional instances they could discriminate in favour of their own citizens. Though this conflict in views can be traced back to the writings of Vitoria and Vattel, it was only in Latin American state practice that it had any significance in earlier times. The claim that its citizens were not given an international standard of treatment became a pretext for intervention by the United States in the affairs of Latin American states. Consequently, Latin American states have steadfastly denied the existence of a rule that mandated a minimum standard of treatment for aliens.

After the decolonisation of African and Asian states, the developed states espoused the view taken by the United States in relation to the rule that there was a minimum standard of treatment for the property of aliens. With the ending of colonialism, there was a greater need to ensure that there was a rule-based system of foreign investment protection as force could no longer be used to settle such disputes as in the past. Newly independent states, like the Latin American states, had denied the existence of a rule mandating a minimum standard of treatment. Asian and African states joined in by contesting the validity of the rule. Some writers from developing countries challenged the very existence of a law on state responsibility in customary international law.[132]

But, the more vigorous challenge to the viewpoint of the developed countries had been mounted earlier by Latin American jurists who, following the lead of Calvo,[133] argued that aliens had only the rights and privileges enjoyed by nationals and can therefore seek enforcement of such rights only before national courts. This doctrine sought to preclude international review by an external body of the standard of treatment accorded to aliens. The principal purpose of the minimum standard rule was the protection of the life and liberty of aliens in situations of turmoil that frequently occurred in some states or at the hands of unprincipled officials.[134] If it had been used exclusively for such a purpose, there could have been a justification for it, but, instead, it became the basis for a system of foreign investment protection which could hinder economic reforms undertaken by developing countries. Since

---

[131]   See, in particular, Article 2(2)(c) of the Charter, which contains in effect a restatement of the Calvo doctrine.

[132]   S. Guha-Roy, 'Is the Law of State Responsibility for Injuries to Aliens a Part of Universal International Law?' (1969) 55 *AJIL* 562.

[133]   Carlos Calvo was an Argentinian foreign minister. He was earlier a professor of public international law, and wrote a multi-volume text in Spanish on international law. The doctrine was adopted at many Conferences of American States (Washington Conference, 1889; Montevideo Conference, 1933). Its offshoot was the Calvo Clause, which gives exclusive jurisdiction over disputes arising from foreign investment contracts to national tribunals. On the Calvo Clause, see D. Shea, *Calvo Clause* (1955); K. Lipstein, 'The Place of the Calvo Clause in International Law' (1945) 24 *BYIL* 130; A. V. Freeman, 'Recent Aspects of the Calvo Doctrine and the Challenge to International Law' (1946) 40 *AJIL* 131; D. Graham, 'The Calvo Clause: Its Current Status as a Contractual Renunciation of Diplomatic Protection' (1971) 6 *Texas International Law Journal* 289; and A. O. Adede, 'The Minimum Standards in a World of Disparities', in R. St J. Macdonald and D. M. Johnston (eds.), *The Structure and Process of International Law* (1983), p. 1001 at pp. 1003–4.

[134]   As formulated by Vattel, the rule was intended to apply to situations where the host state had rudimentary forms of government and was not capable of protecting the alien vigorously. The rule served a deterrent function and justified intervention by the home state for the protection of the alien. It may possibly be extended to mob rule or unstable military rule under dictators as prevailed in many Latin American states. Whether the rule applies to modern governments of whatever ideological persuasion may be questioned. M. W. Gordon, *The Cuban Nationalisations* (1973).

Latin America was one of the first areas of the world to be subject to the application of the minimum standard rule, it was logical that opposition to the rule first came from that region.

3.2 The conflict between the United States and Latin American states

The Latin American view that foreign investors are subject to the laws of the host state alone and have no protection through any external standards is a view which had much support in the international law that existed during the period in which the controversy arose. There was clearly no protection envisaged in international law for contracts made by aliens with the host state.[135] Early twentieth-century US writing on the issue supports the view that there is state responsibility for damage caused to the person of the alien or for destruction of the property of the alien by state forces or as a result of negligence by the host state in providing protection.[136] But, there is no unequivocal support for the proposition that this rule should be extended to foreign investment protection. These writings contain clear statements that breaches of agreements made by US citizens with Latin American states should not be the concern of the state. The idea of foreign investment protection through the principles of state responsibility is a matter of later development.

Because of the importance of the subject, the authorities which support the proposition that international law mandates a national standard of treatment and no more need to be examined at least briefly. A convenient starting-point is the view stated by Sir Henry Strong, the arbitrator in *Rosa Gelbtrunk* v. *Salvador*.[137] The arbitrator observed in his award:

A citizen or subject of one nation who, in the pursuit of commercial enterprise, carries on trade within the territory and under the protection of the sovereignty of a nation other than his own, is to be considered as having cast in his lot with the subjects or citizens of the state in which he resides and carries on business. Whilst on the one hand he enjoys the protection of that state, so far as the police regulations and other advantages are concerned, on the other hand he becomes liable to the political vicissitudes of the country in which he thus has a commercial domicile in the same manner as the subjects or the citizens of that state are liable to the same.

The statement is simply that, once the alien voluntarily takes the risk of investing in a host state, he must bear the risk of potential injury to his investment and must be satisfied with the same standard of compensation as is given to the nationals of the state who suffer the same fate as he does. It is a potentially sound principle of risk allocation. Ralston, commenting on

---

[135] The PCIJ had stated in the *Serbian Loans Case* (1929) PCIJ Series A No. 20, that municipal law applies to state contracts with aliens. In the *Panevezys–Saldutiskis Railway Case* (1939) PCIJ Series A/B No. 76, the PCIJ reiterated that 'in principle property rights and contractual rights of individuals depend in every state on the municipal law and fall therefore more particularly within the jurisdiction of municipal tribunals'. The Mexican Claims Commission usually applied municipal law. Surveying the practice of this Commission, Feller observed that 'international law contains no rules for the controversies involving breach of such contracts'. A. H. Feller, *The Mexican Claims Commission 1923–1934* (1935).

[136] The arbitral and other awards that are used to support the existence of state responsibility for injuries to aliens deal with capricious damage to the person and property of aliens. They do not deal with the taking of property by the state for a public purpose. These cases came later to be used to construct a legal structure for the protection of foreign investment. For representative early cases, see *Neer Claim* (1926) 4 *UNRIAA* 60; *Chevreau Case* (1933) 27 *AJIL* 160; and *Zafiro Claim* (1925) 6 *UNRIAA* 160. These cases, which involved the treatment of individuals in a degrading fashion, are the basis for the construction of an international minimum standard for property protection.

[137] Foreign Relations of 1902, p. 877.

the *dictum* of the arbitrator, stated that it accorded with the practice of the European states at the time.[138] Ralston also cited a passage from the Venezuelan Claims Commission of 1885 which quoted the following view of Fiore with approval:[139]

Protection is illicit and unjustifiable where it has for its purpose to secure in favour of the citizens residing abroad a privileged position. Strong and powerful governments must not take advantage of their superiority and exaggerate the duty of protection by exercising pressure upon weak governments, in order to compel them to favour their citizens and exempt them from certain obligations or grant them privileges of any nature whatever.

Resort to an external standard was made only in circumstances where the internal conditions in the host state were such that no remedies could possibly be expected from the host state. Cushing was almost apologetic in stating that, in such circumstances, there was justification for the home state to intervene. He observed:[140]

As to the exceptions to the general rule, they have grown up chiefly in Spanish America in consequence of the unsettled condition of the new American republics. Great Britain, France and the United States have each occasionally assumed, in behalf of their subjects or citizens in those countries, rights of interference which neither of us would tolerate at home – in some cases from necessity, in others with very questionable discretion or justification.

The passage leaves no room for doubt that interference is an exception to the general rule and was confined to a region, and that too when conditions in the state were unsettled. It also accepts that the justifications for such interventions were often questionable and counterproductive. The exception, however, was to be subsumed when the general principle was broadened by later claims made by the United States. However, on every occasion when such claims were made, the Latin American states objected so that the claims have remained, in the regional context of the Americas, supported only by the consistent practice of the United States. The Latin American states have, almost collectively, been persistent objectors to the formation of any customary practice in the area. It is only in the period when neo-liberalism was in the ascendancy that they have departed from this practice by entering into investment treaties which acknowledged the competence of foreign tribunals to settle foreign investment disputes. After this period of neo-liberal ascendancy, there has been a reversion to the older position emphasising national control over foreign investment.[141]

In the writings of Borchard[142] and Ralston,[143] there does not appear to be any support for the existence of an external standard of protection for foreign investment agreements. Their writings cover the first quarter of the twentieth century. Borchard was convinced that the contractual claims of aliens against the host state should not be espoused too readily by their home states. He justified this position on the grounds that the alien had voluntarily assumed

---

[138] J. H. Ralston, *The Law and Procedure of International Tribunals* (1926), p. 271.   [139] Moore, *Digest*, p. 2965.

[140] Referred to in the *Sambiaggio Case* (1903), cited in J. H. Ralston, *The Law and Procedure of International Tribunals* (1926), p. 272.

[141] The return of the Calvo doctrine has been widely seen, particularly in Latin America, after a series of economic crises following liberalisation.

[142] E. Borchard, *The Diplomatic Protection of Citizens Abroad* (1915).

[143] J. H. Ralston, *The Law and Procedure of International Tribunals* (1926).

a risk in contracting with the foreign state and that, 'by going abroad, he submits impliedly to the local law and local judicial system'.[144] These are views solidly based on the principle of sovereignty of states and the right inherent in such sovereignty to control all economic activity within the state by both aliens and nationals. The only exception to the rule that he recognised was the situation where the local law did not provide an adequate remedy because the local judiciary was corrupt or where the remedy that was provided was too remote.

There is little indication that the picture changed in the next quarter of a century. The United States had insisted on an external standard for the treatment of aliens, but the Latin American states continued to deny the existence of such a standard. In this situation, there was no way that even a regional norm, let alone an international law principle, could have emerged to the effect that there was an international minimum standard for the treatment of foreign investment.[145]

In the context of the relations between the United States and the Latin American states, foreign investment and the claims relating to the international law that protected it were perceived as instruments through which the United States was able to maintain its economic dominance in the region. Foreign investment was seen by Latin Americans as a trojan horse which ensured that American influence could be exerted through the presence of the foreign investment in the various Latin American states.[146] The idea that there were supranational norms which permitted the protection of the foreign investor was anathema to Latin American jurists, who argued that the only protection that existed for foreign investment was to be found in the domestic legal systems of the host states. The United States itself had espoused such a doctrine when it was a recipient of massive capital investment from Europe, but had changed its tack when it became an exporter of capital into Latin America. It could well be that recent events presage another change in the attitudes of the United States.[147] The principle will have its vicissitudes depending on circumstances.[148]

It is the conversion of a principle which was designed to ensure the safety and security of aliens into a system of property protection which has generated conflict. Most of the early cases asserting minimum standards of treatment concerned the personal security of the alien and not his property. When dealing with property, these cases extended protection to property on the basis that such protection was a necessary concomitant of personal security. The rules were developed as safeguards against state violence directed at aliens and not as

---

[144] E. Borchard, *The Diplomatic Protection of Citizens Abroad* (1915), p. 285. Brownlie, who later developed a similar proposition, relied on *Home Missionary Society Case* (1920) 6 *UNRIAA* 42 and the *Yukon Lumber Case* (1913) 6 *UNRIAA* 17 at 20 and on Article 4(4) of the Harvard Draft Convention on the International Responsibility of States for Injuries to Aliens. But, there are awards which go the other way. *Schufeldt Claim* (1930) 5 *AD* 179. The *Delgoa Bay Railway Company Case* (1900) Whiteman, *Digest*, vol. 3, p. 1694, is not a strong case, as the parties had agreed on many issues. *Goldenberg* (1928) *AD* 542 can be distinguished, as it was a wartime case decided on the basis of a treaty.

[145] F. V. Garcia-Amador, *The Changing Law of International Claims* (1984), pp. 356–61.

[146] C. Lipson, *Standing Guard: Protecting Foreign Capital in the Nineteenth and Twentieth Centuries* (1985).

[147] Some writers have argued that, with the United States becoming the largest recipient of foreign investments and being the target of foreign investment arbitrations, especially in the NAFTA context, its attitude would change and it may come to espouse the Calvo doctrine at least in a qualified way. In 2002, Congress mandated that future treaties should not grant foreign investors in the United States greater rights than US investors making investments in the United States. This is very much the Calvo doctrine, brought about possibly by a reaction to NAFTA and an increasing sense of the need for investment protectionism.

[148] A seemingly outrageous suggestion is that the United States itself may be moving towards the Calvo doctrine. This is supported by the fact that it has revived the notion of regulatory expropriation, curtailed the scope of the fair and equitable standard of treatment and proclaimed that the national security preclusion is self-judging in its new model investment treaty.

principles of property protection. It was in later times that the rules, essentially directed at state violence, came to be isolated in order that a system of property protection could be built up. This was resisted by the Latin American states, which have consistently argued that interference with property, particularly in pursuance of economic programmes, fell within the domestic sovereignty of the host state.

The tussle that took place between the United States and the Latin American states became a global one after decolonisation through the claim that the position taken by the United States represented international law. The newly independent states of Africa and Asia joined the Latin American states in denying that the principles of state responsibility for injuries to aliens extends to the protection of direct investments made by aliens. On this point, there is no agreement between developed states and developing states as to what the international law is.[149] At the bilateral level, states have concluded investment treaties articulating a set of rules, which to a large extent adopt the model of property protection desired by the developed states. But, there is strong resistance at the multilateral level to the adoption of similar treaty instruments, which indicates that developing states are reluctant to give up their collective stance that there is no international law on the subject.

During the dispute concerning the Mexican expropriations of US property, the Hull formula that prompt, adequate and effective compensation must be paid to the foreign investor upon expropriation of his property was articulated. The formula articulated what could be described as a component of the minimum standard. But, there was no argument that interference with the alien property itself was unlawful, for the property rights of the alien vested only to the extent of their recognition in the domestic law of the host state. Roth summarised the state of the law on this point in a series of propositions as follows:[150]

(1) General international law gives aliens no right to be economically active in foreign states. In cases where the national policies of foreign states allow aliens to undertake economic activities, however, general international law assures aliens of equality of commercial treatment among themselves.

(2) According to general international law, the alien's privilege of participation in the economic life of his state of residence does not go so far as to allow him to acquire private property. The state of residence is free to bar him from ownership of all or some property, whether movable or realty.

(3) Whenever the alien enjoys the privilege of ownership of property, international law protects his property in so far as his property may not be expropriated under any pretext, except for moral or penal reasons, without adequate compensation. Property rights are to be understood as rights to tangible property which have come into concrete existence according to the municipal law of the alien's state of residence.

This statement of the law, made in 1949 by an American writer, again recognises the sovereignty of the host state and its laws over any foreign investment. There is protection for property rights acquired under the law of the host state but such rights are dependent on

---

[149] This statement must follow from the universalisation of the Calvo doctrine by Article 2(2)(c) of the Charter of Economic Rights and Duties of States. The article received the support of the vast majority of developing states.
[150] A. Roth, *The Minimum Standard of International Law Applied to Aliens* (1949), pp. 185–6.

the host state's laws. The author uses the term 'privilege' rather than 'right' of ownership, which, in Hohfeldian terms, has the significance of indicating that the privilege can be withdrawn by the person or entity conferring it. In the third paragraph, there is reference to an international law standard, reflecting the US claim that there was an external standard as regards the expropriation of alien property. This may have been due to the influence of the Hull formula. But, the Hull formula had never been accepted by the Latin American states.

Clearly, there was a credible case for the minimum standard of treatment being applied to the protection of the life, liberty and property of the alien in the unsettled conditions of many Latin American states from state violence or state-condoned mob violence. There was also a case for the extension of the rule to capricious takings of an alien's property by dictators for their own purpose. There was no support, as a matter of customary international law, for the extension of the concept into the economic sphere to include foreign investment agreements. Indeed, it would have been difficult to prove that, at the time state responsibility for the foreign investment was claimed to have emerged, developed states provided equal treatment to aliens in the economic sphere. Developed states maintained many laws which were racially discriminatory. They continued to discriminate on the basis of race well into the twentieth century.[151]

3.3 The content of the international minimum standard

The content of the international minimum standard is difficult to identify. Apart from the rule relating to compensation for expropriation and the settlement of such issues through a tribunal that sits outside the host state, there does not seem to be any other guidance as to what the content of the standard is. The Hull standard of full compensation is regarded as being incorporated into the minimum standard. The assessment of such compensation by a foreign tribunal, and the requirements that expropriation should be non-discriminatory and for a public purpose are said to flow from the international minimum standard. Apart from the rules relating to compensation for expropriation advanced by the developed states, there does not appear to be any other rule associated with the international minimum standard. The later introduction of the 'fair and equitable standard' led to some controversy as to whether it was a higher standard than the international minimum standard.[152] But, this view has not been accepted by the developed states. The NAFTA Commission issued an interpretative statement indicating that the 'fair and equitable standard' as used in NAFTA did not contemplate a higher standard than the international minimum standard recognised in customary international law.[153] The central issue of the content of the international minimum standard outside the context of expropriation has not been faced. Within the

---

[151] For example, there were laws in the United States forbidding Japanese citizens from buying real estate. McGovney, 'The Anti-Japanese Land Laws' (1943) 35 *California Law Review* 61. Australia maintained a 'white Australia' policy until the 1970s, preventing non-white entry into Australia for residence, let alone ownership of property.

[152] It was regarded as a higher standard by some. F. A. Mann, *Further Studies in International Law* (1990), pp. 234–51.

[153] NAFTA Commission. The issue was raised in some NAFTA awards, which conformed with the interpretative statement, once it was issued. The OECD also had earlier stated the view that 'fair and equitable treatment' is a standard which 'conforms in effect to the "minimum standard" which forms part of customary international law'.

context of the rules on expropriation, the issue of whether full compensation represents international law has remained a contested proposition. Though investment treaties increasingly contain references to full compensation, the question whether they contribute to the creation of customary law on the point remains moot.[154] The international minimum standard evolved as a counter to the standard of national treatment articulated in the Calvo doctrine. Its content was largely determined in the course of the debate on expropriation.

In addition to the question of the standard of compensation, another aspect of the content of the standard related to dispute resolution. Supporters of the minimum standard argued that issues relating to expropriation had to be settled in accordance with an external standard applied by international tribunals. The rule was based on the suspicion that domestic tribunals would not provide objective justice to the foreign investor. It was met with the counter-argument that only domestic tribunals or courts had competence to settle such disputes, and that too only in accordance with the local laws. The emergence of the local remedies rule was, to some extent, a resolution of that conflict.

The local remedies rule requires that, for an international claim to arise from the mistreatment of a foreign investor, there must be a prior exhaustion of the remedies provided to him by the law of the host state.[155] This rule is widely recognised as a rule of international law, and asserts the primacy of the domestic law of the host state to provide a remedy to the foreign investor and thereby avoid an international claim. Exceptions to the rule exist. The foreigner does not have to resort to remedies that are illusory or futile. These exceptions were formulated in the context of Latin American states which were formerly dictatorships, and their significance for modern democratic states is limited. Besides, a denial of remedy by a state is extremely difficult to establish.[156]

There have been attempts to displace the rule through treaties. The ICSID Convention seeks to do this. Developments under the Convention relating to 'arbitration without privity' seek to further the deviation from the rule. Yet, the logical basis of the rule is such that it continues to have vigour. Rooted in state sovereignty, the soundness of the rule that the initial remedy must lie in the host state's laws cannot be lightly shaken. So, when the OECD's Multilateral Agreement on Investment came to be drafted, the option of remedies was provided, confining the foreign investor to local remedies once he had chosen them. Yet, this result is not one which is fully consistent with the local remedies rule, which requires the first attempt at dealing with the issue to be granted to the host state. It is when this option fails that customary international law creates an international claim that could be pursued through international tribunals. The rule also serves the purpose of enabling a local tribunal to identify the dispute and to indicate its views as to the available remedies in local laws and how the matter should be disposed of by local tribunals applying domestic law. The techniques brought about by treaty devices on dispute settlement undermine this salutary purpose of the rule by giving too great an emphasis to the rights of the foreign investor.

---

[154] This issue is more fully explored in Chapter 10 below.

[155] On the rule, see C. F. Amerasinghe, *Local Remedies in International Law* (2nd edn, 2002).

[156] In the *ELSI Case*, the International Court of Justice indicated that a denial of justice will not be lightly assumed.

The bulk of the case law on the international minimum standard concerns physical injury to the person of the individual alien and not damage to his property. The cases that concern damage to the property of aliens dealt with damage that took place during social upheavals and revolutionary situations that posed a danger both to life and to property.[157] It is difficult to extend these cases to situations of taking for the purpose of economic reform. A mental leap was necessary.[158] The extension of the cases to situations of modern strife has been relatively easily accomplished. The category of cases, such as *AAPL* v. *Sri Lanka*,[159] involving damage to alien property during civil strife, demonstrate this. There is greater difficulty in extending the principles developed in cases like the *Neer Claim*,[160] the *Janes Claim*[161] and the *Roberts Claim*[162] to the modern situation of regulatory controls of foreign investment.

In the early cases of physical injury, the common strand that was developed was that a mere error in investigation or a lack of resources to investigate personal crimes will not be a sufficient basis for creating state liability. The reconciliation of the conflict between the Calvo doctrine that asserted national sovereignty and the creation of an international standard to overcome state deficiencies in offering protection to aliens required a balancing factor. This was found in the emphasis in the cases that something more than mere violation of the domestic law was required for state liability to arise. That additional element was expressed in nebulous language. The *Neer* formula was that 'to constitute an international delinquency, the treatment of an alien should amount to an outrage, to bad faith, to wilful neglect of duty or to an insufficiency of governmental action so far short of international standards that every reasonable and impartial man would readily recognise its insufficiency'.[163] That idea is to be found in all the cases of the period, discussing state liability in times of civil strife. Transferring that idea to the application of regulatory mechanisms affecting foreign investment in modern times is fraught with difficulty. Administrative law standards differ. Ascertaining a common standard will prove difficult. Unless some specific content can be given to the international minimum standard in the modern context, the mere assertion that the standard is not static remains rhetorical.[164]

3.4 State responsibility and developing states

In the Latin American context, it would be difficult to establish that there is a law on state responsibility for economic injuries done to aliens. The states of Africa and Asia were in colonial bondage at the time the conflict arose. They did not therefore participate in the making of any law in the area. Even if the theory that states are born into the world of existing international law and are bound by its principles is accepted,[165] it is difficult to

---

[157] There are few cases of property damage. *British Claims in Spanish Morocco* (1926) 4 *UNRIAA* 41.
[158] The leap is now being performed through the usual techniques of arbitral awards and writings of 'highly qualified publicists'.
[159] (1991) 30 *ILM* 577.   [160] (1926) 4 *UNRIAA* 60.   [161] (1926) 4 *UNRIAA* 82.   [162] (1926) 4 *UNRIAA* 77.
[163] It has been suggested that the standard in the *Neer Claim* has undergone modification to suit modern developments. This view is discussed in Chapter 8 below.
[164] See further the discussion in Chapter 7 below.
[165] This is the view supported by D. P. O'Connell, 'Independence and Problems of State Succession', in W. V. O'Brien (ed.), *The New States in International Law and Diplomacy* (1965), p. 7 at p. 12.

establish that state responsibility for economic injuries to alien investors was recognised as a principle of customary international law. Latin American states, as well as African and Asian states, must be taken to be persistent objectors to the formation of such customary international law. Given the existence of such a large number of states objecting to the extension of rules of state responsibility into the sphere of foreign investment protection, it is hardly possible to speak of an international law on state responsibility for injuries caused to the foreign investment of aliens by the host state. It is difficult to establish that these principles had emerged without having a basis in the sources of international law. About the only rule for which there is support in customary international law is the rule that some compensation must be paid for the taking of alien property by the host state. But, this rule developed independently of the law on state responsibility as a result of claims and settlements made by states. It arose as a result of the practice of paying compensation for post-war nationalisations.

3.5 The 'noble synthesis'

In view of the conflict between developed and developing states, there has been a new approach attempted to the issue of state responsibility for injuries to aliens. The new approach seeks to combine the notion of an international minimum standard with the evolving standards of human rights. The principal impetus for this approach was given by the reports of Garcia-Amador, who was Special Rapporteur to the International Law Commission on the subject of state responsibility.[166] A consequence of this development is that the distinction between the minimum standard and the national standard of treatment has now become obsolete and has been replaced by a human rights standard that may be determined by reference to the documents on human rights.[167] From the point of view of ensuring that the alien has rights such as the right to life, liberty, freedom of expression and free movement, the progress that is said to have been made should be welcome. But, the subsequent treatment of the subject of state responsibility in the International Law Commission indicates that the focus had to be shifted away from the difficult issue of state responsibility for injuries to alien investors. When a new draft code was drawn up by the International Law Commission, there was a notable absence of significant reference to the subject of state responsibility for injuries to aliens.[168] The simple reason for this was that agreement on this area would have been difficult to secure.

---

[166] The reports are reproduced in F. V. Garcia-Amador, L. Sohn and R. R. Baxter, *Recent Codification of the Law on State Responsibility for Injuries to Aliens* (1974). It is not likely that the so-called 'noble synthesis' was intended by the Special Rapporteur to provide a system of investment protection. His later writings on the issue of investments indicate his leanings against such a course. See, for example, F. V. Garcia-Amador, *The Emerging International Law of Development* (1990). Over-zealous US glossators on the 'noble synthesis' undermined a worthwhile development in human rights law by attempting to convert it into a scheme for investment protection. It is unlikely that materialism sits well with the idealism involved in the pursuit of human rights objectives.

[167] For developments of this theory, see M. S. McDougall, H. D. Lasswell and Lung Chu Chen, *Human Rights and the World Political Order* (1980), pp. 761–5; R. B. Lillich, *The Human Rights of Aliens in Contemporary International Law* (1984), p. 17.

[168] For the new draft, see James Crawford, *The International Law Commission's Articles on State Responsibility* (2002).

Yet, the question remains whether the human rights standards are relevant to the alien's rights of access to economic activity in his host country or to the protection of his economic interests in that country. On this issue, there have been statements made to the effect that the new human rights standard ensures equal access to the alien on the basis that there is a norm of non-discrimination between the alien and the national that has grown up in international law.[169] Such propositions do not bear close scrutiny. The human rights documents prohibit racial discrimination but have nothing to say on the issue of distinctions made between classes of persons identified on non-racial grounds.[170] Identification of and discrimination between groups on the basis of economic disparities and past inequalities is in fact the basis of affirmative action policies instituted in the constitutional system of many states.[171] In fact, many of the human rights documents preserve the law that discrimination could be made between aliens and nationals as far as access to economic activity is concerned.[172] The assertion of rights of establishment has been accomplished through some investment treaties on a bilateral and regional basis, but the right is not a part of customary international law.[173]

The proposition that there is complete equality between nationals and aliens as to access to economic activity in a host state may be desirable, but at present it does not reflect the position in international law. State practice in both developed and developing countries abounds with examples of discrimination between nationals and aliens as regards ownership of real estate, the practice of the professions, employment in certain spheres and entry into certain businesses.[174] It may well be argued that this position is being encroached upon through treaty law, but it cannot be argued that there is as yet any customary law that requires equal national treatment to be afforded to foreign investors.

Another facet of the argument in seeking to extend the 'noble synthesis' into the area of foreign investment protection is that the right to property is a human right and that this right in the alien is now to be respected so that, where his property is taken over, he must be paid full compensation. The major human rights documents, such as the International Covenant

---

[169] M. S. McDougall, H. D. Lasswell and Lung Chu Chen, *Human Rights and the World Political Order* (1980), p. 773.

[170] See also the *Oscar Chinn Case* (1934) PCIJ Series A/B No. 64, which involved a claim by Britain that its national was not given equal treatment with a corporation created by statute by the host state. The claim was rejected. The Court pointed out that equal treatment was required only between entities in the like group. For more on the question of discrimination, see Z. Kronfol, *Protection of Foreign Investment* (1972), pp. 60–1; H. Kurshid, *Equality of Treatment and Trade Discrimination in International Law* (1968), p. 20.

[171] For example, the Indian Constitution permits affirmative discrimination in favour of scheduled castes and tribes.

[172] Article 2(3) of the International Covenant on Economic, Social and Cultural Rights justifies the denial of economic rights to aliens, and states that 'developing countries, with due regard to human rights and their national economy, may determine to what extent they would guarantee the economic rights recognised in the present Covenant to non-nationals'. The Convention on the Elimination of All Forms of Racial Discrimination permits discrimination between nationals and non-nationals. Article 1(2) reads: 'This Convention shall not apply to distinctions, exclusions, restrictions or preferences made by a State Party to this Convention between citizens and non-citizens.' See further N. Lerner, *The United Nations Convention on the Elimination of All Forms of Racial Discrimination* (1980), p. 30: 'The Convention does not interfere in the internal legislation of any State as far as rights of citizens and non-citizens are concerned.'

[173] US bilateral investment treaties require rights of pre-entry establishment. NAFTA and the ASEAN Framework Agreement on Investment are instances of regional treaties which contain pre-establishment rights. But, they permit wide sectoral exceptions.

[174] See further B. Sen, *A Diplomat's Handbook of International Law and Practice* (1988), p. 350, who observes:
It is now well established that a state may and is free to prohibit or regulate the professional or business activities of an alien even after he is allowed entry into the receiving state. It follows that any professional or business activities carried on by an alien in the receiving state must be in conformity with the local laws, regulations and executive orders as also municipal and other by-laws.
Section 2 of the Declaration on the Elimination of Racial Discrimination clearly permits the making of a distinction between nationals and aliens.

on Civil and Political Rights and the European Convention on Human Rights, do not contain any reference to the right to property. There is a protocol to the European Convention which states it in qualified terms. The case law generated under the provisions on the right to property does not recognise an unqualified right to property. The other human rights conventions which state it do so in qualified terms which recognise the state's right to interfere with property rights in the public interest. In seeking to establish that there is a universal recognition of an unqualified right to property that is basic to making a case, the proponents of the view have scavenged for authority in the most unlikely quarters.[175] The best that has been unearthed is a draft prepared by Baroness Elles as Rapporteur to the Sub-Commission on the Prevention of Discrimination and Protection of Minorities and Aliens. The study was directed at the protection of migrant workers, stateless persons and refugees. The definition of 'alien' for the purposes of the study included refugees, stateless persons, those given asylum, migrant workers, workers who had been transported through clandestine trafficking and women transported from their home states for the purpose of prostitution. The report seeks to protect the property rights of such persons. To extrapolate a scheme for the protection of multinational corporations into this effort at the protection of the meagre property of the flotsam of the human race seems illogical. The need to resort to such illogicality is itself an indication of the meagre nature of the support for the extension of the rules of state responsibility for injuries to aliens to the sphere of foreign investment protection. The relevance of any human rights standard is limited. No one seriously argues that human rights to property can be extended to benefit multinational corporations.[176]

Yet, with the onset of neo-liberalism in the 1990s, a property-centred argument has come into vogue. The Lockean concept of property is sought to be universalised. This concept is based on the idea that the protection of property is so central to the organisation of society that it should be protected through the law in absolute terms. In the United States, the argument has constitutional significance. Since the hegemonic power has a tendency to universalise the views it prefers, there will be a definite effort made to ensure that this particular view of the right to property as an unqualified right receives acceptance. There will, however, be difficulties in the way, as the priority of the public interest over private rights of property is generally recognised in regional systems of human rights as well as in other constitutional systems. In US constitutional law, the issue as to when a regulatory taking can be made by the state without payment of compensation remains unsettled. The devising of a test to distinguish between compensable and non-compensable taking of property has eluded most constitutional systems. The attempt to seek solutions to this through US constitutional law which itself has moved through several phases will not be successful, as different states have different economic priorities and objectives.

During the heyday of neo-liberalism, property protection played an important role in foreign investment policy. The World Bank advanced a notion of the rule of law in which

---

[175] See, for example, R. B. Lillich, 'Duties of States Regarding Civil Rights of Aliens' (1978) 161 *Hague Recueil* 329 at 399–408.

[176] See K. Hailbronner, 'Foreign Investment Protection in Developing Countries in Public International Law', in T. Oppermann and E. Petersmann (eds.), *Reforming the International Economic Order* (1987), p. 99 at p. 105: 'It is doubtful whether humanitarian considerations are relevant in the context of corporate property and foreign investment in general.'

property protection played a central role. The view advanced was that such protection was central to the achievement of economic development. Translated into the legal sphere, the rules of foreign investment protection had to be made rigorous if foreign investment flows were to take place and economic development furthered. This theory has now seen a reversal, but it is a theory that animated many of the rules and opinions that affected the formulation of arbitral awards and the making of investment treaties.

3.6 Damage to property in the course of civil disturbances

Another area that was being addressed in the case law of the period as well as in the literature was the liability of the host state for damage caused during civil strife or like emergencies that took place in the host state. The volatile nature of the political changes that took place in Latin America through insurrections again provided a backdrop for the litigation that took place in relation to such situations. In many cases, damages were claimed for destruction of property by government forces during the quelling of the insurrection. The law was developed largely in the context again of Latin America, though there were cases from outside the region as well.

The starting-point of the discussion was that the foreigner must not expect better protection in times of civil or military strife than the citizens of the host state. The assumption was that the foreigner had entered an unstable country voluntarily and must put up with the perilous conditions there. The position that was taken was that the foreigner 'must be held, in going into a foreign country, to have voluntarily assumed the risks as well as the advantages of his residence there'.[177]

Yet, a competing principle, or perhaps a large exception to the rule, was also emerging, which recognised that, in certain circumstances, there was an affirmative duty to offer protection to the foreign investor in conditions of strife in the country. Two distinct situations were contemplated. The first was where there was destruction during military action by government forces. In these circumstances, there was liability if the action went beyond what was objectively necessary and caused wanton and unnecessary destruction.[178] One has to balance the necessities of the situation under which a military decision has to be made on the spur of the moment and the extent of the destruction caused.

The second situation related to damage caused not by the military forces of the state but by unruly mobs associated with the strife. In some circumstances, these mobs could be associated with the government and hence could be assimilated with the military forces. They could be regarded as extensions of the resources that the government could summon up in order to achieve its purpose. In this case, the situation would share the characteristics of the first category. Agency, a key factor in the imposition of state responsibility, is easier to identify where the link between the mob of rioters and the government can be established.[179]

---

[177] *Upton Case* (1903), cited in J. H. Ralston, *Law and Procedure of International Tribunals* (1926), p. 389.
[178] *AAPL* v. *Sri Lanka* (1992) 17 *YCA* 106; (1991) 30 *ILM* 577.
[179] The case law on the point generated by the Iran–US Claims Tribunal on this is extensive.

But, where the mob is not so associated with the government of the state, a second rule would apply. This principle was stated in terms of a failure to provide protection when the state knew that there was an imminent danger of such destruction of property by the insurrectionists or by a riotous mob.[180] In these circumstances, there was a duty on the part of the state to provide protection to the foreigner and his property. The standard of diligence is required in these circumstances. The standard would vary as to the intensity of the strife, the resources that could be diverted for the purpose of protection and similar factors. It is obvious that the standards that could be maintained in an ordered society cannot be maintained in a state that is constantly faced with civil disorder. The rule has to be applied with a great deal of sensitivity.

The rules of state responsibility for injuries to aliens which grew up in the context of the causing of injury to the person and property of the alien in a capricious fashion by the host state or the failure to provide adequate protection to alien property developed in the context of Latin American relations. Their universal validity is questionable. Even if they are to be accepted as universally valid, it will be difficult to establish that they extend to the protection of foreign investment. The old rules were made in the context of the taking of the real property and physical assets of the foreigner. The modern takings are largely by way of breach of contractual agreements and by the withdrawal of permission to do business. The old law has little to do with takings of property in pursuance of economic programmes. In any event, the law on state responsibility for injuries to aliens that was developed in the Latin American context has been constantly rejected by the Latin American states and subsequently by the African and Asian states so that it is futile to base any arguments on investment protection on principles of state responsibility.

It is for that reason that efforts to resuscitate the notion of denial of justice in recent case law are unfortunate.[181] A denial of justice takes place when the judicial organs of a state act in an unacceptable manner in the eyes of the world by denying justice to an alien. There is a need for a vigorous rule in this area, but it should not be a rule made to justify property protection in the most extreme of cases.[182] But, to use the rule merely because there has been an administrative interference with property rights is uncalled for. The need for the revival has been largely due to the fact that in most states foreign investment has ceased to be a purely contractual matter and has entered the sphere of public law regulation. Given this transference and given the inadequacy of arguments previously built on notions on contract law to cope with the situation, it has become necessary to address the issue through other means. This accounts for the revival of the notion of denial of justice to be applied in circumstances in which the administrative decisions taken by the host state do not conform to external standards of desirable administration. Quite apart from the difficulties of definition of the concept and the unsettled nature of the scope of the principle of denial of

---

[180] *Sambiaggio Case*, 10 *UNRIAA* 499 at 534; *Home Missionary Society Case* (1920) 6 *UNRIAA* 42; C. F. Amerasinghe, *State Responsibility for Injuries to Aliens* (1967), pp. 281–2; I. Brownlie, *The System of the Law of Nations: State Responsibility* (1986), p. 162.

[181] Arguments were advanced in both the *ELSI Case* [1989] *ICJ Reports* 16 and *Amco* v. *Indonesia* on the basis of a denial of justice. See also *Robert Azinian* v. *Mexico* (1998) 5 *ICSID Reports* 269.

[182] This view finds support in the award in *Robert Azinian* v. *Mexico* (1998) 5 *ICSID Reports* 269.

justice, the application of the principle to administrative decision-making is fraught with great difficulties. Standards of desirable administrative practices cannot be imposed by international law on states as much as political philosophies cannot be imposed upon them. It is best to relinquish attempts to build a law on investment protection through notions associated with state responsibility for injuries to aliens and recognise that foreign investment protection is an area distinct from state responsibility for injuries to aliens though it shares some of its features. The better way of constructing the law is through treaties. But, as will be seen, concepts used in treaties refer back to customary international law so that the problem of bridging the gap between the rules of state responsibility and investment protection still remains. A law constructed through alleged custom will be met with the rule that it cannot be binding on persistent objectors. A law bolstered by general principles, by the writings of publicists and by arbitral awards depends on weak sources and is open to the charge of subjectivity in the selection of sources. The creation of norms of investment protection is best attempted through consensual processes.

There is a consciousness among states that the project to build an international law on foreign investment through customary law has been a failure. This accounts for the proliferation of bilateral investment treaties and regional investment treaties. But, these treaties, as will be seen, state the rules between parties, while still leaving room for adequate manoeuvrability for control over investments. They cannot create customary international law. The projects to bring about multilateral agreements on investment have been significant failures indicating the variety of viewpoints that are taken on this issue even among developed states. The law in the area cannot be seen as settled. It contains norms of varying strength. The strength of the norms will also fluctuate with the preferences that are brought about in the ideological, political and economic settings in which they have to operate.

Chapters 5 and 6 below deal with investment treaties. Bilateral investment treaties have grown in numbers, but, contrary to the views of some, despite their numbers, they do not contribute to the creation of customary international law. Rather, they are carefully negotiated compromises between investment protection and sovereign control over foreign investment. Despite the perceived objective of developed states in strengthening the international minimum standard of treatment in these treaties, the treaties do not entirely succeed in achieving that aim at a universal level. They do succeed in ensuring protection as between the parties to the treaties. The attempts at multilateral treaty-making also indicate the entrenched nature of the stances that different states and groupings of states have taken towards this area of the law.

3.7 Validity of conditions on foreign investment

The requirements that are imposed by regulations on foreign investment may now be re-examined in light of the claims as to rules devised to protect alien interests in customary international law. It will be sufficient to deal with three main types of regulation: (1) those on the screening of foreign investment prior to entry; (2) those requiring local equity participation; and (3) those imposing export quotas. It must be remembered that all these rights may be circumscribed if bilateral, regional or multilateral instruments exist or come about which affect their exercise.

3.7.1 Regulations on screening of foreign investments

The only objection to screening is that it discriminates between foreign investors and nationals. Where there is a pre-entry right of establishment provided by a treaty, screening legislation will not be consistent with the treaty obligations as to national treatment.[183] It is clear that discrimination among aliens before and after entry is permissible, provided it is based on rational economic grounds. The screening of foreign investments and the exclusion of investments that are not beneficial to the host economy rest on such economic grounds and cannot therefore be said to be wrongful.[184]

Questions may be raised as to whether foreign investment laws could be designed to keep out nationals of particular states or discriminate between nationals of different states as to entry. The Nigerian decree on foreign investments exempts the application of procedures for screening for nationals of the states of the Organization of African Unity.[185] Nationals of particular states may also be excluded on the basis that there is already a tendency of the economy of the host state to be dominated by the nationals of these states. Unless the discrimination is based on nakedly racial grounds, the discrimination in such instances may, *prima facie*, be lawful as being based on sound economic and political grounds. It is generally accepted that discrimination between categories of persons, where the categorisation is not based on race, is permissible. States also distinguish between their own nationals when it comes to requirements of formation of joint ventures, and mandate that joint ventures be formed in accordance with certain preferential guidelines as to quotas.[186] This, again, is permissible.

A more difficult question relates to the situation where a state discriminates against foreign investors on racial grounds on the basis that foreign investors or nationals belonging to that particular race already dominate the economy of the state and that the influx of more foreign investors of that race would cause resentment within the state and give rise to protests against the investors. For example, Asians were expelled from Uganda and one argument that was made in justification was that they dominated the economy of the state. In Fiji, there is the similar claim that Indians are dominating the economy, though in Fiji the Indians are nationals of Fiji, whereas, in the Ugandan situation, many of the Asians were aliens who were British nationals. In these circumstances, is it possible for a state to enact legislation preventing entry by foreign investors of the particular race or to use screening devices to ensure that they do not enter? The state may be able to justify the exclusion on national security grounds. The presence of the group will lead to protests and instability within the state. There could be economic instability caused if the group of foreign investors were to use their dominance of the economy as a political weapon. The home state of the

---

[183] Such pre-entry rights of establishment are provided for in US and Canadian bilateral treaties as well as in NAFTA.

[184] In the *FIRA Case*, the GATT compatibility of the Canadian screening legislation was considered and upheld.

[185] Such exemptions given within the context of regional associations are a common feature.

[186] The laws of South Africa and Malaysia contain examples.

investors may also use the presence of the investors to exert influence and control over the host state by interfering in its domestic policies. Though these may be justifications, it may be argued that the importance that has come to be attached to the norm against racial discrimination in international relations is such that it must be held to displace such considerations. Yet, there cannot be a blanket rule of such a nature. Much will depend on the exact circumstances of each state's situation. A state should be able to secure its economic independence by ensuring that its foreign investors come from a range of nations. If not, there is a danger that the state could become subject to the economic imperialism of one state or of one racial group. Obnoxious though the idea of exclusion on racial grounds would seem, there may be instances where it would be valid. These instances must be carefully limited to those where the state excludes foreign investors on the ground that, if not for such exclusion, there would be dominance of its economy by the citizens of one state or by one racial group. Such a situation, besides causing disquiet internally, could also lead to dependence on an external power, and the latter could utilise this dependence to its advantage.[187] The issue is complicated by the fact that there are two norms of equal cogency at conflict in this situation. One is the norm against racial discrimination and the other is the norm of economic self-determination and independence. How each situation involving such a conflict is to be resolved will depend on the facts of that situation. The argument based on economic self-determination should not, however, be permitted to cloak an obviously racist decision. The strong abhorrence of racial discrimination in modern international relations must be noted.[188] Precedence must always be given to the principle against racial discrimination.

3.7.2 Local equity requirements

These requirements relate both to foreign-owned companies that existed at the time the requirements were introduced as well as to foreign investments that were to enter after the requirements were introduced. In many African countries, legislation relating to existing companies was passed first. Such legislation, referred to as indigenisation measures, was intended to ensure that control of existing companies passed into local hands in stages, without causing too much of a disruption to the economy. The indigenisation measures were obviously lawful, as a state has a right to reorder the structure of its economic life as it pleases. But, there were issues of adequate compensation that could have been raised in connection with such measures. They required the forced divestment of the shares on the local market. Local buyers may not have had adequate capital resources to pay the real value of the shares. In such a case, the foreign company could not have raised the true market value of the shares on the stock exchange. It had no control over the timing of the sale of the shares. Yet, the issues were not raised as the companies were content to stay on and operate as minority partners in the states. Such accommodation on the part of the foreign companies to the altered situation is a feature of the modern foreign investment scene, for withdrawal may

---

[187] For example, as in Iran, before the ousting of the Shah of Iran, where there existed a largely pro-US government, dependent on US business.
[188] S. Fredman (ed.), *Discrimination and Human Rights* (2001).

mean a loss of access to markets, raw materials and cheap labour and the surrender of existing market advantages to another multinational competitor. This pragmatism is an important factor, which reduces the acrimony in the debate on compensation. A continuing relationship is often more important than monetary compensation in the long-term interests of both the state and the foreign multinational.

Prospective requirements relating to local equity do raise problems of a different kind for international law. Where a corporation enters a state with a commitment progressively to reduce its control by divesting shares to locals, that corporation cannot complain if the host state requires it to abide by its commitments. There can also be few problems relating to the requirement that entry be made with local collaboration. In such instances, there is a voluntary assumption of conditions by the foreign corporation. A state, in pursuance of its sovereignty, is entitled to impose such conditions.

The imposition of conditions relating to the local equity content of the foreign corporation is effected through the public law mechanisms of the host state. Difficult problems will arise when the public authority seeks the termination of the investment on the ground that its conditions have not been adequately met. In these circumstances, the foreign investor would seem to have little safeguard for his interest. Here, the taking of or interference with the property would seem to be done in pursuance of regulatory measures of which the foreign investor had sufficient prior knowledge.

A confrontation of this kind occurred in the *ELSI Case*, decided by the International Court of Justice,[189] and in *Amco* v. *Indonesia*, decided by tribunals constituted under the ICSID Convention.[190] In the former case, the state was held to have acted properly, and in the latter case the foreign investor was awarded damages. Yet, the two disputes indicate that the foreign investor's position is one of weakness when a charge of not conforming to requirements made by administrative authorities is brought against him. In these circumstances, the foreign investor seems to have little remedy, if the host state had followed its internal procedures for dealing with the dispute scrupulously and these procedures met generally accepted standards.

In the *ELSI Case*, a US firm had located in Sardinia, an economically depressed part of Italy. Under Italian law, a foreign company which located in areas which lacked industrialisation was entitled to certain privileges, such as advantages relating to government procurement contracts. But, these privileges were not granted to the US company. The company suffered reversals, and the foreign investor wanted to liquidate the company in an orderly fashion. Under the law of the host state, a company which did not possess sufficient capital assets had to be declared insolvent. When the company announced its plans for an orderly liquidation, the mayor of the city in which it was located temporarily took over administration of the company. His fear was that there would be a loss of employment if the plant was shut down, as contemplated by the company. The Italian courts subsequently held that this requisition by the mayor was unlawful. When the company was finally declared insolvent and sold, it fetched a price well below the minimum bid that had been set. One

---

[189] [1989] *ICJ Reports* 15.   [190] (1983) 23 *ILM* 354; (1988) 27 *ILM* 1281; 1 *ICSID Reports* 509.

question, among other issues, was whether Italy was responsible for the damage caused to the company on the basis that, but for the requisition by the mayor, the investor would have recovered a larger portion of its investment through an orderly liquidation. The mayor was a public official who requisitioned the company to ensure that jobs in his city would not be lost and that there would not be industrial strife at the plant. Here, there was an obvious conflict of interest between the mayor whose interest was in the preservation of jobs in his city and the foreign investor whose interest was to recover as much of his initial investment as possible. The International Court of Justice wriggled out of this difficult issue by making a factual holding that the company was rushing headlong into insolvency at the time of the requisition and that, therefore, the requisition changed nothing.

It would appear that, if the public authority interfering with an investment acted in a procedurally fair manner and in accordance with the host state's law in applying rules the existence of which were known to the foreign investor, there could be no liability arising in the state. It is, however, unclear whether procedural fairness is a matter of internal law or of external standards.[191] The court was reluctant to find that the mayor had acted in an arbitrary manner, despite the fact that the Italian courts had found illegality in the mayor's conduct. The finding of a denial of justice on the basis of a denial of due process may have been a possibility, but both denial of justice and due process are imprecise notions which the Court has seldom applied. Instead, the Court confined itself to the issue of whether there was arbitrary conduct under the relevant treaty between Italy and the United States and found that there was none.

Though the Court was reluctant to use denial of justice as a basis in *ELSI*, in *Amco* v. *Indonesia* an ICSID tribunal awarded damages to the foreign investor on the basis of this doctrine. Here, an issue in dispute was whether the fact that the foreign investor had not capitalised the project in accordance with his commitments justified the termination of the licences required by the foreign investor to operate the project. Such capitalisation commitments are to be made by the foreign investor prior to entry and the reason for the requirement was to ensure that the foreign investor did bring capital into the state from abroad and did not capitalise the project by raising funds on the local market. There will not be much benefit to the host state by the entry of the investor through capital inflows if he were permitted to raise funds on the local market. The best proof of the fact that there was money brought in from outside under the law was certificates issued by the Bank of Indonesia. It was clear that the foreign investor did not obtain such certificates. On the basis of these facts, the government rescinded the licences that had been granted to the foreign investor to operate in Indonesia. The hotel complex that was being constructed by the investor had earlier been occupied by the Indonesian army, which had some interest in the project because the joint-venture partner with whom the foreign investor had fallen out was controlled by an army pension fund.

On these facts, the tribunal performed a neat balancing act by holding that damages should be awarded on the basis of denial of justice. The tribunal held that the foreign

---

[191] K. J. Hamrock, 'The ELSI Case: Toward an International Definition of Arbitrary Conduct' (1992) 27 *Texas International Law Journal* 837.

investor had not been accorded a proper standard of due process. The decision seems unsatisfactory. It would be obvious to any impartial observer that a hearing would have achieved nothing as the foreign investor did not have the certificates from the Bank of Indonesia as to the capitalisation requirements mandated by the law. There was clear evidence that the foreign investor had not capitalised as required. This gave a right to the government to terminate the licences it had given to the foreign investor. On the reasoning of the *ELSI Case*, what was being terminated was an investment in which the investor had rushed headlong into a situation which made the investment ripe for termination. It was only the procedure that was adopted that was irregular. The tribunal focused upon the lack of procedure to find that there was a denial of justice. It is not a step that should have been so lightly taken, for, in modern international law, a finding of a denial of justice is a serious condemnation. The facts in the case did not justify such a condemnation by the tribunal. It is also doubtful whether an arbitral tribunal called upon to decide an investment dispute has sufficient jurisdiction to decide on an issue of state responsibility for denial of justice. This is an issue between the home state of the alien and the host state. Despite the unsatisfactory features of the decision in *Amco* v. *Indonesia*, it may be inferred from the case that a failure to meet the conditions imposed is a valid ground for interference by the state provided due process standards are met.

Both the disputes and the decisions in them seem to indicate that, as long as standards of procedural fairness had been followed, the termination of an investment in accordance with previously declared law will not give rise to any violation of international law. The finding of denial of justice in the *Amco* v. *Indonesia* case seems to have been an easy way of resolving a tedious dispute that had been around the arbitration scene for a long time, but it is unlikely to provide any satisfaction to the state party, which was convinced that it had acted properly. Where measures terminating the investment are taken, the relevant compensation has to be paid. The issue of compensation is dealt with in Chapter 9 below.

3.7.3 Export requirements

The purpose of export requirements has already been explained. They are imposed to ensure that the foreign corporation earns revenue for the host state through exports. Entry is made conditional on the satisfaction of export requirements. Since export requirements are usually administered by the same public authority responsible for granting permission for the initial entry of the investment, the same problems as to the imposition of sanctions arise as in the non-satisfaction of other requirements for entry. As explained above, as long as minimum standards of procedure have been followed, there could be no violation of international law where the sanctions imposed by the local law, including termination, are taken against the foreign investor, subject to the relevant compensation being paid. But, performance requirements, including export requirements, are regarded as trade distortive under the Trade-Related Investment Measures (TRIMS) of the WTO, and hence their validity under this instrument has to be assessed. Their place in a possible multilateral instrument on investment will also have to be given consideration.

The United States has argued that export controls violate standards of free trade. More specifically, the United States alleges that they violate provisions of the General Agreement on Tariffs and Trade (GATT). Their prohibition through trade instruments is justified on the basis of the same argument. The argument is developed on the following lines.

Export requirements to the extent that they lead to exports by subsidiaries that would not have occurred in their absence, have effects similar to export subsidies which artificially increase the supply of the affected product in the world markets and displace more efficient home or third country products and exports of the affected product.[192]

The validity of export requirements under GATT were raised in relation to Canadian investment measures under the Canadian Foreign Investment Review Act 1982, which, among other things, required specific export targets to be indicated when making an application for foreign investment entry into Canada. A GATT panel upheld the validity of the requirements under the GATT.[193] But, the United States has continued to press for reform of this area. As a result, a provision in TRIMS seeks to prohibit export controls.

4. Conclusion

It is evident from this chapter that the state has considerable control over foreign investment which arises from its sovereignty. Foreign investment takes place within the state, and it is the prerogative of the state to control it as it pleases. But, that is not a fact that sits easily with the notion of foreign investment, as home states (as well as foreign investors themselves) are bases of considerable power and have an interest in ensuring the protection of foreign investment. Constraints on the power of the state to deal with foreign investments have been progressively built up through customary international law and through treaties. In the course of building such norms of international law, there has been considerable opposition raised by states. These states have, by no means, all been capital-importing states of the developing world. Though, in the formative stage of customary international law, the world may have been divided into capital-importing developing states and capital-exporting developed states, the division is no longer as clear-cut as it was in the past. The United States is the largest importer as well as exporter of capital. It is also the home of the largest and most powerful multinational corporations which export capital around the world. The interests that a state must now take into account are diverse. A state has to protect its national economy and does so on the basis of intense sovereignty-centred notions. It has to further the interests of its multinational corporations and does so by seeking to create internationally valid norms of foreign investment protection. That situation applies to many states, including the larger states of the developing world like China and India, though internal factors

---

[192] C. N. Ellis, 'Trade-Related Investment Measures in the Uruguay Round: The United States Viewpoint', in S. J. Rubin and M. L. Jones (eds.), *Conflict and Resolution in the US–EC Trade Relations* (1989). See also C. N. Ellis, 'Foreign Direct Investments and International Capital Flows to Third World Nations: United States Policy Considerations', in C. D. Wallace (ed.), *Foreign Direct Investments in the 1990s* (1990), p. 1.
[193] K. R. Simmonds and B. H. Hill, *Law and Practice under GATT* (1989), vol. 3.

may for the present dictate that they resist international norms. The picture will never remain constant. It is for that reason that it is incorrect to speak in terms of a well-established law on foreign investment that is universally accepted, though the tendency in the law has been to speak in terms of such certainty.

In the diverse world of today, correspondingly diverse ideas and interests interact to shape the law. These ideas and interests constantly change. In the 1970s and 1980s, the developing world had sufficient cohesion, born out of its recent release from colonial bondage, to press for new rules on foreign investment. This resulted in the resolutions associated with the New International Economic Order. But, the 1990s witnessed the dismantling of the Soviet Union, the leader of a bloc which had for many years maintained an attitude of hostility to private property. Its existence ensured the maintenance of developing-country views, though the latter views were often not as extreme as those of the communist world. With the collapse of the Soviet Union, new forces were released. Ideologically, economic liberalism was triumphant. The free market was trumpeted as a panacea of development, and measures for the liberalisation of the movement of capital were set in motion. In this period, the developing world lost its old cohesion. The developing states, short of funds for development, began to scramble for foreign investment, as such investments were the only funds available for development. The World Bank and the International Monetary Fund ensured that funds were made available conditional on the acceptance of liberal premises. The law was set on a new course. There was a proliferation of bilateral and regional treaties. There were moves in the OECD to bring about a Multilateral Agreement on Investment (MAI). After the latter's failure, there is an ongoing effort to transfer the project to the WTO.

But, the picture was to change rapidly. A disenchantment with liberalisation and globalisation rapidly set in. The clashes at Seattle and elsewhere demonstrated that civil society was becoming disenchanted with the idea of profits for large corporations at the cost of global poverty and environmental degradation. The increasing political pressure that these groups applied is beginning to have the effect of diverting the attention of the international law on foreign investment away from the traditional area of investment protection into new areas such as corporate responsibility for environmental degradation and human rights violations. These new issues will have an impact on how the law functions in the future as they are also addressed through norms of international law.

The chapters that follow identify the constraints that have been imposed, successfully or otherwise, on the sovereignty of states to deal with foreign investments, which was the subject of this chapter. Chapter 4 deals with the constraints attempted through customary international law. Chapters 5 and 6 deal with constraints created through bilateral and multilateral treaties on investment.

4

The liability of multinational corporations and home state measures

Unlike under the old law, there is now an increasing expectation, particularly among developing countries and non-governmental organisations (NGOs), that home states of multinational corporations should exert control over the activities of their corporate nationals operating overseas. These measures include not only the measures taken to promote the flow of foreign investment into developing countries, but also measures that seek to ensure that multinational corporations do not act to the detriment of host developing states. This chapter concentrates on the latter type of measure.[1] The rationale is that developed states owe a duty of control to the international community and do in fact have the means of legal control over the conduct abroad of their multinational corporations. In moral terms, the activities of multinational corporations eventually benefit the home state's economic prosperity. The argument is that it is therefore incumbent on the home state to ensure that these benefits are not secured through injury to other states or to the welfare of the international community as a whole. The early law concentrated only on the protection of foreign investment through the diplomatic intervention of the home state. However, there is now an evolution of the notion that the home state has duties as well as rights in matters relating to foreign investment which require the home state to intervene to ensure that its multinational corporations act in accordance with emerging standards that require their accountability.

This shift in emphasis is due to a variety of factors. First, the international community's emphasis has been on ensuring that the poorer countries of the world undergo a process of economic development. The instruments fashioned by the developed countries on investment protection are premised on the notion that investment flows will promote economic development. The objective of economic development underlies all investment treaties and measures. This is confirmed by the fact that the most recent of the documents on the issue of investment in which the international community expressed a policy objective, the Doha Declaration of the Third WTO Ministerial Meeting, stated that consideration of an investment instrument had to take the development dimension into account. The touchstone by which norms are to be judged concerns whether economic development is in effect promoted by the observance of a particular norm. In that context, it is interesting to note

---

[1] Home country measures relating to the promotion of investment flows include the provision of risk insurance, the grant of tax exemptions, the provision of information, etc. They are non-binding by nature, and are unilaterally assumed obligations.

that some developing countries have expressed the view that, if there is to be a WTO instrument on investment, it should contain provisions relating to home state measures to control activities considered harmful to the development of host developing states.[2]

Second, there is a new actor in the area – the non-governmental organisation – which seeks to have the emphasis shifted from the notion of the protection of multinational corporations to the idea that these corporations owe a duty of good corporate responsibility. The power of the NGOs was demonstrated when they were able to focus international attention on the Multilateral Agreement on Investment. They are presently actively engaged in the debate on whether there should be a WTO instrument on investment. The activities of NGOs have also brought about spectacular litigation strategies that are directed at the recognition of the parent corporation's responsibility for the activities of its subsidiaries in host states.

Third, the issue also arises in the context of bringing about a multilateral code on foreign investment. The discussion has shifted to whether a complete code would require not only a statement of the rights of protection of foreign investment that a home state can insist upon for its outgoing foreign investments but the duties and obligations that should accompany such outflows. Thus, the movement in this area has resulted in incremental progress towards the recognition of jurisdiction in the courts of the home states over acts of subsidiaries abroad. It is unlikely that the subject can ever be discussed without taking into account the responsibility of the multinational corporations or the responsibility of their host states to ensure that they are held accountable for the violations of norms relating to their conduct in several areas such as human rights or the environment.

As a result of these developments, a series of duties are coming to be recognised by multinational corporations as well as by their home states. These obligations are dealt with in the first section of this chapter. The chapter then goes on to survey the extent to which the home states of multinational corporations have the power to enforce these obligations and the extent to which there is an obligation to enforce them.

1. Obligations of multinational corporations

While international law has recognised that the assets of multinational corporations could be protected through investment treaties and through customary international law, there has been little movement towards the recognition of the obligations of multinational corporations towards host states and the communities in which these corporations operate. The fiction that these corporations do not have personality in international law has often been

---

[2] The paper submitted by China, India, Kenya, Pakistan and Zimbabwe to the WTO Working Group on Investment stated: 'Multinational Enterprises should strictly abide by all domestic laws and regulations in each and every aspect of the economic and social life of the host members in their investment and operational activities. Further, in order to ensure that the foreign investor meets its obligations to the host member, the cooperation of the home member's government is often necessary, as the latter can and should impose the necessary disciplines on the investors. The home member's government should therefore also undertake obligations, including to ensure that the investor's behaviour and practices are in line with and contribute to the interests and development policies of the host member. It is important that the Working Group addresses the issue of the investors' and home governments' obligations in a balanced manner.' WT/WGTI/W/152 (2003). The document can be accessed on the website of the WTO.

used as a reason for the non-development of these rules, though that has not prevented the development of a right of recourse to dispute settlement under treaty. The better reason for the absence of obligations may be that the subject-matters for which obligations may be necessary are matters of relatively recent development in international law. For example, norms in the area of environmental harm (an area of particular concern in this context) are of relatively recent origin in international law. Likewise, the notions of corporate liability for human rights violations have also been slow in evolving. The international rules on bribery have also been slow to evolve. There may be justification in the view that this slow progress was caused in part by opposition to the recognition of such liability by corporations, which have delayed the formation of binding rules through the formulation of soft law prescriptions.[3]

The identification of the areas of activity in which obligations of multinational corporations could arise has been largely effected through international instruments. Because of the divergence of views as to whether these obligations should be enforced against multinational corporations, many of these instruments were aborted, and the few that did come into being contained soft law prescriptions.[4] The same institutions which argued for multilateral codes on investment protection creating rights in multinational corporations were content with calls for voluntary codes of conduct for multinational corporations.[5] Developing countries, on the other hand, have consistently called for the recognition of obligations on multinational corporations. Their views were firmly established during a period in which there was a certain hostility to multinational corporations, and intense study of their conduct in developing states was undertaken by international institutions and other bodies. These concerns were articulated largely in the 1970s and the early 1980s, and may be associated with the general trend among developing countries to seek to change international law in this area through the New International Economic Order. The United Nations Commission on Transnational Corporations (UNCTC)[6] was instrumental in a large number of studies on the issue, and attempted to establish a binding Code of Conduct on Transnational Corporations. Because of divisions among the member states, the code remained in draft form only.[7]

Despite its lack of eventual success, the draft code identified the areas in which the activities of multinational corporations could produce harmful effects on host states. The main emphasis was on development concerns. The use of restrictive business practices and other like practices

---

[3] Misconduct is an area full of voluntary codes of conduct.

[4] Several codes were attempted. Many were aborted. Some remained as non-binding codes. The binding codes were advanced in the context of the UNCTC and the non-binding codes, which probably took the steam out of efforts at binding codes, were advanced by the developed states. There were voluntary codes that were internal to multinational corporations, again taking the pressure off by indicating that corporations were conscious of the problem of their misconduct. M. Baker, 'Promises and Platitudes: Towards a New 21st Century Paradigm for Corporate Codes of Conduct' (2007) 23 *Connecticut Journal of International Law* 123.

[5] The OECD, which wanted a binding multilateral agreement on investment, had drafted a voluntary code of conduct for multinational corporations. There is a certain inconsistency in such trends. Whereas there was a willingness to impose duties on host states through binding codes, there was a reluctance to impose duties on multinational corporations.

[6] The Commission has since been absorbed into UNCTAD. Its downsizing was itself a reflection of attitudes to the question of binding codes. The effort within the UN to draft binding codes was given up in 1992 with the rise of neo-liberalism. The developing countries' interest declined when they started on a course of liberalisation aimed at attracting foreign investment.

[7] In fact, the different groupings of states had their own drafts. The draft is more fully considered in Chapter 6 below.

attracted considerable attention. Involvement in local political disputes and other activities aimed at benefiting groups favourable to foreign business was another issue that was addressed. The avoidance of bribery and other corrupt practices was advocated. There were references to consumer protection and environmental protection. With the decline of hostility to foreign investment in the mid-1980s onwards, the efforts to draft such a code were abandoned and the instruments that were later adopted in profusion emphasised investment protection rather than control of the activities of multinational corporations. The sweep of economic liberalism in the 1990s accelerated this tendency. The fervour for controlling multinational corporations became dormant and the need to attract them became urgent. There were soft prescriptions made in this period, such as the recognition of the norm of non-interference in domestic politics,[8] but no hard rules emerged, except in the field of bribery.[9]

During this period, there were a number of dramatic incidents that illustrated the possibility of the adverse impact of foreign investment on host states.[10] Of these incidents, the worst was the disaster at Bhopal, India, when a gas leak at a plant belonging to Union Carbide, a US multinational corporation, led to a major calamity. The many thousands affected still remain uncompensated. There were other incidents involving environmental degradation and human rights violations which came to light and again focused attention on the issue of the obligations of multinational corporations.[11]

The vigorous pursuit of concerns over the harmful activities of multinational corporations in the developing world would not have occurred were it not for the rise of NGOs concerned with human rights, the environment and development as active players on the international scene.[12] Such developments highlight the fact that NGOs, as well as their targets, the multinational corporations, have the capacity to affect the course of events in this area of international law.[13] Most of the obligations that have been created require action by the

---

[8] APEC's Non-Binding Investment Principles (1994) require foreign investors 'to abide by the host economy's laws, regulations, administrative guidelines and policies'.

[9] The award in *World Duty Free Ltd* v. *Kenya*, ICSID Award, 4 October 2006, contains a survey of the different instruments on bribery.

[10] The coup against Allende and his killing were allegedly engineered by the United States with the involvement of multinational corporations operating in Chile. This led to widespread concerns about the involvement of multinational corporations in the politics of host states.

[11] Starting with Bhopal, there has been an increasing number of major incidents recorded in the literature. For other situations, see Human Rights Watch, *The Price of Oil: Corporate Responsibility and Human Rights Violations in Nigeria's Oil Producing Communities* (1999). The litigation against Unocal relating to its operation in Myanmar (Burma) has been dealt with in other chapters. There is concern with the operations of Freeport-McMoran in Irian Jaya. See also G. S. Akpan, 'Transnational Environmental Litigation and Multinational Corporations: A Study of the Ok Tedi Case' (paper published by the Centre for Energy, Petroleum and Mineral Law, University of Dundee, Scotland, CP 11/98, 1998); and H. M. Osofsky, 'Environmental Human Rights under the Alien Tort Statute: Redress for Indigenous Victims of Multinational Corporations' (1997) 20 *Suffolk Transnational Law Review* 335. George Akpan's PhD thesis at the National University of Singapore contains surveys of the field: G. S. Akpan, 'Multinational Corporations and the Impact of Natural Resource Exploitation in the Host State: The Inadequacy of Legal Protection for Host Populations and Implications for Foreign Investment' (PhD Thesis, Faculty of Law, National University of Singapore, 2002). The issue is raised in F. van Hoof, 'International Human Rights Obligations for Companies and Domestic Courts: An Unlikely Combination?', in M. Castermans-Holleman, F. van Hoof and J. Smith (eds.), *The Role of the Nation State in the 21st Century: Essays in Honour of Peter Baehr* (1998), p. 47. See also M. Kaminga and S. Zia Zarifi (eds.), *Liability of Multinational Corporations under International Law* (2000); J. A. Zerk, *Multinationals and Corporate Social Responsibility* (2006), pp. 160–71; S. Leader, 'Human Rights, Risks and New Strategies for Global Investment' (2006) 9 *JIEL* 657.

[12] There were other institutions, such as UNCTAD, which had commenced work on the issue. But, at the practical level, the work of NGOs accelerated concern with the liability of multinational corporations.

[13] Their impact on international relations has been studied in various works. See, for example, R. O'Brien (ed.), *Contesting Global Governance: Multilateral Economic Institutions and Global Social Movements* (2000); R. Hall and T. Biersteker (eds.), *The Emergence of Private Authority in Global Governance* (2002).

home states of the multinational corporations or their courts and, for that reason, may be considered under the heading of home state measures and obligations. The creation of responsibility in the multinational corporation is not in itself a home state measure, but, if such responsibility has to be enforced through the home state's courts, then it would be fair to characterise such responsibility as involving a home state measure. It is necessary to identify these obligations.

1.1 The obligation not to interfere in domestic politics

This is an obligation that arose from the fear that multinational corporations act in host states in such a manner as to ensure that governments or groups favourable to foreign business retain power. Often, the charge is made that the multinational corporation is a proxy on behalf of the home state to ensure that there is a pliant government, or that the home state encourages interference to ensure that pro-business governments are elected. The often cited instance is the overthrow of the government of Allende in Chile, which had been democratically elected, by a coup engineered, it is alleged, by foreign business groups with the covert support of a foreign government.

Many instruments now include a prohibition on the involvement of multinational corporations in the politics of the host state. The statements contained in them are usually soft law prescriptions. But, the issue does arise in modern law as to whether there is more direct responsibility in circumstances in which there is involvement of a multinational corporation or home state officers for effecting coups or bringing about changes in a host state's governments. Such changes would favour the multinational corporation's continued activity or favour the home state's policies and goals. The movement towards the direct personal responsibility of the corporation's officers for such activity is yet to be fully explored.[14] Whether there is a direct obligation on the home state to ensure that no regime changes are effected will also remain a matter that will be raised and debated.[15]

Multinational corporations, operating particularly in the mining sector, are often caught up in situations where secessionist claims are asserted through violence. In such situations, civil wars can flare up. The tendency has been for the foreign party to side with the state, as its interests are bound up with opposing secession and supporting the state with which it had signed the contract. As these secessionist wars result in efforts by the state to crush the secessionists, violations of humanitarian law often occur. The resulting situation may involve allegations of complicity in these violations by multinational corporations. Victims may subsequently bring claims against the corporation in its home state in respect of these violations. Many claims in the United States brought under the Alien Tort Claims

---

[14] Since the *Pinochet* case, there has been speculation as to the extent of liability for engineering changes of foreign governments.
[15] The situation arose in the Iraq war in 2003, which was about regime change. One argument was that the regime change was effected not because of the threat posed by the government of Iraq but because of the need to ensure supplies of oil from Iraq, thus giving a commercial motive to the war. The extent to which regime changes are permissible for business and investment reasons is raised by the Iraq situation.

Act have such secessionist wars as a backdrop[16] or are connected with other political unrest that implicated the multinational corporation alongside the government in their suppression.

1.2 Obligations relating to human rights

There is increasing literature on the obligation of multinational corporations to abide by human rights standards in the course of its activities in a host state.[17] There is an evident shift away from the old position that shielded multinational corporations from liability for violations of human rights towards a position that recognises liability through the creation of an obligation towards the human rights of the people of the host state.[18] The obligation includes the duty not to support a regime which abuses human rights in the host state, particularly in circumstances in which such abuse works to the benefit of the foreign investor. The obvious situation relates to labour standards which are maintained to ensure that there is a ready supply of cheap labour to the foreign multinational corporation. The activity in this area by the International Labour Organization has been effective in drafting instruments which address the issue of adequate safeguards to protect workers from abuse by multinational corporations.[19] More meaningful are the techniques in the area of human rights that have brought about sanctions against abusive practices affecting both workers and others who are affected by the activities of multinational corporations.

It is untenable that the multinational corporation which seeks rights against host states can shirk obligations under international law towards host states or its people. The rapid movement of the law has been away from this old position that sought to accomplish the sophistry of shielding the multinational corporation from duties but conferring rights upon it.[20] The increased vigilance that NGOs exercise on the conduct of multinational corporations will make this a thing of the past. The strongest movement in the area has been the imposition of liability on multi-national corporations for their human rights violations abroad in the home state's law. Despite the fact that United Nations reports issued on the subject seek a diplomatic compromise, litigation

---

[16] *Saro-Wiwa* v. *Shell* had the Ogoni tribes' claims to their land as its background. *Talisman* v. *Presbyterian Church* had the secessionist civil war in the Sudan as its background. In *AAPL* v. *Sri Lanka*, the context was a civil war.

[17] On the increasing literature on human rights concerns with the operations of multinational corporations, see M. Lippmann, 'Multinational Corporations and Human Rights', in G. W. Shepaher and V. Nanda (eds.), *Human Rights and Third World Development* (1985); B. A. Frey, 'The Legal and Ethical Responsibilities of Transnational Corporations in the Protection of International Human Rights' (1997) 6 *Minnesota Journal of Global Trade* 105; and see further D. Weissbrodt and M. Hoffman, 'The Global Economy and Human Rights: A Selective Bibliography' (1997) 6 *Minnesota Journal of Global Trade* 189; M. A. Geer, 'Foreigners in Their Own Land: Cultural Land and Transnational Corporations – Emergent International Rights and Wrongs' (1998) 38 *Virginia Journal of International Law* 331. For a denial of a linkage between human rights violations and multinational corporations, see W. H. Meyer, 'Human Rights and MNCs: Theory Versus Quantitative Analysis' (1996) 18 *Human Rights Quarterly* 368. A survey of the subject may be found in M. K. Addo (ed.), *Human Rights Standard and the Responsibility of Transnational Corporations* (1999); and N. Jägers, *Corporate Human Rights Obligations: In Search of Accountability* (2002).

[18] The Secretary-General commissioned a study on the subject by appointing a Special Rapporteur on Human Rights and Transnational Corporations and Other Business Enterprise. Professor John Ruggie was appointed the Special Rapporteur in 2005. He initiated studies on the subject, and has issued several reports.

[19] The issue whether such labour standards should form a part of a multilateral code on investment has also been raised. L. Compa, 'The Multilateral Agreement on Investment and International Labor Rights: A Failed Connection' (1998) 31 *Cornell ILJ* 683. The draft OECD code recognised the existence of core labour rights.

[20] A. Clapham, *Human Rights Obligations of Non-State Actors* (2006); S. Joseph, *Corporations and Transnational Human Rights Litigation* (2004); P. Muchlinski, *Multinational Corporations and the Law* (2nd edn, 2008), pp. 509–16.

strategies and political pressure will direct the law towards establishing firm principles of liability for violations of human rights and environmental standards by multinational corporations.

Techniques for imposing direct liability have been possible in US law because of the existence of the Alien Tort Claims Act, an old statute which makes any act considered a tort in international law actionable in US courts. There has been an explosion of litigation against multinational corporations on the basis of this legislation. Though none has so far been successful, the US courts have not yet denied jurisdiction on the ground that the acts complained of were extraterritorial. The plea of sovereign immunity will protect the host state itself from complicity in human rights violations, but the multinational corporation which is complicit in the conduct of the state could be sued for violations of human rights in the US courts. A series of cases has thus resulted. It is possible to deal only with the principal cases in this chapter, but they are considered fully in the extensive literature that has been generated as a result of the litigation.[21]

The litigation involving *Doe* v. *Unocal*[22] is representative. Here, the allegation in a class action was that Unocal, a US multinational corporation, had participated actively or passively in the torture, forced labour and killings of aboriginal people by Burmese military agents in the areas through which passed a gas pipeline Unocal was constructing for the Burmese government. The Burmese government was able to plead sovereign immunity. The focus therefore shifted to the liability of the multinational corporation for being a knowing participant in the alleged activity. This was the theory behind the litigation in several other cases as well. In all these cases, brought under the Alien Tort Claims Act, the courts have held that there is a basis for jurisdiction, though in none of them have they as yet gone on to hold that there could be liability. The link to the parent company in all these situations is that the parent company exercised managerial control and hence had engaged liability for the acts of the subsidiary in the host state. The existence of the parent company within the jurisdiction of the US courts enabled the exercise of personal jurisdiction by the courts over the parent corporations. The Alien Tort Claims Act helps in establishing such jurisdiction but it is not a prerequisite to the pursuit of the strategy behind such litigation. The corporate structure and corporate control are important to jurisdiction. Moral justification is provided by the fact that the parent corporation benefits from the misdeeds of its subsidiaries in host states and should therefore shoulder responsibility for these misdeeds.[23]

In another line of cases involving the association of multinational corporations with past crimes, there is an evident trend towards liability. Thus, the claims of Jewish plaintiffs against IBM and other corporations is based on the allegation that these corporations had helped the Nazi government through furnishing technology and other forms of assistance during the Holocaust in Germany. Many other corporations such as banks benefited from the Holocaust and are subject to claims on that basis. The litigation strategies that are being

---

[21] S. Ratner, 'Corporations and Human Rights: A Theory of Legal Responsibility' (2001) 111 *Yale LJ* 443; J. Davis, *Justice Across Borders: The Struggle for Human Rights in the US Courts* (2008).

[22] 963 F Supp 660 (CD Cal., 1997); there is an extensive list of cases in which the issue has been considered. *Saro-Wiwa* v. *Shell*, 226 F 3d 88 (2nd Cir., 2000); *Beanal* v. *Freeport-McMoran*, 969 F Supp 362 (ED La, 1997). The Bush administration did not favour such litigation and entered *amicus* briefs against such suits. For consideration of these cases, see M. Sornarajah, *The Settlement of Foreign Investment Disputes* (2000); and N. Jägers, *Corporate Human Rights Obligations: In Search of Accountability* (2002), pp. 183–96.

[23] B. Stephens, 'The Amorality of Profit: Transnational Corporations and Human Rights' (2002) 20 *Berkeley JIL* 45.

formulated in these different strands of cases will coalesce to ensure that there will be jurisdiction and liability in parent corporations in respect of human rights abuses which are committed in other states. The line of cases which establish universal jurisdiction over gross human rights violations such as torture and genocide will enhance the acceptance of such jurisdiction over the parent corporation.[24]

These developments are not confined to the United States. The law in England has recognised jurisdiction in the parent company in respect of asbestos-related disease in a worker occurring in the Rhodesian operations of a subsidiary.[25] There is a similar decision recognising parent company liability in Australia.[26] Dutch case law also seems to be moving towards the recognition of liability.[27] The development of the law does not seem to be based on the existence of any legislation such as the Alien Tort Claims Act but rather on the basis of the need to impose control on the activities of the subsidiary through the parent corporation and on the moral liability of the parent for not exercising sufficient control over the subsidiary.

But, the efforts to impose liability on the parent or the assumption of jurisdiction over the multinational corporation on the basis of presence within that jurisdiction will be stoutly resisted by multinational corporations. Courts have also wavered and have usually withdrawn from the brink of imposing liability by finding a want of jurisdiction. The issue is treated as non-justiciable on the basis that finding jurisdiction over corporations on the basis of mere presence may jeopardise foreign policy interests.[28] Powerful companies, it has been suggested, may seek the assistance of the state to invoke such doctrines relating to justiciability in order to escape scrutiny.[29] But, countering these developments are those that seek to expand the scope of universal jurisdiction over gross human rights violations such as torture, mass rape and genocide. Where there is complicity by multinational corporations in such crimes, credibility will be lost if courts permit the argument that national interests override the need to permit the establishment of liability over the offending entities. The general trend in the field of international criminal law may also come to affect this area in the future.[30]

---

[24] Beginning with *Peña-Irala* v. *Filartiga*, 630 F 2d 876 (2nd Cir., 1980), a string of cases in the United States has acknowledged that universal jurisdiction exists over gross human rights violations. These include, principally, torture and genocide. The *Pinochet* case [1999] 2 WLR 827 adds to the impetus of this line of cases. See, in particular, the judgment of Lord Millett, who argued for universal jurisdiction in situations of torture, even in the absence of any law incorporating conventional norms prohibiting torture in the domestic law. See also A. Bianchi, 'Immunity Versus Human Rights: The Pinochet Case' (1999) 10 *EJIL* 237.

[25] *Cape* v. *Lubbe* [2001] 1 WLR 1545.   [26] *Dagi* v. *BHP* [1997] 1 VR 428.

[27] G. Betlem, 'Transnational Litigation Against Multinational Corporations in Dutch Courts', in M. Kaminga and S. Zia Zarifi (eds.), *Liability of Multinational Corporations under International Law* (2000), p. 283. The author suggests that the issue of jurisdiction would be easier in civil law jurisdictions.

[28] Thus, jurisdiction was refused in *Sarei* v. *Rio Tinto*, 221 F Supp 2d 1116 (CD Cal., 2002). In the Bush era, there was a concerted effort to resist litigation under the Alien Tort Claims Act. Despite this, courts have not drawn back from asserting jurisdiction to hear the cases. Though no case has proceeded to decision, the possibility of damages is a strong deterrent to misconduct.

[29] There is litigation in the United States implicating Exxon-Mobil in the human rights violations in respect of the ongoing Aceh separatist rebellion. The judge sought an opinion from the US State Department which, while acknowledging concern with human rights violations, nevertheless stated that the litigation would affect US interests, including interests in the war on terror. The Indonesian ambassador indicated that Indonesia will not accept extraterritorial jurisdiction in respect of events taking place entirely in Indonesia. A similar technique has been employed against Shell in the *Saro-Wiwa* litigation. *Saro-Wiwa* v. *Royal Dutch Shell*, 226 F 3d 88 (2nd Cir., 2000). For the view that such litigation has been made more difficult by current concerns for national security and terrorism, see M. Saint-Saens and A. Bann, 'Using National Security to Undermine Corporate Accountability Litigation' (2003) 12 *University of Miami International and Comparative Law Review* 39.

[30] See further A. Clapham, 'The Question of Jurisdiction under International Criminal Law over Legal Persons', in M. Kaminga and S. Zia Zarifi (eds.), *Liability of Multinational Corporations under International Law* (2000), p. 139.

There are soft law prescriptions relating to the obligation of multinational corporations to respect human rights. But, these prescriptions are not seen as having much effect and are often smokescreens to show that some progress is being made in the direction of dealing with the issues. The establishing of law with sufficient teeth to deal with these issues is what is relevant. It would appear that the law is well set on moving in this direction.[31]

1.3 Liability for violations of environmental norms

The trends in human rights protection have been paralleled in the area of environmental protection. Again, soft law prescriptions exist but are found to be wanting. As in the case of human rights, this too is an area in which NGOs have been active and have sought to bring about strategies that would ensure that there is liability created in the parent corporations in the home state. The Bhopal litigation that arose out of the gas leak at the Union Carbide factory in Bhopal, India, resulted in failure, but, since then, there have been movements in doctrines that were associated with the case which indicate that there is a developing trend towards the recognition of liability for environmental harm caused by subsidiaries. The basis of the refusal of the courts in the Bhopal litigation to entertain the suit against the parent company was the *forum non conveniens* doctrine which itself has undergone sufficient change so as to accommodate future litigation along the lines that were used in the Bhopal situation.

The focus of the literature has been largely on whether controls instituted by the host state on environmental grounds can be regarded as takings which are compensable.[32] This is an issue that is considered later in this book. At this stage, the question must be raised as to whether, assuming they are takings, the existence of liability for environmental harm will reduce the amount of the compensation payable or even require that compensation in excess of the value of the taking be paid by the multinational corporation where the harm is severe. Certainly, if environmental liability exists, then obviously both eventualities are possible. Initially, these are matters for local tribunals to settle. This factor raises the issue as to whether environmental takings, initially at least, are matters to be considered by arbitral tribunals. Where there is no taking of property involved, the issue of the liability of the multinational corporation for the environmental harm arises.

In situations where a treaty protects the investment, a modern trend that has developed in arbitration practice is to determine whether the treatment meted out to the foreign investor is 'fair and equitable'. In applying that standard, it is always relevant to look at the conduct of the foreign investor. If it is the case that the foreign investor had engaged in environmental

---

[31] Resistance to change continues to exist. Much theoretical resistance comes from continued references to corporate responsibility and the raising of hoary ideas of whether or not corporations are capable of committing crimes, especially in the international sphere. See, for example, *Bowoto* v. *Chevron*, 312 F Supp 2d 1229 (2004), where the judge raised the issue of whether private actors could commit international wrongs. These technical issues continue to befuddle the progress of the law, but eventually one can envisage the law taking a course towards liability.

[32] J. M. Wagner, 'International Investment, Expropriation and Environmental Protection' (1999) 29 *Golden Gate University Law Review* 465; T. Walde and A. Kolko, 'Environmental Regulation, Investment Protection and Regulatory Taking in International Law' (2001) 50 *ICLQ* 811; for a general survey, see G. Verhoosel, 'Foreign Direct Investment and Legal Constraints on Domestic Environmental Policies: Striking a Reasonable Balance Between Stability and Change' (1998) 29 *Law and Policy in International Business* 451; M. Anderson, 'Transnational Corporations and Environmental Damage: Is Tort Law the Answer?' (2002) 41 *Washburn LJ* 399.

pollution, it is always relevant to determining fairness whether the interference of the state was justified by the conduct of the foreign investor. Fairness is a concept that cuts both ways and must be assessed in light of the whole situation.[33]

The strategy of investors has been to negate environmental laws through stabilisation clauses in the contract which seek to freeze such controls as at the time of entry and exclude the application of later improvements to environmental standards to the investment. The stabilisation clause, being a contractual device, cannot fetter the legislative sovereignty of a state to extend its control over the investment and to ensure that later standards are applied to the investment. The liability of the foreign investor for environmental harm cannot be excluded by contractual means. The issue for the present, however, is the extent of the obligation of the home state to ensure that its multinational corporations comply with environmental standards in the host state, particularly if these standards are in accordance with the emerging standards of international environmental law.[34] The contention that is advanced here is that, in circumstances in which the environmental harm is prohibited both by the host state's law and by international environmental law, there arises a duty on the part of the home state to ensure that there is compliance by its corporate national making the foreign investment.[35] A duty exists, prior to the making of the investment, to ensure that the multinational corporation does not take the investment abroad. If it has, a duty arises to ensure that correct use is made of that technology or to warn the host state of the potential for harm in the use of the technology. As argued below, there is an obligation on the part of the home state to ensure conformity by its corporate nationals with international law standards wherever the harmful act takes place. The home state, through the link of nationality, has the ability to exercise such control and hence has an obligation to use its powers to ensure compliance.

There is a duty on the part of all states to ensure compliance with standards that are prescribed either in international treaties or in customary international law relating to environmental protection. Home states of multinational corporations have the power of control over these corporations to ensure that they conduct themselves in accordance with the standards in the international law on the environment.[36] There is therefore a duty on the part of the home state to ensure that this is done. The argument that there is state responsibility for failure to do so will be developed in a later section of this chapter.

As in the case of human rights, there has also been an increase in the litigation before the domestic courts of home states alleging violation of environmental standards. The Bhopal litigation was unsuccessful because of the stringent application of the *forum*

---

[33] P. Muchlinski, 'Caveat Investor? The Relevance of the Conduct of the Investor under the Fair and Equitable Standard' (2006) 55 *ICLQ* 527: 'Fairness connotes among other things equity. It leaves open the possibility of looking not only at the conduct of the person who must act fairly but also the conduct of the person who is acted upon.'

[34] On the development of international environmental law, see P. Birnie and A. Boyle, *International Law and the Environment* (2002).

[35] Outside the areas of climate change and biodiversity, there is little authority to support the existence of *erga omnes* obligations in the environmental field. But, when multilateral treaties increase, the areas of *erga omnes* obligations arising from environmental harm could be quickly filled.

[36] There are loose reporting requirements imposed by home country legislation requiring that the environmental standards employed be indicated, but they are confined to activities in the home state. Efforts are being made to extend their scope to activities in other states. H. Ward, 'Legal Issues in Corporate Citizenship' (report prepared for the Swedish Partnership for Global Responsibility, 2003), p. 4.

non conveniens doctrine. But, with new trends resulting in a more liberal application of the doctrine in various jurisdictions, it has become possible to contemplate the imposition of liability on parent corporations for environmental harm that had been caused in host states. These trends will accelerate, giving rise to the establishment of firm principles of liability of parent corporations for environmental harm caused by their subsidiaries.

1.4 The obligation to promote economic development

There is today a resurgence of the international law on development. During the neo-liberal period of the 1990s, growth in this area of the law had faltered. But, the current retreat of neo-liberalism has led to a resurgence of the idea that development in poorer states should once more assume significance. The Doha Development Round signified the return of the promotion of development when the liberalisation premises on which the WTO was founded began to be rethought on the basis of whether the rules on international trade that had earlier been fashioned accorded with the development of the poorer states. This concern will add greater weight to the emergence of a strong international law on development and a reconsideration of the existing principles of international law in light of the principles of economic and other development. The Millennium Development Goals articulated by the United Nations also require movement towards development, and evidence an international consensus on the need to ensure the eradication of poverty and the enhancement of development.

The present instruments on investment are premised on the assumption that foreign investment promotes the economic development of the states into which the investment flows. All bilateral investment treaties and regional treaties on investment contain a prefatory statement to the effect that such development takes place as a result of investment flows. It may be implied from this that multinational corporations which make investments in host states should promote economic development or, at the least, should not conduct themselves in such a manner as to hinder such development. If there is clear evidence that a multinational corporation has hindered development, the argument may be made that the rules of investment protection are not applicable to that investment and therefore that the investment will not be protected. After all, all investment instruments insist that economic development is the objective of foreign investment. As a result, there is an implied obligation on the part of the home state to ensure that its corporate nationals, entering a treaty partner's territory, do not act in such a manner as to harm the economic development of the host state. These may include the avoidance of restrictive business practices and corrupt practices.[37] The idea is encapsulated in the notion of good corporate citizenship.[38]

This view has received support in a coherent body of arbitral awards which have held that investment treaties protect only such investments as can be shown to advance the economic

---

[37] Corrupt practices such as bribery are covered by non-binding codes. An effort to draft a code on restrictive business practices that harm development was made by UNCTAD, but met with developed country opposition.
[38] On this, see UNCTAD, *World Investment Report, 2003*, pp. 164–6.

development of the host state.[39] The preambles to investment treaties often state as their objective the economic development of the host state by means of foreign investment. Therefore, if the foreign investor conducts itself in such a manner as to thwart the development objectives of the host state, then it should lose the protection of the investment treaty. Another group of arbitral awards has emphasised the fact that most of the treaties contain a definition of the protected foreign investments together with a proviso that the protection is expressly subject to the laws and regulations of the host state. Most of these regulations are in the human rights and environmental spheres. This would mean that any multinational corporation which transgresses the rules relating to human rights and the environment will lose the protection of the investment treaty. The more robust view has also been stated that, even where there is no express reference to the laws and regulations of the host state as circumscribing the protected investment, such a limitation will be read into the treaty definition of foreign investment so that any multinational corporation transgressing the laws and regulations of the host state would automatically lose the protection of the investment treaty.

2. Extraterritorial control by home states

The subject of extraterritorial control is usually studied from the point of view of US law, as such control is practised largely by the United States. It is fitting for another reason, as the United States is the home of the largest number as well as of the most powerful multinational corporations. Though other states, in varying degrees, exercise extraterritorial jurisdiction, no state does so as extensively as the United States does. Most of the practice of the United States has been to extend its control through legislation or judicial decisions over matters taking place outside the United States but having an impact within its jurisdiction.[40] In some areas, the extraterritorial legislation of the United States has been influenced by nakedly political objectives.

The most studied instance outside criminal enforcement is the extent to which the United States has arrogated to itself the extraterritorial power to enforce its antitrust laws. In 1945, in the *Alcoa Case*,[41] Judge Learned Hand changed the pre-existing view that the Sherman Act, the principal antitrust legislation in the United States, applied only within the territorial limits of the United States. He announced that a conspiracy, made entirely outside the United States, not to export aluminium into the United States so that the monopoly prices fixed by Alcoa could be continued after the expiration of the lawful monopoly obtained through patents, was a violation of the Sherman Act. If the effects of the conspiracy were felt within the United States, the US courts had jurisdiction over such a conspiracy. As long as the conspirators intended or foresaw the effects on US markets, the jurisdictional test was

---

[39] See *Patrick Mitchell* v. *Congo*; but see the annulment award in *Malaysian Salvors Ltd* v. *Malaysia*.
[40] In criminal matters, such extraterritorial legislation is widely employed by most states in common with the United States. But, it is the employment of such legislation in the economic sphere that has brought the United States into conflict with other states.
[41] *United States* v. *Aluminium Co. of America (Alcoa)*, 148 F 2d 416 (2nd Cir., 1945).

satisfied.[42] The effects rule as to jurisdiction has been followed ever since, despite the fact that it has brought the United States into conflict with other states, many of which have enacted legislation to counter its effects. Unhindered, the US Supreme Court has affirmed the jurisdictional test in *Alcoa* in *Hartford Fire Insurance* v. *California*.[43] These measures do not affect US companies alone but companies belonging to other states as well. But, they indicate that, like Alcoa, which was a US company that had effected the conspiracy through its Canadian subsidiary, it is possible to control US corporations in their activities abroad through the exercise of extraterritorial jurisdiction. It shows that the United States has asserted such powers and is not in any way lacking in the power to control the activities of the subsidiaries of its multinational corporations.

There are other areas in which extraterritorial enforcement has been attempted through legislative and executive measures. These include legislation on export controls which prevents not only US parent companies but also their subsidiaries operating abroad from supplying goods to states considered enemies. The use of that power in connection with the construction of the Siberian gas pipeline, to show displeasure towards the Soviet Union for its invasion of Afghanistan, was widely disapproved of by European states.[44] Likewise, there were freezes of the bank accounts of Iran and Libya in US banks operating overseas. More recently, the Helms–Burton Act sought to prevent companies of third states from trading with Cuba, and imposed sanctions against such trade on companies which do trade. The Liberty and Democracy Act sought to do the same regarding companies trading with Libya and Iran. The assumption of such wide and contested bases of jurisdiction has become common in US law. With such wide powers, it would not be credible to argue that the United States, if so mindful, can control the activities of its multinational corporations in host developing states in such a way as not to harm development or environmental interests.

The absence of sufficient standards of corporate governance has become evident in recent times in the United States. The number of recent corporate scandals involving misreporting of accounts and tax frauds by corporations indicates the seriousness of the lack of corporate standards.[45] The repetition of such practices in developing countries could cause the development of their economies great harm. A reason exists to require that the home states of multinational corporations exercise their undoubted powers to control the activities of their multinational corporations abroad. While the United States and other home states of multinational corporations have done much to emphasise the protection of the investments of multinational corporations, they have done little to ensure that these corporations do not harm the development objectives of poorer states. Some states have argued that there is in

---

[42] M Sornarajah, 'The Extraterritorial Enforcement of US Antitrust Law: Conflict and Compromise' (1982) 31 *ICLQ* 127; generally on jurisdiction, see C. Ryngaert, *Jurisdiction in International Law* (2008).

[43] *Hartford Fire Insurance Co.* v. *California*, 509 US 764 (1993); a softer approach is indicated in *Hoffman-La Roche* v. *Empagran SA*, 542 US 155 (2004), where harm solely to consumers outside the US was held not to be subject to the US antitrust laws.

[44] V. Lowe, 'International Law Issues Arising from the Pipeline Dispute: The British Position' (1984) 27 *German Yearbook of International Law* 54.

[45] There was a succession of business scandals beginning with Enron, which overvalued its stocks, and ending in the global economic crisis which is attributed to banking excesses relating to lending. The tendency of business was to institute self-policing measures and to speak of corporate social responsibility so that the true measure of the problem could be hidden from scrutiny until the global economic crisis made it no longer possible to persevere with the soft approach. A. Neal. 'Corporate Social Responsibility: Governance Gain or Laissez-Faire Figleaf' (2008) 28 *Comparative Labour Law and Policy Journal* 459.

fact an obligation in the home states of multinational corporations to ensure that these corporations do not harm the development objectives of host states. There seems to be some basis for this argument. At the least, it can be argued that the right of diplomatic protection of these corporations is conditional on the multinational corporations conducting themselves in a manner that accords with internationally recognised practices of good corporate citizenship. It can further be argued that there is, as a matter of state responsibility, an obligation on the part of home states to ensure that the subsidiaries of their multinational corporations conduct themselves in a manner that accords with the development objectives of host states. This obligation involves preventing multinational corporations leaving their home states to set up hazardous industries abroad. If they have already set up such industries, it involves the prevention of continued operations through whatever means of control are available. If harm has occurred in a host state, it involves having sufficient laws and providing sufficient means of access to courts to establish the liability of the parent corporation. These may be considered propositions that require further examination.

2.1 State responsibility of home states for failure to control multinational corporations

This section seeks to establish the difficult proposition that a home state of a multinational corporation has a responsibility to ensure that its corporate nationals do not act to the detriment of their host states while abroad.[46] That duty is easier to establish in the case of nationals, but its extension to corporate nationals is more problematic. Yet, the evolving policy objective, at least of some states, is to argue that there should be an obligation on the home state to ensure that there is no deviation in behaviour from the development and other objectives that a host state has set for itself, particularly if those objectives coincide with the objectives of the international community. This section tests that proposition, largely in the context of the obligation to observe human rights standards. It begins with a recapitulation of the rules on state responsibility.

2.2 The existing rules on state responsibility

The right to protect nationals abroad, including (indeed, especially) corporate nationals, has been the focus of attention in the literature on the international law on state responsibility.[47]

---

[46] A credible body of scholarly writing has dealt with this issue. M. Sornarajah, 'Linking State Responsibility for Certain Harms Caused by Corporate Nationals Abroad to Civil Recourse in the Legal Systems of Home States', in C. Scott (ed.), *Torture as Tort* (2001), p. 491; J. Zerk, *Multinationals and Corporate Social Responsibility* (2006); R. McCorquodale and P. Simons, 'Responsibility Beyond Borders: State Responsibility for Extraterritorial Violations by Corporations of International Human Rights Law' (2007) 70 *MLR* 598; S. Seck, 'Home State Responsibility and Local Communities: The Case of Global Mining' (2008) 11 *Yale Human Rights and Development Law Journal* 177.

[47] Despite the efforts of the International Law Commission to shift the focus to other areas, much of the law on state responsibility developed in the context of alien protection. Leading statements of the law on state responsibility for injuries to aliens can be found in C. F. Amerasinghe, *State Responsibility for Injuries to Aliens* (1967); and R. B. Lillich, *International Law of State Responsibility* (1983). The earlier drafts on state responsibility prepared by Garcia-Amador concentrated on alien protection, which was and is a divisive subject in international law. See F. V. Garcia-Amador, *Changing Law of International Claims* (1984).

It has not focused on the protection of the nationals of the host state from the abuses of multinational corporations. This gap has existed in spite of the fact that, in historical terms, the need for protection in the latter situation was more evident. The British and Dutch East India Companies and their likes plundered and pillaged the property of the natives of Asia and Africa with reckless abandon. The native peoples of Latin America, Australia and elsewhere were brought close to extinction so that their lands could be utilised for mining and other purposes by foreign investors. But, international law, which the European states fashioned, was more concerned with the protection of the interests of these corporations and foreign investment interests than with the protection of their victims. An elaborate structure of rules relating to mediate injuries permitting states to espouse the claims of the foreign investors and requiring the payment of prompt and full compensation was progressively built up.[48]

There is of course a power-based explanation for this situation.[49] The powerful states fashioned rules in order to ensure the protection of the assets of multinational corporations and expatriate plantation owners in the weaker states of the world. No inquiry was made into the issue of whether the exercise of this protection should be conditional on the conduct of the foreign citizen or corporation in the host state. An instructive case for the purposes of illustration is the *Schufeldt Claim*.[50] Here, the foreigner had extracted chicle[51] in Guatemala using injurious techniques of bleeding trees. The host state took the position that the trees would have been destroyed if the techniques were continued. The measure taken was for the protection of the industry. The host state advanced this as a reason for the termination of the concession agreement to extract chicle. When the matter went to inter-state arbitration between Guatemala and the United States, the damage caused by the use of injurious techniques was disregarded even in the calculation of damages. Instead, the arbitrator, with touching solicitude for the foreign investor, granted damages for, among other things, the 'anxiety of mind' caused to the foreign investor. There was much concern for the comfort of the foreign investor, none for the host state or its people. However, such instances of disregard for the interests of the developing host state led to the power-based notion of state responsibility being resisted by developing states in several ways. As a result, there has been a significant erosion of the norms contended for by developed states.[52] Yet, the idea of the

---

[48] Its classic statement is in the *Mavrommatis Palestine Concessions Case* (1924) PCIJ Series A No. 2, p. 12. The Court said: 'By taking up the case of one of its subjects and by resorting to diplomatic action or international judicial proceedings on his behalf, a State is in reality asserting its own rights – its right to ensure, in the person of its subjects, respect for the rules of international law.' The converse of this is that a developing state should be able to assert its right of protection of its nationals when an alien causes damage in its state and its nationals are not provided relief in the home state of the alien which has his assets and to which he has repatriated the profits of his operations in the host state.

[49] The role of power in rule formation in international law is coming to be studied in recent times. The work of developing country international lawyers in this area predates the new inquiries that are being made. R. P. Anand, *International Law and Developing Countries* (1987); J. T. Gathii, 'International Law and Eurocentricity' (1998) 9 *EJIL* 184; and M. Sornarajah, 'Power and Justice in International Law' (1997) 1 *Singapore Journal of International and Comparative Law* 28.

[50] (1930) 2 *UNRIAA* 1079; (1930) 24 *AJIL* 799.

[51] Chicle is defined in the *Oxford English Dictionary* as 'a gum-like substance obtained from the bullytree (*Mimusops Globosa*) largely used in the United States for the manufacture of chewing gum'.

[52] In the area of foreign investment, many of the norms advanced by the developed states were dented by the forceful articulation of counter-norms by the developing states.

responsibility of the multinational corporation or its home state for the damage it may cause to the host state or its people has yet to be fully explored.[53]

It may be useful in the context of the possibilities for current international law to reflect on how international law looked in former times. Prior to the ascendancy of the power-based notion of responsibility, it would have been easier to establish that there was a duty to ensure that a national did not act to the detriment of a host state whilst abroad. The right of protection of nationals abroad was conditional on the good conduct of the national.[54] There was forfeiture of protection where a national engaged in censurable conduct abroad. Generally, states recognised this by not acting in support of a citizen who had done wrong whilst abroad.[55] This was a significant acknowledgment of a link between state responsibility and the conduct of the foreign national, but was there an *active duty* to prevent the nationals from engaging in censurable behaviour? There is indeed authority for the view in older international law that a state became responsible to the state which was harmed if the former state was aware of the intention of the national to commit injurious acts against another state and did not prevent him from doing so. So, too, there was a duty on the part of the state to punish a national who committed a crime whilst abroad or to hand him over for punishment. Failure to do so amounted to a tacit approval of his conduct which triggered *ex post facto* responsibility of the state. Jimenez de Arechaga and Tanzi stated the position thus:

> The State which becomes aware that an individual intends to commit a crime against another state or one of its nationals, and does not prevent it or the state which extends protection to the offender by refusing to extradite or punish him gives tacit approval to his act. The State thus becomes an accomplice in his crime and establishes a link of solidarity with him: from such relationship the responsibility of the State arises.[56]

Though this statement is made on reliance of Grotius, there is other, more positivistic authority which also supports their argument. For example, the United States argued for such a rule in the well-known *Alabama Claim*, in which it successfully claimed compensation in respect of a confederate warship built in Britain.[57] There are also a considerable number of older arbitral awards which recognise similar claims based on the responsibility of a state for not being diligent in controlling the acts of its nationals abroad.[58] Borchard distils the following rule from these arbitrations:

---

[53] This is not to say that this has not been explored to some extent in the evolving responses to global environmental problems. See, for example, the Basel and Bamako treaties on the transfer of hazardous wastes. Yet, the treatment of state responsibility in the literature seldom addresses anything but conventional issues of state responsibility of the *Trail Smelter* variety. See, for example, K. Zemanek, 'State Responsibility and Liability', in W. Lang, H. Neuhold and K. Zemanek (eds.), *Environmental Protection and International Law* (1991), p. 187.

[54] The older cases are discussed in E. M. Borchard, *The Diplomatic Protection of Citizens Abroad* (Kraus Reprint Co., 1970; original edition, 1915), pp. 718–20.

[55] Thus, in the *Pelletier Claim* (1887), discussed in Borchard, *Diplomatic Protection*, p. 717, the United States refused to espouse the claim of a man shown to have been guilty of slave trading in Haitian waters. Slavery is subject to universal jurisdiction, as is torture. The refusal of diplomatic protection and the trial of the national for the offence may be mandated in these circumstances by modern law. Where there was a taking of the property of an alien in execution of a criminal fine, this was considered a non-compensable taking. Again, the idea is that the alien loses protection in these situations.

[56] E. Jimenez de Arechaga and A. Tanzi, 'International State Responsibility', in M. Bedjaoui (ed.), *International Law: Achievements and Prospects* (1991), p. 359. They also suggest that 'this theory of state complicity was adopted in several arbitral awards of the nineteenth century and by important writers on the subject'.

[57] (1872) 1 Moore 495.   [58] These are stated in Borchard, *Diplomatic Protection*, p. 217.

A long line of cases has established certain qualification upon the non-liability of the government for the wrongful acts of private individuals. These consist in certain manifestations of the actual or implied complicity of the government in the act, before or after it, either by directly ratifying or approving it, or by an implied, tacit or constructive approval in the negligent failure to prevent the injury, or to investigate the case, or to punish the guilty individual, or to enable the victim to pursue his civil remedies against the offender.[59]

This law, as summarised by Borchard, underwent a change as power-based and state-centred positivism gained sway over international legal thought. It came to be understood that the state could only be held responsible for the acts of its own organs and not for those of its nationals.[60] In other words, the approach, as described by Borchard, of treating states as having a species of direct responsibility through implied approval disappeared as a general principle of attribution. The modern position is stated in Article 11 of the International Law Commission's Articles on State Responsibility in the following terms:

The conduct of a person or a group of persons not acting on behalf of the State shall not be considered an act of the State under international law.[61]

But, significantly, another draft article, Article 8, does retain some notion of this older idea of the possibility of attribution of a national's conduct to the state itself. This article contemplates liability for the acts of persons if they were 'in fact acting on behalf of the State' or where they were 'exercising elements of governmental authority in the absence of official authorities and in circumstances which justified the exercise of those elements of authority'. It may be possible to argue that the rules stated by Arechaga and Tanzi, and Borchard, could be interpreted as having been retained by Articles 11 and 8 in combination, but there is no indication that the situation was even contemplated in the ILC drafting process with respect to those two Draft Articles. The ILC was quite content to go along with the power-based statement which was more concerned with the protection of aliens from injuries by the host state. That being said, the Draft Articles do not speak to substantive rules of law but, rather, only to framework principles of responsibility. Thus, it is generally considered that, even as the Borchardian principle of attribution was expunged from the new understanding of the general law of state responsibility, substantive international law continued to lay down positive duties with respect to the protection of foreigners in the classic type of situation in which there is mob violence directed at the alien which the *host state* did not prevent through due diligence.[62] What we now tend to think of as this 'classic' due diligence rule ceased being a general principle of attribution in the law of state responsibility (according to which negligent control and a failure to provide a process for civil remedies was viewed as creating a kind of direct agency relationship between the home state and its national). It was

---

[59] *Ibid.*

[60] Moore, *International Arbitration*, p. 2082; *Poggioli Case* (1903), in J. H. Ralston, *The Law Procedure of International Tribunals* (1926), p. 847; Borchard, *Diplomatic Protection*, p. 217. There are also cases which recognise liability for the acts of brigands abroad on the basis that there was a duty on the home state to suppress brigandage.

[61] ILC Report (1996), GAOR, 51st Session, Supp. 10, p. 125.

[62] The Iran–US Claims Tribunal dealt with many such situations. See *Shott* v. *Iran* (1987) 16 *Iran–US CTR* 76; *Yeager* v. *Iran* (1987) 17 *Iran–US CTR* 92.

transformed into a specific positive obligation of one branch of substantive law (the law dealing with protection of host states of foreign nationals). In the process, positive duties on the *home state* of these foreigners dropped out of the legal picture – at least in power-based, mainstream international legal thought.

The unprincipled and indeed arbitrary nature of this transformation is apparent. That being so, there would seem to be good reason to argue that substantive international law should be susceptible in light of a policy-based understanding of international law to interpretative development by analogy.[63] While we are quite distant from the old idea of a form of direct responsibility of states for the conduct of nationals abroad, there is no reason why present international law cannot be shaped to extend the substantive duties applicable to the host state of a corporation to the home state of the corporation where the requisite elements of knowledge and control are present. We should therefore not be surprised to find that, recently, challenges to the notion of the one-sided diplomatic protection of the alien corporation through international law despite the atrocious nature of its conduct have (re-) emerged. The idea is back on the table that the home state of a foreign citizen, quite apart from protecting the citizen or corporation, incurs responsibility if it does not prevent him or it from engaging in injurious conduct whilst abroad.[64]

However, the creation of such responsibility has so far been effected either by way of treaties dealing with specific subject-matter (such as the Basel Convention on the Transboundary Movements of Hazardous Wastes) or has been unilaterally accepted by some states concerned to regulate the conduct of their corporations abroad. The case for the existence of such liability in general international law is what this chapter seeks to establish.[65] We can gain a better idea of how easily general international law can embrace home state responsibility by noting some specific instances of the acceptance of such responsibility.

---

[63] The inadequacies in the treatment of the ILC's definition of attribution in the human rights contexts are dealt with, in a different context, in R. Lawson, 'Out of Control, State Responsibility and Human Rights: Will the ILC's Definitions of the Act of State Meet the Challenges of the 21st Century?', in M. Castermans-Holleman, F. van Hoof and J. Smith (eds.), *The Role of the Nation State in the 21st Century: Essays in Honour of Peter Baehr* (1998), p. 91.

[64] *Dicta* in the *Nicaragua Case* [1986] *ICJ Reports* 14 indicate responsibility of a state for acts of persons wholly unconnected with the state if there was control over these persons. Where there is such control, these persons would be equated with an arm of that state's government. The Court said (para. 109): 'What the Court has to determine is whether or not the relationship of the control to the United States Government was so much one of dependence on the one side and control on the other that it would be right to equate the *contras*, for legal purposes, with an organ of the United States Government, or as acting on behalf of that Government.' On the basis of this formulation, the existence of control over multinational corporations acting within the home state to the detriment of the interests of the host state or its people could engage the responsibility of the home state. In the human rights context, the principle was extended in the *Bosnia Genocide Case* [1996] *ICJ Reports* 595, where it was suggested by implication that a state becomes responsible if an individual who had committed a violation of the Genocide Convention was under the control of that state. For such a reading, see S. Rosenne, 'State Responsibility and International Crimes: Further Reflections on Article 19 of the Draft Articles on State Responsibility' (1997) 30 *New York University Journal of International Law and Politics* 145 at 159. *Dicta* in the *Tadic Case* (1997) 36 *ILM* 908 at 933 contemplate the Yugoslav state's liability for atrocities committed by Serbs in Bosnia. See also *Loizidou* v. *Turkey* (1996) 108 *ILR* 443.

[65] There is no doubt that, where the state sends its nationals on a mission abroad to inflict damage in another territory, even if the damage is directed at a third party, there is liability. *Rainbow Warrior Case* (1987) 26 *ILM* 1346. In the *Lockerbie Case*, the specific allegation was that agents sent by Libya had caused the airliner to explode. In both instances, the incidents took place elsewhere, but the acts were of agents of the state whose responsibility was alleged. Agency rather than nationality, and the intention with which the act was done are the factors in the attribution of responsibility. See also the *Nicaragua Case* [1986] *ICJ Reports* 14 for a norm of near-agency for the purposes of the direct attribution of the conduct of rebels in one state to another state supporting those rebels.

Examples of treaty acceptance of such responsibility are to be found especially in the environmental sphere. Thus, for example, the treaties controlling the transport of hazardous waste impose a duty on states to prevent such transport to other states by nationals.[66] Here, a clear treaty obligation arises not to permit citizens and corporations to export hazardous waste to other countries.[67] The law is no longer based on the premise of sovereignty that a developing state can choose to avoid the harm by refusing to accept the waste. It imposes an active duty on the exporting state to ensure that hazardous waste is not sent to other states.[68] But, these treaty obligations still seem to be territorially linked.[69]

The absence of territoriality, however, is not a problem in the emerging international law of human rights which recognises its basic obligations, such as the prohibition of torture, as being owed to the whole of humanity.[70] The meaningfulness of *erga omnes* obligations rests on the idea that state responsibility exists for the violation of any of those obligations which can be directly or indirectly traced to the acts or omissions of the state. The emergence of a duty to prosecute criminals in international law attests the fact that the place of commission of the violation of the obligations is increasingly becoming insignificant.[71] One may argue that the duty becomes more easily established in situations where the criminal is a national of the state. Correspondingly, there is an increasing recognition of a moral, if not yet a legal, duty to prevent the commission of harm injurious to the interests of other states and their peoples. Such a duty is often unilaterally assumed.

The best example of this would be the legislation recently enacted in some states to prevent the organisation of sex tours by their nationals to exploit child prostitutes in foreign states where the problem has become endemic and difficult to control. Here, the problem can only be controlled if both the state from which the tourists originate and those in which child prostitution exists take measures. States like the United Kingdom, Canada and Australia have voluntarily assumed the responsibility of preventing their nationals making such sex tours abroad. Though the legislation contemplates punishment after the event, there is a duty to prevent the tours taking place through denial of passports and other means.[72] The state has the means of preventing harm being caused to other states and persons living within other

---

[66] The Basel Convention on the Control of Transboundary Movement of Hazardous Wastes and Their Disposal (1989) 28 *ILM* 657 (in force, May 1992). See also K. Kummer, *International Management of Hazardous Wastes: The Basel Convention and Related Legal Rules* (1995). For the responsibility of flag states for the discharge of waste by ships on the high seas, see B. D. Smith, *State Responsibility and the Marine Environment* (1988); F. Francioni, 'Exporting Hazard Through Multinational Enterprises: Can the State of Origin Be Held Responsible?', in F. Francioni and T. Scovazzi (eds.), *International Responsibility for Environmental Harm* (1991), p. 275.

[67] See generally R. Risillo-Mazzeshchi, 'Forms of International Responsibility for Environmental Harm', in F. Francioni and T. Scovazzi (eds.), *International Responsibility for Environmental Harm* (1991); and R. Lefeber, *Transboundary Environmental Interference and the Origin of State Liability* (1996).

[68] The Fourth ACP–EEC Convention of Lomé (1989); and International Atomic Energy Agency, Code of Practice on the International Transboundary Movement of Radioactive Waste (1990). The texts of both instruments are in B. Kwiatkowska and A. H. A. Soons (eds.), *Transboundary Movement and Disposal of Hazardous Waste in International Law* (1993).

[69] The obligation is on the state to prevent the physical export of material from its territory, not to prevent export by a national who operates overseas. This is done through a licensing system which requires the prior informed consent of the state to which the export is made.

[70] M. Raggazi, *The Concept of International Obligations Erga Omnes* (1997).

[71] G. S. Goodwin-Gill, 'Crime in International Law: Obligations Erga Omnes and the Duty to Prosecute', in G. S. Goodwin-Gill and S. Talmon (eds.), *The Reality in International Law: Essays in Honour of Ian Brownlie* (1999), p. 199.

[72] Compare the situation of the rugby tours to South Africa during the *apartheid* regime. It was argued that the state should use its prerogative powers to prevent its national teams from travelling for this purpose.

states. There is a duty to prevent such harm. The duty arises not only in terms of morality but also in terms of law. Here, an extraterritorial situation is being controlled by regulating the conduct of nationals abroad. The moral responsibility to control such activities taking place abroad is accepted by the state which uses nationality as the basis for imposing liability on its citizens.[73]

It may be possible to argue that there is not only a moral duty but also a legal duty to take such measures. Beyond the harm caused to children through prostitution itself, the sex tourist is, in the context of sexually transmittable diseases, like a circulating bomb whose conduct can end up harming a wider circle of people than only the children with whom he has 'sex'.[74] There is a duty on the part of his state, which alone has the best means of ascertaining his condition and his proclivities, to prevent the circulation of that person in other states that are less able to deal with the problem.[75] The liability of tourist corporations which knowingly assist in such tours is already provided for in this legislation. The liability of airlines which knowingly carry such tourists must be contemplated. But, what is more important is that states which enact such legislation accept that they have a responsibility to prevent the occurrence of such incidents which directly involve harm to the host state and its people. One can argue that this may indicate a moral responsibility and not a legal one. But, in situations in which the harm prevented is recognised as prohibited by an *ius cogens* principle, it is credible to argue that the responsibility is a legal one.

The above examples[76] clearly demonstrate that, in certain areas, the assumption of responsibility by states for the conduct of their nationals abroad is coming to be accepted. The argument may now plausibly be made that such responsibility must, as a matter of general international law, be recognised in respect of violations of *ius cogens* principles like torture in two situations.[77] The first is where a state knowingly permits its nationals to engage in violations of *ius cogens* principles whilst abroad. The second is where a state gives active assistance to those who are known to violate or are seen as capable of violating such *ius cogens* principles. There are conditions to be satisfied in the traditional law of state responsibility before any liability can be imputed to the state. The manner of the satisfaction of these rules in the situation of imposing responsibility for the acts of multinational

---

[73] Compare the refusal by the United States to issue passports to Mormon missionaries as they would preach polygamy abroad, noted in E. M. Borchard, *Diplomatic Protection of Nationals* (1904).

[74] The link between torture and rape is increasingly being made. Sex with children is rape. In the context of an *ius cogens* principle, there would then be a universal obligation to prevent sex tourism involving paedophiles. In terms of the seriousness of the harm to children, it may be useful, in light of the thematic focus of this book on torture as an example of serious human rights violations, to recall the recent confirmation by the European Court of Human Rights that rape constitutes a form of torture at least for women in state custody: *Aydin* v. *Turkey*. Whether or not private acts of 'sex' are to be considered torture under prevailing international law definitions of torture, the important point is that the kind of abuse of power and associated harm is closely analogous when one considers the conditions under which many children 'choose' to prostitute themselves to foreign tourists. Not only does socio-economic reality and their stage of mental development make their choice illusory, but also we should not forget the jail-like circumstances of much prostitution.

[75] The analogy with the reasoning in the *Corfu Channel Case* [1999] *ICJ Reports* 4 is clear. The International Court of Justice held that Albania, the coastal state of the Corfu Channel, was responsible in law for the mining of the Channel and for the damage caused to vessels as a result of such mining.

[76] There are other examples besides the ones indicated here. Thus, the legislation to prevent bribery abroad by nationals (e.g. the Foreign Corrupt Practices Act) may be a similar instance. Here, again, there may be a slow evolution of international norms prohibiting bribery, which may make it incumbent on home states to act to prevent it. P. M. Nichols, 'Regulating Transnational Bribery in Times of Globalisation and Fragmentation' (1999) 24 *Yale JIL* 257.

[77] There is overwhelming authority for the view that torture is a violation of *ius cogens* principles.

corporations is now canvassed. With respect to the first situation, these rules require the existence of a duty and the ability to control the national from engaging in the proscribed behaviour and the failure to satisfy the duty. The elements of this duty to prevent are the subject of section 3 below. With respect to the second situation, it requires the existence of a link that makes attribution of the conduct of the multinational to the state possible. It will be argued that the home state should be deemed to have implicitly adopted or ratified the conduct of the corporate national if that home state fails to provide for some system of civil remedies for the victims of corporate harm abroad. The legal protection created by this failure should be considered as the requisite active assistance or link needed for attribution – the kind of 'implicit, tacit or constructive approval' spoken of by Borchard.

An alternative argument for the responsibility of the home state could be created on the basis of human rights law. There is a definite commitment on the part of all states to prevent the violation of human rights that take place not only within their territories but anywhere in the world. The statements of rights in the major conventions are not territory-specific.[78] And they impose liability on states not only for violations which they sponsored but also for violations by private persons whose acts have been condoned or encouraged by the state.[79] The argument is possible that a state, whose multinational corporations are known to participate in violations of human rights such as torture, condones such violations as a matter of state policy if they do not take any measures to prevent those violations. A state which profits from the repatriation of the profits which the multinational corporation makes must be credited with the duty to ensure that such profits are made without mass violations of human rights.

2.3 The duty to control nationals abroad

The principles that potentially apply to the control of the conduct of nationals abroad are those relating to responsibility in relation to the acts of private citizens that the state was under a duty to control. As noted earlier, this category has grown up largely in the context of cases involving mob violence against a foreigner within the territory of the host state.[80] The law relating to liability for agents sent out to commit acts of sabotage or abduction is also relevant.

---

[78] For example, Article 3 of the International Covenant on Civil and Political Rights creates a general duty to 'ensure the equal right of the men and women to the enjoyment of all civil and political rights set forth in the present Covenant', whereas Article 2 contains a statement that is territory-specific.

[79] See Reporters' Notes to Article 702, in American Law Institute, *Restatement of the Law: The Foreign Relations Law of the United States* (vol. 2, p. 167). The notes contemplate the possibility of avoiding responsibility by providing domestic remedies against violations.

[80] This area of the law was recognised in modern times in the *Rainbow Warrior Case* (1990) 82 *ILR* 499; and in the *Nicaragua Case* [1986] *ICJ Reports* 14. In the *Rainbow Warrior Case*, a Dutch citizen was killed when French agents sank the *Rainbow Warrior*. The damage was to an alien life and property by aliens sent as agents of France into New Zealand. The New Zealand Minister of Justice said: 'What New Zealand was saying to France on this matter was, in effect, that it was a political imperative that decent arrangements be made for compensation for damage suffered in New Zealand but not by New Zealand.' France paid compensation. G. Palmer, 'Settlement of International Disputes: The Rainbow Warrior Affair' (1989) 2 *Commonwealth Law Bulletin* 585. In *Letelier* v. *Chile*, 488 F Supp 665 (1980), state responsibility (of Chile) for the act of its agent in setting off a car bomb which killed a former Chilean ambassador was recognised. The *Pinochet* case also recognised the liability of a head of state (Chile) for acts of torture committed in Spain. The issue of the liability of Chile was not raised. But, in *Al-Adsani* v. *Kuwait* (1996) 106 *ILR* 536, the English court recognised that Kuwait could be liable for acts of its agents in the United Kingdom if they had caused personal injury to any resident in the United Kingdom.

It is the combination of these two sets of rules which will provide an answer to the issue of home state liability for the acts of a multinational corporation which is associated with torture in a host state. Before dealing with the question of state obligations to control nationals abroad, it should first be noted that *jurisdiction* (i.e. the power or liberty) of a state to control nationals abroad exists in international law. It is relatively common for some legal systems, notably those of civil law countries, to make it a violation of the country's criminal code for a national to commit serious common crimes abroad. Common law jurisdictions tend, as a general rule, to prescribe criminal law rules on a territorial basis.[81] However, it is far less common for states, whatever the nature of their legal systems, to legislate extraterritorially outside the criminal law, with the United States probably being the state most inclined to create legislated exceptions to the presumption of the territorial application of its laws. But, even the United States has been selective in the exercise of this jurisdiction. So far, it has exercised such jurisdiction when it has been advantageous to its interests.[82] It has not exercised such jurisdiction on purely altruistic grounds. Claims before courts that environmental legislation applies to the operation of US companies abroad have uniformly failed, the courts interpreting the environmental legislation as having only a territorial application. It is true that the *Unocal* case establishes that judicial jurisdiction to entertain suits against corporations alleging their participation in torture with a government against its own citizens exists in domestic courts.[83] But, in terms of the jurisdictional foundations of the *Unocal* case, it proceeded largely on the basis that there is universal jurisdiction over *ius cogens* violations of international law such as torture and slavery and not on the basis of nationality, although Unocal is a US corporation. The fortuitous existence of a statute according the US courts jurisdiction, the Alien Torts Claims Act, facilitated the court's assumption of jurisdiction over corporate conduct abroad amounting to breaches of the 'law of nations'. Such legislation does not exist in other states which are home states of multinational corporations.[84]

The issue is whether a state's capacity to control its nationals in respect of their activity abroad must be exercised by a state when the state has knowledge that harm could eventuate to another state or its people. Phrased in this way, it can be seen that the only link that is missing is the absence of a clear positive duty to exercise the jurisdiction to control the conduct of nationals. It is clear that responsibility will arise if there are specific instructions

---

[81] C. Blakesley, 'United States Jurisdiction over Extraterritorial Crime' (1982) 73 *Journal of Criminal Law and Criminology* 1109.

[82] The US export-control legislation applies to corporations operating overseas. Some tax legislation also applies. But, the US courts have consistently held that environmental legislation does not have extraterritorial application.

[83] *Doe I* v. *Unocal*, 963 F Supp 880 (CD Cal., 1997); *Doe I* v. *Unocal*, 27 F Supp 2d 1174 (CD Cal., 1998). The litigation involved claims that the imposition of forced labour, rape and violence on indigenous people in the remote regions of Burma through which Unocal was constructing a pipeline involved liability of the Burmese state as well as of Unocal. The responsibility of the state was alleged on the basis that the Burmese army was involved in the atrocities, and that of Unocal flowed from complicity in the atrocities. For a description of the litigation in respect of the massacre in East Timor brought in Boston against an Indonesian military officer who had come to the United States to study management at Harvard, see R. Clark, 'Public International Law and Private Enterprise: Damages for a Killing in East Timor' (1996) 3 *Australian Journal of Human Rights* 21. The action was based on the Alien Tort Claims Act (1879) and the Torture Victim Protection Act (1992). For environmental litigation, see *Beanal* v. *Freeport-McMoran*, 969 F Supp 362 (ED La, 1997).

[84] A point made by the English courts in another context in *Al-Adsani* v. *Kuwait* (1996) 106 *ILR* 536.

given to nationals to engage in the harmful behaviour abroad.[85] Such instructions in effect create an agency relationship such as is contemplated by Draft Article 8 of the ILC's Draft Articles on State Responsibility, resulting in the nationals acting on behalf of their state. But, where such instructions are absent, can a state's mere knowledge of the harmful behaviour of its national be sufficient to trigger responsibility if the state fails to do what is necessary to cause the harmful conduct to cease?[86] Finally, how far do the home state's positive obligations go in situations where it is not alleged that the national's employees are the direct agents of harm but rather that the national is benefiting from a foreign state's human rights violations which have been committed in order to advance a joint project involving both the national and that state? In other words, in the situation such as the one in *Unocal*, is there a duty on the part of the United States to prevent Unocal acquiescing in the Burmese government's torture and rape of local people as alleged in that case?

The argument is that such a duty *can* be constructed under present international law. As already indicated, the intentional sending of nationals or agents abroad to cause harm involves state responsibility. To extend this to situations where there is actual or constructive knowledge that harm will be caused by nationals requires but a small leap in the law. This leap is justified by existing doctrines. There is a general duty in international law not to cause harm to other states. Where a state knows that the activities of its nationals will cause, or are causing, harm to other states or their peoples, it is consistent with this duty that it should prevent such harm. As a matter of general principle, if the state has the right to have its nationals protected abroad, a concomitant duty to ensure that the nationals act in a manner consistent with international norms should be recognised. Additionally, in a situation such as that alleged in *Unocal*, the home state of the foreign investor benefits from the foreign investment through the repatriation of the company's profits. The profits are enhanced by the forced labour that is secured by torture and repression. The fact that the home state itself benefits in this way casts a duty on the state to ensure that the company's profits (which are in a sense also profits for the home state) are not secured through means that violate international norms.

The home state has the ability to ensure that its nationals who operate abroad as foreign investors act in a manner consistent with international norms through the exercise of jurisdiction on the basis of nationality. If tax legislation and other legislation such as antitrust legislation can be extended in this manner, then the creation of a duty to exercise such jurisdiction to secure fundamental norms of international law cannot be regarded as unjustified. Some states reached out in this manner to prevent corruption and bribery in international business by their national corporations even before agreement on multilateral treaties began to be reached under the auspices of regional and sectoral organisations like the OAS

---

[85] The *Nicaragua Case* [1986] *ICJ Reports* 14 provides obvious authority. There need not even be the link of nationality; the mere existence of control of a group would suffice. The ICJ held that control over the *contras* was absent, and that state responsibility could not be imputed to the United States. Nationality makes control easier to establish, particularly in circumstances where the national's activities are known to the home state and the home state profits from them directly or indirectly.

[86] And, further, is advance knowledge not of actual harm but of the *risk of harm* sufficient to trigger the duty to control the national in order to prevent the harm before it occurs?

and the OECD.[87] The prohibition of bribery has not nearly as much support in international policy as the prohibition of torture. Indeed, in the hierarchy of public policy norms, the prohibition of bribery comes well below the violation of human and environmental rights. The minimum effect of a state being unprepared to prevent the violation of international public policy norms, is that it must lose its right of diplomatic protection of its nationals. The theory of foreign investment that was articulated in the past justified the protection afforded to business on the ground that the home state made sure that the business practices of the multinational corporations it sent abroad were above board, thereby entitling the state to give the corporate national its maximum protection. This policy fails in situations in which the multinational corporation engages in practices that violate *ius cogens* norms against torture or engages in other practices which violate international public policy.

There must be a satisfaction of the existing rules on state responsibility before a state is subjected to responsibility. As the International Court of Justice stated in the *ELSI Case*, an allegation of state responsibility should not be lightly made.[88] Hence, the rules on state responsibility must be clearly satisfied before an allegation of state responsibility for the conduct of its nationals is raised. Knowledge must be attributable to the home state with respect to the acts of the nationals in question. This will ordinarily be difficult to satisfy, as a state cannot know beforehand what its nationals who go abroad seek to do. But, where a multinational corporation, as in the *Unocal* situation, is alleged *currently* to be violating the human rights of peoples abroad, the situation will be sufficiently widely known for the state to have imputed knowledge of the situation. There is not merely a jurisdictional power to control but a duty to control the activities of the national corporation in these circumstances.[89] The issue then becomes one of whether the state took reasonable steps to prevent the harm where advance knowledge of likely harm can be shown or to stop an ongoing violation of human rights.

Returning to the parallel provided by the law on state responsibility for the activities of loosely organised mobs which attack foreigners, the law has been worked out on the basis that, if the state had knowledge of the situation, a duty to protect the aliens is triggered. If an attack by a mob was foreseeable, then a duty of protection is owed to the alien. State responsibility arises from the failure of the territorial state to provide such protection, liability flowing from the omission to act in a situation where the law creates a duty to act.[90] Even if a standard of strict liability is not the basis of state responsibility, a due diligence fault requirement will be satisfied in these circumstances where a capacity to exercise control exists but there was a failure to exercise that control. Since a capacity to

---

[87] Foreign Corrupt Practices Act; see also Article 2 of the OECD Convention on Combating Bribery of Foreign Public Officials in International Business (1997).

[88] *ELSI Case* [1989] *ICJ Reports* 15.

[89] In the *Sambiaggio Case* (1903) 10 *UNRIAA* 499, Arbitrator Ralston said: 'Governments are responsible, as a general principle, for the acts of those they control.' Control of the conduct of multinational corporations through the nationality principle is possible, and the United States has used such control in many areas, such as the export of technology. See also Article 30 of the Charter of Economic Rights and Duties of States (1974): 'All states have the responsibility to ensure that activities within their jurisdiction *or control* do not cause damage to the environment of other states or areas beyond the limits of national jurisdiction.' Emphasis added.

[90] *Home Missionary Society Case* (1920) 6 *UNRIAA* 20; R. Pisillo-Mazzeschi, 'The Due Diligence Rule and the Nature of the International Responsibility of States' (1992) 35 *German Yearbook of International Law* 46.

control exists in the home state with respect to a multinational corporation which operates abroad, the same rules can therefore be extended to render home states liable when they are aware of the conduct of their multinational corporate nationals and do not curb such conduct through the means available to the state.

International law requires that there must be an exercise of governmental authority before a state can become responsible. It may be argued that there is no governmental authority in the situation of a multinational corporation whereas there is such authority in the agent who is sent to commit sabotage abroad, as in the *Rainbow Warrior* situation, in which French security agents were sent abroad to sabotage one of Greenpeace's vessels while in port in New Zealand. But, international law recognises very clearly that governmental authority may be exercised either by act or by omission.[91] Whether or not conduct by omission breaches international law depends on whether there is a positive duty placed by substantive international law on the state (i.e. a duty to act in a certain way and/or with a view to achieving a certain result). Again, the classic mob situation illustrates the way out of this supposed difficulty. The mob is by no means the agent of the government. The requirement of governmental authority is provided in these cases by the failure of the governmental authorities to act in the situation of danger to the alien posed by the mob.[92] It is the failure to exercise due diligence to protect the alien from which governmental complicity in the episode arises. Likewise in the case of the multinational corporation, responsibility arises due to the failure of the state authorities to prevent it from engaging in human-rights-abusive conduct abroad. The theory of liability that has evolved primarily in arbitral case law on mob violence provides the necessary body of general principles for establishing the liability of the home state for the torture and other human rights violations engaged in by multinational corporations. We would do well to remember that the application and development of these principles in some cases also involved the making of leaps in legal reasoning from general principles to concrete contexts no less creative than what is being contended for here.

Some may argue that distance is a constraining factor in the attribution of state responsibility to home states for corporate conduct abroad. In most instances of state responsibility, the state held responsible had caused injury to the alien resident within that state's territorial limits. But, this common *factual situation* of territoriality cannot be understood as having given rise to any *legal* rule that proximity to the act is necessary. Proximity has never been isolated as a limiting rule by any writer.[93] In any event, it would be completely inconsistent with the willingness of international law to extend responsibility to states for extraterritorial acts of its nationals where there is some direct agency or similar kind of link. For example, in

---

[91] It is generally recognised in the law of state responsibility that an omission to act to prevent harm entails responsibility.

[92] *Youmans Claim* (1926) 4 *UNRIAA* 110; *Zafiro Claim* (1925) 6 *UNRIAA* 160 (where liability was imposed on the basis that a naval officer did not stop looting by the mob 'with sufficient promptitude'). This case is relevant to the situation under discussion, as liability was imposed on the basis that an unruly Chinese crew of a privately owned ship that was requisitioned by the United States was let loose to riot in an area of the Philippines that had no civil administration.

[93] Nor have the older cases required that the injurious acts should have taken place on the territory of the state held responsible. For example, in the *Zafiro Claim* (1925) 6 *UNRIAA* 160, responsibility of the United States in respect of acts of vandalism of a Chinese crew under the command of a US naval officer in a port city of the Philippines (which was, at the time, not under the control of any authority). The presence of the officer at the scene of the injury was held not to be necessary.

Short v. *Iran*,[94] it was contemplated that, if the Ayatollah Khomeini, who had yet to come to Iran, had instigated hostile acts towards the US nationals resident in Iran whilst still in exile in France, his incoming government would be responsible for those acts. And states have been held responsible for sending agents to engage in abduction abroad and for sending saboteurs into another state.[95] It is true that the existing principles of state responsibility will have to be extended creatively to cover state responsibility for corporate misconduct. But, as was argued earlier, if the need and will to achieve a pressing policy objective is to be placed at the centre of the evolution of international law, achieving it by adapting and extending existing law is a legitimate means to do so.

Another challenge might take the form of the question of why there should be state responsibility in these circumstances. This question has already been answered implicitly. The imposition of state responsibility on the home state is one means of providing for control over the conduct of a multinational corporation whose conduct otherwise remains unregulated in modern international law – and arguably is increasingly unregulated as economic globalisation pressures sap the will and capacity of states to regulate corporate conduct within their borders for fear of losing investment.[96] The paradigm being argued for will throw the onus of control onto home states which not only are able to bear that burden but which also have a moral duty to bear it because they and their societies profit from the overseas operations of their multinational corporations. It is clear that they have the ability to control such activity as they have claimed wide extraterritorial powers of control over these corporations in several areas. Home state responsibility will help in the creation of an international law which prevents human rights abuses by these corporations which exert considerable power and influence over the course of international relations without being subjected to any meaningful control.

Finally, of specific interest to the civil liability theme of the present book is that an important aspect of such state responsibility is that the wrongdoing state then comes under a duty to provide a remedy to the victim. The failure to provide a remedy again leads to an independent basis of state responsibility. To this issue we now turn in the final section of this chapter.

2.4 State responsibility and the duty to provide remedies to victims

It has been demonstrated that state responsibility arises from the breach of a duty to control the human rights violations of a multinational corporation abroad. When such a breach occurs, a duty on the part of the home state to provide a remedy to the victims of its misconduct then arises. More specifically, the contention is that, in the Bhopal- or Unocal-type situations, there is an obligation on the home state to provide a remedy through the domestic courts. This again is a contention that initially seems difficult to establish, but, once it is conceded that there is a duty to prevent nationals from causing harm to people in other states, the obligation can be made out as a matter of law.

---

[94] (1987) 16 *Iran–US CTR* 76.   [95] *Rainbow Warrior Case* (1987) 26 *ILM* 1346.
[96] The voluntary codes which exist hardly provide the function of control.

The current paradigm of the duty to provide an effective local remedy is the situation of an alien who suffers injury at the hands of the host state. The duty to provide access to local courts in order to receive an effective remedy is already well recognised in the law.[97] It follows (at least at the level of consistency of the policy justifications underlying the law) that, once the primary obligation to prevent harm abroad is accepted as applicable to the home states of multinational corporations, the law must be shaped to ensure that the home state provides a remedy. That is, at least where the home state itself has breached duties to control in situations of adequate knowledge of the corporate national's conduct abroad, the duty to provide a remedy to the victims seems to follow as a matter of basic considerations of justice.

Significantly, the existing law is not a blank slate on this, and in fact contains the kernel of a duty to provide access to the home state's courts whether or not the home state itself bears responsibility for a failure to control the corporate national prior to or during the harm. There is sufficient authority that a state which does not provide a remedy against the wilful harm caused to other states by a national becomes responsible to the state which suffered the harm.[98]

It must finally be noted that the duty to provide a remedy to victims may exist in general international human rights law, quite independently of any argument relating to state responsibility for the state's own involvement in or failure to prevent human rights violations.[99] There is a generic duty to provide remedies for human rights violations.[100] There is a credible argument to be made that there is not only a duty to provide a remedy but that, in the case of violations of *ius cogens* norms, like torture committed by nationals abroad, emerging international law recognises a positive duty to prosecute the offenders. If such a positive duty exists, then it must follow that failure to perform it engages the responsibility of states.

3. Conclusion

Globalisation is supposed to be moving at a rapid pace, but, historically, the process of globalisation has always been accompanied by a process of fragmentation which involves the withdrawal of people into their own cultures and values in order to face the onset of new global values. This process of fragmentation is seldom studied. The violence which is generated by the clash will be a concern of the future. The potential for violation of human rights in this clash has also been seldom studied. There is a paucity of norms in international law which provide for the control of such violence.

---

[97] C. F. Amerasinghe, *Local Remedies in International Law* (1990).

[98] The rule is usually discussed in the context of the requirement either to punish or to hand over a national who has committed a crime abroad. There is no reason why the rule should not be applied to situations of human rights violations which involve acts like torture, which are considered criminal in most legal systems.

[99] The view is canvassed in R. Pisillo-Mazzeschi, 'International Obligations to Provide for Reparation Claims?', in A. Randelzhofer and C. Tomuschat (eds.), *State Responsibility and the Individual* (1999), p. 149.

[100] *Velasquez Rodriguez* (1988) 9 *HRLJ* 212 (where the Inter-American Court of Human Rights recognised the duty of states to prevent violations and remedy or punish such violations after their commission). Recognition of human rights requires positive action by states, including access to courts for remedies.

The process of globalisation itself is a power-based process which seeks to secure the rights of business to the detriment of the rights of people. The positivist basis of the rules on state responsibility were formulated so as to enhance this process which stressed the rights of the foreign investor and eclipsed the earlier law which did recognise the fact that responsibility could arise in the home state for the conduct of a national abroad. The Draft Articles on State Responsibility of the International Law Commission continue this trend by their emphasis on power-based solutions to state responsibility. Yet, the development of an international law of human rights is based on the competing notion of idealism in the law which requires the recognition of the responsibility of the state for the violation of the more basic human rights giving rise to *erga omnes* obligations wherever they take place as long as they can be directly or indirectly attributed to that state. There is clear evidence of the impact of this competing objective. The progress towards the stabilisation of this norm may be incremental but the signs are that, once a breach is made, the law will quickly develop to ensure this progress, notwithstanding the establishment views stated in the ILC's Draft Articles. Work remains to be done in combining the different strands which are moving towards supporting the growth of such a law.

5

Bilateral investment treaties

There was a massive proliferation of bilateral investment treaties in the 1990s. A World Bank study stated that in 1994 there were over 700 such treaties.[1] By the end of the millennium, the figure had moved towards 2,600 treaties.[2] It has now exceeded that mark.[3] Investment chapters are also included in free trade agreements.[4] Obviously, states which participate in the making of these treaties consider them to be necessary for a variety of reasons, the most important being the belief that they promote the flow of foreign investment. The question whether they do in fact promote foreign investment flows has been subjected to considerable doubt in recent literature.[5] Yet, the treaties continue to be made, though there is a decline in their numbers in recent times. Other reasons are advanced for their making. One is their signalling function. The making of such treaties is an indication that a state previously committed to certain ideological stances inimical to foreign investment has changed its policy and is now prepared to accept standards of protection of investment and international arbitration to settle investment disputes. The activity of China and Vietnam, erstwhile communist states wedded to a concept of public ownership of property, is illustrative of this signalling function. The former East European states, liberated from communist ideology, also signed many such treaties. But, such treaty activity is also explicable on the basis of the need of these

---

[1] R. Dolzer and M. Stevens, *Bilateral Investment Treaties* (1996), p. 1. According to a list of treaties that appears in (1989) 4 *ICSID Rev* 189, the first bilateral investment treaty was that concluded between Germany and Pakistan in 1959. The list refers to 308 treaties that had been concluded by the end of 1988. The treaties are collected together in a looseleaf publication. ICSID, *Investment Promotion and Protection Treaties* (1983). They are also listed on the websites of UNCTAD and ICSID. The texts of the various treaties are also made available.

[2] The first bilateral investment treaty was signed in 1959. By the end of 1970, only 53 bilateral investment treaties had been signed (although many of them were still relatively weak – compared to now – in terms of protections and dispute settlement). Their number began to grow slowly during the 1970s (when 71 bilateral investment treaties were signed), increased during the 1980s (when 243 bilateral investment treaties were signed) and really took off in the 1990s (between 1991 and the end of 2000, 1,549 treaties were signed), for a total of 2,636 bilateral investment treaties at the end of 2007, involving 179 countries. Bilateral investment treaty activity declines thereafter. The 1990s were the period of the ascendancy of neo-liberalism. This accounts for the growth in the number of treaties during this period.

[3] UNCTAD, *World Investment Report, 2003*, puts the figure at 2,153. It has charts pointing to the treaty activity peaking in the mid-1990s and declining in the first years of the new millennium. Later counts bring the figure close to 2,700. But, this does not include free trade agreements containing investment chapters. The Energy Charter Treaty is a sectoral investment treaty with a large membership. It also is not included in the count.

[4] These free trade agreements usually contain provisions of investment treaties that are cobbled together. Thus, Chapter 11 of NAFTA is essentially the then existing model bilateral investment treaty of the United States cobbled into a free trade agreement.

[5] The literature on this is large. See, for example, J. W. Salacuse and N. P. Sullivan, 'Do BITs Really Work? An Evaluation of Bilateral Investment Treaties and Their Grand Bargain' (2005) 46 *Harvard ILJ* 67 at 78.

countries to enhance their competitive positions.[6] The assumption is that developing countries, competing with each other to attract investment, make investment treaties in order to ensure that they recognise the same standards of protection as other developing states similarly placed. This may provide explanations as to why there are newcomers, like India,[7] on the scene. It may also be supported by the fact that the granting of incentives like tax breaks are replicated within a region, indicating that, once one state grants an incentive, it is quickly copied by other states within the region.[8]

But, these explanations belie the fact that often pressure, advice or convenience are the reasons for the making of treaties. It is well known that investment insurance will not be granted by official agencies of developed states unless an investment treaty has been agreed with the host state.[9] International financial institutions bring pressure to bear on developing states to sign treaties when they seek loans. Bodies like the United Nations Commission on Trade and Development (UNCTAD) advise that such treaties be signed. There is also the suggestion that investment treaties are signed because they provide photo opportunities with visiting dignitaries. Certainly, there seems to be evidence of a low level of understanding of the implications of such treaties and their consequences by developing states until their impact is felt.[10]

The explanations given in the literature generally concentrate on why developing countries sign such treaties. The same question should be asked with respect to developed countries as well. The assumption that 'the impetus for investment treaties is host country driven'[11] does not tie in with their history or purpose. The history is that the move for investment treaties began with developed countries in response to the calls for a New International Economic Order made by developing states. The law became uncertain as a consequence. The purpose of investment treaties was to preserve some of the norms that the developed states advanced as customary international law. Developed countries made these treaties because their favoured rules on investment protection had been subjected to attack. Germany, which signed the first treaty and now has a large number of such treaties, actively sought overseas investment in the process of its reconstruction after the Second World War. Developed states also compete for markets and for natural

---

[6] Z. Elkins, A. T. Guzman and B. Simmons, 'Competing for Capital: The Diffusion of Bilateral Investment Treaties' (2008) *University of Illinois LR* 265; E. Neumayer and L. Spess, 'Do Bilateral Investment Treaties Increase Foreign Direct Investment to Developing Countries?' (2005) 33 *World Development* 1567 at 1582; M. Hallward-Driemeier, 'Do Bilateral Treaties Attract FDI? Only A Bit ... And They Could Bite' (World Bank Development Research Group, Working Paper No. 3121, 2003); J. Tobin and S. Rose-Ackerman, 'Foreign Direct Investment and the Business Environment in Developing Countries: The Impact of Bilateral Investment Treaties' (Yale Law and Economics Research Paper No. 293, 2005); K. P. Gallagher and D. Chudnovsky, *Rethinking Foreign Investment for Sustainable Development: Lessons from Latin America* (2009).

[7] Though a latecomer to liberalisation, India has now signed a large number of treaties. D. Krishnan, 'Indian and International Investment Laws', in B. Patel (ed.), *India and International Law* (2008), vol. 2, p. 277.

[8] Tax incentives within the Asian region are an example. Once a state introduces an incentive system or changes it, it is quickly followed by other states, a fact which can be explained by competition for investment.

[9] OPIC, the US government agency which insures foreign investments, will not provide insurance to foreign investors who invest in states with which the US has no investment treaty. Demands are also made by the IMF that investment treaties be made as a condition for granting loans. D. Kaldermis, 'IMF Conditionality as Investment Regulation' (2004) 13 *Social and Legal Studies* 103.

[10] Thus, a former Attorney-General of Pakistan candidly admitted that there was little or no understanding of the nature of the treaties in government departments until arbitrations were brought against Pakistan.

[11] Z. Elkins, A. T. Guzman and B. Simmons, 'Competing for Capital: The Diffusion of Bilateral Investment Treaties' (2008) *University of Illinois LR* 265 at 298.

resources. They are keen to ensure that investments that flow into states which have political and other risks are protected by rules. When China opened up its economy, the size of its markets, the availability of cheap labour and its natural resources were attractions but there was a need to counteract the political risk to investment. The making of treaties with China was an obvious advantage.

Multinational corporations seek to manufacture at locations where cheap skilled labour as well as cheap resources are readily available. The law follows such investments, and it is logical that developed states will want to protect their multinational corporations in the countries they enter. They seek to make treaties in order to bring about a climate in which their foreign investors feel confident. Multinational corporations also act as pressure groups to ensure that changes favourable to their interests are brought about through treaties so that their investments are protected and their profits can be repatriated.[12]

The underlying reasons for the treaty activity of any one state does not remain constant. China again provides an example. It was in earlier times a recipient of capital. When it announced its 'open door' policy, there was a need to signal this fact, and it signalled its willingness to give guarantees of protection by signing treaties. It married this with its existing philosophy by confining arbitration to disputes as to the quantum of compensation and required a compulsory period of negotiation prior to arbitration. China's more recent treaties are, however, premised on the fact that the current significant outflows of foreign investment from China need to be protected.[13] Its newer treaties are becoming very similar to those which Western industrialised states sign.[14]

The more important reason for the proliferation of these treaties in the 1990s was that neo-liberalism became the accepted economic wisdom during this period.[15] The hegemonic leadership of the United States, along with the international financial institutions, drove this philosophy.[16] For a period, international law itself became instrumental in ensuring that rules were made that would favour the spread and acceptance of the model of trade and investment that neo-liberalism favoured. This accounts for the fact that many of the instruments of the World Trade Organization promote the liberalisation not only of trade but also of areas linked to it such as intellectual property and the trade in services.[17] The rise in the number of the investment treaties in the period is also evidence of the wholesale acceptance of neo-liberal philosophy during this period. With the more recent retreat of neo-liberalism, however, one witnesses a decline in the number of treaties being made. The retreat is also evidenced by the fact that even the model treaty of the United States contains changes which agitate the purists of investment protection. This signifies

---

[12] In international trade, the instrument on intellectual property, TRIPS, was brought about by pressure exerted by pharmaceutical companies intent on securing effective global intellectual property protection.

[13] A Chinese foreign investor has now brought an ICSID arbitration on the basis of a bilateral investment treaty between China and Peru. *Tza Yap Shum* v. *Peru*, ICSID Case No. ARB/07/6 (Decision on Jurisdiction and Competence, 19 June 2009).

[14] See the treaties with Germany and the Netherlands signed in 2007; and the treaty with Columbia signed in 2008.

[15] J. Stiglitz, *The Roaring Nineties* (2006).

[16] The tenets of this philosophy came to be known as the 'Washington Consensus': see N. Serra and J. Stiglitz (eds.), *The Washington Consensus Reconsidered* (2008). For a favourable view of neo-liberalism as the foundation of the law, see K. Vandevelde, 'Sustainable Liberalism and International Investment Regime' (1998) 19 *Michigan JIL* 373.

[17] The linkage itself illustrates the force of neo-liberalism.

a return by the United States and Canada to a sovereignty-centred approach born out of their experience of being at the wrong end of several NAFTA arbitrations. The experience of these arbitrations are reflected in the US and Canadian treaties. These modern treaties are said to strive for a balance between the regulatory powers of the state and the interests of the foreign investor. They provide for circumstances of preclusion of liability, defences based on the need to protect public interests through the exercise of regulatory powers and national security exceptions. They also withdraw areas such as taxation from the scope of arbitration, and require their settlement through consultation mechanisms. They have moved so far away from the original object of investment protection that the purist would wonder whether they are of any use any more. The balance that is struck makes it difficult to base decisions on these treaties – so much so that it will accentuate rather than reduce the deep schisms that have already begun to appear in investment arbitration. It could well be that there is a return to the normlessness that existed at the time when bilateral investment treaties were seen as the way out of the morass caused by the clash between the norms preferred by developed states and the norms of the New International Economic Order advanced by developing states. Yet, despite such changes, treaties still remain a significant part of the international law on foreign investment. The significance of these treaties needs closer assessment.

1. Introductory survey

In the 1980s, bilateral investment treaties were considered a relatively new phenomenon in the international investment scene.[18] They seek to set out the rules according to which investments made by the nationals of the two states parties in each other's territory will be protected. Writers are divided as to the effect of these treaties. Some writers believe that these treaties give 'important support for those standards of customary international law which had seemed to be slipping away'.[19] For such an assessment to be made, one must be

---

[18] For the literature on the subject in the 1980s and the 1990s, see J. Voss, 'The Protection and Promotion of European Private Investment in Developing Countries' (1981) 18 *CMLR* 363; A. Asken, 'The Case for Bilateral Investment Treaties', in South West Foundation, *Private Investors Abroad* (1981); F. A. Mann, 'British Treaties for the Promotion and Protection of Foreign Investment' (1982) 52 *BYIL* 241; K. Kunzer, 'Developing a Model Bilateral Investment Treaty' (1983) 15 *Law and Policy in International Business* 273; M. S. Bergman, 'Bilateral Investment Treaties: An Examination of the Evolution and Significance of the US Prototype Treaty' (1983) 16 *New York University Journal of International Law and Politics* 1; D. A. Cody, 'United States Bilateral Investment Treaties: Egypt and Panama' (1983) *Georgia Journal of International and Comparative Law* 491; J. E. Pattison, 'The United States–Egypt Bilateral Investment Treaty: A Prototype for Future Negotiation' (1983) 16 *Cornell ILJ* 305; K. J. Vandevelde, 'The Bilateral Investment Treaty Program of the United States' (1988) 21 *Cornell ILJ* 201; UNCTC, *Bilateral Investment Treaties* (1988); J. W. Salacuse, 'BIT by BIT: The Growth of Bilateral Investment Treaties and Their Impact on Foreign Investment in Developing Countries' (1990) 24 *International Lawyer* 655; K. J. Vandevelde, *United States Investment Treaties: Policy and Practice* (1992); 'The Development and Expansion of Bilateral Investment Treaties' (1992) *ASIL Proceedings* 532; A. Guzman, 'Why Do LDCs Sign Treaties That Hurt Them? Explaining the Popularity of Bilateral Investment Treaties' (1998) 38 *Virginia JIL* 639; K. J. Vandevelde, 'Investment Liberalisation and Economic Development: The Role of Bilateral Investment Treaties' (1998) 36 *Columbia Journal of Transnational Law* 501; K. J. Vandevelde, 'The Economics of Bilateral Investment Treaties' (2000) 41 *Harvard ILJ* 469; S. Gross, 'BITs, Non-NAFTA MITs and Host-State Regulatory Freedom – An Indonesian Case Study' (2003) 24 *Michigan JIL* 893. A bibliography can be found in (1992) 7 *ICSID Rev* 231.

[19] E. Denza and S. Brooks, 'Investment Protection Treaties: The United Kingdom Experience' (1987) 36 *ICLQ* 908 at 912. White seems to agree with this view. G. White, 'The New International Economic Order: Principles and Trends', in H. Fox (ed.), *International Economic Law and Developing States* (1992), vol. 2. The view was stated by Mann that such treaties contribute to the development of customary international law: F. A. Mann, 'British Treaties for the Promotion and Protection of Foreign Investment' (1981) 52 *BYIL* 241. But, in a later contribution, his enthusiasm for such treaties was somewhat muted: F. A. Mann,

convinced as to the existence of a customary international law in the field covered by bilateral investment treaties. It is doubtful whether there ever was much customary international law on the point. The existence of such customary international law is difficult to establish, as a large part of the world's community of states objected to the creation of such customary law, particularly during the early decades of bilateral investment treaty practice.[20] It may be claimed that the treaties stabilise pre-existing practices and will contribute to the creation of customary principles in this area in the future. The stridency with which the claim that these treaties create customary law may be due to the fact that the treaties provide a means for creating a universally applicable body of law when attempts at creating a multilateral treaty on investments failed. But, this failure is in itself due to an absence of a belief in the existence of universal principles on the subject. In the circumstances, the notion that a customary body of law has emerged is illusory. The debate justifies a closer examination. Such an examination is made in the last section of this chapter.

The opposing view is that the states making such treaties create *lex specialis* as between themselves, and in doing so are motivated by the uncertain state of the existing international law on foreign investment protection. It is, of course, possible that, if there is a concordance of standards in these bilateral investment treaties, such standards could become customary international law. For, it is well established that principles in bilateral treaties can become international law because they evidence the consistent agreement of states as to the existence of principles just as much as multilateral treaties do. They are also evidence of the customary practices of states.[21] But, there is so much divergence in the standards in bilateral investment treaties that it is premature to conclude that they give rise to any significant rule of international law.[22] Though the outer shell of bilateral investment treaties looks similar, thus contributing to the claim that they create customary international law, a deeper examination would indicate that the contents of the treaties vary so greatly that each must be considered a carefully balanced accommodation reached after negotiation between the parties.[23] Even an examination of the practice of a single

'Foreign Investment in the International Court of Justice: The ELSI Case' (1992) 86 *AJIL* 92. German lawyers concede that the German treaties (which provide the model for European practice) do not constitute customary international law or even state practice, but show 'that there are reciprocal interests between the investor and the host state leading to a mutually agreed standard of protection'. A. Weber, 'Investments Risks and International Law', in T. Oppermann and E. Petersmann (eds.), *Reforming the International Economic Order* (1987), p. 36 at p. 37. The view among US lawyers also seems to be that the treaties contribute to customary law. This is a parochial view, based largely on an examination of US treaties. It is summarily dismissed in the preliminary award in *UPS* v. *Canada*, UNCITRAL Arbitration Proceedings (NAFTA) (Award on the Merits, 24 May 2007), para. 97: '[W]hile bilateral investment treaties are large in number, their coverage is limited . . . and in terms of *opinio iuris* there is no indication that they reflect a general sense of obligation.'

[20] The 1960s and 1970s were the heyday of the New International Economic Order, through which developing states canvassed a system that stood in opposition to the normative system favoured by developed states.

[21] S. Rosenne, *Developments in the Law of Treaties* (1989), p. 124: '[T]he law generative role of the international treaty may be its most important function, and its most durable.' But, the law-creating function of bilateral treaties is diminished by the fact that most of them have an impact on domestic legal systems and are prone to be interpreted differently by national courts. Extradition treaties and double taxation treaties are examples. Due to the differences in interpretation, the opportunity for standards emerging from such treaties is reduced.

[22] The present writer took this view in 1986 See M. Sornarajah, 'State Responsibility and Bilateral Investment Treaties' (1986) 20 *JWTL* 79. Despite the growth in the number of bilateral investment treaties, there has been no reason to change this conclusion. More recent studies also indicate that it is premature to regard these treaties as creating customary law. J. W. Salacuse, 'BIT by BIT: The Growth of Bilateral Investment Treaties and Their Impact on Foreign Investment in Developing Countries' (1990) 24 *International Lawyer* 655 at 660, states that the purpose of the treaties was to establish 'specific legal rules' as between the parties.

[23] The US treaties are very similar to each other. But, US treaty practice does not make international law (or, so one assumes).

state like China would indicate that its treaties varied at different times, and that they were motivated by different considerations as circumstances changed.[24] These treaties are best seen as creating *lex specialis* between the parties rather than as creating customary principles of international law.[25] Yet, the widespread belief in their significance among international lawyers and the fact that they have the potential for the creation of customary principles of international law contribute to the importance of these treaties. More importantly, the treaties are the basis of a rapidly increasing body of arbitral awards explaining and interpreting the standards of protection contained in them. The awards and the commentaries based on them have been a rich source of the law on the subject. The treaties assume great significance as a result. Since many differences have arisen as to the interpretation of similar provisions in these treaties, there is some scepticism expressed as to the legitimacy of the investment protection that has been created by the treaties.

Another feature of bilateral investment treaties is that they are made between unequal partners.[26] They entrench an inequality that has always attended this area of international law. They are usually agreed between a capital-exporting developed state and a developing state keen to attract capital from that state. The observation that developing countries make such treaties among themselves does not obscure the fact that one of these countries is an exporter of capital *vis-à-vis* the other.[27] The rationale for the treaty itself is the promise of protection for the capital that is so received. Though the treaty contemplates a two-way flow of investments between the states parties to the treaty, it is usually only a one-way flow that is contemplated and feasible in reality in the context of the disparities of wealth and technology between the two parties. There is an insufficient *quid pro quo* in that the two-way flow that is openly stated as the basis of the treaties is often a fiction. There are interesting problems that arise as a result of this inequality of bargaining power. It is unrealistic to expect some of the developing countries which are signatories to these treaties to have government legal departments sophisticated enough to understand the nuances in the variations in the language that is used in these treaties.[28] There may be a basis for the suspicion that these treaties are signed in the belief that they will result in the inflow of foreign investment. They do not contain any firm obligation on the part of the

---

[24] N. Gallagher and W. Shan, *Chinese Investment Treaties: Policy and Practice* (2009). C. Congyan, 'China–US BIT Negotiations and the Future of Investment Treaty Regime: A Grand Bilateral Bargain with Multilateral Implications' (2009) 10 *Journal of International Economic Law* 1.

[25] *AAPL* v. *Sri Lanka* (1992) 17 *YCA* 106; (1991) 30 *ILM* 577. Both the award and the dissent make frequent references to the investment treaty between the United Kingdom and Sri Lanka being *lex specialis*. The award, in particular, contrasted the rules of the treaty with customary principles.

[26] J. W. Salacuse, 'BIT by BIT: The Growth of Bilateral Investment Treaties and Their Impact on Foreign Investment in Developing Countries' (1990) 24 *International Lawyer* 655 at 663, observed: '[I]n reality, an asymmetry exists between the parties.' See also J. E. Alvarez, 'The Development and Expansion of Bilateral Investment Treaties: Remarks' (1992) 86 *ASIL Proceedings* 532 at 552, where he said: 'BIT partners turn to the United States with the equivalent of an IMF gun pointed at their heads; others feel that, in the absence of a rival superpower, economic relations with the one that remains are inevitable. For many, a BIT relationship is hardly a voluntary, uncoerced transaction.' He goes on to describe the treaty as 'a one-way ratchet designed to benefit multinationals' (*ibid.*, p. 555).

[27] For example, when Singapore makes a treaty with Bangladesh, Singapore is seeking to protect the low-technology, labour-intensive industries its foreign investors relocate in Bangladesh. The existence of these treaties does not diminish the fact that there is an inequality in the relationship as there are no mutual flows of investments which take place.

[28] This is particularly so in view of the very unexpected interpretations that are now being placed on the NAFTA provisions on foreign investment. The meaning of the so-called umbrella clauses provides an interesting example of creative extrapolations: *SGS* v. *Pakistan* (2004, unreported).

capital-exporting state to ensure that such flows actually take place. In the belief that foreign investment flows will be forthcoming, there is a surrender of sovereignty on the part of the state that hopes to receive the capital by way of foreign investment. Sovereignty is ceded as the foreign investment subject to the treaty receives external protection from international dispute-settlement mechanisms and is insulated from the reach of the local laws to a considerable extent.

From the perspective of reforming these treaties, there is now a greater awareness of the inequality that is involved in these treaties and the requirement to bring about a balance. Thus, the commentary to the new model bilateral investment treaty of Norway[29] states that the new model was premised on 'a desire to lead the development from one-sided agreements that safeguard the interests of the investor to comprehensive agreements that safeguard the regulative needs of both developed and developing countries, making investors accountable while ensuring them predictability and protection'.[30] However, Norway's perception is not shared by all developed countries.[31] The basic inequality that attends these treaties will remain, as it is an essence of the treaty. There is an obvious lack of a need for such treaties to be made between developed states.[32] Yet, such an essential balance would be brought about by the fact that developed states see the need to protect their own domestic interests in the face of changing investment patterns which see massive influxes taking place from the newly industrialising countries like China, India and Brazil. Faced with this change, the newer treaties of the developed states are evincing a movement towards preserving regulatory space to interfere with foreign investment arrangements if public interests so dictate. This changed perception will require developed states to move away from the emphasis on protection of investments. Yet, the inequality in the bargaining power will not diminish significantly, as enforcement resources will continue to remain unequal.[33]

Despite the existence of inequality, there is an external validity to these treaties. States which conclude them must be presumed to have intended to be bound by them. It is unlikely that, if any doctrine of unequal treaties does exist outside the field of coercion, it could be applied to the situation of bilateral investment treaties.[34] Bilateral investment treaties are voluntary, and there is no element of coercion involved in their making.[35]

---

[29] Due to widespread disagreement, this new model did not come into existence.   [30] Note to the draft.

[31] Norway itself has shown reluctance to act on the model.

[32] NAFTA's investment provisions may be cited against this view. But, these investment provisions were directed at Mexico, though they had unintended consequences of resulting in disputes involving the United States and Canada.

[33] There is obviously greater sophistication in the legal resources a developed state can muster to deal with investment issues.

[34] On unequal treaties, see I. Detter, 'The Problem of Unequal Treaties' (1966) 14 *ICLQ* 1069, who regarded capitulation treaties entered into between China and European powers as unequal and subject to annulment. Parallels can be drawn between, on the one hand, the capitulation treaties which wholly insulated European traders from the scope of local laws and, on the other hand, bilateral investment treaties the purpose of which is to insulate foreign investors at least partially from the scope of local laws.

[35] Whether the approach of the United States, which has a pre-announced model bilateral treaty from which it does not permit significant variations, makes the situation different is an issue that must be raised. The charge that the treaties are unequal may gain credence if signing them is made a condition for aid, for access to preferential treatment in trade matters and for the granting of loans. In *Santa Elena* v. *Costa Rica* (2000) 39 *ILM* 317; (2002) 5 *ICSID Reports* 153, the award mentions that the dispute was arbitrated under the treaty because of the possibility of aid being refused under the Hickenlooper Amendment.

The developing state which enters into such treaties does so freely, in the belief that such treaties will promote the flow of foreign investments from the other contracting state.[36] Unless there is compelling evidence of coercion, one must proceed on the basis that these treaties are voluntarily made. Such evidence may exist where the signing of the treaty is made conditional on the granting of aid, loans or trade preferences.[37]

The significance of these treaties for the international law on foreign investment is no doubt tremendous. But, care must be taken not to overstate their importance. For one, there is a slowing down of treaty-making with the retreat of neo-liberalism. Treaties may not be extended beyond their termination dates, or, when extended, their provisions may come to be renegotiated. The fact that their existence had led to large numbers of investment claims resulting in heavy damages in excess of the reserves of affected states will lead to a rethinking of their utility.[38]

Developing states will also be wary of the claims that are made on the basis of these treaties. The exorbitant claim that the treaties create customary international law has already been dismissed. But, other avenues of creating universal norms through the backdoor on the basis of investment treaties should be noted. One would be to argue that a regime of investment protection is created. This creative use of the regime theory argues that the establishment of definite rules of protection and treatment with a dispute-resolution system through a network of bilateral investment treaties creates a regime on investment protection.[39] It is highly unlikely that such a regime has come about simply because, as in the case of customary international law, there is simply a lack of concordance in the treaty principles. Another technique employed to argue for the same result uses the most-favoured-nation clauses in the treaties to argue that the best standard of protection with a near-universality of acceptance may be created through the exercise of isolating the best standard that is to be found in the different treaties and arguing for their incorporation in existing treaties through the most-favoured-nation clause, thereby creating a network of norms that apply universally. These different techniques of creating universally applicable norms are considered more fully in the next chapter.

Before dealing with modern bilateral investment treaties, it is useful to examine the treaties of 'friendship, commerce and navigation' which were the precursors to the bilateral investment treaty. The experience that was gained with these treaties shaped the formulation of bilateral investment treaties.

---

[36] Nevertheless, suspicions will be raised as to their real nature. Asante skirts close to calling them unequal treaties. Doubts are raised as to whether the nuances in the different terminology that is used are understood by developing country advisers. In some instances, high officials in the developing state are even unaware that such treaties have been concluded. S. K. B. Asante, 'International Law and Investments', in M. Bedjaoui (ed.), *International Law: Achievements and Prospects* (1991), p. 667 at p. 675. Many are made as a result of advice given by international financial institutions or are made because of conditions attached to loans granted by these institutions.

[37] OPIC, an insurance scheme established by the US government, does not insure foreign investments flowing into states which do not have investment treaties with the United States. There is evidence in the publications of the World Bank that the Bank promotes investment treaties. Anecdotal evidence suggests that loans are made conditional on signing investment treaties.

[38] It has been suggested that, in the case of Pakistan, the awards given in three disputes exceeded the foreign exchange reserves of that country.

[39] J. W. Salacuse, 'The Treatification of International Investment Law' (2007) 13 *Law and Business Review of the Americas* 155.

2. Treaties of friendship, commerce and navigation

Bilateral treaties for the protection of trading interests have been in existence from early times.[40] The progenitors of the modern bilateral investment treaty were the treaties on 'friendship, commerce and navigation' (FCN) which were concluded from the eighteenth century onwards.[41] The United States concluded such treaties in large numbers with its allies, and many of them have been the subject of both domestic and international litigation.[42] One clear purpose of these treaties is to tie many states of the world to alliances with the United States. The treaties were not confined to commerce. They extended to military matters such as access to ports and navigation through internal waters. The early treaties were designed at a time when commerce was largely restricted to trading in goods by merchants and did not contemplate direct investment by corporations.[43]

The treaties emphasised the protection that should be accorded to individual aliens, as trading was largely done by individuals establishing themselves overseas for the purposes of trade. This may indicate a linkage between trade and investment, a much searched-for link in modern times in formulating a thesis that trade and investment are interlinked and must therefore be provided for in instruments attached to institutions that are linked with trade. The treaties dealt with a variety of matters concerning alien treatment, including freedom of worship and travel within the host state. The FCN treaty contained almost a charter of the rights that the alien was to enjoy in the host state, often listing his due process and procedural rights in the case of arrest and criminal trial. Post-Second World War treaties were more investment-specific, and provided for the making of investments by corporations and for the freedom of establishment in the host state. To the extent that the early FCN treaty was not specific to investment, the FCN treaty may not be the precursor of the modern bilateral investment treaty, but its investment provisions contain many features which are now found in a more refined way in bilateral investment treaties. The wide use of the most-favoured-nation clause in the FCN treaty was taken over into later bilateral investment treaties. The treaties made after the Second World War provided for national treatment as regards entry and establishment for corporations of the state

---

[40] H. Neufeld, *The International Protection of Private Creditors from the Treaty of Westphalia to the Congress of Vienna* (1971); see also *Sumitomo Shoji America Inc.* v. *Avagliano*, 457 US 176 (1982), for a discussion by the US Supreme Court of the history of these treaties.

[41] A treaty between France and the United States concluded in 1778 is reputed to be the first such treaty. See further K. J. Vandevelde, *United States Investment Treaties: Policy and Practice* (1992).

[42] The United States relied on the FCN treaty with Italy for developing many of its propositions as to liability in the *ELSI Case* [1989] *ICJ Reports* 15. There were also frequent references to the treaty with Iran in the awards of the Iran–US Claims Tribunal. But, other states' use of these treaties to enable the International Court of Justice to assume jurisdiction over the United States has caused considerable concern. The FCN treaty was used by Nicaragua to bring its case against the United States before the Court in *Nicaragua* v. *United States* [1984] *ICJ Reports* 352. Iran now has a claim regarding the shooting down of a civilian airliner before the Court, where jurisdiction is also sought to be established on the basis of an FCN treaty. In *Sumitomo Shoji America Inc.* v. *Avagliano*, 457 US 176 (1982), the treaty was used in its defence by a Japanese company charged with discrimination in employment practices.

[43] For the treaty practice of the United States, see D. Foster, 'Some Aspects of the Commercial Treaty Program of the United States – Past and Present' (1946) 11 *Law and Contemporary Problems* 647; H. Walker, 'Modern Treaties of Freedom, Commerce and Navigation' (1958) 42 *Minnesota LR* 805; H. Walker, 'Post-War Commercial Treaty Program of the United States' (1958) 73 *Political Science Quarterly* 57; R. Wilson, *United States Commercial Treaties and International Law* (1960).

parties.[44] The dispute-settlement mechanisms in FCN treaties were considerably strengthened in the later bilateral treaties. The experience of the FCN treaties certainly helped to formulate later bilateral investment treaties which dealt with the more specific needs of foreign investors.

FCN treaties belonged to a different age and contained many features which would not be accepted by many states in modern times. They provided for an unlimited right of entry and establishment of business. They provided early instances of the right to entry and establishment which are now recognised in modern investment provisions such as those in Chapter 11 of the North American Free Trade Agreement (NAFTA) and in US bilateral investment treaties. The FCN treaties were undoubtedly measures for spreading the influence of the major powers. They were concluded with smaller, less powerful states, which could be tied to the larger power in the context of the bipolar world that existed at the time the treaties were signed. With changes in the economic and power balances and in the internal structure of the states, FCN treaties came to be used in ways quite unintended by the powerful state which secured the treaty. Thus, the FCN treaty between Japan and the United States, which permits access to and establishment in the Japanese market, has come to be used by Japan for making claims of access to US markets at a time when there was a dramatic change in the economic balance between the two states.[45] Not only is access claimed on the basis of the treaty, but claims are also made as to exemptions from domestic laws such as those on non-discrimination in employment.

Nicaragua has used the dispute-settlement provisions of its FCN treaty with the United States to establish jurisdiction in its claims against the United States regarding the military intervention of the United States in Nicaragua's internal affairs.[46] Similar use of an FCN treaty was made by Iran in the *Oil Platforms Case*. The fact that worms may turn and the treaty may be used against the more powerful party will lead to a rethinking of the usefulness of these broadly framed treaties. The past is instructive for the future. It appears that the provisions of the NAFTA dispute-settlement procedure are having consequences quite unintended by the parties to the agreement. Several claims have been made against Canada and the United States on the basis of the investment provisions of NAFTA, testing the limits of the treaty, and these developed states are largely taking refuge in

---

[44] In *Sumitomo Shoji America Inc. v. Avagliano*, 457 US 176 (1982), it was held that the foreign corporation could incorporate in the host state which was party to the treaty as a result of the freedom of access provided by the FCN treaty, and thereafter it acquires the nationality of the state of incorporation, thus becoming entitled to the same treatment as other corporate nationals.

[45] The arguments based on the treaty bestowing powers on a company to use its own employment practices were used by the defendant Japanese company in *Sumitomo Shoji America Inc. v. Avagliano*, 457 US 176 (1982). The Supreme Court sidestepped the argument by holding that the Japanese company was a US corporate national as it had incorporated in the United States, and that it could not therefore claim the treaty rights. This would mean that a Japanese employer, choosing not to incorporate in the United States, could violate US laws against discrimination with impunity. The result was never thought of at the time of the treaty simply because the economic dominance of Japan was not contemplated at the time. In a later case, *Fortino v. Quasar Co.*, 950 F 2d 389 (1991), the right of a Japanese subsidiary to employ Japanese personnel in preference to Americans was recognised on the basis of the provisions of the FCN treaty. The decision has been criticised: S. Mozarsky, 'Defining Discrimination on the Basis of National Origin under Article VII(1) of the Friendship Treaty Between United States and Japan' (1992) 15 *Fordham ILJ* 1099.

[46] *Nicaragua Case* [1984] *ICJ Reports* 352.

the same arguments relating to sovereignty and regulatory control which developing states have made in the past. With reverse flows of foreign investment from the newly industrialising states into the developed world, existing investment treaties will increasingly be used by investors of these states against their developed host states.[47] Apart from this, the FCN treaty has few bases for comparison with the more focused investment treaties of modern times.

The history of FCN treaties also demonstrates that, at different periods of time, changes to treaties would take place and that the use to which the treaties are put will also change. FCN treaties, while they were extant, showed variations which can be explained as responses to changes in circumstances. That they could be put to use by friends who later become adversaries is evident from the cases brought against the United States on the basis of these treaties by Nicaragua and Iran. Thus, treaties could have unintended consequences and unintended uses subsequent to their making.

This is also the case with the later investment treaties which the United States made. Model investment treaties are redrafted with the benefit of earlier experiences. This is evident from studies of the practice of US investment treaties. The various models of these treaties underwent changes in response both to past experience as well as to changing circumstances.[48] The original model underwent changes after the period of liberalisation giving rise to a new approach.[49] It would appear that the purists are disappointed with the new 2004 model treaty which dismantles many of the inflexible investment protection standards of the 1992 model treaty. It roots the fair and equitable standard firmly in the customary law international minimum standard. In light of the experience in *Metalclad*, which was argued on the basis of sovereign regulatory control, the new model circumscribes the category of indirect expropriations and affirms the rule on regulatory takings, states a national security exception and excludes some categories of dispute, such as tax disputes, from arbitration. Knowing that they are among the largest recipients of investment capital and that they are exposed to investment arbitration has helped to concentrate the minds of Europe and the United States, which has led to a rethinking of the investment treaty system and a search for what commentators describe as more balanced treaties. The question is whether there could be balance between two mutually exclusive notions.

---

[47] An interesting instance of the use of the UK–India treaty is the arbitration brought by an Indian investor against the UK alleging discrimination in the law practice he had established in the UK: *Sanchetti* v. *United Kingdom*. A Court of Appeal judgment regarding stay of proceedings relating to contractual claims under the lease was refused on 11 November, 2008. (*Sanchetti* v. *City of London* [2008] EWCA Civ 1283). The complaints involved racial discrimination and harassment by the City of London against the claimant, an Indian solicitor who had set up practice in London. There is also a case pending against Germany: *Vattenfall AG* v. *Federal Republic of Germany* (Request for ICSID arbitration filed on 30 March 2009).

[48] The changes can be studied through the writings of Kenneth Vandevelde whose writings reflect the gamut of changes that the US treaties have undergone. K. Vandevelde, *United States Investment Treaties: Policy and Practice* (1992); K. J. Vandevelde, 'Investment Liberalisation and Economic Development: The Role of Bilateral Investment Treaties' (1998) 36 *Columbia Journal of Transnational Law* 501; and, more recently on the 2004 model investment treaty of the United States, see K. Vandevelde, 'Comparison Between the 2004 and the 1992 Model Investment Treaties' (2008) 1 *Yearbook of International Investment Law* 257. For a conservative reaction to the 2004 model, see S. Schwebel, 'The US 2004 Model Bilateral Investment Treaty: An Exercise in the Regressive Development of International Law', in *Liber Amicorum Robert Briner* (2005).

[49] In *Methanex*, the United States made arguments which were sovereignty based. They were arguments heavily reminiscent of the New International Economic Order rhetoric.

3. Reasons for making bilateral investment treaties

There were several unsuccessful attempts at multilateral treaties on foreign investment protection.[50] The reasons for the failure of these attempts are obvious. The issues that relate to foreign investments made by large multinational corporations give rise to sensitive issues of sovereignty, exploitation of natural resources and internal economic policies. It is unlikely that developing states will commit themselves readily on such issues in a binding multilateral treaty, though developed states will be keen to realise such a treaty.[51] In the decades after decolonisation, developing states have been striving to bring about a New International Economic Order (NIEO), one facet of which is national control over all foreign investment. Though the vigour of the movement for the NIEO has now dissipated, there has been no urgency among developing states to dismantle the gains that resulted during that period. Hence, it is unlikely that developing states will surrender their efforts to establish national control as the prevailing general standard by subscribing to a multilateral treaty which strikes at the principle of national control. The efforts at drafting multilateral instruments on investment will continue, but the possibility of agreeing strong rules in such an instrument remain a distant possibility. This is particularly so after the global economic crisis which commenced in 2008. There is a return to regulatory control of the economy in both the developed and the developing world. It is unlikely, in that context, that states will be willing to be constrained by a multilateral treaty on investment, or, for that matter, by bilateral treaties with inflexible rules.

Yet, bilateral treaties are different in that they are made on an *ad hoc* basis, and their ability to give rise to general principles is remote. In addition, such treaties could be negotiated in such a way as to suit the mutual interests of the parties, whereas a multilateral treaty cannot be. Bilateral solutions become necessary simply because of an absence of a consensus on multilateral norms.[52]

The rules on investment protection became considerably diffuse in the post-colonial era as a result of concerted attacks by developing states on the rules contended for by developed states. Contractual regimes on the basis of which foreign investments were made were being replaced by new contractual techniques that were favourable to national control of the investment. The rules of state responsibility and the minimum standards of treatment of aliens were being attacked not only by Latin American states but also by other developing states. The norm of prompt, adequate and effective compensation in the event of the expropriation of foreign property, which had been consistently supported by the developed states, was threatened by a competing notion of appropriate compensation. Whereas the previous tendency had been to create doctrines that favoured the insulation of

[50] See Chapter 6 below. Early attempts are described in G. Schwarzenberger, *Foreign Investments and International Law* (1969), pp. 109–20.

[51] The keenness of the developed states is also suspect after the experience of the effort at the OECD's multilateral agreement on investment, which was an effort made entirely by developed states to create a multilateral agreement. Discord broke out among the developed states on several provisions. This is dealt with in Chapter 6 below.

[52] For a similar view in a different context, see A. Carty, 'Critical International Law: Recent Trends in the Theory of International Law' (1991) 2 *EJIL* 66.

foreign investment through theories of internationalisation of foreign investment, there were now competing norms such as the doctrine of permanent sovereignty over natural resources, economic self-determination and national control over all economic activities. These norms sought to localise the foreign investment process by vesting control in the hands of the host state. Though much of the acrimony that attended the debate has subsided, the ideas that were generated in the course of the tussle of norms still persist. They led to regulatory legislation in the developing world, controlling the entry of investments and their subsequent operation within the host state. The system of norms so constructed stood in stark opposition to the system of norms that were favoured by the developed states that emphasised the protection of foreign investment. The legislation that was enacted during the period remains largely intact, despite the period of neo-liberalism that led to the explosion of investment treaties. This disjunct between national laws and international obligations is a reason for much of the difficulties that arise in the area. Unless the treaties had provisions preserving the local laws and regulations, the situation was ripe for disputes.

In this confused state of conflicting norms, bilateral investment treaties provided the parties with the opportunity to set out definite norms that would apply to investments made by their nationals in each other's territory. It would be wrong to subscribe to the thesis that the treaties stabilised customary international law. If there was a definite conviction as to the existence of customary international law in the area, there would have been little need for such frenetic treaty-making activity on investment protection. There was an absence of significant customary international law in this area simply because it would be difficult to show that there was free consent on the part of all the developing states to the creation of any customary principles in the area. If there was such customary international law, many developing states would regard themselves as persistent objectors who were not bound by the customary law. If there was customary international law on investment protection, there was no need to confirm time and time again what already existed by making bilateral investment treaties. States, which entered into investment treaties, were not engaging in such a stultifying exercise by repeatedly confirming what already existed. On the contrary, knowing the confused state of the law, they entered into such treaties so that they could clarify the rules that they would apply in case of any dispute which arose between them.

The view that there has been an absence of a rapid development of international law to meet the needs of foreign investment was stated by the International Court of Justice in the *Barcelona Traction Case* in the following terms:

Considering the important developments of the last half-century, the growth of foreign investments and the expansion of international activities of corporations, in particular of holding companies, which are often multinational, and considering the way in which the economic interests of states have proliferated, it may at first sight appear surprising that the evolution of the law has not gone further and that no generally accepted rules in the matter have crystallised on the international plane.[53]

---

[53] [1970] *ICJ Reports* 3.

There was a need for rapid development of the law in this area, but such development was not forthcoming because of the conflicts which were inherent in the area of foreign investment. Hence, states had to resort to the second-best solution by making bilateral investment treaties to ensure that, as between them at least, there would be definite rules relating to foreign investment. This is a better explanation for the rapidity with which such treaties have come about on the international scene than the explanation that they merely confirm existing customary international law or create new customary international law.

In recent times, the states of the old Soviet bloc, now turning towards a market economy and foreign investment, have begun making bilateral investment treaties with capital-exporting countries. The practice began even when communism was still in place as the Eastern bloc countries were desperately short of capital and looked to foreign investment to provide it. The remaining communist states have also made several investment treaties. China, which announced its 'open door' policy in 1984, signed over 100 such treaties within a short period.[54] Vietnam has also joined the trend. There are also treaties between developing countries.[55] In the case of the remaining communist states and the former communist states, the reasons for this treaty activity may be to dispel perceptions that they are high-risk countries because of past ideological commitments that opposed the influx of foreign investments and the notion of private ownership of property.[56] The treaties have a signalling function in that they are addressed to the investment community to indicate a major change of policy undertaken by a country in relation to foreign investment.[57] But, having faced a spate of arbitration awards against them, some of these states are now having second thoughts about the utility of these treaties.[58]

The sudden spurt of treaty-making in the 1990s was due to a variety of factors. The lack of funds for economic development consequent upon the loan defaults in the previous years caused sovereign lending by banks to dry up. The flow of aid also dwindled due to recession in the developed economies as well as due to changes of policy. Economic liberalism being the prevailing philosophy in the United States and Europe, there were

---

[54] UNCTAD, *World Investment Report, 2003*.

[55] Two such treaties are the treaties between Singapore and Sri Lanka and between Thailand and Bangladesh. In these treaties, too, it is a one-way relationship that is contemplated, Singapore and Thailand being capital-exporters while Sri Lanka and Bangladesh are recipients of capital. The reason for the flow may be that Singapore and Thailand are relocating less technology-intensive industries to Sri Lanka and Bangladesh as the latter are sources of cheap labour and also products made in these countries are able to obtain greater access to the markets of developed states due to the generalised system of preferences (GSP). Singapore was removed from the GSP list on the ground that it had become an industrialised country. Developing states which fear such graduation will seek to invest in other less developed countries in the hope of making use of cheaper labour and preferential access terms. They will need protection for their investments. The essential asymmetry involved in the investment treaties still remains, despite the fact that the treaties technically are between developing countries.

[56] See K. R. Propp, 'Bilateral Investment Treaties: The US Experience in Eastern Europe' (1992) 86 *ASIL Proceedings* 540.

[57] Thus, the Argentinian treaties, made in the 1990s, signalled a departure from the Calvo doctrines, which Argentina had hitherto adhered to, and a policy of assumption of international obligations in respect of investment flows into the country as regards investments from the treaty partners. It is a signal to other capital-exporting states of a willingness to sign similar treaties with them and to be accommodating to foreign investment from them. The change from the Calvo doctrine to the acceptance of investment treaties led to a spate of arbitrations against Argentina following the measures it took to deal with its economic crisis in 2002. This prompted Argentina to rethink its strategy as to investment treaties. It has resisted enforcement awards by seeking annulment. Recently, it did not deposit the sum necessary to suspend the enforcement of the *Sempra* award involving US$75 million. The stay of enforcement was lifted on 7 August 2009.

[58] The Czech Republic in particular has had to cope with several arbitrations. Some of them involved inconsistent awards arising from the same fact situation. Pakistan and the Philippines are other states which have had difficulties in rationalising the utility of the treaties after the awards made against them.

vigorous efforts made to promote the free market and liberalisation of the international economy. One phenomenon of these trends was the increase in bilateral investment treaties in the 1990s. They were seen as instruments that accomplished liberalisation in the sphere of foreign investment, not because they contained any norms on liberalisation itself,[59] but because of the belief that protection of foreign investment increased the flow of foreign investment.[60] The flow of foreign investment funds was seen as conducive to economic development. The view that securing foreign investment protection through investment treaties facilitated such flows was a reason given for the increase in the number of bilateral investment treaties.[61]

Though the number of these treaties may be increasing, their contents indicate the adoption of a variety of standards depending on the negotiating positions of the states involved. The treaties concluded in the 1990s show the vigour of the liberalising tendencies of economic liberalism. Yet, these treaties are disparate as to content. Only US and Canadian treaties provide for pre-entry establishment.[62] The repatriation of the profits of multinational corporations once they have gained entry is guaranteed through the provision of a right of repatriation in these treaties. The standards of protection are also intended to promote the flow of foreign investment. Often, the same state will accept varying standards on areas such as compensation for expropriation, the repatriation of profits and the arbitration of disputes that arise. The developed state will seek to extract as much protection for the investor as possible but often concedes the fact that this may not be possible. These concessions are seen in the exceptions to the general propositions contained in the treaties. Thus, the treaty may recognise the right of the foreign investor to repatriate profits, but also contain a provision that, in exceptional circumstances, such as a foreign exchange shortage, a state party may restrict repatriation to a percentage of the profits. The developing state will seek to concede as little as possible, ensuring that the treaty is consistent with its foreign investment laws and its national interests. Its interests always lie in giving up as little of its sovereign rights of control over the foreign investment as possible and preserving as much regulatory control over foreign investment as possible. In the reconciliation of these mutually incompatible aims, vague terms often come to be used in the treaties, making the protection they give to the foreign investors meagre. For this reason, each treaty must be taken as a bargain that has been struck between the parties, depending on their relative strengths and mutual dependence. This may also explain the reasons why the terms in the treaties differ to a considerable extent.

There are also differences that reflect the period in which the treaties were made. The provisions in the early treaties are often less stringent and formulated in nebulous

---

[59] Treaties, like the US treaty, which contained provisions on the right of entry and establishment were liberalisation treaties. Canada, Japan and South Korea began making such treaties. But, it was possible to exclude sectors from such pre-entry national treatment involved in the right of entry and establishment.

[60] Except for US and Canadian treaties, investment treaties seldom accepted pre-entry national treatment as an obligation.

[61] This is an untested hypothesis. Southeast Asian states which have received large investments from the United States do not have investment treaties with that country. Stability and other factors have a greater influence on investment flows than do investment treaties.

[62] With Japan and South Korea joining in later.

terms. The treaties show increasing sophistication as the practice develops. Thus, new dispute-settlement techniques are tried out, but there is doubt as to whether the full ramifications of the words used were really understood by both parties. There is also the suspicion that the making of the treaties was a condition for the granting of loans and rescue packages that were put together by financial institutions.

The claim is made that these treaties boost investor confidence in the host state and that as a result more investment flows take place. This is an untested claim. It is empirically untestable whether states will receive more investments if they conclude such treaties.[63] Many smaller developing states have signed a large number of treaties without witnessing significant inward investment flows. Nevertheless, the principal reasons for developing countries concluding such treaties is the belief that they will lead to greater investor confidence by dispelling any impression of risk associated with the country in the past. States with a record of nationalisation see such treaties as a panacea for their past deeds. Thus, Sri Lanka, after the fall of its socialist government which had embarked on a course of nationalisation, entered into seven treaties in three years, whereas it took Singapore and Malaysia twelve years to accomplish the same. There is nothing to show that there were greater investment flows into Sri Lanka than into Singapore and Malaysia as a result of these treaties. In reality, attracting foreign investment depends more on the political and economic climate being favourable to such foreign investment than on the creation of a legal structure for its protection.

The assumption behind the treaties is that the framework for protection they create leads to increased flows of foreign investment. This assumption is coming to be questioned. Institutions which have assiduously promoted investment treaties have expressed scepticism of the proposition that there is a correlation between investment treaties and flows of investment. They now seem to take the view that other factors such as political stability and economic circumstances play a greater role in promoting investment.[64]

4. Features of bilateral investment treaties

The structure of different bilateral treaties has a basic similarity. The treaty begins with a prefatory statement as to the aims of the treaty, which are usually the reciprocal encouragement and protection of investment flows between the two states. This is followed by an identification of the types of property which are protected and the nature of the link of nationality to one of the parties that entitles the foreign investor to the protection of the treaty. The standard of treatment to be accorded to the foreign investor is established.

---

[63] UNCTAD, *World Investment Report, 2003*, p. 89: 'An aggregate statistical analysis does not reveal a significant independent impact of bilateral investment treaties in determining FDI flows. At best, bilateral investment treaties play a minor role in influencing global FDI flows and explaining differences in their size among countries.' Similar conclusions are drawn in the World Bank, *World Development Report*, p. 129: 'Countries that had concluded a BIT were no more likely to receive additional FDI than were countries without such a pact.'

[64] As indicated earlier, there is increasing economic literature on this, but the debate as to the effect of the treaties is inconclusive. The dominant view, however, seems to be that there is little evidence of the treaties leading to significant inflows of foreign investment.

The right of repatriation of profits is asserted. There are statements on the nature of the compensation, if any, to be provided to the foreign investor for loss occurring during wars and civil riots. The standard of compensation in the event of a takeover of the foreign investor's property is identified. The procedure for the settlement of disputes arising from the investment by arbitration is stated. These are standard contents in all bilateral agreements. But, there are variations of the statements of the rules that are to be applied as between the parties on each of these areas. To understand these variations, it is necessary to analyse the contents of these treaties separately. The variations indicate the impossibility of customary principles arising from these treaties, however many of them there are.[65]

4.1 The statement of the purpose of the treaty

Every bilateral investment treaty begins with a declaration as to the purpose of the treaty. This is usually stated to be the reciprocal encouragement and protection of investments. The statement disguises the important fact that the flow that is contemplated is in reality a one-way flow of investment from the developed state to the developing state. The treaty starts with an inexactitude. There is an inequality inherent in the very process of making a treaty between the giver and the receiver. As pointed out earlier, there is an erosion of sovereignty by one party without a corresponding erosion in the other party. This erosion of sovereignty is based on an unprovable belief that greater investment flows will take place once the treaty is signed.

The extent to which this important consideration affects the whole process of making bilateral investment treaties is yet to be analysed, though writers have referred to the asymmetry inherent in the making of such treaties.[66] Sometimes, bilateral investment treaties are secured by the holding out of promises or threats of trade sanctions. Sometimes, the making of the treaty is made a condition for a loan. In this latter case, the problem of inequality becomes accentuated. Though it has not been suggested that these treaties are invalid because of their unequal nature, it is easy to foresee a state, pushed into a corner in an investment dispute, taking this path and arguing that the treaty is invalid. In such circumstances, the better view would be that, despite any argument as to inequality, the treaties, for whatever reason, were freely entered into and are valid. The motive of a state for entering into a treaty does not affect the validity of the treaty. The inequality in the bargaining power of the states is also irrelevant. However, where there had been inducements held out to the weaker state for making the treaty, the situation may be different. It would be interesting to speculate as to the

---

[65] There are no bilateral investment treaties between developed countries. The reference made to the existence of treaties between developing countries does not affect the fact that one of them is an exporter and the other a receiver of foreign investment. Two receivers of foreign investments do not sign such treaties.

[66] Thus, J. W. Salacuse, 'BIT by BIT: The Growth of Bilateral Investment Treaties and Their Impact on Foreign Investment in Developing Countries' (1990) 24 *International Lawyer* 655 at 662, observed:

A BIT purports to create a symmetrical legal relationship between the two states, for it provides that either party may invest under the same conditions in the territory of the other. In reality, an asymmetry exists between the parties to the bilateral investment treaties since one state will be the source and the other the recipient of any investment flows between the two countries.

effect of the treaty where the level of understanding of the treaty as between the officials of the state was different.[67]

An issue may arise as to whether the prefatory statement creates a positive duty on the part of the capital-exporting state to encourage its investors to take investments to the other party. Such a positive duty is not created by the prefatory clause itself, but there may be a duty on the part of the capital-exporting state to facilitate the making of investments in the host state by giving, at the least, the same assistance and facilities that are given to nationals making foreign investments in other states. Thus, where other investors are permitted to insure with the state insurance scheme for foreign investors, the state could be said to be under a duty to grant insurance to a foreign investor.[68] Where the parties undertake to encourage investment flows in a separate article rather than in the prefatory statement, the duty to encourage flows of foreign investment may be stronger.[69] But, the content of such a duty cannot be assessed, as the amount of the investment that should be encouraged under the treaty cannot be quantified. The duty so created is not a positive duty. It is satisfied so long as a state does not impede the flow of investments to the other contracting party.

The prefatory statement usually contains a statement of the beliefs of the parties that the flows of foreign investment between them are mutually beneficial to their economic development. One question that may arise is whether the treaty protection will apply to all investments or only to such investments as can be shown to contribute to the economic development of the host state. Can it be argued that the host state can escape its obligations by showing that a particular foreign investment coming from the capital-exporting state did not in fact contribute to its economic development or that it was positively harmful to such development and therefore fell outside the protection of the treaty? Can it be said that the prefatory statement showed that it was never the intention of the parties to protect an investment which did not promote economic development?

Within a few short years, views have been stated in arbitral awards that the fact that no development took place or that the investment had no potential for economic development would be a reason to deny the protection of the treaty to the particular foreign investment.[70] Whereas in the heyday of neo-liberalism, the assumption was readily made that all foreign investment was beneficial, it would appear that there is a new trend to determine whether or not the intention of the parties stated in the preamble that economic development should result from the flow of the foreign investment is emerging in the more

---

[67] Treaty law does not go behind the treaty and examine such issues. The fiction is that states are equal. This is an absurdity when most investment treaties between developing and developed states are made by persons unskilled in international law, on the one side, and a team of sophisticated lawyers and economists, on the other.

[68] Such insurance is not provided if foreign investors invest in states without treaties, which in itself is an inducement for developing states to make such treaties.

[69] Can a state argue that the treaty could be rescinded because this duty has not been satisfied? If so, how can the amount of investment that must be encouraged be quantified? Can a developing country justify its breach of the treaty on the ground that the failure of the developed state party to encourage a sufficient flow of foreign investments was a prior breach which gave it the right to regard the treaty as invalid? These are problems that arise, given the vague nature of some of the provisions of the investment treaties.

[70] For example, the *ad hoc* committee's decision in *Patrick Mitchell* v. *Congo*. The issue as to whether the investment must contribute to development for it to qualify for protection of the treaty is considered below.

recent arbitral awards. The awards are not in agreement, but it is a change in attitudes that must be recognised. The change is consistent with the principle stated in Article 31 of the Vienna Convention on the Law of Treaties that the preamble to a treaty indicates the context of the agreement and is relevant for its interpretation. The preamble will have increasing significance. A recent study by UNCTAD of investment treaties mentions that an increasing number of countries include specific language in the preamble to their treaties 'aimed at making clear that the objective of investment promotion and protection must not be pursued at the expense of other key public policy goals, such as the protection of health, safety, the environment and the promotion of internationally recognised labour standards'.[71] These encapsulate notions of development and it could well be that they would provide a genesis for the emergence of defences to liability in circumstances where it can be shown that the conduct of the foreign investor was harmful to the economic development of the host state.

The literature on the subject of bilateral investment treaties is usually laudatory of foreign investment. It takes the single view that foreign investment is beneficial and fashions rules as to its protection. This view has yet to change to accommodate the position that there could be different perceptions of foreign investments and that the law should not be guided by a single view on foreign investment. Such tussles as to whether only such investment as proves beneficial to the economic development of the host state – the premise which underlies the investment treaties – will be given due weight is one the law will increasingly face in the future.

4.2 Definitions

All the treaties seek to define some of the terms that are used in the treaty, and the definitions contained in them have some common elements that will contribute to the understanding of the usage of terms in international investment law. In addition, they also indicate the understanding states have on issues such as corporate nationality and thereby contribute to the stabilisation of theories that may be evolving in such areas. These are innovative features in the treaties. Some of the common terms that are defined in the treaties are considered below.

4.2.1 Investments

All treaties contain definitions of investments. Investments are usually defined as broadly as possible. They dispel any lingering doubts that may exist from early ideas that intangible property is not protected by international law. Many early texts contain the idea that the intangible property of an alien is incapable of protection by international law, presumably because the creation of intangible property is dependent on the laws of the host state. Rights to intellectual property such as patents, copyright and know-how, which are the intangible assets referred to most often in the context of international investment,

---

[71] UNCTAD, *Bilateral Investment Treaties 1995–2006: Trends in Investment Rule Making* (2007), p. 3.

vest in a person only to the extent that the local law recognises such rights. Hence, there was a view that the host state had absolute control over intangible property, as such rights were dependent on the law of the host state for their recognition. Rights of protection for shareholders were also seldom referred to. These rights were also created by reference to an entity whose existence depended on the law of the state of incorporation. Verdross, writing in 1931, excluded from his definition of property recognised by international law, 'so-called literary, artistic and industrial property'.[72] But, increasingly, it came to be recognised that the protection of intangible rights was central to investment protection. The concession agreement which was the principal vehicle of foreign investment in the mineral resources sector created contractual rights which were intangible. The idea that in these contractual situations what was being protected was an intangible contractual right and not the physical assets took time to evolve.[73] A series of cases dealt with the protection of such rights. In *Le Courturier* v. *Rey*,[74] the assets confiscated in France included trademarks. The dispute in the *Carl Zeiss Stiftung* cases[75] litigated in England and elsewhere also concerned trademarks. Many of the new forms of foreign investment contracts involved the transfer of intangible rights. Licensing agreements, management contracts and consultancy contracts had intangible assets as their subject-matter. Protection of foreign investment increasingly meant the protection of not only the physical assets of the investor but also the intangible assets that he took into the venture, which were often as valuable as or more valuable than the physical assets. It was possible to capitalise new ventures by transferring intangible assets such as technology or know-how to the ventures. Yet, as in domestic law, the original idea that rights in property related to physical property was difficult to shake off.

Bilateral investment treaties leave no room for doubt that they include intangible assets within the definition of property and often spell out the types of intangible assets protected by the treaty. Article 1 of the United Kingdom treaty with Singapore may be taken as representative of the types of property listed as protected by such treaties in some early treaties. The term 'investment' is defined as including: (1) movable and immovable property and property rights such as mortgages, liens and pledges; (2) shares, stocks and debentures in companies and other interests in companies; (3) claims to money or to any performance under contracts having a financial value; (4) intellectual property rights and goodwill; and (5) business concessions including concessions relating to natural resources. But, as treaty practice advances, the definition becomes more refined and seeks to capture new instruments that are associated with the making of investments within the definition of investment.

---

[72] A. Verdross, 'Les Règles Internationales Concernant le Traitement des Etrangers' (1931) 37 *Hague Recueil* 364; see also G. White, *Nationalisation of Foreign Property* (1961), pp. 421–30; in the *Chorzow Factory Case* (1928) PCIJ Series A No. 17, however, much emphasis was placed on the protection of know-how that was transferred in the calculation of the damages claimed by Germany.

[73] See Chapter 1 above. See also I. Brownlie, 'Legal Status of Natural Resources in International Law' (1979) 162 *Hague Recueil* 255; N. Schrijver, *Permanent Sovereignty over Natural Resources: Balancing Rights and Duties* (1997). Some treaties show little regard for the notion of permanent sovereignty over natural resources. Thus, the Australia–Vietnam treaty defines property that is protected to include contractual rights 'to engage in agriculture, forestry, fisheries and animal husbandry, to search for, extract or exploit natural resources and to manufacture, use and sell products'.

[74] [1910] AC 262. [75] [1967] 1 AC 853.

The US model bilateral investment treaty contains a longer list which includes, in addition to the five categories listed above, 'licenses and permits issued pursuant to law, including those issued for manufacture and sale of products' and 'any right conferred by law or contract, including rights to search for or utilise natural resources, and rights to manufacture, use and sell products'. These additions are not merely taken out of excessive caution, but are a recognition of the fact that many of the rights which the foreign investor obtains in host states are administrative law rights based on permission to conduct certain activities in the host state. The whole course of the foreign investment may depend on the existence of such public law rights. The investment will cease to be of much value if rights such as the right to export or repatriate profits initially granted are later withdrawn by the administrative agency which grants them.[76] The protection of such acquired rights and privileges is seen as a task of the bilateral investment treaty, and the US model seeks to achieve this by extending the definition of property to include these public law rights acquired under the host state's law in the definition of property. Whether the freezing of a decision taken in pursuance of the exercise of a discretionary power, though feasible in terms of law, is wise in terms of practice remains to be seen. The objection to it is that it excessively curtails the regulatory power of a state. The idea that the first exercise of a discretionary power is binding for all time is one that sits uneasily with administrative practice. Administrative decisions are made by a state having the public interest in mind. Whether a treaty should be able to fetter that discretion will always be a contentious issue. Many states overcome this problem by confining the investments that are protected by the treaty to investments which are made in accordance with their laws and regulations on investment.[77] This introduces even greater subjectivity and uncertainty into the treaty as local laws and regulations may be changed. The content of the treaty obligations could be manipulated simply through changes to laws and regulations.

From the point of view of the capital-exporting state, the stance adopted in the US model treaty safeguards the interests of US nationals given the increasing tendency to subject investments to screening and other administrative mechanisms instituted in the host state. The US treaties provide for open entry to US investments as well as for the protection of those investments.[78] But, the host state is unlikely to view the inclusion of the privileges it confers on the foreign investor under its public law as rights that are protected by an international treaty. The effect of the treaty would be to make the public law rights irrevocable once granted. This defeats the very notion of public law rights which are granted with the public interest in mind and become defeasible when they are no longer in the public interest. It is well accepted that any matter that falls within the domestic sphere can

---

[76] Some of the issues in *Amco* v. *Indonesia* concerned such administrative controls. The fact that the rights of the foreign investor are dependent on administrative decisions has been pointed out in Chapter 3 above.

[77] The formula used in Australian and Indonesian treaties is that only such investments 'made in accordance with the laws, regulations and policies, from time to time in existence' are protected. This introduces indeterminacy into the treaty, as a state could remove protection from an investment simply through a change of policy, regulation or law.

[78] The idea that the right of establishment must be provided for is taken over from the FCN treaties. See note by H. Golsong, (1992) 31 *ILM* 124. The FCN treaties had political objectives which dominated their economic objectives. The link between politics and investment has always been close but unobserved.

be brought within the sphere of international law by making it the subject of a treaty. But, it is unlikely that a state will lightly surrender its public law powers relating to the regulation of foreign investment. The inclusion of these public law rights will mean that rights that are granted in connection with the exploitation of natural resources cannot later be withdrawn without violating the treaty. The extent to which a state is willing to lose its regulatory powers over foreign investment through the creation of treaty rights in the foreign investor lies at the crux of the problem in this area. It also provides a setting for the theoretical conflict between those who believe that the expectations of the foreign investor at the time of entry should be protected through the life of the investment and those who believe in the right of the state to alter the bargain with the foreign investor in light of changing circumstances so as to reflect the public interest.

In the case of the protection of concession agreements, the consistency of a position that brooks no change to the original bargain with the notion of permanent sovereignty over natural resources, which some authorities regard as an *ius cogens* principle, will have to be considered.[79] It may well be argued that the removal of the public law rights of the host state relating to natural resources has no effect in law on the ground that it is contrary to an *ius cogens* principle.[80] There could be problems regarding other public law rights which the bilateral investment treaty seeks to ensure the continuity of, once granted. The treaty will remove the discretion of the granting state to interfere with this public law grant for the duration of the treaty. Whether such a freezing of the right created in pursuance of its discretionary power was contemplated by the developing state at the time it signed the treaty is conjectural. There is continuing disquiet expressed as to the extent of the sovereignty that has been unwittingly transferred over inherently sovereign functions through the treaty device.

There is little doubt that bilateral investment treaties contribute to the development of a concept of property in international law.[81] Its identification and inclusion of various types of intangible property is an important step towards the formulation of such a concept. The protection of tangible property was an easy notion to fit into the scheme of alien protection, as such property was often taken into the host state by the alien himself. In the case of intangible property, the difficulty was created by the fact that the right to such property depended on the extent to which the domestic law itself recognised it. It is now coming to be recognised that, once the right to such intangible property has been acquired under the domestic law of the host state by the alien, the acquired rights could be converted into rights protected by international law through bilateral investment treaties. In the absence of such treaty protection of such intangible rights, the old view that they are rights dependent on the law of the host state and may be extinguished in accordance with the law of the state must still be valid.

---

[79] See note 40 above.
[80] A treaty, conflicting with a peremptory norm of international law, is invalidated to the extent of the conflict by Article 53 of the Vienna Convention on the Law of Treaties. There is some authority for the view that the doctrine of permanent sovereignty over natural resources is a peremptory norm of international law. I. Brownlie, 'Legal Status of Natural Resources in International Law' (1979) 162 *Hague Recueil* 245 at 255.
[81] In earlier times, there was some doubt as to whether international law had a notion of property. The concept of territory was quite distinct.

But, the philosophical bases of the concept of property that is involved in various bilateral investment treaties differ markedly and influence the manner in which the treaty itself is formulated. The US treaties clearly give expression to a notion of property as an absolute and indefeasible right. Such a view is consistent with US constitutional thinking on the right to property. This notion is a unique product of US history. Transported to the United States, the Lockean notion of property as an indefeasible right of the individual found a hospitable home in the context of the history of a country in which land was cleared by labour and wrested from hostile natives and the elements by personal effort. It is this concept of property which finds expression in US investment treaties and US policies on investment protection which have influenced international law. It is not a notion of property that one finds in the English law. Nor is it to be found in the legal systems of the Commonwealth based on the English law. Like European systems, the common law recognises that the right to property is always defeasible in the public interest. This schism between attitudes to property is reflected in the bilateral investment treaties as well and to a large extent in the differing attitudes to investment protection. The arbitral awards that are made on the basis of investment treaties will increasingly reflect these different attitudes to property and its protection.

The neo-liberal view was that property protection was essential to economic development. The sanctity of transactions involving property and the ease and certainty of the transfer of property was regarded as essential for economic progress. The investment treaties seemed to adopt a similar attitude towards the protection of foreign investment. The idea was that it was essential for development that protection was afforded to foreign investment. This inflexible notion of property protection underlay investment treaties as well as arbitral awards interpreting the treaties. But, with the decline of neo-liberalism, the notion that the right to property was an indefeasible right also began to recede. An inflexible right to property that is contained in some investment treaties would sit uneasily with the statement of that right in constitutional systems.[82]

4.2.2 Limitation on the definition of investment

Though investments are defined as widely as possible, many bilateral investment treaties confine the benefits of the treaty only to investments approved by the state parties to the treaty.[83] This limitation, at once, creates two categories of foreign investment originating from the same state party, one which is protected by the treaty because it is approved by the

---

[82] See further Tom Allen, *The Right to Property in Commonwealth Constitutions* (2000). The balancing of social interests with individual interests is commonplace in European law. On the jurisprudence of the European Court of Human Rights, see *Kozacioglu* v. *Turkey* (Judgment, 19 February 2009).

[83] This limitation is to be found in the treaties made by Southeast Asian states. The treaties of Singapore and Malaysia contain the requirement that the investment must be approved for the purposes of investment. The newer Malaysian treaties offer protection only to investments made in accordance with the 'laws, regulations and policies' of Malaysia. In *Grueslin* v. *Malaysia* (2000) 5 *ICSID Reports* 483, the tribunal ruled that jurisdiction under the treaty could not be invoked by investors who did not have specific approval. Malaysia suffered an economic crisis and took exchange-control measures. But, foreign investors, like the claimant in *Grueslin* v. *Malaysia*, were not able to obtain relief. The comparison with Argentina, where investment was not so restrictively defined, is instructive. The liberalisation treaties Argentina signed did not contain such restrictions. The parties who do not qualify as investors or whose investments do not fall within the definition of investments will not be able to invoke the dispute-settlement provisions of the treaties. *Yaung Chi Oo Ltd* v. *Myanmar* (2003) 42 *ILM* 540; (2003) 8 *ICSID Reports* 463.

state party which receives the investment, and one which is not because it lacks such approval. Discrimination between investments is inherent in this situation.[84] This category of investment which is not approved by the host state is protected by whatever principles of investment protection there are in international law. Approved investments are entitled to the special protection devised by the treaty regime. The recognition of a distinction between approved investment and other investment itself indicates the *lex specialis* nature of bilateral investment treaties, for unapproved investments are subject to general norms of investment protection, if any exist, whereas approved investments are subject to the treaty regime.[85] The investments covered by the different treaties differ according to definition. In these circumstances, it is wishful thinking to contemplate the possibility of customary international law emerging from these treaties, a point that needs constant reassertion only for the reason that the view that investment treaties create customary law seems so tenacious despite the paucity of any evidence supporting it except the opinions of individual writers.

The distinction between approved and other investments comes about as a result of the systems for screening foreign investment entry maintained by host state laws. Some states require approval for all incoming foreign investments. Others maintain an open door for all foreign investments but give special privileges only to investments that secure approval. The approval is usually given only to such investments as are considered particularly beneficial to the host state and are subject to the satisfaction of conditions that may be imposed. Difficult problems could arise where the approval is later withdrawn by the state for non-satisfaction of the conditions. Does such withdrawal result in the investment losing the protection of the investment treaty as it will cease to be an approved investment? It would be better if this problem were to be ironed out by the treaty itself. One solution is to require that such withdrawal of approval is not made except on objective factors and that the investor can resort to domestic tribunals to test whether there was justification for the withdrawal of the approval.

Some treaties seek to meet the situation by treating the right of entry and establishment that is granted by the screening authority as investment rights to be protected by the treaty. It is a neat solution, but it is unlikely to be accepted by states which are keen on devising effective systems of investment screening. The whole object of the system is to keep out investments that do not promote the economic objectives of the state. The termination of investments that are seen to be inconsistent with these objectives will also be seen as necessary for the functioning of the scheme. The subjection of the right of termination to external scrutiny by submitting it to the protection of a bilateral treaty regime will therefore be resisted by many developing states.

---

[84] Such discrimination is based on objective, economic factors and does not offend any norm against discrimination involved in the provision of national treatment to all foreign investors. It is unlikely that racial discrimination is involved in such situations.

[85] This approval procedure proved crucial in *Yaung Chi Oo Ltd* v. *Myanmar* (2003) 42 *ILM* 540; (2003) 8 *ICSID Reports* 463, where the arbitral tribunal refused jurisdiction on the ground that there was no specific approval in writing as required by the ASEAN Investment Protection Treaty (1987). Also, where the regulatory laws of the state are not adhered to by the investor, he will lose the protection of the treaty, if the treaty had confined protection to investments that ensured conduct according to the regulations of the host state.

In view of these problems, a wider limitation on the type of investment that is subject to the protection of the treaty is emerging. This focuses on the issue of the internal laws and regulations of the host state. The limitation is to provide protection to the investments, however broadly defined, only if they are made according to the laws and regulations of the host state.[86] Some provisions indicate that the investments must continue to function according to the laws and regulations of the host state. Some even contemplate future changes to these laws and regulations and insist that only those foreign investments that comply with these laws and regulations 'from time to time in existence' will qualify for protection.[87] This indicates that many of the treaties which contain such limitations are uncertain as to the types of investment that they protect. For the host state could manipulate this through its own internal laws and regulations. Such treaties contain an internal device which leads to uncertainty. However elaborate their treatment or protection standards may be, the initial statement of the investments covered by the treaties in such uncertain terms makes these treaties quite unstable and subject to the caprices of each state party to the treaty. Such treaties err on the side of preserving the host state's right to regulation without balancing it with the right to protect the foreign investment. Even this short survey demonstrates the disparity as to the types of investment that different treaties protect.

4.2.3 Portfolio investments

In some treaties, portfolio investments are included in the definition of investments. Portfolio investments must be distinguished from primary shares in companies which are the vehicles for the foreign investment.[88] These are not shares that are ordinarily traded.[89] Portfolio investments are instruments which are either directly connected with the companies (such as shares) or are only indirectly connected with the companies (such as promissory notes and bonds). They are used in order to raise capital for ventures, and are freely circulated through stock exchanges or through other markets or means. The argument for the inclusion of portfolio investments is that they are an important means of encouraging capital flows, and that it is in the interests of developing states that their flows should be encouraged. The argument against including portfolio investments is that their inclusion in investment treaties means that the host state owes a duty of protection to unascertainable holders of these instruments whose identities would continuously change. In addition, because of the fact that they can be rapidly pulled out of a state, the value of such investment has come to be questioned in view of the financial crises that have been precipitated in the past through the sudden exodus of portfolio capital. *Fedax* v. *Venezuela*[90] is an interesting decision. The domestic holders of promissory notes, who were not entitled to any

---

[86] *Fraport* v. *Philippines* (ICSID, 2007); *Inceysa* v. *El Salvador* (ICSID, 2006).

[87] The formula is to be found in the Australia–Indonesia investment treaty and in some of the older Australian treaties.

[88] As where a foreign investor becomes a shareholder in a joint-venture company the creation of which is mandated as the form of entry of foreign investment by the host state.

[89] This distinction is unfortunately not made in some of the literature which asserts, on the basis of the protection of shares in companies like joint-venture companies which are the vehicles of foreign investment, that portfolio investment is protected. This is erroneous.

[90] (1998) 37 *ILM* 1378.

protection, transferred the notes to foreign citizens of a state with an investment treaty, who then became entitled to claim against the state on the basis that the treaty protected portfolio investments. The case illustrates the problems that attend the inclusion of portfolio investments in investment treaties. Policy on portfolio investment varies. While there are treaties which include portfolio investments, there are also treaties which expressly exclude them.[91] There are widely drafted formulations which clearly take in portfolio investments as much as there are treaties which specifically exclude portfolio investments from their scope. States which have experienced economic crises will be wary of protecting portfolio investments. It would be easy to withdraw portfolio investments from a state. The Asian economic crisis was precipitated by such sudden withdrawal of large portfolio investments. The beneficial effects of portfolio investments may not be seen as sufficient to permit protection to be given them.

4.2.4 Corporate nationality and the protection of shareholders

The definition of a company in bilateral investment treaties runs counter to the traditional notions in international law. The general rule relating to the diplomatic protection of corporations making investments in foreign countries was stated in the *Barcelona Traction Case*.[92] According to the International Court of Justice in that case, a corporation has the nationality of the state in which it is incorporated, and only the latter state has the right of diplomatic intervention on behalf of the corporation. This is a rule based in logic, for a corporation cannot have an existence outside the legal system which created it. This rule, however, did not permit the protection of shareholders of companies. In the *Barcelona Traction Case*, the Court denied that Belgium had *locus standi* to maintain an action against Spain to protect the interests of Belgian shareholders of a Canadian company whose investments in Spain had been affected by Spanish judicial and administrative measures. The Court, in reaching this much criticised conclusion, referred to the growth of multinational corporations within the global economy and expressed surprise that there had been little development towards securing greater protection for investments by multinational corporations.

The Court indicated clearly that a means of protection of shareholders was to be found through bilateral and multilateral arrangements on investment protection.[93] The increase in the number of bilateral investment treaties in the 1970s may also be a result of the decision in the *Barcelona Traction Case* which created doubts as to the possibility of the protection of shareholders in the absence of bilateral or multilateral treaties.[94] Shareholder protection was becoming important due to the insistence of many foreign investment

---

[91] The ASEAN Framework Agreement on Foreign Investment contains an article which specifically excludes its application to portfolio investments.

[92] [1970] *ICJ Reports* 1. The separate judgment of Judge Oda in the *ELSI Case* [1989] *ICJ Reports* 15 contains an affirmation of the rule.

[93] Para. 90.

[94] The *Barcelona Traction Case* recognised that there could be treaty protection of shareholders: [1970] *ICJ Reports* 1, paras. 54 and 61. Judge Tanaka, in his separate opinion, was willing to regard shares as property (pp. 127 and 134). The technique of regarding shares as property is widely used in bilateral investment treaties. On shareholder protection, see further J. M. Jones, 'Claims on Behalf of Nationals Who Are Shareholders in Foreign Companies' (1949) 20 *BYIL* 227; C. Staker, 'Diplomatic

codes which limited the entry of foreign investments except through locally incorporated joint ventures formed in association with domestic entrepreneurs or state entities. There has been an increase in the number of such foreign investment codes. This has meant that much of the foreign investment would have to be made without the diplomatic protection of the home states of the foreign investors. The situation had to be remedied, and it was remedied to a large extent by a growth in the number of bilateral investment treaties redefining investments to include intangible property such as shares and including tests of corporate nationality other than incorporation. Again, the departure that these treaties make from customary international law is clear. The treaties remove any doubt that may have existed in customary international law as to shareholder protection by defining investments to include shares. The intention clearly was to include primary shares.[95] The second method through which shareholder protection is effected relates to the definition of corporate nationality. Customary international law shows no inclination to depart from incorporation as the test of corporate nationality.[96] There are technical problems with the international protection of such corporations because the corporation itself is a creature of domestic law and depends for its existence on domestic law. It can be destroyed at will by the domestic system which created it. For this reason, international law did not interfere with corporate personality in any significant manner. It was also logical that, since the creation of the corporation depended on the will of the state as expressed in its domestic law, the corporation should have the nationality of the state in which it was created.

Some of the bilateral treaties seek to establish alternative tests of corporate nationality for the purposes of protection under the treaty. They specify that a company incorporated in one contracting party will be protected by the other party provided the seat of control of the company is located in the other contracting party or where there is control or a substantial interest in the company by the nationals of the other party.[97] This alternative test is to be

Protection of Private Business Companies' (1990) 61 *BYIL* 155; G. Sacerdoti, 'Barcelona Traction Revisited: Foreign-Owned and Controlled Companies in International Law', in Y. Dinstein (ed.), *International Law at a Time of Perplexity: Essays in Honour of Shabtai Rosenne* (1989), p. 699.

[95] This point is made again to assert the view that portfolio investment was never intended to be covered by the reference to shares in companies. The history of the inclusion of shares suggests that it was done to get over the problem raised in the *Barcelona Traction Case.*

[96] Besides the *Barcelona Traction Case* and the separate opinion of Judge Oda in the *ELSI Case* [1989] *ICJ Reports* 15, which was affirmed in *Diallo Case*, ICJ (Judgment, 24 May 2007), there are arbitral awards in which incorporation has been held to be the test of corporate nationality. The problem of corporate personality has arisen in arbitral jurisprudence, particularly before ICSID tribunals. ICSID has accepted that, where a foreign investor incorporates his company in the host state, ICSID will not have jurisdiction unless the host state clearly indicates that it was still willing to consider the company as a foreign national. A clear waiver clause was required. *Holiday Inns* v. *Morocco* (1980) 51 *BYIL* 123. But, in more recent awards, an inference of waiver has been drawn from the circumstances. *Amco* v. *Indonesia* (1983–90) 1 *ICSID Reports* 389. National courts have used incorporation as the test of nationality of foreign companies. *Sumitomo Shoji America Inc.* v. *Avagliano*, 457 US 176 (1982); *Compagnie Européene de Petroles* v. *Sensor Nederland BV* (1983) 22 *ILM* 320. The issue of what amounts to effective management for the purposes of the ASEAN Investment Treaty is discussed in *Yaung Chi Oo Ltd* v. *Myanmar* (2003) 42 *ILM* 540; (2003) 8 *ICSID Reports* 463. The ASEAN Investment Treaty requires both incorporation and management for corporate nationality. This is drawn from the treaty practice of the Philippines.

[97] Thus, the Singapore–UK treaty provides that a company incorporated in Singapore is to be regarded as a British company if the majority of the shares of the company are held by British nationals. The *siège social* theory of corporate nationality, which attributes nationality to the state of the seat from which the corporation is controlled, is followed in many civil law legal systems. The Netherlands and Denmark use the incorporation test. For Denmark, see *Centros Ltd* v. *Ehverves-og Selskabsstyrelsen* [1999] 2 CMLR 551. Ireland, being a common law jurisdiction, also uses the test of incorporation. It would appear that European Community law is veering towards an incorporation test.

found largely in the treaties made by European states and by those states which have legal systems based on the civil law tradition. They accord with the *siège social* theory of corporate nationality that has wide currency in the civilian systems.[98] A third type of test is used in the Algiers Accord creating the Iran–US Claims Tribunal, which regarded a corporation as protected only if over half the shares in the corporation were held by nationals of a contracting party and the corporation is controlled by such nationals. This formulation was used to overcome difficult issues where the corporation is controlled by persons holding dual nationality.[99] Some treaties require both incorporation and effective management to be located in the state which is party to the treaty.[100] Australian and Dutch treaties seek to confer protection on companies incorporated in a state other than the party to the treaty in which their nationals have shares. All these different formulations also introduce uncertainties into the area as there is no uniformity in the definition of the protected company. The corporation has the duty to indicate that it is entitled to protection under the treaty because it was established in the contracting state and it took the investment into the other contracting state.

Corporate nationality has been used in some recent awards to create new and expansionary principles which can hardly be regarded as grounded in theory. These views are guided more by expediency and a belief that the system of investment protection should become as wide as possible. These new views on determining corporate nationality fall well outside the careful manner in which the law was developed and will create strains on the system as states will begin baulking at the extensions they contain. The new views on corporate nationality are discussed when considering the relevance of corporate nationality to the jurisdiction of arbitral tribunals. It is sufficient to deal with the conventional issues that arise with corporate nationality in this chapter.

Depending on the investment laws of the host state party to the treaty, the investment could be made through a wholly owned subsidiary of the foreign corporation or through a joint venture. The treaty would ensure protection for wholly owned subsidiaries of multinational corporations which are incorporated in a host state party and which could easily be identified as a foreign-controlled corporation. The situation in which the multinational corporation invests through the formation of a joint venture in the host state party, however, requires a different solution. The protection of joint-venture interests will still remain a problem in many states. The foreign party may have to be the minority shareholder, who will not therefore have control over the joint-venture corporation.[101] If the shares of the minority foreign shareholders are affected through the procedures prescribed in the internal constitutional documents of the joint-venture company in accordance with the laws of the host state, there can be little protection given through

---

[98] Problems have arisen in EC law on the issue of corporate nationality. For a discussion, see Peter Behrens, 'International Company Law in View of the Centros Decision of the ECJ' (2000) 1 *European Business Organization Law Review* 125.

[99] Extensive case law was generated by the Iran–US Claims Tribunal on this point.

[100] The Philippines treaties contain this formula. The ASEAN Investment Treaty also contains this formula. It was one of the issues considered in *Yaung Chi Oo Ltd* v. *Myanmar* (2003) 42 *ILM* 540; (2003) 8 *ICSID Reports* 463.

[101] Though there has been considerable movement away from minority shareholdings, there are states which still insist on control remaining with local entities.

diplomatic intervention. The fact that the bilateral investment treaty provides protection for shareholdings by including them in its definition of investments may provide an avenue for such protection. In *AAPL* v. *Sri Lanka*,[102] an ICSID tribunal decided that an appropriately worded bilateral investment treaty will confer protection on a minority shareholder in a joint venture. Such a treaty will protect the shares and other interests in the joint venture company but possibly not the assets of the company.[103]

Though some of the bilateral treaties seek to grapple with the problem raised by corporate nationality, there is no consistency in the solutions adopted by them which could give rise to any uniform principle. One can find a wide array of solutions in different treaties. The Japanese treaty with Sri Lanka uses a test of 'control or decisive influence' in determining corporate nationality but leaves the application of the test itself to the *bona fide* decision of the party in whose territory the investment is made.[104] The practice of even single states varies. Thus, the Singapore–UK treaty defines a UK company as a company incorporated in the United Kingdom whereas the Singapore– Germany treaty defines a German company as one 'having its seat in the Federal Republic of Germany'. UK practice is also inconsistent on this point. Whereas the incorporation theory is preferred in the treaty with Singapore, the UK–Philippines treaty opts for a theory of control when it defines a protected company as one 'actually doing business under the laws in force in any part of the territory of that Contracting Party wherein a place of effective management is situate'.[105] The absence of uniformity of approach in these bilateral investment treaties to the problem of protecting companies again indicates that they cannot provide the basis upon which common principles or customary law can evolve on the issues of corporate nationality and shareholder protection in international law. They merely represent a consensus of opinion as between the two parties to the agreement as to such issues. They are negotiated in the context of legal preferences shaped by legal attitudes that exist within the legal systems of the different parties to such treaties. Thus, civil law countries have preferred to use the *siège social* theory whereas common law states have approached the treaty negotiations with the under- standing that the norm is the test of incorporation. But, even such an explanation of the variations cannot find uniform support, for there are common law countries which have used the *siège social* theory.[106]

---

[102] (1992) 17 *YCA* 106.

[103] [1970] *ICJ Reports* 1; the separate judgment of Judge Oda in the *ELSI Case* [1989] *ICJ Reports* 15 contains affirmation of this rule. See also *AAPL* v. *Sri Lanka* (1992) 17 *YCA* 106; (1991) 30 *ILM* 577, para. 90, where it was held that the physical assets of a company incorporated in a host state are not protected by a bilateral investment treaty as the assets belong to a national of the host state. In such circumstances, the foreign investor can only rely on shareholder protection. [1970] *ICJ Reports* at 47. The newer awards do not clarify this point. Presumably, the protection of the assets of the company must be the task of the majority shareholders in a situation of government interference rather than that of a foreign minority shareholder who must be satisfied with the protection of his shareholding in the company. But, the logic of this view is doubtful as the value of the shares would depend on the assets of the company. There is a lack of clarity in working out a solution to this problem.

[104] Article 12(2) of the Japan–Sri Lanka treaty.

[105] The Philippines uses control and management as the preferred test. This has passed into the regional ASEAN Investment Treaty as well.

[106] This is particularly so in multilateral treaties where several legal traditions are brought into play. Thus, the ASEAN Treaty on the Protection and Promotion of Investments (1987) uses the test of effective management. Some members of ASEAN (Malaysia and Singapore) are common law states.

In any event, neither test will be meaningful where the laws of the host state make it mandatory that foreign investment can enter only through the incorporation of a joint venture with a local partner or that minority participation must be progressively achieved. In this case, neither test of corporate personality will afford much protection to the foreign investor. The strengthening of protection for shareholders is necessary in such circumstances. But, even this may not provide much relief for the foreign investor in circumstances where the host state takes over control of the company without affecting the shareholding in the company, as where it intervenes to appoint a new management. The company cannot be protected simply because it is a corporate national of the host state and the shareholdings cannot be protected as they have not been affected.[107] A state could also take over management of a company, without affecting the company or its shareholdings.[108] In these circumstances, protection will depend on the manner in which the taking of property is defined in the treaty. These issues are considered later in the context of what amounts to a taking of property.[109]

4.3 Standard of treatment

There are a variety of standards of treatment provided for in bilateral investment treaties. They would usually contain one article on treatment standards but that article would identify several different standards of treatment. These include national treatment, a fair and equitable standard of treatment, an international minimum standard of treatment and full protection and security. There would be references to the most-favoured-nation standard of treatment, but the operation of this standard is not internal to the treaty as it depends on the identification of standards of treatment in other treaties so that the best standard offered could be determined. It is this best standard that flows through the most-favoured-nation clause to the foreign investor. Unlike the other treatment standards, the most-favoured-nation standard has significance to jurisdiction as well. Chapter 9 deals with the violation of these different standards of treatment. It is sufficient at this stage to describe the issues which arise in connection with each of these treatment standards.

4.3.1 National standard of treatment

There has been considerable disagreement between states on the question of state responsibility for injuries to aliens. Many Latin American countries and other capital-importing countries have argued for the national standard of treatment of aliens. Article 2(2)(c) of

---

[107] Mann made the point as follows: 'The shares in a company incorporated in a host country are not usually affected by any measures taken there. It is the company itself that is the victim.' F. A. Mann, 'Foreign Investment in the International Court of Justice: The ELSI Case' (1992) 86 *AJIL* 92 at 100. Technical arguments may be made that such interventions are takings in that they lead to depreciation in the value of shares. But, such arguments contemplate the existence of sophisticated stock markets in the state.

[108] Interference with management of a company is regarded as a taking as it affects the property rights of the foreign investor. This view has been accepted in many arbitral awards. *Revere Copper & Brass Inc.* v. *OPIC* (1980) 56 *ILR* 258 at 290–3 and 295. There are many awards of the Iran–US Claims Tribunal which considered the issue. These are dealt with in Chapter 8 below.

[109] See Chapter 10 below.

national treatment VS IMS

Bilateral investment treaties

the Charter of Economic Rights and Duties of States articulates the national treatment principle. Capital-exporting states, however, have argued that aliens should be treated in accordance with an international minimum standard. If the national treatment principle is accepted, protection for the foreign investor will become minimal as legislation that affects property enacted uniformly to apply to all in the state irrespective of nationality will leave the alien without any remedy in international law.

Capital-exporting states have rejected this view, arguing for a minimum standard of treatment to be accorded to aliens. The recognition of a minimum standard of treatment will permit international scrutiny of the treatment of the foreign investor by the host state. However, unlike in the past when national treatment was rejected altogether because such treatment was in the case of some countries lower than the minimum standard contended for by the capital-exporting states, in modern times national treatment may have its advantages as states reserve many of their economic sectors and privileges to their nationals. In addition, national treatment at the stage of entry is regarded as an important right, as it entitles the foreign investor to a right of entry and establishment in the host state. Treaties which aim at liberalisation contain such pre-entry rights of establishment. The granting of national treatment after entry may confer advantages on aliens, as it will grant them the same privileges enjoyed by nationals. For this reason, there is a tendency among developed states to support national treatment as a relevant standard and to approach the issue of international responsibility on the basis of discrimination resulting from the failure of the host state to provide national treatment to the foreign investor. In fact, the violation of national treatment is emerging as a significant cause of action arising from investment treaties.[110]

The existence of a national treatment standard could provide a basis for the argument that performance requirements such as export quotas or local purchase requirements should not be imposed upon the foreign investor, at least after entry has been made. Such requirements are not imposed on local entrepreneurs, and it is to be expected that the national treatment standard would require that it not be imposed on foreign investors as well. National treatment standard may as a result work against the imposition of performance standards unless such performance requirements are exempted from the national treatment standard.[111]

Yet, treaties that refer to national treatment often have specific provisions excluding performance requirements, and often spell out the types of performance requirement that are excluded. The inclusion of national treatment will also mean that the existence of an economically valid reason for discrimination between nationals and foreign investors

---

[110] Thus, under NAFTA, there are a significant number of cases which have been instituted on the basis of a violation of national treatment, principally between the United States and Canada. See, for example, *S. D. Myers* v. *Canada* (2000) 40 *ILM* 1408; (2002) 121 *ILR* 7; *UPS* v. *Canada*, UNCITRAL Arbitration Proceedings (NAFTA) (Award on the Merits, 24 May 2007); and *Marvin Feldman* v. *Mexico* (2002) 7 *ICSID Reports* 318; (2003) 42 *ILM* 625.

[111] *ADF* v. *United States*, ICSID Case No. ARB(AF)/00/1 (NAFTA) (Award, 9 January 2003) is a NAFTA case in which the issue was raised as to performance requirements, in this case the 'Buy American' statutes, being a violation of national treatment standards.

may not provide a justification for the discrimination. The trade-related term 'in like circumstances' is used to limit the effect of the national treatment requirement. It is difficult to understand the nature of such a limitation in the context of investment. A large multinational corporation as an investor is never 'in like circumstances' because of its size and vertically integrated global organisation. If this is a basis for discrimination, then the granting of national treatment becomes pointless. But, it is the precise reason why foreign multinational corporations should be discriminated against. There is a dilemma presented by the unthinking extension of notions of trade law into the area of investment. The two areas do not mix that easily. Another exception, again from the trade arena, relates to the exceptions of discrimination based on national security, public health or morals. Again, there is no precedent in investment law relating to the interpretation of these exceptions.

Recent writings on economics suggest that a state should be able to discriminate in favour of its own investors. These writings point out that most developed states adopted such discriminatory policies in the course of their own development and are now seeking to deny the benefits of such policies to developing countries. As a result, some views take the position that the preferences given to the nationals over foreign investors should remain.[112] Developed states could adopt similar stances in response to the global economic crisis of 2008 onwards. In the United States, the Congress has voiced concern about investment treaties giving greater protection to foreign investors than to US nationals.

Wide sectoral exceptions are used, particularly where the treaty provides for pre-entry rights of national treatment and rights of establishment. Thus, in the case of NAFTA, which requires both pre-entry and post-entry national treatment, Mexico incorporated all the sectors from which it excludes foreign investment under its Foreign Investment Law as sectors that are exempted from the obligation of national treatment. The list is of considerable length. The use of a negative list of sectors is a common practice. Thus, for example, the Canada–Thailand investment treaty contains in its appendix the Thai investment laws, which list the sectors into which foreign investment is not permitted and the sectors into which foreign investment is permitted in partnership with its nationals. Where states have investment codes with such negative lists, it is sensible to include that list of sectors as industries that are not subject to national treatment. Since some investment treaties are made subject to the existing laws and regulations of the host state, discriminatory rules based on economic criteria will be captured in the treaties so that the discrimination will not violate the treaty standards.

National treatment seems a sensible answer in view of the increase of administrative controls over foreign investment. National treatment may, however, rebound on the foreign investor. A harsh measure taken against one's own nationals may be extended to the foreign investor and be justified on the basis of national treatment. For this reason, it is necessary to include other standards of treatment in the treaty.

---

[112] Ha-Joon Chang, *Kicking Away the Ladder: Development Strategy in Historical Perspective* (2005).

4.3.2 Fair and equitable standard

Treaties refer to 'fair and equitable treatment' to be accorded to the nationals of the contracting parties. This phrase is vague and is open to different interpretations. The content of this standard has caused much anxiety.[113] It was at one stage thought that the standard was a higher standard than the international minimum standard. But, in NAFTA litigation, the wide interpretation given to the formula resulted in the NAFTA Commission issuing an interpretative note declaring that the fair and equitable standard was no more than the international minimum standard of customary international law. The letters attached to the Singapore–United States Free Trade Agreement also take the position that the phrase 'fair and equitable treatment' as used in the treaty should be taken to refer to the international minimum standard of treatment. The new model investment treaties of both the United States and Canada repeat this formula. The resulting practice makes the phrase 'fair and equitable treatment' otiose at least as far as these treaties are concerned. But, there has been a burgeoning number of arbitral awards seeking to make the fair and equitable standard the most important provision in the investment treaty, virtually absorbing all other claims that can be made under the treaties. For this reason, these trends deserve a fuller treatment. The discussion of the phrase and the arbitral awards interpreting it is made in Chapter 9. At this stage, it is sufficient to note that the fair and equitable treatment standard has been expanded to include notions of transparency and legitimate expectations of the foreign investor. But, as has been pointed out, if notions of fairness are to be taken into account, they would make the context in which the fairness is to be assessed relevant so that the standard would require taking into account whether or not the state interference was in response to the malpractices of the multinational corporation. The evaluation of the standard may not be as one-sided as its original proponents had intended it to be. After the expansive interpretation, some arbitrators have sought to ensure that the basis on which these expansions are made are kept within strict limits, requiring the expectations to be reasonable in the context of the particular circumstances. Discussion of these issues is left to Chapter 9.

4.3.3 Most-favoured-nation treatment

A clause that is now commonly included in bilateral investment treaties was handed down from old FCN treaties, and provides for most-favoured-nation treatment, enabling the nationals of the parties to profit from favourable treatment that may be given to nationals of third states by either contracting state. The inclusion of most-favoured-nation treatment presents the difficulty that the foreign investor could latch onto more favourable treatment provided in past or future treaties. Already, a precedent for this has been established in relation to dispute settlement. It has been held that it is possible for a foreign investor who is protected by an investment treaty with a most-favoured-nation clause to use a better dispute-settlement provision in a treaty made by the respondent

---

[113] UNCTAD, *Fair and Equitable Treatment* (1999).

state with a third state.[114] This would be particularly the case where a multilateral or regional treaty is concluded. If a state enters into a multilateral treaty which contains a most-favoured-nation clause, the number of states that could utilise a more favourable provision in a future bilateral investment treaty could become greater. This may be an unintended result, and care must therefore be exercised to avoid this. As a result, the scope and use of most-favoured-nation clauses in investment treaties have attracted controversy. This issue is dealt with in a later chapter of this book.

Where a state belongs to a regional organisation, and as a result the state gives special privileges to other member states of the organisation, it will seek to exclude those privileges from applying to a state with which it makes a bilateral investment treaty by the automatic operation of the most-favoured-nation clause. This will be stated in the treaty itself. It cannot therefore later be argued that measures conferring privileges under these regional arrangements should be conferred upon foreign investors on the basis of the most-favoured-nation clause.

4.3.4 *Full protection and security*

The treatment provision also includes the provision of 'full protection and security' to the foreign investment. It has been held in arbitral awards that this again adverts to customary law standards which require either that the state's forces should not be utilised to harm the foreign investor's property or that the state should give protection from violence against the interests of the foreign investor if such violence could be reasonably anticipated.[115] Again, there has been a tendency to expand the scope of the provision well beyond its moorings in customary law to include a wider notion that the clause mandates the maintenance of conditions of stability for the investment. This issue requires more detailed treatment. It is dealt with in a later chapter of this book.

4.4 *Performance requirements*

Treaties made by the United States and Canada in particular have sought to do away with performance requirements. Performance requirements are imposed by host states in order to ensure that the foreign investor exports a percentage of his production, buys local products and services, and employs local labour. From the point of view of developing countries, the imposition of such requirements enhances the value of the foreign investment. Thus, the requirement of export ensures that more foreign exchange is earned for the host state than profits made for the foreign investor through sales on the local market. Such profits will be repatriated, causing a possible loss to the foreign investor which could be balanced against profits made on exports. Another reason for the export requirement is that it preserves the market for local entrepreneurs. Local entrepreneurs are likely to be

---

[114] *Maffezini* v. *Spain* (2000) 5 *ICSID Reports* 396; (2004) 40 *ILM* 1129. For the most recent award, see *Tza Yap Shum* v. *Peru*, ICSID Case No. ARB/07/6 (Decision on Jurisdiction and Competence, 19 June 2009).
[115] *American Machine Tools* v. *Zaire* (1997) 36 *ILM* 1531; *Wena Hotels* v. *Republic of Egypt* (2002) 41 *ILM* 896.

driven out of the market if they are obliged to compete with foreign multinational corporations able to produce goods at a lower cost. This effect will mean that incipient local industry will be strangled. Export requirements are justified on the basis that such a crowding-out effect will be avoided.[116] Multinational corporations are averse to export requirements, as they require internal competition within the production systems of the multinational corporation. The use of local content requirements will ensure that local products are utilised in the manufacture of products made by the foreign investor and not imported from abroad. The employment of local personnel also ensures one of the presumed advantages of the foreign investment.

Some economists suggest that developed countries adopted performance requirements in their own economic development and are now denying it to developing countries. They argue that the very strategies regarding performance requirements which developed states now seek to prohibit helped the developed states to rise to their present economic eminence. There is a general refusal to accept performance standards for the reasons that have been stated.[117]

But, these arguments are countered by the developed countries on the basis that performance requirements distort international trade. To some extent, the Trade-Related Investment Measures (TRIMS) instrument of the WTO is based on the prohibition of performance requirements on the basis of this argument. Unlike TRIMS, which prohibits only trade-related performance requirements, the investment treaties which address the issue of performance requirements seek to prohibit them altogether. The provision of national treatment will also require that these restrictions be done away with as they are not imposed on nationals. Economic literature is not conclusive on whether performance requirements enhance the developmental goals of host states. Though studies concentrate on the trade-distortive effects of such requirements, there are studies which show that the use of performance requirements has ensured the harnessing of the foreign investment to the economic objectives of the host state.[118]

4.5 Repatriation of profits

The main objective of all foreign investment is to make profits and to repatriate those profits to the home state. If repatriation of the profits is prevented by the host state, this purpose of the foreign investor will be frustrated. Protection of the right to repatriate profits becomes an objective of investment treaties. Repatriation of profits is necessary for the foreign investor, who may have to service loans, buy equipment and machinery and pay for services. Many of the treaties contain absolute statements protecting the right of repatriation. This is unrealistic, as problems will arise when a contracting party has

---

[116] See further UNCTAD, *World Investment Report, 2003*.

[117] Caribbean Community (CARICOM) countries, for example, produced a document, entitled 'Guidelines for Use in the Negotiation of Bilateral Treaties', which states that CARICOM countries should not accept any prohibition of the use of performance requirements.

[118] For policy debates on performance requirements, see UNCTAD, *World Investment Report, 2003*, pp. 119–23.

exchange shortfalls necessitating currency controls. Absolute rights of repatriation are included in treaties in the over-zealous belief that such situations will not eventuate. Situations like the Asian financial crisis do occur. The Argentinian financial crisis resulted in a number of investment disputes, which raised issues as to whether these crises give rise to situations of necessity justifying the suspension of the right of repatriation and other interventions. When such crises occur, an absolute right of repatriation in a treaty will cause difficulties for the state experiencing the crisis.

Some UK treaties provide that the right of repatriation of profits may be restricted 'in exceptional economic or financial circumstances'.[119] In other UK treaties, there is a requirement that the repatriation of a percentage of the profits (usually 20 per cent) should be permitted every year in circumstances of foreign-exchange difficulties. The UK formulation is preferable. Absolute rights of repatriation cannot bind a state in times of financial crisis. It may be argued that circumstances of financial crisis call for the application of the doctrine of *clausula rebus sic stantibus*, making the provision on absolute rights of repatriation defeasible as a result of the different situation that had arisen. In situations of extreme balance-of-payment difficulties, it could be argued that the general doctrine of necessity suspends the treaty obligation to permit repatriation, at least until the situation improves. Several arbitral awards arising out of the Argentinian crisis have dealt with the issue, but they are inconclusive as to whether the defence will succeed.[120]

The more realistic approach is to adopt the solution found in UK treaty practice and create an obligation to permit the repatriation of at least a percentage of the profits and the remainder when circumstances permit. The repatriation clause will usually include not only the profits that are made but all other payments such as fees or other entitlements that are paid to the foreign investor and his employees. Again, practice on the right of repatriation varies in the treaties.

Exceptions are sometimes made in relation to delays occurring due to reporting requirements or seizures of assets that may be made by courts to satisfy debts. These exceptions are provisions that relate to the laws of one of the contracting parties. They are not related to balance-of-payment difficulties that are experienced by developing state parties to such treaties but exceptions that cater to the requirements of the laws of the developed state parties.

4.6 Nationalisation and compensation

Nationalisation poses the greatest threat to foreign investment. Capital-exporting states have sought to circumscribe the right of a state to nationalise foreign property by regarding at least certain types of taking of alien property as unlawful. It is now generally accepted that a state has a right to nationalise foreign-owned property, subject to exceptions. The change from illegality to legality of state takings of alien property had much to do with the fact that the nature of taking had undergone significant change. Whereas

---

[119] Not all UK treaties contain such provisions. The treaty with Jamaica is an example.
[120] The issue is dealt with in Chapter 12 below.

previously takings were largely confiscations motivated by the greed of dictators in power or were racially motivated, modern state takings are done in pursuance of economic reforms on the basis of sincerely held ideological views or policy grounds. Though vestiges of the old law still remain to cater for the occasional takings that are racially motivated or motivated by the greed of ruling coteries, modern law tends to regard takings by the state as lawful, unless the contrary can be established. There is broad agreement that the exercise of the right should not be discriminatory and should have a basis in public purpose.

The conditions relating to public purpose and non-discrimination are stated in all bilateral investment treaties, and there can be little doubt that these conditions form part of customary international law. It is such customary law that is reiterated in these treaties. In this respect, the treaties do not create new customary law but reinforce existing customary law as found in the practice of developed states. In modern international law, the force of these exceptions to the legality of nationalisations is somewhat muted, as the subjective view of the state that the nationalisation serves a public purpose is given great weight.[121] A discriminatory nationalisation is illegal, but discrimination may be difficult to establish in circumstances in which there is an ostensible economic reason for the nationalisation, as the state could argue that the economic reason was the predominant reason behind the nationalisation.

The treaties indicate that the provisions relating to expropriation apply not only to outright takings but also to 'creeping expropriation' or the slow erosion of the alien's ownership rights through regulatory measures. Thus, US bilateral investment treaties define expropriation to include 'any measure or series of measures the effect of which would be tantamount to expropriation or nationalisation'. Chapter 11 of NAFTA, a regional treaty, contains the same formulation. It has received extensive interpretation.[122] In the earlier US treaties, examples are given of such indirect takings: confiscatory taxation, total or partial compulsory sale, and impairment or deprivation of management, control or economic value.[123] Later treaties do not contain such illustrations, presumably in the belief that they are unnecessary or in the belief that they may limit the effect of the language. Indirect taking is regarded as bringing about results akin to a physical taking without actual interference with the property itself. The phrase 'tantamount to a taking' has caused considerable problems. In the context of NAFTA, it has been read as not adding to the meaning of indirect taking. It is another clause in the investment chapter of NAFTA that has become otiose as a result of interpretation. It is left out altogether in the US model investment treaty of 2004. These matters are dealt with in Chapters 8 and 9, dealing with expropriation.

The issue of compensation is controversial, and, on this issue, bilateral investment treaties make law as between the parties but make no contribution to the formation of common norms of international law. Capital-exporting states, particularly the United

---

[121] *Marvin Feldman* v. *Mexico* (2002) 7 *ICSID Reports* 318; (2003) 42 *ILM* 625, para. 136.   [122] See further Chapter 8 below.
[123] United States–Egypt treaty (1982).

States, have steadfastly adhered to the standard of 'prompt, adequate and effective compensation' as the standard of compensation that must be satisfied in the event of nationalisation. The standard would require, at the least, the payment of the full value of the property that had been taken over. Developing countries have collectively articulated the standard of 'appropriate compensation'. This latter standard is a flexible standard that would permit a state to take into account factors such as the profits made by the foreign investor, the duration of the period during which the profits were made, and similar factors, in assessing the compensation. Developing countries have also expressed the view that the tribunals of the host state should be the sole arbiters of the amount of compensation. Given the existence of this conflict between states, bilateral investment treaties have become the means by which the parties could agree on the standard of compensation that is to be used as between themselves. Some writers advocated the use of bilateral investment treaties to settle the issue of compensation as between the parties, given the uncertainty as to the existence of a standard in international customary law. Thus Eli Lauterpacht, referring to the alleged existence of a customary law standard of 'appropriate compensation', observed:[124]

The evidently discretionary and objectively unpredictable content of this standard is as good a reason as any for recognising the virtue of the use of specially agreed bilateral treaty standards.

Bilateral investment treaties are not made with the aim of subscribing to the formulation of a uniform standard of compensation, but are instead efforts by the parties to agree on the standard on which they would compensate in the event one of them nationalises the property of a national of the other. The imputation of any more grandiose motive to such treaties is misplaced.

However, heavy reliance is placed on bilateral investment treaties to argue that the standard of prompt, adequate and effective compensation has been reinforced in these treaties. A former legal adviser to the US Department of State relied on bilateral investment treaties to argue that the standard of prompt, adequate and effective compensation has been reinforced by these agreements. He observed:[125]

States have shown their real practice by establishing a network of international treaties. Provisions controlling compensation in expropriation are often contained in bilateral friendship, commerce and navigation (FCN) treaties. In the case of the United States, many of these are with developing nations. They contain provisions calling for compensation in terms equivalent to the traditional standard, although there are slight drafting variations. The history of these agreements indicates that the parties recognised that they were thereby making the customary rule of international law explicit in the treaty language and reaffirming its effect.

The old FCN treaties were drafted before the alternative standards came to be articulated. In the new investment treaties that the United States has made, it appears to have taken

---

[124] E. Lauterpacht, 'Issues of Compensation and Nationality in the Taking of Energy Investments' (1990) 6 *Journal of Energy and Natural Resources Law* 241.
[125] D. Robinson, 'Expropriation in the Restatement (Revised)' (1984) 78 *AJIL* 176.

an inflexible stance on the issue of compensation and not permitted any 'drafting variations'. Its new bilateral investment treaties require the payment of prompt, adequate and effective compensation and refer to the standard of valuation being 'the fair market value of the expropriated investment immediately before the expropriatory action was taken or become known'. The US model treaty of 2004 also asserts the standard.

As regards the treaty practice of other states, the requirement of 'prompt, adequate and effective' compensation is frequently used, but there are departures from the formula in some treaties. In UK treaties, the formula is often used, but there are other formulations in use as well. It will be too facile to explain these departures as drafting variations, for every state will seek consistency in its practice, and there is an obvious advantage to the capital-exporting state in insisting on the standard of prompt, adequate and effective compensation. But, in the UK treaties, whatever formula is used to describe the compensation, there follows a valuation standard stated in a clause which reads as follows:

Such compensation shall include market value of the investment expropriated immediately before the expropriation became public knowledge, shall include interest at a normal commercial rate until date of payment, shall be made without delay, be effectively realisable and be freely transferable.

It can be argued that this standard of valuation indicates an obligation to pay full compensation.

In the treaties to which Singapore is a party, there are wide variations in the statements relating to compensation. The prompt, adequate and effective formula is referred to in the treaties with the UK and Switzerland, but the alternative formula of 'just' compensation is used in the treaties with the Netherlands and Germany. In the treaty with France, the agreement is to pay as compensation, 'the commercial value of the assets on the day of the expropriation'. This formula does not take into account the fact that the value of the property may have depreciated as a result of an earlier announcement of the expropriation. In most Dutch treaties, there is a reference to 'just' compensation. Australia, a relative newcomer to the area of bilateral investment treaties, has been able to secure the inclusion of the prompt, adequate and effective formula in all its treaties. Its treaty with China contains such a formula. But, its neighbour, New Zealand, was able to secure in its investment treaty with China a formula which simply refers to 'compensation which shall be effectively realisable'. Treaties between developing countries also contain the prompt, adequate and effective formula.[126] Bargaining strengths and negotiating strategies have much to do with the variations that appear in all these treaties. Since the variations are attributable to such strengths and strategies, they cannot be dismissed as 'drafting variations' so as to make them fit an *a priori* conclusion. But, as a general proposition, one may conclude that the more recent treaties tend towards using the Hull formula of prompt, adequate and effective compensation. No definite conclusions can be drawn from this trend.

---

[126] There is no uniform practice. The treaty between Egypt and Thailand (2000) speaks of compensation without any qualifying adjectives, though it later speaks of market value.

The practice that can be analysed will support different claims depending on the predisposition of the person drawing the conclusions. The use of the formula of 'just compensation' in a significant minority of treaties cannot be dismissed as 'drafting variations'. It can also be a compromise formulation adopted by some states in light of the conflict that has been generated in the area. A writer in the field has pointed out that 'it would seem foolhardy, if the argument that the nineteenth-century customary law being recreated by these treaties is pressed too far, to maintain that "just", "full", "equivalent" and "adequate" have exactly the same meaning'.[127]

Quite apart from the relative bargaining strengths of the parties, the period in which the treaty was drafted has relevance. At a time when there is an availability of investment funds, capital-importing states will be reluctant to agree to higher standards of compensation. But, treaties that are concluded at a time when there is a dearth of such capital will contain higher standards such as the Hull formula. The ascendance of a free market philosophy in a given period may also favour the acceptance of such a formula. This may explain why the more recent treaties, concluded at a time when there was intense competition for foreign investment and a relatively widespread acceptance of a free market philosophy, contain more frequent references to the Hull formula. So, too, when high-risk states conclude treaties with states having large investment capital, they are likely to include the Hull formula. Thus, China and Vietnam have cast aside their ideological objections and included the Hull formula in many of their treaties simply because they are keen to attract investments and keen to dispel impressions that they are high-risk countries. This demonstrates a readiness to respect the property rights of the foreign investor even though the property rights of the nationals may not be as well protected. This paradox is not restricted only to developing countries, for constitutional experts in developed countries have pointed out that the protection given to foreign investors by investment treaties is of a higher standard than that given by the laws of the developed states.[128]

There is also a double standard that is apparent in the conduct of many developing states. On the one hand, they maintain stances that oppose the Hull formula in international fora, but, on the other, they are busy making bilateral treaties containing the formula. This inconsistency can be explained on the basis that, while these states subscribe to a particular norm of international law at the global level, they are nevertheless prepared to accord a higher standard of protection to the nationals of states with which they conclude bilateral investment treaties in the hope of attracting investments. They subscribe to a general standard of appropriate compensation at the international level but are prepared to negotiate higher standards on a case-by-case basis. This is a pragmatic approach dictated by circumstances. The charge of inconsistency may therefore be misplaced.[129]

---

[127] C. F. Amerasinghe, 'Issues of Compensation in the Taking of Property in the Light of Recent Cases and Practice' (1992) 41 *ICLQ* 22.

[128] The argument has been made that the protection under the US investment treaties for foreign investment is greater than that given by US domestic laws. For Canada, see D. Schneiderman, *Constitutionalising Economic Globalization* (2007).

[129] A. Guzman, 'Why LDCs Sign Treaties That Hurt Them: Explaining the Popularity of Bilateral Investment Treaties' (1998) 38 *Virginia Journal of International Law* 639. Guzman and his colleagues have explained the phenomenon on the basis of

The inclusion of the Hull formula in treaties between developing states also constitutes a paradox. The explanation for these treaties is that they are not only intended to attract investments from richer developing states but are also aimed at multinational corporations already operating in the state. Thus, a treaty between Singapore and Vietnam is aimed not only at Singaporean nationals and companies which have now acquired the capacity to invest overseas but also at multinational corporations already operating in Singapore. These corporations will have incorporated in Singapore and hence are entitled to the benefit of the treaties as corporate nationals of Singapore. The strategy of a state like Vietnam could well be to attract such corporations through making investment treaties with states like Singapore which have already been able to attract good foreign investments. This constitutes Singapore as an export platform for the region, and Singapore will not be unhappy with the situation as there will be revenue flows moving through Singapore.[130] The treaty may also attract other multinational corporations to set up in Singapore and then proceed to Vietnam and thereby invoke the protection of the investment treaty. The inclusion of the Hull formula in these treaties is for strategic reasons. Yet, the argument that these treaties stabilise the Hull formula must be seen as having merit, despite the fact that they do not provide any conclusive evidence of the acceptance of the formula as customary international law.

The motives for the inclusion of the Hull formula as well as the variations that appear in the different treaties as to the standard of compensation make these treaties unsafe bases on which to make the argument that they contain evidence that there is sufficient acceptance of the Hull formula to make it part of customary international law. There is a lack of unanimity in the practice of states on the point. It must, however, be conceded that the large majority of treaties contain the Hull formula. But, this is no more than about half the treaties that had been concluded in 1992 when the count was last made.[131] The rest have different formulas to indicate the compensation payable. The definite conclusion that these treaties support the Hull formula is untenable.

Besides, many of these treaties in which the Hull formula appears qualify the types of investment that are protected. Thus, quite uniformly in Southeast Asian treaties, only 'approved' investments are protected by the Hull formula, if used. This leaves aside the large number of investments which do not have approval. In such a situation, these treaties cannot create customary international law. Likewise, many states, China, Australia and Indonesia included, protect only investments which are made in accordance with their laws and regulations. In the context of these qualifications, the nature of the investments that are protected by many treaties made by large groups of states is so qualified that they cannot meaningfully contribute to any customary practice as to the Hull formula. In these

---

competition for foreign investment. Unless states give protection, they fear that they would lose out on foreign investment flows to their competitors. Z. Elkins, A. T. Guzman and B. Simmons, 'Competing for Capital: The Diffusion of Bilateral Investment Treaties' (2008) *University of Illinois LR* 265.

[130] Other small states use this strategy. Mauritius and the Netherlands use this strategy and permit foreign companies to use the protection their treaties afford them through the simple technique of incorporation of companies and acquiring corporate nationality through these means.

[131] This was the position in 1992. See World Bank Group, *Legal Framework for the Treatment of Foreign Investment* (1992), vol. 1, p. 48. But, the newer treaties refer to the Hull formula more frequently, so that the proportion may now be different.

cases, the Hull formula becomes a higher standard that protects a desirable type of investment made under the regulations of the host state rather than all investments.

A contemporary controversy pertains to the extent to which regulatory intervention can be characterised as a 'taking or an act tantamount to a taking' under the expropriation provision in investment treaties. This issue has displaced compensation as the central issue in expropriation law. Some arbitral decisions which have construed the phrase used in the treaties seem to indicate that the regulatory character of the taking is no reason for regarding the taking as non-compensable. This view has created controversy, as it would mean that takings motivated by environmental and other concerns will have to be compensated. There have been reactions against this view. This issue is discussed more fully in Chapter 8 below.

4.6.1 Compensation for destruction during wars and national emergencies

Investment treaties contain provisions for compensation in the event of damage to the foreign investor's property as a result of war, civil unrest or other national emergencies. They provide for national treatment of the foreign investor so that, if nationals of the state are compensated for such losses, then the foreign investor will also have to be compensated on the same standard. The treaties also provide for liability where the armed forces requisition the foreign investor's property or where such property is destroyed by the armed forces. However, liability for such destruction is excluded where the destruction occurs during combat action or was required by the necessity of the situation. These provisions have been used in a dispute involving Sri Lanka and a national of Hong Kong which was submitted for arbitration to the International Centre for the Settlement of Investment Disputes. The award in *Asian Agricultural Products Ltd (AAPL)* v. *Sri Lanka*[132] is the first dispute in which an international tribunal had an opportunity to deal with the provisions of a bilateral investment treaty. It has significance not only for the provision on compensation for damages caused during wars and national emergencies but also for bilateral investment agreements generally. A central theme in the award is the interplay between customary principles and the treaty principles on destruction by government agents.

The dispute arose as a result of the destruction of the shrimp culture farm AAPL had established in a joint venture with a local company, as a result of a military action taken by the armed forces of Sri Lanka against Tamil insurgents fighting for a separate state. The tribunal's jurisdiction was based on the provision on dispute settlement in the bilateral investment treaty, again making the award of significance for the development of the law on bilateral investment treaties. It was the first occasion on which an arbitral tribunal exercised jurisdiction on the basis of a provision in a bilateral investment treaty providing for such jurisdiction. The issue was whether the foreign investor was entitled to compensation for the destruction of the property.

The claimant's argument was presented on the basis that the bilateral investment treaty created a higher standard of protection, so that there may even arise strict liability

[132] (1992) 17 *YCA* 106.

in the event of destruction of a foreign investor's property. This was rejected by the arbitral tribunal, which held that the inclusion of terms such as 'full protection' in bilateral investment treaties does not refer to any standards higher than the minimum standard of treatment required by general international law. The tribunal then went on to consider whether there could be liability under the provision of the treaty which stated that a party will be liable where the foreign investor suffers losses as a result of his property being requisitioned or as a result of destruction of his property by the armed forces of a contracting party 'which was not caused in combat action or was not required by the necessity of the situation'. The tribunal held that the action taken by the Sri Lankan armed forces leading to the destruction of the foreign investor's property was directed against the Tamil guerrillas and qualified as combat action which attracted the application of the exception to liability. But, the tribunal held that the bilateral investment treaty included the standards of protection of general international law to which the foreign investor could have resort as these standards are incorporated in bilateral investment treaties. The rule that was applied by the tribunal was that, in times of civil conflicts, there was a duty on the part of the host state to confer adequate protection on foreign investments and that a failure to give such protection will engage the liability of the state. This rule was extracted as a proposition of customary international law which formed a part of the bilateral investment treaty. It was on the basis of the failure to provide the protection required by general international law that the tribunal awarded compensation to the foreign investor.

On this reasoning, bilateral investment treaties are *lex specialis* which stand apart from general international law, entitling the foreign investor to the protection of both the standards of general international law as well as the standards contained in the treaty itself. In this case, the two standards worked in tandem, for the foreign investor was able to invoke the protection of the general international law before the tribunal only because the bilateral investment treaty had created jurisdiction in the tribunal. But, an issue which the tribunal failed to answer was whether the tribunal could assume jurisdiction on the basis of the treaty and apply rules that were not stated in the treaty itself. The tribunal was assuming virtually limitless jurisdiction by dealing with the problem through customary international law. A tribunal concerned essentially with investment law could find itself out of its depth when it concerns itself with general international law. Could the tribunal in *AAPL* v. *Sri Lanka* have looked into the question as to whether the war in Sri Lanka was a war of national liberation and, hence, akin to an international war? Could it then have gone into issues of protection of property under the laws of war? Surely, arbitral tribunals which are constituted for investment disputes are not designed to deal with such problems. Its personnel are not selected on the basis of their competence in these matters.[133]

The award of the tribunal indicates that bilateral investment treaties could raise problems of vital national interests before international tribunals and that sometimes these

---

[133] For the criticism that personnel on these tribunals have little acquaintance with international law, see C. F. Amerasinghe, 'The Prawn Farm Arbitration' (1992) 2 *Sri Lanka Journal of International Law* 12.

problems may not be directly involved with the investment. If the fighting of a civil war becomes the concern of an arbitral tribunal that was created essentially to settle commercial disputes, then there is an unexpectedly large genie being released from the bottle. In the civil-war-type of situation like that in *AAPL* v. *Sri Lanka*, issues such as the characterisation of the war, the legality of the force used to suppress it and other like matters that may concern the internal sovereignty of the state could have been raised. An issue of investment thus opens the possibility of the conduct of the hostilities being queried by an international tribunal which is not designed to deal with such political matters. The US experience with FCN treaties rebounding to provide jurisdiction for Nicaragua and Iran to score juridical triumphs can be expected to be repeated many more times. This may lead to capital-exporting countries being more cautious in embarking upon bilateral investment treaties. The issue as to whether there is a doctrine of arbitrability which prevents arbitral tribunals constituted to deal with foreign investment disputes straying into other fields over which they have little or no competence is fairly raised in situations like that in *AAPL* v. *Sri Lanka*.

If there is no national emergency declared in local law, it is unlikely that a state can use this provision to justify measures of deprivation of property. In *Funekotter* v. *Zimbabwe*,[134] Zimbabwe sought to justify the grabbing of land by its war veterans from white farmers as an emergency situation. The tribunal, besides pointing out that there was no declaration of emergency, also held that the provision relating to emergency situations merely requires that, if nationals are compensated, then like compensation must be paid to foreign investors. It does not create any defence to liability for the taking of property. The provision does not create an exception analogous to necessity.

4.7 Protection of commitments

Investment treaties contain clauses which require the parties to keep commitments that are made to each other's nationals. Thus, the treaty between the United Kingdom and the Philippines contains the following clause:

Each Contracting Party shall observe any obligation arising from a particular commitment it may have entered into with regard to a specific investment of nationals or companies of the other Contracting Party.

The reference to 'particular commitment[s]' made to the foreign investor may mean that guarantees such as the guarantee against expropriation without compensation or guarantees as to repatriation of profits made in investment codes, which are *general* commitments, are not covered by the clause. It may, however, be possible to argue that these general commitments are addressed to the particular foreign investor as well and hence fall within the protection of the clause.

The clause may refer more specifically to the contractual commitments that a state or a public entity like the investment board screening the application of the investor prior

---

[134] ICSID Case No. ARB/05/06; 22 April 2009.

to entry may have made in the course of initial contacts with the foreign investor. Liability will arise where these commitments are not met. They could also refer to contractual commitments made to the foreign party. Thus, where there are stabilisation clauses in the contract, it could credibly be argued on the basis of the provision in the bilateral investment treaty that future changes to the law in the host state adverse to the interests of the foreign investor should not be applied to the contract. But, a difficulty with the argument is that such contracts are not made directly by the state. They are made by state entities and the stipulations and guarantees given by the state entity may not bind the state. The state will argue that these guarantees are not binding on it and that the treaty protection does not apply to contractual guarantees made by state entities. But, administrative commitments, such as those relating to the grant of permits necessary to do business effectively, may be protected by this treaty provision.

In any event, there has in recent times been much debate as to the validity of the clause which has come to be known as the 'umbrella clause' because of its catch-all nature. The original controversy appeared in the two awards concerning SGS.[135] Two diametrically opposing positions were taken, with the award involving Pakistan holding that the clause cannot be the basis of a claim and the one involving the Philippines holding the contrary. Since then, there have been several awards which have agreed with one or other of the two initial awards. The issue of the validity of the umbrella clause as a basis of claims requires more detailed analysis in light of the divisions that are apparent in the awards.

4.8 Dispute resolution

Many bilateral investment treaties provide for the resolution of disputes arising from the foreign investment by specifying arbitration in a neutral forum as the method of resolution of the dispute.[136] There are several different types of clause creating different obligations as to such arbitration. At the lowest level, the clauses merely direct the parties to arbitration as a way of resolving disputes arising out of foreign investment transactions. In these treaties, there is merely a prescription of arbitration as a method of settlement of the dispute without in any way creating an obligation on the part of any party to submit compulsorily to arbitration. At the highest level, the treaties entitle the foreign investor unilaterally to initiate proceedings before an ICSID tribunal. The existence of such provisions in bilateral investment treaties is a major step that has been taken to ensure the protection of the foreign investor by enabling him to have direct access to a neutral forum for the settlement of disputes that could arise between him and the host state. It has been suggested that this technique of permitting the foreign investor to take up his own dispute 'depoliticises' the process, as the dispute does not become a dispute between the home state and the host state. The two states could continue their relations as if the dispute did not affect their mutual relations.[137]

---

[135] *SGS* v. *Philippines*, ICSID Case No. ARB/02/6 (Award, 29 January 2004); *SGS* v. *Pakistan*, ICSID Case No. ARB/01/13, (2004) *ICSID Rev* 307.

[136] W. Peters, 'Dispute Settlement Arrangements in Investment Treaties' (1991) 22 *Netherlands Yearbook of International Law* 91.

[137] I. Shihata, 'Towards a Depoliticisation of Foreign Investment Disputes: The Roles of ICSID and MIGA' (1986) 1 *ICSID Rev* 1.

This idea of 'depoliticisation' raises the issue as to whether the foreign investor is enforcing the right of protection which the state has under the treaty or whether he has a fresh right created in him as a result of the treaty. There is significance in having an answer to this issue, as the foreign investor can be reined in by the state if he exceeds his claims or if the arguments that are made are in excess of what the state had intended. The historical origins of the right in the law on diplomatic protection would favour the view that the right that is being enforced is in effect a right of the home state of the foreign investor rather than a right that inheres in him. Increasingly, the technique of being able to interpret the treaty so as to affect the rights of the foreign investor even while a claim he makes goes through arbitration will be a feature of investment treaties, demonstrating the fact that the right that is being enforced is the right of the state.[138] The enforcement of the right is outsourced to the foreign investor but it remains the right of the host state. The existence of the subrogation clause in the treaty which provides for the state to assume the claim after paying off the foreign investor also indicates that the claim that arises is in pursuit of the violation of the right of the state and not of the foreign investor.

A foreign investor, justifiably in many instances, will not have confidence in the impartiality of local tribunals and courts in settling any dispute that may arise between him and the host state. Arbitration, in a neutral state before a neutral tribunal, has traditionally been seen as the best method of securing impartial justice for him. Where an international treaty backs him up by creating an obligation on the host state to submit to arbitral proceedings brought against it by the foreign investor, a major step could be said to have been taken towards investment protection. Bilateral investment treaties take such a step with varying degrees of success. It would, once more, be wrong to say that there is any uniform pattern in the nature of the obligation to arbitrate created by the different treaties. There is no uniform pattern or commitment to arbitrate which emerges from the different treaties. The superficial similarity in many of the provisions is deceptive.[139]

In some treaties, there is a period during which conciliation of the dispute should be attempted prior to arbitration. Treaties concluded by China uniformly contain such a provision indicating the Chinese preference for conciliatory solutions over litigious ones. The requirement of a period in which negotiations must be attempted is becoming usual in treaty practice. Unless a time limit is attached to such a requirement to negotiate, the reference to arbitration may be frustrated by the adoption of delaying tactics.

Most dispute-settlement provisions in investment treaties refer to ICSID arbitration.[140] These treaties work in tandem with the ICSID Convention in creating jurisdiction in an ICSID tribunal. But, care must be taken to examine each provision so as to discover the precise extent of the commitment to create such jurisdiction. Broches, who studied the

---

[138] While the arbitration was going through, the NAFTA parties asked the NAFTA Commission to issue an interpretation, and this then affected the outcome of the arbitration. The tribunal, despite brave posturing, did not question the right of the NAFTA Commission to issue such an interpretation. The technique of consultation between the parties as to the meaning of provisions, particularly in tax matters, is becoming increasingly common in treaties.

[139] A thorough survey is made in A. Parra and I. Shihata, 'Provisions on the Settlement of Investment Disputes in Modern Investment Laws, Bilateral Investment Treaties and Multilateral Treaties on Investment' (1997) 12 *ICSID Rev* 287.

[140] Because of disenchantment with annulment procedures in ICSID, other tribunals are resorted to as well. Treaties provide for resort to other tribunals, particularly *ad hoc* tribunals using UNCITRAL Rules.

provisions containing references to ICSID arbitration, pointed out that the mere references
to ICSID in these treaties did not give jurisdiction over individual disputes to ICSID.[141]
Whether such jurisdiction is created will depend on the precise wording used in the
treaty. Broches makes a distinction between four types of arbitration provision in bilateral
investment treaties. The first type merely states that the dispute 'shall, upon agreement by
both parties, be submitted for arbitration by the Centre'. Such a clause does not constitute
consent to arbitration in the absence of an agreement after the dispute had arisen. The
second type, which requires 'sympathetic consideration to a request [for] conciliation or
arbitration by the Centre', does not amount to consent but, according to Broches, it may
imply an 'obligation not to withhold consent unreasonably'. The third type of clause
requires the host state 'to assent to any demand on the part of the national to submit for
conciliation or arbitration any dispute arising from the investment'. Refusal to assent
may amount to an international wrong, but the clause itself does not create jurisdiction in
ICSID. The fourth type of clause creates jurisdiction in the Centre by giving consent in
anticipation of the dispute. This clause, which is usually found in the treaties concluded
by the United Kingdom, reads:

Each Contracting Party hereby consents to submit to the International Centre for the Settlement of
Investment Disputes for settlement by conciliation or arbitration under the Convention on the
Settlement of Investment Disputes between States and Nationals of Other States ... any legal disputes
arising between that Contracting Party and a national or company of the other Contracting Party
concerning an investment of the latter in the territory of the former.

Such a clause creates jurisdiction in ICSID. Broches is cautious in speaking about the
fourth type of clause, and it is best to cite his words as to the effect of such a clause:

Provisions of this kind, subject to the conditions stated therein and subject further to their compatibility with the Convention, will enable the investor to institute proceedings against the host state
before the Centre and may entitle the host state to avail itself of the same remedy against the investor.

An ICSID tribunal assumed jurisdiction on the basis of a provision in an investment
treaty for the first time in *Asian Agricultural Products Ltd (AAPL)* v. *Sri Lanka*. The
provision in the UK–Sri Lanka treaty on the basis of which such jurisdiction was
assumed is a standard type used in UK treaties, and has been reproduced above as an
example of the fourth type of clause adverted to by Broches. Neither party contested the
jurisdiction assumed by the tribunal on the basis of the treaty. Since *AAPL* v. *Sri Lanka*,
there have been several instances in which jurisdiction has been assumed by ICSID
tribunals on the basis of provisions in investment treaties.[142] The large majority of
investment arbitrations are now based on jurisdiction obtained on the basis of treaty

---

[141] A. Broches, 'Bilateral Investment Treaties and Arbitration of Investment Disputes', in J. Schulsz and J. A. van den Berg (eds.),
       The Art of Arbitration: Liber Amicorum Pieter Sanders (1982).
[142] *AMT* v. *Zaire* (1997) 36 *ILM* 1531; *Tradex* v. *Albania* (1999) 14 *ICSID Rev* 161; *Československá Obchodní Banka* v.
       Slovakia (1999) 14 *ICSID Rev* 251. C. Schreuer, *The ICSID Convention: A Commentary* (2001), pp. 210–23. The volume of
       litigation before ICSID skyrocketed after this new basis of jurisdiction, which had obviously existed in the past, was
       'discovered', in *AAPL* v. *Sri Lanka* (1992) 17 *YCA* 106; (1991) 30 *ILM* 577. Commentators on the UK treaties had not

provisions. This also indicates that the large majority of investment treaties fall under the fourth category mentioned by Broches. They create compulsory jurisdiction at the instance of the foreign investor. There are also NAFTA awards in which jurisdiction was based on the equivalent provisions in that treaty.[143] Whether or not the assumption of such jurisdiction is proper, there is little doubt that many precedents have been established for the assumption of such jurisdiction.[144]

The enforcement of an ICSID award is provided for in the ICSID Convention. The situation of non-ICSID awards depends on the New York Convention on the Enforcement of Foreign Arbitral Awards, which deals with enforcement of awards in international commercial arbitration. Many treaties make reference to the New York Convention. It is doubtful whether the New York Convention, which was designed for the enforcement of arbitral awards made in disputes arising from private traders, could be used to serve the purpose of disputes involving sovereign states. If an obligation to abide by the arbitral award is created by the investment treaty, any reference to the New York Convention must be regarded as a surplusage. There does not appear to have been any awards against states enforced under the New York Convention.

4.9 Arbitration and the exhaustion of local remedies

One further problem which arises in connection with the existence of the arbitration provisions in these treaties is whether, despite the existence of these provisions, there is still a duty on the part of the foreign investor to exhaust all the local remedies provided by the host state before resorting to international arbitration.[145] Some of the arbitration provisions themselves recognise the local remedies rule, which requires the prior exhaustion of all the remedies provided for by the law of the host state before resorting to international remedies. Some impose a time limit and permit the international arbitration after the time limit has expired. The remarks of the International Court of Justice in the *ELSI Case* on whether there is a duty to exhaust local remedies when there is an FCN treaty between the parties is pertinent to bilateral investment treaties as well.[146] The Court

---

adverted to the possibility at the time the UK treaties such as those with Sri Lanka and the Philippines were drafted. Care must be taken to ensure that the investment from which the dispute arises qualifies the conditions that are imposed by the treaty regarding approval, licences, etc. *Yaung Chi Oo Ltd* v. *Myanmar* (2003) 42 *ILM* 540; (2003) 8 *ICSID Reports* 463.

[143] Most NAFTA tribunals, given the strength of the provision on dispute settlement, have rightly assumed jurisdiction on the basis of the provision. Given existing trends, they have not felt it necessary to discuss the issue. When jurisdiction is contested in NAFTA cases, it is not contested on the basis that the provision does not create jurisdiction in the tribunal but on issues pertaining to the standing of the claimant, lack of finality or time bars. *Mondev* v. *United States* (2003) 42 *ILM* 85.

[144] The present author expressed disquiet about the situation in M. Sornarajah, 'Power and Justice in International Investment Arbitration' (1997) 14 *Journal of International Arbitration* 103. There have been recent writings which also indicate that the readiness of arbitral tribunals to infer jurisdiction from treaties may cause concern as to whether there is in reality consent. In the absence of actual consent, there will be an unwillingness on the part of states to accept the awards that are made. Since the awards are difficult to enforce due to a multiplicity of factors such as sovereign immunity and the act of state doctrine, it would be counter-productive for awards to be made in cases where actual consent by the state is difficult to find. See further E. Gaillard, 'Commentary' (2002) 18 *International Arbitration* 247 at 249: 'In recent years, around 70 per cent of ICSID cases were based on bilateral or multilateral investment treaties, not a specific agreement. In all other cases, the state therefore consented to ICSID arbitration only by entering into the investment treaty, not by a specific agreement. It is difficult in this context to sustain an argument based on the supposed consent of the state.'

[145] C. F. Amerasinghe, *Local Remedies in International Law* (1990).

[146] M. Adler, 'The Exhaustion of Local Remedies Rule After the ICJ's Decision in ELSI' (1990) 39 *ICLQ* 641.

observed that the local remedies rule is such a fundamental principle of international law that it cannot be excluded except by express words having that effect. A view has been forcefully stated by Judge Schwebel that the presence of an arbitration clause excludes the need to exhaust local remedies.[147] It is sufficient to point out that this view sits uneasily with the view of the Court that even a treaty such as an FCN treaty should not be considered as ousting the local remedies rule. Yet, it is sometimes claimed that an arbitration clause in a contract can have this effect. This is clearly not possible. This conclusion is supported by the fact that many bilateral investment treaties, despite providing for arbitration, still require the exhaustion of local remedies. Thus, for example, the UK–Jamaica treaty permits submission of disputes to ICSID arbitration only if 'agreement cannot be reached through pursuit of local remedies in accordance with international law'. There are also treaties which require exhaustion of local remedies but specify a time limit for such exhaustion. These treaties recognise the primacy of the rule of exhaustion and of the jurisdiction of the local tribunals over the dispute but effect a compromise between the competence of the local tribunal and the foreign investor's preference for international arbitration by imposing a time limit for local remedies to be exhausted. This latter type of treaty again confirms the existence of a duty to exhaust local remedies despite the fact that they also make provision for international arbitration of the dispute. There are a very few treaties which expressly provide that local remedies need not be exhausted. This indicates a consciousness that securing the exclusion of the rule is advantageous to the foreign investor. Yet, most treaties are silent on this issue. Where a treaty is silent on the question of exhaustion of local remedies, it may be assumed that the reference to arbitration is subject to the rule.

Where the treaty is silent on the issue, it is imperative that it be interpreted in a manner that least derogates from the sovereignty of the parties to the treaty. The local remedies rule is a recognition of the judicial sovereignty of the state over issues that fall within its jurisdiction. It should not be lightly disregarded. This conclusion is supported by the fact that, in the *ELSI Case*, the International Court of Justice dealt with a similar issue regarding the FCN treaty and observed that it was 'unable to accept that an important principle of customary international law should be held to have been tacitly dispensed with, in the absence of any words making clear an intention to do so'.

The absence of any indication regarding the local remedies rule may simply be due to the fact that its negotiation would have provoked too much controversy and raised all the arguments relating to the Calvo doctrine, which required that foreign investment disputes be decided exclusively by the domestic courts. It is a doctrine that has been universalised through the adoption of Article 2(2)(c) of the Charter of Economic Rights and Duties of States. The local remedies rule was at least a compromise. It is unlikely that capital-receiving states will desire to do away with a rule which was in their interest and which has general acceptance. The local remedies rule should therefore be implied into bilateral

---

[147] S. Schwebel and G. Wetter, 'Arbitration and Exhaustion of Local Remedies' (1966) 60 *AJIL* 484; S. Schwebel and G. Wetter, 'Arbitration and the Exhaustion of Local Remedies Revisited', in *Festschrift for Joseph Gould* (1989).

investment treaties which are silent on the issue, even where there is provision in them for international arbitration of the dispute. It was implied in circumstances where there was provision for the dispute to be decided by the International Court of Justice. There is no reason why it should not be implied in circumstances where the dispute is referred to an inferior tribunal. The fact that an arbitration clause which is supported by treaty obligations still requires the exhaustion of local remedies considerably weakens the view of Judge Schwebel that the mere existence of an arbitration clause providing for settlement of the dispute by an international tribunal dispenses with the need to exhaust local remedies. The foreign investor had consciously undertaken the risk of establishing contacts with the legal system of the host state and should not be permitted to remove himself from it merely by inserting an arbitration clause into his contract.

However, the situation is different where the dispute arises directly from a violation of the treaty rather than from a violation of the contract in pursuance of which the dispute arises. Where a treaty violation arises, the dispute may be directly submitted to arbitration, without resort to local remedies. It has also been held that this treaty right cannot be excluded by a contractual provision.[148] This seems to be a sensible distinction. It concedes that the contract and the treaty operate in two distinct realms, the first in national law and the second in treaty law. Where a state has entered into a treaty which gives an automatic right to arbitration to the foreign investor in respect of violations of rights given to him by treaty, it is appropriate that the state should subject the dispute to arbitration. This view is now so established in arbitration practice that it is too late to be contested.

4.9.1 Arbitration between states

The treaties provide that, if disputes were to arise between the two parties, the dispute should be submitted to arbitration. Whether this is a desirable provision in bilateral investment treaties is doubtful. The inclusion of this provision may make many internal political matters of a state subject to arbitration. The decision in the *Nicaragua Case* demonstrated how an FCN treaty, concerned largely with commerce, could give rise to jurisdiction in an international tribunal over a wide range of matters involving the conduct of foreign policy. The *AAPL* v. *Sri Lanka* case, discussed above, shows how matters involving the conduct of civil and secessionist wars could arise before a tribunal which was created to deal with investment disputes. In the case of a more specific treaty such as the bilateral investment treaty, an arbitration clause may create a wider base of jurisdiction. Since the promotion of conditions favourable to the flow of investments is the stated objective of the treaty, hostile acts that undermine that objective could become arbitrable. This has the potential for creating jurisdiction in an arbitral tribunal created under the treaty to review the policies of a contracting state. The implications of this possibility are as yet unclear. There may be a reluctance on the part of more powerful states to conclude treaties with wide language because of such possibilities, but this has the consequence of not being able to give investments adequate protection. The state will

---

[148] The reasoning is that treaty rights exist independently of the contract.

have to balance these factors in deciding whether to conclude such treaties and, if it does so, how restrictive the language it uses should be. There is no perfect treaty provision which will take all these factors into account.

4.9.2 Subrogation

Modern bilateral investment treaties provide for subrogation of the claims of the foreign investor in the home state. This enables the home state to succeed to the investor's claims against the host state after paying out the claims through the insurance schemes for foreign investments run by the home state. The major capital-exporting nations provide such insurance facilities for corporations which make investments overseas. In a sense, this promotes the outflow of investments. Though it is suggested that such outflows are made for the altruistic purposes of promoting investment flows into less developed parts of the world, the fact is that national interests are served by these outflows. Quite apart from the exported capital earning more than it would if it had stayed at home, there is repatriation of profits that will benefit the home state. Where the foreign investment is in the resources field, this assures the home state a ready source of such resources. There is also the fact that an extension of investment and trade overseas brings with it an extension of power, and this serves the foreign policy goals of the home state. The facilitation of foreign investment flows through insurance promotes the goals of the home state.

Subrogation of the home state, in place of the foreign investor who had suffered damage and has been paid off by the insurance agency, achieves another goal. It enables the home state to pursue the claims of the foreign investor as if it had suffered the loss itself. This substitution has a deterrent effect on the host state, as it would be loath to tangle directly with a powerful home state. Technically, the home state will have to pursue the foreign investor's claim in exactly the same manner as the foreign investor himself would have. There has as yet been no rush on the part of home states to utilise subrogation. The prejudice it would cause to the diplomatic relations between the two states deters resort to such extreme measures. Subrogation acts as a subtle threat, but it will not be put to extreme use.

4.10 Safeguard provisions and exceptions

Investment treaties usually contain safeguards and exceptions to the standards of protection and standards of treatment that they offer to foreign investors. These exceptions have assumed significance in the more recent treaties largely because of changed circumstances. The environmental and human rights lobbies have been active against investment treaties which emphasise protection alone without any regard to the environmental and human rights consequences of foreign investment. Besides, once developed states became targets of foreign investment arbitration, these states realised the need for sovereign regulation of certain areas of public concern. As a result, they began making exceptions of those areas of concern. The new model treaties of Canada and the United States contain many exceptions, indicating that foreign investment protection is not the only objective of the treaties and that such protection would not be granted at any cost. The result of this change would introduce many defences to liability of the host state for violations of the treaty standards.

The existence and variety of these safeguards and exceptions themselves defeat any claims as to the possibility of customary international law developing from these treaties. The nature of these safeguards and exceptions in relation to the treaty as a whole and in relation to specific provisions must be carefully scrutinised in order to determine the precise balance that has been struck in each treaty.

The treaty as a whole is affected where the definition of the protected investment is limited by qualifications. It has been seen that some treaties confine protection to investments specifically 'approved in writing' for the purposes of protection by the treaty. Other treaties contain formulations such as investments 'made in accordance with the laws and regulations' of the host state or the wider formula, 'made in accordance with the laws and regulations from time to time in existence'. These treaties preserve sovereign rights. The wider preservation of laws and regulations which contemplate the application of future amendments being included considerably weakens the scope of the treaty because of the implied suggestion that the contracting state could move an investment out of the scope of treaty protection simply by making a subsequent amendment to its laws on investment. In Indian treaties, this exception is stated in a separate article.

Early Canadian treaties, following the US model, contain an exception relating to the environment, but this provision has been considered to be merely hortatory. But, in the latest US and Canadian model treaties, there are stronger provisions regarding environmental protection. Borrowing from trade treaties, there are provisions which protect the health, morals and welfare of the public. Again, these provisions preserve significantly the regulatory powers of the host state. There has been an obvious movement away from the model of the investment treaty which emphasises only protection of the foreign investment. The effect has been to bring about a balance in such a manner as to preserve the regulatory function of the state.

Safeguard provisions are intended to preserve at least a degree of regulatory space. But, such space is preserved more effectively by provisions which are attached to the definition of the investment that is protected. A more effective way to preserve regulatory space is to confine the protection of the treaty only to those investments which conform to the regulatory regime of the host state. Such a limitation also achieves the objectives of economic development, as the regulatory framework exists to promote such development. The extent of the regulatory space that can be preserved depends on the bargaining strength of each state.

However, what is crucial in the new developments is that there is a move towards balancing the interest in investment protection with the interest of the state in preserving its public interest. This view, however, is one that hides the fact that it is not easy to achieve this balance. Once safeguards in the public interest are created, the fact is that the object of investment protection gets diluted. Comfort may be taken from the fact that a tribunal has to decide whether the exception should be applied. But, this will lead to greater uncertainty as tribunals will have to rely on subjective perceptions of whether the safeguard measures or exceptions apply. There will be inconsistency in their decisions. Worse still, the situation is fraught with opportunities for charges of bias. The critic may hazard the view that a treaty that seeks a balance may end up achieving nothing of substance other than to take the law back to square one. The inevitable acceptance of safeguards and exceptions pushed the law in this area into uncharted territory.

4.11 Succession of governments and bilateral investment treaties

One important issue that arises in connection with bilateral investment treaties is whether a government of a state different from that which made the treaty could, at a later date, claim that it is not bound by the treaty because it subscribes to an ideology or an economic strategy that is antithetical to foreign investment. The issue could arise particularly where the subsequent government was installed as a result of a revolutionary change. The new government could argue that the investment treaty stands in the way of the implementation of its economic programme as it imposes more stringent requirements such as the payment of immediate and full compensation for the termination of existing foreign investments. The argument could also be made that the revolutionary change was a changed circumstance which justified termination of the treaty. It is unlikely that such arguments could succeed in the present state of international law. A change of government, even through a revolution, cannot amount to a 'change that radically transforms the obligations under the treaty'.

The situation where the treaty is made by a non-representative government consisting of an elite that has ties with foreign investors and is replaced by a democratic government which seeks to do away with the privileges granted by treaties and other means to a group of foreign investors is more difficult. There may, in addition to arguments based on changed circumstances, also be an argument based on the fact that the previous government was an undemocratic government making a treaty that did not accord with the general interests of the people. It is unlikely that such an argument, despite the moral merits involved in it, could succeed. It may be possible to make arguments based on self-determination and related principles, but it is unlikely that the law would look beyond the fact that a treaty was made and that its obligations are binding on succeeding governments. If self-determination is taken to include the existence of a freely elected government and thus has the nature of an *ius cogens* principle, there may be room for the argument that a treaty concluded by a coterie in power is not binding on a succeeding government which has the democratic mandate of the people. But, the notion of self-determination has not developed in international law to cover such a situation. Such arguments, despite their moral merit, may not have legal validity.

5. New concerns in bilateral investment treaties

The globalisation protests against multilateral investment agreements were generated by the fact that these agreements showed little concern for the environmental and human rights interests involved in foreign investment. The charge was that investment agreements focused entirely on the protection of the interests of the foreign investor and did not concern the interests of the international community or the host state in the protection of the values that were of concern to them. These values generally involve the areas of environmental protection, human rights and economic development. The protests against globalisation have also focused attention on these areas. The non-governmental organisations (NGOs) working in these fields have ensured that these criticisms remained alive. Though initially made against the Multilateral Agreement on Investment promoted by the OECD, these criticisms have become directed at all types of investment treaty.[149] Those who argue along these lines would want to ensure that the regulatory function of the state in areas such as environmental protection are retained, that the state should have a defence to any claims made by foreign investors on the basis of the protection of its interests and that the state should also have the means of recourse to the same dispute-settlement mechanisms provided in the treaty in the event of the violation of its interests. Only the ASEAN Investment Treaty contemplates the possibility of such an action being brought against a multinational corporation.[150] The reaction is justified, for investment treaties have nearly always provided for the interests of multinational corporations without taking into account the possible harm that may be caused by such corporations and the plight of the developing state that stands powerless in the face of this problem. For this reason, the criticisms and the effect they have had in bringing about changes to investment treaties, both regional and bilateral, may be dealt with at this stage.

5.1 Environmental concerns

Environmental groups have regarded multinational corporations as having been responsible for pollution caused particularly in developing countries, where environmental standards are lax. As a result of lax laws, multinational corporations see developing countries as havens where they may make profits without having to bear the costs associated with compliance with the strict regulatory standards they face in their home states. NGOs believe that investment treaties deter actions being taken against polluters as the treaties ensure that infringements of existing rights of investors are regarded as expropriations under the treaties.[151] The argument has also been made that investment treaties secure the export of highly polluting industries into the developing world. For this reason, these groups have argued that investment treaties should contain exemptions to allow host states to protect the environment.

---

[149] The activities of NGOs such as the International Institute for Sustainable Development (IISD) in this area should be noted. The IISD has drafted a code, which seeks to take factors such as environmental protection and human rights into account.

[150] There are, however, instances where states have brought arbitrations against foreign investors for not abiding by contractual obligations. See, for example, *Republic of Indonesia* v. *Newmont* (unreported, *ad hoc* award under UNCITRAL Rules, 2009).

[151] This is borne out by cases such as *Santa Elena* v. *Costa Rica* (2000) 39 *ILM* 317; (2002) 5 *ICSID Reports* 153.

Few investment treaties have responded to this concern. US and Canadian treaties do contain provisions addressing environmental concerns. Such provisions may also be found in NAFTA. Article 1114(1) of NAFTA reads:

Nothing in this Chapter shall be construed to prevent a Party from adopting, maintaining, or enforcing any measure, otherwise consistent with this Chapter, that it considers appropriate to ensure that the investment activity in its territory is undertaken in a manner sensitive to environmental concerns.

But, in *S. D. Myers v. Canada*,[152] the tribunal, which interpreted this provision, said that its nature was merely 'hortatory'. The tribunal did not consider that the Canadian defence – that Canadian hazardous waste should be disposed of in Canada and not sent across the border into the United States for disposal – had any merit. This view was taken despite the fact that Canada's action to prevent the export of the waste was consistent with obligations under the Basel Convention on the Transboundary Movements of Hazardous Wastes. The tendency of tribunals has been to read down the effect of the rare environmental provisions that are to be found in investment treaties, thus preserving the original basis of these treaties as investment protection treaties.

But, the provisions of the model investment treaties of the US and Canada contain far stronger statements of the exception to liability for interference with the foreign investment on environmental grounds. Article 10 of the Canadian model treaty, which contains the general exceptions, states:

1. Subject to the requirement that such measures are not applied in a manner that would constitute arbitrary or unjustifiable discrimination between investments or between investors, or a disguised restriction on international trade or investment, nothing in this Agreement shall be construed to prevent a Party from adopting or enforcing measures necessary:
    (a) to protect human, animal or plant life or health;
    (b) to ensure compliance with laws and regulations that are not inconsistent with the provisions of this Agreement; or
    (c) for the conservation of living or non-living exhaustible natural resources.

This article ensures that a wide range of environmental concerns fall within the exception. It also preserves the validity of all domestic laws and regulations on the environment. No longer can the provision be dismissed as 'merely hortatory'. Importantly, the Canadian treaty also contains a prohibition against the reduction of environmental standards as a means of attracting foreign investment. It entitles Canada to ask for a consultation with the host state if it believes that this has been done.

In most treaties, such an environmental exception has not been spelt out. In these situations, the tendency has been to disregard environmental concerns and emphasise the protection of the foreign investment. But, since an interference justified on the basis of environmental protection will amount to a regulatory interference, the changing legal perceptions will require the nature of the interference to be taken into account in assessing liability. The efforts by Norway at taking environmental protection into account in their

---

[152] *S. D. Myers v. Canada* (2000) 40 *ILM* 1408; (2002) 121 *ILR* 7.

treaties may indicate the direction that could be taken by some investment treaties. In explaining the change, the explanatory note stated:

[E]conomic interests have been weighed against a number of other important social considerations, including resource administration and the environment, in a collective assessment of advantages and disadvantages for Norway of concluding new investment agreements. In order to conduct a satisfactory environmental protection policy, it is of decisive importance that national authorities have a right to employ effective instruments relevant to meet the needs dictated by environmental problems at any given time. Freedom of action and flexibility in the use of instruments are important over time. For the Government, it has therefore been a primary consideration to ensure that investment agreements are drafted in such a way that they do not limit the freedom of action of the environmental protection authorities in providing national instruments for protection of the external environment.

As stated, even if the treaty does not contain such a change, it would be that in the context of changing attitudes, a governmental interference on environmental grounds will be treated as a regulatory interference that is justifiable.

5.2 Human rights

As with the environment, human rights are seldom, if at all, referred to in bilateral investment treaties. But, violations connected with the suppression of dissent against particular projects initiated by multinational corporations have come to light in recent years. Recent litigation before domestic courts against parent companies of multinational corporations allege violations of human rights committed by agents of those multinational corporations in association with the political elites of developing countries illustrates the extent of the problem. Investment treaties may deter a state from interfering to correct a human rights situation that may have arisen. Often, however, the state, or the elites which control it, are also participants along with the multinational corporation in the human rights abuse. Succeeding governments may, however, want to remedy the situation but may be deterred from doing so by the fact that such interference may be regarded as an infringement of the investor's rights under the treaty.

There are few treaties which address this issue. The saving of issues of health, morals and public welfare, a formula that is used in international trade law, has found its way into some investment treaties. But, the scope of the use of the phrase in investment treaties has yet to be determined. In international trade, tribunals have not given the term such a scope as would enable the interests contained in the formula to trump the interests of free trade.[153] There is little cause to believe that the situation will be any different when the phrase is considered in relation to investment treaties. The general trend to interpret these treaties as giving primacy to investment protection will probably be continued. But, the seeds of discontent will multiply as a result.

---

[153] See, for example, the *Thai Tobacco Case* (1991) 37 GATT BISD 200, where the ban on cigarettes by Thailand, justified on health grounds, was given short shrift.

Many states, particularly in Asia and Africa, walk on tightropes when it comes to adopting ethnic policies. Repeated race riots have damaged their economies. Their laws attempt to forestall problems by allocating the economic pie in accordance with ethnic policies devised to reduce tension by ensuring that the majority have an economic role. These policies are enforced by legislation.[154] Investment treaties sit uneasily with such social experiments as they contain national treatment standards that may require that the best national standards are given to foreign investors. There is an obvious need to remove those provisions favouring the disadvantaged sections of the community from the scope of the investment treaties, but, so far, there have been few efforts made in this regard. The South African treaties attempt this by providing that their affirmative action programmes are exempt from national treatment.[155]

Human rights will assume greater significance in the future and will therefore have to be accommodated within investment treaties. The tendency of elites in many states geared to neo-liberalism has been to attract foreign investment even at the cost of human rights. Studies by NGOs in the field show that many natural resource projects are entered into despite the fact that they would have adverse human rights consequences, particularly on aboriginal peoples.[156] Besides, because these projects involve water, electricity and other essential items, the prices that have to be paid under the build, operate and transfer agreements under which the projects are undertaken are fixed by the foreign investor.[157] They are prohibitively high, denying the local people the means of access to life-sustaining resources. Whether later governments will be deterred by investment treaties from breaking agreements related to these projects raises an interesting question. If the violations of human rights involve rights that are protected by *ius cogens* principles such as the prohibition of genocide, torture or racial discrimination, interference with them cannot be prohibited by a bilateral treaty. The Vienna Convention on the Law of Treaties requires that *ius cogens* principles should be given precedence over such treaties.[158] Where lesser types of human rights are involved, these have to be taken into account in making a balanced decision, the protection of investments under the investment treaty not being the only criterion. Where treaty norms conflict, the tribunal has a definite duty in terms of international law to decide which norm is to be given priority. The issue also arises whether arbitrators who are appointed to decide investment disputes have sufficient expertise to decide such questions of international law. It is one of the reasons why the

---

[154] Malaysia has had such a policy for some time. In South Africa, land redistribution and other schemes envisage that economic power will be slowly transferred to the native people of that country.

[155] The clause in the South African treaties, after providing for exemptions from national treatment, lists as an exception: 'any laws or other measure the purpose of which is to promote the achievement of equality on its territory or to advance persons or categories of persons, disadvantage by unfair discrimination in its territory'. The Black Empowerment Act enables discrimination in favour of the black citizens who had suffered discrimination under the *apartheid* regimes.

[156] Amnesty International, 'Understanding Corporate Complicity: Extending The Notion Beyond Existing Laws' (AI Index POL/34/001/2006).

[157] This is indicated by the nature of the disputes which have arisen. For example, *Biwater Gauff* v. *Tanzania*, ICSID Case No. ARB/05/22 (Award, 24 July 2008) and *Baywater Irrigation District* v. *Mexico*, ICSID Case No. ARB(AF)/05/1 involved water disputes. *Himpurna* v. *Indonesia* (2000) 25 *YCA* 13; and the *Hubco* arbitration in Pakistan involved power projects.

[158] This issue is discussed in M. Sornarajah, *The Settlement of Foreign Investment Disputes* (2000), pp. 186–92. See also A. van Aaken, 'Fragmentation in International Law: The Case of International Investment Law' (2008) 19 *Finnish Yearbook of International Law* 128.

issue is avoided. The legitimacy of an award of a tribunal which shows a lack of concern for the competing norms based in human rights is to be doubted. States may well refuse to give effect to such awards, and the legitimacy of the awards may be tested through some other means.

5.3 Economic development

The premise on which investment treaties are made is that foreign investment leads to economic development and that foreign investment treaties lead to greater flows of foreign investment. Both assumptions are coming to be contested. There is no evidence to show that investment treaties have led to greater flows of foreign investment into states making them. Many states, particularly the least developed states, have liberalised their foreign investment laws and made a large number of investment treaties without witnessing the expected flows of foreign investment.[159] The institutions that were formerly advocating these treaties now have studies indicating that the evidence that they lead to positive flows of foreign investment is non-existent and conjectural.[160] Since the underlying assumption of these treaties is that flows of foreign investment lead to economic development, there is no reference to economic development in the treaties nor do they contain any meaningful provisions as to the promotion of such economic development. The role of the capital-exporting partner in promoting flows of foreign investment is not stated as an obligation in the treaties, but instead is referred to in permissive language.

But, the movement for the inclusion of development provisions in investment treaties will gather increasing momentum. The Doha Declaration of the WTO Ministerial Meeting, which mandates the study of investment as a possible discipline under the WTO, requires that the issue be studied in the context of development. Such concessions will highlight the need to ensure that investment treaties contain provisions addressing issues of economic development and a movement away from the investment-protective models of economic liberalism to models that contemplate the elimination of the harmful effect of foreign investment while protecting beneficial investment.

The issue of economic development is intertwined with that of corporate responsibility and good corporate governance. It is obvious that a company that does not practice such responsible conduct cannot contribute to the economic development of the host state. Every positive aspect of foreign investment has a negative aspect as well. If foreign investment does bring about the transfer of technology, there is the possibility that such technology is unsuitable because it is not labour-intensive or is obsolete. In addition, it is also the basis on which restrictive practices such as tie-in provisions,[161] restrictions relating to geographical markets and restraint of competition are practised. If there is employment creation, the employment is at lower wage levels and at a cost that bears no

---

[159] Ghana provides the classic example.
[160] M. Hallward-Driemeier, 'Do Bilateral Investment Treaties Attract FDI? Only a Bit .... And They Could Bite' (World Bank Development Research Group, Working Paper No. 3121, 2003).
[161] These provisions require that goods to be used with the technology be purchased only from the transferor.

relation to the price of the manufactured goods. If there is any upgrading of the infrastructure, this is usually a cost borne by the host state. Environmental pollution and hazardous technology impose costs on the host state. When a situation like Bhopal occurs, the costs are too horrendous ever to be redeemed. In that context, the idea of the absolute protection of foreign investment that is offered by current investment treaties sits uneasily with the possibility of adverse effects. In several instances, the entry of foreign investment could have beneficial effects, but it could also have the opposite effect. A treaty premised on the notion that all foreign investment is uniformly beneficial is not one based on sound foundations.

5.4 *International concerns*

Quite apart from the concerns of the host state, foreign investment within a state raises international concerns as well. It is evident that international law has moved to recognise the fact that matters that fall within the domestic concern of states can implicate international values and that in these situations the international community has a right to ensure that changes are brought about in the domestic situation. The classic modern situation is the movement that has taken place in the area of human rights. No longer can a state claim that gross violations of human rights taking place within its territory are of domestic concern only and do not concern the rest of the international community. The international law on foreign investment has also moved in the same direction, adopting values that it has drawn from associated areas of international law. Though foreign investment is a process that takes place entirely within the host state's territory, the host state cannot avoid the scrutiny of the international community. It cannot avoid the overriding power of international rules over domestic law that justifies the conduct.

There are instances in which international law values have supported changes in foreign investment arrangements, and other instances in which these values have been used as a justification for effecting changes in existing foreign investment arrangements. Thus, for example, in *International Bank of Washington* v. *OPIC*,[162] the blanket measures changing the environmental law were held to justify the breach of a foreign investment agreement. The federal government's interference with a foreign investment contract on the ground that the sand-mining project involved potential damage to the Great Barrier Reef, an area classified under the World Heritage Convention, was held to be justified by the domestic courts. Likewise, the creation of a new state through the assertion of self-determination measures was held to rescind obligations arising from a foreign investment contract.[163] Then there are decisions which indicate that obligations are subject to higher values of the international community. If so, the question has to be raised as to whether investment treaties must accommodate these higher values or make reference to them.

---

[162] (1972) 11 *ILM* 1216.   [163] *Société des Grands Travaux de Marseille* v. *Bangladesh* (1980) 5 *YCA* 177.

But, the provisions of bilateral investment treaties have not been interpreted in that manner at all. In *S. D. Myers* v. *Canada*, the Canadian argument was that, in requiring Canadian hazardous waste to be disposed of in Canada, Canada was complying with the international community's values articulated in the Basel Convention on the Transboundary Movements of Hazardous Wastes. But, the argument was rejected on the ground that NAFTA provisions on national treatment were violated. In *Santa Elena* v. *Costa Rica*, the tribunal held that a foreign investment contract to convert a coastal area into a tourist resort had priority over a later decision of the state to preserve the unique wildlife of the region by converting the area into a nature reserve. In *SPP* v. *Egypt*, the issue was raised as to whether the protection of a cultural site which was listed under the World Heritage Convention justified the termination of a project to build a tourist complex at the site.[164] These decisions, made under investment treaties, indicate that there is insensitivity to international values in tribunals which obtain jurisdiction over the dispute through dispute-settlement mechanisms in investment treaties.

The issue arises as to whether matters of international concern relating to the environment or human rights are *ius cogens* principles which trump the rights of foreign investors under investment treaties unilaterally to institute arbitral proceedings. The argument can credibly be made that there are some values in international environmental law and human rights law that are so fundamental that the propositions of investment treaties which are designed to protect large multinational corporations should give way to them. There is also room for the further proposition that these issues should not be dealt with by arbitral tribunals that are created under investment treaties which have only a narrow mandate to decide issues that arise from the foreign investment. Instead, tribunals that reflect the interests of the international community as a whole should deal with such disputes. There must be a doctrine of arbitrability created which ensures that issues that concern the international community as a whole should not be disposed of by arbitral tribunals which draw their jurisdiction from the will of only the parties to the dispute before them.

5.5 Regulatory space and bilateral treaties

All treaties constrain sovereignty. Investment treaties constrain sovereign rights of control over the intrusive process of foreign investment which takes place entirely within the territory of the host state. To this extent, the erosion of sovereignty in such treaties is considerable. But, it is trite law that a treaty can control events that are entirely internal and domestic. In Chapter 3 above, it was shown that states have various techniques of controlling foreign investment, and thus the state can promote its own development objectives. The issue arises as to whether the right to control investment by the host state is lost as a result of investment treaties. The answer depends on the type of treaty that is made. Where the treaty is of the type that the United States makes, with rights of entry and national treatment, then the erosion of the regulatory space becomes

---

[164] This case did not arise under a treaty.

considerable. But, in other treaties, there is always a negotiated balance between the right of regulation by the host state and the rights of protection and treatment given to the foreign investor.

Many treaties preserve the regulatory regimes of the host state by confining the scope of the treaty or by defining the foreign investment that is protected in a restrictive manner. This point bears repetition. In most Southeast Asian treaties, the practice has been to extend protection only to 'investments specifically approved in writing'. This ensures that only investments that are regarded as particularly beneficial to the state are given approval for the purposes of protection. In other treaties, the formula is to extend protection only to investments 'made in accordance with the laws, policies and regulations' of the host state.[165] It is evident that there is a desire to ensure that the regulatory regime plays a role in defining the extent of the treaty protection. It is evident that only investment which conforms to the state's regulatory structure will receive protection under such treaties. Another formulation is so subjective as to tilt the balance entirely in favour of the host state. This contains the subjective formula that the investment that is protected is an investment 'made in accordance with the laws, policies and regulations from time to time in existence'.[166] Such a formulation, while fully preserving regulatory space, deprives the treaty of all its protective content, as the host state could defeat the treaty's protection simply by changing its laws. The existence of this concern over the preservation of the regulatory space and the manner in which it has been achieved in different treaties indicates that a carefully negotiated balance is struck in every bilateral investment treaty. The preservation of regulatory space is achieved in individual provisions in the treaties through various methods. Thus, limitations on the right of repatriation of capital in times of economic difficulties and on the safeguard provisions in some treaties are examples of preserving regulatory space in specific areas.

5.6 Bilateral investment treaties and customary international law

The view is stated that the large number of bilateral investment treaties that have been signed in recent years has led or will lead to the creation of customary principles of international law on the protection of foreign investment. The frequency with which this view is stated is puzzling in view of the fact that the evidence and the theory are against the possibility of investment treaties creating customary international law. It is necessary therefore to consider again the reasons why investment treaties cannot create customary international law.

The obvious starting-point is the reason for the treaties. Had the rules on investment protection in international law been clear, there would have been no reason for such treaties. The accepted reason for the treaties is that as a result of the drive for the New International Economic Order by the developing states, there had been a lack of clarity as

---

[165] The Malaysian model treaty, 2002. A similar formula is used in recent Chinese treaties.
[166] This formulation is widely used in the newer treaties of Australia and Indonesia.

to the rules, with two competing sets of norms accepted by two sets of states as constituting the rules on foreign investment protection. It was in this context that investment treaties came into play so that states could bilaterally decide on what rules of protection would apply. These treaties were intended to be *lex specialis*, the general rules being unclear.

The treaties do not deal with all foreign investment but only with those that fall within their definition. Thus, some treaties require that the investment be an 'approved investment' for purposes of protection, and some require that they be made 'in accordance with the laws and regulations' of the host state. Once this limitation is accepted, there will be a different set of rules applying to investments which fall outside the definition. So, the conclusion must be that the treaties, being specific to the types of foreign investment they cover, cannot create customary law which is of general application.

The element of *opinio iuris* necessary is also diminished when one considers the reasons for the making of these treaties. Clearly, many states make these treaties without understanding their significance. They make them because others make them and they have to compete with the others, or because they are told to do so by grant- and loan-making institutions. These circumstances hardly give rise to the *opinio iuris* that is necessary to create custom.

It is not possible to show uniformity as to norms even in the practice of just one state. The model treaty of the United States has undergone changes in light of experience and changed circumstances. As the United States becomes one of the largest capital-importing countries, its treaties will show a greater awareness of this fact. Similarly, the newer Chinese treaties show the reverse process at work. As China becomes a capital exporter, it will be more conscious of stricter norms of investment protection. That being so, it is difficult to support the idea that there is customary practice when there is a lack of concordance in the practice of even one state within the short period the treaties have been in existence.

Even definite rules in investment treaties may have difficulty in establishing themselves as principles of customary law. The obvious candidate is the rule that there must be prompt, adequate and effective compensation upon expropriation, the 'Hull formula' supported consistently by the United States. Not all treaties adopt this formula. It is true that the large majority of newer treaties do so. But, they still may not have the force to change the rules that developing countries had asserted together in the past.

With the increasing tendency to create exceptions to liability, the possibility of inflexible rules on investment protection arising becomes remote. The insistence on the idea that the treaties create customary international law is due to the creation of inflexible rules on investment protection that can be applied universally now that the means of creating them through multilateral treaties have ended. It is essentially a neo-liberal project. But, the scope for inflexible rules has also lessened with the acceptance of wide exceptions to liability in the treaties. If the treaties do create custom, then it is obvious that the exceptions also have to be taken on board. Once the scope for exceptions increases, the drive for acceptance of the treaties as customary law will subside.

6. Conclusion

There has been intense activity in the area of bilateral investment treaties. This activity results from a convergence of factors. Developing states are intent on attracting foreign investment, and there is competition for the investment that is available. In the absence of clear rules on investment protection, capital-exporting states have found it desirable that they should give as much protection as possible to their investors by negotiating treaties with clear rules. This accounts for their desire to enter into these treaties. They are preferred by new industrial states which did not have much influence on developing states. This accounts for the large number of treaties which a country like Germany has entered into. The German treaties also indicate that they have no consistent pattern, again showing the desire on the part of that state to emphasise more the forming of an investment relationship than the form of the treaty. The wide divergence in the terms of the German treaties indicates this factor. Given this wide divergence in the practice of even a single state, it is unlikely that these treaties can give rise to any significant customary international law on foreign investment protection. Bilateral investment treaties are *lex specialis* as between the parties, and they are likely to remain so. It was once thought that their momentum may be somewhat reduced by the fact that the nature of the uses to which they could be put have not been explored yet. Indeed, Vagts pointed out, 'so far as the literature discloses, [bilateral investment treaties] have not yet been put to the test so that we do not know how much they enhance the security of foreign investment'.[167] But, passage of time has shown that investment treaties have been very effective in providing relief to the foreign investor. The *AAPL* v. *Sri Lanka* case shows that such a treaty is effective in conferring jurisdiction on international arbitral tribunals. Since then, the caseload of ICSID has multiplied largely on the basis of the invocation of jurisdiction on the basis of the provisions in bilateral investment treaties. The explosion of litigation under NAFTA also demonstrates that, from the point of view of the foreign investor, creative litigation strategies can be employed to secure the rights of foreign investors. But, the issue now is whether there has been too rapid a movement in favour of the protection of the rights of the investor without heeding the interests of the host state and its environmental and other interests. A reaction will set in if there is further movement in favour of protection without assuaging the valid concerns of those who argue the case for environmental protection, human rights and economic development. Unless investment treaties come to reflect a balance between the rights of the foreign investors and the regulatory concerns of the host state, their future viability will continue to be contested. This concern will become particularly acute as evidence keeps mounting that such treaties do not lead to greater flows of foreign investment into a host state or that they do not necessarily lead to economic development. The question will then be raised more stridently as to why there is so great a surrender of sovereignty in favour of

---

[167] D. Vagts, 'Protecting Foreign Investment: An International Law Perspective', in C. Wallace (ed.), *Foreign Investment in the 1990s* (1990), p. 102 at p. 112.

the interests of the foreign investor when the *quid pro quo* that the host state receives is tenuous and uncertain. If the fervour for economic liberalism dies down, the challenges to investment treaties will become more strident.

It could be that a tipping-point has now been reached. The model treaties of the United States and Canada have sought to achieve a balance, but the opening up of new defences may indicate disenchantment in that the original purpose of investment protection has become much diluted. The Norwegian model treaty also sought a balance. The ASEAN Comprehensive Treaty reflects an attempt to accommodate the inconsistent objectives of regulatory control with investment protection. The new generation of treaties are moving away from the original purpose of investment protection. The trend was accelerated by excessively pro-investor interpretations[168] and the manifestly expansive arguments that claimants put upon treaty formulations.

The proposition that foreign investment flows are beneficial to economic development is based on the tenets of economic liberalism. It is this assumption that has driven the sudden growth in the number of foreign investment treaties in recent times.[169] But, with its decline, the fervour for investment treaties has noticeably diminished. In the process of reversal of the excessive interpretations placed on the treaties by arbitral tribunals, states are making new types of treaties purporting to bring about a balance. But, this effort may result in the object of investment protection being so emasculated that the purpose of the treaty may become meaningless. The result is that the law will return to the same state of normlessness that prevailed prior to the making of investment treaties.

---

[168] Efforts have been made to show that the interpretations of the arbitrators were not biased. S. D. Franck, 'Empirically Evaluating Claims about Investment Arbitration' (2007) 86 *North Carolina Law Review* 1. But, in doing so, authors merely look at the results of arbitrations and not at the nature of the pro-investor doctrines created by arbitrators on the basis of treaty interpretation.

[169] For the view that developing states are overwhelmed by economic theories that are formulated in the West, see O. Mehmet, *Westernising the Third World: The Eurocentricity of Economic Development Theories* (1999).

6

Multilateral instruments on foreign investment

If states were in agreement as to the norms that constitute the international law of foreign investment, it would have been possible to agree a multilateral agreement on foreign investment stating the substantive rules which apply in the area. The fact that no such multilateral agreements exist is due to the existence of conflicting approaches to the problem of foreign investment protection and the existence of contending systems relating to the treatment of foreign investment. Several attempts have been made at bringing about a comprehensive code on foreign investment,[1] but they have resulted in failure simply because of the ideological rifts and clashes of interests that attend this branch of international law. Most drafts have been made with the objective of providing as much protection as is possible to foreign investment. These have been rejected by capital-importing states. The entry into the picture of non-governmental organisations (NGOs) further complicates the picture. They object to multilateral agreements which concentrate on investment protection exclusively without addressing issues relating to environmental degradation or the human rights violations associated with foreign investment. Some of these organisations take the view that the development interests of the poor are not addressed through such instruments, which seek only to protect the rights of rich multinational corporations. The entry of NGOs as major players in the area has further complicated the issue of making such agreements. It is relevant to note that NGOs which supported the rights of foreign investors have been active in the field for a longer period of time.[2] But, voices against confining the drafting of investment treaties to investment protection alone have increased as a result of the growing strength of the environmental and human rights groups entering this sphere.[3] They provide support to developing countries, which do not support multilateral codes which restrict their

---

[1] The first attempt was the foreign investment provisions in the Havana Charter (1948), which contemplated the establishment of an International Trade Organization. It did not eventuate due to the objection to the provisions by business groups and the eventual refusal of the United States to participate in the process of the establishment of such an organisation. J. E. S. Fawcett, 'The Havana Charter' (1949) 5 *Yearbook of World Affairs* 320.

[2] The International Chamber of Commerce is one such non-governmental organisation. In 1972, it drafted Guidelines for International Investments. A private group drafted what came to be known as the Abs–Shawcross Convention. It was espoused by Germany and submitted to the OECD. For a discussion of the draft, see Lord Shawcross, 'The Problems of Foreign Investment in International Law' (1961) 102 *Hague Recueil* 334; for the text, see (1968) 7 *ILM* 117.

[3] This phenomenon is new. Though these non-governmental organisations have existed for a considerable time, their concern with the investment field probably dates from the organised protests against the OECD's attempt to formulate a multilateral agreement on investment (1995–8). The abandonment of the project is at least partly due to the organised protests.

ability to regulate foreign investment significantly and which deny them the power to negotiate treaties bilaterally. The fear also is that, once a multilateral treaty is created, higher standards could be obtained through bilateral negotiations.[4]

There have also been instruments which contained rules favouring the interests of developing states.[5] These have been rejected by developed states. Most of these instruments came about when there was a movement to curb the power of multinational corporations. There was a period in which these corporations were seen as undermining the sovereignty of the states in which they operated. That period also coincided with the movement towards the creation of a New International Economic Order giving greater control over foreign investment to developing states. In that context, codes were drafted by, in particular, a specially created United Nations body, the United Nations Commission on Transnational Corporations (UNCTC). These codes were resisted by developed states, which put forward an alternative version. The efforts within the UNCTC to draft a code of conduct did not succeed. Developing countries, which in the 1990s gave up their call for a New International Economic Order and instead adopted policies of liberalisation, gave up the effort to create a code of conduct on multinational corporations in 1992.[6] The first section of this chapter describes the efforts at drafting multilateral investment codes.[7]

Among the more recent efforts to draft instruments on investment are the Guidelines on Foreign Investment proposed by a study group of the World Bank, and the Multilateral Agreement on Investment (MAI) attempted by the Organization for Economic Co-operation and Development (OECD). The Guidelines were drafted in 1992. They were non-binding, as the expert group felt that the time was not ripe for a binding multilateral code on investment. This was despite the fact that, in the 1990s, there was a general fervour for a liberalisation of the regime for foreign investment. There was a proliferation of bilateral and regional treaties on investment. The developing countries had for various reasons given up the attempt to create a New International Economic Order and instead were courting foreign investors by granting them high levels of protection both through their domestic law as well as through investment treaties. In 1992, the developing states also gave up on the project to draft a code on multinational corporations. They had begun to court these corporations in order to obtain foreign investment. Certainly, this was the optimum time to negotiate and agree a multilateral code. The OECD, perhaps rightly, thought that the time was ripe to push through a binding code on foreign investment. Its project for a Multilateral Agreement on

---

[4] This has happened in the area of intellectual property, where, after TRIPS, developed states negotiated bilateral intellectual property treaties establishing higher standards of protection than in TRIPS.

[5] There was an attempt to draft a code of conduct on multinational corporations by the now defunct United Nations Commission on Transnational Corporations. The attempt failed due to its non-acceptance by developed states.

[6] This coincided with the rise of neo-liberalism. It is possible to identify a chain of events that took place. The fall of the Soviet Union, the drying up of aid, the lack of funds from private banks, the sudden competition for foreign investment coming from the former Eastern European satellite states of the Soviet Union and the assumed success of the East Asian states based on foreign investment combined to compel a change of direction towards neo-liberalism.

[7] The World Bank study lists the multilateral instruments made up to the date of the study. The inclusion of human rights documents in the list is selective. It includes the Universal Declaration of Human Rights and the European Convention on Human Rights. But, the relevance of these documents is confined to the statement of the right to property only. If the right to property is relevant, a fuller list containing the variations on the statements of this right should have been included. For the list, see World Bank, *Legal Framework for the Treatment of Foreign Investment* (1992), vol. 1, pp. 63–72.

Investment (MAI) began in 1994, but was soon to run aground as the fervour for liberalisation subsided and the anti-globalisation protests took hold. The MAI became the first target of these protests and was the catalyst enabling the coming together of a diversity of interests opposed to globalisation. The negotiations involved only the developed states, and this was in practice the wrong strategy. It should be remembered that the world had just seen the establishment of the WTO, with its instruments on intellectual property and services which were to the disadvantage of the developing world. It could well be that a world enamoured with neo-liberalism could have accepted a code on investment as well. But, the moment had passed. A crippling economic crisis in Asia in 1997 catalysed disenchantment with neo-liberal policies.[8]

With the failure of the MAI, the focus has now shifted to the WTO. The Second Ministerial Conference of the WTO, held in Singapore, mandated the consideration of an agreement on investment under the auspices of the WTO. The matter was not considered at the Third Ministerial, in Seattle, where massive demonstrations against the WTO muted consideration of the issue. At the Doha Ministerial Meeting, the decision was made to consider the possibility of taking up the subject of investment, but with the 'development dimension' in mind. By the time of the Cancun Ministerial Meeting in September 2003, a group of developing countries had coalesced. They put together a paper expressing the view that, if a multilateral code were to come into existence, it should not concentrate solely on the protection of investment. The code should also have regard to the prohibition of misconduct of multinational corporations, the active promotion of investment flows and other matters of interest to economic development. As other issues, such as agriculture, dominated the meeting, the investment issue was not considered. After much debate, the issue of investment was given up. The strategy of including within the instrument the misconduct of multinational corporations worked. Obviously, in the future, when a multilateral code comes to be discussed, the same argument will be made that any such code should address both the protection of foreign investment as well as the avoidance of harm to the host state by imposing liability for such harm on multinational corporations. It is, however, unlikely that home states of multinational corporations would agree to such a code. The area covered by this chapter is both current and controversial.

1. The international norms on multinational corporations

The study of multinational corporations in international law is rather recent,[9] though they have been actors on the international scene for a long time. The major trading companies that

---

[8] The Suharto government, which advocated liberal foreign investment, fell. In neighbouring Malaysia, the technique of overcoming the crisis was through exchange controls. In Thailand, a policy of strengthening native industries was adopted. The move away from neo-liberalism and a move towards regulation had started earlier in Southeast Asia, making it able to better withstand the later global crisis.

[9] For book-length treatments of the subject, see P. Muchlinski, *Multinational Corporations and the Law* (2nd edn, 2008); and C. Wallace, *The Multinational Enterprise and Legal Control: Host State Sovereignty in an Era of Economic Globalization* (2002). S. Amarasinha and J. Kokott, 'Multilateral Investment Rules Revisited', in P. Muchlinski, F. Fortino and C. Schreuer, *Handbook of International Investment Law* (2008).

existed in Europe, such as the East India Company and the Dutch East India Company, though they were not multinational corporations in the modern sense, were the progenitors of imperial rule. The modern multinational corporation is better integrated due to superior means of communication and is more cohesive due to integrated modes of production. They are responsible for all the investment flows that take place.[10] The largest of these multinational corporations command financial assets in excess of those controlled by some states. Their role in domestic and international affairs cannot be under-estimated. As major repositories of power, they advanced rules and codes of conduct which suited their interests. They have the capacity to influence the course of international events and to shape principles of international law.

It has been a defect in the theory of international law that this fact has not been accommodated in theoretical constructs of the law. The idea of the open seas was formulated at the behest of trading companies so as to ensure that they had open access to the seas to favour their maritime trading interests.[11] The system of appointing diplomatic agents for the protection of nationals owes its origins to the system of agents appointed by corporations to look after their commercial interests.[12] Colonies were first conquered by corporations before they were attached to an imperial system. State-centred theories of international law have, however, never recognised the fact that trading corporations have been forces within the international system with the capacity to generate international norms of behaviour or, at least, to have an influence on the shaping of the forms these rules take.[13] The power of the companies continued long after the imperial states took over from the trading companies and established their sovereignty over the colonies. In the Middle East, oil diplomacy, upon which power depended in the twentieth century, was pursued as much by the major oil corporations as by their home states.[14] It was evident that the system of investment protection through contractual means was devised largely through the activity of individuals and organisations that were keen on protecting the interests of these corporations. The law that was built up through private means of law-making focusing on arbitral awards that result from consensual procedures of decision-making and the writings of scholars who were desirous of building up of a system of investment protection through the instrumentality of international law. Multinational corporations are thus able to make law by using low-order sources of international law, arbitral decisions and the writings of 'highly qualified publicists'.

The power of the old trading corporations like the British East India Company pale into insignificance when compared with the power of the multinational corporation in the

---

[10] Technically, every individual is capable of making foreign investments. At least one modern investment dispute arose from an investment made by a single investor: *Vacuum Salts* v. *Ghana*. But, it is seldom that large investments are made by a single investor, though large multinational corporations are often controlled by single individuals or by families.

[11] It is no secret that Grotius, who is sometimes credited as being a disinterested founder of international law, was in the employ of the Dutch East India Company when he formulated the theory of the freedom of the seas.

[12] A. Nussbaum, *A Concise History of the Law of Nations* (1954), p. 125.

[13] It is incredible that the United Nations Rapporteur on Multinational Corporations and Human Rights still believed in his 2008 report that multinational corporations do not have personality in law and hence cannot be subject to binding codes. This flaw taints his approach to the subject.

[14] D. Yergin, *The Prize: The Epic Quest for Oil, Money, and Power* (1991).

modern world. The old trading corporation was a dinosaur with a small head and a huge body in the sense that actual control over subsidiaries in far-flung lands could not in practice be exercised by the parent company due to inadequate communication facilities. The control exercised by the parent company over its subsidiaries in the case of a modern multinational corporation is far more effective due to speedier methods of communications and the transferring of assets and personnel. The influence that the multinational corporation can exert on states and on the international community is commensurate with the increase in this power. Many multinational corporations command capital assets far in excess of the states in which they operate. It is not difficult to understand how they can affect trends in both international and domestic politics. The need for regulation of this private power through the instrumentality of international law is a necessary fact which has not been adequately addressed, largely because the existence of such power itself ensures that no control is brought about.[15] The curtain of positivism provides obvious advantages.

At one stage, developing countries saw the need to control the power of multinational corporations. They sought to influence the United Nations bodies which they controlled to formulate rules of conduct for multinational corporations. These efforts were part of the package to bring about the New International Economic Order. These efforts began at a time when the developing states had sufficient cohesion and sufficient confidence in being able to achieve new rules through their unity. The general belief that multinational corporations were undermining the sovereignty of states also had a hold in Europe at the same time. The dependency theory – that multinational corporations were instrumental in keeping the economies of peripheral states in a state of perpetual dependence – still had hold in Latin America. In that context, it was possible to talk of bringing about binding codes of conduct to regulate the activities of multinational corporations. The circulation of petro-dollars ensured that there was sufficient money available for developing countries. It is in that context that the effort was made by the UNCTC[16] to draft a Code of Conduct on Transnational Corporations.

But, the fervour for the New International Economic Order was to diminish. With aid drying up and a loan crisis emerging due to a failure to meet payments on petro-dollar loans, foreign investment capital became the only available capital for economic development. All developing countries began to compete with each other for the limited foreign investment that was available. Hostility to multinational corporations ended, and they began to be heavily courted. Changes in ideology also occurred with the fall of communism. With the new states resulting from the break-up of the Soviet Union embracing free market notions, the competition for foreign investment among developing countries increased. The ascendancy of neo-liberalism speeded the process of the liberalisation of trade regimes, resulting in the formation of the WTO. Though, in 1992, the World Bank judged rightly that the world

---

[15] Through the employment of devices such as soft, non-binding codes and heavy advertising campaigns, attention is deflected from the need for control. The very institutions like the OECD, which want strong, binding measures on foreign investment protection, argue for soft codes for the regulation of the conduct of multinational corporations.

[16] The UNCTC was established in pursuance of a study of the problem of multinational corporations. A group of eminent persons was appointed by ECOSOC Res. 1721 (LIII) to study the problem. The group recommended the setting up of the UNCTC, which was established in 1974. The group justified its continued interest in the issue on the ground that 'certain practices and effects of transnational corporations had given rise to widespread concern and anxiety in many quarters and a strong feeling has emerged that the present *modus vivendi* should be reviewed at the international level'.

was still not ripe for a binding code on foreign investment and brought out a set of guidelines instead, the OECD, just a few years later, embarked upon the framing of a binding Multilateral Agreement on Investment (MAI). 1992 was also the year in which the UN effort to draft a code of conduct for multinational corporations was shelved.[17]

The picture was to change again. The MAI soon became the focus of protests. They were generated largely by human rights and environmental groups which claimed that the instrument focused entirely on the protection of multinational corporations without addressing the fact that they were also responsible for much of the human rights abuses and environmental degradation that takes place around the world. Around that time, there was also growing disenchantment with globalisation, which had been trumpeted as a force that integrated the world and ensured human progress.[18] Suddenly, there was discontent with the process. It was seen as driving a wedge between the rich and the poor not only on a global scale but also within the developed states themselves. As one commentator put it, the process of globalisation had so divided society on an economic basis that the Third World had moved into the First World.[19] The battles that ensued on the streets of Western capitals whenever the economic organisations connected with neo-liberalism met signalled the growing opposition to the idea of bringing about regimes on foreign investment that gave protection to multinational corporations without controlling their faults. The protesters had organised themselves so effectively that they were able to exert sufficient pressure on their governments to pull out of the negotiations of the MAI.

But, the issue of investments then moved into the WTO. It was tasked with the formulation of an instrument on investment which would then be fitted into the existing structure of the WTO with its dispute-settlement mechanism. The assurance to the developing world and to the discontented was that the issue of investment would be considered in the context of economic development. The text of the Doha Ministerial Meeting of the WTO assures that this would be done in formulating an instrument. Though work on the process of considering an instrument had begun, some states had already come out strongly against the making of such an instrument. Finally, a coalition of developing states drafted an instrument on investments, very reminiscent of the UNCTC Code, which linked the protection of foreign investment and the liability of multinational corporations for environmental, human rights and other misconduct. With that, the developed states thought it prudent to discontinue the efforts at pursuing a multilateral instrument on investment through the WTO. Some would see in this episode a return to Third World cohesion in matters of investment. The coalition was led by China, India and Brazil, three emerging industrialising powers. But, the question whether it was the return to Third World cohesion or a practical means of avoiding the imposition of firm norms that would reduce regulatory control at a time when developing states were industrialising should be considered more carefully.

---

[17] The UN Centre for Transnational Corporations thereafter was absorbed into UNCTAD, and UNCTAD itself was to undergo transformation from being an active sponsor of Third World viewpoints to performing mundane functions like commissioning studies on investment. The reduction of the UNCTC and the transformation of UNCTAD are themselves visible evidence of the transformation of power equations in the field.

[18] J. Stiglitz, *Globalization and Its Discontents* (2002).   [19] Caroline Thomas, *Globalization and the South* (1997).

The four principal instruments that have been attempted, all of which resulted in failure, tell the tale of these movements. The first is the OECD's draft code of conduct on multinational corporations. The second is the World Bank Group's non-binding guidelines on foreign investment. The third is the OECD's MAI. The fourth effort was to move the issue into the WTO. The following sections describe the principal features of some of these efforts. In the course of doing so, all four efforts are captured. The efforts at drafting an instrument demonstrate the constantly shifting ebb and flow of attitudes to foreign investment. The OECD code was attempted at a time when developing countries were weak. The UNCTC code was attempted during the highpoint of Third World cohesion, as part of the NIEO package. During the period of neo-liberalism, the World Bank drafted its Guidelines on Foreign Investment in 1992 and the OECD attempted the MAI in 1995. The WTO discussed its instrument at a time when fervour for neo-liberalism was ending. It is clear that the text of a code will depend very much on the dominant views of the time. With the ending of the neo-liberal period and the economic crisis of 2008 requiring new regulatory controls, states are unlikely to agree a multilateral code that restricts their control over economic sectors. As a result, further attempts at such codes may not be made for a long time to come. The effort will likely shift towards cobbling together principles extracted from bilateral investment treaties and elevating them into multilateral principles either on the basis that they are customary law or on the basis of the most-favoured-nation clauses in the treaties.

2. The Draft Codes on Multinational Corporations

The UNCTC Draft Code on Multinational Corporations, like the OECD's Multilateral Agreement on Investment (MAI), never received acceptance. But, both are important, as they indicate the differences that exist between states, and their respective conceptions of what constitutes the ideal code for investment. Both documents were drafted at a time when the political climate was favourable to their drafting. The UNCTC's Draft Code was attempted at a time when there was considerable hostility to multinational corporations and a determination among developing countries to control foreign investment. The OECD's MAI was drafted at a time when the fervour for liberalisation was at its highpoint, and it came to a halt when that fervour subsided. Both efforts, and the contents of the codes that were drafted, are described in this section, along with the intervening attempts. We commence with a description of the UNCTC's Draft Code.

2.1 Description of the UNCTC Draft Code

The final version of the Draft Code contained seventy-three paragraphs. Unlike the MAI, which was an investment protection document only, the UNCTC Draft Code was a comprehensive document which addressed the conduct of multinational corporations. It was premised on preventing misconduct by multinational corporations, not on the protection of their investments. The philosophy behind the two instruments were different. This gap in perceptions has proved to be unbridgeable.

The major provisions of the code may now be noted.

2.1.1 The preamble

The preamble to the Draft Code states that the object of the Code is to 'maximise the contributions of transnational corporations to economic development and growth and to minimise the negative effects of the activities of these corporations'. It is clear that the code is based on the premise of the report of the Group of Eminent Persons on Multinational Corporations that multinational corporations can promote economic development provided they are harnessed to the economic goals of the state and provided the negative impacts of their investments are avoided. It thus rejects the classical economic theory on foreign investment that foreign investment uniformly promotes the economic development of the host state. As a result, the premises on which foreign investment protection has hitherto been built stand rejected. Economic liberalism, which was to gather strength in the 1990s and fuel the move towards the MAI, is based on the premise that what is good for development deserves protection. The Draft Code contains an implicit rejection of that argument, and therefore presents an ideological counter to the premises on which the developed states have built up their norms on foreign investment protection. The preamble, though not contested by the developed states during drafting, stands as a rejection of the policy of the developed states in constructing their instruments on foreign investment. It is in marked contrast to other international instruments on investment, such as bilateral investment treaties or the ICSID and MIGA Conventions, which are prefaced by the classical view that foreign investment is uniformly beneficial to economic development. These instruments do not advert to the 'negative effects' of foreign investment or the need to minimise them.

2.1.2 Definition

There was some early dispute as to the definition of the transnational corporation. The developed states required the inclusion of state corporations in the definition of transnational corporations, whereas developing states preferred that the definition be confined to private corporations. There was no consensus as to the inclusion of state corporations within the definition of multinational corporations. This debate will become relevant when sovereign wealth funds make foreign investments in developed states. They will claim protection of the investment treaties on the ground that they are to be treated like private foreign investors or multinational corporations.

2.1.3 Respect for national sovereignty

Article 7 of the Draft Code states that transnational corporations shall respect the national sovereignty of the countries in which they operate and the right of each state to exercise permanent sovereignty over its natural resources. The succeeding articles flow from the principle of sovereignty. They seek to spell out the fact that the foreign corporation which operates in the territory of the host state should recognise the sovereignty of the host state. They require foreign corporations to accept and abide by the laws of the host state and ensure that they do not act in any way that is inconsistent with the economic objectives of the host state.[20] The sovereignty of the host state is not absolute, for the Code later refers to the duty of the state to fulfil in good faith the international obligations that it has undertaken. The qualification is consistent with the reference to sovereignty in the other documents associated with the New International Economic Order. Thus, the Charter of Economic Rights and Duties of States also refers to the requirement that international obligations are fulfilled in good faith. But, the content of the international obligations is a matter of controversy. It obviously includes obligations in multilateral and bilateral treaties. But, whether it includes contractual agreements between transnational corporations and their host states and limitations created by customary international law is a matter of dispute.[21]

The reference to permanent sovereignty over natural resources originates from a long string of General Assembly resolutions which have asserted a state's right to control the exploitation of its natural resources. The doctrine is too well entrenched now, as a result of its acceptance in constitutional provisions as well as in the new forms of contract that have been devised so as to reflect the host state's right of control. Though contested, there is some serious support in the literature for the rule to be considered an *ius cogens* principle.

2.1.4 Renegotiation of contracts

An obligation is created to renegotiate contracts where the contractual equilibrium which existed at the time of the contract has been altered by a fundamental change of circumstances.[22] This is a departure from the hoary doctrine of *pacta sunt servanda* upon which developed states have placed so much store in building up a theory of internationalisation of foreign investment contracts.[23] But, renegotiation is more sensible as a technique for avoiding disputes and for ensuring that the relationship remains viable in the context of changed circumstances. There is a growing body of opinion which believes that a renegotiation clause should be read into foreign investment contracts of long duration. The inclusion of the duty to renegotiate in the Draft Code is consistent with this view.[24] Again, one can see that the genesis of many of the ideas which underlay the Draft Code was in the resolutions that accompanied the New International Economic Order and the writings that supported it. To that extent, there was a definite effort being made to bring about norms opposed to those that had hitherto been articulated in the area.

2.1.5 Non-interference in domestic affairs

The Draft Code imposed a duty on transnational corporations not to interfere in the domestic politics of the host state. Nor should transnational corporations attempt to persuade their

---

[20] Articles 8–10.

[21] S. Tiewul, 'Transnational Corporations and Emerging International Legal Standards', in P. de Waart, P. Peters and E. Denters (eds.), *International Law and Development* (1988), p. 105 at p. 113, suggests that it does include limitations created by customary international law. But, there is a reluctance to spell this out in the code itself. Resolution 1803 (1962) on the Permanent Sovereignty over Natural Resources contained the obligation by affirming that 'foreign investment agreements freely entered into by or between sovereign states shall be observed in good faith'.

[22] Article 12.   [23] On the theory, see Chapter 2 above.

[24] The *Aminoil* arbitration showed the relevance of changed circumstances and the view that the contract cannot remain unresponsive to changed circumstances. For writings which favour the view that renegotiation should be implied in all foreign investment contracts of long duration, see M. Sornarajah, 'The Supremacy of Renegotiation Clauses in International Contracts' (1988) 6 *JIA* 97; and N. Nassar, *Sanctity of Contracts Revisited* (1995).

home states to intervene on their behalf in a manner inconsistent with the latter's obligations under the Charter of the United Nations and the Declaration on Friendly Relations Between States.[25] The inspiration for these articles is the fear on the part of developing states that transnational corporations will use their economic power to influence domestic politics. There was also the fear that they would induce their home states to interfere with the internal politics of host states to bring about political climates favourable to them, as they did in the past. The role of companies like the British East India Company in imperial history is not forgotten. A contemporary example of such interference was in Chile, which resulted in the overthrow of the government of President Allende who had nationalised the copper mines without paying compensation. The role of foreign corporations as well as their home states in the military coup that ensued and the replacement of the Allende government by a right-wing dictatorship favourable to foreign business induced a general fear that the situation could be repeated in other states. There was a feeling that reformist governments which seek to institute economic policies that may be unfavourable to foreign business may meet with a similar fate.

The requirement of non-interference is an established principle of international law. In the *Nicaragua Case*,[26] the International Court of Justice rejected the US argument that the growing influence of communist power in Nicaragua was a matter which concerned all the states of the region. The Court indicated that it was not permissible under international law for one state to dictate the economic system that another state should possess. This, the Court recognised, is a matter entirely for the internal sovereignty of the state. But, the multinational corporation is already present within the state, and often it cannot meaningfully participate in business activities unless it acquires and wields some domestic political influence. It is the degree of such political influence that is the issue. The fear of developing states is that the influence that is acquired could be used to ensure that governments partial to the interests of foreign investors are maintained in power.[27] There is also the fear that the home state will use the multinational corporation to influence the course of politics in the host state. From the human rights angle, the fear has been expressed that multinational corporations form alliances with local ruling elites and ensure that governments favourable to business are kept in power even through repression. The issue is the right balance between acquiring the necessary influence to function as an effective business organisation in the host state and interfering in the political affairs of the state.

The Draft Code seeks to recognise the difficulty posed by this issue. It seeks a reconciliation of the conflict by stating that legitimate activities permitted by the laws and regulations of the host state are not forbidden. But, the acquisition of the right type of political influence necessary for the multinational corporation to function is not a matter of law or regulation.

---

[25] Articles 16–20.   [26] [1984] *ICJ Reports* 352.

[27] An expanding list of cases under the Alien Tort Claims Act are premised on the assistance given to dictatorial governments by multinational corporations in quelling dissent or secessionist movements. For example, *Saro-Wiwa* v. *Shell* alleged the oil company's involvement in killings associated with dissent by the Ogoni tribes-people in the oil-producing area of Nigeria. *Mobil Oil* involved alleged support to quell the secessionist movement in the oil-rich Aceh province of Indonesia. Talisman, a Canadian oil company, had to move out of Sudan due to protests in Canada for investing in a region affected by a secessionist war quelled through ruthless violence by the government. The cases indicate that dictatorial governments in resource-rich countries are supported by investors seeking stability.

The question is not adequately addressed by the Draft Code as it would depend on the circumstances of doing business in each state.

Developed states will be touchy in recognising the rule on non-interference as it is an admission of their past acts of interference through multinational corporations and requires abjuration of future interference. The acceptance of the rule may mean the acceptance of the existence of covert interference in international affairs in the past as well as in the present. States will be unwilling to have such a construction placed on their acceptance of the rule. As regards future involvement, states will not be keen on evolving principles which could be used against them. The issue of the recognition of the rule of non-interference will pose problems.

Yet, it addresses one of the issues that plagued the drafting of the OECD's MAI, that of unconcern for human rights. The rule of non-interference imposes an obligation on the multinational corporation not to assist in the repression of the people by the ruling elite so as to promote business. To the extent that the rule promotes such an interest, it will have appeal to human rights groups which will campaign for the inclusion of such a rule in a code on investments. But, they may desire that the rule be stated as a more proactive obligation and not be confined to the passive obligation of mere non-interference. The nature of the instances in which complicity in human rights abuses have been indicated show some active participation or knowing condonation of the abuses. There is a need to impose a positive duty to prevent such abuses.

Since the drafting of the UNCTC's Draft Code, the prohibition of interference in domestic affairs by multinational corporations has been taken further by other instruments. But, the latter are largely non-binding codes. The OECD Guidelines for Multinational Enterprises require as a general policy that the multinational corporation have regard to the laws of the host state and abstain from political activities in the host state. The notion of an obligation to protect affected persons from abuses by multinational corporations has been advanced. But, it is a notion that has appeared at a time when the idea itself has proved unworkable in the primary situation for which it was devised.[28]

2.1.6 Abstention from corrupt practices

The use of bribery to achieve the objectives of the multinational corporation has also caused general concern. These concerns have been dealt with in most codes. Several scandals involving multinational corporations indicate that the practice was widespread. The United States passed legislation against the use of bribery by their nationals in the conduct of foreign business, though the enforcement of that legislation has not been pursued due to the feeling that it places US businesses at a disadvantage.[29] Later amendments to this legislation have relaxed the heavy penalties that the original legislation contemplated.

---

[28] The idea of a responsibility to protect (or 'r2p', its catchy acronym) was stated in response to situations of extreme human rights violations justifying humanitarian intervention, such as in Kosovo or Rwanda. The failure to act in Darfur and Sri Lanka dents the chances of its being taken seriously. The idea, however, has been adopted by John Ruggie, the UN Rapporteur on Transnational Corporations and Human Rights.

[29] Foreign Corrupt Practices Act (1977) 15 USC § 78m.

The OECD has formulated non-binding codes on illicit payments. The fact that the codes are non-binding indicates that there is a softer approach to the issue of the corrupt practices of multinational corporations. It is an idea that does not sit well with the increasing clamour for the imposition of responsibility on multinational corporations for their misdeeds. It would appear that institutions of developed states are favouring multinational business by not advocating instruments that impose definite liability for the corrupt practices of multinational corporations. It may smack of double standards that an institution that worked for a binding agreement on investments wants a mere non-binding code of ethics on the corrupt practices of multinational corporations.

Domestic legal systems regard bribery as criminal. But, in developing states, enforcement is lax because these states are often ruled by the same elites which receive the bribes. Contracts tainted by bribery are regarded as illegal.[30] The Draft Code creates a definite duty on the part of multinational corporations to refrain from making payments to public officials as a consideration for the performance of their duties and also requires a register to be kept of payments made to officials.[31]

Since the Draft Code, there have been dramatic movements in the area of bribery, and a universal consensus developing that it must be prohibited through criminal sanctions. The rapidity with which the law has moved in this area is not matched by other areas of misconduct where softer prescriptions are still preferred. The reason may well be that, where bribery is used in international business, there is no level playing field for competition so that multinational corporations themselves are affected. In such a situation, it is in the interest of the multinational corporations that the level playing field is maintained through the elimination of bribery. The selectivity in norm enforcement is evident. It is explicable only on the basis of practical consideration.

Both the OECD Code and the UN Code on bribery advocate strong sanctions and make prosecution easier through shifts in the burden of proof. One result is the development of an international public morality that requires the nullification of any contract that had been obtained through bribery.

2.1.7 Economic and other controls

There follows a series of articles which deal with the economic, financial and social controls that the host state could institute in respect of the activities of the multinational corporation. Many of these matters are provided for in other international instruments. These issues include transfer of technology,[32] restrictive business practices,[33] labour

---

[30] *Lemenda Trading Co. Ltd* v. *African Middle East Petroleum Co. Ltd* [1988] 1 All ER 513. [31] Article 21.

[32] On the issue of the transfer of technology, UNCTAD had sought to formulate a draft code, which became bogged down as a result of ideological divisions. The code sought access to technology by developing countries and the elimination of restrictive business practices involved in the transfer of technology such as grant-back and tie-in provisions, geographical divisions of markets and export restraints. For the text of the draft code, see UNCTAD, 'Draft International Code of Conduct on the Transfer of Technology', UN Doc. E/1990/94 (1990).

[33] The effort to identify and provide for the restrictive practices of multinational corporations has met with a degree of success, at least to the extent that a General Assembly resolution on the subject was voted without dissent. See generally M. Sornarajah, 'Towards an International Antitrust Law' (1982) 22 *Indian Journal of International Law* 1; J. Davidow and L. Chiles, 'The United States and the Issue of the Binding or Voluntary Nature of International Codes of Conduct Regarding Restrictive Business Practices' (1978) 72 *AJIL* 247. There is a distinction between these early efforts at creating codes on restrictive businesses

relations,[34] transfer pricing, consumer protection[35] and environmental protection. Duties are imposed on multinational corporations to avoid harmful practices in the areas identified.

The imposition of these duties recognises the need for the assertion of accountability of the multinational corporation for harm that is caused in the course of its operations. The major criticism of the OECD's MAI was that its emphasis was entirely on the protection of the multinational corporation without addressing the issue of the multinational corporation's social responsibility and accountability for harm.[36] There is increasing litigation addressing issues of corporate fraud,[37] participation in genocide,[38] participation in torture[39] and environmental harm.[40] In view of these developments, it would seem hollow that a code on multinational corporations should come to be drafted without addressing the issues of responsibility for harm that is caused during the operation of the foreign investment. The difficulty of combining foreign investment protection with ideas of social accountability is that such protection will be considerably diluted if combined with notions of accountability. But, for that reason, the issues raised cannot be avoided. An instrument that is made on the basis of foreign investment protection alone will lack credibility.

2.1.8 Disclosure of information

There is a broad disclosure requirement that is imposed in the Draft Code. It requires information to be made publicly available of financial and other matters relating to the operations of multinational corporations. This may not be too onerous a duty as the company law of most states will require such disclosures to be made. New laws made after successive corporate scandals in the United States and Europe mandate such disclosures.[41] Most states have modelled company disclosure laws on the ensuing regulatory controls. Similarly, the duty to make disclosures is now a feature of many foreign investment codes that require that foreign investment should be made through joint ventures. Many of these codes mandate that feasibility studies of the proposed foreign investment projects should be made. Such feasibility studies should contain full disclosure of information.

2.1.9 Treatment of transnational corporations

This section of the Draft Code contains four parts, which seek to recognise the duties owed by the host state to the multinational corporation. Its brevity stands in marked contrast to the length

---

practices and the efforts at creating codes on competition. The latter codes, attempted initially as a part of the Singapore Issues in the WTO, are intended to bring about competition globally with the aim of maintaining free trade. The UN efforts were, however, intended to control the practices of multinational corporations deemed detrimental to development.

[34] International Labour Organization, Tripartite Declaration of Principles Concerning Multinational Enterprises and Social Policy (1977).

[35] There is a General Assembly resolution incorporating guidelines on consumer protection. For the text, see UN Doc. ST/ESA/170 (1986); see also OECD, Guidelines for Multinational Enterprises and the Protection of Consumer Interests (1999).

[36] UNCTAD Series on Issues in International Investment Agreements, 'Social Responsibility' (UNCTAD/ITE/IIT/22, 2001).

[37] Particularly after the unearthing in 2002 of the accounting practices of Enron in the United States.

[38] A. Ramasastry, 'Secrets and Lies: Swiss Banks and International Human Rights' (1998) 31 *Vanderbilt Journal of Transnational Law* 325.

[39] *Doe* v. *Unocal*, 27 F Supp 2d 1174 (CD Cal., 1998).

[40] *Beanal* v. *Freeport-McMoran*, 969 F Supp 362 (1997); *Jota* v. *Texaco*, 157 F 3d 153 (2nd Cir., 1988).

[41] Successive scandals leading to spectacular collapses of large companies like Enron in the United States and Parmalat in Europe led to regulatory legislation, such as the Sarbanes–Oxley Act in the United States, requiring strict disclosure.

at which the duties owed by the multinational corporation to the host state are set out. This is, no doubt, a concession to the developed states and their demands for a 'balanced code'. The question now is whether the concessions go far enough to appease the interests of the developed states. The four matters that are included in this section of the Draft Code are: the recognition of international legal rules and principles relevant to the treatment of multinational corporations; the requirement of compensation for nationalisation; jurisdiction; and dispute settlement.

3. The outstanding issues

The Draft Code has been described above. Though consensus had been reached on many of the provisions in the Code, there were issues on which no consensus could be reached. These are referred to as the 'outstanding issues' in the successive reports of the Secretary General which have identified and discussed them.[42]

3.1 The relevance of international law

Developing countries have generally rejected the relevance of international law to the making of foreign investments, except where commitments relating to such investments have been created by treaty. The developed states have, however, adopted a strategy of insulating foreign investment from the scope of domestic law, subjecting it instead to minimum standards of treatment which they claim are required by international law. The dispute between the two groups of states has been stated in the following terms:[43]

The industrialised Western countries insist that the code must unequivocally stipulate the applicability of international law in the relations between the governments and transnational corporations. The developing countries, while recognising that states may have multinational obligations in this area, are reluctant to accept the term 'international law' because of its traditional connotations, and have instead proposed a formula calling for states to fulfil, in good faith, their international obligations in this area. The Western countries have however rejected the term 'international obligations' or 'international legal obligations' on the ground that it does not expressly include obligations founded on customary international law. Some of the developing countries contend with equal fervour that beyond the norms provided in the code, they are unable to recognise 'vague' and 'imprecise' principles of customary international law in the area of foreign investment.

Since the strategy towards foreign investments in the New International Economic Order was to ensure the primacy of host state control, the position of the developing states was to downplay the significance of international law. The argument was that there were no clear doctrines on state responsibility for the treatment of foreign investment because there was opposition to this view, particularly by the Latin American states through the assertion of the Calvo doctrine which asserted the host state's right of control over foreign investment. The

---

[42] UNCTC. 'Outstanding Issues in the Draft Code of Conduct on Transnational Corporations', UN Doc. E/C.10/1985/S/2 (1985).
[43] S. Asante, 'International Codes of Conduct and NIEO', in *Proceedings of the First Yugoslav International Seminar on Legal Aspects of the New International Economic Order* (1986), p. 245 at p. 247.

socialist states had also resisted the relevance of international law to foreign investment. The resolutions on permanent sovereignty over natural resources as well as the Charter of Economic Rights and Duties of States had also asserted the primacy of host state control. Consistent with this view, the developing states took the position that international law was not relevant to foreign investment. This view was reflected in the early versions of the Draft Code.

A compromise formulation was adopted in the final version of the Draft Code. It is contained in the section of the Draft Code entitled 'General provisions relating to the treatment of transnational corporations'. It stated:

In all matters relating to the Code, States shall fulfil, in good faith, their international obligations, including generally recognised and accepted legal rules and principles.

This compromise formula will not satisfy the standards of foreign investment protection that developed states seek. The duty is to protect 'international obligations'. Such obligations will not include foreign investment agreements, as international obligations can only arise from agreements between states.[44] The developed states argue that customary law protects obligations arising from such agreements as well. The compromise formula will apply to multilateral and bilateral treaties on foreign investment protection, but it is not clear whether it applies to the foreign investment agreements themselves. In this sense, the formulation in the Draft Code means very little, as there is already an international obligation to fulfil treaty commitments. It does not accept the theory that foreign investment contracts become internationalised and are subject to the protection of customary international law.

Neither does it accept the view of the developed states that there is a body of customary international law that is relevant to the issue of investment protection. It makes reference only to international obligations, though it recognises that such obligations could arise from 'generally recognised and accepted international legal rules and principles'. The reference to 'generally accepted international legal rules' gives scope for the recreation of the argument as to whether claims relating to the existence of a minimum standard of treatment have such wide acceptance in international law as to amount to 'generally accepted international rules'. The fact is that the existence of an international minimum standard in connection with the protection of aliens generally has been consistently opposed by the Latin American states. It has also been rejected by the developing states as a whole because the context of the protection of the assets of foreigners indicates an absence of the general acceptance required for these rules to be regarded as having any significance for the purpose of this formulation in the Draft Code. The draft, even with the compromise formula, will probably not satisfy the developed states.

3.2 Non-interference in domestic affairs

The inclusion of a provision of non-interference in domestic affairs also proved to be a contentious issue. This provision is not found in later investment agreements, though the

---

[44] This interpretation was accepted by a group of experts who met at The Hague to consider the draft code. See 'Report on the Hague Summit on the United Nations Code of Conduct on Transnational Corporations' (annexed to UNCTC, 'Work Related to the Code of Conduct on Transnational Corporations', UN Doc. E/1989/28 Rev.1).

Asia–Pacific Economic Cooperation's Principles on Investments, a non-binding set of guidelines, contained a provision on non-interference in domestic affairs and adherence to the laws of the host state. The OECD Guidelines on Multinational Corporations, another non-binding instrument, also contain a provision on non-interference. But, the UNCTC Draft Code sought to create an affirmative obligation. The formulation had the difficulty that it would have to balance, on the one hand, the right of a multinational corporation, which needs to have some interaction with the host government in order to function effectively within the ordinary economic and political process of the state, and, on the other, the obligation of a multinational corporation not to interfere directly in the course of government within the state. The final formulation in the Draft Code reads:

Transnational corporations shall not interfere in the internal affairs of host countries, without prejudice to their participation in activities that are permitted by the laws, regulation or established administrative practices of host states.

It is unlikely that observing 'laws, regulations or administrative practices of the host states' will provide sufficient scope for the exercise of the influence necessary to secure the ordinary business advantages a multinational corporation seeks. There is a divergence between the myth system maintained by the 'laws, regulations or administrative practices' which business, both domestic and foreign, should follow in influencing governments and the operational code which demands that other avenues be used in securing these advantages. It is unlikely that the matter can be satisfactorily reduced to a written formula. The general rule of non-interference must be stated, but the drafting of the exception to it is a matter of great difficulty. Too broad an exception will undermine the rule. Too narrow an exception will not satisfy those who insist on its inclusion.

The insistence on a need for the rule may diminish as multinational corporations come to be perceived as independent agents acting in their own interests rather than in the interests of their home state. The perception of these corporations as mere agents of the interests of their home states will diminish with time when it is seen that they have their own interests to pursue. On occasion, corporations see advantage in linking themselves with their host states, sometimes even to the detriment of their home states.[45] The importance of the rule is also reduced by the fact that the usual form of entry into most states is through joint ventures with local participation. Where influence is sought to change economic or other policies, the local partner to the joint venture could secure such influence. This would be particularly so where the local partner is a state corporation, in which case the leverage on the government will already exist. The government, in turn, could ensure that the local joint-venture partner reflects the policy objectives it has set out for the business. The increase in the number of multinational corporations, the growing ability of developing states to bargain with them on a competitive basis and the nature of the administrative and other controls that host states have instituted to oversee the process of foreign investment are trends which will lessen the

---

[45] An extreme instance is the Angolan civil war where Gulf Oil, a US company, was protected by Cuban forces supporting the government from rebels supported by the United States.

scope of political and other interference by multinational corporations. These trends may diminish the significance of the rule of non-interference in the future.[46] Developed countries will come to accept the rule of non-interference, and developing countries will see little significance in the rule as they will have instituted sufficient internal controls to ensure non-interference.[47]

Multinational corporations are actors on the international scene and have the capacity and power to influence the policy of governments, particularly their policies on international trade. There appear to be no norms preventing multinational corporations from engaging in such international activity. The question of whether host states could exert pressure upon a subsidiary present within its territory in order to ensure that the parent company does not influence the international policies of its home state in a manner hostile to the interests of the host state is also a matter on which there are no legal norms.

3.3 Permanent sovereignty and international obligations

Another outstanding issue is whether the reference to respect by transnational corporations for the permanent sovereignty of host states over their natural resources should be qualified by reference to international obligations that may have been undertaken in respect of them. As regards treaty obligations relating to natural resources, the need for the rule does not arise as it is well recognised that these rights could be surrendered by treaty between the two sovereign states, unless of course the view that the doctrine on permanent sovereignty forms an *ius cogens* principle is recognised.[48] Developing states will seek to establish the idea that permanent sovereignty over natural resources is a principle of *ius cogens* in international law and is not defeasible even by treaty. Developed states, on the other hand, resist this view and also insist that international obligations could be contained in the foreign investment contract on the basis of which dealings in the natural resources were commenced in the host state by the multinational corporation. The theory of internationalisation of the foreign investment contract is the basis of this argument, and the preservation of the obligations created by the contract for the duration of the contract is an aim of the developed states. The right to permanent sovereignty is stated in an unqualified manner in the Draft Code, though there is a reference later in the Code to the duty of the host state to respect its international obligations. Again, a central question would be whether these obligations include the contractual obligations between the foreign investor and the host state or whether they are confined to treaty obligations.

---

[46] But, in some states, the influence of certain companies is well entrenched. Nigeria and the oil companies operating there provide an example. In these circumstances, the foreign corporation would be reluctant to let go of its historical role, as this would invite competition into the industry it controls. Elite participation alongside the foreign corporation increases the maintenance of such control over politics.

[47] Complacency, however, is not desirable. Studies show that multinational corporations could so command projects in essential sectors that they become dominant actors on the economic and political scene of the host states.

[48] Some writers, including Brownlie, recognise the doctrine as constituting *ius cogens*.

4. The regional agreements

4.1 NAFTA

Though there are other regional agreements on investments which had been concluded earlier,[49] the agreement which has attracted the most attention and provided a model for the OECD's Multilateral Agreement on Investment is Chapter 11 of the North American Free Trade Agreement (NAFTA). The case law that NAFTA has generated and the extensive commentary it has received makes it the most important of the regional treaties that have been made in this area.[50] The controversy that has surrounded the making of NAFTA and the jurisprudence that it has generated will have an impact on the development of the law, though it must be kept in mind that NAFTA's provisions are not necessarily repeated in other investment treaties. For this reason, caution must be exercised in using the jurisprudence generated by NAFTA.

NAFTA's provisions on investment are the same as those which appear in the earlier United States–Canada Free Trade Agreement.[51] The latter, in turn, are no different from the provisions which appear in the US model bilateral investment treaty existing prior to the drafting of NAFTA. To this extent, NAFTA contains provisions which are preferred by the United States. Essentially, they embody the investment protection regime which the United States has developed with consistency over many years. The focus therefore has been on ensuring that there is an emphasis on high standards of treatment of foreign investment and its protection. The scope it leaves for sovereign control over foreign investment is limited.

The main features of Chapter 11 of NAFTA may be stated, emphasising its differences from the normal run of bilateral investment treaties. As indicated, the provisions in Chapter 11 are the same as in the model bilateral investment treaty of the United States. NAFTA contains strong treatment provisions. It provides for both pre-entry[52] and post-entry national treatment. It provides for most-favoured-nation treatment and the better of the national and most-favoured-nation treatment standards. It asserts an international minimum standard, and provides for 'full protection and security' of the investment. It provides for the right of repatriation of profits and the transfer of funds associated with the investment. It deals with expropriation, defining it widely to include direct and indirect takings and anything 'tantamount to an expropriation'. It creates strong procedures for securing compliance. Though these procedures are not innovative, as thought by some US writers,[53] the

---

[49] Of these, the ASEAN Treaty on the Protection and Promotion of Foreign Investment, 1987, is significant in its coverage (in that it involves eleven states) and scope (in that it involves compulsory dispute settlement). The later ASEAN Investment Treaty, introducing the concept of an 'ASEAN Investor', considerably enlarges the scope of the treaty. The 'ASEAN Investor', defined to include any company incorporated in an ASEAN state, is granted pre-entry rights of establishment and national treatment.

[50] L. Dawson (ed.), *Whose Rights? The NAFTA Chapter 11 Debate* (2002); H. Mann, *Private Rights, Public Problems: A Guide to NAFTA's Controversial Chapter on Investor Rights* (2001).

[51] For a record of the anxieties of the Canadian negotiating team in relation to the investment provisions of the treaty, see M. Hart, *Decision at Midnight* (2001).

[52] Meaning that the treaty creates a right of establishment in the foreign investor.

[53] US writers have referred to the dispute-settlement mechanism of providing a unilateral remedy to the foreign investor as innovative. This is not entirely correct. Such remedies were provided in earlier US investment treaties as well as in UK and other treaties. The first case in which the remedy was invoked related to the UK treaty with Sri Lanka in *AAPL* v. *Sri Lanka* (1992) 17 *YCA* 106; (1991) 30 *ILM* 577. It is, however, true to say that it is the first treaty to provide for such a remedy in a treaty that involved two developed states.

treaty provides for unilateral dispute resolution at the instance of the foreign investor against the host state, if a cause of action is created. It is the first time that a treaty with at least two developed-state parties has contained such a provision.[54] From this novelty proceeds the fact that the focus of much of the case law generated under NAFTA has dealt with treatment standards and regulatory takings, thus somewhat shifting the concerns of the law in a new direction. It also developed novel theories on expropriation considerably expanding the scope of the concept. In both the area of treatment as well as in expropriation, parties had to react by curbing this zeal for expansionism through reinterpretation and the creation of restrictive counter-arguments.[55]

A large part of the case law that has arisen under NAFTA has focused on whether interference with the rights of the investor on the ground of environmental protection could amount to a compensable taking. A view has been stated that the provisions of NAFTA have reduced the regulatory powers of the state to such an extent that even the making of non-binding policies that have an impact on foreign investment through the depreciation of its value could amount to a taking.[56] Such a view has led to concern among environmental and other groups with the provisions of NAFTA. The jurisprudence under NAFTA has fed this anxiety. There is clear controversy as to the impact of NAFTA. The position regarding regulatory taking in the context of the cases under NAFTA as well as other jurisprudence is considered in Chapter 8 below.

4.2 The ASEAN agreements

The ASEAN Investment Protection Agreement (1987) (the 'ASEAN Agreement') is a significant agreement which creates a system of protection within the ASEAN region. It also binds the new members of ASEAN, and applies to their existing investments if specific written consent for such a purpose has been given. One specific feature of this agreement is that it contemplates the unilateral right of the host state to invoke the dispute-settlement provisions of the agreement against the foreign investor. It was followed by the Framework Agreement on the ASEAN Investment Area (1998) (the 'ASEAN Framework Agreement'), the aim of which was to liberalise the flows of foreign investment within the ASEAN region. This agreement created the concept of an 'ASEAN Investor', defined as a national of an ASEAN state or a corporation organised in such a state. But, there was no fit between the two instruments. Though the intention was that the two instruments would be read together, this was not made clear in the texts.

The first tribunal that was set up under the ASEAN Agreement was in *Yaung Chi Oo Ltd* v. *Myanmar*. The highly dogmatic interpretation of the requirements of the treaty for the

---

[54] One fear is that the concerns and the analysis made in accordance with the constitutional standards of property protection in rich states will drive the law in the future. This may be detrimental to the interests of developing countries where different social and political notions of property may be more appropriate.

[55] The two classic instances are the reinterpretation of the fair and equitable treatment standard as no different from the international national minimum standard by the NAFTA Commission and the upholding of the US argument in *Methanex* v. *United States* that regulatory expropriations are not compensable.

[56] H. Mann and K. von Moltke, *NAFTA's Chapter 11 and the Environment* (1999).

invocation of jurisdiction made by the tribunal whittles down the possible scope of the treaty. The tribunal also considered the impact of the ASEAN Framework Agreement, which sought to liberalise the movement of investment within the ASEAN region. The aim of the latter treaty was to enable the free movement of investment assets among the ASEAN states. The tribunal thought that the provisions of the ASEAN Framework Agreement were 'programmatic', a view that may have accorded with ASEAN trends in the 1980s but not with the trends towards liberalisation that were taking place around the world when the ASEAN Framework Agreement was agreed. It is unfortunate that the tribunal was not able to interpret the agreement in accordance with the prevailing mood of the times when the agreement was made or in accordance with the intention of the drafters. This was a setback to the development of the law in the ASEAN region.

This setback has, however, been remedied by a new Comprehensive Investment Agreement (2009) which seeks to combine liberal movement of ASEAN investment within the region with the protection of such investment. This instrument, being the most recent of regional agreements on investments, deserves closer scrutiny. The purpose of the agreement as stated in the preamble is to 'increase intra-ASEAN investments and to enhance ASEAN's competitiveness in attracting inward investments into ASEAN'. Though the agreement tracks the usual provisions of investment treaties, there are several innovative features in it which need to be identified. Primarily, it seeks to strike a balance between protection of investment and the preservation of regulatory control in the national interest.

It remains a liberalisation treaty in that it permits pre-entry national treatment so that an investor from one ASEAN state will have access to the markets of other ASEAN investment states. This can be subjected to sectoral limitations through listing these sectors with the ASEAN Investment Council created by the agreement, but there is a commitment to progressively liberalise in these sectors. Another feature is that it treats government-owned corporations on a par with private corporations.

There are only two treatment standards recognised, apart from most-favoured-nation treatment. These are fair and equitable treatment and full protection and security. It takes the bold step of eliminating the old international minimum standard. It also avoids the nebulous nature of the fair and equitable standard and full protection and security – both concepts which have received expansionary definition by arbitral tribunals – by defining them. Article 11 states as follows:

1. Each Member State shall accord to covered investments of investors of any other Member State, fair and equitable treatment and full protection and security.
2. For greater certainty:
   (a) fair and equitable treatment requires each Member State not to deny justice in any legal or administrative proceedings in accordance with the principle of due process; and
   (b) full protection and security requires each Member State to take such measures as may be reasonably necessary to ensure the protection and security of the covered investments.

One has to assume that the definitions are exhaustive. This would mean that the fair and equitable standard captures what was referred to as 'denial of justice'. This would make it imperative that local remedies before the host state's courts are exhausted before recourse is had to the remedies under the agreement. Thus, only a denial of justice resulting from an absence of due process results in liability. But, unfortunately, the definition of full protection and security is circuitous and does not deal with the expansive meaning attributed to it to the effect that a failure to ensure stable conditions for the foreign investment is a violation of full protection and security. This indicates a failure of the drafters to take account of developments that have taken place in arbitral jurisprudence regarding the interpretation of full protection and security. The provision on expropriation is also truncated, in that, apart from making the licensing of patents compulsory, the article on general exceptions provides for a wide category of measures which are not to be treated as violations of the agreement. The protection provisions are not as strong as they would be in a traditional investment treaty, which has stronger provisions on standards of treatment.

The protection of investment is balanced with the need to preserve the regulatory and other interests of the host state. For a region that has witnessed economic crises and acted in different and creative ways to deal with them, it is natural that attention should be given to balance-of-payment crises. The suspension of obligations during times of crisis is justifiable under the agreement. Provision is made to preserve regulatory freedom where public morals, health, welfare, the environment and national security make interference necessary. The list of exceptions is long, and is set out in Article 17 ('General exceptions'):

1. Subject to the requirement that such measures are not applied in a manner which would constitute a means of arbitrary or unjustifiable discrimination between Member States or their investors where like conditions prevail, or a disguised restriction on investors of any other Member State and their investments, nothing in this Agreement shall be construed to prevent the adoption or enforcement by any Member State of measures:
   (a) necessary to protect public morals or to maintain public order;
   (b) necessary to protect human, animal or plant life or health;
   (c) necessary to secure compliance with laws or regulations which are not inconsistent with this Agreement, including those relating to:
       (i) the prevention of deceptive and fraudulent practices to deal with the effects of a default on a contract;
       (ii) the protection of the privacy of individuals in relation to the processing and dissemination of personal data and the protection of confidentiality of individual records and accounts;
       (iii) safety;
   (d) aimed at ensuring the equitable or effective imposition or collection of direct taxes in respect of investments or investors of any Member State;
   (e) imposed for the protection of national treasures of artistic, historic or archaeological value;
   (f) relating to the conservation of exhaustible natural resources if such measures are made effective in conjunction with restrictions on domestic production or consumption.
2. Insofar as measures affecting the supply of financial services are concerned, paragraph 2 (Domestic Regulation) of the Annex on Financial Services of the General Agreement on Trade in Services in Annex 1B to the WTO Agreement ('GATS') shall be incorporated into and form an integral part of this Agreement, mutatis mutandis.

The next provision contains a subjective statement to the effect that nothing in the Agreement could be considered as preventing a state from taking any action which it considers necessary for the protection of its essential security interests. The debate will, of course, be whether the exceptions and the subjective national security provision are so broad that they take the substance out of the protection provisions. Efforts at balanced treaties will always have this difficulty. As bilateral investment treaties also now provide for exceptions to liability and greater regulatory control, there will be changes taking place in this area. The nature of the law resulting from these newer treaties will be very different from those under the existing treaties which have largely concentrated on the protection of foreign investments.

5. The Multilateral Agreement on Investment

In 1992, a group of experts from the World Bank studied the possibility of a multilateral agreement on investment. But, they thought that the time was not ripe for such an agreement. Instead, they drafted a set of guidelines, the World Bank Guidelines on Foreign Investment.[57] Just a few years later, in 1995, the OECD attempted to draft a multilateral agreement on investment.[58] It was an effort to draft a code among developed countries, and this fact alone makes it unique. NAFTA involved two developed states, but the MAI involved all the members of the OECD. The OECD membership consists of developed states. Some developing states attended the discussions. The strategy was to bring about a multilateral agreement among the developed states and have the developing states accede to it afterwards. Given the ascendancy of neo-liberal tenets in the mid-1990s, it was thought that a code which emphasised those investment protection rules supported by the developed states could easily be drafted among the developed states first and then later presented as a *fait accompli* to the developing world. The agreement would then be opened for accession by non-OECD countries. It was also thought that, once finalised, the agreement could be taken over by the World Trade Organization.[59]

The draft the Multilateral Agreement on Investment (MAI) is similar in most respects to the investment provisions of NAFTA.[60] In that sense, it also bears a resemblance to the US model investment treaties on which NAFTA was based.[61] It was initially drafted in secrecy.[62] But, when the provisions became widely known, it immediately became the

---

[57] The Guidelines are analysed fully in the first edition of this work.

[58] It is generally regarded as having commenced with the G-7 Summit in Halifax in 1995 and ended with the G-7 Summit at Birmingham in 1998.

[59] Though this is referred to, it is difficult to see how the MAI, as drafted, would have meshed in with the WTO. The WTO would, for example, have no competence to deal with such matters as the right of establishment of foreign investors. The OECD was the preferred forum for the developed states because of the success of the developing states at watering down the Trade-Related Investment Measures under the WTO. S. Canner, 'The Multilateral Agreement on Investment' (1998) 31 *Cornell JIL* 657. The article also refers to the strategy of final integration of the MAI into the WTO.

[60] R. Geiger, 'Towards a Multilateral Agreement on Investment' (1998) 31 *Cornell JIL* 467, states an official position on the drafting of the MAI.

[61] There were differences, but they were not substantial. Because negotiations were not completed, the draft contained different alternative formulations. But, the factors which drove both documents were the same.

[62] This is now denied. But, academics found it difficult to obtain copies when it was being drafted. All contacts with officials concerning the document at the early stages were rebuffed on the ground that the document was secret. This was an early error.

target of attack by environmental and human rights groups which objected to the emphasis on the protection of multinational corporations without providing for protection against the environmental and human rights abuses of which they were capable. The last years of the 1990s saw the emergence of disenchantment with economic liberalism and the force of globalisation to which it had given a free rein. The Asian economic crisis also increased fears that unrestricted liberalisation of the international economy may be harmful. There was a cause needed for the outlet of these feelings, and the MAI was the most opportune cause available. Opposition to the MAI was galvanised on a global scale through the same forces of instant communication that makes globalisation possible. Disparate groups were able to coordinate opposition to the MAI on a global scale. The mounting dissent affected the governments of Europe, who then began to distance themselves from the project of drafting the MAI. They did not want to displease their electorates.

Quite apart from the impact of this opposition, there were cracks appearing within the developed states as to the rules that the MAI should contain. The conflict between the United States and the European Union over the Helms–Burton Act – which sought to impose secondary boycotts on European and other companies trading with Cuba – was seen as an instance of the United States wanting unilateral rules when it suited its interests. There was also the fear that the advances that had been negotiated within NAFTA may be dismantled if less was negotiated under the MAI. But, there were more direct conflicts such as the desire of Canada and France to protect their cultural industries from US influence. There was a fear that unrestricted access to markets, which the MAI intended to achieve, would lead to the swamping of these industries by the US entertainment industry. There were internal problems rather than the efforts of the NGOs by themselves which finally scuttled the MAI. Other incidents also added to the rethink of the viability of the MAI from the point of view of each state's own interests.

Around the same time, *Ethyl* v. *Canada*[63] was decided under NAFTA. It concerned an attempt to ban the use of an additive to petroleum, which was suspected of being pollutive and harmful to humans. The sole manufacturer of the substance in Canada was a US corporation. It sought to bring a suit on the ground that consideration of a ban was tantamount to a taking under NAFTA. The case was seen as NAFTA infringing on the power of states to interfere with foreign investment in order to protect the environment or to act in the interests of the health of the people. More broadly, the case was seen as limiting the sovereignty of the state to perform essential functions relating to the protection of internal values in order to ensure the protection of the interests of the foreign investor. The fears that this case created fuelled the arguments against acceptance of the MAI.[64]

---

[63] (1999) 38 *ILM* 708.

[64] The impact of *Ethyl* v. *Canada* is stated by Jan Huner, who played a leading role in negotiating the MAI, in the following terms: 'Decisive, because some of the points raised by the environmental groups convinced many Negotiating Group members that a few draft provisions, particularly those on expropriation and on performance requirements, could be interpreted in unexpected ways. The dispute between Ethyl Corporation and the Canadian government illustrated the point that the MAI negotiators should think twice before copying the expropriation provisions of the NAFTA.' J. Huner, 'Lessons from the MAI: A View from the Negotiating Table', in H. Ward and D. Brack (eds.), *Trade, Investment and the Environment* (2001), p. 242 at p. 248.

While the dissension among and within the developed states indicated that fears of losing sovereign control over an intrusive process such as foreign investment underlay the downfall of the MAI, the developing countries would have had even greater problems with the formulations in the MAI. Some developing countries did participate in the discussions as observers. Others offered comments from the sidelines, but, on the whole, developing countries were absent from the proceedings. But, the objections of the developing countries could be anticipated from the comments made by developing-country officials and scholars.[65] The MAI was premised on one view of economic development, that foreign investment was so beneficial that its protection was necessary in order to ensure its flow, which in turn would promote economic growth. One version of the preamble to the MAI spoke of the wish to 'establish high standards for liberalisation of investment regimes and investment protection with effective dispute-settlement procedures'. That singular vision of foreign investment is not accepted by all developing states. Developing states want to be able to choose between the different models and find one which suits them best. Whereas the institutions controlled by the developed countries have identical prescriptions and conditions for development, each developing country wants to assert its own right to choose the model which it considers best for itself. The regime that the draft MAI sought to impose restricted this choice. That would have made the MAI unpalatable to developing states.[66]

There were specific provisions in the MAI which would have been objected to as well. The right of establishment contained in the MAI is at the heart of the liberalisation of investment flows. The provision on national treatment applies to both the pre-entry phase as well as to the post-entry phase.[67] This provision would sit uneasily with the screening legislation which most developing states still maintain. They believe that they should have the right to reject deleterious foreign investment and regulate the investment that is permitted entry so as to maximise and harness the benefits of the investment to the host economy. The opportunity for doing so would be lost if uncontrolled access to foreign investment were permitted. In the treaty practice of a large number of states, specific provisions preserve this right. In Southeast Asian treaties, only 'approved' investments are given treaty protection. In the practice of China, Australia and an increasing number of other states,[68] only investments made 'in accordance with the laws and regulations of each Contracting Party from time to time in existence' are granted protection. Given the existence of this limitation even in the heyday of liberalisation, it is unlikely that the MAI would have made much progress with these states. There were standstill provisions permitting existing sectoral reservations from national and most-favoured-nation treatment and rollback

---

[65] A. Ganesan, 'Development Friendliness Criteria for a Multilateral Investment Agreement' (1997) 6 *Transnational Corporations* 139. C. Huiping, 'Comments on the MAI's General Principles for the Treatment of Foreign Investors and Their Investments: A Chinese Scholar's Perspective', in E. Niewenhuys and M. Brus (eds.), *Multilateral Regulation of Investment* (2001), p. 67.

[66] For accounts of various interests that opposed the MAI, see S. Picciotto and R. Mayne (eds.), *Regulating International Business: Beyond Liberalization* (1999).

[67] The whole range of activities associated with investment is spelt out, and includes 'establishment, acquisition, expansion, operation, management, maintenance, use, enjoyment and sale or other disposition of investment'. Chapter III on Treatment of Investors and Investments: National Treatment and Most Favoured Nation Treatment, para. 1.

[68] The formula is coming to be used widely. It appears in the more recent treaties of Malaysia and Indonesia.

provisions, though their eventual elimination was required. The European Union issued a lengthy list of such sectoral reservations during the negotiations. Most states focused on the telecommunications and transportation sectors. France and Canada held out for the total exclusion of the cultural sector. The developed states did not exhibit much unity on this core issue of the MAI.

National treatment after entry is also an important feature of the MAI. Again, this would pose problems for a large number of developing states, which often seek to protect fledgling industries and actively promote local entrepreneurship. A strategy of building up small enterprises within the economy could not be adopted unless extensive sectoral exceptions were made. Developing countries also operate large sectors of their economies through state corporations which are monopolies by definition. Privatisation of state corporations is an aim of economic liberalism, but it is not an aim which appeals to all developing states. There are increasing reservations expressed about the efficiency levels of post-privatisation economic activity even in developed states. There is also a tendency in developing states as well as in developed states to give ethnic groups preferential treatment on the basis of purely political or historical considerations.[69] It would be difficult to accommodate these constitutional preferences with a system of national treatment for foreign investors. These preferences are not driven by economic considerations on which the premises of liberalism rest. It is inappropriate to regard economic factors alone as the driving forces behind policy on foreign investment. There are equitable, historical and other considerations which a state has to accommodate in fashioning policy on foreign investment.

The MAI also prohibits performance requirements. These are widely employed by developing countries. The Trade-Related Investment Measures (TRIMS) instrument of the WTO prohibits certain performance requirements. But, it permits those that developing countries usually employ in regulating foreign investment, such as entry through joint ventures, employment of a specific quota of nationals and a minimum level of equity participation. The MAI provided a more comprehensive list of prohibited performance requirements and applied them to a greater range of activities. The MAI prohibited export requirements, domestic content requirements, domestic purchase requirements, the tying of imports to the value of exports, requirements relating to the transfer of technology, territorial exclusivity in export, the compulsory location of research and development activities, the entry of investment through joint ventures and a requirement to hire local personnel. These are all requirements that developing host states wish to impose in the belief that they secure the advantages of foreign investment. Developing countries would have had to dismantle much of their local investment codes in order to accommodate such a long list of prohibitions within their laws. The exceptions seek to secure advantages for developed states rather than to cater for the needs of developing countries. Economists point out that these very performance requirements now sought to be prohibited were used by developed states in their own ascent to developed status.[70]

---

[69] Reference has already been made to the studies of the role of ethnicity in shaping foreign investment rules. In developed states, such as Canada and Australia, such preferential treatment is given to the aboriginal people of these states.

[70] Ha-Joon Chang, *Kicking Away the Ladder: Development Strategy in Historical Perspective* (2005).

The dispute-resolution provisions of the MAI are more extensive than those commonly used in investment treaties. They provide for both state-to-state and investor-to-state arbitration. Like other treaties containing provisions relating to the prior consent of the host state, the MAI also provides for the prior consent of the contracting parties to arbitration. There is a minor change in that a contracting party may at the time of ratification or accession require the foreign investor to be confined to the remedy of his choice. That is, the foreign investor will have to discontinue other proceedings if he chooses arbitration. This is not a major hurdle from the point of view of the foreign investor as his preferred choice would be arbitration rather than domestic proceedings in the host state. It seems to be a light-hearted parody of something akin to the local remedies rule, creating the impression of a disadvantage to the foreign investor. The so-called election of the procedure or the fork-in-the-road principle has hardly deterred the foreign investor from having his preferred choice of procedure.[71]

The MAI included sections containing general safeguards and exceptions. These provisions commence with the statement that they 'shall not apply to Article IV, 2 and 3 (expropriation and compensation and protection from strife)'. The exceptions relate largely to war and public order situations. The fact that expropriation is saved even from measures which provide a total justification in customary international law will not prove acceptable to many states. The MAI also avoids the issue as to whether a regulatory interference with foreign investment on environmental or human rights grounds should be considered an exception. The other exceptions deal with the curtailment of financial flows resulting from the investment on balance-of-payment grounds, which again contain more stringent standards than are usually contained in bilateral investment treaties.

The MAI failed for a variety of reasons. There have been various assessments of the causes of its failure. The role of the NGOs is regarded by some as the reason for its failure.[72] Others regard the MAI as not being strong enough, so that the multinational business community did not give it its wholehearted support. If it were any stronger, the MAI would have proved unacceptable to more states. The seeds of the failure of the MAI lay in the fact that there was insufficient agreement within the developed world on the norms of investment protection. France broke off first. The incoming Labour government in the UK was concerned about the non-inclusion of environmental safeguards. Canada joined France in its concern over cultural industries. As much as the NAFTA experience illustrates that the instrument could have a life quite unforeseen by the parties and lead to discomfort for the parties, the long years of negotiation of the MAI showed the developed states that the rules that they seek to impose on the developing world may prove too onerous to bear when applied to themselves. They could not brook the loss of sovereignty that the MAI entailed. With the failure of the MAI, attention has shifted to the possibility of creating an investment

---

[71] The distinction between contractual remedies and remedies under the treaty principles has made it possible for the foreign investor to choose both types of remedy. The 'fork in the road' provision is used in other treaties as well. But, the provision has not yet deterred the use of arbitration despite resort to other procedures. See *Compañía de Aguas del Aconquija SA and Vivendi Universal v. Argentina*, ICSID Case No. ARB/97/3.

[72] A. Rugman, 'New Rules for International Investment: The Case for a Multilateral Agreement on Investment (MAI) at the WTO', in C. Milner and R. Read (eds.), *Trade Liberalization, Competition and the WTO* (2002), p. 176.

instrument under the auspices of the WTO. The impact of the experience with the MAI will last for a considerable time. The debate is no longer about investment protection alone but about the wider implications it has for globalisation. The future possibility of a multilateral code on investment is bleak. The same coalitions that moved against the MAI are still around and will coalesce to work against the acceptance of any measure that is driven by liberal economic theory on foreign investment alone without taking into account factors such as development, poverty, human rights and the environment.[73] But, if this is done, and a balanced code brought about, as in the case of the ASEAN Agreement, doubts would be raised as to whether it achieves its purpose of creating an effective scheme of investment protection. The balance is as elusive as the past efforts at a multilateral code.

6. The WTO and foreign investment

The Havana Charter of 1948 for the International Trade Organization (ITO), which was to have come into existence along with other institutions at the end of the Second World War, contained provisions on investment.[74] Articles 11 and 12 of the Havana Charter dealt with investment. Article 11 stated that no member 'shall take unreasonable or unjustifiable action' against investment, and assured 'just and equitable treatment'. Article 12 provided members with the right to take appropriate safeguards against foreign investment and 'to determine whether and to what extent and upon what terms it will allow future foreign investment'. This part of the article would have been acceptable to developing countries, as it stated basic norms that they later articulated. But, the second part of Article 12 contained the genesis of the developed-country position. It stated that 'members undertake to provide reasonable opportunities for investments acceptable to them and adequate security for existing and future investments, and to give due regard to the desirability of avoiding discrimination as between foreign investments'. In the event, the ITO never came into existence.[75] But, the few developing countries that existed at the time objected to the provisions on investment on the ground that they were based on rules preferred by the developed states. The conflict had begun early. The GATT, which was a truncated version of the ITO, was concerned largely with trade in goods and the elimination of tariff barriers, and dealt with investment issues only peripherally. This ensured that international trade law developed separately from international investment law in the intervening period between the ITO and the WTO.

---

[73] M. Sornarajah, 'The Impact of Globalisation on the International Law of Foreign Investment', Simon Reisman Lecture, 2002, Ottawa (2002) 12 *Canadian Foreign Policy* 1.

[74] C. Wilcox, *A Charter for World Trade* (1948). The developing countries opposed the provisions on the ground that they articulated the preferred rules of the developed states. C. Lipson, *Standing Guard: Protecting Foreign Capital in the Nineteenth and Twentieth Centuries* (1985), pp. 86–7; P. S. Watson, J. Flynn and C. Convell, *Completing the World Trading System* (1999), pp. 237–57; M. Koulen, 'Foreign Investment in the WTO', in E. Niewenhuys and M. Brus (eds.), *Multilateral Regulation of Investment* (2001), p. 181; T. Brewer and S. Young, 'Investment Issues at the WTO: The Architecture of Rules and the Settlement of Disputes' (1998) 1 *Journal of International Economic Law* 457.

[75] This was largely due to US opposition. A. Eckes, 'US Trade History', in W. Lovett, A. Eckes and R. Brinkman (eds.), *US Trade Policy, History, Theory and the WTO* (1999).

The only issue relating to investment presented to a GATT panel was the challenge by the United States to Canada's Foreign Investment Review Act. This legislation instituted a screening process for incoming foreign investment in Canada. The legislation has many features common to the screening legislation that is used in developing countries. The United States challenged it on the ground that it constituted a GATT violation. The specific challenges concerned the requirements that the foreign investors should export a percentage of their manufactured goods, purchase materials for manufacture from Canadian sources and utilise Canadian resources to manufacture finished products in Canada. The GATT panel found that the GATT did not prevent Canada from exercising its sovereign right to regulate foreign investment. But, it made specific findings. It found that the requirement to purchase Canadian goods to the exclusion of foreign goods was discriminatory as foreign products were given worse treatment, and hence violated Article III(4) of the GATT. The panel found against the view that the export requirement violated Article XVII of the GATT. It did not make a finding on the issue of the local manufacture of products from Canadian materials.

It has been suggested that it was the GATT panel ruling in this case that forced Canada to move away from the policy of the Foreign Investment Review Act to a more permissive policy, which culminated in NAFTA.[76] This is to read too much into the case. The decision did not affect developing states to any significant degree, as they continued to maintain screening restrictions and performance requirements. There has been no suggestion that these screening devices violated the GATT. The matter was not even tested out and, if the *FIRA Case* was such a success as it is made out to be, there would have been challenges to screening legislation elsewhere.

6.1 Investment in the Uruguay Round

In the Uruguay Round, definite efforts were made to introduce measures relating to investment into international trade. The WTO instruments which affect investment directly and which create competence in the WTO to deal with investment issues are the Agreement on Trade-Related Aspects of Intellectual Property Rights (TRIPS), Trade-Related Investment Measures (TRIMS) and the General Agreement on Trade in Services (GATS). Other instruments deal with investments indirectly. Thus, the Agreement on Government Procurement requires that there be no discrimination in sourcing materials for purchase by the host government as between foreign investors and local manufacturers. But, the more significant instruments are those which affect investments directly.

6.2 GATS

Of these instruments, the most significant is GATS. It deals with services and defines services supplied by foreign firms within a state as covered by it. Of the four modes of

---

[76] C. Wilkie, 'Origins of NAFTA Investment Provisions: Economic and Policy Considerations', in L. Ritchie (ed.), *Whose Rights? The NAFTA Chapter 11 Debate* (2002), p. 7 at p. 14. Wilkie suggests that the case indicates that 'the artificial divisions between international trade and investment policy would no longer enjoy protection under international rules'. If this was a lesson, it was not learned by developing states, which continued with the screening of incoming investments.

supply that are covered by GATS, one is the provision of services 'through commercial presence' in the territory of a member. This 'commercial presence' could be created through the establishment of a juridical person or through a branch or office for the supply of services within the territory of a member state.[77] Thus, GATS covers foreign investment in the services sector. It accounts for a large share of foreign investment, and thus establishes WTO competence in a substantial sector of the economy of every member state.[78] GATS considerably liberalises entry barriers in the services sector, which were previously high.

Unlike bilateral and regional investment treaties, which apply a top-down approach in that sectors have to be excluded from standards that are stated, GATS adopts a bottom-up approach requiring the commitments in the services sector to be listed in each member state's schedule. There is, however, an understanding that there will be a progressive liberalisation. The schedules contain sector-specific disciplines.

The core principles of GATS are non-discrimination and national treatment, but these principles are not general in scope.[79] They arise only from specific commitments made by the parties. Though the liberalisation of entry is sought as a target, this does not take place as it does in an investment treaty like NAFTA which requires pre-entry rights of establishment. Access can still be controlled in those sectors not included by the state in its schedule. In that sense, free trade in services is a distant prospect.[80]

National treatment applies only to those service sectors which are listed in each state's schedule, and then only to the extent that no conditions are attached. To that extent, national treatment does not as yet pose a problem for measures that discriminate between foreign investors and local entrepreneurs, unless the state feels confident that competition within the sector is possible and should be promoted by inclusion in its schedule. If the sector is subject to GATS, then there is a prohibition of restrictions on the number of service suppliers allowed, the value of the transaction or assets, the total quantity of service output, the number of persons employed, the type of legal entity through which the service is supplied and limits on foreign equity. These prohibitions will no doubt come to affect regulatory legislation on foreign investment when liberalisation processes advance and more sectors are listed in the schedule.

The general most-favoured-nation provision also poses problems. GATS permits members to list exemptions to most-favoured-nation treatment upon entry into force of agreements. The exemptions are to last for no longer than ten years. The exemptions have been explained on the basis that 'an unconditional most-favoured-nation rule would allow competitors located in countries with relatively restrictive policies to benefit from their sheltered markets while enjoying a free ride in less restrictive export markets'.[81] But, the more pressing issue from the point of view of investment is whether the most-favoured-nation provision applying to GATS, which has a wider membership, can be used to latch on to the advantages that are provided in an instrument like the MAI, NAFTA or even bilateral investment treaties. This would mean that advantageous provisions like the

---

[77] Article 1 of the GATS.　　[78] B. Hoekman and M. Kostecki, *The Political Economy of the World Trading System* (2001), p. 239.
[79] Countries could list exemptions from the general MFN standard.
[80] B. Hoekman and M. Kostecki, *The Political Economy of the World Trading System* (2001), pp. 257–8.　　[81] *Ibid.*, p. 253.

investor–state dispute resolution provisions in investment treaties could come to be used on the basis of the most-favoured-nation clause. This may be another reason for the popularity of exemptions from the most-favoured-nation rule applying to GATS.[82]

GATS is instructive for the making of an instrument on investment. It will be seen as a possible model for such an instrument as the instrument could then be sold to the reluctant members as merely extending an existing instrument which affects investments into the whole of the area. GATS is also seen as a weaker instrument which states could accept, as the exclusion of sectors is permissible. But, this exclusion is time-limited and there may be some exercise of power in ensuring the listing of more sectors. The fear is that, once the breach is made, the breach could be made wider to allow a large number of sectors to pass through. It is this fear that will hold back an instrument on investment which is modelled on GATS.

6.3 TRIPS

The Agreement on Trade-Related Aspects of Intellectual Property Rights (TRIPS) deals with standards of protection of intellectual property. Since intellectual property is defined as falling within investments in regional and bilateral investment treaties, the link between TRIPS and investment treaties is clear. TRIPS mandates standards of protection that should be transposed into national law. Intellectual property rights are created in domestic law, and apply within the system which creates it. In that sense, the instrument rightly requires that violations of these standards should be addressed through domestic law. It is only a failure to address them in that manner that would result in the violation of the international obligation. Investment treaties, on the other hand, do create international obligations, which protect intellectual property as investment. TRIPS is largely intended to address the problem of piracy, and, to that extent, it is not aimed at investment protection.

The matter may become significant in the context of compulsory licensing. Compulsory licensing was a matter insisted upon by developing states during the TRIPS negotiations, and it was conceded. In the context of drugs, the issue becomes an important one as to whether drugs that are needed could be subjected to compulsory licensing in the host state. It would appear that different answers may flow from the different treaty regimes. Under the TRIPS regime, the case for compulsory licensing could be made out. Under a strong investment treaty regime, the possibility of compulsory licensing amounting to a taking of property becomes a real issue.[83] Under a weaker investment regime, there is less scope for this.[84]

Developing countries are also concerned about the extent to which foreign multinational companies utilise their indigenous knowledge without rewarding its holders. The lack of

---

[82] M. Koulen, 'Foreign Investment in the WTO', in E. Niewenhuys and M. Brus (eds.), *Multilateral Regulation of Investment* (2001), p. 288. A. Wimmer, 'The Impact of the General Agreement on Trade in Services on the OECD Multilateral Agreement on Investment' (1996) 19 *World Competition* 109.

[83] For a discussion of these issues, see A. Z. Hertz, 'Shaping the Trident: Intellectual Property under NAFTA, Investment Protection Agreements and at the World Trade Organization' (1997) 23 *Canada–United States Law Journal* 261.

[84] Thus, in investment treaties which preserve the laws of the host state being applied to the investment, the possibility of compulsory licensing being considered expropriation is remote.

protection that international instruments provide for such a situation is seen as an instance of unequal treatment that regimes like TRIPS impose upon developing states. The Convention on Biodiversity addresses the issue by seeking to provide protection for indigenous knowledge, but the United States is not a party to the Convention. In the two areas of compulsory licensing of drugs and the protection of indigenous knowledge, there is much opportunity for conflict. The acceptance of TRIPS itself can only be seen as an intrusion that was achieved in the context of the acceptance of economic liberalism as well as the exercise of pressure.

TRIPS also is the document which has proved to be the battleground between the interests of developed and developing states in recent times. There is little doubt that the instrument was brought about largely due to the pressures exerted by pharmaceutical companies for patent protection for their drugs. It was possible to push the document through during a time when neo-liberal philosophies held sway. But, with the decline of this particular wisdom, dissent against TRIPS began to mount. When the issue of cheaper generic drugs for diseases like AIDS for use in afflicted developing countries arose, the developing countries made the matter the focus for demanding change. They won that particular battle, and parallel imports of generic drugs and less onerous provisions for compulsory licensing became permissible. This signalled the beginning of a retreat of neo-liberal norms and a possible recovery of developing-country unity to reverse some of the laws that had been made in the neo-liberal period which were detrimental to their interests.[85]

6.4 TRIMS

The Trade-Related Investment Measures (TRIMS) instrument of the Uruguay Round deals directly with foreign investment. It is, however, not a comprehensive document, as it deals only with certain types of performance requirement.[86] The *FIRA Case* had dealt with this issue previously, and established the limited competence of the GATT in issues of foreign investment. The TRIMS agreement is not seen as extending beyond what had been established in that case nor as building up on the foundations established in it. It is based on measures related to investments which cause 'trade-restrictive and distorting effects', thus cautiously establishing a link between foreign investment and international trade in goods. TRIMS relates back to the GATT by stating that 'no member shall apply any TRIM that is inconsistent with the provisions of Article III (on national treatment) and Article XI (on quantitative restrictions) of GATT'. The annex to the agreement contains an illustrative list of measures.

The main aim of TRIMS is to prohibit the use of performance requirements. Not all such performance requirements are prohibited, only those that fall within the narrow focus of the

---

[85] On the role of the pharmaceutical industry in bringing about TRIPS, see S. Sell, *Private Power, Public Law: Globalisation of Intellectual Property Rights* (2003).

[86] E. Burt, 'Developing Countries and the Framework for Negotiations on Foreign Direct Investment in the World Trade Organization' (1997) 12 *American University Journal of International Law and Policy* 1015; P. Civello, 'The TRIMS Agreement: A Failed Attempt at Investment Liberalisation' (1999) 8 *Minnesota Journal of Global Trade* 97.

limitation provided by the linkage between TRIMS and the old GATT provisions. It is unlikely that there will be an extension of the list of the prohibited performance requirements, as developing countries are opposed to such an extension. There is a growing view among developing-country economists that performance requirements aid economic development and were in fact used by developed states in the past. They take the view that developing countries should not be denied the benefits of using techniques which developed countries had used with success in the past.[87]

7. An investment regime under the WTO

The existing WTO instruments are piecemeal considerations of aspects of foreign investment. Various WTO Ministerial Meetings have proposed the consideration of a comprehensive instrument under the WTO. A Working Group on the Relationship Between Trade and Investment was set up at the Singapore Ministerial Meeting in 1996. The Doha Ministerial Meeting mandated that regard should be had to the development dimension of the problem and to the experience of other agencies, in particular the United Nations Commission on Trade and Development (UNCTAD). In light of the rich experience and debate on treaty- and instrument-making that has been attempted so far, the issues that could arise may be anticipated. This section outlines those issues. Though the efforts were given up due to the opposition of developing states, the course of the development of the would-be instrument is instructive.

7.1 The definition of investment

The developing-country position was that only long-term investments should be included. This may be more consistent with the Doha mandate, which speaks of 'long-term cross-border investment, particularly foreign direct investment, that will contribute to the expansion of trade'. Such investment would exclude portfolio investment, which, though it promotes the liberalisation of capital flows, is nevertheless short term and may be damaging to developing countries. The Asian economic crisis of 1997 was precipitated by the sudden withdrawal of portfolio investment. The Malaysian answer was to institute currency controls. The regulatory power of the state over portfolio investments is seen as essential by developing countries. Many developing-country instruments, in particular the ASEAN Framework Agreement on Investment, exclude portfolio investment from the definition of investments. There are, however, bilateral investment treaties which include portfolio investment.[88] It is unlikely that developing countries will agree to the inclusion of portfolio investment in the definition of foreign investment in a future WTO instrument. They would prefer to ensure that only long-term interests or those interests enmeshed into their

---

[87] Ha-Joon Chang, *Kicking Away the Ladder: Development Strategy in Historical Perspective* (2005).
[88] The arbitral award in *Fedax* v. *Venezuela* (1998) 37 *ILM* 1378 demonstrates the potential instability caused by the inclusion of portfolio instruments within the definition of foreign investment.

economies through associations such as joint ventures are given protection.[89] They would also prefer to protect greenfield activity rather than mergers and acquisitions of existing ventures. The former could be easily accommodated within the existing economic frame-work whereas the latter would create problems for local entrepreneurs.

Developed countries are likely to favour a broader, assets-based definition of foreign investment, which could include portfolio investments as well. They would prefer a comprehensive definition of tangible and intangible assets, as is found in instruments such as NAFTA. But, even NAFTA excludes some assets such as claims to money. The idea that there should be a comprehensive list of investments and that they could thereafter be dealt with on a case-by-case basis in the substantive provisions is not a good one, for, once the door is opened, the bargaining power is lost. The definition of investment itself remains a thorny problem to be overcome at the very outset, as progress will not be made unless this initial issue is overcome.

7.2 Definition and preservation of regulatory control

Much of the debate on investment instruments focuses upon the extent to which it is possible to grant liberalisation, treatment and protection to foreign investments on the basis of external standards contained in treaties yet, at the same time, ensure that there is regulatory control to protect the host state's interests. It is for this reason that many states define the investment to ensure that only such investments that operate within the framework of their regulatory structure are given the protection of the treaty. Thus, Australian and Indonesian bilateral investment treaties contain a provision that only investments 'made in accordance with the laws and regulations from time to time in existence' are given the protection of the treaty. China adopts a similar formula. India uses a formula which ensures that the operation of foreign investment is always subject to the laws of India. Thailand often attaches its laws on foreign investment to the treaties it signs.[90] In the practice of most Southeast Asian states, only investments 'approved in writing' are given protection by investment treaties. All this means that the initial screening mechanisms and the conditions they impose as well as other laws, including environmental laws, are preserved and only such investments as operate in accordance with these laws and regulations are entitled to the protection of the treaty. It is unlikely that states which adopt such practices in preserving their regulatory legislation will come to the party if the multilateral instrument does not also preserve the right of the state to regulate foreign investment. Developed states will resent this position for, if regulation were to be permitted, the scope for binding external standards will be significantly eroded. The Doha Ministerial Meeting stressed that development issues should be approached in a balanced manner, and therefore the preservation of the right of regulation in the interests of developing states will be an important issue.

---

[89] The IMF definition which defines foreign investment as being one with more than a 10 per cent interest in a company may favour their approach.

[90] See, for example, the Canada–Thailand treaty.

7.3 Definition of investor

This again is a controversial issue. In the case of natural persons, it does not pose problems (apart from the issue of dual nationality). The issue as to whether permanent residents should be included or not is not a major problem, as many developing states already include permanent residents in their bilateral investment treaties as persons whose investments are protected.[91] It is the position of the multinational corporation which is the more important one, as they are the major investors and investment treaties are primarily concerned with protecting their investments.

Practice differs among states as to the criterion to be used for corporate nationality. States often insist that foreign companies should enter and operate through locally incorporated companies. The company so incorporated then becomes a local corporate national, which would not normally qualify for protection by an investment treaty. But, this problem is overcome by the recognition of the foreign interests in the shares of the locally incorporated company. This situation is wrongly considered as protection of portfolio investments in some official publications. All that happens is that the primary shareholdings in the local company are protected. For purposes of ICSID arbitration, the host state will have to acknowledge that the locally incorporated corporation is in reality a foreign company, though an inference to this effect is drawn in certain circumstances.

Corporate nationality also becomes a problem, as different legal traditions use different tests for such nationality. Common law jurisdictions use the incorporation test, and civil law jurisdictions use the *siège social* theory. This distinction has come to be reflected in the treaty practice of the different states. Again, in a multilateral agreement, this difference in approach will be an issue unless states can agree on a single test in the interest of uniformity.[92]

7.4 Treatment standards

The WTO has an essentially liberalising mission. In the context of the WTO, it is difficult to envisage an instrument which does not have liberalisation as its ultimate objective. In that sense, the instrument will ultimately, if not immediately, have to provide for pre-entry national treatment. That idea will be stressed by developed states but will not be acceptable to developing states. It will mean that their screening procedures, based on the view that some types of investment are welfare-reducing and deleterious to developmental goals, could not be maintained. Economic liberalism tends to view all foreign investment as uniformly beneficial and to postulate a balanced stance relating to their treatment and protection, but this is not a view that finds favour with developing countries which have had a long experience of harmful investments. Those who argue for pre-entry establishment rights point out that, as in the case of GATS, a bottom-up approach could be adopted with positive lists of sectors open to entry and other conditions attached. But, this is not the

---

[91] See, for example, the model treaty of Malaysia.   [92] This is a large topic, but space does not permit a longer treatment.

preferred approach of developing countries which have usually used negative lists in their investment laws, enabling the exclusion of sectors that are kept for their own nationals and gradually increasing the amount of foreign participation in others. Pre-entry national treatment is used only by the United States and Canada in their bilateral investment treaties. The European states do not use them. It is unlikely that there will be agreement on this issue between the developed states themselves. The standard had to be dropped from the OECD's Multilateral Agreement on Investment. Developing states will resist their imposition. The world is not yet ready for such an idea.

Post-entry national treatment will also present problems. The continued regulation of the multinational corporation after it enters the host state in order to control its activities is perceived as necessary by developing states. The flow of funds associated with the investment, the protection of local entrepreneurship from competition, the use of local management and labour, the export of products and the utilisation of local raw materials are some of the matters that host states wish to control. This raises the issue of performance requirements, which would also be unlawful on the additional ground that they violate national treatment standards. Regulatory control will also be affected in that there may be a problem in exercising control over foreign investment without exercising control over local investment. Again, it is unlikely that national treatment will prove acceptable to developing countries. The suggestion that exceptions could be made on the basis of development needs will not prove acceptable, as such exceptions cannot be exhaustive and broad exceptions will not be supported by states which desire national treatment on the ground that the uncertainty which results makes the inclusion of national treatment futile.

It is possible to argue that the introduction of a provision like Article XX of the GATT could solve the problems regarding preservation of the regulatory framework of the host state. This is unlikely to happen. The uncertainties involved in the interpretation of Article XX have been manifested in the GATT/WTO jurisprudence.[93] The provision for non-trade-related values such as protection of the environment, national security, the promotion of human rights and labour standards will be objected to as undermining the strength of the protection and treatment provisions of an investment instrument. The introduction of the GATT phrase 'like circumstances' to provide leeway to regulatory schemes is also possible, but regulation is seen as a right by most countries and not as an exception where 'like circumstances' exist.[94] The phrase 'like circumstances' is used in later versions of the OECD's MAI, supposedly to permit regulatory discrimination. Towards the end, the negotiators of the MAI recognised the need to 'preserve the necessary scope for non-discriminatory regulation'.

7.4.1 Most-favoured-nation treatment

The inclusion of the most-favoured-nation standard may universalise all the specifically negotiated advantages that are given in bilateral investment treaties and, for that reason, such

---

[93] For example, the *Thai Tobacco Case* (1991) 37 GATT BISD 200.
[94] These issues are discussed in the context of NAFTA in the separate opinion in *S. D. Myers* v. *Canada* (2000) 40 *ILM* 1408; (2002) 121 *ILR* 7. They were also considered in the chairman's interpretative package released during the MAI negotiations. OECD, Chairman's Note on Environment and Related Matters on Labour (9 March 1988), DAFFE/MA (98) 10.

a move will not find favour with many states.[95] The effects of a multilateral treaty that includes a most-favoured-nation clause are difficult to contemplate, as it universalises every provision of every bilateral investment treaty. Its operation will differ from that in the GATT context. In the case of most-favoured-nation treatment, the general practice is to exclude from the scope of the clause regional agreements which give partners in regional arrangements preferential treatment. It is uncertain how such an exclusion would fit into a multilateral agreement on investment.

Treatment standards have become important in NAFTA litigation. This litigation employs strategies which use the treatment standards in NAFTA to argue that state regulations violate these standards. The linking of GATT approaches to arguing violations of standards is evident in many of the cases.[96]

7.5 Performance requirements

Only a few GATT-related performance requirements were caught by the TRIMS. The investment instrument that is contemplated by the WTO will take in a wider variety of performance requirements, which, in the eyes of the United States, are all trade-distortive. The developing countries, on the other hand, believe that certain performance requirements are necessary, and point out that they have been used at various stages of the developed states themselves in their own economic development. There are studies which indicate that certain performance requirements were used by developed states as part of their economic development, and that it would now be unfair to ban their use by developing states. The issue is still fresh and, despite the practice in US treaties of identifying and proscribing the use of performance requirements, it is unlikely that such a practice will be acceptable to developing countries in a multilateral instrument. India and China have already indicated strong stances on this. An issue akin to performance requirements is that of incentives, which are often tied to performance requirements so as to ensure that these requirements are balanced against each other. Again, views differ as to the economic value of incentives, but it is unlikely that developing countries can be persuaded to forego the granting of such incentives. Incentives, other than tax incentives which are employed by developing states, are given by developed states as well.

7.6 Expropriation

Expropriation has historically been a thorny issue. The expansive views that have been presented in the NAFTA litigation have caused anxiety to developed countries, and developing countries which have been at the receiving end of the stick on these matters will not be happy with the inclusion of definitions of expropriation that are capable of such expansion.

---

[95] In *Maffezzini* v. *Spain* (2001) 40 *ILM* 1129, a tribunal held that a more favourable provision of any treaty made by a party will flow through the most-favoured-nation clause in a treaty.

[96] See *UPS* v. *Canada*, UNCITRAL Arbitration Proceedings (NAFTA) (Award on the Merits, 24 May 2007); *Methanex* v. *United States* (pending); and *S. D. Myers* v. *Canada* (2000) 40 *ILM* 1408; (2002) 121 *ILR* 7.

With this proviso, developing countries have generally accepted that some appropriate compensation should be paid for any taking effected by the state. The formulation of the provision on expropriation will also be fraught with difficulty.

Any provision on expropriation must now provide safeguards that would ensure the use of environmental protection measures. The United States, the principal proponent of the watertight provision, seems to agree with this position, as is evidenced by the way in which it is arguing the *Methanex* v. *United States* case. Its argument seems to proceed on the basis that, where there is a general measure taken to protect the interests of the community through the legislative process, such a measure should not be regarded as an expropriation. The general exception of measures taken to protect health, morals and the environment that are used in the sphere of international trade will have to be accommodated within the provision. This will take care of the concern of the different groups that have come out in opposition to the formulation of the protection of the interests of multinational corporations without taking into account poverty eradication, environmental protection and human rights protection. If this were to happen, the protection aspect of the investment treaty will be considerably weakened.

7.7 *Balance-of-payment safeguards*

There are a variety of transfer-of-funds provisions which appear in bilateral investment treaties. It may be observed that they vary from the strict standards of repatriation of profits favoured by multinational corporations and developed countries to ones which are more accommodating of the balance-of-payment difficulties that could be encountered in the event of an absolute right of repatriation of profits and liquidated assets. Given the succession of economic crises that have buffeted developing states, it is unlikely that a model favouring an absolute right of repatriation of profits will be acceptable to developing countries or could be said to be in accordance with development objectives. Neither could it be said to fit in with the Doha mandate that the provisions of an investment instrument must take into account the development dimension. The right to regulate capital outflows becomes central to the issue of balance-of-payment safeguards. The imposition of currency controls, which was the Malaysian solution to the Asian financial crisis of 1997, was decried by the International Monetary Fund, which had later to accept that it was indeed a possible solution to the problem. The curtailment of this power of regulation cannot be said to promote the development dimension.

7.8 *Dispute resolution*

This is again a contentious issue. The investment treaties now provide unilateral remedies to the foreign investor. It is said that this is not possible under the WTO system, as only inter-state remedies are possible under the WTO dispute-settlement mechanism. This is used as an argument for multilateral treaties on investment, as states will not readily go in to bat on behalf of investors, and thus risk the displeasure of other states, unless there are heavyweight policy reasons for doing so. This is not entirely true. The United States is the home of the world's largest multinational corporations. They have enormous power to ensure outcomes that are favourable to them. Many of the cases that have been brought before the dispute-resolution system of the WTO were clearly brought at the instance of particular multinational corporations. The *Fuji* v. *Kodak* case is an example: it is apparent that the case protected the interests of one multinational corporation, Kodak, but involved no general heavyweight policy issue.

The internal laws of the United States also mandate that the United States Trade Representative (USTR) can be compelled by the US courts to take up the claims of any individual investor whose interests have been violated by a foreign state acting contrary to treaty standards. Hence, the USTR is obliged to institute proceedings before the WTO dispute-settlement bodies where a US corporation alleges a violation. The enormous resources of the United States will be brought to bear almost without expense in settling the claims of the multinational corporation. This is a matter that will concern developing states. The same concerns expressed in the case of the United States may also apply in the case of other capital-exporting developed states.

8. The right to regulate foreign investment

The right to regulate foreign investment from entry to exit lies at the root of conflicts concerning the making of an investment instrument. It runs through every aspect of the provisions of the instrument from definition to dispute settlement. Customary international law recognised that the entry of foreign investment was entirely a matter for the sovereign prerogative of the state. Liberalising instruments on foreign investment seek to change this view. Developed states themselves are disunited on this point. When the OECD's MAI was being negotiated, France and Canada sought a cultural exception that would have prevented the US entertainment industry from entering these states and dominating their cultural industries. On a wider scale, the objections are even greater. Developing states maintain screening legislation in order to exclude investments they perceive as harmful to their economies. This is a right that is unlikely to be given up.

The regulation of the operation of the foreign investment after entry is also regarded as a right of the host state, as foreign investment, unlike trade in goods, is an essentially intrusive activity which takes place entirely within the territorial boundaries of the state. Its regulation is seen as vital by developing countries. Again, during the negotiation of the OECD's MAI, the protests, which came largely from Western NGOs, were motivated by the fact that the MAI did not have sufficient regard to the protection of the environment and other social concerns such as human rights and labour standards, all of which the multinational corporations were seen as capable of disregarding.

The chairman of the negotiations was conscious of this criticism. He issued a package which was intended to 'achieve a balance between MAI disciplines and other important areas of public policy of concern to MAI Parties and to avoid unintended consequences on normal regulatory practices'. One suggestion was to include preambular provisions that would contain references to conventions that contain environmental and labour standards.[97] Preambular provisions are not binding, though they may be of interpretative significance. The need to preserve some scope for non-discriminatory regulation was recognised. An absolute oxymoron of a provision was suggested to accomplish this feat. The provision is worth reproducing, for it demonstrates the draftsman's inability to reconcile the two competing forces of effective protection of foreign investment with the recognition of the right of regulation in the host state. The suggested provision read:

A Contracting Party may adopt, maintain or enforce any measure that it considers appropriate to ensure that investment activity is undertaken in a manner sensitive to health, safety or environmental concerns, provided such measures are consistent with this agreement.

It is abundantly clear that this provision is practically meaningless. It contains the language of Article XX of the GATT, but, in addition to the fact that such language presents difficulties in interpretation, the inconsistency of aims in the provision is obvious. It illustrates the difficulty of marrying the underlying philosophy of liberalisation in an instrument like the MAI with the preservation of the right of regulation. These are difficulties that developed countries faced between themselves in drafting an instrument on investment.

When it comes to the inclusion of the developing countries and the taking into account of the development dimension, as the Doha Declaration directs, the problems become compounded. For developing countries, the right of regulation lies at the root of foreign investment policy. Most of the domestic laws on foreign investment are premised on this fact. No multilateral investment instrument can be agreed unless this fundamental inconsistency is resolved. Its resolution will prove difficult as no solution will prove acceptable to all groupings of states. The optimum moment for bringing about a solution was at the high point of economic liberalism, but this moment has now passed. Until another such occasion arises, this hope will remain unrealised. As in the past, efforts will be continued. The issue of the right to regulation will remain a stumbling block that cannot be avoided. The Doha Declaration mandates that the investment solutions should 'reflect in a balanced manner the interests of home and host countries, and take due account of the development policies and objectives of host governments as well as their right to regulate in the public interest'. Finding that elusive balance is what the game is about. The obvious starting-point is to ditch the ideas that underlay the OECD's MAI. These ideas were rejected by the developed states which participated in the negotiations, and they will be rejected by the developing states, with the NGOs (a reality of modern international relations) still hovering over the issues. A new approach, sensitive to the needs of development, will recognise the significance of the right to regulation and ensure its meaningful accommodation in the new instrument.

The NAFTA litigation has certainly caused some concern as to whether investment protection has gone too far. The litigation strategies evidence a disregard of the state's

---

[97] In *S. D. Myers* v. *Canada* (2000) 40 *ILM* 1408; (2002) 121 *ILR* 7, Canada unsuccessfully argued that its regulation of the waste-disposal industry was supported by the Basel Convention on the Transboundary Movement of Hazardous Waste.

right to regulation which discomforts the United States and Canada to such an extent that interpretative devices have been used to ensure that the regulatory rights of the state are not diminished. In that context, it is unlikely that there would be a keenness to draft a comprehensive investment instrument which does not recognise the right to regulate.

9. Conclusion

Each of the eight areas that have been detailed in section's 7.1 to 7.8 above contain issues of concern to developing countries. The drafting of effective rules relating to these areas will adversely affect the interests of developing countries and diminish their right to regulate foreign investment. If the instrument is inspired by the tenets of economic liberalism, as NAFTA seems to have been, then the diminution of the right to regulation will be near complete. NAFTA does contain exceptions relating to the environment, but already tribunals have held that these seemingly wide exceptions have only hortatory significance.[98]

The only way that an acceptable investment instrument can be created that takes into account the Doha prescription relating to the development dimension is to ensure that there is plenty of scope for the right to regulate foreign investment so that a state is given sufficient leeway to harness the foreign investment to its development objectives. This would mean that, in the eight areas identified above, there must be sufficient flexibility to accommodate the interests of developing states. But, such flexibility is unlikely to be acceptable to developed states. The battle-lines are clearly drawn.

---

[98] *Pope and Talbot* v. *Canada* (2002) 41 *ILM* 1347.

7

Settlement of investment disputes: contract-based arbitration

The previous chapters have indicated how efforts have been made through diplomatic means and through treaty means to bring about the protection of foreign investment. Diplomatic means are the older of the two. There are definite rules on the basis of which diplomatic intervention to protect the interests of the foreign investor could be made. They are the genesis of what some states regard as customary international law. Where diplomatic intercession fails, the same rules become the basis on which litigation could be brought against the recalcitrant state before an international tribunal or the International Court of Justice. There have been very few cases that have been brought before the International Court of Justice or its predecessor.[1] Where a large number of foreign investment disputes arise from a single incident, states may choose to set up Claims Commissions to deal with them. In these circumstances, an international tribunal is established pursuant to an instrument akin to a treaty with clear means of enforcing the awards it makes.[2]

Investment treaties, as has been seen, have also devised their own methods of dispute settlement. They usually enable the foreign investor to invoke remedies through arbitration at his own instance, the state being taken to have expressed its consent through the treaty provision. In a sense, an attempt has thus been made to create a regime of investment protection. But, in the absence of a multilateral treaty, such a regime will not come about. Yet, there is a system of protection that is provided through a network of investment treaties which works through a compliance mechanism provided through arbitration. The existence of a specialised international body dedicated to providing arbitration of investment disputes, the International Centre for the Settlement of Investment Disputes, set up by the World Bank-sponsored Convention for the Settlement of Disputes between States and Nationals of Other States, greatly enhances the system. Besides this arbitration system, there are other arbitration centres which deal with investment disputes and are referred to in investment treaties.

But, well before the emergence of the investment treaty system in 1959, there was an earlier system of investment protection which the multinational corporations had virtually devised by themselves for the protection of their investments. This system worked entirely on

---

[1] For a consideration of the cases decided by the International Court of Justice and the Permanent Court of International Justice, see M. Sornarajah, *The Settlement of Foreign Investment Disputes* (2000), pp. 315–33.
[2] The obvious recent examples are the Iran–US Claims Tribunal and the United Nations Compensation Commission set up after the 1990–1 Gulf War.

the basis of contractual structures of protection that were negotiated with the host state at the time of the entry of the investment. Virtually every foreign investment entry is accomplished through a contract, except where entry is made through a merger or acquisition. The contract is negotiated with the host state or its agency at the time of entry. The idea then was to ensure that contractual techniques of protecting the terms of the contract and the assets that flow on the basis of the contract are protected through devices that are built into the contract. This would also require the application of a law other than the law of the host state in order to ensure that the contractual protection can operate in practice. The host state's law will not be sufficient, as it could easily be changed by the host state. However, the contractual technique of protection had first to be ironed out. Next, an elaborate theory had to be built to ensure that the contractual structure receives protection. International law, or at least some supranational system of law, was thought to be the best system for protecting the contract. Great effort was put into structuring this system of investment protection. This chapter discusses the manner of the creation of this system of contractual protection that was so tied up with the use of arbitration. Arbitration emerges as the central feature of the system. It was ideas derived from this system of arbitration, which still continues to exist as a distinct means of settling foreign investment disputes, which fertilised the law on foreign investment arbitration under investment treaties. Though a fashion has emerged in the literature to deal with investment arbitration under treaties as unique, the genesis of this type of arbitration lies in arbitration that arose from foreign investment contracts unsupported by treaties, at a time before investment treaties first appeared. So, this chapter begins a consideration of the settlement of disputes through arbitration with a discussion of arbitration under contract, which continues to be of signifi-cance despite being overtaken in volume by arbitration of investment disputes under treaties. The technique of protection achieved was important from the point of view of international law. From a theoretical perspective, it is important to show that multinational corporations, though essentially private actors denied personality in international law,[3] nevertheless had sufficient power to manipulate the low-order sources of international law, such as judicial decisions, the writings of highly qualified publicists and the general principles of law, to construct the system of protection they desired. The system had a substantial compliance mechanism that permitted enforcement of arbitral awards by domestic courts. All these strategies sought to invoke either international law, or a supranational system specially created for the purpose, in order to give legitimacy to the contractual scheme.

The initial view promoted was that a taking in violation of a foreign investment contract was illegal.[4] The illegality presupposed the application of the foreign investment contract

---

[3] It demonstrates incidentally that positivist international lawyers were wrong in denying that entities other than states did not have personality in international law. It may also be that they maintained this stance so that these corporations, active from colonial times as sources of power, could cloak their activities under the veil that lack of personality provided to them. It entailed a lack of responsibility as well.

[4] The case for the UK government in the *Anglo-Iranian Oil Company Case* was built on the basis that, though a state has a right to nationalise, the nationalisation is illegal if it is done in violation of an existing contractual commitment. See the opinion prepared for the drafting of the UK memorandum by Sir Hersch Lauterpacht in H. Lauterpacht, *Collected Papers* (1978), vol. 4, p. 25 at p. 29. The high point of the view was the award of Professor Dupuy in *Texaco v. Libya* (1977) 53 *ILR* 389. In *Aminoil* (1982) 22 *ILM* 976, the case for the oil company was built on the view that a taking in violation of the stabilisation clause in the concession agreement was invalid. This view gained support in the separate opinion of Sir Gerald Fitzmaurice in *Aminoil*.

being founded in international law. This view has lost support as theory did not support the notion that a breach of a foreign investment contract *per se* would be an illegality in terms of international law.[5] But, the existence of an agreement in which the state makes a commitment not to take the property of the foreign investor for a certain period of time has always had some significance in the law. The view is that such agreements are akin to treaties and their violation is unlawful. There is little support for this view in modern times. But, variations of this theme still continue to exist. The argument is sometimes made that the violation of contractual rights enhances compensation. Because the old view still continues to have echoes in modern law, it is necessary to consider the ramifications of the notion that the foreign investment agreement itself has a status in law and that its violation brings about certain consequences, principally remedies provided by arbitral tribunals.

Foreign investment agreements are usually the basis on which entry is made into the host country. They are also the basis on which dispute settlement through arbitration is resorted to when parties are in conflict. The bargaining power of the foreign investor is at its greatest at the moment of entry, when he is best able to secure terms favourable to himself. Prudence requires that these terms be reduced to the form of a contract. The agreement secures the basis on which the expectations of the foreign investor are to be protected. But, the agreement also contains an 'obsolescing bargain'[6] in the sense that the bargaining power of the foreign investor diminishes as the foreign investment project progresses. Once the investment has been made and the project is under way, the foreign investor becomes a captive of the host state. Unless he takes measures to ensure his continuing usefulness to the project, the host state will seek to change the initial terms on which entry was made by the foreign investor. The ability of the state to interfere with the foreign investment is enhanced by the fact that it has the legislative machinery of the state at its disposal and, at least as far as municipal law is concerned, a theory of legislative supremacy to interfere with any domestic event.

It is crucial for foreign investment protection that a counterbalancing theory which neutralises the power of the state to interfere with foreign investment contracts is constructed. It is an interesting facet of the law that this counterbalancing theory, which sought to stigmatise a taking in violation of a foreign investment agreement as illegal or, at least, as inviting the condemnation of the law by requiring the payment of higher compensation, was built up largely through mechanisms devised by foreign investors and those supporting their endeavours. It is a fiction to say that international law is a law between states. Power in international relations is not exercised by states alone but by individuals and conglomerations of individuals, and the fiction of international law that it is a law between states merely hid this fact and avoided the scrutiny of these actors. Many of the legal techniques, particularly in the field of foreign investment, were created through the exercise of private power.

---

[5] The debate on this no longer takes place. For the old debate, see C. F. Amerasinghe, *State Responsibility for Injuries to Aliens* (1967).

[6] R. Vernon, 'International Investment and International Trade' (1966) 2 *Quarterly Journal of Economics* 80.

Capital-exporting states supported the formulation of the theory but were not direct participants in the initial efforts to build it. To this extent, this area, at least in its early stages, may evidence a rare instance of an attempt at private power being used to create public international law.[7] The sources which were used to create the rules of protection were the teachings of highly qualified publicists and arbitral awards. They were weak sources, which could be utilised by private power.[8] The capital-importing states, against whose interests the system was created, did not have recourse to any means of countering the creation of these laws.[9] The method of investment protection depended on the nature of the foreign investment contract which initiated the process of foreign investment and the inclusion in it of certain types of clauses. The contractual structure on which the theory of foreign investment protection was erected requires examination.

1. Contractual devices for foreign investment protection

The first rule concerned with liability for breach of foreign investment agreements did not appear until late in the twentieth century. Technically, defaults on debts made by foreign citizens amounted to breaches of contract, but the manner of the settlement of such disputes was through negotiation and persuasion and as a last resort through military intervention to secure payment. It may be possible to extract a principle that such practices gave rise to a rule that a loan contract must be honoured, but the practice on intervention to extract payment of debts was insufficiently uniform to give rise to any rule. Latin American states resisted the formation of any rule relating to liability for debts or any rule that military intervention could be justified on the basis of the enforcement of liability for debts.[10]

Writing in 1943, Hackworth stated the US position in the following terms:[11]

Generally speaking, the Department of State does not intervene in cases involving breaches of contract between a foreign state and a national of the United States in the absence of showing a denial of justice ... The practice of declining to intervene formally prior to a showing of denial of justice is based on the proposition that the Government of the United States is not a collection agency and cannot

---

[7] It is not suggested that there was a conspiracy to build such a law. Once formulated, the advantage of the system was perceived by foreign investors and their advisors. The imitation effect played a role, and theory came to be formulated to preserve what was achieved. Political scientists, unlike lawyers, are not averse to dwelling on the role of private power in foreign investment protection. It is also instructive to compare the manner in which the *lex mercatoria* has been constructed to apply in private international transactions. Again, the movement is one that has progressed due to the vigour of the support of publicists and business organisations.

[8] This is a strong claim to make. It subjects many respected academics to a charge of an absence of neutrality in the pursuit of their disciplines. Such a charge is not intended. The need for investment protection is obvious. The idea that there should be external protection for foreign investment contracts was generated by a genuinely felt need to counterbalance the legislative power of the host state. Given the commitment to notions of sanctity of contract, it would be logical to build up a theory of investment protection through international law. But, the role of private power in accentuating this trend, while it must not be exaggerated, was considerable, for the initial contracts that had to be devised on the basis of building up such protection were devised by lawyers for foreign investors. Once the idea took hold, rationalisations of the idea of investment protection came to be made and passed into more serious efforts to formulate theory.

[9] They had to wait until they were powerful enough within the General Assembly to pass resolutions asserting their economic sovereignty.

[10] The Latin American jurists formulated the Drago doctrine, which forbade the use of force to recover debts.

[11] Hackworth, *Digest of International Law* (1943), vol. 5, p. 611.

assume the role of endeavouring to enforce contractual undertakings freely entered into by nationals with foreign states.

States were extremely reluctant to intercede in situations of breach of contract, except where state responsibility arose as a result of denial of justice in the host state. It was recognised that a mere breach of contract to which a state was party did not, *per se*, engage the state in responsibility. In the period after the Second World War, there is clear evidence of an attempt to change this rule. The ending of colonialism and the outlawing of the use of force meant that capital-exporting states could not use military pressure as a means of securing the interests of citizens who had contractual claims against other states. In this state of help-lessness, there was a need quickly to develop principles which would ensure that contractual claims could be enforced through supranational means. It is evident that these means were formulated initially not by states but by foreign investors and by associations favourable to them. It was they who stood in immediate need of protection. By this time, foreign invest-ments were made largely by multinational corporations which had sufficient capacity in terms of power, if not in terms of law, to act in their own interests.

The early devices relating to the contractual protection of foreign investment were worked out in the context of investments made in the extractive industries, principally the oil industry. In the extractive industries, the usual form of entry was through the concession agreement. The concession agreement came close to being a transfer of sovereignty over whole tracts of land for long periods of time. The agreement ensured total control over the transaction by the foreign investor. These forms of investment were possible only in situations in which the government of the host state was not powerful enough to protest or was subject to the control of the home state of the foreign investor. The states which granted the concessions were either colonies or protectorates. In some instances, the absolute rulers who controlled their states were dependent on the foreign power for the continuation of their hold on the reins of power. When power came to be transferred to the host state and its people on decolonisation, new techniques of foreign investment had to be devised which would reflect the interests of the host state and involve an internal balance between the interests of the host state and the foreign investor. The change that has come about in the contractual structures also required a reconsideration of the issue of investment protection. Whereas, previously, these states would not have dared to court the displeasure of the home state of the foreign investor, the situation had now changed. Political and military pressure could not ensure the security of the foreign investor or the supply of the necessary natural resources for the furnaces of European industry. The use of such pressure was unwise due to the anti-colonial sentiments that had become prevalent. In addition, the founding of the United Nations and the outlawing of war by its Charter made the use of military pressure no longer feasible. The Iraqi War of 2003 indicates that there is a weakening of the United Nations system and that the solitary hegemonic power may still use force in order to achieve its ends. Yet, it must still be accepted that there remain constraints on the use of force in modern international law. When such constraints came to be recognised, it became necessary to devise other means to ensure investment protection based on some semblance of legality. This was sought to be effected largely by the construction of a distinct legal system which would give security to existing and future concession agreements. Before examining the construction of this new structure of protection, the basic contractual form on which this elaborate theory was built and the clauses which were used in this contractual form need to be examined.

1.1 The essential clauses

Though the terms of the early concession agreements vary, their core features were similar. These early concession agreements were to last for a long period of time. They were to be immune from interference by the home state during this period. They would contain a 'stabilisation clause' seeking to freeze the law as it was at the time of the entry of the investment and to ensure that later changes to the law did not apply to the concession. They usually contained a choice-of-law clause which would seek to exclude the application of the domestic laws of the host state and subject the contract to some nebulous external standard such as 'general principles of law' or 'standards that prevail within the industry'. The object of the latter technique was to ensure the application of a system which could not be unilaterally altered by the home state as its own laws could have been. In return for the resources extracted, the home state was to receive in return a payment of royalties calculated on the basis of the amount of resources extracted. The later importance of the structure of some of the clauses involved in the concession agreement requires a more careful study to be made of them. It must also be kept in mind that there were many agreements which did not contain all or some of the clauses described here. At this stage, the clauses are described, and some of the theoretical difficulties associated with them identified. The use made by them of arbitral tribunals will be discussed thereafter.

1.1.1 The stabilisation clause

The aim of the stabilisation clause was to ensure that future changes in the legislation of the host state did not vary the terms of the contract on the basis of which entry was made. The foreign corporation stood at a disadvantage in any agreement it made with the host state, as the host state had the legislative power to alter the impact on the contract of any event that took place within its territory or to affect any contractual right or right to property that was located within its territory. Such a power flowed from its sovereignty. It was in the interests of the foreign corporation to neutralise this power. The stabilisation clause was introduced into the agreement to effect this.[12] The basis of the stabilisation clause was that the state was bound by the agreement contained in the clause not to apply any later changes to its laws to the particular contract or to alter the terms of the contract directly by legislation. The clause sought to freeze the law of the host state at the time of the entry of the foreign investor, and to

---

[12] Generally, see E. Paasivirta, 'Internationalisation and Stabilisation of Contracts versus State Sovereignty' (1989) 50 *BYIL* 315; T. W. Walde and G. Ndi, 'Stabilising International Investment Commitments: International Law Versus Contract Interpretation' (1996) 31 *Texas International Law Journal* 215. It has been pointed out that the stabilisation clause is inconsistent with the choice-of-law clause, because the stabilisation clause is an implicit acceptance that the host state's law, in the stabilised form, applies to the contract. A. El Kosheri and T. Riad, 'The Law Governing a New Generation of Petroleum Contracts' (1986) 1 *ICSID Rev* 259.

make the law so frozen the law that controls the foreign investment. The stabilisation clause is intended to immunise the foreign investment contract from a range of matters, such as taxation, environmental controls and other regulations, as well as to prevent the destruction of the contract itself before the contract expires. There are a variety of types of stabilisation clause but, however drafted, the main purpose of the stabilisation clause is to prevent the application of changes in the law to the contract.[13] Some clauses contemplate the possibility of changed conditions and provide for renegotiations in light of these changes so that the contractual equilibrium existing at the time of the conclusion of the contract is restored. These clauses are also not stabilisation clauses in the strict sense.[14]

Doubts have been raised as to whether a contractual clause can achieve the effect of fettering the legislative sovereignty of a state for a lengthy period of time.[15] The state, in theory, must act in the public good as it perceives it to be at any given time. It may not be possible, as a matter of constitutional theory, for a state to bind itself by a contract made with a private party, particularly a foreign party, to fetter its legislative power. It is trite law that a legislature is not bound by its own legislation and has the power to change it. That being so, a provision in a contract cannot bind the state. As a matter of constitutional theory, a stabilisation clause may not be able to achieve what it sets out to do. It may not serve as anything more than a comforter to the foreign investor, who may derive some security from the belief that there is a promise secured from the state not to apply its future legislation to the contract. This conclusion would hold unless an alternative rationale can be found to give the stabilisation clause greater force. There was a need for a theory which would confer validity on the stabilisation clause by ensuring that its force was derived from some external source that stood higher in the hierarchy of validity than domestic law. The structuring of such a theory was necessary to ensure that the objective behind the stabilisation clause was achieved.

The theory of internationalised contracts sought to achieve this effect. The inclusion of the stabilisation clause was seen as evidencing the intention of the state party to the agreement not to subject it to its domestic law but to subject it to some external system which would ensure the validity of the stabilisation clause and the contract which contains it. The stabilisation clause, along with other clauses which gave rise to such an inference, played an important role in enabling the inference to be drawn that the foreign investment contract was not subject to the domestic law of the host state.

Some examples of a stabilisation clause are apposite. The stabilisation clause involved in the concession agreement between Texaco and Libya which was relevant to the *Texaco* v. *Libya* arbitration,[16] read as follows:

---

[13] Some clauses seek to ensure that, though the foreign investor complies with the changes to the law, the cost of such compliance is carried by the host state. This seeks to allocate the risk of the change to the host state, and is not, properly speaking, a stabilisation clause. However, it secures from the point of view of the foreign investor the same degree of protection as the stabilisation clause, and neutralises the effect of the change.

[14] There may be a general duty to renegotiate in light of changed circumstances. Prudence dictates such a duty. State intervention will result in the absence of such a renegotiation. Arbitral awards support the existence of such a duty of renegotiation.

[15] In *Aminoil* v. *Kuwait* (1982) 21 *ILM* 976, the tribunal suggested that the clause may be valid if it is limited to a reasonable period of time.

[16] (1977) 53 *ILR* 389.

The Government of Libya will take all steps necessary to ensure that the company enjoys all the rights conferred by the concession. The contractual rights expressly created by this concession shall not be altered except by the mutual consent of the parties.

This is not a direct stabilisation clause which spells out that future legislative changes cannot apply to the agreement. But, it creates an obligation to secure the consent of the foreign party before effecting any changes by legislation or otherwise to the contractual regime. It seeks to neutralise sovereignty by creating the need for the consent of the foreign party to changes that are to apply to the agreement. But, since it provides for negotiation between the parties as to changes to be effected to the contract, it provides at least an avenue through which the parties could renegotiate and establish a new contractual balance in light of any new circumstances. To this extent, an indirect stabilisation clause may not prove as objectionable as a direct stabilisation clause which precludes the making of any changes to the agreement.

A more direct form of stabilisation clause was contained in the contract involved in the *Aminoil* v. *Kuwait* arbitration.[17] It read as follows:

The Shaikh shall not by general or special legislation or by administrative measures or by any other act whatever annul this Agreement except as provided in Article 11. No alteration shall be made in terms of this Agreement by either the Shaikh or the Company except in the event of the Shaikh and the Company jointly agreeing that it is desirable in the interests of both parties to make certain alterations, deletions or additions to this Agreement.

The fact that the state party agreed to such a wide stabilisation clause is an indication of a promise not to interfere with the working of the foreign investment process during the period of its duration.

After a dispute arises between the foreign investor and the host state, the validity of the stabilisation clause becomes a subject of debate. States have always queried whether such a blanket surrender of sovereignty through what is in effect a contract located under their own laws can curtail their legislative sovereignty. There are two main ways in which the stabilisation clause could be attacked. One is to query the *vires* of the officials who made the contract on behalf of the state party. The contract would usually have been made by officials of a state entity or of a ministry. They would usually lack the powers to commit the state to any definite obligation, particularly the obligation not to use the legislative powers of the state in a particular manner.[18] The second objection to the stabilisation clause is that the legislative powers of a state cannot be fettered by a mere contractual provision, particularly where the exercise of such power is necessary to secure a public benefit. In ordinary terms, both objections have a great deal of validity. These objections are met. The first objection on *vires* is met with the rule which states that, once the contract is made, a state is not permitted to rely on its internal laws to contest its validity. The origins of this rule are obscure. Judge Cavin justified it in the *Sapphire* v. *NIOC* arbitration on the basis that a foreigner cannot be

---

[17] (1982) 21 *ILM* 976.

[18] A French court in *SPP* v. *Egypt*, 3 *ICSID Reports* 101; (1983) 22 *ILM* 752 held that a state does not become a party to a contract merely because officials of a state entity and the minister responsible for the entity signed the contract.

expected to know all the laws of a state.[19] Why a sophisticated multinational corporation with its own in-house legal department should have this privilege when every alien who enters a foreign state is presumed to know and abide by the law of his host state is unclear.[20] The second objection is met with the theory that the foreign investment contract is subject to a supranational system which can bind the local legislature much in the same way that a treaty can bind the state. This observation likens the foreign investment agreement to a treaty, which obviously it is not.[21] In any event, a foreign investment agreement in the natural resources sector has to contend with the principle of permanent sovereignty over natural resources. There is a view gaining support that this doctrine prevents a foreign investment agreement binding the legislative competence of a state. In any event, the analogising of a foreign investment to a treaty is far-fetched.[22] The foreign investor does not have personality in international law. Some writers have sought to overcome this problem by arguing that the defect of personality in the foreign investor could be cured by the state conferring personality on the foreign investor. This is stretching logic to breaking point. It is far-fetched to argue that the multinational corporation has personality when it suits its interests and that it does not have personality when it does not, as where liability is sought to be imposed on it for misconduct or to institute a code of conduct through international instruments.

But, the issue is whether the cumulative effect of other clauses, introduced along with the stabilisation clause, seeking to externalise the agreement will make a difference and strengthen the internationalisation of the contract. A discussion of this issue must await a consideration of the other clauses.

1.1.2 Choice-of-law clause

The principle of party autonomy is used in order to ensure that the foreign investment agreement is not subject to the laws of the host country which can be changed at will by the sovereign party. The assumption is that, as in the case of other international contracts, parties have autonomy to choose the law which is applicable to the foreign investment contract. On the basis of party autonomy, the foreign party to the agreement will choose a system other than the domestic law of the host state.[23] The choice of another state's domestic law is possible but will cause affront to the host state. Besides, such a choice will not have the

---

[19] (1963) 35 *ILR* 136.

[20] However, a rule is entrenched in practice, particularly in International Chamber of Commerce arbitrations, to the effect that a state cannot set up an *ultra vires* defence on the basis of its own laws. *Framatome* v. *Atomic Energy Organization of Iran* (1984) 111 *Journal du Droit International* 58; (1983) 6 *YCA* 94.

[21] Treaties are seldom made with stabilisation clauses. In any event, they are subject to doctrines which make the obligations defeasible due to changed circumstances.

[22] State interference with contracts in the public interest have generally been recognised as valid in English law. As to public contracts, see *Amphitrite* v. *R.* [1921] 3 KB 300. An Australian lawyer has observed that 'the exercise of statutory powers is not inhibited in any way by the prior existence of contractual arrangements which might be detrimentally affected if those statutory powers were to be exercised'. E. Campbell, 'Legal Problems Involved in Government Participation in Resource Projects' (1984) *Yearbook of the Australian Mining and Petroleum Law Association* 126 at 144. English courts have recognised foreign legislation interfering with state contracts located within the foreign state's jurisdiction. *Czarnikow Ltd* v. *Rolimpex* [1979] AC 351; *Settebello* v. *Banco Totta e Acores* [1985] 1 WLR 1050.

[23] On party autonomy, see J. D. M. Lew, *The Applicable Law in International Commercial Arbitration* (1978); P. E. Nygh, *Party Autonomy in Private International Law* (1998).

desired effect of subjecting the contract to a system which is higher in the hierarchy than the domestic system of the host state. This hierarchical notion is important for the achievement of the strategy of investment protection that is attempted. Another municipal system will have only an equal and not a superior force. The choice of international law may be possible, but the theoretical difficulty is that, even if an entity with no status in international law may choose international law as the law applicable,[24] there is no body of international law applicable to contracts between states and foreign private entities. Given this difficulty, the strategy has been to opt for the choice of some nebulous system of supranational principles and indicate the means for the creation of the rules of such a system. The formula often is to refer to 'general principles of law'. The assumption is that, because these principles cannot be unilaterally changed by the host state as its domestic law can be, they will provide a measure of protection to the foreign party.

There are two problems with this assumption. The first involves the status of the doctrine of party autonomy. The idea of party autonomy is exalted to a position of near absoluteness in private international transactions such as export transactions. But, it may not have the same degree of exclusivity in the case of large transactions which involve state parties. The involvement of the state introduces into the contract a party which has to have paramount regard to national interests and give only secondary regard to the carrying out of the contract. Besides, the nature of the foreign investment contract differs from the types of contract in relation to which the doctrine of party autonomy was developed. Unlike export transactions, which have a uniform degree of contact with several jurisdictions, the foreign investment contract has contact predominantly with the host state. It is of long duration. The carrying out of any major industrial project attracts the application of many regulatory controls, such as those relating to planning, environmental protection, customs controls and similar areas of public law. Such laws are bound to affect a major industrial project being carried out within the state. They will be regarded as mandatory provisions of the law, and it is well accepted in every legal system that mandatory laws cannot be evaded by the mere technique of choosing a foreign law as the law applicable to the contract. In the natural resources sector, there are likely to be even greater controls relating to pricing, taxation and the environment. It is very unlikely then that party autonomy itself can support the idea that the application of the domestic law to a foreign investment transaction can be excluded altogether by the choice of some nebulous system of law.[25] Much of the case law in this area arose at a time when host states did not have foreign investment codes. Most host states now have sophisticated laws regulating foreign investment, particularly in the natural resources sector.

---

[24] As a matter of private international law, such a choice may be possible. But, English law has always required there to be a definite and ascertainable system in which the agreement is rooted. Hence, the choice of equity or an honourable code as the applicable system has been resisted by the English courts. The civil law systems have taken a different attitude to this issue. But, as a jurisprudential proposition, a contract must be founded on ascertainable rules so that the parties may know the extent of their obligations. A system with a variable content can hardly be the basis of a contractual obligation. In *Deutsche Schachtbau- und Tiefbohrgesellschaft mbH* v. *Ras Al-Khaimah National Oil Co.* [1988] 3 WLR 230; [1988] 2 All ER 833, the enforcement of an award involving such a clause was considered. It would appear that there is a move towards regarding concession agreements as *sui generis* in this respect.

[25] See further M. Sornarajah, *International Commercial Arbitration* (1990), pp. 102–60.

The second factor is that there are numerous authorities in the first half of the twentieth century identifying the domestic law of the host state as the law applying to the foreign investment transaction. In the *Serbian Loans Case*,[26] the Permanent Court of International Justice indicated that international law has no relevance to a transaction involving a state and a private party, and that reference should be made to a municipal system to settle problems arising from such a transaction. It is clear that, at the time of that decision at any rate, the application of any system other than the municipal system of a state to such transactions was contemplated.

There are many other authoritative statements supporting the view that a municipal system, in particular the municipal system of the state party, will apply to the transaction involving the state and a foreign private party. In *Kahler* v. *Midland Bank*, in 1950, Lord Radcliffe stated that, in the case of a contract between a state and a foreign private party, the state's law 'not merely sustains but, because it sustains, may modify or dissolve the contractual bond'.[27] The view that the host state's law applies was stated in several arbitral awards made in the 1950s. If the law had changed to permit the choice of some other system, then the change must be identified in some concrete fashion. If a rule of international law had emerged on the matter to permit a choice of a system other than that of the domestic law of the host state, its evolution must be identified clearly. The source from which it emerged must be shown with a sufficient degree of precision. This is an onus which may be difficult to satisfy. Whether the onus has been satisfied is discussed below.

1.1.3 Arbitration clause

The third clause, the inclusion of which is said to give rise to an inference that the foreign investment agreement has been subjected to an external system, is the arbitration clause. An arbitration clause is included in the contract so as to allow the choice of a neutral forum for the settlement of disputes which arise from the agreement. The foreign investor will not have much confidence in the ability of the courts or other tribunals of the host state to settle any disputes that arise from the contract in an impartial manner. The choice of the domestic court of another state will not be appropriate, as there could be problems of sovereign immunity. The choice which is preferred by the foreign investor is an arbitral tribunal which would sit outside the host state and would be constituted in accordance with the arbitration clause. In older agreements, arbitration clauses made reference to *ad hoc* tribunals. These tribunals could be tailor-made by the parties for the arbitration of the types of dispute that could arise from the contract. In any event, until the creation of the International Centre for the Settlement of Investment Disputes (ICSID),[28] there were no tribunals with expertise in settling disputes which arose from foreign investment transactions involving states and private parties.[29]

---

[26] (1929) PCIJ Series A No. 20.   [27] [1950] AC 24 at 56.

[28] ICSID was created by a World Bank-sponsored convention, the Convention on the Settlement of Investment Disputes Between States and Nationals of Other States. The Convention came into force in October 1966.

[29] The International Chamber of Commerce has dealt with disputes arising from state contracts. As the awards are not made public, the visibility of its activity is diminished. However, there are now studies of the practice adopted by ICC tribunals. In more recent times, national chambers of arbitration, like the Stockholm Chamber of Arbitration, have begun to play a role. *Ad hoc* arbitration, especially under UNCITRAL Rules, is also resorted to. These are not specialist institutions like ICSID, which is dedicated to the arbitration of foreign investment disputes.

An *ad hoc* tribunal is created in accordance with the procedure for its constitution, which will be set out in the arbitration clause. Since disputes involving state contracts constitute a specialised area of arbitration, it was usual to create *ad hoc* tribunals for the settlement of such disputes. This gave the parties greater freedom in selecting arbitrators as well as the place and procedure of the arbitration. It is also possible in a contract to refer such disputes to specific arbitral institutions. These institutions, however, are private institutions and do not have any specialised knowledge of the area. ICSID arbitration is exclusively for disputes arising from state contracts.[30] ICSID is a body created by an international convention. The fact that it was created by sovereign will distinguishes it from private arbitral institutions. It is important to keep this in mind, particularly in view of the fact that these private institutions often arrogate to themselves, without any basis in theory or law, the powers possessed by ICSID.[31]

The arbitration clause should specify the extent of the jurisdiction that is conferred on the arbitral tribunal. The nature of the jurisdiction of the tribunal depends on the clause and the contract that contains it. Where the arbitrator exceeds the jurisdiction so given and makes pronouncements outside the scope of the clause or acts otherwise than in accordance with the clause, the award may be void for excess of jurisdiction. ICSID has its own procedures for annulment of awards made in excess of jurisdiction.

In general arbitral practice, it is accepted that an arbitration clause survives the termination of the contract. The issue is whether this general principle applies to the arbitration of state contracts as well. Where a state seeks to terminate the agreement unilaterally by legislation, at least from the state's point of view, the arbitration clause will be terminated along with the whole contract. The legislative act is an act of sovereignty, and a state which resorts to such an act will rarely concede that the arbitration clause in the contract survives the termination of the contract by legislation. The survival of an arbitration clause after the termination of the contract is possible in a private transaction because the termination is seldom brought about by legislative act.

However, in the case of an arbitration clause referring disputes to ICSID, the position that an arbitration clause in a state contract is effaced by legislation that affects the contract is not tenable. There is an obligation created by the ICSID Convention to submit disputes to ICSID for settlement. The fact that the contract was terminated by legislation cannot mean that an international obligation was extinguished. Legislation cannot have such an effect. In the case of a reference in the arbitral clause to ICSID, the survival of the arbitration clause, even

---

[30] For a survey of the ICSID Convention, see J. Cherian, *Investment Contracts and Arbitration* (1975); for recent assessments of ICSID, see M. D. Rowat, 'Multilateral Approaches to Improving the Investment Climate of Developing Countries: The Cases of ICSID and MIGA' (1992) 33 *Harvard ILJ* 103; J. Paulsson, 'ICSID: Achievement and Prospects' (1991) 6 *ICSID Rev* 380; and S. J. Toope, *International Mixed Arbitration* (1990), pp. 219–62. Clearly, the most important work on the subject now is C. Schreuer, *The ICSID Convention: A Commentary* (2nd edn, 2009). It is, however, very much an official commentary. See also M. Sornarajah, *The Settlement of Foreign Investment Disputes* (2000).

[31] Thus, for example, in *SPP* v. *Egypt*, 3 *ICSID Reports* 101; (1983) 22 *ILM* 752, a tribunal constituted by the International Chamber of Commerce claimed the power to apply international law as the law applicable to the contract using Article 42(1) of the ICSID Convention as the basis. The fact that the parties to the ICSID Convention gave such a power by the article to ICSID tribunals does not mean that private tribunals have such a power. An ICSID tribunal is an international arbitral tribunal set up by convention; private tribunals, such as ICC tribunals, are set up by the exercise of party autonomy. In the case of a state contract, one of the parties is a non-sovereign who lacks capacity to constitute an international tribunal in the proper sense.

after the termination of the contract by whatever means, is protected by an international obligation created by treaty. The situation may be otherwise in the case of *ad hoc* arbitration or references to private arbitral institutions. This fact accounts for the failure of state parties to appear before such arbitral tribunals and for the fact that, in most cases, *ad hoc* arbitral tribunals have had to proceed to an award unilaterally. Yet, in the case of *ad hoc* tribunals as well as other institutional tribunals, an obligation to arbitrate despite the extinction of the foreign investment by legislation could arise when that obligation is supported by a bilateral or regional investment treaty.[32]

But, arbitrators do not accept the distinction that is made in the last paragraph between ICSID arbitration and other types of arbitration. Instead, they argue that the arbitration clause survives the termination of the contract to create jurisdiction in the arbitral tribunal, whether or not the arbitral tribunal is an *ad hoc* tribunal or one created by treaty. The proposition was stated in the following terms by Arbitrator Mahmassani in the *Liamco* award:

> It is widely accepted in international law and practice that an arbitration clause survives the unilateral termination by that state of the contract in which it is inserted and continues in force even after that termination. This is a logical consequence of the interpretation of the intention of the contracting parties, and appears to be one of the basic conditions for creating a favourable climate of foreign investment.

This is a sound proposition as far as private international arbitrations are concerned. The validity of the proposition has been established beyond doubt as far as such arbitrations are concerned by Judge Schwebel in no uncertain terms in a long survey of arbitral practice.[33] But, whether it applies in circumstances where a contract located in a state is absolutely extinguished by legislation still remains a moot point. For, unlike private contracts which are broken by the choice of private parties or terminated by other external events, the act which terminates a concession agreement is a public act of a sovereign state. A sovereign state which decides to perform that public act will seek to destroy the contract, arbitral clause and all. In these circumstances, it might be too facile to argue that the arbitral clause survives the unilateral termination of the agreement by the legislative act of the state, unless it is protected by a treaty. States certainly do not seem to think so, for they seldom appear before arbitrators who seek to establish their jurisdiction on the basis of the survival of the arbitration clause. The point remains at least a moot one for the moment. It must, however, be conceded that a reference to an ICSID tribunal is kept alive by the operation of the treaty provision on the arbitral clause. The same would apply where there is an international obligation created by an investment treaty which protects other forms of arbitration.

Given the structure of foreign investment contracts, and the fact that it involves states and foreign parties, an elaborate theory of foreign investment protection was created by arbitral tribunals and writers who supported its creation. Put simply, the contract that is concluded between the state and the foreign party goes through a transmogrification which enables it to

---

[32] See, for example, *Yaung Chi Oo Ltd.* v. *Myanmar* (2003) 42 *ILM* 540; (2003) 8 *ICSID Reports* 463.
[33] S. Schwebel, *International Arbitration: Three Salient Problems* (1986).

move out of the sphere of the domestic law of the host state onto a higher plane of supranational law, variously identified as transnational law, general principles of law and international law. This near-mystical effect is achieved on the basis that the inclusion of clauses, such as a stabilisation clause, a choice-of-law clause and an arbitration clause, which are aimed at establishing external points of contact for the contract, justifies this change. It is this theory of the internationalisation of state contracts on which contractual techniques of foreign investment protection depend to which attention must next be turned.

ICSID arbitration must, once more, be treated differently for purposes of discussion. The ICSID Convention itself elevates a contract which contains an arbitral clause referring disputes to ICSID to a different level. Likewise, the significance of investment treaties is that they do effectively provide a foreign investor with a variety of protection in situations requiring dispute settlement, depending on the precise wording in the provisions of each treaty.

2. The internationalisation of state contracts

The removal of the foreign investment transaction from the sphere of the host state's law and its subjection to an immutable, supranational system is seen as essential for the protection of foreign investment under the theory of internationalisation. The contract acquires stability when it is removed from the legislative control of the state authority and its other sovereign powers. This neutralisation of the power of the state to change the contract is seen as essential to the stability of the foreign investment contract. It is an idea which also contains the seeds of conflict. It is futile to expect a state not to interfere at some stage with the conduct of a transaction which takes place essentially within its territory, involves substantial income and endures over a long period of time. Yet, the formulation of the theory and the nature of the authority which supports it must be examined with care.

2.1 The origin of the theory of internationalisation

The origin of the theory of internationalisation is firmly rooted in three early arbitral awards made in disputes arising from three concession agreements involving petroleum resources and some writings of scholars.[34] In the hierarchy of norms of international law, the awards of

---

[34] It is possible to find old arbitrations in disputes arising from state contracts in which the arbitrator used external standards as an added justification to support conclusions he had arrived at on the basis of the host state's law. However, they do not provide authority for the exclusive application of external standards. Thus, in the *Delgoa Bay Railway Case* (1900) Whiteman, *Damages*, vol. 3, p. 1694, the dispute arose from an agreement to build a railway in a Portuguese-held territory. The arbitrator found Portuguese law to be the applicable law, but also stated that Portuguese law 'did not contain any particular provision on the decisive points that would depart from general principles of the common law of modern nations'. Also, in referring to the principles of damages, there is a mention of 'universally accepted principles'. In the *Schufeldt Claim* (1930) 5 *AD* 179; 24 *AJIL* 799, the law of Guatemala, which was the state party to the agreement, was applied, but there was reference to the fact that the relevant law was the same in all legal systems. In the *Lena Goldfields* arbitration (1936), a contract for mining gold was involved. The tribunal upheld the argument that the dispute should be settled according to general principles. V. V. Veeder, 'The Lena Goldfields Arbitration: The Historical Roots of Three Ideas' (1998) 47 *ICLQ* 747. Such references are not efforts at creating a universal system applicable to state contracts but merely efforts on the part of tribunals to show that their award should be accepted as it accords with conclusions that would have been arrived at by applying the legal systems of the other party or any other legal system.

arbitral tribunals or the writings of highly qualified publicists are not significant sources of law, and any theory of international law based entirely on such sources will be tainted with the weakness of the sources on which it is built. The same could be said of the writings of highly qualified publicists that emerged during and after this period supporting the techniques that were used in these arbitrations to externalise the state contract.

In each of the three arbitrations, there are *dicta* that, ordinarily, the law applicable to the concession agreements will be the law of the host state in whose territory the transaction is located. None of the concession agreements involved contained an express choice-of-law clause. Applying ordinary techniques of conflict of laws, the arbitrator in these circumstances will have to infer the law applicable to the agreement by looking at the state with which the contract had its closest connection. The use of such a technique would lead to the inescapable conclusion that the law applicable was the law of the host state. The resources which were the subject-matter of the agreement were located and the contract was performed in the state. The arbitrators conceded this point. Thus, in the *Qatar* arbitration,[35] the arbitrator, Sir Alfred Bucknil, said that the subject-matter of the contract, together with the fact that the state was party to the contract, made Islamic law applicable to the contract. In the *Abu Dhabi* arbitration,[36] Lord Asquith said:

This is a contract made in Abu Dhabi and wholly to be performed in that country. If any municipal system of law were applicable, it would, *prima facie*, be that of Abu Dhabi.

The arbitral tribunal in the *Aramco* arbitration[37] reached a similar conclusion. Professor Sauser-Hall, who was the arbitrator, observed:

The law in force in Saudi Arabia should be applied to the content of the concession because this state is a party to the agreement, as grantor, and because it is generally admitted, in private international law, that a sovereign state is presumed, unless the contrary is proved, to have subjected its undertakings to its own legal system. This principle was mentioned by the Permanent Court of International Justice in its judgment in the *Serbian Loans Case*.

There was unanimity in these arbitral awards that the law applicable to the concession agreements should be the law of the host state. It was a conclusion indicated by the state of authority in the 1950s when these awards were made.

But, the arbitrators argued that Islamic law, which would have otherwise applied as the domestic law of the host state, was not sophisticated enough to deal with transactions involving exploration for oil. At that time, there does not seem to have been any other legal system considered to be mature which contained any law on petroleum contracts. The law would have had to be created by analogy.

Instead, there was much work done by European Arabists to establish that Islamic law did not contain any principles on petroleum contracts.[38] The proposition is now contested by

---

[35] (1953) 20 *ILR* 534.   [36] (1951) 18 *ILR* 144.
[37] (1958) 27 *ILR* 117. For a fuller discussion of the change attempted, see M. Sornarajah, *The Settlement of Foreign Investment Disputes* (2000).
[38] J. N. D. Anderson and N. J. Goulson, 'The Moslem Ruler and Contractual Obligations' (1958) 33 *New York University Law Review* 917, however, argued that there was, in fact, Islamic law on the issue, and that it supported sanctity of contract.

Middle Eastern experts on petroleum law.[39] There was no law specific to petroleum contracts in European law either. The law had to be constructed by analogical reasoning, and this could well have been done with Islamic legal principles too. But, after having come to the conclusion that Islamic law could not apply, the arbitrators concluded that, in the absence of any relevant principles in the domestic law, they should apply general principles of law to fill the lacunae.

There were important academic writings which also began to support the thesis that, in situations in which there was an absence of any law in the host state, general principles of law could be used to fill the lacunae. The most significant of these writings was an essay written by Lord McNair, who supported the application of general principles to concession agreements.[40] Lord McNair was careful to confine his view to the situations in which the law of the host state lacked any significant principles which could apply to the agreement.[41] But, he was taken by others as supporting a wider proposition that general principles of law applied to concession agreements because the transnational nature of the agreements warranted the application of such neutral principles. Since general principles of law were a source of public international law, an easy transference was possible to the formulation of the rule that contracts between states and foreign private parties were subject to public international law.

A European writer, Verdross, claiming to be the initiator of the theory, suggested that foreign investment contracts with states were quasi-international agreements akin to international treaties and that international law applied to such agreements.[42] There was an array of writers who followed suit, making the claim that international law applied to agreements between states and foreign private parties.[43] One aspect of the theory was dependent on the characterisation of such transactions as economic development agreements. This idea depended on the policy reason that transfers of wealth to developing countries were beneficial to these countries. It was further argued that the entirely altruistic reasons (namely, economic development) for which foreign investments are made are worthy of protection by international law.[44] It is interesting to note that the same justifications are advanced for investment treaties in more recent times. In both situations, the rationale rests on untestable hypotheses.

The theory of internationalisation, though it continues to be advanced in modern writings, can be dismissed as having no merit. No one seriously suggests that agreements made with

---

[39] A. Z. El Chiati, 'Protection of Investment Agreements in the Context of Petroleum Agreements' (1987) 204 *Hague Recueil* 1.

[40] Lord McNair, 'The General Principles of Law Recognised by Civilised Nations' (1957) 33 *BYIL* 1.

[41] Thus, it is clear from passages in the article that Lord McNair was addressing situations in which, if the normal rule that the host state's law is applied, the situation would result in the contracts being governed by a 'system of law which had not yet been developed to deal with this particular type of transaction' ((1957) 33 *BYIL* 1 at 4). See further R. Jennings, 'State Contracts in International Law' (1961) 37 *BYIL* 156; J.-F. Lalive, 'Contracts Between a State or a State Agency and a Foreign Company' (1964) 18 *ICLQ* 987.

[42] A. Verdross, 'Quasi-International Agreements and International Economic Transactions' (1964) 18 *Yearbook of World Affairs* 230.

[43] P. Weil, 'Problèmes Relatifs aux Contrats Passés Entre un Etat et un Particulier' (1969) 128 *Hague Recueil* 95. For a discussion, see S. J. Toope, *International Mixed Arbitration* (1990), pp. 75–90.

[44] J. Hyde, 'Economic Development Agreements' (1962) 105 *Hague Recueil* 271. For recent support, see G. T. Curtis, 'The Legal Security of Economic Development Agreements' (1988) 29 *Harvard ILJ* 317; but see I. Pogany, 'Economic Development Agreements' (1992) 7 *ICSID Rev* 1. For the rejection of the argument based on economic development agreements by an arbitral tribunal, see *Amoco International Finance Co.* v. *Iran* (1987) 15 *Iran–US CTR* 189.

developed nations are subject to anything other than the law of the state. It would be offensive to the notion of the equality of states to suggest that the same principle does not apply to agreements made with developing countries. To overcome this difficulty, it is argued that agreements made in developing countries are different as they are intended to lead to the development of the host states. The idea that foreign investment is motivated by altruistic motives of developing the economy of the host state is such an absurdity that it can hardly be the basis of any rule that deserves even a casual consideration. Transnational corporations which make overseas investments are not charitable institutions doling out largesse but are companies in search of profits to be distributed among their shareholders. The argument based on the view that they bring benefits to developing states merely shows the paucity of justifications possessed by international lawyers, all of whom, of course, will claim a high degree of rectitude, scholarship and impartiality, in formulating theories to advance the cause of foreign investors from their states.[45]

There are obvious defects with the theory that international law could apply to foreign investment transactions. The foreign party to the transaction, at least in the eyes of positivist international lawyers, does not have sufficient personality in international law to enter into relations with a state or to be a possessor of rights in international law. There may come a time when international personality may broaden to include multinational corporations, which are significant actors on the international economic scene, but no serious writer on the subject had recognised, at the time the theory was formulated, that such an evolution had already taken place. It is evident that private power does possess sufficient instruments through which it could assert itself in the realm of international law, even in periods where positivism held sway and emphasised the idea that international law was based entirely on the consent of states.

Another defect in the theory that international law applies to foreign investment transactions is that there is no body of international law on the subject of state contracts. The notion that general principles of law could be used to supply the lacunae is hardly an answer to this criticism. The extraction of law on the basis of such a weak source of law in such a controversial area is unsatisfactory. The principles which have been extracted have been challenged as being based on subjective choices of individual arbitrators and scholars predisposed to building up a system of investment protection. There is also a selective use of principles. Thus, the often advocated proposition relating to sanctity of contract, enshrined in the phrase *pacta sunt servanda* and advocated by the proponents of the theory of internationalisation, is not reflected in any major system of contract law in an absolute manner. In every contract system, absolute sanctity of contract has given way to conflicting principles relating to the protection of the weaker party to the contract. There has been an increase in the number of vitiating factors the law of contract recognises, based on the acceptance of the idea that the law should take into consideration the relative bargaining strengths of the parties.[46] In light of these developments, the maintenance of a doctrine of

---

[45] See S. J. Toope, *International Mixed Arbitration* (1990), pp. 82–4, who also rejects the notion of economic development agreements as having no merit.

[46] For developments in the English law, see J. Cartwright, *Unequal Bargaining: A Study of Vitiating Factors in the Formation of Contracts* (1991).

nineteenth-century contract law that contracts have sanctity and the transference of this doctrine without taking account of the fact that the exceptions to it in modern law have increased significantly is an exercise in partiality. The search for general principles of contract law, even if possible, has not been attempted in an impartial manner but in a manner that is designed to promote the interests of investment protection to the detriment of the interests of the host state.[47]

Besides, the foreign investment contract has now ceased to be a private law agreement to which general principles of the law concerning private contracts could be extended. There has always been an effort to counter the making of an analogy between state contracts and private contracts by pointing out that the state contract was more akin to administrative contracts. Obligations arising from administrative contracts were defeasible in the public interest. Unfortunately, the early efforts concentrated on pointing out the similarities between state contracts and the *contrat administratif* of French law. Since French law developed a law on administrative contracts quite early, the comparison was a natural one to make. This argument was, however, rejected on the ground that the *contrat administratif* was a peculiarity of French law. Hence, it was argued, the principle could not be regarded as a general principle of international law.[48] The idea that a contract made by a state is defeasible in the public interest is demonstrably common to all legal systems.[49] This, again, is an illustration of the selectivity of the arguments used by the scholars who support the theory of internationalisation of contracts.[50]

Whatever the position may have been in the past, recent developments in legal systems indicate that there has been a rapid development of the notion of administrative contracts in all major legal systems.[51] There is a more credible basis now than previously to argue that contracts made by states with private parties are universally recognised as defeasible in the public interest and that no illegality can be attached to its breach by the state provided it can demonstrate a public purpose for the breach.

Quite apart from this analogy of foreign investment contracts to administrative contracts in municipal systems, the foreign investment contract itself has undergone an important transformation. The nature of the foreign investment agreement is increasingly taking on a

---

[47] Christine Gray, referring to remedies given by arbitral tribunals, made the point that there has been no systematic borrowing by arbitral tribunals from municipal law or a coherent theory on which such borrowing rested. C. Gray, *Judicial Remedies in International Law* (1990), p. 7. One may go further and suggest that expediency has been the main factor in the choice of municipal law principles. They are chosen from specific legal systems when support can be found for the view of the arbitrators in analogies from these systems. For the view that an improper choice of general principles amounts to an excess of power on the part of the tribunal, see E. Paasivirta, *Participation of States in International Contracts* (1990), p. 64.

[48] Thus, in *Texaco v. Libya* (1977) 53 *ILR* 389, para. 57, Arbitrator Dupuy, a distinguished French professor of international law, suggested that 'the theory of administrative contracts is somewhat typically French' and that it should not be accepted as forming part of international law. But, Professor Bernard Audit of the University of Paris has rejected the view that the idea is French. B. Audit, *Transnational Arbitration and State Contracts* (1988), p. 108. He observes: 'These arguments make the form unduly prevail over substance. Comparative law indicates that everywhere contracts concluded by public authority are not altogether governed by the same regime as purely civil contracts.'

[49] S. J. Toope, *International Mixed Arbitration* (1990), p. 73; E. Paasivirta, *Participation of States in International Contracts* (1990), pp. 194–5.

[50] There was greater receptivity to the view that administrative contracts are recognised generally in most legal systems in *Aminoil* (1982) 21 *ILM* 976 at 1022, and in *BP* (1977) 53 *ILR* 976 at 349.

[51] A. A. Fatouros, 'The Administrative Contract in Transnational Transactions: Reflections on the Uses of Comparison', in *Ius in Privatum: Festschrift für Max Rheinstein* (1969), vol. 1, p. 259.

public law character in both developed and developing countries. Writers have noted that petroleum agreements that are entered into in Europe are based more in public law than in private law.[52] The production-sharing agreements which are the model universally employed by developing countries permit constant supervision of the whole process of oil exploration and sale by state oil corporations. In the other areas of foreign investment, the increasing use of pre-entry screening and other administrative controls over the whole process of foreign investment makes the area more one of administrative law than one of pure contract law.[53] Theories that have been built in the past on the basis of contract may be inapposite to deal with the encroachments that administrative law has made into the process of foreign investment. The theory of internationalisation which is contract-centred may be a casualty in these developments. This theory will be unable to accommodate modern developments satisfactorily. Despite these theoretical problems, the theory of internationalisation continues to be accepted in arbitral jurisprudence and in the writings of publicists.

The more extreme variety of the theory of internationalisation is that the very nature of the foreign investment contract gives rise to the inference that it is subject to a supranational system of law.[54] Whereas the less extreme version will look to the existence of clauses such as a choice-of-law clause indicating the subjection of the contract to general principles of law and an arbitration clause indicating dispute settlement by a foreign tribunal as factors giving rise to an inference that the parties had an intention to internationalise the contract, the extreme theory infers internationalisation merely from the nature of the contract.

The argument that is advanced is that the foreign investment transaction has contacts with several states besides the host state. The capital for the project may have been raised from banks in several countries. The shareholders of the multinational corporation which makes the agreement may be nationals of different states. The argument states that, in these circumstances, the relevant law cannot be only that of the host state. It must be international law or some supranational system. In these circumstances, even if there is an express choice of law which indicates the applicability of some other law, that express choice must give way to the application of international law as the proper law of the agreement. The reasoning was that in view of the enormous capital risks involved in the project, it was unlikely that the foreign investor would have consciously subjected his investment to the laws of the host state.[55] The less extreme version of the theory states that, even if the host state's law is the relevant law, it is still subject to the standards of international law, so that, if it conflicts with the standards of international law, it must give way to those standards.[56]

---

[52] See R. W. Bentham, 'The International Legal Structure of Petroleum Exploration', in J. Rees and P. Odell (eds.), *The International Oil Industry* (1987), p. 57. He pointed out that, in the UK, petroleum licences are part contracts and part instruments of public law (*ibid.*, p. 61). The situation is similar in the case of Norwegian oil contracts, which include express clauses permitting changes by legislation.

[53] This is a point stressed by Gus Van Harten in his book, *Investment Treaty Arbitration and Public Law* (2007).

[54] *Revere Copper & Brass Inc.* v. *OPIC* (1978) 17 *ILM* 1321.

[55] The arbitrations which form the basis of this extreme theory of internationalisation are *Sapphire* v. *NIOC* (1964) 35 *ILR* 136; *Texaco* v. *Libya* (1977) 53 *ILR* 389; *Revere Copper & Brass Inc.* v. *OPIC* (1978) 17 *ILM* 1321; and *Elf Aquitaine* v. *NIOC* (1982) 11 *YCA* 112.

[56] *Aminoil* v. *Kuwait* (1982) 21 *ILM* 976; *SPP* v. *Egypt*, 3 *ICSID Reports* 101; (1983) 22 *ILM* 752.

This internationalisation has important consequences. The arbitral tribunals which formulated the thesis have identified these consequences. The first is that the host state cannot thereafter rely on its own laws to argue that the agreement is a nullity. The rule was stated in the *Sapphire* v. *NIOC* arbitration by Judge Cavin.[57] The assumption that was made was that a foreign multinational corporation could not be expected to acquaint itself with all the laws and regulations of the host country that would apply to the agreement. This is a fascinating assumption, given that a multinational corporation has all the resources and expensive advisers to do the necessary research. Besides, like any alien or alien entity, it had entered the state voluntarily and should acquaint itself with and obey all the laws of that state like any other alien. That is a basic principle of international life. Somehow it does not seem to apply to multinational corporations, for the self-evident proposition has had to be stated in guidelines and in treaties.[58] But, it is the rule stated by Judge Cavin which has become the accepted one. The rule that has been formulated has now passed into the Swiss legislation on international commercial arbitration.[59] One explanation of the rule suggests that it has a basis in good faith. It is difficult to accept such an explanation. If the agreement was defective under the host state's law and the foreign party knew or ought to have known of the defect, it is hardly possible to argue that the agreement should be regarded as valid on the basis of good faith.[60] It is basic to all legal systems that aliens entering a state should abide by the laws of that state. If it were otherwise, aliens could transgress the law, particularly the criminal law, of a state and escape liability by pleading ignorance. Legal systems cannot permit such a defence to aliens. Similarly, it should be expected that an alien corporation, particularly a multinational corporation, which usually does not lack access to good legal advice, should know of the capacity of the party with which it seeks to conclude agreements.[61] Such agreements are based on the law of the host state. State entities, which are usually the parties to such agreements, are created by legislation which is publicly available, and the extent of the powers of these corporations can be easily ascertained by looking at the legislation. Legal instruments on foreign investment increasingly recognise the duty of the foreign investor to abide by the laws of the host state.[62] However, secret instructions or regulations concerning the limitations on such powers will not bind the foreign party.

---

[57] (1963) 35 *ILR* 136.

[58] Thus, the APEC Guidelines on Foreign Investment require the foreign investor to abide by the laws of the host state. The ASEAN Comprehensive Agreement on Investment also imposes this affirmative duty. Investment treaties also require foreign investors to make the investment in accordance with the laws of the host state. Failure to do so will mean that the investment loses the protection of the treaty. *Fraport* v. *Philippines* (ICSID, 2007). The rules in ICSID arbitrations seem to be in conflict with those developed by tribunals like the ICC tribunal. As long as the internal rules are transparent, there would appear to be a duty to abide by the rules of the host state in making the investment or to be aware of the ascertainable powers of the bodies with which the foreign investor contracts.

[59] Section 177 of the Act on International Commercial Arbitration. Judge Cavin, who was arbitrator in *Sapphire* v. *NIOC* (1963) 35 *ILR* 136, was a distinguished Swiss judge and jurist. A connection is not suggested. The rule was probably derived from the rule in the law of treaties that a state cannot rely on its internal law to establish that it did not have competence to enter into the treaty, if all the external formalities of treaty-making have been satisfied.

[60] See C. J. Olmstead, 'Economic Development Agreements' (1961) 49 *California LR* 607, who states that the position in these circumstances is similar to the *ultra vires* contracts of corporations in domestic law. Inconvenient views such as this are conveniently ignored by writers who support the theory of internationalisation or are dismissed as tendentious.

[61] The draft United Nations Code of Conduct for Transnational Corporations makes it mandatory for multinational corporations to abide by the law of the host state. It is to be inferred from the provision that such a corporation has an understanding of the laws of the host state. A recent arbitral award, *Biloune* v. *Ghana Investment Board* (1993) 95 *ILR* 184 contains the unfortunate suggestion that the letter of the law can be overlooked in light of practice (para. 80).

[62] See, for example, the APEC Guidelines on Foreign Investment.

The second principle that is created relates to the immutability of the foreign investment agreement. When the theorists supporting internationalisation argue that international law or general principles of law or some other supranational system applies to foreign investment agreements, the only norm of law that they are all able to identify is *pacta sunt servanda*. Its application does not rest on the assimilation of foreign investment agreements to treaties, which assimilation has been demonstrated to have an inadequate theoretical basis; instead, it is claimed that the norm is a general principle of law. Those who support the view that international law applies to such agreements will argue that it is a rule of international law, as general principles are a source of international law.

There are several difficulties in accepting *pacta sunt servanda* as a general principle of law. Sanctity of contract may have been the basis of agreements in nineteenth-century law, but both it and the notion of absolute free will as the basis of contract law have been subject to challenge in the twentieth century.[63] Quite apart from the statutory erosion of the notion of free will, there are other notions such as inequality in bargaining power, economic duress and equitable estoppel which have affected the traditional notions of contractual sanctity. The passing-off of the sanctity of contract as an inflexible norm of contractual systems is contestable. Again, there seems to be a selection of principles to favour the building up of a system of investment protection. A system of investment protection built on such questionable premises can hardly provide adequate protection for foreign investors.

In addition, there are general principles which apply to state contracts which may, in effect, work against the notion of sanctity of contract. The notion of sanctity of contract is taken from laws applicable to private contracts, whereas foreign investment agreements are public contracts concluded with a state or a state agency vested with a monopoly so that it can promote the interests of the public and the state through trade and industry. It is a notion common to all major legal systems that contracts concluded by states or state entities are subject to the public interest and that a state may terminate such contracts if the public interest so requires. This idea was dismissed as a peculiarity of French law, but a French lawyer has pointed out that the defeasibility of state contracts in the public interest is a notion that is common to all legal systems.[64] If that proposition is accepted, then the idea of sanctity of contract will have to give way to the idea of the defeasibility of state contracts in the public interest. The elevation of general principles of law to the status of international law of investment protection may rebound against the interests of those seeking to internationalise foreign investment agreements, as equally cogent principles contrary to the notion of sanctity of contract could be developed.

The application of international law does not secure the foreign investment agreement to the extent desired by the proponents of the internationalisation theories. The proponents of the theory rely on static notions of international law and seek to ignore the strides that international law has taken in devising doctrines which seek to confer protection on the economic interests of the developing state. International law has also moved into areas such

---

[63] P. Atiyah, *The Rise and Fall of the Freedom of Contract* (1979).
[64] B. Audit, *Transnational Arbitration and State Contracts* (1988).

as environmental protection, economic development and human rights which impact on the protection of investments by multinational corporations and question whether the emphasis on protection accords with other interests of the international community. If international law does indeed apply to state contracts, it is obvious that any state contract which conflicts with any fundamental norm of international law will be invalid.[65] If this is so, then the notion of immutability of contracts will conflict with emerging principles of economic sovereignty and international development law and will, to that extent, be invalid. The rapid growth of international environmental law imposes duties on multinational corporations not to violate the standards contained in them. International environmental law supports the regulatory controls exercised by states to ensure environmental protection. The clash in this area has become particularly acute.[66] Arbitrators should not be one-sided by selecting only those norms of international law which promote investment protection. Likewise, norms of the international law on development will have to be addressed. Thus, the principle of economic self-determination is an offshoot of the notion of self-determination which in itself is a principle enshrined in the United Nations Charter and elevated, at least by a group of writers, to a principle of *ius cogens* in modern international law. One of the offshoots of the principle of economic self-determination is the doctrine of permanent sovereignty over natural resources. This doctrine, though regarded by some as a weak principle because it is contained in a General Assembly resolution, is regarded by many to be in itself an *ius cogens* principle. The latter view seems to be more cogent, for the principle itself logically flows from the notion of territorial sovereignty which forms the basis of the international legal order. The idea of state sovereignty and non-interference with the exercise of sovereignty has been asserted consistently. The International Court of Justice asserted the proposition that a state can choose the economic ideology it prefers without interference by other states.

The detailing of the economic aspects of sovereignty by both the International Court of Justice and the General Assembly in numerous resolutions emphasising the right of total control over the running of the economy and the management of resources considerably diminishes the argument that the application of international law to foreign investment contracts provides protection to such contracts. The contrary may, in fact, be the case.

It may be argued, as in fact has been done, that these contrary norms are weak norms or are at best *lex ferenda*. But, the difficulty with this argument is that the notion of internationalisation and the extraction of *pacta sunt servanda* also rely on the weakest norms of international law. The theory of internationalisation relies on the writings of publicists (and the publicists are by no means in agreement on the point) and on a few, usually uncontested, arbitral awards. Both are weak, manipulable sources, and, indeed, the suspicion that writings of publicists are mercenary sources cannot be easily avoided.[67] The notion

---

[65] The point is made by C. J. Olmstead, 'Economic Development Agreements' (1961) 49 *California LR* 607, who instances a state contract to engage in the slave trade, and observes that such a contract will be invalid as being contrary to basic norms of international law.

[66] *Metalclad* v. *Mexico* (2000) 5 *ICSID Reports* 209; (2001) 40 *ILM* 55; *Santa Elena* v. *Costa Rica* (2000) 39 *ILM* 317; (2002) 5 *ICSID Reports* 153.

[67] The study of international arbitration by two Canadian scholars, Dezalay and Bryant, seeks to confirm this. See Y. Dezalay and G. Bryant, *Dealing in Virtue: International Commercial Arbitration and the Construction of a Transnational Legal Order* (1996).

of sanctity of contract, which has been demonstrated not to be an absolute principle in modern contract systems, depends on general principles of law, which are also a weak source of law. A contractual system of investment protection constructed on the basis of weak norms which are contested by other weak norms cannot inspire much confidence.

The stabilisation clause, one of the clauses on the basis of which the theory of internationalisation is raised, has aroused the concern of human rights groups.[68] These groups were concerned that the presence of such clauses would not permit changes to be made to protect human rights concerns such as labour conditions, fair wages and the environment. Since taxation of windfall profits would also be prevented, the fear was that the benefits of natural resource exploitation in times of high profits would not be used equitably to promote the welfare of the people of the host state. As a result, campaigns were mounted to change these clauses.

Another facet of internationalisation relates to the remedy that is provided. Since the assimilation of the foreign investment contract to a treaty between states is the basis of the theory of internationalisation of foreign investment agreements, it is claimed that an arbitral tribunal before which a dispute involving a breach of the agreement is brought, has the power to order specific performance of the agreement.

Specific performance in these circumstances will appear to be an illusory remedy, especially for an arbitrator. For, short of the use of military power, which an arbitrator does not have at his disposal, an order for specific performance cannot be executed. Even in cases of breach of international treaties, the usual order is for damages. Specific performance is seldom ordered by international courts, except in the case of territorial disputes where the order that territory be transferred to the rightful owner can be the only means of resolving the dispute.[69] Yet, in the case of foreign investment disputes, the exorbitant claim is made that the arbitral tribunal can order specific performance. The only reason for this is that it could facilitate the pursuit of the fruits of the concession that has been taken over through the domestic courts into whose jurisdiction such property is later taken.[70] Here, again, theory is twisted to suit the convenience of foreign investment protection.

The theoretical objections cannot be overcome merely by defining the supranational system applicable as some system other than public international law. Some authorities, when faced with the difficulty of applying public international law, have suggested the development of some intermediate system such as transnational law to apply to foreign investment contracts. This suggestion recognises the theoretical difficulties in applying international law to a contract, and hence is a rejection of the notion of internationalisation.

---

[68] For the Amnesty International report on the BTC pipeline, see 'Human Rights on the Line: The Baku–Tbilisi–Ceyhan Pipeline Project', Amnesty International (2003), www.amnesty.org.uk/business/; and see the Amnesty International report on the Chad–Cameroon pipeline project, 'Contracting Out of Human Rights: The Chad–Cameroon Pipeline Project' (2005), POL 34/12/2005, www.amnesty.org.uk/business/.

[69] C. Gray, *Judicial Remedies in International Law* (1990), pp. 16–17. Though initially confined to treaty and contractual obligations, her discussion tends to the general view that such orders cannot be made against governments. This cannot stand as an unqualified proposition. Specific performance can be the only remedy in territorial disputes. *Temple of Preah Vihear Case* [1982] *ICJ Reports* 1. But, it is difficult to extend specific performance to areas outside territorial disputes. It would be too artificial to assimilate a dispute relating to a concession agreement involving land to a territorial dispute.

[70] See M. Sornarajah, *Pursuit of Nationalized Property* (1986).

But, the attempt to construct a separate regime has been unsuccessful, for these writers also have to rely on general principles of law to build the principles applicable to the agreement. This, it has been shown, depends entirely on the subjective prejudices of the persons seeking to extract the general principles applicable to the agreement. The problem with the construction of a transnational law to apply to such foreign investment agreements is the identification of a juridical base for the system. Without the consent of states, such a system cannot be established. The system at present exists only in the imaginings of writers partial to its creation.

2.2 The ICSID Convention and international law

Arbitration under the ICSID Convention is distinct and should not be confused with *ad hoc* arbitration or with arbitration conducted by private arbitral institutions. Yet, the two are often confused. ICSID, as indicated above, is a specialist organisation tasked with the settlement of investment disputes and, unlike other arbitral tribunals, operates on the basis of an international convention. Its juridical status is as an international institution, whereas other arbitral tribunals are either private bodies, creatures of single sovereigns or of the immediate parties to a dispute as in the case of *ad hoc* tribunals. In the area under discussion, reference is frequently made to Article 42(1) of the ICSID Convention, which reads as follows:

The Tribunal shall decide a dispute in accordance with such rules of law as may be agreed by the parties. In the absence of such agreement, the Tribunal shall apply the law of the Contracting State party to the dispute (including its rules on the conflict of laws) and such other rules of international law as may be applicable.

Clearly, the article contemplates the relevance of international law to the resolution of disputes by the ICSID tribunal. But, the use of the technique of choice of law is conferred on a tribunal created by an international convention by its member states. Whatever the interpretation of the article may be, the mandate is given by the states which are parties to the Convention to the tribunal created by the Convention to apply the particular technique of choice of law created by the article. It is not a mandate that is given to private tribunals. A tribunal constituted by the International Chamber of Commerce, a private body which is in no way akin to the ICSID (which is created by the will of sovereign states), is referred to Article 42 in justifying its use of the same choice-of-law technique as contained in that article. In their rush to pretend to greater powers than they really possess, these tribunals seem to sacrifice principle and rush headlong into areas into which they have no mandate to trespass. They can hardly be regarded as bodies capable of deciding on issues relating to the declaration or application of principles of international law.

As much as it is an error for tribunals not created by an international convention to imitate the powers of ICSID, it is also an unwelcome development that in many ICSID arbitrations an effort is being made to marry ICSID jurisprudence with the internationalisation theory.

This effort is apparent in awards such as *Benvenuti et Bonfant* v. *Congo*,[71] which are based on the theory of internationalisation.

The ICSID Convention has sought to establish a system which remains neutral and finely balanced between the interests of the foreign investor and the host state. It requires an initial consideration of the domestic laws of the host state. It may be that this was a disguised effort to get developing states to agree to the Convention. If so, this would be to attribute improper motives to the framers of the Convention. The ordinary meaning of the words in the article do require that primacy should be attached to the domestic laws of the state party to the dispute. But, there has been an undisguised effort to tilt the law towards the internationalisation theory. Examples of this trend include: the greater willingness to find jurisdiction in the face of problems presented by corporate personality; regarding unilateral guarantees as indicating support for assuming jurisdiction; the use of denial of justice as a basis for damages even though there may be jurisdictional problems of awarding damages on this ground; and a willingness to be involved in matters of war and peace to give relief to the foreign investor. The alacrity with which ICSID tribunals are willing to find jurisdiction from bilateral investment treaties is another feature which will bring the ICSID system into contention. Though these trends have been in keeping with the times over the last decade of the high point of liberalisation, a backlash will set in once the fervour for liberalisation subsides.

ICSID tribunals have also subscribed to the theory of internationalisation by taking the view that the reference to international law gives that system a supervisory role. Though much of the jurisprudence generated by ICSID is based on jurisdiction obtained on the basis of investment treaties, it is important to remember that ICSID was originally fashioned to deal with cases arising from investment contracts. Indeed, Article 42 relating to applicable law contemplates the situation of contractual choices of the applicable law. It was only after *AAPL* v. *Sri Lanka* in 1992 that treaty-based arbitration became prolific. Contract-based arbitration under ICSID still continues, though there are now fewer cases.[72] It is also the case that cases arising from the same facts are sometimes brought under both treaty and contract.[73] It is now well established that the causes of action under the two types of arbitration are distinct,[74] though on one view of the umbrella clause[75] and in certain situations (particularly of expropriation),[76] it may well be that there could be overlap between the two types of arbitration.

2.3 The continued relevance of contract-based arbitration

As indicated above, ICSID arbitration under investment treaties is the most prominent form of investment arbitration as a result of the large volume of cases resulting from alleged

---

[71] (1982) 21 *ILM* 740.

[72] For example, *World Duty Free Company Ltd* v. *Kenya*, ICSID Case No. ARB/00/7 (Award, 4 October 2006).

[73] For example, *SPP* v. *Egypt*, 3 *ICSID Reports* 101; (1983) 22 *ILM* 752; *Fraport* v. *Philippines* (ICSID, 2007).

[74] *Compañiá de Aguas del Aconquija SA and Vivendi Universal* v. *Argentina*, ICSID Case No. ARB/97/3.

[75] If the view in *SGS* v. *Philippines* is accepted, that commitments given by the host state are covered by the umbrella clause, then, clearly, contractual commitments, particularly the stabilisation clause, will be covered by the treaty obligation. *SGS* v. *Philippines*, ICSID Case No. ARB/02/6 (Award, 29 January 2004).

[76] An expropriation would be a breach of the foreign investment clause and any stabilisation clause in it.

violations of investment treaty provisions. The importance of treaty-based investment arbitration is enhanced by the fact that there is a considerable literature dedicated to the subject, largely because it has become a lucrative area of legal practice.[77] This impression is further enhanced by works purporting to deal with international investment law but confining the treatment largely to problems in investment arbitration arising from treaties.[78] While this, no doubt, represents the present reality that much of the vital force in the area comes from ICSID arbitration and arbitration based on investment treaties,[79] it does not fit in with the historical reality or with the fact that there is much investment arbitration that still takes place outside the treaty system. As mentioned, ICSID itself continues to deal with cases based on contract. Other arbitral centres deal with contract-based claims.[80] With many states in Latin America pulling out of the ICSID system and yet others threatening to terminate investment treaties, it could well be that contract-based arbitration may become prominent once more. Even if this does not eventuate and contract-based arbitration continues at the present rate, it will still have a prominent place in investment law. In certain sectors, contract-based arbitration has always been the preferred choice as it enables the parties to construct their own means of investment protection.[81] In states which do not have investment treaties[82] or are not members of ICSID,[83] contract-based investment arbitration will remain the system of dispute settlement. There may also be circumstances in which the foreign investor's home state does not have an investment treaty with the host state.[84]

Foreign investment arbitration before certain arbitral institutions has over the years developed characteristics of its own. A favoured system is the arbitral system of the International Chamber of Commerce, which has had much experience in the field and has developed distinct rules. The arbitral awards made by such institutions are not readily available, though commentaries[85] and shorter versions of some awards have been published. Some rules, for example that *ultra vires* cannot be pleaded in respect of agreements and that invalidity should not be pleaded in reliance of a host state's law, are well accepted in arbitration under the International Chamber of Commerce. For this reason, arbitration

---

[77] The titles of the books that have emerged give the impression that investment arbitration is confined to treaty-based arbitration. See C. McLachlan, L. Shore and M. Weiniger, *International Investment Arbitration* (2007); and C. Dugan, D. Wallace, N. Rubins and B. Sabahi, *Investor–State Arbitration* (2008).

[78] For example, R. Dolzer and C. Schreuer, *Principles of International Investment Law* (2008).

[79] Treaty-based arbitration could take place under the rules of other arbitral institutions or through *ad hoc* arbitration as many investment treaties do mention these alternatives. Indeed, many treaty-based arbitrations have been held outside the ICSID system.

[80] The ICC arbitration scheme has attracted a significant number of cases. Other centres, including relatively new centres like the Singapore International Arbitration Centre deal with investment arbitration.

[81] The strong association of contract-based arbitration with the petroleum industry is clear. The creation of what some writers term the *lex petrolia* still presents a strong basis for contract-based arbitration. The *lex petrolia*, if it does exist, depends largely on contract forms, arbitral awards interpreting them and writings on the subject.

[82] Brazil, now an industrialising state, is the most prominent state not to have investment treaties. In some states, for example, Colombia, the constitutionality of investment treaties is doubted.

[83] Some states have preferred to remain outside the ICSID system. For example, Mexico is not a party to the ICSID Convention.

[84] The United States does not have investment treaties with several states such as Indonesia which are averse to signing treaties with pre-entry national treatment. Recent contract-based arbitrations concerned investments made by US companies in Indonesia (*Karaha Bodas Co.* v. *Perusahaan Pertambangan Minyak Dan Gas Bumi Negara*, 465 F Supp 2d 283 (SDNY, 2006); *Himpurna* v. *Indonesia* (2000) 25 *YCA* 13; and *Phaiton Energy*).

[85] P. Leboulanger, 'Some Issues in ICC Awards Relating to State Contracts' (2004) 15(2) *ICC International Court of Arbitration Bulletin* 93.

under the International Chamber of Commerce has gained considerable acceptance in the field.

Ad hoc arbitrations also have currency despite the shift towards treaty-based arbitrations. Since such arbitrations can be tailor-made to suit the contract, parties sometimes prefer to include reference to such arbitration. It is relevant to note that some high-profile arbitrations in recent times have been conducted by *ad hoc* tribunals. Information about them is not available as readily as in the case of ICSID arbitrations. Yet, these arbitrations remain important to international investment law. For the reasons already stated, the importance of these types of contract-based arbitrations may grow in the future.

The tussle in contract-based arbitration between the interest of the multinational corporations to create a supranational law and the interest of the host states to ensure the exclusive relevance of national law will continue. Many host states have attempted to exclude the jurisdiction of contract-based arbitral tribunals through anti-suit injunctions prohibiting the conduct of the arbitrations issued by their national courts.[86] These injunctions have been routinely ignored by arbitral tribunals on the ground that they are external institutions grounded in supranational law and that domestic courts do not have jurisdiction over them.[87] The tribunals have also tended to recognise the existence of a supranational law whether it be international law or *lex mercatoria* as the applicable law.

Since the awards are enforceable under the New York Convention on the Enforcement of Foreign Arbitral Awards, there is a powerful compliance mechanism available to the system which may also make it attractive. The working out of the compliance system was demonstrated in the sequel to the *Karaha Bodas* arbitration,[88] which arose from a project for the creation of thermal energy from gas fields in Indonesia. The award made in Geneva was enforced against the assets of the Indonesian state corporation, Pertamina, held in New York, simultaneous proceedings being brought against assets held in Hong Kong and Singapore. The courts were inclined to allow assets to be seized so that the award could be enforced. Sovereign immunity no longer poses a problem to enforcement, as the contract would readily be regarded as a commercial contract, despite the fact that it may have many sovereign features. This aspect of enforcement also makes contract-based arbitration attractive to foreign investors.

2.4 Lex mercatoria and state contracts

A new avenue enabling the protection of foreign investment through the creation of international norms has been opened up by the international commercial arbitration of private transnational business disputes. In such arbitration, *lex mercatoria* is recognised

---

[86] In Pakistan, such an antisuit injunction was issued in relation to the *Hubco* arbitration. Indonesian courts issued such injunctions against the *Himpurna* and the *Phaiton Energy* tribunals. A Bangladesh court issued one against the ICC proceedings in *Saipem*. See further E. Gaillard (ed.), *Antisuit Injunctions in International Arbitration* (2005).

[87] In *Himpurna v. Indonesia* (2000) 25 *YCA* 13, the tribunal, which was sitting in Jakarta, Indonesia, changed the venue to The Hague after an Indonesian court issued an antisuit injunction.

[88] *Karaha Bodas Co. v. Perusahaan Pertambangan Minyak Dan Gas Bumi Negara*, 465 F Supp 2d 283 (SDNY, 2006).

as a body of rules which could be applied to international commercial transactions. There is no accepted definition of *lex mercatoria*, but it generally refers to a body of commercial rules that are applied frequently by international arbitrators who short-circuit the need for determining the law applicable to the dispute by discovering a commercial legal principle which is a common denominator of all the legal systems possibly applicable to the dispute, or by discovering some trade usage or custom that may be relevant, and converting that into a legal principle. The argument is that, as a result of an accumulation of arbitral awards and the consistency with which arbitrators have adopted certain doctrines, a system of law applicable to transnational business disputes has now been created.

There are many defects with this thesis. It has been pointed out that *lex mercatoria* does not have any principles that are clearly identifiable, and the ones that have been stated as principles of the system are so obvious that they could have been used without any resort to such a nebulous theory. The sources from which the law is to emanate and the ease with which private bodies may foist principles of law onto the whole international community made scholars wary of the theory. There are no objective criteria by which the principles of this so-called legal system can be identified and no benchmark by which it could be tested except its acceptance by a select group of European arbitrators and scholars who promote it through their writings. The steadfast tradition in the English law of resisting *lex mercatoria*, on the ground that it creates a system of private justice dependent on individual notions of what the law is, seems to be on the wane.[89]

The relevance of this development in the field of private international commercial arbitration and the distinct field of the arbitration of disputes arising from state contracts is that there seems to be an effort to coalesce the ideas of *lex mercatoria* and the idea of the internationalisation of state contracts and the application to it of a supranational system of law. The unity is seen in the manner of the extraction of the norms of both systems. General principles of law and arbitral awards form a substantial basis for both *lex mercatoria* and the use of a supranational system for dispute resolution in state contracts. The writers who favour the creation of both systems appear to come from the same stable. An advantage is seen in seeking to bolster both systems at the same time, as the same private power centres in the international arbitral systems support the creation of both principles.

However, both systems are characterised by the same defects. They depend on uncertain norms. The few arbitral awards which purport to apply the system come out with rules like good faith which could have been applied without resort to any convoluted notion like *lex mercatoria*. Both contain the idea that a small group of persons can foist a system on the whole world by an esoteric process to which others are not privy. The claim is that, as a result of an accumulation of arbitral awards and the consistency with which arbitrators have adopted certain doctrines, a system of law applicable to transnational business disputes has now been created.

---

[89] Its best representations were in the writings of Lord Mustill on the subject.

2.5 Umbrella clauses and internationalisation

There has been revived interest in the internationalisation theory as a result of recent awards involving so-called umbrella clauses in investment treaties.[90] These are provisions found towards the end of some investment treaties containing a catch-all statement that conditions and privileges that are negotiated by the parties to an investment agreement will be protected by the treaty. This provision, which has generally been ignored by commentators from the inception of these treaties, has been given special significance in the two awards which considered it and arrived at opposite conclusions. Since then, there have been other awards essentially dividing behind these two views. The significance of the umbrella clause is that it establishes a situation very similar to the one that the stabilisation clause was intended to establish, namely, to protect the commitment that was made to the foreign investor at the time of the contract not to change the bargain by subsequent legislation.

The argument that the umbrella clause has significance was roundly rejected by the award in *SGS* v. *Pakistan*. The matter was left more open in *SGS* v. *Philippines* which seems to incline towards the opposite view. The eventual result in the award was inconclusive on this point. It is difficult to see how a clause, hitherto regarded as insignificant, can have the effect of enhancing the obligations contained in contractual documents. As the award in *SGS* v. *Pakistan* points out, if such an extensive meaning was to be given to the clause, it would render the carefully negotiated provisions of the investment treaty nugatory. Besides, the idea that a yet-to-be-identified multinational corporation, which lacks international personality, could create fresh international obligations in a state through a contract lacks a theoretical basis in international law, which carefully regulates the extent to which rights may be created in third parties, normally states, to treaties. Lengthy statements are made on this subject on the basis of little study of the theoretical implications of the expansive propositions that are advanced on the basis of clauses that seem to create only rights between the parties.

2.6 Arbitration based on investment legislation

It is possible for an arbitral tribunal to be created on the basis of the foreign investment legislation of the host state. In this situation, the legislation would merely provide the consent of the host state in advance of any dispute with a current or future investor to submit to arbitration under the auspices of an arbitral institution specified in the legislation. Very often, ICSID is specified in the legislation, though other tribunals can also be chosen. The classic illustration is provided by *SPP* v. *Egypt*, where the basis of the jurisdiction of the tribunal was founded in the Foreign Investment Law of Egypt. Once jurisdiction is so founded, the law that the tribunal must apply in settling the dispute has to be decided on. The very fact that jurisdiction has to be found in the legislation may point to the absence of a contractual arbitration clause or a choice-of-law clause. In such circumstances, the tribunal

---

[90] *SGS* v. *Philippines*, ICSID Case No. ARB/02/6 (Award, 29 January 2004); *SGS* v. *Pakistan*, ICSID Case No. ARB/01/13, (2004) *ICSID Rev* 307.

will have to be guided either by its own procedural laws or by having recourse to techniques of choice of law in the absence of an express choice by the parties. In the case of the ICSID tribunal, it would be guided by Article 42 of the ICSID Convention, which would require the application of the host state's law supplemented by international law. Other tribunals will have to determine the applicable law by resorting to choice-of-law techniques.

3. Conclusion

The attempt to create an international law on investment protection through purely private means did succeed to a large extent, despite the fact that its theoretical foundations were slim. It indicates not only the power of multinational corporations to create law but also the existence of avenues through which international law can be used as an instrument of private power through weak sources of law such as the awards of arbitral tribunals and the writings of highly qualified publicists. The role of the latter, who are but individuals with partialities to certain views either because they believe firmly in them or because it is lucrative to do so, requires a view of international law not as a scientifically neutral discipline but as a manipulable device which serves the interests of power.

The process of internationalisation continues, in the sense that there are still awards being made purely on the basis of the internationalisation theory. But, the opportunity for such awards is receding, largely because there are more sophisticated and theoretically sounder bases for the invocation of arbitration for the settlement of foreign investment disputes. Whereas, in the past, the invocation of arbitration was based on the consent of the parties expressed through a clause in a foreign investment agreement, increasingly arbitration in the field of foreign investment has become treaty-based. The role of investment treaties in promoting arbitration has been instrumental in the increase in the number of arbitrations in this area, particularly ICSID arbitrations. While treaties provide a sounder jurisdictional foundation for arbitral tribunals, the law that is sought to be applied still continues to be 'international law' represented by the solitary principle of *pacta sunt servanda*. It has been demonstrated that this carry-over from the internationalisation theory has insecure foundations. But, it would not create even a dent in the theory to point this out, as the trends in the field are such that it is not theory which matters but pragmatism dictated by power and self-interest.

8

Treaty-based investment arbitration: jurisdictional issues

Consent of the parties is the basis of all arbitration. In contract-based arbitration, the consent is specific to disputes arising from the contract. It is usually expressed in the arbitration clause. In treaty-based arbitration, the consent of the state is said to be given to all present and potential investors who satisfy nationality criteria and whose investment is protected by the treaty in advance of the dispute. The rule can be so simply put. But, much dispute has arisen as to the jurisdictional criteria that have to be satisfied before an arbitral tribunal can proceed to the merits of a case. In virtually every treaty-based dispute that has arisen, the jurisdiction of the tribunal has been queried. So, it is necessary to examine the jurisdictional criteria that need to be established. Since most treaty-based arbitrations take place before ICSID tribunals,[1] the rules are best stated on the basis of ICSID arbitration, which is likely to provide the standard for other types of treaty-based arbitration.[2]

As may be realised, with an increase in the number of claims, states have invested much effort in exploring the methods of excluding jurisdiction, and have met with a measure of success. Cases are fought with tenacity, and states are resistant to the use of treaties for the imposition of responsibility. This, again, raises doubts as to the utility of treaties as an investment protection device.

There is no doubt that, in light of the experience accumulated in contesting jurisdiction, states will continue to argue against the assumption of jurisdiction, and will strengthen provisions in the investment treaties negotiated in the future to enable them to better challenge jurisdiction. Many treaties also have a procedural requirement to the effect that recourse to arbitration should be preceded by a period of negotiations aimed at an amicable settlement.[3] In light of experience, states have devised procedural rules that may make

---

[1] Treaties usually refer to ICSID arbitration. But, because of annulment procedures under ICSID and other possible faults, treaties now provide an option to the foreign investor to have recourse to other forms of arbitration. The most popular of the alternative forms is *ad hoc* arbitration under the UNCITRAL Rules. The US model treaty attempts to include a virtual code on arbitration. For ICSID arbitration, the rules of the ICSID Convention also have to be satisfied for jurisdiction to be created. On this subject, see C. Schreuer, *The ICSID Convention: A Commentary* (2nd edn, 2009).

[2] Many treaties, as stated in note 1 above, provide the investor with alternatives to ICSID arbitration which include arbitration before the Stockholm Chamber of Commerce, other institutions and *ad hoc* arbitration using the UNCITRAL Rules. Because these tribunals are not based on a convention which limits their scope to investment arbitration, the precise problems that arise before ICSID tribunals may not arise before these alternative tribunals. For ICSID arbitration, the requirements of the ICSID Convention as well as the investment treaty have to be satisfied, whereas, for other tribunals in whom jurisdiction is created by treaty, the treaty requirements alone have to be satisfied.

[3] The significance of this provision is dealt with below.

recourse to arbitration more difficult, for example by requiring prior recourse to local remedies. Others remove issues such as taxation from the scope of arbitration, subjecting disputes concerning these issues to different mechanisms.

One preliminary matter may be disposed of. There must of course be a legal dispute for any claim to be maintained. As in the case of any legal claim, the dispute must involve a claim as to the violation of a right or obligation by the state party. So, for a contractual dispute, there must be a violation of the rights or obligations under the contract and, in the case of a treaty-based dispute, there must be a violation of the rights created in the foreign investor by the treaty against the host state. It is now accepted that contractual disputes are distinct from treaty-based disputes, though there may be instances of overlap.

The rights must be against a state or a state entity for the claim to be made in an investment arbitration. Otherwise, it is obvious that a tribunal cannot have jurisdiction under an investment treaty which involves measures taken by a state affecting a foreign investor. *UPS* v. *Canada* illustrates this point.[4] There, the claims related to measures taken by CanadaPost, a monopoly supplier of postal services in Canada and a public corporation, in creating a subsidiary for the collection and delivery of parcels. The subsidiary directly competed with UPS, an American company operating in the parcel delivery sector. CanadaPost took steps, such as permitting post offices to be collection points for parcels, which conferred benefits on its subsidiary. The claim by UPS was that such measures were a violation of the national treatment principle. The tribunal held that CanadaPost was not acting as a state entity in promoting the interests of its subsidiary but as an entity engaged in a commercial venture. It is essential that the claim is brought against a state entity exercising public functions that can be attributed to the state for there to be a violation of the treaty rights of the foreign investor. A dispute that could be characterised as a dispute between two private actors engaged in commercial rivalries cannot be the subject of investment arbitration based on treaty rights.

Tribunals have classified the jurisdictional issues that have to be established before a tribunal can assume jurisdiction under an investment treaty referring disputes to ICSID. These are (i) that there should be jurisdiction as to the subject-matter of the dispute (*jurisdictio ratione materiae*); (ii) that there should be jurisdiction on the basis of the standing of the claimant to sue (*jurisdictio ratione personae*); (iii) that there should be jurisdiction based on the consent of the parties (*jurisdictio voluntatis*); and (iv) that the dispute must satisfy the time limits in the treaty as to standing as well as to the arising of the cause of action (*jurisdictio temporis*).[5] Of these, the limitations relating to subject-matter and personal standing are the most important and are considered in this chapter.

Consent of the parties is constructed on the basis of the treaty. The treaty provision is said to contain a unilateral offer to arbitrate made to all foreign investors of the other state party. When a dispute arises, the request for arbitration is treated as an acceptance of the offer,

---

[4] *UPS* v. *Canada*, UNCITRAL Arbitration Proceedings (NAFTA) (Award on the Merits, 24 May 2007).
[5] These requirements have been stated in several jurisdictional awards. See *Phoenix* v. *Czech Republic*, ICSID Case No. ARB/06/5 (Award, 19 April 2009), para. 54. There are critical dates as to the existence of the nationality requirements as well.

creating the arbitration agreement.[6] As to the time factors involved, the treaty will stipulate whether or not investments made prior to it will be given the protection of the treaty. The facts as stated by the claimant are generally taken as correct when assessing jurisdiction, except where there is dispute as to one of the essential requirements for jurisdiction, for example as to the nationality of the claimant. In that situation, the burden of satisfying the tribunal as to the fact is on the claimant.[7]

1. Jurisdiction ratione materiae

The subject-matter of the dispute must be capable of being submitted to arbitration. It must satisfy the requirements of both the treaty and the ICSID Convention. This limitation would not apply to *ad hoc* arbitration and possibly to other types of institutional arbitration. The ICSID Convention has wider application and is based on assumptions that were made to secure wide participation. So, it does have certain stricter rules on consent and the satisfaction of nationality links than in the case of other arbitral institutions. It has provisions for withdrawal from the system under the Convention, indicating again the importance of state consent. This is illustrated by the current debate surrounding the withdrawal from the ICSID Convention of the Latin American states. There is a divergence in policy between the ICSID Convention which was drafted in 1965 at a time when developing countries were cautious towards foreign investment and had to be cajoled into acceptance of the Convention and the 1990s when investment treaties were made in the context of an intense fervour for liberalisation. This divergence in policies underlies many of the problems that befuddle the area today.

1.1 The definition of investment

It is essential, both in terms of Article 25 of the ICSID Convention as well as in terms of the investment treaty in question, for the dispute to arise from an investment. Article 25 of the ICSID Convention does not contain a definition of an investment, but merely requires that the dispute should arise from an investment. Investment treaties adopt different techniques for defining an investment. Some contain exhaustive lists.[8] Others contain illustrative lists. But, tribunals have not been guided to any significant extent by these lists as the problems that have arisen cannot be fitted neatly into categories mentioned in the treaties.[9] Tribunals have,

---

[6] The idea of 'arbitration without privity' may be appealing but theoretically inaccurate. There cannot be arbitration without privity. The idea results from *AAPL* v. *Sri Lanka* (1992) 17 *YCA* 106; (1991) 30 *ILM* 577, and, since that case, a proliferation of arbitrations has resulted from the theory of an offer to all nationals of the other state. Whether this was ever intended by the state has never been questioned. Eminent commentators have written on the British treaty which was the basis of *AAPL* v. *Sri Lanka* without noticing the momentous change the case brought about. Whether the *stipulation alteri* (not recognised in English law because of difficulties about consideration) was thought of between two common law states, and whether international law recognises such rights being created in potentially non-existent entities, are problems never addressed. But, the problems that the explosion of cases has caused will have to be addressed by states.

[7] *Phoenix* v. *Czech Republic*, ICSID Case No. ARB/06/5 (Award, 19 April 2009).

[8] Chapter 11 of NAFTA, based on the older model investment treaty of the United States, is such a treaty.

[9] In *Československá Obchodní Banka* v. *Slovakia* (1999) 14 *ICSID Rev* 251, para. 66, a tribunal held that the submission of a transaction to ICSID arbitration creates a strong presumption that 'the parties considered the transaction to be an investment within the meaning of the ICSID Convention'. But, surely, that does not relinquish the task of the tribunal finding whether or not there was an investment, the parties' intention not being conclusive on the point.

however, been able to identify some characteristics which could be considered in identifying the types of activity that would qualify as investments. Indeed, the issue is a relatively new one, the first time it was taken up being in *Fedax* v. *Venezuela* in 1997. It shows that, with the explosion of claims against states, states began to explore fresh avenues of defending the claims. Arbitrators reacted to these arguments in different ways. This characterises the course of treaty-based arbitration, which, in its recent history, has found innovative strategies of litigation and counter-strategies of defence, resulting in considerable schism within the subject.

There is a continuum of international transactions starting with the international sales transaction, which obviously does not qualify as an investment,[10] and ending with the foreign investment transaction, which does. Between the two ends of this spectrum, there are a variety of transactions, such as distribution agreements, franchising arrangements, licensing agreements, provision of services,[11] management contracts,[12] contracts of design,[13] 'build, operate and transfer' agreements,[14] technology transfers, construction of highways,[15] the building of plants for electricity, gas supply[16] and water supply,[17] oil contracts,[18] joint ventures and the establishment of wholly owned subsidiaries. As indicated in the footnotes to the last sentence, there are awards which have considered many contracts in this spectrum of transactions. Somewhere along this spectrum, the transaction loses its similarity with the sales transaction and assumes features of the foreign investment transaction. The problem is to identify the stage at which this transformation takes place and the characteristics that a transaction must have in order to be considered an investment transaction.

In *Salini*,[19] an attempt was made to identify the characteristics of an investment. The *Salini* test has often been followed by other arbitral tribunals. It identified the characteristics of an investment as involving: contributions in money, in kind or in industry; long duration; the presence of risk; and the promotion of economic development.[20] The *Salini* tribunal

---

[10] *Joy Mining Machinery* v. *Egypt*, ICSID Case No. ARB/03/11 (2004).

[11] In *SGS* v. *Philippines*, ICSID Case No. ARB/02/6 (Award, 29 January 2004) and *SGS* v. *Pakistan*, ICSID Case No. ARB/01/13, (2004) *ICSID Rev* 307, contracts for the supply of customs-inspection services were regarded as investments without over-much scrutiny. In *Malaysian Salvors Ltd* v. *Malaysia*, the award held that a salvage contract was one for the supply of services and not an investment. But the award was annulled. In *Patrick Mitchell* v. *Congo*, the Annulment Board considered the running of a law firm as not amounting to an investment.

[12] *Wena Hotels* v. *Egypt*, ICSID Case No. ARB/98/4 (2005).

[13] In *Autopista Concessionada de Venezuela* v. *Bolivarian Republic of Venezuela* (2001) *ICSID Reports* 417, the state did not contest the contention that a contract to design, construct and maintain roads was an investment. There are many decided cases in which the issue could have been raised but was not. For example, in *SGS* v. *Philippines*, ICSID Case No. ARB/02/6 (Award, 29 January 2004), the customs-inspection services took place entirely outside the Philippines (though the contract included the supply of computer systems to the Philippines customs). An early case, *Atlantic Triton* v. *Guinea* (1986) 3 *ICSID Reports* 13, involved converting ships into fishing vessels. The point at issue – whether the completed vessels were suitable for the purpose – was a purely commercial issue. It seems that, as experience is gathered and states seek ways of defending themselves, arguments are raised on issues such as the definition of investment.

[14] *Salini Costruttori SpA* v. *Morocco*, ICSID Case No. ARB/00/4 (Jurisdiction Award, 23 July 2001), (2001) 42 *ILM* 577.

[15] *Pantechniki SA Contractors & Engineers* v. *Albania*, ICSID Case No. ARB/07/21.

[16] *Saipem* v. *Bangladesh*, ICSID Case No. ARB/05/07 (2007).

[17] *Bayinder Insaat Turizm Ticaret ve Sanayi* v. *Pakistan*, ICSID Case No. ARB/03/29 (2005).

[18] Oil concessions contracts were described as quintessential investments in *RSM Production Corporation* v. *Grenada*, ICSID Case No. ARB/05/14 (Award, 13 March 2009). Commitment to bring in resources for exploration was held to be a sufficient investment (para. 243). This seems a strained interpretation.

[19] *Salini Costruttori SpA* v. *Morocco*, ICSID Case No. ARB/00/4 (Jurisdiction Award, 23 July 2001), (2001) 42 *ILM* 577.

[20] Professor Schreuer has identified an additional criterion, the generation of profits: C. Schreuer, *The ICSID Convention: A Commentary* (2001), p. 140. But, this additional criterion would apply to all types of international business transactions, or indeed any and every business transaction. See also the second edition of his work: C. Schreuer, *The ICSID Convention: A Commentary* (2nd edn, 2009), pp. 130–4.

suggested that the factors should be taken in totality, though for convenience they may be treated individually. The criteria laid down seem helpful, but they are common to almost every international transaction. Even an international sales transaction involves long duration as goods have to be transported across boundaries. Clearly, an investment transaction has a longer duration, particularly in the natural resources, manufacturing and construction sectors. Duration again cannot be specified, but long duration is a characteristic of foreign investment.[21] Risks – the avoidance of which is the function of documentary credits, insurance and a definite indication of when property passes – also exist in the sales transaction., though the risks are undeniably greater in traditional investment transactions. But, there is a distinct feature to the risk involved in a foreign investment transaction that is protected by an investment treaty, which is the risk of governmental intervention. A mere commercial risk will not suffice. It is this identifying factor – a political or economic risk that arises from a governmental measure – that distinguishes the risk involved in an investment apart from the risk involved in other types of contract. A contract of services also involves contributions in kind and in industry, and could contribute to economic development. The need for economic development is stated in the preambles to both the ICSID Convention and the investment treaties. There is, however, disagreement on the precise requirements of this characteristic, as discussed later. Generally, the criteria that are identified in *Salini* have come to be accepted.

The fact is that there has been an effort in modern times to move the law away from the traditional types of foreign investment such as those in the natural resources sector which are characterised by long duration and provisions to avoid governmental intervention and where protection is justified on the basis of economic development. In the early stages of development of this area of the law, the law was concerned largely with these types of contracts in the natural resources sector which now would clearly be identified as investment transactions. The law then moved away from this older provision, as it was felt that the newer types of foreign investment standards also needed protection. This move was secured by the newer investment treaties which contain expansive notions of investment in an attempt to capture within the definition a whole host of intangible rights which may not have fitted in with older notions of investment which existed at the time when the ICSID Convention was drafted. In 1964, when the Convention was being drafted, the existence of disagreement resulted in the concept being left undefined, with the acceptance that there are 'outer limits' to the definition. The 'outer limits' remained unidentified. In the course of the movement away from the traditional paradigm, the meaning of investment has also become purposefully diffused. With the emphasis coming to be placed on liberal movements of capital, investment treaties sought to include within the ambit of investment all rights and incidental transactions that pertained to the transfer of capital assets into another state. There is consequently a conflict taking place between the traditional meaning of investment in the ICSID Convention and the newer, wider meaning that seeks to accommodate within the

---

[21] In *Salini*, the construction was to last for thirty-two months but took thirty-six months. *Salini Costruttori SpA* v. *Morocco*, ICSID Case No. ARB/00/4 (Jurisdiction Award, 23 July 2001), (2001) 42 *ILM* 577.

concept a wider category of transactions in the hope of bringing them within the scope of investment protection provided by the treaties. Consequently, there has been a division of opinion among arbitral tribunals as to the precise meaning of investment. The fit between the meaning in the Convention and that in the investment treaties has become inexact. The objects and purposes of the Convention and the investment treaties are not wholly identical, the Convention having the purpose also of inducing a greater number of developing states to participate in the system it was creating, which, in 1964, was not an easy task.[22]

When it comes to ICSID arbitration, the difficulty is enhanced by the fact that the Convention was drafted at a time when the meaning of investment did not go beyond the conventional meaning of a long-term contract for the exploitation of resources or a project contract. In both, the foreign investor was present within the territory of the host state, a situation contemplated in customary international law as well. The investment treaties, however, sought to extend the categories of foreign investment, thus resulting in a lack of fit between the meaning of investment under the Convention and the meaning in the investment treaties. It will be said that meanings evolve, but there is a problem that has to be recognised. The view that the consent of the parties to ICSID arbitration indicates their understanding that the particular transaction was an investment is an inference that some tribunals have drawn. It has to be objectively shown that there was in fact an investment. The objective understanding of an investment under the Convention does not fit in with the wide definition of an investment in investment treaties. Therein lies a crack which tribunals have tried to paper over, depending on their inclinations and subjective preferences.

The course of the ICSID arbitration in *Malaysian Salvors* v. *Malaysia* is illustrative of the divisions that have come about. In his award, the sole arbitrator made a survey of the existing ICSID awards which had dealt with the definition of investment. The claimant, a British company, had entered into a contract for the salvage of a historical wreck, the *Diana*, which had sunk off the Malaysian coast in 1817. The arrangement was that the claimant would have a right to share in the proceeds of the sale of the recovered items. The Malaysian Archaeological Commission, however, decided to withhold pieces from the auction because of their historical significance. Items of porcelain originating in China and being taken by a British ship had historical significance not only to Malaysia but also to other peoples.[23] The claimant, having failed before the Malaysian courts, alleged violation of the UK–Malaysia investment treaty before an ICSID tribunal consisting of a sole arbitrator.[24] The sole arbitrator canvassed the existing authorities on the definition of an investment under the ICSID Convention and the investment treaty. There was little doubt in the minds of the sole arbitrator and three other arbitrators at the annulment phase that the indicia of the definition in the investment treaty were satisfied, as that definition included a claim to money and to performance under a contract having financial value; the contract involved intellectual

---

[22] Article 31 of the Vienna Convention requires a treaty to be interpreted 'in good faith in accordance with the ordinary meaning to be given to its terms in their context and in light of its object and purpose'.

[23] This raises an interesting issue of arbitrability: whether the issue should be settled by arbitration arising from a contract when the subject-matter may involve global or regional interests that transcend the immediate interests of the parties.

[24] Mr Michael Hwang of Singapore was the Sole Arbitrator.

property rights; and the right granted to salvage may be treated as a business concession conferred under contract. The transaction qualified as an investment on these several grounds, but the issue was whether it qualified as an investment for the purposes of the ICSID Convention. The sole arbitrator found that 'it is unnecessary to discuss whether the Contract is an "investment" under the [treaty]'. The annulment committee essentially found fault with this,[25] but the sole arbitrator was quite right in concluding that, if the Convention definition was not satisfied, there was little point in proceeding to an analysis of the treaty definition, as both had to be satisfied for jurisdiction. Clearly, the annulment committee was in error in its conclusion on this point. The fact that the transaction falls within the wide treaty definition cannot by itself be sufficient.

The annulment tribunal depended on its own capricious reasoning as to what the intention of the parties to the treaty was. It stated:[26]

It cannot be accepted that the Governments of Malaysia and the United Kingdom concluded a treaty providing for arbitration of disputes arising under it in respect of investments so comprehensively described, with the intention that the only arbitral recourse provided between a Contracting State and a national of another Contracting State, that of ICSID, could be rendered nugatory by a restrictive definition of a deliberately undefined term of the ICSID Convention, namely, 'investment', as it is found in the provision of Article 25(1). It follows that the Award of the Sole Arbitrator is incompatible with the intentions and specifications of the States immediately concerned, Malaysia and the United Kingdom.

This is reasoning from the investment treaty but not an interpretation of the term 'investment' in the Convention which probably had to be done without recourse to the investment treaty as the Convention stands alone. Quite apart from the fact that the annulment committee had no authority to embark on such analysis, the question remains whether such reasoning is tenable and whether a treaty requirement could be read in light of an interpretation placed on another treaty. The vigorous dissent to the award makes this point cogently.[27] The result is that the definition of investment remains an unresolved problem due to the schisms that have developed regarding the definition between various arbitral tribunals. This is accentuated by the fact that there is disagreement on whether economic development is a requirement of an investment protected by the ICSID Convention and by investment treaties.

The reasoning of the majority of the annulment committee in *Malaysian Salvors* was that the parties to the investment treaty would not have subjected investments under the treaty if they believed that the ICSID system would not be able to protect all investments and would therefore have been of the belief that every investment subject to the treaty is protected. But, it could well be that Malaysia, the capital-importing party, submitted to ICSID jurisdiction only because ICSID arbitration is available solely to investments that protect economic

---

[25] Para. 61 of the Annulment Award.   [26] Para. 62 of the Annulment Award.
[27] The dissent was by Judge Shahabudeen. Of the four arbitrators who considered *Malaysian Salvors*, two wanted to refuse jurisdiction on the ground that the requirement of an investment was not satisfied. In this sense, the result was unsatisfactory.

development.[28] An annulment committee is not entitled to engage in creative reasoning. Even so, the reasoning it attempted may be fallacious.

1.2 Economic development as a characteristic of investment

Economic development has been stated to be a criterion in the majority of the cases that have dealt with the issue of the definition of investment. There are two awards which are contrary to this view, namely, the award in *Salini* (which has been followed on the requirement of economic development by other awards)[29] and the annulment committee's report in *Malaysian Salvors*, which has also found support in one other award.[30] But, the annulment committee may have gone beyond its reach in stating this view.[31] Nevertheless, the question is raised and needs to be examined. This is a crucial issue, which, as the dissent in the annulment committee's report in *Malaysian Salvors* states, is intertwined with the classic dispute between the capital-importing and capital-exporting states:

What this case hinges on is a perception of the objectives of ICSID: Was the jurisdiction of ICSID meant to be solely dependent on the will of the parties? Or, was it meant to be dependent on the will of the parties subject to conformity with the overriding objectives of ICSID as a body concerned with the economic development of the host State? The former may be referred to as the 'subjectivist' view, the latter as the 'objectivist' view. The cleavage marks a titanic struggle between ideas, and correspondingly between capital exporting countries and capital importing ones.

The very essence of the system of investment protection, whether it is treaty-based or contract-based, is economic development. The system of protection involves a considerable erosion of sovereignty. States concede sovereignty only in the belief that the resulting investment flows will promote economic development. Subjection to foreign arbitration involved in the ICSID system is achieved at the cost of a surrender of sovereignty, and this is justified by the belief that economic development will take place as a result. It is the basis on which successive ICSID officials have explained the system. It is for this reason that Schreuer states that economic development is 'the only possible indication of an objective meaning of the term "investment"'.[32] The intention behind the Convention was explained by the Executive Board of the World Bank on the ground that 'adherence to the Convention by a country would provide additional inducement and stimulate flow of private international investment into its territories, which is the primary purpose of the Convention'. The ICSID system itself will become redundant if it is not so confined. Being a subsidiary body of the World Bank, ICSID would not have any competence to supply arbitration services to a system that was not connected with economic development, which falls within

---

[28] This is particularly so as Malaysian investment treaty practice carefully limits treaty protection to approved investments.

[29] *Jan de Nul NV* v. *Egypt*, ICSID Case No. ARB/04/13 (Decision on Jurisdiction, 16 June 2006); *Phoenix* v. *Czech Republic*, ICSID Case No. ARB/06/5; *Patrick Mitchell* v. *Congo*.

[30] *LESI SpA and Astaldi SpA* v. *Algeria*, ICSID Case No. ARB/05/3: 'Il ne paraît en revanche pas nécessaire qu'il réponde en plus spécialement à la promotion économique du pays, une condition de toute façon difficile à établir et implicitement couverte par les trois éléments retenus.'

[31] A point made in the dissent of Judge Shahabudeen in *Malaysian Salvors*.

[32] C. Schreuer, *The ICSID Convention: A Commentary* (2001), as cited in *Patrick Mitchell* v. *Congo* (Annulment), para. 31.

its mandate. The supply of general arbitration services, as the majority of the *ad hoc* annulment committee in *Malaysian Salvors* seems to contemplate, falls clearly outside the mandate of both the World Bank and ICSID.

While the limitation applies to ICSID arbitration, it clearly does not apply to other arbitral institutions which are referred to in dispute-settlement provisions of investment treaties. But, investment treaties uniformly refer to economic development as the objective of the treaties. There may be an inherent limitation in the investment treaties to the effect that protection is confined to investments that promote economic development. The obvious view is that, if an ICSID tribunal is to have jurisdiction, the subject-matter of the investment must be capable of promoting the economic development of the host state, in addition to satisfying the other criteria for a foreign investment.

1.3 Does portfolio investment qualify as investment?

The *travaux préparatoires* of the ICSID Convention show that the overwhelming concern was with foreign direct investment. Indeed, the early efforts were directed to replacing the customary international law which was concerned entirely with direct investment. Again, as far as the ICSID Convention is concerned, the issue may arise whether disputes as to portfolio investments will qualify as investment. In the case of arbitration before other tribunals, the definitions in the investment treaties seem broad enough to capture portfolio investments. This is, however, a tentative conclusion before analysing the policy debate on the issue.

Portfolio investment is unstable, as it can be withdrawn at any time. It may not satisfy the requirement of long duration, as the ability to withdraw anticipating adverse fluctuations is an essential feature of portfolio investments. The Asian economic crisis in 1997 was widely regarded as having been caused by the sudden withdrawal of portfolio funds from Asian states. Such instability cannot promote economic development. Such investment also does not satisfy other characteristics of foreign investment, such as presence within the state. No relationship with the government is established. The investor does not enter the host state, nor does he exercise control over his investment. There is no transfer of technology or creation of employment associated with such investment. On the whole, portfolio investment lacks the characteristics that justify the policy of protection of foreign investment. It is for that reason that some investment treaties specifically exclude portfolio investments from the scope of their protection.[33]

Yet, there is specific reference in investment treaties to instruments which could be regarded as portfolio investments. There are references to shares, stocks, claims to money and a series of other intangible rights, which give rise to the inference that portfolio investments or other easily transferable instruments in the nature of portfolio investments are protected. This was a haphazard development that piggy-backed on the protection of investments that were created during the period of fervour for liberalisation. But, the

---

[33] See, for example, the ASEAN Investment Protection Treaty (1987).

instruments that are listed are those associated with companies. It may nevertheless create an obligation to protect these types of investment, though whether such protection could be achieved through ICSID arbitration is open to doubt unless it can be shown that the holders entered the state and exercised management and other functions related to the running of the company.

Fedax v. *Venezuela* is the first case in which the issue was considered, though not with sufficient rigour. Promissory notes (which were the type of investment involved in the dispute) were initially sold by the Venezuelan government to a Venezuelan company. Anticipating that their value would diminish, the Venezuelan company transferred the promissory notes to the claimant, a Dutch company incorporated in the Netherlands Antilles. When measures taken by the Venezuelan government affected the value of the promissory notes, the claimant sought damages under the Netherlands–Venezuela bilateral investment treaty. Venezuela objected to the jurisdiction of the ICSID tribunal on the ground that the promissory notes could not be regarded as investments. The tribunal assimilated the promissory notes to loans, as they were issued in acknowledgment of services that the original holder, the Venezuelan company, had provided to the Venezuelan government. The tribunal held that the promissory notes were investments. Obviously, when originally granted, the notes were not *foreign* investments, as they were granted to a local company which could not have resorted to ICSID arbitration. Simply by transferring them to a foreign party, the original nature of the notes, in the understanding of the tribunal, underwent a change. Quite apart from this transformation, the loans that are usually referred to form part of a package of company instruments associated with the making of a foreign investment. It was not so in this case. *Fedax* has the distinction of being the first in a line of expansionary awards associated with liberalisation and the trend to extend standing before investment tribunals to as wide a category of transactions as possible. It may have initiated a trend that could eventually lead to the dismantling of the system of investment arbitration, at least in Latin America.

This expansionary trend became common after state companies were privatised during the era of liberalisation. Shares bought by foreign interests in existing state entities came to be regarded as protected investments. When their value was affected during economic crises, a series of awards held that they were entitled to protection under the investment treaties.[34] This line of cases also gives rise to the impression that portfolio investments are protected by ICSID arbitration and by investment treaties. This is not necessarily so. The shares were in established projects, but had other indicia of investments such as entry into the host state, long duration, an absence of ready transferability and the aim of economic development (as the state entities were involved in the operation of vital sectors of industry). The mere fact that entry was made into the sector through the purchase of shares is not determinative of the issue whether as a general rule portfolio investment is protected.

The initial reason for the protection of shares and other company-related instruments was the *Barcelona Traction Case*, which denied protection to the state of nationality of the

---

[34] These awards were in cases arising out of the Argentine economic crisis.

shareholders and confined it to the state of incorporation of the company. The purpose of the inclusion of shares in investment treaties was to deal with the situation in *Barcelona Traction*, not to make all portfolio investments subject to treaty protection. That purpose became stronger when developing-country entry laws required investments to be made through locally incorporated companies. Protection of the shares of the companies and other instruments associated with the functioning of these companies became important. Hence, there was recognition of the need for protection of shareholders as primary shareholders in companies. This does not mean that treaties protect all shareholders, including those who purchase secondary shares on a stock exchange.

The problem became more acute when privatisation took hold. Several Argentinian cases raised the issue whether the shareholdings in privatised state companies could be protected. Most held that they could be. An issue is whether the minority shareholder who voluntarily buys shares in the host state's company is subject only to the protection of such shareholder's rights under the company law of the host state or whether he has additional protection under the investment treaties. It is not an issue that has been squarely faced. Participation in a company involves acceptance of decisions taken collectively by the shareholders. That principle comes into conflict with a foreign shareholder's interests being different and its protection by investment treaties.[35] Portfolio capital may contribute to the assets of a state, but could also be withdrawn rapidly when conditions become uncertain, thereby pushing an incipient crisis into a full-blown one. The uncertainty it creates will hamper rather than encourage development. Such capital inflows are associated with ordinary business risk rather than with the type of risks that investment treaties guard against. They are not subject to state regulation to the same extent as foreign investment. As such, a state may not feel justified in giving protection to such investments.

1.4 Pre-contractual expenses as investment

It is clear that pre-contractual expenses, such as the drawing up of tender documents, and expenses incurred in connection with entry, do not qualify as investment. They do not confer sufficient advantages on the host economy to justify protection. They are expenses forming part of the ordinary business risks that foreign investors take. The function of investment treaties is not to insure such risks. The award in *Mihaly* v. *Sri Lanka* indicated as much. There must have been a definite contract on the basis of which an investment could proceed. The crucial factor in the dispute, as the tribunal pointed out, was that the respondent took great care to point out that none of the documents conferring exclusivity to the claimant created a contractual obligation. Preparatory steps towards contractual obligations may involve expenditure on the part of the investor but it does not qualify as an investment for the purposes of the ICSID Convention. Where steps have been taken towards the creation of contractual obligations, the fact that the contract was incomplete as to some provisions may

---

[35] See further *Gami Investments* v. *Mexico* (Award, 15 November 2004).

not matter, and tribunals may hold that sufficient progress has been made to convert the process into an investment.[36] The *Mihaly* tribunal did not exclude the possibility that pre-investment expenses could have been capitalised after the contract as part of the investment. The fact that the expenses were of economic value and could have amounted to an investment under the investment treaty is of no avail. Such expenses do not fall under the concept of investment under the ICSID Convention.[37] Where the investment treaty refers to non-ICSID arbitration, it would be possible for the tribunal to rely on the broader definition of investments contained in treaties.[38]

1.5 The qualification of investment as subject to local laws and regulations

Many states make investment treaties which define those investments that are protected as investments made 'in accordance with the laws and regulations' of the host state. Some further qualify the laws and regulations as 'from time to time in existence'. The reason for the provision is that states making such investment treaties have restrictions as to entry and subsequent operations and wish to confer protection only on investments that conform to these laws, and thus seek to ensure that only investments that promote their economic development and interests enter the state.[39] There is thus a link between this qualification and the aims of economic development stated in the preambles to their treaties.

There is a view that, even in the absence of such a qualification in the treaty, the treaty applies only to investments that are made in accordance with the laws of the state party, as there could not have been an intention to protect investments that transgressed these laws. It is a perfectly logical view.[40] If the investments had been made otherwise than in accordance with the law, there is scope for the inference that there has been a deliberate disregard of the laws of the host state. There is also room for the view that the investment would not be of a kind that would promote the economic development of the host state, as the host state's laws are intended to admit only such investments which do so. Where there is obvious fraud in obtaining entry, the initial licence or the contract on the basis of which the entry was made would themselves be invalid and could not therefore support a claim.[41] There could have

---

[36] *Mihaly* was so distinguished in *PSEG Global Inc.* v. *Turkey* (2005) 44 *ILM* 465. See also *Zhinvali Development Ltd* v. *Georgia*, ICSID Case No. ARB/00/1, where the contract was still in the process of negotiation. In a non-treaty case, an agreement to obtain a petroleum licence was held to be an investment. *RSM Production Corporation* v. *Grenada*, ICSID Case No. ARB/05/14 (Award, 13 March 2009). R. Hornick, 'The Mihaly Arbitration: Pre-Investment Expenditure as a Basis for ICSID Jurisdiction' (2003) 20 *JIA* 189; C. McLachlan, L. Shore and M. Weiniger, *International Investment Arbitration: Substantive Principles* (2007), pp. 178–80.

[37] Compare the separate opinion of Arbitrator Suratgur. Incidentally, if the argument of the annulment committee in *Malaysian Salvors* were to be accepted, then this should have significance in altering the result.

[38] Thus, in *Petrobart* v. *Kyrgyz Republic* (2005), a case under the Energy Charter Treaty, a contract to sell gas over a twelve-month period was held to be an investment by a Stockholm Chamber of Commerce tribunal. The Treaty included 'trade, marketing and sale' within its definition of investment.

[39] Anna Joubin-Brett, 'Admission and Establishment in the Context of Investment Protection', in A. Reinisch (ed.), *Standards of Investment Protection*, (2008), p. 9.

[40] *Inceysa Vokkisoletana* v. *El Salvador*, ICSID Case No. ARB/03/26 (Decision on Jurisdiction, 2 August 2006). But, see *Middle East Cement Shipping and Handling Co.* v. *Egypt*, ICSID Case No. ARB/99/6 (12 April 2002).

[41] *Marvin Feldman* v. *Mexico* (2002) 7 *ICSID Reports* 318; (2003) 42 *ILM* 625.

been no intention by the state parties to protect such investments. The legality of the investment is a pre-condition for its protection.[42] The inclusion of the provision is a means by which a state can preserve its regulatory control over the foreign investment, particularly at the entry stage. In any event, rights to property are created by the host state's laws, and it is these rights that are to be protected by the investment treaty. To that extent, the domestic law is always relevant, and the extent of these rights as described in the domestic law has to be ascertained before an examination can be made of whether they are also protected by the treaty.[43]

Fraport v. *Philippines*[44] demonstrates the application of this requirement. The respondent state claimed that the claimant had violated a domestic law which required the foreign investor not to control more than 40 per cent of the shares in the investment company which was the vehicle for the foreign investment. The setting up of a locally incorporated company was a requirement of the foreign investment laws of the Philippines. Defeating the requirement through the creation of an elaborate corporate structure that hid the extent of the foreign control was held to be a violation which took the investment out of the ambit of protection of the investment treaty.

1.6 Good faith limitations

Awards in which attempts have been made to defeat the host state's laws also raise good faith limitations to jurisdiction.[45] Absence of good faith may indicate an abuse of process either in seeking to obtain jurisdiction through improper means or by some taint, such as fraud,[46] in the manner in which the original investment was made. It is possible to argue that, at this stage, the tribunal will consider whether deciding the case would involve public policy considerations. A request for arbitration based on a false claim of ownership of the investment has been considered to be an abuse of process.[47] Notions of abuse of process and good faith open up further possibilities for contesting jurisdiction where there has been misconduct on the part of the foreign investor. But, such misconduct has to be at the stage of the entry of the investment. Subsequent misconduct may affect the merits of the case but not jurisdiction.

---

[42] *Tokios Tokelés* v. *Ukraine*, ICSID Case No. ARB/02/18 (Decision on Jurisdiction, 29 April 2004); *Ioannis Kardassopoulos* v. *Georgia*, ICSID Case No. ARB/05/18 (Decision on Jurisdiction, 6 July 2007).

[43] For the relevance of domestic law, see Z. Douglas, 'The Hybrid Foundations of Investment Treaty Arbitration' (2003) 74 *BYIL* 151. This would be particularly so in the case of intangible intellectual property rights which rely for their creation and recognition entirely on municipal law. In *Tradex* v. *Albania* (1996) 5 *ICSID Reports* 43, local law, which covered investments made after 1990, was used to protect the investment, though the investment treaty was made in 1994.

[44] *Fraport* v. *Philippines*, ICSID Case No. ARB/03/25 (16 August 2007). *Aguas del Tunari* v. *Bolivia*, ICSID Case No. ARB/02/3 (Decision on Jurisdiction, 21 October 2005) also considered the situation and came to the seemingly opposite conclusion. But, the decision is criticised as expansionist, and possibly is unlikely to carry much weight.

[45] *Amco* v. *Indonesia*, ICSID Case No. ARB/81/1 (Award, 20 November 1984); *Plama Consortium Ltd* v. *Bulgaria*, ICSID Case No. ARB/03/24 (Award, 27 August 2008); *Inceysa* v. *El Salvador*, ICSID Case No. ARB/03/26 (Award, 2 August 2006); *Phoenix* v. *Czech Republic*, ICSID Case No. ARB/06/5 (Award, 15 April 2009).

[46] *Inceysa* v. *El Salvador*, ICSID Case No. ARB/03/26 (Award, 2 August 2006).

[47] *Phoenix* v. *Czech Republic*, ICSID Case No. ARB/06/5 (Award, 15 April 2009), para. 113; *Europe Cement Investment & Trade SA* v. *Turkey*, ICSID Case No. ARB(AF)/07/2 (ECT) (Award, 13 August 2009).

1.7 Investments 'approved in writing'

Some states, particularly Southeast Asian states,[48] require that the investments be 'approved in writing' before they qualify for protection. This contemplates the existence of a competent authority to approve the investment to which an application has to be made.[49] In *Philip Grueslin* v. *Malaysia*, jurisdiction was refused on the ground that the investment had not gained approval as required in the treaty. The case arose from investments in the nature of portfolio investments made in Malaysia, which had taken measures following the Asian economic crisis of 1997 to curtail the repatriation of profits. It is instructive that similar measures taken in Argentina resulted in a spate of arbitrations while Malaysia and other Asian states were spared such litigation because of the limitation requiring approval for the investment to be protected. For the restriction to operate, there must be a distinct approval authority.[50] Otherwise, the fact that there had been a licence in writing provided to the foreign investment may suffice.[51]

1.8 The time factor

Investment treaties usually protect investments made after the date the treaty comes into force, unless they specifically refer to the protection of existing investments. Treaties often contain a specific provision to the effect that the protection 'shall not apply to disputes or claims arising before its entry into force'. Where a dispute had 'crystallised' before the treaty had come into force, jurisdiction will be denied.[52] It is very clear that the fact that the investment no longer exists because it has been terminated has no effect, for termination is one of the eventualities which the treaty itself was designed to protect.[53] The time of the acquisition of ownership of the assets may also be relevant when a company involved in a pre-existing dispute is acquired. In this situation, the relevant time period is after the acquisition.[54]

Where the dispute arises after termination of the treaty, the treaty itself would provide a means of dealing with this situation by indicating a time period within which the dispute must arise in order to be protected. Treaties can specify that they continue to be valid for a

---

[48] As a result, the requirement appears in the ASEAN investment treaties. States such as Malaysia and the Philippines adopt this approach. Singapore has discontinued the approach. But, the new ASEAN Investment Treaty of 2009 contains the requirement. The requirement again considerably limits the possibility of investment arbitration.

[49] Investigations disclosed that few of the states having this provision had nominated an approving authority or had mechanisms or forms for securing this approval. On this basis, it was argued in *Yaung Chi Oo Ltd* v. *Myanmar* (2003) 42 *ILM* 540; (2003) 8 *ICSID Reports* 463 that securing approval from some licensing authority would be sufficient approval. The tribunal accepted this argument.

[50] During the *Yaung Chi Oo* arbitration, the counsel found that most ASEAN states did not maintain any procedure for approval and that none had been sought by foreign investors in the region. The new ASEAN Investment Agreement requires a transparent procedure for approvals.

[51] *Yaung Chi Oo Ltd* v. *Myanmar* (2003) 42 *ILM* 540; (2003) 8 *ICSID Reports* 463.

[52] The crystallisation of the dispute itself is a difficult notion. A dispute may have existed for a long time but may have crystallised after the treaty came into force, in which case jurisdiction could be exercised. Compare *Maffezini* v. *Spain* (2000) 5 *ICSID Reports* 396; (2004) 40 *ILM* 1129 and *Empresa Luchetti SA* v. *Peru* (2005) 20 *ICSID Rev* 2005.

[53] *Jan de Nul Dredging International* v. *Egypt*, ICSID Case No ARB/04/13 (2006).

[54] *Phoenix* v. *Czech Republic*, ICSID Case No. ARB/06/5 (Award, 19 April 2009).

certain period of time after the treaty has been terminated.[55] Difficult questions arise when a party seeks to withdraw from the treaty or withdraws from the ICSID Convention which is indicated as the tribunal in the dispute-settlement provision of the investment treaty. This situation has arisen in respect of some pending cases as a result of the withdrawal of Bolivia and Venezuela from the ICSID Convention.

1.9 Negotiations

Many treaties, following the lead of Chinese treaties, now require that there be a period of negotiations after a dispute has arisen before recourse can be had to arbitration. There may be cultural predispositions towards negotiated settlement, which host states prefer. Investors may prefer it too, as the continuation of a harmonious relationship may be a more desirable objective than a termination in the context of hostility. This requirement thus ensures that negotiations are attempted. There must be a good faith attempt to secure a settlement.[56]

1.10 The 'fork in the road' and waiver

Treaties often confine the foreign investor to the remedy that he has chosen. To a large extent, this is a compromise that forestalls recourse to a multiplicity of claims being brought in respect of the same dispute before different tribunals or courts. The treaty requires the investor to make an election of the means of redress and thus confine the investor to one form of redress. There are three possible methods of recourse to remedies that the investor himself could invoke. The first is through the domestic courts, which is preferred by the host state as it involves the application of local law and is, in any event, in the eyes of many, mandated by the rule requiring the exhaustion of local remedies, which an investment treaty may seek to dispense with.[57] The second is the dispute settlement that the foreign investor negotiated in the contract, which is usually arbitration before an overseas institution or *ad hoc* arbitration. The third is the mechanism in the investment treaty that protects his investment. A 'fork in the road' provision in a treaty seeks to confine the foreign investor to one remedy by precluding resort to others if he is shown to have made a prior election. Provisions on waiver or a defence relating to waiver have a similar effect of seeking to confine the foreign investor to his earlier choice. In a sense, where one of the procedures resorted to has already been completed, the situation is akin to the consideration of a *res judicata* plea, as one tribunal has to decide to what extent it is bound

---

[55] For example, the Dutch Model Treaty, Article 14(3): 'In respect of investment made before the date of the termination of the present Agreement, the foregoing Articles shall continue to be effective for a further period of fifteen years from that date.' The period varies. The German Model Treaty specifies twenty years.

[56] On cooling-off periods, see *Occidental* v. *Ecuador*, London Court of International Arbitration (Award, 1 July 2004); *Western NIS Enterprise Fund* v. *Ukraine*, ICSID Case No. ARB/04/2 (Order, 16 March 2006); and *Biwater Gauff* v. *Tanzania*, ICSID Case No. ARB/05/22 (Award, 24 July 2008).

[57] The rule is required for diplomatic protection. Few treaties still require that local remedies be exhausted prior to arbitration. Some require that local remedies be pursued for a specified period before recourse to external arbitration.

by an earlier decision of a court or tribunal belonging to a different system. The principles used to dispose of a defence based on waiver are very similar to those used in considering *res judicata*.

Generally, tribunals have been averse to the defence that there has been a prior election of a procedure. In the case of the prior use of the local courts by the foreign investor, the dispute that is formulated by a foreign investor in arbitration invoking jurisdiction on the basis of the investment treaty arises before a tribunal belonging to a supranational legal order. Parties are likely to be different, inasmuch as the dispute before the domestic court will be brought by the locally incorporated company, usually a joint-venture company, which was the vehicle for the foreign investment, whereas the foreign investor would usually be the parent company. In these circumstances, there would be no identity between the parties. The cause of action before the domestic courts will also be likely to be different, particularly if the remedy was of an administrative kind.[58] Where, however, the domestic court's judgment is grossly unfair, that in itself is a violation of the international minimum standard required by the treaty.

Likewise, an existing award under a contractual arbitration provision also does not preclude a subsequent treaty-based investment arbitration, as the causes of action may be different. The reasoning here is that the tribunal in the contract-based arbitration is confined to disputes resulting from breaches of the contractual provisions whereas a treaty-based tribunal is concerned with violations of the treatment standards of the treaty, expropriation or other rights under the treaty such as the repatriation of profits. The distinction between contractual claims and treaty claims made in the *Vivendi* annulment award has generally been accepted by other tribunals.[59] But, there could be circumstances where the two types of claim shade into each other. An expropriation could be both a breach of contract as well as a breach of a treaty, and, likewise, the manner of the breach may amount to a breach of the fair and equitable standard of treatment.

The situation where there is an umbrella clause in the treaty protecting all assurances, including contractual assurances, given to the foreign investor will also make the two types of claim similar. This situation would raise the distinction between a contract claim and a treaty claim in a starker form. The contract may include an exclusive dispute-settlement clause or a waiver of other methods of remedy. In this situation, the issue arises whether there could still be treaty arbitration, particularly one based on an umbrella clause. The issue has created conflict in the opinions of different tribunals. One view is that the treaty claims exist independently of the will of the foreign investor and cannot be waived by him. This view is reminiscent of the view taken in the *North American Dredging Company Case*[60] that the insertion of a 'Calvo Clause' in a contract cannot prevent diplomatic intervention, which is the right of the state. But, this analogy would not be appropriate, as the whole purpose of

---

[58] See, for example, *CMS Gas Transmission Co* v. *Argentina* (2003) 30 *ILM* 788; (2005) 44 *ILM* 1205; *Genin* v. *Estonia* (2002) *ICSID Rev* 395; *Occidental* v. *Ecuador*, London Court of International Arbitration (Award, 1 July 2004).

[59] *Compañiá de Aguas del Aconquija SA and Vivendi Universal* v. *Argentina*, ICSID Case No. ARB/97/3 (Annulment Decision, 3 July 2003); *PSEG Global Inc.* v. *Turkey* (2005) 44 *ILM* 465.

[60] (1947) 4 *UNRIAA* 26.

the treaty is to privatise the process of dispute settlement by giving the foreign investor a right to arbitration. If the latter assumption is correct, then the right can be waived by an exclusive arbitration clause. If, however, the right is regarded as the right of the home state, it is clear that it cannot be disposed of by the foreign investor through contract.

1.11 Most-favoured-nation clause

The jurisdictional award in *Maffezini*[61] was regarded as opening up infinite possibilities of jurisdiction, in that it held that it was permissible to use the most-favoured-nation clause in a treaty with a host state to latch onto more favourable dispute-resolution provisions it had made in other investment treaties with third states. The possibility opened up by this technique would have been immense and quite unintended by states which had inserted the clause in the treaty. *Maffezini* was the product of the liberal expansiveness of the period, and there have been embarrassed reversals of the view in later awards.[62] A line of awards has queried the reasoning in *Maffezini* on the ground that arbitration required a clear and unambiguous consent and not consent through the construction of treaty terms.[63] The view that is taken in this later line of awards is that there must be a clear and express indication that the most-favoured-nation provision should apply to dispute settlement as well. In the circumstances of a treaty-based arbitration, construction has to be done in terms of the line of decisions since *AAPL* v. *Sri Lanka*. If the technique in *Maffezini* is correct, then a tribunal can extend the process by constructing consent to its jurisdiction, thereby undermining consent of the parties as the basis of arbitration. Such adventurism is unwarranted.

1.12 Exhaustion of local remedies

Treaties vary as to how this rule of customary law is to be adopted. Some treaties expressly exclude the need for exhaustion of local remedies. Some prescribe a time during which local remedies are to be attempted. In the latter case, there must be a good faith effort to pursue the remedies. A few commentators still insist on the exhaustion of all available remedies before arbitration can be commenced. These limitations have usually resulted in recourse to most-favoured-nation clauses. In some instances, tribunals have held that the most-favoured-nation clause could be used. This may be due to the fact that the clauses which specify a time for domestic remedies unduly add to the costs of a remedy.[64]

---

[61] *Maffezini* v. *Spain* (2000) 5 *ICSID Reports* 396; (2004) 40 *ILM* 1129.

[62] *Maffezini* involved the Argentine–Spain treaty, which required an attempt at settlement be made through the local courts for eighteen months. The claimant was permitted to use the Chile–Spain treaty, which contained a six-month period. *Maffezini* was confirmed in *Ross-Invest* v. *Russia* (2007).

[63] *Plama* v. *Bulgaria* (Jurisdiction Award, 8 February 2005), (2005) 44 *ILM* 721; *Telenor Mobile Communications* v. *Hungary*, ICSID Case No. ARB/04/15 (Award, 13 September 2006); *Berschader* v. *Russia*, Stockholm Chamber of Commerce Case No. 080/2004 (Award, 21 April 2006); *Yaung Chi Oo Ltd* v. *Myanmar* (2003) 42 *ILM* 540; (2003) 8 *ICSID Reports* 463; *Tza Yap Shum* v. *Peru*, ICSID Case No. ARB/07/6 (Decision on Jurisdiction and Competence, 19 June 2009).

[64] *Maffezini* v. *Spain* (2000) 5 *ICSID Reports* 396; (2004) 40 *ILM* 1129; *Siemens* v. *Argentina* ICSID Case No. ARB/02/8.

2. The investor as claimant

Claims under investment treaties can be brought by physical persons or by corporations. Though claims have been brought by individuals or families, the large investors in the more important sectors of global business are multinational corporations. As a result, the large majority of claims are brought by corporations, and the nature of their corporate organisations, their ability to move business around the globe and the fact that the concept of corporate nationality can be manipulated by lawyers has made corporate claims more complex from the jurisdictional point of view. These issues are considered in this section.

2.1 Natural persons

Natural persons take investments overseas, and such investments are protected by treaties made by their home states. The claimant must show that he has standing under the treaty to bring a claim by establishing that he is a national of the state party to the treaty under which he claims.[65] As in customary international law, there are few problems when it comes to the nationality of physical persons, apart from dual nationality and proof of citizenship at the time the claim was made. The nationality requirement of the investment treaty has to be satisfied. Nationality is a matter of proof under the domestic law of the state whose nationality is claimed.[66]

Problems of dual nationality often arise and are usually settled through the application of traditional principles of international law. The principle of dominant or effective nationality is the determinative criterion of nationality in these circumstances.[67] In the case of a claim before ICSID, the ICSID Convention itself states that the dispute must be between the state and a foreign national so that an investor having the nationality of the state cannot bring a claim against it, even if he happens to have at the same time the nationality of another state.[68] Article 25(2)(a) of the Convention states the requirement of foreign nationality in clearer terms, refusing jurisdiction to any person who, at the relevant dates, also had the nationality of the state against which the claim is made.

2.2 Juridical person: corporate nationality

The treaty formulations and the theories behind them have been explained in Chapter 7 on investment treaties. As indicated, states use different techniques of identifying corporate

---

[65] Some states extend protection to their permanent residents as well.

[66] *Soufraki* v. *United Arab Emirates*, ICSID Case No ARB/02/07 (7 July 2004).

[67] *Nottebohm Case* [1955] *ICJ Reports* 4; C. F. Amerasinghe, *Jurisdiction of International Tribunals* (2003), pp. 276–80. The issue has been dealt with in many awards of the Iran–US Claims Tribunal. The tribunals adopted the test of effective nationality. A. Sinclair, 'Nationality of Individual Investors in ICSID Arbitration' (2004) 6 *International Arbitration Law Review* 191; F. Orrego Vicuña, 'Changing Approaches to the Nationality of Claims in the Context of Diplomatic Protection and International Dispute Settlement' (2000) 15 *ICSID Rev* 340.

[68] *Champion Trading* v. *Egypt*, ICSID Case No. ARB/02/9 (Award, 27 October 2006). The test of effective nationality, according to *Champion Trading*, will not be used in situations where it would lead to 'a result which is manifestly absurd or unreasonable', as where a state uses a *ius sanguinis* principle of nationality for over four generations. The situation of dual nationality does not exist in the case where a person is only a permanent resident in another state. *Karpa* v. *Mexico*.

nationality. The preferred test is the test of incorporation, a company having the nationality of the state in which it is incorporated. International law indicates a preference for the place of incorporation to determine the nationality of the corporation.[69] European states have generally favoured the *siège social* theory, which determines nationality by looking for the place where the seat of its effective management is located. Some treaties combine both tests.[70] The test of incorporation is used in the ICSID Convention. The test used in both the investment treaty and the ICSID Convention has to be satisfied if the claim is brought before an ICSID tribunal. The cases considered by ICSID have generally arisen from treaties using the incorporation test of nationality.[71]

2.3 Locally incorporated company

The foreign investment laws of many states require that investment entry should be made through a locally incorporated company. This would make the locally incorporated company a corporate national of the host state and thereby move it out of protection. It would, in theory, be subject to local law. For this reason, it has been necessary to devise a means of protection for the locally incorporated vehicle of the foreign investment. The investment treaty approaches this problem in two principal ways. Many treaties would regard the locally incorporated company as protected if it is controlled from abroad by the parent company. The second way is to protect shareholdings in the locally incorporated company. In this way, the treaty gets over the problem in the *Barcelona Traction Case*,[72] which held that the shareholders of a foreign corporation could not be protected by their home state, such protection being within the sole prerogative of the state of incorporation.

The ICSID Convention gets over the problem of the locally incorporated corporation by stating that the host state could, by agreement, regard the locally incorporated company as a foreign corporation if it is controlled from abroad. Article 25(2)(b) treats the locally incorporated company as a foreign juridical person if, 'because of foreign control, parties have agreed it should be treated as a national' of another state for the purpose of the Convention.[73] This agreement would normally be in writing. Logically, in the absence of such an agreement, such a corporation would be treated as a local corporation and ICSID jurisdiction would be denied as ICSID does not provide for arbitration between a national and his own state.[74] But, since *Amco v. Indonesia*, the existence of an ICSID arbitration clause in a contract between the foreign investor and a state entity has been regarded as sufficient to infer consent of the state to treat the locally incorporated company as a foreign juridical person for the purposes of ICSID arbitration. Some investment treaties contain

---

[69] *Barcelona Traction Case* [1970] *ICJ Reports* 3; *Diallo Case*, ICJ (Judgment, 24 May 2007); *Guinea v. Congo*, ICJ (Judgment, 24 May 2007).

[70] For example, the ASEAN Investment Protection Treaty and the treaties made by the Philippines.

[71] For an example of the consideration of the alternative test, see *Yaung Chi Oo Ltd* v. *Myanmar* (2003) 42 *ILM* 540; (2003) 8 *ICSID Reports* 463.

[72] [1970] *ICJ Reports* 3.

[73] *Klockner* v. *Cameroon* (1983) 2 *ICSID Reports* 16. The fact of foreign control has to be proved. *Vacuum Salts* v. *Ghana* (1994) 4 *ICSID Reports* 329.

[74] *Holiday Inns* v. *Morocco* (1980) 51 *BYIL* 123.

provisions which require locally incorporated companies to be treated as foreign companies, in which case the treaty provision must be taken as advance consent.

These provisions have been interpreted, often expansively, by various tribunals. The expansive interpretation goes well beyond what would appear to be the intention of the parties making the treaties. For this reason, it is necessary to look more closely at some of the extensions made through interpretation. They may lend credence to the view that the expansionary tendency is explicable on the basis of the neo-liberal preferences of some arbitrators.

2.4 The wholly owned company

Where the investment is made by a company wholly owned by the foreign investor, its overseas investments are entitled to the protection of any investment treaty made by the state of its incorporation. But, some states are averse to their treaties being used as vehicles for protection and specify a minimum percentage of shareholdings before their investment treaties could be invoked. These states may require that over 50 per cent of the shares should be held by nationals for the corporation to qualify for protection. Other states are not averse to providing protection to any company that is incorporated in its territory. Their strategy is to attract companies by offering the protection of their investment treaties so that they would bring capital into their countries and use it as a platform from which they could launch themselves into the region. The smaller states of the world adopt this strategy due to locational and other advantages they have.[75] The use of incorporation as a means of establishing nationality has led to two contentious techniques that have provoked controversy. These relate to the idea that corporations could migrate, meaning that a foreign investor could, after making the investment, locate the company which controls the investment in a state which has a favourable investment treaty and thereby obtain jurisdiction under that treaty. The second relates to the phenomenon of 'round-tripping', where nationals of a state take capital from their state into another state with which it has an investment treaty, vest that capital in a company they incorporate there, and bring it back into their home state as a foreign investment, claiming the protection of the investment treaty between their home state and the state of incorporation of their company. These two strategies need discussion.

2.5 The migration of companies

The idea that companies, having made a foreign investment from one state, could migrate to another state with the aim of securing the protection of that state's investment treaty is an idea that received acceptance from a tribunal in *Aguas del Tunari* v. *Bolivia*.[76] The case

---

[75] Thus, Singapore serves as a platform for China and Southeast Asia, Mauritius for India, and the Netherlands for Europe. The Netherlands, unlike other European states, adopts incorporation as the test of nationality.

[76] *Aguas del Tunari* v. *Bolivia*, ICSID Case No. ARB/02/3 (Jurisdiction Award, 21 October 2005).

caused much controversy generally because of the environmental and other social interests it attracted, and focused adverse attention on the nature of the expansionary doctrines on jurisdiction that the tribunal articulated. Dubbed the 'water war', it became entangled in the anti-globalisation movement and became a focus of attack on neo-liberal policies of privatisation and the market economy. The expansionary view that the tribunal took of jurisdiction through migration of companies exposed it to the criticism that it too engaged in support for neo-liberal trends. The claimant prudently settled the case without any payment involved after the jurisdictional phase.[77]

The claimant, Aguas del Tunari, a consortium of companies specially created for the purpose, secured a contract to supply water and sewerage services to the city of Cochabamba in Bolivia. Aguas Del Tunari belonged to a complex corporate chain. Its founding stockholder was an American company, Bechtel Enterprises Holding Ltd. It owned International Water Ltd, which was incorporated in the Cayman Islands. In turn, International Water Ltd owned 55 per cent of the shares of Aguas del Tunari. There was a restructuring of the corporate holdings, during which time there was a 'migration' of the holding company from the Cayman Islands to Luxembourg, which in turn was controlled by a company incorporated in the Netherlands.[78] The argument of the claimant was that Aguas del Tunari was now protected by the Netherlands–Bolivia treaty, as it was directly or indirectly controlled by a Dutch corporate national.

It was clear that, at the time of the investment, the claimant, a Bolivian corporate national controlled by a Cayman Islands company, was without protection.[79] After problems arose with the investment, the restructuring led to 'migration' from Luxembourg to the Netherlands so that the Dutch investment treaty with Bolivia could be invoked. The tribunal, by a majority,[80] rejected Bolivia's view that this 'migration' was a fraudulent device to secure jurisdiction under the treaty with the Netherlands. It also rejected the argument that the controlling company was really the American company, and that the Dutch company was inserted into the structure merely to obtain jurisdiction. There has been much criticism directed at the award, as it extended corporate nationality in a manner that could not have been within the intention of the parties making the treaty.[81] It merely ensured that a clever legal strategy was given effect. In the process, it destroyed the credibility in the system of investment arbitration.

As in other situations, there has emerged a division of opinion among arbitral tribunals on the issue of 'migration' of companies. In *Banro v. Congo*,[82] the 'migration' of the claimant company, originally incorporated in Canada, was to the United States. Canada was then not

---

[77] Bolivia bought Bechtel's share in Aguas del Tunari. The 'water war' led to the election of Eva Morales as President of Bolivia, and triggered off the subsequent Bolivian displeasure with ICSID.

[78] There is a diagram in the award, at para. 71, illustrating the new holding structure. Basically, it was that 55 per cent of Aguas del Tunari was with the Luxembourg company (formed through migration from the Cayman Islands) which was 50 per cent owned by the Dutch company, which in turn was 100 per cent owned by Bechtel, the US company.

[79] Bolivia had a treaty with the United Kingdom, but most UK treaties do not extend to the Cayman Islands, a British dependent territory, where companies are incorporated for tax and other reasons of convenience. The United States–Bolivia investment treaty could not have been used as it was signed after the dispute had arisen.

[80] Arbitrators Caron and Alvarez were in the majority; Arbitrator Alberro-Semerena wrote a dissenting award.

[81] C. McLachlan, L. Shore and M. Weiniger, *International Investment Arbitration: Substantive Principles* (2007), pp. 155–60.

[82] (2002) *ICSID Rev* 380.

a party to the ICSID Convention. The 'migration' was carried out immediately prior to the institution of the claim, so that ICSID jurisdiction could be obtained through incorporation in the United States. The tribunal denied jurisdiction.

There were no assets that moved from the Netherlands to Bolivia to justify the use of the Netherlands–Bolivia investment treaty for protection. The clear purpose of the treaty was to protect such flows of assets. Here, there was only a paper transaction that changed the holding structure creating a chain through several companies connecting the Dutch company over which stood other American companies which were the real controllers of the investments in Bolivia. There was no actual control by the Dutch company, but the satisfaction of the mere formality that it stood higher in the corporate structure. By restructuring just prior to an anticipated dispute, an investor could secure an advantage, simply through the process of migration in a manner that would not have been within the contemplation of either party to the treaty. Quite apart from encouraging forum shopping, the primary purpose of economic development which underlies the investment treaty system is defeated by legal manipulation of the form of wording in the treaties without heed to their purpose. Read along with the 'round-tripping' in *Tokios Tokelės* v. *Ukraine*, the notion of 'migration' in *Aguas del Tunari* indicates bias towards neo-liberalism and the sacrifice of the intention of the parties to further legal schemes that advance narrow interests involved in the area.

2.6 Shopping for jurisdiction

The 'migration' of companies and other strategies are employed in order to gain the advantages that the uncertainties relating to corporate nationality provide. Some tribunals, willing to take a formalistic view of corporate nationality that would satisfy the wording in the treaties, are willing to permit such techniques to be used to establish jurisdiction. One way of securing an advantage would be to locate a corporation in the chain of corporations in the preferred state with an advantageous treaty in anticipation of the dispute and claim the nationality of that state for the purposes of treaty protection and arbitration. This was attempted in *Aguas del Tunari*, where there was no treaty protection in the original place of incorporation. In *Fedax* v. *Venezuela*, the transfer of the loan notes meant that an investment that originally had no treaty protection became entitled to protection. No company was involved. *Tokios Tokelės* v. *Ukraine* is another case in which the nationals who had no treaty protection and who were not entitled to ICSID arbitration were given such protection through incorporation in another state. In *Phoenix* v. *Czech Republic*,[83] a similar effort was made.

Such jurisdiction shopping goes well beyond the purposes of both the ICSID Convention and the investment treaties. States have reacted to these developments by introducing denial-of-benefits clauses. But, even where these clauses do not cover the situation, such flagrant

---

[83] *Phoenix v. Czech Republic*, ICSID Case No. ARB/06/5 (2009).

abuse of the objectives for which the treaties were made by the parties should not be given effect to. The sudden change of location for purposes only of dispute settlement can in no way be said to promote the economic development of the states making the treaties. The party against which arbitration proceedings are brought could not have consented to jurisdiction in the circumstances, even if the wording of the treaty is satisfied. The purpose of the treaty is defeated by such textual interpretation. These are instances of legal sophistry that will affect the credibility and legitimacy of the system.

What was attempted in Phoenix v. Czech Republic was novel. A Czech citizen who had a dispute with the Czech government, took Israeli citizenship. He then repurchased companies in the Czech Republic which he had previously owned, and then sought to continue his dispute with the Czech government using the investment treaty.

2.7 *Round-tripping and corporate nationality*

'Round-tripping' is a technique which nationals of a state use in order to protect their investments from interference by their own states. It involves an investor transferring funds to another state and then redirecting the funds into his own home state, thus securing the protection as well as the advantageous treatment that may be given by the law of the home state to foreign investors.[84] One such advantage is that the funds, when vested in companies incorporated in the host state, may become entitled to the diplomatic protection of that state as well as to the protection of its investment treaties.

This possibility was raised in *Tokios Tokelės* v. *Ukraine*. In this dispute, a company incorporated in Lithuania alleged violations by Ukraine of the Lithuania–Ukraine treaty. Ninety-nine per cent of the shares in the Lithuanian company were owned by two Ukrainian nationals, and the company itself was managed by one of them.[85] The respondent state contested jurisdiction on the ground that the treaty's purpose was to protect foreign investors and not nationals of the state, and that ICSID jurisdiction itself was based on the fact that there was a dispute between a state and a foreign national. Giving the claimant in this situation the right to invoke the investment treaty and the ICSID Convention defeats the purposes behind both instruments.[86] The respondent state argued that the corporate veil should be lifted so that the true state of the ownership of the Lithuanian company by its nationals could be ascertained and jurisdiction declined on this basis. The tribunal, however, chose not to look at the purpose of the investment treaty but only its wording. It held that incorporation was determinative of nationality, and that the claimant was a Lithuanian investor in terms of the treaty. The tribunal held that the '[c]laimant is a thing of real legal existence that was founded on a secure basis in the territory of Lithuania'.[87] The tribunal

---

[84] The technique is used by Chinese nationals, thus distorting the true extent of the foreign investment flows into China, as it is difficult to separate the funds of these nationals from true foreign investment flows.

[85] The other manager was the Lithuanian owner of 1 per cent of the shares.

[86] Ukraine also maintained that ICSID case law favoured the control test rather than a test of incorporation. The basis of this argument is not clear.

[87] Para. 30 of the Award.

held that the control test was not relevant, and the fact that no substantial activity of the claimant took place in Lithuania was equally irrelevant.[88]

2.8 Denial of benefits

States have taken various measures in an attempt to ensure that such techniques are not successful. Some treaties have required actual control of the companies from within a state party, so that the mere formality of incorporation does not suffice and benefits are denied to a corporation which is in reality controlled from a third state.[89] As indicated, many treaties require that there be effective management instituted from the place of incorporation in order for corporate nationality to be satisfied. More modern treaties have a denial-of-benefits clause addressing the specific situation, which permit a state to deny the benefits of the treaty to a company which is not controlled from the state of incorporation. This gets over the problem that mere satisfaction of the formalities involved in incorporation does not satisfy corporate nationality. The denial-of-benefits clause need not be worded in permissive terms in order for it to have effect.[90] In more recent treaties, the denial-of-benefits clause is worded in definite terms, thus ensuring that there is actual control. It is evident that, as states become conscious of trends in international arbitration, they make treaty provisions so as to ensure that their intentions prevail over the preferences of arbitrators by tightening treaty provisions. This trend would, however, eventually result in treaties becoming so emasculated that they offer little meaningful protection to investors.

2.9 Protection of minority shareholders

In customary international law, it was the corporation, not its shareholders, which was protected. The distinction between the corporation and the shareholders drawn in the *Barcelona Traction Case* continues to hold, and has been confirmed more recently by the International Court of Justice in *Diallo*. Investment treaties reverse this trend by providing protection to shareholders. Where the company in which the shareholder holds shares is taken over[91] or his shares are divested compulsorily, there is little doubt that he could claim protection under the investment treaty. Here, there is a direct interference with the shares of the foreign investor.

A difficulty is created where measures are taken which adversely affect the company as a whole. In these circumstances, a foreign shareholder may be left without protection,

---

[88] Some treaties do require this as an element. They would require both incorporation and management to be located in the state before protection could be claimed. Some treaties provide that a state may refuse to give the benefits of the treaty to a company that does not have substantial activity in the territory of the treaty partner. These treaties are discussed in paras. 33–4. These are to be found in the 'denial of benefits' provision of the treaty.

[89] *Generation Ukraine* v. *Ukraine* (2005) 44 *ILM* 404. In *Yaung Chi Oo Ltd* v. *Myanmar* (2003) 42 *ILM* 540; (2003) 8 *ICSID Reports* 463, effective management was considered, and it was held that the satisfaction of the requirements of domestic company law such as the publication of annual reports was sufficient to establish effective management.

[90] *Plama* v. *Bulgaria* (Jurisdiction Award, 8 February 2005), (2005) 44 *ILM* 721.   [91] *Amco* v. *Indonesia*.

particularly if he is a minority shareholder and the majority agree to the measures that are taken or the majority shares are held by a state corporation.[92] In these circumstances, protection of the shares becomes necessary. The disputes following the Argentine economic crisis illustrate this situation clearly.[93] Many of the disputes arose in respect of privatised companies in which foreign investors held shares. The measures taken to control the economic crisis affected the profitability of these companies. The issue was whether, in these circumstances, the foreign investor had a basis for a claim. The view that has been taken is that, even in these circumstances, where the foreign owner of the privatised shares may be a minority shareholder, it would have a remedy as a shareholder under the investment treaty. This, of course, creates a curious situation, as the majority shareholder may be confined to a remedy under the domestic law or may accept the measures that have been taken. It could be argued that the minority shareholder took the risk that the other shareholders would take a different approach to the situation and that he should be committed to that situation unless there is a remedy under the domestic law. Investment tribunals have been averse to this view, holding that the foreign shareholder whose shares are protected by an investment treaty is entitled to a remedy.

3. Conclusion

The basic rule regarding the jurisdiction of an international tribunal is that such jurisdiction depends entirely on the consent of the parties. This rule has been extended through the technique of the construction of consent, as used in *AAPL* v. *Sri Lanka*.[94] Whether this technique is tenable and whether it is consistent with the structure of the ICSID Convention may have to be rethought when the issue of withdrawal of consent comes to be decided. The ICSID Convention permits withdrawal of consent, and this has been done by some Latin American states. The validity of such withdrawal will also test out the theory of the construction of consent through the notion of an investment treaty containing a permanent offer to arbitrate.

But, whatever the merit in that extension may be, it triggered an expansionist boom in investment arbitration that may end up destroying the system if carried too far. The killing of the goose that lays so many golden eggs may be thoroughly unwise. Arbitrators and lawyers may now be inclined to show restraint and rein in the tendency towards expansion

---

[92] Some investment laws compel the foreign investor to be a minority shareholder in a joint-venture company established as the investment vehicle: *Amco* v. *Indonesia*. Investment treaties address such situations by providing for protection of such minority shareholdings.

[93] *CMS Gas Transmission Co* v. *Argentina* (2003) 30 *ILM* 788; (2005) 44 *ILM* 1205; *Sempra Energy International* v. *Argentina*, ICSID Case No. ARB/02/16 (Award, 28 September 2007); *El Paso* v. *Argentina*, ICSID Case No. ARB/03/15 (Decision on Jurisdiction, 27 April 2006).

[94] The term 'arbitration without privity' may be appealing but theoretically inaccurate. What was done was to construct consent through an implied offer contained in the investment treaty and regard the request for arbitration as an acceptance of the offer. The implied offer in several treaties was commented on by Mann and other eminent scholars, none of whom spotted that the treaties contained such an offer until *AAPL* v. *Sri Lanka* came along. It could well be that the proliferation of cases, the resulting jurisdictional challenges and adventurism on the part of tribunals extending both jurisdiction and the substantive law have now considerably undermined the system of investment arbitration.

that has been so prevalent in recent years. But, these expansionary episodes show how arbitrators, inspired by a particular vision, could continue to expand the scope of jurisdiction well beyond what states had intended to confer on them. The resulting chaos would give salutary lessons as to the need to rein in such adventurism in judicial activism that is intended to secure a one-sided notion of justice conducive only to the interests of the foreign investor.

9

Causes of action: breaches of treatment standards

The usual cause of action in investment disputes has hitherto been the taking of property. Though, as was claimed, customary international law recognised an international minimum standard of treatment of a foreign investor, the violation of this standard outside the context of the taking of property was seldom discussed. The growth of such a customary law was dealt with in Chapter 4 above. It forms a prelude to the discussion here. That chapter dealt with the manner in which the creation of an international standard was effected and the conflicts which attended it. But, investment treaties have sought to iron out such conflicts and provide recognition of certain standards of treatment of investments as between the parties to such treaties. It is only with the spelling out of the different standards of treatment in the investment treaties that the breach of treatment standards has become a distinct head of liability distinct from the taking of property. In more recent disputes, the failure to provide treatment according to standards prescribed in investment treaties has become important, especially in the context of Chapter 11 of the North American Free Trade Agreement (NAFTA). The vigour with which disputes have arisen between the two developed-country participants in NAFTA, largely on the basis of treatment standards and novel theories of the taking of property, has opened up new possibilities in the field.[1] Litigation strategies have taken a new turn as creative interpretations have been used to find new arguments in order to impose liability in foreign investment transactions. Whereas previously the targets of arbitration were developing countries, the new battleground opened up by NAFTA makes two developed states the targets of the mechanisms and legal standards of investment protection they themselves used against developing states in the past. Developed states seldom engage in direct takings, but do employ discriminatory and protectionist practices against foreign investors. The litigation that has emerged against Canada and the United States has largely focused on the provisions in NAFTA which make arguments possible that such practices are tantamount to takings or violate treatment standards. Both the strategies of litigation that are fashioned as well as the defences that the vaster legal resources of these states employ against them will have an impact on shaping the law in this area. There will be a spill-over effect of this experience into disputes arising from other treaties, thereby making

---

[1] Commentators agree that the extensive use of these provisions against Canada and the United States was unforeseen. D. Price, 'Investor–State Dispute Settlement: Frankenstein or Safety Valve?' (2000) 26 *Canada–US Law Journal* 107.

the jurisprudence under NAFTA of general relevance. Sophisticated theories of litigation tested out in the context of NAFTA will be extended to disputes involving developing states, which may not have the legal resources to meet these arguments effectively.

The NAFTA provisions on investment closely track the provisions of the older US model bilateral investment treaty. There are, however, significant drafting differences.[2] Provisions on treatment standards along similar lines are also to be found in other bilateral investment treaties. Language variations in these treaties will have significance, but the broad content of the standards is generally the same.[3] The law that is created in the context of NAFTA and the debates that take place as a result will have a profound impact on the international law of foreign investment. The tendency to transport the thinking on takings in US constitutional law into the interpretations of NAFTA is strong.[4] There is a likelihood that the jurisprudence that emerges will seep into international law, as similar provisions exist in other bilateral investment treaties. The techniques that are used in NAFTA litigation and the responses of arbitral tribunals to them will influence the decisions that are made by other tribunals. To the extent that NAFTA tribunals state that they are applying standards of international law, there is a likelihood that their decisions will affect the whole corpus of international law in the area. This is despite the fact that NAFTA tribunals caution that their references even to customary law relate only to customary law as between the parties, raising the tantalising possibility of customary international law existing as between just three states of the world.[5] The cross-fertilisation of thinking is already evident in the case law that is emerging.[6] It is for this reason that this chapter is devoted to a study of the failure to abide by treatment standards as creating a cause of action. Causes of action arise not only from the NAFTA provisions but also from the provisions in other investment treaties. Special attention, however, is devoted to the new awards made under NAFTA and the potential impact they have on the law. It must, however, be remembered that, though treatment standards have featured more heavily in recent NAFTA decisions, they are by no means absent in other types of arbitration. Thus, in *Genin* v. *Estonia*,[7] an ICSID arbitration, the only allegations concerned violation of treatment standards. In other ICSID cases, there have been increasing references to violations of treatment standards. But, such references are used to bolster

---

[2] Particularly in relation to Article 1105 of NAFTA, which deals with treatment standards.

[3] If they are not, the possibility is raised by *Maffezini* v. *Spain* (2000) 5 *ICSID Reports* 396; (2004) 40 *ILM* 1129, that the most-favoured-nation clause in any treaty could be used to entitle a litigant to the better standards in another treaty involving the same treaty partners.

[4] Two US scholars have argued that NAFTA jurisprudence on taking goes beyond the notions of US law. V. Bean and J. Beauvais, 'Global Fifth Amendment? NAFTA's Investment Protection and the Misguided Quest for an International "Regulatory Takings" Doctrine' (2003) 78 *New York University Law Review* 30.

[5] See *Mondev* v. *United States* (2003) 42 *ILM* 85, para. 120; *ADF* v. *United States*, ICSID Case No. ARB(AF)/00/1 (NAFTA) (Award, 9 January 2003), para. 178: 'Thus, it [Article 1105] clarifies that so far as the three NAFTA Parties are concerned the long-standing debate as to whether there exists such a thing as a minimum standard of treatment of non-nationals and their property prescribed in customary international law is closed.' The assumption is that the debate continues for the rest of the world.

[6] It is evident that such cross-fertilisation takes place. The personnel of arbitral tribunals are usually persons who have experience sitting on other tribunals which deal with investment issues. Thus, members of the Iran–US Claims Tribunal now sit on ICSID tribunals and bring with them the experiences gained while on the earlier tribunal. This is an inevitable process. The impact of the takings cases decided by the Iran–US Claims Tribunal is beginning to be felt in this area, despite the fact that the wording of the treaty creating the tribunal on takings was different.

[7] ICSID Case No. ARB/99/2 (2001).

findings relating to taking.[8] Often, the claims relating to takings fail but the claims relating to taking standards succeed. Chapters 10 and 11 below deal with takings of property. Takings and the issue of compensation for such takings remain the principal cause of action. Though NAFTA perspectives on these aspects are important, they can be accommodated under existing viewpoints. This chapter builds upon the earlier consideration of treatment standards in customary international law and is principally concerned with the standards in treaties as well as the interaction of these treaty standards with customary international law. A recapitulation of the customary standards is made before considering the treaty formulation of these standards.

1. The customary international law standards

In Chapter 4 above, the effort on the part of the United States to create an external standard of foreign investment protection was outlined. The resistance to the creation of such a standard and the assertion of control by national standards by developing states was also examined. Modern tribunals concede the existence of this 'long-standing and divisive debate' between states.[9] Some tribunals have openly acknowledged the fact that two distinct systems existed and that the major tradition pretended that only one existed.[10] The outcome of this was that there was no clear international law standard that had emerged. However, arbitral tribunals had independently created 'law' through their awards asserting the existence of an international minimum standard of treatment of aliens, including foreign investors. The standards created were disputed, for, as long as the collective stances of developing countries supporting the instruments associated with the New International Economic Order remained unaltered through the adoption of a multilateral instrument on investment, there can be no truly international standard relating to the treatment of foreign investment. In the absence of such a treaty, the second best option is to settle the controversy relating to treatment standards as between the parties through regional or bilateral investment treaties. The continuous quest for the creation of external standards through the instrumentality of international law has been carried on through such treaties. The effort to create a multilateral treaty that would have embodied these standards and made them acceptable universally has failed each time it was attempted.

The struggle to create such an international standard of treatment is manifested in several ways. The first is the articulation of the standard in the official positions taken by developed states. As indicated, these positions have little chance of creating customary practice, as there is evidence of resistance to the standard by developing states. The second is the

---

[8] For example, *Middle East Cement Shipping and Handling Co.* v. *Egypt*, ICSID Case No. ARB/99/6 (12 April 2002), para. 143, where there is a suggestion that a failure to give notice prior to the auction of the investment property amounted to a violation of the fair and equitable standard of treatment.

[9] *Mondev* v. *United States* (2003) 42 *ILM* 85, para. 120: '[I]t is clear that Article 1105 was intended to put at rest for NAFTA purposes a long-standing and divisive debate about whether any such thing as a minimum standard of treatment of investment in international law actually exists.'

[10] See the preliminary award in *UPS* v. *Canada*, para. 90, criticising the Sohn–Baxter codification on state responsibility for not recognising the competing system of state responsibility.

argument that is continuously pressed that the incorporation of the standards in investment treaties is evidence of customary international law. Again, this is not a tenable argument, as investment treaties are premised on different objectives, and the internal balance that is achieved between sovereign control over investments and the competing notion of the international standards from which there can be no deviation differ from treaty to treaty. It is true that some of the more powerful states are able to secure treaties with very little deviation from their model treaties, but these treaties are too few in number to create customary international law. With an increasing array of defences to liability coming to be included in the investment treaties, the possibility of the emergence of inflexible standards of protection seems increasingly remote.

The most that can be said is that investment treaties generally recognise treatment standards and some of them refer explicitly to the standards as they exist in customary international law. Thus, they seek to bolster the existence of customary international law standards of treatment the creation and maintenance of which are the avowed objective of most developed states. There is a view that a technique of *renvoi* operates in the area, as reference has to be made to customary international law in order to give effect and meaning to the standards of treatment that are incorporated into the treaties.[11] This view will give the alleged rules of customary international law continuing validity. As a result, an opportunity has been created for arbitral tribunals to interpret these provisions, sometimes creatively, giving rise to further support for the idea of the existence of a customary standard in international law. This interaction takes place largely in the context of the opportunity to interpret appropriate provisions in investment treaties. What follows is an analysis of the different treatment standards in the context of recent arbitral jurisprudence.

2. The violation of national treatment standards

In the age of globalisation and liberalisation, the emphasis has been on national treatment at both the pre-entry and the post-entry phases of investment. The object of national treatment under the Calvo doctrine was entirely different. It evolved as a counter to the external international minimum standard advocated by the United States.[12] The doctrine confined the foreign investor to the standards applicable to local investors. There was an assumption that such standards were lower than those which prevailed in the investor's home state and those which both the foreign investor and the home state would have desired. It is not to be confused with national treatment that is advocated in the more recent investment treaties. In modern international law, the national standard has assumed a much desired form. At the pre-entry stage, national treatment, if permitted, creates a right of entry into the host state,

---

[11] *AAPL* v. *Sri Lanka* (1992) 17 *YCA* 106; (1991) 30 *ILM* 577.

[12] The US practice also required national treatment but expected the national treatment to conform to 'the established standards of civilisation'. E. Root, 'The Basis of Protection of Citizens Residing Abroad' (1910) 4 *ASIL Proceedings* 16 at 20. In that sense, national treatment is the primary obligation, liability arising where such treatment fails to conform to the international minimum standard.

unhindered by its screening laws,[13] and a right of establishment of business. Post-entry national treatment entitles the foreign investor to be treated equally with national entrepreneurs. It thus becomes an instrument of liberalisation of movement of capital.

The emergence of new meanings that are attributed to old standards of treatment as well as their expansion is what makes the emergence of treatment standards as a new cause of action relevant to the modern law. State responsibility arises from the violation of these standards. Such responsibility is seen not as a static concept but as a continuously evolving one.[14] It is not as if some of the standards had not existed in the past; rather they have been dusted off and given new vigour through philosophical and political underpinnings. The neo-liberalism that motivates modern investment treaties promotes the free flow of investments around the world. The treaties that are motivated by this philosophy therefore require that all movements of foreign investment must take place with the least amount of restrictions. With that objective, the investment treaties made by the United States and Canada have stressed that there should be free access of foreign investment into the markets of the contracting states.[15] The treaties made by the European states have generally eschewed such an approach, limiting national treatment only to the post-entry phase. Though states have made treaties on the acceptance of national treatment at the pre-investment phase, they have done so on the basis that they could exempt certain sectors from such national treatment. All states, including the United States, have exempted a variety of sectors from the scope of pre-entry national treatment. The idea is that they start with the general proposition regarding free movement of investment but make exemptions of sectors to which the proposition does not apply. It is a technique taken over from trade instruments. The statement of national treatment as applicable to both phases is a change that has been made in these treaties. The change is clearly attributable to the acceptance of neo-liberal views.

Regional treaties have also adopted notions of pre-entry national treatment. Chapter 11 of NAFTA is by no means the only regional investment treaty that stresses liberalisation as well as the protection of foreign investment. Regional treaties such as the ASEAN Framework Agreement on Investment also contain provisions that seek to confer protection as well as liberalise flows of foreign investment. The new ASEAN Treaty on Investment which replaces the earlier document is also based on regional liberalisation, stressing free movement of investments within the ASEAN region. The earlier ASEAN treaty sought to create the concept of an 'ASEAN Investor' and ensures that this investor, who could be either a national of an ASEAN member state or a company incorporated within an ASEAN state, has freedom of movement within the ASEAN region.[16] This treaty was replaced in 2009 by the

---

[13] These laws would have to be dismantled at least to the extent that they are inconsistent with the pre-entry national treatment provision. The formulation would permit the exclusion of sectors from the standard. Many treaties have extensive lists of excluded sectors. States can continue to exercise screening and other procedures limiting entry to these sectors.

[14] See *Mondev* v. *United States* (2003) 42 *ILM* 85, para. 116: 'In particular, both the substantive and procedural rights of the individual in international law have undergone considerable development. In light of these developments, it is unconvincing to confine the meaning of "fair and equitable treatment" and "full protection of security" of foreign investment to what those terms – had they been current at the time – might have meant in the 1920s when applied to the physical security of the alien.'

[15] But, the newer versions of the US and Canadian treaties contain subjective national security provisions, exceptions relating to health and the environment and other safeguards which attenuate considerably the notion of liberalisation.

[16] The provisions of this treaty have been interpreted in *Yaung Chi Oo Ltd.* v. *Myanmar* (2003) 42 *ILM* 540; (2003) 8 *ICSID Reports* 463.

ASEAN Comprehensive Investment Treaty which continues the notion of free movement of investment within the ASEAN region.[17] The treaty is the most recent of the regional treaties. Its attempt at balancing liberalisation with national regulatory objectives indicates the difficulty in achieving such a balance without sacrificing the protection objectives of the treaty and creating considerable doubts as to the extent to which the objectives of protection and liberalisation are achieved.

The basis of national treatment is non-discrimination between the foreign investor and a local investor conducting similar business. For discrimination to be found in this context, there must always be a comparison made between the two types of investor operating in the same sector and competing with each other. The comparison must be between persons in like circumstances. Few treaties state such a limitation explicitly, but it is of the essence of discrimination law.[18] The better treatment of the national who is alike and operates in like circumstances, unless there is a justification, would involve a violation of the treaty standard.[19] Non-discrimination may also be required by the drafting of a contractual provision to this effect or where the local laws promise such non-discrimination to the foreign investor.[20] The discussion here concerns only treaty provisions.

The awards that have been made also demonstrate that there is an emphasis on national treatment. The operation of national treatment at the pre-entry phase has yet to be considered in an award.[21] The creation of such a right will require the dismantling of regulatory legislation which tests foreign investment to determine whether it will benefit the host state and avoid harmful effects such as environmental pollution. It is clear, however, from the practice of states that have permitted pre-entry rights that many industrial and natural resources sectors could be exempted from such entry rights.

The list of sectors that are excluded by Mexico from the pre-entry national treatment provision of Chapter 11 of NAFTA is long. In the case of the 2009 ASEAN Comprehensive Investment Treaty, there is provision for reserving sectors from national treatment, but there is also an obligation to open these reserved sectors within specified time periods. Usually, the treaties contemplate a process in which the list of excepted sectors is progressively narrowed. Some treaties fix time limits for the removal of sectors from the list. It will be interesting to see whether these time limits are adhered to.

National treatment at the post-entry phase is more common. It has implications for economic development. The granting of special preferences to new industries may not be

---

[17] Though liberalisation is indicated, the protected investment is defined as one admitted in accordance with the laws, regulation and national policies and specifically approved in writing. This provision allows scope for restrictions on entry and discrimination as to the types of investment permitted for protection of the treaty. The interaction of this provision with the national treatment provision leaves the extent of national provision uncertain. There is still scope for discretion as to entry and approval for protection. Since 'national policy' is also introduced as relevant, further uncertainty is created as national policies will differ. In addition, each state can maintain a list of reserved sectors.

[18] Thus, for example, in laws relating to racial discrimination, it is possible to discriminate in favour of disadvantaged groups, as they are not in like circumstances with other groups due to the historical disadvantages they had suffered.

[19] Some tribunals regard the identification of a comparator as important. The reference *Consortium RFCC* v. *Morocco*, ICSID Case No. ARB/00/6 (Award, 23 December 2003) to identical circumstances may be excessive. It is unlikely that due to size and deep pockets, the foreign investor is likely to be identical to local investors.

[20] For such a situation, see *Aguaytia Energy* v. *Peru*, ICSID Case No. ARB/06/13 (Award).

[21] The NAFTA case, *UPS* v. *Canada*, UNCITRAL Arbitration Proceedings (NAFTA) (Award on the Merits, 24 May 2007), raised issues of pre-entry national treatment, but the issue was not decided.

possible unless exceptions have been made. If ethnic groups within the state are to be given preference because of positive discrimination programmes,[22] this too may violate national treatment provisions. It would be difficult to formulate such exceptions.[23] The constitutional validity of the national treatment of a foreigner may also be a problem in that equal rights are usually conferred by constitutions only on citizens.[24] Perfect national treatment is an objective that is seldom achieved. States seek to protect local investors by providing incentives and directing that government agencies purchase their products,[25] and exclude entry because of the fear that local businesses would get 'crowded out'.[26] There may be sufficient economic justifications for taking such measures. Such discriminatory treatment may be justifiable on the ground that the foreign investors may not be in like circumstances in most cases. Size, dominant position and capacity for predatory pricing may by themselves make the foreign investor different from local investors. Merely being in the same sector may not be sufficient to show that the national investor and the foreign investor are in like circumstances.[27]

The application of like circumstances is to be found in trade treaties, and principles may be borrowed from international trade law when comparisons are made.[28] Sectoral and market classification will play an important role in determining discrimination, for the idea of like circumstances requires the drawing of the circle in which the comparison is to be made. Such a task involves considerable subjectivity. In *Occidental v. Ecuador*,[29] the comparison was not made between those in like sectors, the tribunal finding a violation of national treatment when the claimant, an exporter in the oil sector, was not given tax concessions which were given in unrelated sectors such as the export of flowers and seafood. There is discretion in the arbitral tribunal in drawing the circle within which the comparison is made. Where, as in *Occidental*, the circle is drawn too widely, the reasoning in the award becomes weak.[30] It also narrows the scope for policies that a state can make in order to promote development within targeted sectors, as it creates the fear that investors in entirely unrelated sectors could argue that they have been discriminated against. To that extent, national treatment curbs the regulatory freedom of the state.

---

[22] See, for example, Malaysia and South Africa. There are similar programmes for native peoples in Australia and Canada, and for 'backward' tribes and castes in India. The South African treaties contain provisions exempting its affirmative action programmes from the scope of national treatment.

[23] In some treaties, national treatment is postponed until a level of economic development is reached. But, this is a nebulous formulation which requires later decision as to when such an event occurs.

[24] For example, the rights under the Indian Constitution are conferred only on its citizens. Treaties may confer more favourable rights on foreign investors. In these situations, too, constitutional problems could arise.

[25] A ground of complaint in *ADF* v. *United States*, ICSID Case No. ARB(AF)/00/1 (NAFTA) (Award, 9 January 2003).

[26] This fear is a reason why foreign supermarket chains are kept out of developing countries. The small corner shops will not be able to withstand the competition.

[27] *UPS* v. *Canada*, UNCITRAL Arbitration Proceedings (NAFTA) (Award on the Merits, 24 May 2007). Market characterisation may become relevant. The drawing of a market could be done broadly or narrowly, depending on the product or activity in question. On these issues, see *Marvin Feldman* v. *Mexico* (2002) 7 *ICSID Reports* 318; (2003) 42 *ILM* 625.

[28] J. Pauwelyn and N. Di Mascio, 'Non-Discrimination in Trade and Investment Treaties: Worlds Apart or Two Sides of the Same Coin' (2008) 102 *AJIL* 48.

[29] London Court of International Arbitration, Final Award, 1 July 2004.

[30] The award has been criticised on this basis. See A. Bjorklund, 'National Treatment', in A. Reinisch, *Standards of Investment Protection* (2008), p. 29 at p. 40. In *Marvin Feldman* v. *Mexico* (2002) 7 *ICSID Reports* 318; (2003) 42 *ILM* 625, the circle was drawn narrowly.

In considering discrimination, some tribunals have held that the intent or purpose of the measure is not relevant and that the impact alone matters.[31] This is a view that further restricts the discretion of the state. It is necessary to identify the purpose of the measure to ensure likeness, for there could have been justification in taking the measure that affected the foreign investor as where the measures had been taken because of the violation of pollution or labour standards. In that case, the foreign investor would cease to be in like circumstances. The tribunals which disregard the intent or purpose behind the alleged discriminatory measure, define the law in a manner that restricts legitimate regulation by the state. Though there is a duty on the state not to discriminate, it is not a rule that creates strict liability on violation. The tribunal is still under a duty to assess the legitimacy of the discrimination. It must allow a margin of appreciation to a state to take policy measures so that, in looking at the legitimacy of the measure in hindsight, the tribunal could permit some leeway in determining whether there were good social and economic grounds on which the measures could have been taken. There must, however, have been transparency in taking the measures. *Ex post facto* rationalisations would not be sufficient.[32]

National treatment provisions may also have an impact on the imposition of performance requirements.[33] As explained earlier, these requirements are imposed on the foreign investor to ensure that the host state gains the maximum benefit from the foreign investment. Such performance requirements include the requirement that export earnings be achieved through the export of a percentage of manufactured goods, that local products be incorporated into the manufactured items, and that there is employment of local personnel. Some laws also require the foreign investor to locate in prescribed zones or direct that he establishes in regions which are in need of industrialisation. Such requirements are enforced through local laws and regulations, which may have to be disapplied if national treatment is to be provided to the foreign investor. The welfare-enhancing potential of such requirements may be lost if national treatment for foreign investment is to be implemented. Performance requirements are directly prohibited in many treaties, but their violation of national treatment standards could be raised as a ground of liability as well.

Such a situation occurred in *ADF Group Inc.* v. *United States*.[34] A contention of the claimant, a Canadian company which had contracted for the supply of steel girders to be used in the construction of a highway in the United States, was that the 'use of domestic material' policy mandated by statute was a violation of the national treatment standard. The supply contract was made with the main contractor for the construction of the highway. The main contract was between the Virginia Department of Trade and a US company. It was a term of the supply contract that the laws on the use of domestic materials be complied with. ADF proposed that some of the work on the fabrication of the steel girders produced in the United

---

[31] For example, *Siemens* v. *Argentina* ICSID Case No. ARB/02/8; *S. D. Myers* v. *Canada* (2000) 40 *ILM* 1408; (2002) 121 *ILR* 7.

[32] In *S. D. Myers* v. *Canada* (2000) 40 *ILM* 1408; (2002) 121 *ILR* 7, the justifications advanced by Canada were *ex post facto*. The idea that the prohibition violated the Basel Convention was clearly a splendid afterthought. The issue was addressed in *UPS* v. *Canada*, UNCITRAL Arbitration Proceedings (NAFTA) (Award on the Merits, 24 May 2007), where the tribunal felt that, to be relevant, the justifications must precede the measure.

[33] The issue is addressed in *ADF* v. *United States*, ICSID Case No. ARB(AF)/00/1 (NAFTA) (Award, 9 January 2003).

[34] *ADF Group Inc.* v. *United States*, ICSID Case No. ARB(AF)/00/1 (NAFTA) (Award, 9 January 2003).

States be done in Canada. The Virginia Department of Trade ruled that such fabrication would not be in compliance with the 'buy America' provisions and could not therefore be permitted. The main contract had a 'buy America' clause which would be violated, and the federal government would not reimburse the state government for the costs of the highway if the provision was violated. A waiver of the provision was refused on the ground that there were local providers of steel fabrication within the United States. As a result, ADF had to incur greater costs by subcontracting the fabrication of the steel. It fulfilled its contractual obligations but brought NAFTA proceedings against the United States on the ground that there were violations of NAFTA standards on national and fair and equitable standards of treatment. But, the tribunal found that there was no violation of the national treatment standard, as all that the regulations required – a requirement that applied just as much to US as to foreign operators – was that the steel that was to be used in government projects should be fabricated in the United States. On the argument that the requirements were performance requirements as to local content, the tribunal held that, if so, the exception relating to procurements by a state party applied to excuse the state from liability.

There have been several disputes under NAFTA which have been based on the violation of the national treatment standard at the post-entry phase. *S. D. Myers* v. *Canada*[35] is a case in which a violation of national treatment was found. It involved an attempt by the Canadian government to prevent hazardous waste being disposed of by the claimant's waste-disposal system in Ohio in the United States, just across the border from Canada. The government intended to have the disposal done at a Canadian plant in Alberta, far away from the source of the waste. The issue was whether the Canadian policy was in violation of the national treatment provisions of NAFTA. The tribunal held that it was.

UPS v. *Canada*[36] was a NAFTA case brought largely on the basis of the violation of the national treatment standard. UPS, a US provider of courier services, alleged violation of the national treatment standard when CanadaPost, a monopoly provider of postal services, permitted its subsidiary, which runs a courier service, to collect parcels from post offices. This facility was denied to UPS and other courier services, and was therefore a violation of the national treatment standard of NAFTA. The tribunal found that it did not have jurisdiction to hear the claim. In *Occidental* v. *Ecuador*,[37] the tribunal upheld a claim as to violation of national treatment standards when tax concessions available in certain export sectors were not made available to the claimant who operated in the oil sector.

The arguments raise interesting issues. The first is that, as a result of national treatment standards in an investment treaty, the foreign investor is placed on a footing that is not only equal to the host state's citizens but is superior in that the rights of equal treatment are protected, not by local courts as in the case of the citizen, but by international tribunals. In addition, such rights are protected not in accordance with local laws but in accordance with external standards. This brings in the second issue, as to whether rights emanating from the local laws applying to a local situation should be subject to scrutiny by an external tribunal,

---

[35] NAFTA/UNCITRAL Tribunal, 21 October 2002.
[36] *UPS* v. *Canada*, UNCITRAL Arbitration Proceedings (NAFTA) (Award on the Merits, 24 May 2007).
[37] London Court of International Arbitration, Final Award, 1 July 2004.

bypassing the local courts.[38] Thus, the old issue of local remedies is raised. But, the significance here is that the bypassing of the local court system is seen as a constitutional violation inasmuch as a local dispute is taken at once to an international tribunal, without the domestic courts having a chance to decide on the issues in dispute. The arguments that have been raised, quite apart from the significance of domestic constitutional law to investment treaties, are reminiscent of the old debate as to the place of local remedies in a system of investment protection.[39]

There could be legitimate reasons for discriminatory treatment. In *Marvin Feldman* v. *Mexico*,[40] the failure to provide tax rebates which were granted to nationals was explained on the basis that the foreign investor was not able to produce the necessary invoices. Justification for the discrimination could also be provided if it was based on sound policy considerations.[41]

Methanex v. *United States* was premised on the violation of national treatment standards and not on the provision on taking alone. The claimant alleged that the ban on the use of methanol, a chemical additive, in petroleum on the ground that it was a pollutive substance was motivated by a desire to discriminate in favour of a domestic producer of another chemical additive. *Methanex* thus raises the issue of national treatment in a direct form. In *Methanex*, the tribunal refused to treat the two substances as being alike, again illustrating that much depends on how widely the market is drawn. There is an obvious discretion in the tribunal in this respect. The validity of the discrimination was the basis of the defence that is made to the charge. The existence of a justification is also a factor in the drawing of the market. Methanol was found to have health risks which justified it being treated differently from other chemical additives. *Methanex* also raises the issue of regulatory controls which are addressed to foreign investors.

Unlike in developed states, a foreign investor entering a developing state would almost always be the dominant producer in its sector. This dominance factor by itself sets the foreign investor apart from national investors. Where regulatory control has to be exercised, it will almost always be directed at the foreign operator and not at a small-scale national operator. Discrimination based on size is likely to affect foreign investors exclusively. Such discrimination may be necessary in the interests of certain types of regulation such as environmental regulation, where the pollution caused by a very large company requires control whereas pollution caused by smaller operators could be absorbed. National treatment therefore works to the detriment of the exercise of regulatory control over certain types of activities. Likewise, antitrust concerns are likely to arise in respect of large operators with a dominant position in the market. These large operators are more likely to be foreign investors than local companies.[42] Avoidance of liability will require that exceptions be

---

[38] Or, in the situation of *Loewen* v. *United States* (2003) 42 *ILM* 811, whether decisions of local courts should be pronounced upon by foreign tribunals without the appellate process being exhausted.

[39] Mexico has argued that the local remedies rule is valid in the context of NAFTA: *Marvin Feldman* v. *Mexico* (2002) 7 *ICSID Reports* 318; (2003) 42 *ILM* 625, para. 70. See also *Loewen* v. *United States* (2003) 42 *ILM* 811, para. 43. This may presage the revival of the local remedies rule.

[40] (2002) 7 *ICSID Reports* 318; (2003) 42 *ILM* 625.   [41] *Gami Investments* v. *Mexico* (2004) 44 *ILM* 545.

[42] Antitrust interference is a clear instance of regulatory taking. However, the issue remains whether it could violate national treatment.

provided for certain types of regulatory interference. But, the prior identification of such exceptions is an impossible task, so that exceptions cannot be meaningfully formulated. Too wide an exception will make national treatment meaningless. Too restrictive an exception will not safeguard state interests.

2.1 *Performance requirements and national treatment*

Performance requirements will also be inconsistent with national treatment standards. The imposition of performance requirements, as already explained, is necessitated by the host state's desire to obtain the benefits of the foreign investment to the fullest extent possible. The screening laws of host states enable the imposition of these requirements at the time of entry or at a later stage when the foreign investment project has commenced operation.[43] Many of these requirements constitute the basis of the control that the host state exercises over the foreign investment process.

The requirement that the foreign investor operate only through a locally incorporated joint venture is common in many developing states. So are requirements relating to the hiring of local personnel, the use of local raw materials in the finished product and the export of a percentage of the goods manufactured by the foreign investor.[44] These requirements are intended to secure the advantages of the foreign investment for the host economy. But, the imposition of these requirements will violate national standards of treatment, as they are not imposed on local entrepreneurs. If they are imposed equally on local investors, there can be no valid complaint of discriminatory treatment.[45] Performance requirements are expressly prohibited in many investment treaties. But, this is unnecessary, as the inclusion of national treatment will have this effect because national treatment will certainly be violated if performance requirements are imposed only on foreign investors. Again, technically, it may be possible to exempt the imposition of performance requirements from the scope of national treatment, but this appears not to have been done. The states which in their domestic laws impose performance requirements have not addressed this issue in their investment treaties which grant national treatment.[46] But, it is possible to argue that, where the definition of protected investments in a treaty are those investments made in accordance with the laws and regulations of a state, the treaty does not prohibit the imposition of performance requirements through these laws and regulations. Likewise, there could be other strategies adopted to ensure that performance requirements are not covered by the national treatment standards of the treaty.

In *ADF* v. *United States*,[47] the tribunal found that the performance requirement requiring the use of steel fabricated in the United States may be a violation of the NAFTA provisions

---

[43] The imposition of such requirements at a later stage may amount to an act tantamount to a taking on a wide interpretation that the imposition of performance requirements may affect the profit-making capacity of the venture.

[44] In *ADF* v. *United States*, ICSID Case No. ARB(AF)/00/1 (NAFTA) (Award, 9 January 2003), para. 91, the claimant argued that the 'Buy American' policies in the United States were performance requirements prohibited by NAFTA.

[45] *ADF* v. *United States*, ICSID Case No. ARB(AF)/00/1 (NAFTA) (Award, 9 January 2003).

[46] Where the treaties confine their protection to investments made in accordance with the laws and regulations of the participating states, this issue relating to national treatment may not arise.

[47] *ADF* v. *United States*, ICSID Case No. ARB(AF)/00/1 (NAFTA) (Award, 9 January 2003), para. 161.

seeking to prohibit performance requirements. But, the tribunal went on to hold that the practice was saved by the exception that such performance requirements may be imposed in cases of procurement contracts by any party. The exception applied equally to procurements made by sub-national entities. The tribunal took a dourly positivistic stance in making an exact interpretation of the terms of the treaty, indicating that there will be a reluctance to expand the scope of national treatment in such a manner as to limit the adoption of regulatory policies by a party. Of course, tribunals could differ as to the approach they take, but, in these situations, a strict construction limiting the scope of the treaty to the intention of the parties is justified as it would not upset the balance between liberalisation and regulation which the parties had struck in the treaty.

In economic literature, there is considerable debate as to the value of performance requirements. Investment treaties which prohibit them are based on the view that they distort trade and impose discriminatory standards on foreign investment.[48] The other view is that performance requirements are necessary for economic development. This view is based on the fact that developed countries used such performance requirements in their own progress towards development. This view is that the same techniques of development should not now be denied to developing countries. Performance requirements capture the additional benefits of foreign investment to the host state, and, it is argued, for that reason, their use should be permitted.

2.2 National treatment and infant industries

States may want to protect local entrepreneurs from foreign firms which, because of their dominant size and deep pockets, can run them out of business. Infant industry protection ensures that a state has the right to nurse its local industries to a level where they can withstand competition from foreign sources. This has been used as an argument for tariff protection being given to local firms. Most of the developed states practised such protection for their incipient industries at earlier stages of their development. It is used in international trade as an argument that justifies the differential treatment of developing countries. In the case of foreign investment, since penetration of the market has already taken place, the need for such protection in the face of competition from the foreign investor may be more urgent. The danger would be that the foreign investor could emerge as the dominant entity within the local market after driving out the weak local competition.[49] The granting of national treatment to the foreign investor will deny the state the ability to protect local business, as such protection will be regarded as involving violations of the national standard of treatment. Again, the issue arises as to whether provision must be made for an exception in the case of states treating foreign investors differently because of the need to protect local industries from the competition of foreign investors. Unless the investment treaty so

---

[48] US treaties have favoured prohibiting the use of performance requirements.

[49] The writings of Stiglitz, Ha-Joon Chang and other economists favour the infant-industry protection argument. They believe that these techniques, adopted in their own early stages of development by the developed states, should not be denied to developing states.

provides, there will be a violation of the treaty if the protection given to the local industry is not given to the foreign investors as well. A solution would be to exclude sectors which require protection from the scope of the treaty or to preserve regulatory controls relating to competition and similar factors from the scope of national treatment.

2.3 Subsidies, grants and national treatment

Many treaties, including NAFTA, exclude 'subsidies or grants provided by a Party or a state enterprise, including government-supported loans, guarantees and insurance' from the scope of national treatment.[50]

2.4 Ethnicity and national treatment

There will be difficulty in accommodating laws which give preferences to certain sections of the local population with national treatment to foreign investors. Thus, in South Africa, there is a programme to ensure that a certain percentage of the mining sector is controlled by native South Africans. The Black Empowerment Act is based on the idea that the effects of past discrimination practised against the original people of South Africa should be reversed by a policy of positive discrimination in their favour. There are similar views in other countries, Malaysia being another example. Often, foreign investments are made with minorities which control economic power. Such situations cause friction between ethnic groups within the state and lead to strife. Discriminatory laws may be necessary to deal with such a situation. The perfect market cannot be reconciled with inter-ethnic harmony in many developing countries.[51] Such laws will be difficult to reconcile with national treatment. They are usually dealt with through the provision of exceptions for such laws.

2.5 Conclusion

The thrust of liberalisation has largely focused on national treatment at both the pre-entry and the post-entry phases. But, it would appear that even states that have advocated liberal policies regarding the movement of foreign investment have been reluctant to provide complete national treatment. There is a gap between aspiration and the pragmatic concern that, if fully implemented, national treatment may harm the ability to regulate the economy. That is a concern which is felt by developed countries which, judging by cases like *ADF* v. *United States*, provide for performance requirements and ensure that their programmes are protected through exceptions for government procurement contracts in their treaties. The concern of developing countries in the case of national treatment will be greater as their economies will not be able to withstand competition from foreign investors, unless carefully regulated. For this reason, there will always be a balance maintained between national

---

[50] NAFTA, Article 1108(8).
[51] A. Chua, *World on Fire: How Exporting Free Market Democracy Breeds Ethnic Hatred and Global Instability* (2003).

treatment and the ability to regulate the entry and subsequent operation of the foreign investment. How the balance is struck in the different treaties is a matter that the parties decide and, judging by awards such as *ADF* v. *United States*, the language of the treaties will be construed carefully in determining the extent of the national treatment that is permitted.

3. International minimum standard treatment

Chapter 4 dealt with the division of views among states as to the existence of an international minimum standard of treatment.[52] That division has continued into modern times, and it cannot be said with certainty that there is an international minimum standard of treatment of foreign investment in customary international law, the violation of which results in state responsibility. The content of this international minimum standard as far as foreign investment is concerned is also difficult to identify. But, where there is a treaty on investment which makes reference to an international minimum standard, the treaty conclusively establishes the existence of the standard as between the parties. Thus, in *ADF* v. *United States*,[53] the tribunal said that the relevant provision in NAFTA on the international minimum standard, Article 1105(1), 'clarifies that so far as the three NAFTA Parties are concerned, the long-standing debate as to whether there exists such a thing as a minimum standard of treatment of non-nationals and their property prescribed in customary international law, is closed'.[54] The view is a repetition of what the tribunal in *Mondev* v. *United States*[55] had stated. It is an acceptance of the view that there is a customary international law at variance with that claimed to exist by states which have participated in the treaties[56] and have created obligations as between themselves as to the existence of an international minimum standard of treatment. Impliedly, it accepts the possibility of the existence of two sets of customary international law, one recognising the existence of an international minimum standard and the other not. There were very few norms of property protection developed as international minimum standards. Most of them dealt with the treatment of the physical person of the alien. The tribunals were conscious of the fact that a gap had to be filled between cases in the first half of the twentieth century, which dealt with the protection of the physical person of the alien through the creation of an international minimum standard, and the modern treaties, which seek to extend that concept to investment protection.[57] The issue will always be whether such a mandate to fill this gap was intentionally given to arbitral tribunals.

Tribunals have asserted that they do have a creative function to perform. They have stated that the concept of an international minimum standard is not a static one but is capable of

---

[52] See further A. O. Adede, 'The Minimum Standards in a World of Disputes', in R. St J. MacDonald and S. Johnston (eds.), *The Structure and Process of International Law* (1986), p. 1001.

[53] *ADF* v. *United States*, ICSID Case No. ARB(AF)/00/1 (NAFTA) (Award, 9 January 2003), para. 178.

[54] J. C. Thomas, 'Reflections on Article 1105 of NAFTA' (2002) 17 *ICSID Rev* 21.

[55] *Mondev* v. *United States* (2003) 42 *ILM* 85. Para. 120 reads: '[I]t is clear that Article 1105 was intended to put at rest for NAFTA purposes a long-standing and divisive debate about whether any such thing as a minimum standard of treatment of investment in international law actually exists. Article 1105 resolves this issue in the affirmative for NAFTA Parties.'

[56] This is certainly the case for Mexico, which has historically opposed the existence of an international minimum standard. Prior to NAFTA, Mexico had not signed any investment treaties.

[57] The *Mondev* tribunal acknowledged that the awards in the 1920s, on the basis of which the international minimum standard was built, 'applied to the physical security of an alien'. *Mondev* v. *United States* (2003) 42 *ILM* 85, para. 116.

being developed in a modern context.[58] The difficulty in this approach is whether the tribunal will perform a near-legislative function, which it has consistently stated it does not have,[59] in identifying areas of international minimum standard. The content of the international minimum standard, when it comes to investment protection, will always be problematic. One knows that there is such a standard, but what the standard contains and what its modern limits are, are unclear.

There are three instances in which the old cases on state responsibility may provide guidance as to the international minimum standard. These relate to compensation for expropriation, responsibility for destruction or violence by non-state actors, and denial of justice. In the context of investment treaties, the relevance of the provision on international minimum standards outside these three areas is to be doubted. Of these three areas, two are separately provided for in almost all investment treaties. Compensation for expropriation forms the centrepiece of any investment treaty. There would usually be a lengthy article stating the circumstances relating to a legal taking and the standard of compensation to be paid for such taking. Responsibility for destruction by non-state actors is also specifically provided for in the provision which requires 'full protection and security'. This leaves only denial of justice, a concept directed at misconduct by the judicial organs of a state from which state responsibility arises. The classic situation of a denial of justice is where the judicial organs of a state acted in a definite and grossly excessive manner that indicated a clear injustice evident to any reasonable observer. It is not an ordinary error of law which courts often commit but such an excessive error as to invite condemnation. One can see that the definition abounds with uncertain criteria with ordinary error and excessive error not being clearly distinguishable. Denial of justice is a nebulous notion, and has seldom been the basis of an award, because of the extreme reluctance of tribunals to find that judicial organs of states had acted improperly.

The rule was that the judicial impropriety had to be of such a degree as to shock the conscience. The standard of misconduct is described by using negative superlatives which require an inordinate degree of deviance on the part of the judicial organs of the state before responsibility in the state can arise.[60] There has been a reluctance on the part of tribunals to find such a degree of impropriety as would justify the imposition of state responsibility. One has to struggle to find a role here for the international minimum standard as stated in treaties. The international minimum standard is then a concept that contains a limitation because treaties limit its meaning to the circumstances in which it was recognised in customary international law as conceived by the principal capital-exporting states.

The United States had assiduously built up the idea of an international minimum standard.[61] When confronted with the use of the standard against itself, the United States has argued that a claimant alleging the violation of the standard should show the violation of a specific rule of

---

[58] This view is stated in *ADF* v. *United States*, ICSID Case No. ARB(AF)/00/1 (NAFTA) (Award, 9 January 2003), para. 180, citing *Mondev* with approval.

[59] NAFTA tribunals have done so when considering the interpretative statement of the NAFTA Commission.

[60] For a recent statement, see *Azinian* v. *Mexico* (1998) 5 *ICSID Reports* 269, paras. 102–3.

[61] The international minimum standard can be clearly traced in US practice. The early commentators on the practice supporting such a standard were US scholars. Though its statement in the texts on international law is widespread, it is a doctrine whose roots lie in US practice.

customary international law incorporated in the international minimum standard.[62] Despite the fact that the *Mondev* tribunal was effusive in describing the increasing spread of investment treaties, these treaties cannot contribute to the identification of the content of an international minimum standard, as none of the treaties seeks to describe the content of this standard.[63] They merely make reference to the standard. The tribunal's assertion that this numerical explosion of treaties must have some meaning hardly gives content to the standard.[64] The number of repetitions of the same notion is immaterial if the content of it is not identified. Emptiness multiplied several times over can still produce only emptiness. The paucity of content in the international minimum standard outside the three areas, two of which are separately provided for in treaties, cannot be rectified by the mere fact of its repetition in a growing number of investment treaties.[65] The fact is that, even in the customary international law, which was developed in cases like the *Neer Claim*,[66] the content of the international minimum standard outside the abuse of the physical security of the alien was minimal. The grafting of the idea onto a system of property protection is recent, and the uncomfortable fact is that the content of the standard is yet to be identified. It is unhelpful to suggest that the lapse in the system of identification of a standard can be rectified by having recourse to general principles of law.[67] Neither is it helpful to say that these standards have 'an evolutionary potential'. The question is how they are to evolve and what guidance is to be had and from whom as to their evolution. On property protection, it would be extremely difficult for these standards to evolve from general principles, for, as between the Western legal systems, the principles of property protection vary so markedly that it would be difficult to identify common norms that could be passed off as general principles.

There has been an effort in recent times, both in awards[68] as well as in academic literature, to lower the threshold of the international minimum standard. Whereas the *Neer Claim*, decided in 1926, had required a high standard for denial of justice to be established, on the basis of language used in the *ELSI Case*, it has been suggested that the violation of the standard through a denial of justice need not be of an inordinately high level. There is no indication that the International Court of Justice in *ELSI* sought to signify a change. Yet, its statement of the standard is used as the peg to hang the change. It is suggested that, in modern times, the standard of injustice needed to find a denial of justice is lower. Why that should be so is not explained. Presumably, the desire for property protection trumps the traditional view that there should be no easy finding of a denial of justice. Such a finding

---

[62] *ADF* v. *United States*, ICSID Case No. ARB(AF)/00/1 (NAFTA) (Award, 9 January 2003), para. 182.

[63] This is based on the personal study of African and Asian treaties.

[64] The *Mondev* tribunal, (2003) 42 *ILM* 85, para. 117, said: 'It would be surprising if this practice and the vast number of provisions it reflects were to be interpreted as meaning no more than the *Neer* Tribunal (in a very different context) meant in 1927.'

[65] The present count puts the number at an inordinately high level. There is no indication that the International Court of Justice in *ELSI* sought to signify a change. UNCTAD, *World Investment Report, 2003*.

[66] (1926) 4 *UNRIAA* 60. None of the other cases popularly associated with minimum standards involved the protection of property. *Roberts Claim* (1926) 4 *UNRIAA* 77; *Chevreau Case* (1931) 27 *AJIL* 153.

[67] The suggestion appears in footnote 176 to *ADF* v. *United States*, ICSID Case No. ARB(AF)/00/1 (NAFTA) (Award, 9 January 2003).

[68] For example, *Mondev* v. *United States* (2003) 42 *ILM* 85 initiated this trend. It was not the view taken by the states involved. The view rests entirely on the opinions of individual arbitrators. In *Saluka Investments* v. *Czech Republic* (Award, 17 March 2006), the Czech Republic also supported the view that *Neer* represented the law. This is the view of states as opposed to those of arbitrators.

would convert an investment tribunal virtually into an appellate body entrusted with the task of scrutinising domestic law to find an injustice. A tribunal may not be competent to perform such a task. Neither would the parties have intended it to perform such an appellate task. Yet, the prevailing sentiment seems to favour the tribunal performing such a task.[69]

Some tribunals seem inclined to accept the US view, stated in the context of its new-found role as a respondent in litigation involving foreign investment, that, when a violation of an international minimum standard is alleged, there must be a specific violation of the standard that is identified in terms of customary international law. In other words, there is no scope for creating new categories of violation of these standards by tribunals outside existing customary international law. Since the international minimum standard was created almost entirely by the practice of the United States, this view must be given considerable weight. Whatever creative role an international tribunal may have in treaty interpretation, when considering the international minimum standard, there is a limiting factor provided by the alleged rules of customary international law, the existence of which the treaty parties accept.

If it were not for this limiting factor, arbitrators could adopt expansionary views as to the content of the international minimum standard. Earlier cases such as *Metalclad* v. *Mexico* indicated the potential for such an expansionary view. It is for this reason that Canada and Mexico intervened in later disputes against the United States to support the view that there is a limitation to the effect that a specific rule of pre-existing customary international law must be shown to have been violated. There must be a pigeonhole into which the case can fall. The difficulty with this approach is that, outside expropriation, there seems to be no identifiable pigeonhole apart from denial of justice into which an allegation of violation of the international minimum standard could be fitted. The brave face that the *Mondev* tribunal put on the concept not being static sounds hollow if the specific rules of the standard cannot be identified. It is for this reason that the more expansive formulation contained in treaties relating to the 'fair and equitable standard' of treatment becomes important. They hold out the possibility, as some claimants have argued on the basis of limited academic writing, that it is a standard that is additional to existing standards of customary international law. This view, though originally triumphant, has now been beaten back.

Some of the beating back of that view is attributable to the views taken by the United States. When, in *Pope and Talbot* and other NAFTA cases,[70] the argument was raised that the fair and equitable standard was a ceiling, referring to a higher standard, and that the international minimum standard was the floor, indicating a lower minimum standard, the NAFTA parties disagreed. They sought an interpretation from the NAFTA tribunal that the fair and equitable standard was pegged to the international minimum standard. The NAFTA tribunal gave an interpretation which accorded with the views of the NAFTA parties. The US model investment treaty of 2004 ties the fair and equitable standard to the international

---

[69] In *International Thunderbird Gaming Corporation* v. *Mexico*, UNCITRAL (NAFTA) Arbitration Proceedings (Award, 26 January 2006), the tribunal referred to the *Neer* standard without any effort to reduce the standard.

[70] In *Pope and Talbot* v. *Canada* (2002) 41 *ILM* 1347, the tribunal showed an inclination towards the view first stated by Francis Mann that the fair and equitable standard was a higher standard. While the case was pending, the NAFTA Commission issued its Interpretative Note saying this was not the case.

minimum standard, much to the dismay of some US commentators. But, the formula is now used not only in US treaties but also in other investment treaties as well. It puts an end to the incipient expansionary notions that some arbitrators were embarking on. It is appropriate to consider the fair and equitable standard next, as it has a link with the international minimum standard in modern treaties.

4. Fair and equitable standard of treatment

Many investment treaties provide that a fair and equitable standard of treatment is to be provided to investors and their investments, in addition to the international minimum standard and full protection and security. The content of this clearly nebulous provision has become a focal point of discussion, particularly as claimants have placed emphasis on this standard of treatment in NAFTA litigation. As the possibility of establishing expropriation has become more difficult, there has been an effort to shift liability into an as-yet-unexplored standard that appears in most investment treaties. There are two general views. The first is that the fair and equitable standard does not add anything more to the international minimum standard but merely affirms it.[71] The second is that the fair and equitable standard expands the scope of the international minimum standard by allowing future tribunals to create new standards when the situation demands, so that justice may be done for the foreign investor who suffers unfair treatment at the hands of the host state.[72] It is an autonomous standard which absorbs arbitrary conduct injurious to the foreign investor.

The expansive view would mean that any discriminatory measure that the host state adopts could be regarded as offensive to the standard of fair and equitable treatment. It has been used in circumstances where transparency as to laws or intentions were shown to be lacking.[73] The more expansive notion is that the standard is violated if assurances giving rise to a legitimate expectation in the foreign investor are violated. The possibility of such expansion was clearly the approach of the World Bank Guidelines which made reference to the standard.[74]

Until NAFTA, despite the fact that the phrase has been used in a large number of treaties, it had not been analysed by any tribunal because it was not made the basis of any claim. Vasciannie observed, in 1999, that 'the pronounced reliance on the fair and equitable standard in treaties has not been matched by judicial consideration of the meaning of the

---

[71] S. Vasciannie, 'The Fair and Equitable Standard in International Investment Law and Practice' (1999) 70 *BYIL* 99 at 104. The origin of the phrase is usually traced to the OECD Convention of 1967. The OECD at that time supported the narrow view, and regarded the fair and equitable standard as not distinct from the international minimum standard. OECD, 'Council Resolution on the Draft Convention for the Protection of Foreign Property' (1967) 7 *ILM* 117. But, it took the opposite, expansive view when the MAI came to be drafted in 1998.

[72] The most expansionary of these views is the one taken by Francis Mann, that it is a standard above and beyond the international minimum standard of treatment and is distinct from any existing international law. This view, stated in 1981, could not have anticipated the manner in which it was later employed in NAFTA litigation. F. A. Mann, 'British Treaties for the Promotion and Protection of Foreign Investment' (1981) 52 *BYIL* 241. Mann's analysis was based on the UK treaty with the Philippines. He spoke of the standard as involving an 'overriding obligation' which not only prohibited discriminatory treatment but embraced within it other standards of treatment as 'specific instances of this overriding duty'.

[73] *Metalclad* v. *Mexico* (2000) 5 *ICSID Reports* 209; (2001) 40 *ILM* 55. [74] Guideline III (2).

standard in particular cases'.[75] But, in several of the NAFTA cases, commencing in almost the same year, the phrase has been the focus of the claims. In the early litigation under NAFTA, there was a clear preference for the expansive interpretation of the phrase. This would increase the ability of NAFTA tribunals to review every act of the state against standards, which do not have a definite content or a reference point against which their validity could be tested. It would enable the tribunals to create new law binding on the parties. The tribunals had set themselves on such a course.

In the intervening period from 1999 to the present, arbitral tribunals have sought to fill what was a vacuous concept with a new meaning quite unintended by the parties at the time of the making of the treaties. In *Metalclad* v. *Mexico*, the absence of transparency in the rules applicable to the circumstances in which licences were granted was said to violate the standard. Expansive language was used as to the obligation to ensure that laws, regulations and administrative rulings are promptly made available to the foreign investor.[76] A British Columbia court reviewed the award at the instance of Mexico. Canada supported the application for review made to the court by Mexico. The British Columbia court ruled that the transparency requirement was not inherent in the Article 1105 formulation of fair and equitable standards by reference to customary international law but was imported from outside the investment provisions of Chapter 11 of NAFTA.[77] The court therefore ruled that there was an excess of jurisdiction in the finding that the transparency requirement was a part of Article 1105's reference to fair and equitable standards. The court also ruled that the finding on treatment also affected the finding on expropriation on the basis of the cancellation of the licence. The court, however, upheld the *Metalclad* tribunal's finding that the Mexican decree involved in the dispute amounted to an expropriation. The decision of the British Columbia court strikes a blow against the expansive interpretation of the standard of fair and equitable treatment. But, events since the judgment have shown that the adherents of the expansionary view were in no way deterred.

The NAFTA provisions on investment were generally regarded as being aimed at Mexico, the developing-country partner in the regional association. The impact of the *Metalclad* award was not as evident as when the NAFTA provisions came to be used against Canada and the United States, challenging their regulatory legislation as inconsistent with the standard of fair and equitable treatment. The reaction of the states was then to secure a limitation on the possibility of tribunals using expansive theories of fairness and equity to scrutinise the validity of their regulatory schemes affecting foreign investment.

S. D. Myers v. *Canada*[78] demonstrated the possibilities of a NAFTA tribunal sitting in judgment on the regulatory schemes of the parties. The case involved Canadian export prohibitions of hazardous waste material for disposal in the United States. S. D. Myers, a US company which alone carried out such waste disposal by exporting the waste to its plants in

---

[75] S. Vasciannie, 'The Fair and Equitable Standard in International Investment Law and Practice' (1999) 70 *BYIL* 99 at 162.
[76] Paras. 76 and 99. Mexico failed to ensure a transparent and predictable framework for Metalclad's business planning and investment. The totality of these circumstances demonstrates 'a lack of orderly process and timely disposition in relation to an investor of a party acting in the expectation that it would be treated fairly and justly in accordance with NAFTA.'
[77] The transparency provision that the tribunal referred to is in Article 1802, which does not form part of Chapter 11.
[78] *S. D. Myers* v. *Canada* (2000) 40 *ILM* 1408; (2002) 121 *ILR* 7.

Ohio, argued that the prohibition was discriminatory and violated both national treatment and the fair and equitable standard of treatment. The claimant ascribed the prohibition to the Canadian interest in promoting the Canadian waste disposal industry. The tribunal found a violation of both the national treatment standard and the fair and equitable treatment standard. However, it limited violations of the fair and equitable standard to situations in which there was arbitrary treatment that was 'unacceptable from an international perspective'. The *Myers* tribunal was conscious of the need to limit the scope of the standard to violations of customary international law. It was conscious of the reference to the limiting words in Article 1105 ('in accordance with international law') when construing the extent of the standard. But, this caution was cast to the winds in *Pope and Talbot* v. *Canada*.[79]

Pope and Talbot involved a consideration of whether the implementation by regulation of a softwood lumber agreement between the United States and Canada through permits allocating quotas was a violation of the treatment standards of NAFTA. The tribunal made three separate awards. The first award was an interim award which dealt with issues of whether the right of access to lumber markets in the United States was an investment and whether regulatory measures could amount to expropriation. The tribunal concluded in the interim award that the regulatory measure involved did not amount to an expropriation. That award ruled out a claim on expropriation and left the only possibility of liability to arise from the violation of the treatment standards.

The second award found that the system did not discriminate between domestic and foreign investors. Hence, the regulation did not violate the national treatment standard. It then went on to consider whether Article 1105, which refers to treatment 'in accordance with international law, including fair and equitable treatment and full protection and security', was violated. The issue that arose for interpretation was whether the reference to fairness was over and above the international minimum standard that was required by international law. The tribunal accepted that the language of Article 1105 'suggested otherwise', but that it was possible to read the phrase as requiring a standard higher than the international minimum standard as having an 'additive character'.[80] On this view, the fair and equitable standard would be a higher standard than the international minimum standard.

When it came to the identification of the contents of the standard, the tribunal relied heavily on the policy objectives behind NAFTA, which was to 'create the kind of hospitable climate that would insulate [investors] from political risks or incidents of unfair treatment'. One might think that that was also the purpose behind the creation of the international minimum standard as well, and indeed of all investment treaties. Yet, having created this platform which the tribunal thought was unique to the fair and equitable standard, it went on to hold that existing precedents on the content of the international minimum standard did not contain any limitations on the standard of fairness. After so concluding, the tribunal found that Canada had not breached any obligation except in connection with the 'verification review process' administered by one division. In this respect, the tribunal found that the

---

[79] *Pope and Talbot* v. *Canada*, NAFTA/UNCITRAL Tribunal (26 January 2000) (2002) 41 *ILM* 1347.
[80] Para. 110 of the second award.

claimant was subjected to threats, was denied information, was obliged to incur unnecessary expense in obtaining information, was obliged to expend legal fees, suffered as a result of reviews not being conducted in the most convenient place,[81] and suffered loss of reputation in government circles.[82] Such conduct went 'well beyond the glitches and innocent mistakes that may typify the process' and amounted to a violation of the fair and equitable standard. After finding this violation, the tribunal announced that the third award would deal with the issue of the damages to be paid to the claimant. It can be readily seen that the tribunal claimed wide jurisdiction to examine the details of the domestic procedures that were used in a state that had an advanced system of administrative justice that was subject to review by an experienced supreme court. Clearly, the reasoning would have given investment arbitral tribunals wide control over administrative decisions within the state.

Prior to the third award,[83] the NAFTA Commission delivered its 'Notes of Interpretation of Certain Chapter 11 Provisions'. It stated that the 'concepts of "fair and equitable treatment" and "full protection and security" do not require treatment in addition to or beyond that which is required by the customary international law minimum standard of treatment of aliens'. The tribunal was, as a result, faced with having to assess the impact of this interpretative note on its second award. The tribunal doubted whether the note was an interpretation or an amendment of the article. It also doubted that it could have retroactive effect. The tribunal reconsidered the interpretation of the fair and equitable standard, and took the view that it could not be a static concept frozen in a manner stated in the *Neer Claim*. But, having said that, it failed to spell out the content of the new standard, other than repeating the official commentary to the OECD's Draft Convention in 1967 that the standard requires treatment 'at least as good as that accorded by a state to its own investors'.[84] Since this formulation makes the standard no different from post-entry national treatment which is contained in most investment treaties, the inclusion of the standard on the meaning so attributed becomes as much a surplusage as it is to say that it is the same as the international minimum standard. The tribunal reaffirmed its view that the manner in which the verification review took place violated the standards of fair and equitable treatment. Having done so, the damages awarded were paltry, reflecting the expenses involved in the verification review and the expenses of the hearing on interim measures.[85]

The tribunal in *Pope and Talbot* may have made a bold attempt to breathe content into the fair and equitable standard, but it will be opposed by states simply because of the fact that the creators of the standard themselves are faced with the constant threat of their regulatory structures being reviewed by international tribunals. Tellingly, the tribunal in *Pope and Talbot* examined the *travaux préparatoires* of the treatment provisions in NAFTA and found no indication of the meaning attributed to the term by the interpretative note of the NAFTA Commission. The purpose of introducing the fair and equitable standard was clearly to broaden the scope of the standards beyond what was required in the international minimum

---

[81] Which in this case was outside Canada, in Portland, Oregon.   [82] Second award, para. 181.
[83] The second award was made on 10 April 2001. The note of the NAFTA Commission was released on 31 July 2001. The third award was made on 31 May 2002.
[84] The difficulty with the approach is that the national investor is confined to the courts of the state, whereas the foreign investor can invoke arbitration overseas which seems to hold the state to a higher and moving standard.
[85] The total amount awarded was US$461,566. Canada has sought a review of the award before its federal courts.

standard in international law. There was little authority for expanding the scope of the minimum standard beyond the twentieth-century cases, particularly in relation to property protection. It may well be that a need was felt by capital-exporting states to create a more embracing standard to give protection to their investors. But, when the technique of protection was turned against them, the situation became uncomfortable and there was a need for a quick back-tracking, leading to the exposure of the implications of the efforts in *Pope and Talbot*.

Initially, it seemed unlikely that other tribunals will take an expansionist view of the fair and equitable standard.[86] In one of the first ICSID cases in which the standard was made the focus of the litigation, the tribunal took the view that was taken by the NAFTA Commission well before the Commission issued its note, indicating that the Commission was not without support in law for taking the view it did. *Genin* v. *Estonia*[87] also involved a challenge to the exercise of regulatory control. The allegation was that the revocation of a banking licence violated the fair and equitable standard in the United States–Estonia investment treaty, which is similar to Chapter 11 of NAFTA.[88] The tribunal was sensitive to the fact that the regulation took place in a nascent economy unused to the exercise of such controls in a vital economic sector. Once such an approach is adopted, the subjectivities involved in the situation make the fairness standard not a universal standard but a movable standard depending on the circumstances.[89] The tribunal also recognised the primacy of the regulatory laws of the host state and the need for the foreign investor to comply with them. The general provisions of an investment treaty cannot obviously negate the thrust of the specific regulatory laws intended to deal with problems in the economy.[90] The tribunal did not think that discriminatory treatment was always significant, unless of course it could amount to a violation of national treatment.[91] Referring to the content of the fair and equitable standard, the tribunal stated:[92]

While the exact content of this standard is not clear, the Tribunal understands it to require an 'international minimum standard' that is separate from domestic law, but that is, indeed, a minimum standard. Acts that would violate this minimum standard would include acts showing a wilful neglect of duty, an insufficiency of action falling far below international standards or even subjective bad faith.

---

[86] In the preliminary award in *UPS* v. *Canada*, para. 97, it was stated that the fair and equitable standard was not an addition to the international minimum standard. The Interpretative Note of the Commission was held not to be necessary to arrive at such a result. The side letters attached to the Singapore–United States Free Trade Agreement indicate that treatment standards are to be read in light of customary international law. For the text, see www.ustr.gov/new/fta/Singapore/final.htm.

[87] *Genin* v. *Estonia* (2002) 17 *ICSID Rev* 395.

[88] Chapter 11 is in reality the model investment treaty of the United States cobbled into NAFTA.

[89] To quote: '[T]he Tribunal considers it imperative to recall the particular context in which the dispute arose, namely, that of a renascent independent state, coming rapidly to grips with the reality of modern financial, commercial and banking practices and the emergence of state institutions responsible for overseeing and regulating areas of activity perhaps previously unknown.' Para. 31.

[90] Para. 36.

[91] Para. 51. Citing authority, it suggested that discriminatory treatment by itself did not offend customary international law, though it would violate national treatment. See further *CME* v. *Czech Republic*, UNCITRAL Arbitration Proceedings (Award, 14 March 2003) and *Lauder* v. *Czech Republic*, UNCITRAL Arbitration Proceedings (Final Award, 3 September 2001), available on the website of the Department of Finance of the Czech government.

[92] Para. 50.

Of the three instances given, wilful neglect of duty and insufficiency of action falling below international standards are clearly traceable to the customary international minimum standard. They are extensions of principles in cases like the *Neer Claim* to the situation of property protection. The third – subjective bad faith – is without authority. The tribunal found that the standard of fairness is the same as the minimum standard, but it too had difficulty giving content to the two standards. In any event, the tribunal found no violation of any standard of treatment. It accepted the respondent state's explanation that 'the circumstances of political and economic transition prevailing in Estonia at the time justified heightened scrutiny of the banking sector', again affirming the relevance of the context of each situation.

4.1 *Violation of legitimate expectations*

In 1999, the United Nations Commission on Trade and Development (UNCTAD) published a survey on bilateral investment treaties, in which it stated, referring to the fair and equitable standard, that 'there is little authority on its application'.[93] But, since then, there has been an independent development of the fair and equitable standard in some ICSID awards, stressing particularly the notion of legitimate expectations of the foreign investor at the time of entry of the investment.[94] The development in this line of cases is that there could be liability for breach of the fair and equitable standard in circumstances where the assurances made to the foreign investor both in the contract as well as in non-contractual documents, in the law of the host state[95] and even possibly verbal communications of high officials of the state that give rise to legitimate expectations in the foreign investor. The course of development of this notion requires analysis, as it seems clearly to be an extension that has been made through arbitral jurisprudence. As one commentator put it, it can be traced to awards that were made in the last few years.[96]

Sometimes, it is said that the idea is drawn from domestic legal systems and that it is a general principle of the law.[97] But, as a general principle, legitimate expectations provides only procedural protection, requiring that an expectation created by administrative conduct

---

[93] UNCTAD, *Bilateral Investment Treaties in the Mid-1990s* (1998), p. 54.
[94] *Metalclad* v. *Mexico* (2000) 5 *ICSID Reports* 209; (2001) 40 *ILM* 55; *Tecmed* v. *Mexico* (2006) 10 *ICSID Reports* 54; *MTD* v. *Chile* (2007) 12 *ICSID Reports* 6; *Occidental* v. *Ecuador*, London Court of International Arbitration (Award, 1 July 2004); *CMS Gas Transmission Co* v. *Argentina* (2003) 30 *ILM* 788; (2005) 44 *ILM* 1205; *Waste Management* v. *Mexico* (2001) 40 *ILM* 56; *International Thunderbird Gaming Corporation* v. *Mexico*, UNCITRAL (NAFTA) Arbitration Proceedings (Award, 26 January 2006); *Saluka Investments* v. *Czech Republic* (Award, 17 March 2006); *LG&E Energy Corporation* v. *Argentina* (2007) 46 *ILM* 36; *Enron Corporation* v. *Argentina*, ICSID Case No. ARB/01/03 (Award, 22 May 2007); *Sempra Energy International* v. *Argentina*, ICSID Case No. ARB/02/16 (Award, 28 September 2007); *Bayinder Insaat Turizm Ticaret ve Sanayi* v. *Pakistan*, ICSID Case No. ARB/03/29 (2005); and *Parkerings-Compagniet AS* v. *Lithuania*, ICSID Case No. ARB/05/8 (Award, 11 September 2007).
[95] *LG&E Energy Corporation* v. *Argentina* (2007) 46 *ILM* 36, para. 130.
[96] C. Schreuer, 'Fair and Equitable Treatment in Arbitral Practice' (2005) 6 *Journal of World Investment and Trade* 357; R. Dolzer, 'Fair and Equitable Standard: Key Standard in Investment Treaties' (2005) 39 *International Lawyer* 87; I. Tudor, *Fair and Equitable Standard in the International Law of Foreign Investment* (2008).
[97] See F. Orrego Vicuña, 'Foreign Investment Law: How Customary Is Custom?' (2005) *ASIL Proceedings* 98, who compared it with English law principles: '"[F]air and equitable treatment" is not really different from the legitimate expectations doctrine as developed, for example, by the English courts and also recently by the World Bank Administrative Tribunal.' But, in English law, the notion of legitimate expectations is a rule of procedure requiring that a hearing be given if an expectation is to be violated. This is a clear misunderstanding of the English law. Professor Orrego Vicuña has sat as arbitrator in a large number of

should not be violated unless a hearing is given to the person who had that expectation. The principle has rarely been used as a substantive principle because of practical difficulties. Governments make assurances as to policies on taxation, agriculture and other areas. Administration would become difficult if, at each change of policy to suit new circumstances, the state has to pay damages to affected parties. It is an error to state that there is a general principle of law that violations of legitimate expectations give rise to substantive remedies. That does not appear to be the case, in English law at any rate. It is unlikely that such a rule can be maintained in any system. Yet, it is precisely such a rule that has been developed in the recent ICSID cases which declare it to be a substantive rule, justifying the award of damages for its breach.

The breadth of the rule stated in some awards is staggering and could not have been agreed to by the states concluding the treaties. There are statements that the standard requires stable conditions to be maintained so that the foreign investor could obtain profits through the life of the investment.[98] It is as if a stabilisation clause is read into every contract. In other cases, what is protected is in effect the foreign investment contract or some informal contract that is brought about by assurances. Parties did not make the treaty to provide for contractual protection. There are problems even with the umbrella clause. But, the effect of the interpretation of the fair and equitable clause as an autonomous, free-standing provision protecting foreign investment is that a rule of protection extending beyond the contractual protection is created.[99] This goes well beyond the intention of the parties.

The reaction of the NAFTA parties to this expansionary view has been noted. The view is maintained that the NAFTA position does not extend to other investment treaties which do not tie the fair and equitable standard to customary international law. But, many of the newer treaties do contain such tying provisions.[100] *Gami Industries v. United States* is one of the recent NAFTA cases to decide the issue. The award dealt with fair and equitable treatment, and considered the existing non-NAFTA cases as well. It agreed, not surprisingly, with the view that there was no independent standard of fair and equitable treatment outside customary law.

cases contributing to the views on legitimate expectations. For the English law on the subject, see P. Craig, *Administrative Law* (5th edn, 2005), pp. 639–56. The one case in English law in which legitimate expectations were held to create a substantive principle has since been distinguished by subsequent cases. *R. v. North and East Devon Health Authority, ex parte Coughlan* [2001] QB 213. The extension in *Coughlan* was explained in later cases as follows: 'Here lies the importance of the fact in the *Coughlan* case that few individuals were affected by the promise in question. The case's facts may be discrete and limited, having no implications for an innominate class of persons. There may be no wide-ranging issues of general policy or none with multi-layered effects, upon whose merits the court is asked to embark.' *Begum v. Returning Officer for the London Borough of Tower Hamlets* [2006] EWCA Civ 733 (para. 68, citing and approving earlier *dicta*). It is evident that courts will not don the garb of the policy-maker and determine the correctness of policies. Craig also wrote a work on *European Union Administrative Law* (2006), in which he considered the position in European law. He pointed out that the European Court of Justice would balance overriding public interests with the expectations of individuals (*ibid.*, p. 649). It is unlikely that, in matters of general public interest, the individual interest could override the policy decisions a state takes.

[98] In *Occidental*, the tribunal required 'stability of the legal and business framework' as part of the fair and equitable standard. *Occidental v. Ecuador*, London Court of International Arbitration (Award, 1 July 2004), para. 183. In *CMS*, the tribunal required 'a stable framework'. *CMS Gas Transmission Co v. Argentina* (2003) 30 *ILM* 788; (2005) 44 *ILM* 1205.

[99] In the Argentine cases (*CMS Gas Transmission Co v. Argentina* (2003) 30 *ILM* 788; (2005) 44 *ILM* 1205; *Siemens v. Argentina* ICSID Case No. ARB/02/8), what were in effect protected through the notion of legitimate expectations were the contractual or quasi-contractual commitments made to the foreign investor.

[100] Apart from the model treaties of the US and Canada, newer treaties like the ASEAN Comprehensive Agreement on Investment (2009) refer to the standard in the context of customary law. This is strange, as the ASEAN states had little custom on the issue. But, see also the Indian treaties and the Chinese treaties. For China, see N. Gallagher and W. Shan, *Chinese Investment Treaties: Policy and Practice* (2009).

The NAFTA episode is instructive in that states will not permit intrusive supervision of their regulatory mechanisms by international tribunals on the pretext of inquiring into the fairness of the use of the regulation. The approach of the ICSID tribunal in *Genin* v. *Estonia* indicates that many tribunals will be loath to pass judgment on the regulatory mechanisms and their use. They would prefer to let each state be the judge of the manner in which such mechanisms are employed, unless there is such a gross violation of procedural norms that shocks the sense of justice.[101] The adventurism in building up new rules of what are regarded as standards of governance through fair and equitable treatment collides with other notions such as the rule that the foreign investor must take the rules of a state as he finds them.[102] In any event, if there have been administrative faults, the domestic system would afford the opportunity for its correction. Unless there had been recourse to these methods, it is difficult to see responsibility arising, except in a situation of denial of justice. If the latter is the case, then the situation of denial of justice is already captured within the international minimum standard.

Tribunals, however, have continued to develop the fair and equitable standard, despite the resistance of states. They have searched widely for support for the construction of the law through the fair and equitable standard in notions of good faith, transparency and expectations of consistency.[103] They have looked for it in even-handedness and justice,[104] forgetting the fact, that in similar circumstances, the national investor is not so protected. But, states as well as other agencies have resisted the idea that liability should be imposed and the regulatory powers of the state be stymied through the creation of doctrines that have no basis in the treaty itself or in the intention of the parties.

This is evident from *Biwater Gauff* v. *Tanzania*, which involved an investment in water supply. It ran into problems during the performance of the contract. The minister responsible had made adverse comments as to the operation of the investor. The tribunal held that these ministerial statements provided the context for the decline of the relationship between the investor and the government,[105] and held that there was a violation of the fair and equitable standard. These awards open up considerable uncertainty as to the scope of responsibility.

Despite brave assertions that the law on state responsibility for injuries to aliens has not remained static, there has been little demonstration as to the basis of how this law is to be extended to protect foreign investment or what the content of the law is. Merely to assert that tribunals can recognise a violation when they see it, does not take the law any further. Though treaties have used an abundance of standards, the extent of the protection they create is a matter of uncertainty because of the paucity of jurisprudence and the difficulty of identifying the content of these standards. Now that Canada and the United States have retreated on assertions of new and expansive standards, the area may return to the quiescence of the past. Their attitude, as the principal backers of both the international minimum

---

[101] The latter situation would be accommodated within denial of justice.
[102] C. McLachlan, L. Shore and M. Weiniger, *International Investment Arbitration: Substantive Principles* (2007), p. 236 citing the *Oscar Chinn Case* (1934) PCIJ Series A/B No. 63.
[103] *Tecmed* v. *Mexico* (2006) 10 *ICSID Reports* 54.   [104] *MTD* v. *Chile* (2007) 12 *ICSID Reports* 6.
[105] Compare *Ethyl* v. *Canada*, where a ministerial statement was alleged to result in depreciation of the shares of the claimant, and hence to amount to expropriation.

standard and the fair and equitable standard in treaty practice, will deprive the latter standard of any content, if it indeed did have any. In light of these developments, it would be difficult to view the fair and equitable standard as distinct from the international minimum standard which was created in customary international law largely on the basis of US practice in Latin America. The NAFTA cases also reiterate the idea that the practice that they apply is confined to the region, leaving the old conflicts on the subject alive in the rest of the world. But, the NAFTA developments have not been mirrored under other investment treaties where standards continue to be interpreted expansively by tribunals. As the NAFTA states did, other states are also bound to react. Such reaction is evidenced by, for example, the omission of the fair and equitable standard from some treaties or the adoption of the NAFTA formula of tying it to the customary standard.

4.2 Denial of justice

The customary law of state responsibility recognised that the actions of the judicial organs of the state could engage the state in liability if they so exceeded the norms of proper judicial conduct or showed such prejudice as would shock the conscience of the outside world. Inordinate judicial impropriety was required to engage the liability of the state through the conduct of its judicial organs. This seems to have been well settled in the law on state responsibility. In the *ELSI Case*, the International Court of Justice pointed out that it was not the misapplication of a rule of law but the violation of *the* rule of law that engages state responsibility.

In modern law, the idea has been revived in some arbitrations. The *Loewen Case*[106] is the most direct instance where litigation was brought on the basis of a denial of justice. There are other tribunals which have considered whether judicial or quasi-judicial acts of states violated the treatment standards in treaties. The *Loewen Case* is symptomatic of the possible problems of the revival of notions of denial of justice under treaty standards. The more direct argument was that the sum awarded in that case by way of punitive damages was tantamount to expropriation. But, the claimant also alleged that the award of damages was in breach of the treatment standards in NAFTA.

A denial of justice is the central concept of the international minimum standard of customary international law. The ideal circumstance in which it operates is the existence of a final judgment of the host state that is grossly and inordinately unjust. This is a high standard for the foreign investor to satisfy. It is a reason why there has been a need to resort to the hitherto dormant standard of fair and equitable treatment. But, it would be difficult to see how in terms of strict international law responsibility could arise for an administrative fault unless a domestic court had finally denied a remedy in respect of that fault. *Glamis Gold* v. *United States* highlights this problem. States cannot be credited with a departure from their understanding of what they perceived to be rules of customary international law unless there are clear words to that effect. It is unlikely that any state would have agreed to

---

[106] US$600 million were awarded as punitive damages by the Mississippi courts in a civil suit for defamation.

relinquish its power of regulation indefinitely into the future by subjecting its discretion to the whims of an arbitral tribunal consisting of three persons at a distant venue.

4.3 Due process and administrative irregularity

The notion of denial of justice has also surfaced in the *dicta* and writings on the subject in the form of absence of due process, lack of transparency, absence of good faith and violation of legitimate expectations in exercising administrative functions associated particularly with licences involved in foreign investment.[107] They are usually asserted in the arguments of the claimants but have, on one occasion at least, been upheld by a tribunal. Thus, in *Middle East Cement Shipping and Handling Co.* v. *Egypt*,[108] the tribunal held that the seizure and auction of the property of the claimant without notification was a violation of the fair and equitable standard and full protection and security required by the investment treaty between Egypt and Greece. But, there was also a finding of expropriation, and this seems to have been the sole basis for the award of compensation. The due process that is required for expropriation is distinct from the lack of due process which amounts to a violation of a treatment standard.[109] The due process requirement for expropriation is usually specifically provided for in the expropriation provision of the investment treaty.

But, the effort to include violation of due process within the fair and equitable standard is evident in many awards. Thus, in *Waste Management* v. *Mexico*,[110] the tribunal held that the standard is infringed when the conduct of the state 'involves a lack of due process leading to an outcome which offends judicial propriety – as might be the case with a manifest failure of natural justice in judicial proceedings or a *complete lack of transparency and candour* in an administrative process'. The problem with such formulations is that, unless a final court pronounces on these matters, the attribution of responsibility to the state would not be theoretically acceptable.

Another instance of a domestic administrative law principle being used relates to references that are found to legitimate expectations. Such ideas are clearly borrowed from domestic administrative law. The attempt to import the whole body of principles of administrative review into the arbitration of investment disputes through the fair and equitable standard is a visible factor. In *ADF* v. *United States*,[111] arguments were made based on a failure to meet the legitimate expectations of the claimant, but the tribunal did not consider the issue, finding that the expectations indicated were not raised by the defendant state.[112] In *Genin* v. *Estonia*,[113] too, there are references to lack of procedural safeguards in the exercise of regulatory functions, but there were no adverse findings on these grounds. Lack of transparency may be another ground that is advanced as amounting to a violation of the fair and equitable standard.

---

[107] On the good faith requirement, see *ADF* v. *United States*, ICSID Case No. ARB(AF)/00/1 (NAFTA) (Award, 9 January 2003), para. 116.
[108] ICSID Case No. ARB/99/6 (2002), para. 143.
[109] *Amco* v. *Indonesia* (1983–90) 1 *ICSID Reports* 189 illustrates the situation where the due-process requirement is not satisfied prior to an expropriation.
[110] (2001) 40 *ILM* 56.   [111] *ADF* v. *United States*, ICSID Case No. ARB(AF)/00/1 (NAFTA) (Award, 9 January 2003).
[112] Para. 189; there were also references to good faith requirements.   [113] (2002) 17 *ICSID Rev* 395.

It is evident that the rules on which liability is being created are not based on international law principles but rather on notions that are imported from possibly faulty understandings of English or US administrative law.[114] These principles cannot be imported into a treaty through a wide interpretation of the fair and equitable standard in investment treaties. In addition, arbitral tribunals were not created under investment treaties to sit in judgment on the manner of the exercise of discretionary power by domestic administrative organs. The tribunal in *ADF* v. *United States* asserted this when it said that the 'tribunal has no authority to review the legal validity and standing of the US measures here in question under the US internal administrative law'.[115]

It would appear that the tribunals are beating back the trend to argue that all administrative irregularity should be regarded as unfairness under the treatment standards. On the odd occasion that the absence of a requirement of notice is stated as a violation of fairness, it is usually provided as a throwaway addition to a finding based on expropriation but has not yet been an independent ground for awarding damages on the basis of expropriation.[116] It is unlikely that states will accept such an expansive intrusion into their administrative decision-making.

5. Full protection and security

In their provisions on treatment standards, investment treaties include the requirement that the foreign investment should be given 'full protection and security'.[117] This standard has a firmer basis in customary international law as developed by the United States. It has been recognised, in a long series of awards, that the failure to provide protection to an alien who is threatened with violence creates responsibility in the host state.[118] The principles of such customary international law, as found in the practice of some states, can be taken as being settled. The precedents in the Iran–US Claims Tribunal on this issue are many, and the law was stated in the different cases by the Tribunal on the basis of customary international law. Cases decided by ICSID tribunals in this area are also based firmly on precedents which existed in the past.[119] In *Saluka* v. *Czech Republic*, the tribunal confirmed that the standard was concerned with the diminution of the physical security of the investment.

---

[114] It is difficult to accept that any system would adopt such administrative inflexibility that some of the arbitral tribunals mandate. As indicated, English law does not accept the rule relating to legitimate expectations as giving rise to a substantive remedy.

[115] *ADF* v. *United States*, ICSID Case No. ARB(AF)/00/1 (NAFTA) (Award, 9 January 2003), para. 190, following *Mondev* v. *United States* (2003) 42 *ILM* 85, para. 136.

[116] *Middle East Cement Shipping and Handling Co.* v. *Egypt*, ICSID Case No. ARB/99/6 (12 April 2002), para. 143.

[117] G. Cordero Mos, 'Full Protection and Security', in A. Reinisch (ed.), *Standards of Investment Protection* (2008), p. 131.

[118] *Ibid.*

[119] *AMT* v. *Zaire* (1997) 36 *ILM* 1531; *Wena Hotels* v. *Egypt* (2002) 41 *ILM* 896. See also *CME* v. *Czech Republic*, UNCITRAL Arbitration Proceedings (Award, 14 March 2003), para. 613; and *Lauder* v. *Czech Republic*, UNCITRAL Arbitration Proceedings (Final Award, 3 September 2001), decided under the Stockholm Chamber of Commerce Rules. Both decisions are available on the website of the Department of Finance of the Czech government. In *Lauder* v. *Czech Republic*, UNCITRAL Arbitration Proceedings (Final Award, 3 September 2001), para. 54, there was a finding of arbitrary treatment. But, the two awards, on the same facts, are inconsistent on many findings relating to treatment standards. In *Desert Line Projects LLC* v. *Yemen*, ICSID Case No. ARB/05/17 (Award, 6 February 2008), there was a threat to physical security and reputation. Moral damages were awarded. In *Pantechniki SA Contractors & Engineers* v. *Albania*, ICSID Case No. ARB/07/21 (Award, 30 July 2009), where, during a spontaneous riot, there was widespread property damage which included the property of the foreign investor, no damages were awarded.

But, in some recent awards, full protection and security has been delinked from its early customary roots and given a new meaning promoting the stability of the investment. This tendency parallels the similar tendency of viewing the fair and equitable treatment as involving investment stability. This expansionary interpretation is made in a line of cases, so that any interference with the legal and economic stability of the investment would amount to a violation of the standard of full protection and security. Obviously, this expansionist move would make the parallel development which seeks to include economic stability in the fair and equitable standard otiose. For this reason, some tribunals have indicated that the stability of the investment climate is a part of the fair and equitable treatment and is not to be included in full protection and security.[120] Yet, a distinct body of awards treats the full protection standard as violated even if there is no damage to the assets but investment stability is destroyed.[121] Obviously, it cannot be the wording of the treaty that induces such an interpretation. It is a distinct philosophy of property protection that seeks to construct a new basis for the protection of investments, many of which are not in tangible form so that a physical object can be affected.[122] Hence, an extension is made of the full protection standard to include within it measures that affect the depreciation in the value of the investment as a result of the measures taken by the state.

They do not involve any extension of the law as found in the practice of states. They are based on the existence of a duty of protection to be afforded to aliens and state responsibility arising from the failure to fulfil that duty either wilfully or negligently. The standard that is owed is no higher under an investment treaty.[123]

6. Conclusion

The short interlude in experimenting with expansionist views on treatment standards has resulted in these views suffering a setback. Tribunals have now found limiting factors in customary international law, but the content of the treatment standards nevertheless remains uncertain. The fact that the liability arising from treatment standards was tried out in litigation involving developed states was fortunate, as the problems involved were exposed quite early. Investment treaty formulations were originally intended to be a sword to be used against developing countries. Their use against developed countries was not foreseen. The nature of the exorbitant claims exposed the extent to which treatment standards could curtail the regulatory powers of the state over foreign investments. Developed states found such restrictions to be unpalatable and reacted with vigour to find guiding principles for their limitation.

The interlude also exposed the democratic legitimacy of arbitral tribunals being able to exercise extensive supervisory control over decisions of judicial and administrative organs

---

[120] *Eureko* v. *Poland*, Ad Hoc Arbitration (Partial Award, 19 August 2005), paras. 248–53.

[121] *Asurix* v. *Argentina*, ICSID Case No. ARB/01/12 (Award, 14 July 2006); *Occidental* v. *Ecuador*, London Court of International Arbitration (Award, 1 July 2004).

[122] The cases involving the extension have involved shareholdings in companies which cannot be subject to physical destruction.

[123] In *AAPL* v. *Sri Lanka* (1992) 17 *YCA* 106; (1991) 30 *ILM* 577, the argument that a form of strict liability is created by the investment treaty was rejected.

of the state. There have been challenges mounted to the constitutionality of the investment treaties on the ground that vital issues of domestic policy are being pronounced upon by external tribunals dealing on the face of it with disputes of an essentially commercial nature. Indeed, many arbitrators deciding these disputes are drawn from commercial arbitration and have little acquaintance with the public law issues that are really at the core of such disputes.[124] There is also the criticism that arbitrators are bent on imposing, through their awards, a standard of governance drawn from neo-liberal tenets. They articulate standards of constitutionalism that favour the accumulation of principles that lead to property protection globally.[125] It is almost as if the absence of a multilateral treaty is to be remedied through the accumulation of principles formed through the accumulation of arbitral decisions. However, the project, if there was one, has resulted in so many internal schisms that it is unlikely to succeed.

There is also concern that tribunals are able to pronounce on matters that are well beyond the area of investment. Tribunals are able to pronounce on issues that transcend the interests of the parties to the dispute and have a wider significance for the international community as a whole. Such issues arise where, for example, a state seeks to regulate environmentally hazardous activity[126] or to deal with issues affecting the conduct of a civil war.[127] They have dealt with issues concerning international conventions like the Convention on Biodiversity,[128] the Convention on the Protection of Cultural Heritage[129] and the Basel Convention on the Transboundary Movements of Hazardous Wastes,[130] which are areas that would be expected to fall beyond the purview of investment tribunals, especially if they consist largely of commercial lawyers with no training in those areas. The extent of the powers with which arbitral tribunals could be vested in these circumstances will remain a moot point and will increasingly come to be questioned. The fact that many of these situations involve developed countries shifts the focus away from developing countries and invites the attention of scholars in the developed world to anxieties that have been raised by developing countries and their lawyers in the past. Quite apart from the fact that some of the disputes involve issues concerning the health and safety of the people of the state, they may also implicate *ius cogens* principles of international law. If so, the question again arises whether they are the sorts of issues that should be settled by investment arbitrators who are not likely to have the competence or the training to deal with issues affecting humanity in general. Whether this gives rise to the existence of a principle of arbitrability in investment arbitration is an interesting question to pursue.[131] It is obvious that the system of investment arbitration has to operate in the context of international law, very much as the system of international trade operates within the context of international law.[132] As the tribunal in

---

[124] This point is developed in the writings of Gus Van Harten. See his *Investment Treaty Arbitration and Public Law* (2007).

[125] D. Schneidermann, *Constitutionalising Economic Globalisation: Investment Rules and Democracy's Promise* (2008).

[126] *Santa Elena* v. *Costa Rica* (2000) 39 *ILM* 317; (2002) 5 *ICSID Reports* 153; *S. D. Myers* v. *Canada* (2000) 40 *ILM* 1408; (2002) 121 *ILR* 7.

[127] *AAPL* v. *Sri Lanka* (1992) 17 *YCA* 106; (1991) 30 *ILM* 577.

[128] *Santa Elena* v. *Costa Rica* (2000) 39 *ILM* 317; (2002) 5 *ICSID Reports* 153.

[129] *SPP* v. *Egypt*, 3 *ICSID Reports* 101; (1983) 22 *ILM* 752.   [130] *S. D. Myers* v. *Canada* (2000) 40 *ILM* 1408; (2002) 121 *ILR* 7.

[131] See M. Sornarajah, *The Settlement of Foreign Investment Disputes* (2000), pp. 188–91.

[132] *Phoenix* v. *Czech Republic*, ICSID Case No. ARB/06/5 (Award, 19 April 2009), para. 77.

Phoenix v. *Czech Republic* put it, 'to take an extreme example, nobody would suggest that ICSID protection should be granted to investments made in violation of the most fundamental rules of protection of human rights, like investments made in pursuance of torture or genocide or in support of slavery or trafficking of human organs'. But, the concept of *ius cogens* now extends beyond the categories recognised in the *Barcelona Traction Case* with several other candidates in the environmental and human rights sphere for canonisation as *ius cogens* principles.

It is interesting to see that the same sovereignty-centred arguments that were raised by developing-country lawyers – with much overt ridicule from developed-country lawyers – are now the refuge of those who argue cases for developed-state respondents, as well as of an increasing band of academic commentators. The birds have come home to roost. With the increasing penetration of the developed world by developing-country sovereign wealth funds, developed countries now want to dismantle their pre-entry national treatment standards and deny easy access to these funds, especially where vital sectors of their industry are concerned. There is already a backlash against the attempts to widen the interpretation of the fair and equitable standard of treatment by pegging that standard to standards in customary international law. The expansion of the full protection and security standard has also been similarly curbed. The retreat from aggressive protection of foreign investment now comes more from the developed states of the world. Times are changing, and there is a response to the change.

10

The taking of foreign property

What constitutes an act of taking of foreign property in international law was once clear but has now come to be befuddled with difficulty as a result of the progressive expansion of the concept of taking. In the past, the law was discussed in the context of outright takings of the property of the alien. There was no difficulty in characterising the act of physical dispossession as a taking. After colonialism came to an end, there was a spate of nationalisations intended to regain control of the economy from the companies of the erstwhile colonial powers. After the initial rush of nationalisations, there was a movement away from the wholesale takings of industrial sectors to the targeting of specific companies. Developing countries instituted changes regarding the manner of entry of foreign investment. There was greater administrative control over investment. The vehicle of foreign investment was often a mandatory joint-venture company incorporated in the host state. The company became a corporate citizen of the host state and thus more amenable to its control. The process of foreign investment itself came to be enmeshed in a host of regulations which directed it to economic development objectives and environmental protection. In this context, the notion of what constituted a taking had to change. The focus was on the manner of governmental interference with the contracts on the basis of which the original investment was made or on the running of the corporate vehicle through which the investment was made. The system of investment protection would become undone if there was no response to this changing situation.

The controversy has been compounded by the formulations in investment treaties which refer to three types of taking: direct, indirect and anything 'tantamount to a taking' or 'equivalent to a taking'. Previously, the focus of attention in this area was on the issue of compensation and, to a lesser extent, on the question of whether a breach of a foreign investment agreement in itself gives rise to responsibility. The attention has now shifted to the more basic question of what scope of a taking against which the law, or more specifically the treaty, grants its protection. The problems have been compounded by the fact that the law, originally developed in order to give protection to investments operating in developing countries, is now being used against developed countries as a result of treaties like NAFTA. With the increase in free trade agreements, the chances of developed countries becoming targets of litigation involving takings is likely to increase. As a result, the thinking on the law relating to takings in advanced constitutional systems is likely to encroach into this field, which was designed with entirely different motives in mind. This chapter is concerned with the issue as to what acts of the state may be characterised as amounting to takings, and with the circumstances in which such takings would be considered unlawful.

Though, at one stage of the development of the law, the question of compensation was linked to the legality of the nationalisation, the modern view is that the question of legality is independent of the payment of compensation. It is recognised that the state has a right to control property and economic resources within its territory to enhance its economic, political and other objectives. Once this right is acknowledged, it must be conceded that the taking of property by a state is *prima facie* lawful. Non-payment of compensation does not make an otherwise lawful nationalisation unlawful.[1] It is generally accepted that a lawful taking creates an obligation to pay compensation, whereas an unlawful nationalisation creates an obligation to pay restitutionary damages. In the calculation of damages for an unlawful nationalisation, the tribunal takes a more liberal view and proceeds on the basis that compensation should be calculated as for any other illegality in international law. However, the issue of compensation for nationalised property is a celebrated cause of controversy among writers on international law. A separate chapter is devoted to the consideration of compensation for the nationalisation of foreign property and damages for unlawful nationalisation.[2] Though the controversy does not affect much of the modern law, yet, understanding it is key to understanding the nature of the conflicts that affect this area of the law.[3]

1. What constitutes taking?

A distinction must be made between confiscation, expropriation and nationalisation of property. The terms are often used interchangeably, but it is best, for the sake of clarity, that precise meanings be attributed to these terms. Confiscation is the capricious taking of property by the ruler or the ruling coterie of the state for personal gain. This was common in states ruled by dictators and oligarchies. Such takings happen, though less frequently, in modern times.[4] Much of the law on state responsibility was developed in the context of the law relating to the confiscation of property, which had no benefit to the state but helped only to enrich the ruling elite.[5] Unfortunately, the law so developed was extended indiscriminately to other types of taking. Most of the early law was also developed in the context of

---

[1] The scope for the illegality of an expropriation in modern law is confined to situations where the expropriation was discriminatory or lacked a public purpose.

[2] See Chapter 11 below.

[3] The leading writings on the subject are: G. C. Christie, 'What Constitutes Taking of Property in International Law' (1962) 38 *BYIL* 307; B. Weston, 'Constructive Takings under International Law: A Modest Foray into the Problem of Creeping Expropriation' (1975) 16 *Virginia JIL* 103; R. Higgins, 'The Taking of Property by the State' (1982) 176 *Hague Recueil* 259; R. Dolzer, 'Indirect Expropriation of Alien Property' (1986) 1 *ICSID Rev* 41; and UNCTAD, *The Taking of Property* (UNCTAD Series on International Investment Treaties, 2000).

[4] *Siderman de Blake* v. *Argentina*, 965 F 2d 699 (1992), where the court suggested that the taking of the property had a 'discriminatory motivation based on ethnicity'. Such takings are clearly illegal.

[5] There were also cases of looting and pillaging by mobs or the army, for which liability was attributed to the state. *British Claims in Spanish Morocco* (1926) 2 *UNRIAA* 620. The Zimbabwe situation, where there are land grabs, resembles this situation. It was dealt with in *Funnekotter* v. *Zimbabwe*, ICSID Case No. ARB/05/6 (Award, 22 April 2009).

Latin America. The taking of property by army-ruled states to replenish the personal coffers of military dictators and their coteries must be distinguished from the later takings in that region that were associated with a revolutionary zeal to redistribute property. The latter had an economic motive, whereas the former had none. Clearly, there was justification in the view that a confiscatory taking motivated by caprice should be regarded as unlawful. The law that was developed on the basis of confiscation has no relevance to the situation in which a state takes property with the object of effecting an economic programme. Nationalisation referred to a situation in which a state embarks on a wholesale taking of the property of foreigners to end their economic domination of the whole economy or of sectors of the economy. This was common in the period after decolonisation when states in Africa and Asia sought to regain control of their economies by taking over the assets of companies controlled from the former colonial powers. Again, the law that was developed in this context had a special flavour and is best confined to the precise period in which these types of taking took place. There is no doubt that ideas that were developed in the context of such takings were carried through to the future. The assertion of national control that was implicit in nationalisation had a continuous force that applies in modern times. The justice-related notions that were articulated cannot be confined in time. Yet, the rhetorical flavour of the law that was developed has little relevance today. There is a temporal quality that attaches to the phenomenon of taking in various periods. In modern times, the law on taking has taken a different turn. The incidents that occur are best described as expropriation, which is a specific term that could be used to describe the targeting of individual businesses for interference for specific economic or other reasons. Many of them involve the use of existing regulatory mechanisms. This, of course, does not mean that takings of the types that were common in the past do not take place now.[6]

Confiscation in the earlier periods concerned the property of individual traders who had gone overseas in search of wealth and stood powerless in the face of the organised might of the totalitarian dictators who ruled some of their host states.[7] The moral dimensions involved favoured the alien in such circumstances, and the evolution of a law protecting the interests of the individual trader was justifiable. The picture is quite different in modern times when the foreign investor is often a multinational corporation, which can often muster greater power than the host state and is backed by the even greater power of its home state. In this changed situation, it would be invidious to use the law formulated in the context of the confiscation of the property of the adventurous individual trader to cater to the situation of the large multinational corporation of the modern age.

The early law on taking was worked out in the context of the formative period of the relations between the United States and the Latin American states.[8] In Latin America, where

---

[6] Dictatorial takings may take place in some states even now. The recent case of *Yaung Chi Oo Ltd* v. *Myanmar* (2003) 42 *ILM* 540; (2003) 8 *ICSID Reports* 463 was argued on the basis that it was such a taking. Of the same variety is the Zimbabwe case, *Funnekotter* v. *Zimbabwe*, ICSID Case No. ARB/05/6 (Award, 22 April 2009).

[7] There is the issue of whether the voluntary taking of the risk of investing in such states should be taken into account.

[8] For the view that the rules on the minimum standard constitute regional law, see P. Trimble, 'International Law, World Order' (1990) 42 *Stanford LR* 811 at 835. See also C. Lipson, *Standing Guard: Protecting Capital in the Nineteenth and Twentieth Centuries* (1985).

colonial relationships did not exist, there was a need for the assertion of norms for the protection of foreign investment. The United States sought to assert such norms, and the Latin American states resisted their imposition. Some of the Latin American takings were carried out by elites for their personal benefit, but some, like the Mexican expropriations of 1917 and 1938, were carried out in pursuance of economic reforms. The US assertions of norms often did not seek to make a distinction between the two. Both types of taking were regarded as being in violation of international law, and therefore compensable.[9] The distinction that had to be drawn between these types of taking became sharper in the post-colonial period. The states of Asia and Africa had been under colonial domination. In those states which were not, investment protection was achieved through capitulation treaties which ensured that the foreign investor was insulated from the reach of the local law and through the establishment of local regimes of property protection favourable to the foreign investor.[10] The development of international norms was not thought to be necessary in these circumstances. Takings in pursuance of economic programmes came to be debated after the Russian revolution. The Eastern bloc states maintained that such taking was non-compensable. In the first half of the twentieth century, there were two regions, Eastern Europe and Latin America, where European attitudes to state taking were questioned. With the independence of Africa and Asia, two more regions were added, and there were four regions in the world which stood outside the European sphere in articulating attitudes to taking which were quite different from those that the European states preferred. Their attitudes to notions of property were also different. Notions of taking differed in accordance with the different philosophical standpoints as to property. In that context, it is futile to suggest that any customary international law could have developed on the point, despite the suggestions of some writers to the contrary. Of the four groupings in the world, only one supported the notion of full compensation for expropriation.

In modern law, as suggested above, it is best to refer to takings by states as 'expropriation', as in most instances these takings are carried out for an economic or other public purpose. The term 'nationalisation' should be confined to across-the-board takings that are designed to end or diminish foreign investment in the whole economy or in sectors of the economy. In dictatorial regimes, there could still be capricious, confiscatory takings but the opportunity for such taking is rare. In the present world climate, which is favourable to foreign investment, it is unlikely that nationalisations will occur unless there is some

---

[9] P. E. Sigmund, *Multinationals in Latin America: The Politics of Nationalisation* (1990). Arbitral tribunals were in sympathy with takings done to effect economic programmes, but glossed over the distinction. See, for example, *De Sabla v. Panama* (1934) 28 *AJIL* 602, where the taking was effected in pursuance of land reform. The tribunal stated: 'As the public statements of its high officials show, it was endeavouring throughout this period to bring order out of a chaotic system of public land administration. In such a period of development and readjustment, it is perhaps inevitable that unfortunate situations like the present one should arise. It is no extreme measure to hold that if the process of working out the system results in the loss of private property of aliens, such loss should be compensated.'

[10] The existence of notions of community of property in native systems was anathema to colonial powers. They soon replaced these notions with notions of individual property ownership. A. G. Hopkins, 'Property Rights and Empire Building' (1980) 40 *Journal of Economic History* 787, quotes a British governor of The Gambia as having said:

On what do the English capitalists rely for their security? Of course on the prestige of English power. On the knowledge that English troops and guns are stationed in different positions along the Gambia – and also I am happy to add on the more civilised and juster notions of the rights of property which the continued presence of Europeans and the spread of legitimate commerce is producing.

political upheaval resulting in ideological change within a state.[11] One could argue that the Latin American states, which have become disenchanted with the neo-liberal economics they had adopted in the 1990s, will in the course of their retreat from neo-liberalism spark off nationalisations. There is evidence of this happening at least in some sectors.[12] Economic nationalism still remains a potent force, and its triumph could still lead to the wholesale nationalisation of foreign investments.[13] Expropriation, the targeting of a specific business, will be the more usual form of governmental interference with which the law has to be concerned. It, in turn, is divided into three principal categories in the modern law. This results from treaty definitions which distinguish between direct and indirect takings and include a third category identified as anything 'tantamount to a taking' or 'equivalent to a taking'. The assumption is that such a definition accepts the existence of three distinct types of expropriation. A view has been expressed that the phrases 'tantamount' or 'equivalent' to a taking do not create a third category because the dictionary meanings of tantamount or equivalent simply require the act to be the same as or similar to direct and indirect takings.[14] But, the fact is that they continue to be used widely in treaties and must at least be taken to expand the meaning of the term 'taking'. The significance of the category is that it became a focus for widening the scope of expropriation law well beyond its moorings, but the response of the states to such expansionary efforts has been to return the law to its previous position in customary law.

1.1 New forms of taking

In identifying categories of taking, it is necessary to know something of the history. This related not only to the political circumstances of the different periods, but also to the evolution of ideas as to property and as to the control of foreign investment. In the early period, takings involved the direct seizure of physical property, which belonged to the foreign investor. The law was developed in the context of such takings. The period of post-colonial nationalisations also involved direct takings of property. In the period after these spectacular, across-the-board nationalisations, takings of property have been motivated by specific reasons and have been directed against individual corporations. Where such takings are direct, no issue of identification arises. But, a characteristic of taking in the later period was that there was no change effected to the rights of possession of the physical property of the foreign investor. There is a diminution of his property rights that is accomplished without dispossession necessarily taking place. It is only when the taking is indirect that difficulties

---

[11] The last real instance of this was the overthrow of the Shah of Iran and the consequent taking over of US businesses, resulting in the Iran–US Claims Tribunal. Economic nationalism still remains a potent force and could lead to nationalisation of the whole economy of a state.

[12] In Venezuela and other states, this is happening in the petroleum sector, where old arrangements are being replaced with greater state control. There is a shift towards the left in Latin America. It has resulted in some arbitrations. For example, *Phillips Petroleum* v. *Venezuela* (pending).

[13] The Iranian revolution and the effects of it on American business, culminating in the setting up of the Iran–US Claims Tribunal, was the last instance of a nationwide taking of foreign business.

[14] *S. D. Myers* v. *Canada* (2000) 40 *ILM* 1408; (2002) 121 *ILR* 7.

arise. There are diverse ways of affecting property interests such that the definition of indirect taking becomes difficult. These types of taking have been identified as 'disguised expropriation',[15] to indicate that they are not visibly recognisable as expropriations or as 'creeping expropriations',[16] to indicate that they bring about the slow and insidious strangulation of the interests of the foreign investor. In *Middle East Cement Shipping and Handling Co.* v. *Egypt*,[17] indirect expropriation was described as 'measures taken by a state the effect of which is to deprive the investor of the use and benefit of his investment even though he may retain nominal ownership of the respective rights'. In *Lauder* v. *Czech Republic*,[18] the tribunal stated that such taking 'does not involve an overt taking but effectively neutralises the enjoyment of property'. It is sometimes referred to as 'constructive taking' so as to emphasise the idea that results akin to taking are produced though externally the situation remains unchanged. Such descriptions, while providing catchy labels for takings outside the obvious situation of direct takings of physical property, do little to further the identification of indirect takings which will attract the application of the international law on expropriation. The best approach to the discussion is to group the types of indirect taking that have been discussed in the literature and the arbitral awards that have dealt with the question. It is this approach which is used in this work. By doing this, an assessment can be made as to the different claims that exist as to the circumstances that qualify as a taking.

The awards of the Iran–US Claims Tribunal have been a fruitful source for the identification of such types of taking.[19] The Tribunal dealt with types of taking that took place in the context of a revolutionary upheaval following the overthrow of the Shah of Iran, and the propositions the Tribunal formulated may not have relevance outside the context of the events that attended that upheaval. Also, one has to be cautious in making any generalisations on the basis of *dicta* in the awards of this tribunal as its constituent documents gave the Tribunal power to deal not only with direct takings of physical assets but also with 'all measures affecting property rights'.[20] It is clear that such a wide definition of taking will not be acceptable in general international law for the reason that many normal activities of states, such as taxation, affect property rights and cannot ordinarily be expected to give rise to claims of expropriation or scrutiny by international tribunals. Also, dispossession was often voluntary because it was unsafe for Americans to remain in Iran due to the situation. Since many who previously sat as arbitrators on the Iran–US Claims Tribunal now sit on

---

[15] Judge Fitzmaurice in *Barcelona Traction Case* [1971] *ICJ Reports* 3.

[16] R. Dolzer, 'Indirect Expropriation of Alien Property' (1986) 1 *ICSID Rev* 41; B. Weston, 'Constructive Takings under International Law' (1975) 16 *Virginia JIL* 103. Creeping expropriation may be more appropriate to denote the slow and progressive measures adopted to initiate attrition of ownership and control rights. See *Tecmed* v. *Mexico* (2006) 10 *ICSID Reports* 54, para. 114, which emphasises that such expropriation takes place 'gradually and stealthily'.

[17] ICSID Case No. ARB/99/6 (2002), para. 107. The sentence goes on to equate creeping expropriation with the phrase 'tantamount to a taking', in investment treaties.

[18] *Lauder* v. *Czech Republic*, UNCITRAL Arbitration Proceedings (Final Award, 3 September 2001). The authorities used for such expansive notions of taking are virtually incestuous. Often, the arbitrators who sat on a tribunal that made such an expansive interpretation later cite the authority they created in later arbitrations.

[19] For a survey of the jurisprudence, see G. Aldrich, *The Jurisprudence of the Iran–US Claims Tribunal* (1996); C. Brower, *Iran–US Claims Tribunal* (1998).

[20] Article 2(1) of the Claims Settlement Declaration (19 January 1981).

foreign investment arbitral tribunals, there is a tendency to transfer the ideas developed by the former into other foreign investment disputes. This transference without closer analysis of each situation would be improper, as a wider mandate was given to the Iran–US Claims Tribunal than is generally the case with tribunals deciding foreign investment disputes. Nevertheless, the guidance provided by the Iran–US Claims Tribunal on many issues relating to takings cannot be ignored.[21] The dissection of ownership rights that was effected in some of the cases decided by the Tribunal will have an impact on future discussions of the subject. The analysis by the Tribunal of property damage caused during mob violence as creating state responsibility will also continue to be valuable in that particular category of liability.

The increase in concern with 'creeping expropriation' in modern literature and arbitral awards is that a state could sometimes diminish property rights without affecting the direct ownership of the investment. Neither is the act of expropriation a single act of finality which either takes away a right or diminishes an interest of the foreign investor. It could be a slow, insidious erosion of such rights and interests set in motion by an initial act and spreading over a period of time.

Indirect expropriation takes place within a wide variety of circumstances. Examples of it can be catalogued. It cannot be identified through a single principle. The factors that can be isolated are that there is a diminution in the value of the interest of the foreign investor in the assets, and that the time period over which this occurs is often longer than necessary for a single act. But, these are not factors that contribute to the formulation of a single rule that describes the process. Thus, where the management of a company is taken over, the company, its assets and its shareholdings are not affected but the foreign investor's control over the operations of the company is diminished. A similar result follows where a licence to operate is withdrawn or where such a withdrawal restricts or prevents profit-making activities, for example where exports are restricted. With the increase of administrative control over foreign investment, there has been an increase in the use of such techniques of interference with the rights of the foreign investor. The assimilation of indirect expropriation to direct expropriation is seen as crucial, as it builds a platform for an analysis of the remedies that are to be provided.[22] Much of the analysis of the law has depended on a dissection of the notion of property.

1.2 The ideas of property

The philosophical underpinnings of property have also become important in the analysis of takings. Roman law recognised the unbundling of property rights into its constituent components.[23] Property was seen not as a single right of ownership but as involving a

---

[21] The best analysis of the jurisprudence of the Tribunal is to be found in G. Aldrich, *The Jurisprudence of the Iran–US Claims Tribunal* (1996).

[22] In *Biloune* v. *Ghana Investment Board* (1993) 95 *ILR* 184, para. 75, the tribunal held that no distinction should be drawn between direct and creeping expropriation. The decision was followed in *Metalclad* v. *Mexico* (2000) 5 *ICSID Reports* 209; (2001) 40 *ILM* 55, para. 108.

[23] The usual Roman law formulation is that ownership constituted *ius utendi, fruendi et abutendi* (the right to use, enjoy and destroy or dispose). It provided the inspiration for the definition of taking in the Harvard Draft Convention on International Responsibility for Injuries to Aliens (1961) 55 *AJIL* 554. Article 10 of the Draft defines a taking of property as including 'not

series of rights relating to its use and enjoyment. The growth of modern law, particularly administrative law, has resulted in the rediscovery of the idea that, when government interference occurs, it targets only some of the rights in the bundle of rights that constitute ownership and thereby reduces the value of the ownership in the property. This provides a launching pad for the extensive view that any diminution in the value of property as a result of a governmental measure could amount to a taking.

The notion of indirect expropriation is based on the unbundling of property rights. Though such a notion was known from Roman times and has been referred to in philosophical writings in England, the concept became familiar in the case law of the United States in the jurisprudence on the taking of property. It is in the United States – and that too more recently[24] – that the dissection of property into its component rights has been carried out with a high degree of finesse. The issue then becomes one of whether this dissection should be carried into the jurisprudence on taking in international law.[25]

The different types of taking were refined in the awards of the Iran–US Claims Tribunal. One suspects that the analysis, particularly of the US arbitrators who sat on the Tribunal, followed the legal techniques that had been developed in US law. To that extent, the views that were taken in these awards, though based on logical premises, should not be taken as fully reflecting the international law position. To a large extent, they reflected philosophical predispositions to certain views relating to property developed in US law that may not be acceptable in other legal systems. Yet, the fact is that, once made, the sway they have had in the determination of the course of the law has been strong. The precedents have found their way into the awards of other arbitral tribunals.

The precedents that have been generated have a basis in a distinct US theory of property which not only permits the dissection of the concept of property with finesse but also ensures that individual property is protected in more absolute terms than would be the case in other legal traditions. Perhaps because of the fact that, in early America, individual property had to be won and defended against the odds, this notion of absolute property has become a hallmark of US law.[26] It is widely justified on the basis of the statements of the English philosopher, John Locke, some of whose statements identified the protection of individual property as the central function of a political society. The thinking is reflected in the US Constitution, which states that there must be just compensation paid when the state takes the property of the citizen. In the formative stages of the United States, the taking of

---

only an outright taking of property but also any such unreasonable interference with the use, enjoyment, or disposal of property as to justify an inference that the owner thereof will not be able to use, enjoy, or dispose of the property within a reasonable period of time after the inception of such interference'.

[24] The taking jurisprudence in the United States was dormant until the decision of Justice Holmes in *Penn Central Transportation Co* v. *New York City*, 438 US 104 (1978). It became more pronounced only in the 1980s. There was greater latitude shown towards state taking in the formative years of the United States. The experience of the United States in the field must be approached with caution. The tendency has been to foist modern US notions of property onto the international scene. A similar tendency may be seen with the jurisprudence of the European Court of Human Rights interpreting the provision of the right to property.

[25] Either a hegemonic state ensures that its own principles are adopted in international law or, in the alternative, an explanation may be that the principles of the law of the hegemonic state become so pervasive as to be adopted in international law.

[26] This is admittedly a contentious statement. The takings jurisprudence in US law does not show sufficient consistency to suggest that the notion of property was not a changing concept.

property for the purposes of the state went uncompensated on the theory that the permissible exercise of a state's police powers was a necessary feature of government. As the United States progressed into an economic power, there was a re-emergence of the view that there must be just compensation paid whenever a state interferes with the enjoyment of the property rights of the individual.[27] But, when it came to regulatory takings, courts were still reluctant to categorise them as compensable. They refused to formulate a categorical rule. Instead, they preferred a rule which weighed the relevant circumstances of each case to determine whether or not compensation should be paid.[28] In the course of making these judgments, US courts made fine dissections of what constituted these property rights.

This tradition is not reflected in other legal systems. The traditional societies favoured community of ownership of property and would have found notions of individual ownership unacceptable. Western law that was transplanted in colonial times has displaced these traditional notions. Yet, the traditional notions survive in cultural attitudes to property in these communities. Within the traditions of European systems, different notions of property prevail. The competing notion that property must serve a social function and that individual rights are subject to the prior right of society to secure common goals had a wider acceptance in the European systems of law. It is this view that is reflected in the judgments of the European Court of Human Rights. The European Convention on Human Rights itself did not originally contain a right to property. The First Protocol to the Convention states the right. Constitutional systems also indicate a variety of approaches to the protection of property. Canada had much difficulty in fitting a notion of property into its Bill of Rights. It exists in Canadian law only as a matter of inference. The Nigerian Bill of Rights, the model for many Commonwealth constitutions, identifies the circumstances in which the right to property becomes defeasible in the social interest.[29] The African Charter of Human and Peoples' Rights subjects the right to property to the public interest.

Yet, there is a clear project to foster in the international regime, as the centrepiece of foreign investment protection, a theory of absolute protection of foreign investment which sits uneasily with the constitutional systems that are recognised in different parts of the world. In each age of globalisation, the hegemonic power has sought to project its own vision of property onto the world. The United States incorporates in its treaty practice the absolute vision of property protection and works through international institutions and other means to achieve this purpose.[30] But, as its own power recedes, the newer version of the US model investment treaty (2004) displays a movement away from this absolute convention to subject the right to protection to a variety of exceptions related to the public interest and

---

[27] Again, this is too sweeping a statement. The most recent US Supreme Court decision shows the extent of the disagreement on these issues in US law. *Tahoe-Sierra Preservation Council Inc.* v. *Tahoe Regional Planning Agency*, 122 S Ct 1465 (2002).

[28] *Palazzolo* v. *Rhode Island*, 533 US 606 (2001); the law was largely developed in the context of real property interests.

[29] For a recent comparative study, see T. Allen, *The Right to Property in Commonwealth Constitutions* (2000).

[30] The US vision incorporated in its treaty practice has been adopted by Canadian treaty practice, though Canada's internal laws do not contain such absolute visions of property protection.

national security. The treaty practice of some states is thus at loggerheads with the constitutional principles of states with which they conclude the treaties.[31] The proliferation of
investment treaties which include an absolute concept of individual property rights,
especially that of a foreign investor to the exclusion of similar rights for citizens, will
provoke internal controversy and lead to the assertion of sovereignty-centred arguments. It
will raise the issue as to whether these treaties, made largely by bureaucrats, do not
constrain the democratic wishes of the people of the state.[32] In any event, as the regulatory
powers of the state are seen to diminish as a result of extensive interpretations placed on the
language in the treaties, the response of states will be to reassert their regulatory powers
and indicate clearly that there was no intention to abdicate such powers through the
investment treaties.

The tendency to dissect the rights that are inherent in the ownership of property may
accelerate as a result of decisions made under NAFTA and the US treaties. There are
views being expressed that the awards made under NAFTA are more intent on property
protection and have constructed more rigorous theories of absolute property rights than
even the decisions of US courts.[33] But, these tendencies have been checked by the
reaction of the NAFTA parties to cases like *Metalclad*, which sought to extend the
meaning of expropriation beyond customary law notions to include any measure that
leads to depreciation of the value of property or violation of reasonable expectations of
benefits. Subsequent awards did not follow *Metalclad*, perhaps sensing the reaction of
the NAFTA states.[34]

As the same arbitrators and arbitral institutions are often involved in the settlement of
other foreign investment disputes, the tendency to use theories made under NAFTA will
ensure that the trends become widespread. As far as taking is concerned, expansive theories
will be tried out in litigation. Some of them may be accepted in arbitral awards. The *dicta* in
the *Metalclad* award illustrate the expansive scope given to expropriation. The tribunal in
that case defined expropriation thus:[35]

[E]xpropriation under NAFTA includes not only open, deliberate and acknowledged takings of
property, such as outright seizure or formal or obligatory transfer of title in favour of the host State,
but also covert or incidental interference with the use of property which has the effect of depriving the
owner, in whole or significant part, of the use or reasonably to be expected economic benefit of
property even if not necessarily to the obvious benefit of the host State.

---

[31] Some writers believe that US treaty practice in relation to NAFTA does not conform to the narrower concept of property rights in
the US Constitution. V. Been and J. Beauvais, 'The Global Fifth Amendment? NAFTA's Investment Protections and the
Misguided Quest for an International "Regulatory Takings" Doctrine' (2003) 78 *New York University Law Review* 30.

[32] Canadian scholars such as D. Schneiderman have commented on the 'new constitutionalism' that is driven by such treaties. The
treaty standards mandate that existing constitutional balances are redrawn to accommodate the new standards of property
protection to be afforded to foreign investors who are provided with most-favoured-nation treatment and national treatment
standard as well as an external standard provided through customary international law. See D. Schneiderman, 'Investment Rules
and the New Constitutionalism' (2000) 25 *Law and Social Inquiry* 757.

[33] V. Bean and J. Beauvais, 'The Global Fifth Amendment? NAFTA's Investment Protection and the Misguided Quest for an
International "Regulatory Takings" Doctrine' (2003) 78 *New York University Law Review* 30.

[34] For example, *Marvin Feldman v. Mexico* (2002) 7 *ICSID Reports* 318; (2003) 42 *ILM* 625.   [35] Para. 103.

The wide definition is by no means confined to awards under NAFTA.[36] The theory of litigation in the *Ethyl* v. *Canada*[37] and *Methanex* v. *United States*[38] was that any depreciation of the assets of the foreign investor amounted to a taking. They demonstrate the potential that the wide formulation of the provisions in the treaties have. The inclusion of phrases such as 'tantamount to a taking' or 'equivalent to a taking' gives rise to the impression that the treaties intend to widen the scope of taking. States will resist the broadening of the definition of taking because of the fact that the legitimate activity of governments may be hindered if over-broad definitions are accepted. The expansionary view of expropriation has already begun to cause concern to the developed states, which now find themselves defendants in expropriation claims based on such broad views on expropriation.[39] As rich countries like the United States and Canada find themselves at the wrong end of the stick, they will contest broad definitions of taking with vigour. As a consequence, in *Pope and Talbot* v. *Canada*,[40] the tribunal upheld the Canadian contention that the phrase 'tantamount to a taking' did not add anything to the concept of taking. The subject is one which no longer concerns developing countries only. It is fortunate that harsh law which could have been developed by maverick arbitrators could now be checked by developed states, who now have an interest in doing so. A law that was largely aimed at developing countries now implicates the interests of developed states as well. It is likely that developed countries will respond by making the same sovereignty-centred arguments that developing countries have been wont to make when faced with intrusive decisions by international tribunals in this area. It will be interesting to see whether the arguments the developed countries use in their own defence will succeed when developing countries use them.[41]

The expansive interpretation of expropriation may have been a passing phase induced by a fervour for building up standards of governance through investment protection that was evidenced in the law during the ascendancy of neo-liberalism. After this period, there seems

---

[36] Thus, in *Middle East Cement Shipping and Handling Co.* v. *Egypt*, ICSID Case No. ARB/99/6 (12 April 2002), para. 107, the tribunal defined creeping expropriation as follows: 'When measures are taken by a state the effect of which is to deprive the investor of the use and benefit of his investment even though he may retain nominal ownership of the respective rights being the investment, the measures are often referred to as a creeping or indirect expropriation or, as in the BIT, as measures "the effect of which is tantamount to expropriation". As a matter of fact, the investor is deprived by such measure of parts of the value of his investment.'

[37] (1999) 38 *ILM* 708. The claimant company, a US investor in Canada, was the sole manufacturer in Canada of a petroleum additive. A Canadian minister announced in Parliament that he was contemplating a ban on the substance, as it was a pollutant. The litigation was brought on the basis that the announcement led to a depreciation in the value of the shares of the claimant company and thereby amounted to a taking. The tribunal upheld jurisdiction, but the dispute was settled as a result of Canada agreeing to pay damages.

[38] The facts of *Methanex*, which has not yet been decided, are similar to *Ethyl* v. *Canada* (1999) 38 *ILM* 708. Studies showed that the additive that Methanex, a Canadian company, manufactured in California was injurious to health. There was a ban on the manufacture of the additive. The allegation was that the ban amounted to a taking as a result of the effect it had on the internal and overseas sales of the substance.

[39] The United States, in *Metalclad* v. *Mexico* (2000) 5 *ICSID Reports* 209; (2001) 40 *ILM* 55, para. 27, rejected the view that the phrase 'tantamount to an expropriation' created a new category of expropriation.

[40] (2002) 41 *ILM* 1347.

[41] The cynic will have regard to the development of the concept of an economic development agreement. A foreign investment agreement made in a developed country is subject to its own laws. The same agreement made in a developing country becomes an economic development agreement subject to a supranational law. The distinction was justified on policy grounds. The *Metalclad* approach has been used in non-NAFTA cases. See *CME* v. *Czech Republic*, UNCITRAL Arbitration Proceedings (Award, 14 March 2003), where the tribunal held that the 'commercial value of the investment' was destroyed. The decision is available on the website of the Department of Finance of the Czech government.

to have been a tightening of the law which required a 'substantial deprivation' of property rights for there to be an expropriation.[42]

Quite apart from the categorisation of taking, one further issue that has become important is the identification of a category of taking described as 'regulatory' taking for which no compensation needs to be paid. The law has always recognised this category. It has always been recognised that ordinary measures of taxation, or the imposition of criminal penalties or export controls, do not constitute taking that is compensable. Legislation creating regulatory regimes in areas such as antitrust, consumer protection, securities, environmental protection, planning and land use are more common in developed states.[43] It is well recognised that interference on the basis of such legislation does not constitute compensable taking in situations in which public harm has already resulted or is anticipated. To pay compensation would be to reward a wrongdoer or to recognise an absence of overwhelming public interest in the use of property. These regulatory takings are regarded as essential to the efficient functioning of the state. The problem is to find a rational basis for the distinction between regulatory, non-compensable taking and other forms of taking. The new awards indicate that many takings that would earlier have been characterised as regulatory takings are now being subjected to compensation.[44] Thus, in *Santa Elena* v. *Costa Rica*,[45] the tribunal stated:

Expropriatory environmental measures – no matter how laudable and how beneficial to society as a whole – are in this respect, similar to any other expropriatory measures that a state may take in order to implement its policies: where property is expropriated, even for environmental purposes, whether domestic or international, the state's obligation to pay compensation remains.

But, it could well be that such views have changed as a result of the fresh articulation of the regulatory taking exception.

This blanket statement that compensation is payable for any environmental measure that is taken is unlikely to be accepted even by developed states. The US Supreme Court has decried the possibility of the creation of such a *per se* rule relating to the taking of property. In most states, domestic law would not accept such an absolute statement. The passage articulates a rule for which little authority can be found. The issue has become a hotbed of dispute because of the growth of environmental movements that seek to ensure that interference by states motivated by environmental concerns are not deterred through the characterisation of such interference as compensable takings. The issue as to the distinction between compensable taking and regulatory taking is also considered in this chapter.

But, since *Methanex*, it has to be accepted that there is a definite category of regulatory expropriation which is non-compensable. The formulation of this category by the *Methanex* tribunal is as follows:

---

[42] *Pope and Talbot* v. *Canada* (2002) 41 *ILM* 1347.
[43] The exception is stated in the American Law Institute's *Restatement (Third) on Foreign Relations Law of the United States* (1987).
[44] *Metalclad* v. *Mexico* (2000) 5 *ICSID Reports* 209; (2001) 40 *ILM* 55.
[45] (2002) 15 *ICSID Rev* 72. The passage quoted was cited and followed in *Tecmed* v. *Mexico* (2006) 10 *ICSID Reports* 54.

A non-discriminatory regulation for a public purpose, which is enacted in accordance with due process, and which affects, *inter alios*, a foreign investor or investment, is not deemed expropriatory and compensable unless specific commitments had been given by the regulating government to refrain from such regulation.

This formulation would embrace almost every expropriation that has a public purpose. The exception as to specific commitments seems unsupported by authority. It may preserve stabilisation clauses, but there is no policy reason why a stabilisation clause should stand in the way of a state taking a measure that is evidently in the public interest. In any event, stabilisation clauses are contractual means of protection, and whether a treaty protects contractual provisions or other commitments is not clear. When the rule on regulatory taking was formulated in *Saluka* v. *Czech Republic*, no exception was stated regarding specific commitments. The formulation is that 'states are not liable to pay compensation to a foreign investor when, in the normal exercise of their regulatory powers, they adopt in a non-discriminatory manner *bona fide* regulations that are aimed at the general welfare'. Again, the width of the proposition is so great that expropriation law will become redundant if the proposition is taken at face value, as a modern state seldom takes property unless there is a general welfare reason justifying the taking. The problem of the extent of non-compensable, regulatory takings will remain contentious for some time, as the criteria for a meaningful identification of such takings will prove elusive. But, increasingly, there will be pressure exerted to include within regulatory takings those takings which are justified on the basis of environmental protection, human rights standards, protection of health and morals, and national security. This is inevitable, as modern treaties clearly identify these instances as providing an exception to liability and also include clear statements to the effect that regulatory takings are not subject to compensation. The recognition of regulatory takings knocks a massive hole in the law on expropriation. The issue is revisited in this chapter. The manner in which later tribunals have dealt with the issue requires consideration.

The types of taking, other than the obvious situation of a direct taking of physical assets, that could amount to expropriation have been identified in the literature and in arbitral awards. The question as to what amounts to a taking cannot be answered easily. The circumstances in which takings could arise can, however, be described and discussed. They could be grouped as follows for convenience of discussion: (1) forced sales of property; (2) forced sales of shares in an investment through a corporate vehicle; (3) indigenisation measures; (4) taking over management control of the investment; (5) inducing others to take over the property physically; (6) failure to provide protection when there is interference with the property of the foreign investor; (7) administrative decisions which cancel licences and permits necessary for the foreign business to function within the state; (8) exorbitant taxation; (9) expulsion of the foreign investor contrary to international law; and (10) acts of harassment such as the freezing of bank accounts or promoting strikes, lockouts and labour shortages. These different types of taking and their significance to international law are considered below.

All these instances involve conduct by the state. Unless the conduct of those committing the acts is directly attributable to the state, the taking cannot involve state responsibility.[46] In the old law, the cases largely considered the circumstances in which the acts of officials and agents could be attributed to the state. In the modern law, the issue has largely been whether acts of regulatory agencies and sub-national entities such as municipalities can be attributed to the state. In the case of direct taking, it would be easy to find clear evidence of the link between the state and the taking. In the case of indirect taking, the link may be difficult to find, but it must be found, for otherwise the requirement of attributability of the taking to the state would not be satisfied. The law that is being applied is no different from the old law on attributability. The test is whether knowledge and the power of control over the regulatory or sub-national body exercising authority over the foreign investment existed but was not exercised so as to protect the interests of the foreign investor.[47]

1.2.1 Forced sales of property

A distinction must be drawn between forced sales of the foreign investment which are brought about by civil unrest or economic downturns and those brought about by a state policy such as the indigenisation of the economy. In the former situation, the alien may extricate himself from his business difficulties by selling his assets cheaply, or he may abandon his property altogether. It is a situation faced in common by all in business, national and foreigner alike. A state cannot be held responsible for such conduct on the part of the foreign investor, unless it has taken measures that affect the investment.[48] But, if the unrest is engineered by the host state and the violence is directed at the foreign investors for the specific purpose of ensuring that they leave the host state, clearly there is a situation that involves a taking. Where the foreign investor abandons the property or makes a quick sale of the property in these circumstances, there is no voluntary conduct on his part. The conduct is induced by the state. State responsibility could therefore arise in such a situation.[49]

Some of the authority in this area comes from cases where the conduct of the state was motivated by considerations of race. Where there is racial discrimination that motivates conduct, this gives rise to a separate head of liability. However, no comfort is provided to the individual who has suffered as a result. For him, the fact that the taking of his property is a clear illegality in terms of international law provides no better protection than a claim for damages. It could well be that a claim on these grounds is easier to establish if the circumstances show a clear policy of discrimination against foreigners of a particular race or group.

---

[46] See *Amco* v. *Indonesia* (1985) 24 *ILM* 203, para. 158, where the tribunal said: '[A]s a *conditio sine qua non* there shall exist a taking of private property and … such taking shall have been executed or instigated by a government, on behalf of a government or by an act which otherwise is attributable to a government.' *UPS* v. *Canada*, UNCITRAL Arbitration Proceedings (NAFTA) (Award on the Merits, 24 May 2007), where the tribunal found no responsibility as CanadaPost was acting commercially and not as a state agency.

[47] *Genin* v. *Estonia* (2002) 17 *ICSID Rev* 395; *Metalclad* v. *Mexico* (2000) 5 *ICSID Reports* 209; (2001) 40 *ILM* 55; *Compañiá de Aguas del Aconquija SA and Vivendi Universal* v. *Argentina*, ICSID Case No. ARB/97/3 (2003).

[48] Unless there is some contractual obligation on the part of the state or its organ to protect the property. *United Painting Company Inc.* v. *Iran* (1989) 23 *Iran–US CTR* 351 at 366–70; the instance of state measures to deal with the crisis is provided by the Argentinian economic crisis. But, the extent to which economic necessity will provide a defence remains contentious.

[49] There could also be an argument that the duty to give full protection and security to the investment is violated.

Illegality flows from the fact that the presence of racial discrimination negates the requirement that a public purpose is necessary for a lawful taking.[50]

The *ELSI Case*[51] contemplates another category of forced sales. Where the rules of a state require that a company facing bankruptcy should be dissolved, the forced dissolution of the alien company will not amount to a compensable taking by the state. The failure had not been brought about by the state but by external circumstances or by the ineptness of the alien investor himself. In these circumstances, the state has its own interests to protect. In such a situation, the foreign investor's company will inevitably become insolvent, and the state merely steps in to protect its own interests by taking over the failing company. In *ELSI*, there were the interests of the employees of the company to consider, as well as the state's policy of industrialisation of an economically depressed area which it was keen to protect. This is a classic regulatory taking situation.

There was also pre-existing legislation which permitted state interference in failing companies. In these circumstances, the interference was not considered to be a compensable taking by the state, even though the local courts had held that the administrative measures taken by the state were not lawful. But, some modern investment treaties protect against abuse of the process of liquidation.[52] The protection usually appears in the treatment provision of the treaty. There must be a demonstration that the ordinary process of justice attended the liquidation process and that there was nothing that could be seen as a denial of justice. The mere fact that there is a court-ordered liquidation may not provide legitimacy to the taking. The court may be used as an instrument to effect the taking, in which case, clearly, the liquidation could amount to a taking depending on the circumstances.[53]

1.2.2 Forced sales of shares

The question whether there could be diplomatic protection and state responsibility where wholly foreign-owned companies incorporated in the host state are taken over has been clouded by problems relating to corporate personality in international law.[54] Such companies, incorporated in the host state, have personality only under the law of the host state and are corporate nationals of the host state. The *Barcelona Traction Case*[55] relied on this proposition when the International Court of Justice denied standing to Belgium to espouse the claims of a company incorporated in Canada and operating in Spain. The much criticised

---

[50] *Osthoff* v. *Hofele*, United States Ct Rest App 111 (1950); *Poehmann* v. *Kulmbache Spinneri AG*, US Ct Rest App 701 (1952); and *Zwach* v. *Kraus Bros*, 237 F 2d 255 (2nd Cir., 1956), are discussed in the context of forced sales. They arose from expulsions of aliens motivated by racism.

[51] [1989] *ICJ Reports* 15.

[52] Thus, the ASEAN Investment Treaty (1987) states that: 'Each contracting party shall, within its territory, ensure full protection of the investments made in accordance with its legislation by investors of the other Contracting Parties and shall not impair by unjustified or discriminatory measures the management, maintenance, use, enjoyment, extension, disposition or *liquidation* of such investments' (Article IV(1), emphasis added).

[53] In *Yaung Chi Oo Ltd* v. *Myanmar* (2003) 42 *ILM* 540; (2003) 8 *ICSID Reports* 463, the claimant argued that the liquidation proceedings before the Myanmar courts were themselves an act of taking. But, the tribunal did not find on this.

[54] On corporate nationality, see D. Ijalye, *Extension of Corporate Personality in International Law* (1978); I. Seidl-Hohenveldern, *Corporations in and under International Law* (1987).

[55] [1970] *ICJ Reports* 3; for a discussion of earlier views on the protection of shareholders, see J. M. Jones, 'Claims on Behalf of Nationals Who Are Shareholders in Foreign Companies' (1949) 26 *BYIL* 225.

decision held that Belgium could not espouse the claims of the Belgian shareholders and that Canada alone had the right to protect the company.

The company had been declared bankrupt in Spain and its assets sold. The interests of the foreign and local shareholders in the company were destroyed as a result. The effect of the judgment of the International Court of Justice was that the company could be protected only by the state in which it was incorporated. The interests of the shareholders would thus receive indirect protection but the shareholders themselves could not receive protection directly from the states of which they were nationals. The Court proceeded on the basis that, since there were no adequate rules on the subject of corporate personality in public international law, questions relating to corporations would have to be decided in accordance with the relevant principles of municipal legal systems. There were exceptions to the general rule that there could not be direct diplomatic protection of shareholders. The Court accepted that there could be such protection in circumstances in which the company itself had ceased to exist under the law of the state of the company's nationality and the shares had been divided *pro rata* among the shareholders or in circumstances in which a lifting of the veil was justified, for example where there had been an illegal act aimed at the company.[56] Mann summarised the effect of the judgment in the following terms:[57]

No rule of customary international law has yet come into existence which would confer a right of diplomatic protection on a state merely by reason of the fact that the value of its nationals' shareholdings and thus its own economic resources suffer damage.

In the three decades that have passed since the judgment, there has been no evolution of international law which would entitle the foreign shareholders of a company to receive protection directly from the state of which they are nationals except through treaty law.[58] The significance of investment treaties is that they remedy the defects of customary international law on this point by recognising that shareholders of foreign companies are protected against government interference through procedures and remedies that are devised by the treaties. The brave redefinition of property to include shareholdings attempted by Judge Tanaka in the *Barcelona Traction Case* does not provide the answer. It may reflect the need for protection, but it does not provide a solution to the problem as to whether the redefinition will also include shares in companies. Too much judicial creativity having regard to teleological factors may provoke dissent.

The International Court of Justice recognised that treaties provide the answer. The Court observed in the *Barcelona Traction Case* as follows:

[I]n the present state of the law, the protection of shareholders requires that recourse be had to treaty stipulations or special agreements directly concluded between the private investor and the state in which the investment is placed. States ever more frequently provide for such protection, in both

---

[56] Para. 92.

[57] F. A. Mann, 'Protection of Shareholders' Interests in the Light of the Barcelona Traction Case', in F. A. Mann, *Further Studies in International Law* (1990), p. 217 at p. 233.

[58] C. Staker, 'Diplomatic Protection of Private Business Companies: Determination of Corporate Personality for International Law Purposes' (1990) 51 *BYIL* 155. *Diallo Case*, ICJ (Judgment, 24 May 2007).

bilateral and multilateral relations, either by means of special instruments or within the framework of wider economic relations.

One possible reason for the increase in bilateral investment treaties is the need to provide for shareholder protection. These treaties recognise that shares are included in the definition of treaties.[59] In the absence of treaty protection, international law does not appear to provide relief to shareholders of a company whose shares have been affected as a result of state intervention. But, after the *Barcelona Traction Case*, the UK government asserted its right to protect the shareholdings of nationals in a foreign corporation. The rules regarding international claims issued by the UK government take this view:

> Where a United Kingdom national has an interest as shareholder or otherwise, in a company incorporated in another state and of which it is therefore a national, and that state injures the company, Her Majesty's Government may intervene to protect the interests of the United Kingdom national.

Many bilateral treaties now contain provisions which contemplate the protection of shareholders. They alter the rule in the *Barcelona Traction Case* which is based on the rule that corporate nationality depends on incorporation. The primacy of that rule has been confirmed in later developments.[60]

Shareholder protection becomes important because of the requirement found in host state laws that entry by the foreign investor be made through an incorporated joint venture company formed in association with a local entrepreneur or state company. The foreign partner will usually be only a shareholder of such a company, and the protection of his investment in the company would be on the basis that he is a shareholder. The foreign investor or his home state will ordinarily have no standing to protect the company or its assets. The only way in which the investment could be protected through international law mechanisms is to confer treaty protection upon the shareholding of the foreign investor.[61] The effect of this would be that, even where the management of the company is taken over as a result of state interference but shareholdings are kept intact, there will be no taking in respect of which the foreign shareholder can invoke protection. This will not be an acceptable result from the point of view of the foreign investor for the profits of the company may diminish considerably in the absence of a vigorous management. It is quite possible that the treaty is widely worded so as to include the right to management and control within the definition of an investment, provided the shareholdings were such as to create management rights in the foreign investor. In any event, investment treaties usually cover contractual rights. This would be so where the foreign investor had made entry through a corporate joint

---

[59] Some would specifically include portfolio investments. This has been discussed in earlier chapters.

[60] Corporate nationality features heavily in the jurisprudence of ICSID. Article 25 of the ICSID Convention recognises the incorporation test, but permits the state of incorporation to treat the company as a foreign company for the purposes of arbitration. There are many awards dealing with the interpretation of the provision. For a statement of the law, see C. Schreuer, 'Diplomatic Protection of Private Business Companies' (1990) 51 *BYIL* 155.

[61] See *ELSI Case* [1989] *ICJ Reports* 15, para. 106: 'While there may be doubt whether the word "property", in Article V, paragraph 1, extends, in the case of shareholders, beyond the shares themselves, to the company or its assets, the Chamber will nevertheless examine the matter on the basis argued by the United States that the property to be protected under this provision of the FCN Treaty was not the plant and equipment the subject of the requisition, but the entity of ELSI itself.'

venture. The joint venture contract should have provided for such management and control rights, in which case they will become protected.

Another factor to note is that the shareholder protection that has evolved through treaties should not be taken to include portfolio investments. The developments that have taken place seem to confer protection only on primary shareholders and not those down the line to whom the shares may have been transferred. Though no conclusive view can be formed on this, the evolution of the law suggests that there was no intention on the part of states to create protection for portfolio investments. There are treaties which provide for the protection of portfolio investments.

1.3 Privatisation and forced sales

The present era has witnessed a fervour for the privatisation of publicly owned companies in the Western world. The same fervour is to be found in many other regions of the world. Since many privatisation measures do not restrict shareholdings by foreigners, there are likely to be many foreign investors who have bought shares in foreign privatised public companies. Attitudes to privatisation display a certain ambivalence, and political parties which have opposed privatisation may renationalise them when the opportunity presents itself. Such renationalisation will raise many issues of shareholder protection in developing countries, which may find themselves unable to raise sufficient funds to compensate the foreign shareholders adequately if they are to effect the renationalisation quickly. Renationalisations can be expected to be effected through forced sales on the local stock markets on which the real value of the shares cannot be raised for the obvious reason that the sales will be confined to the local investors and there will be a flood of the shares on the stock exchange. The question will arise as to whether such forced sales amount to takings or whether the situation is akin to one of interference with portfolio investments, in which case the shareholders will have to bear the risk of loss or seek remedies provided by the local law. The buying of shares during privatisation is more akin to the making of a portfolio investment and the answer, resulting from the analogy, may be that there would be no taking by the state in these circumstances. But, the Argentinian cases suggest that, even if there may be expropriation involved, there could be liability for violation of treatment standards.

1.3.1 Indigenisation measures

Indigenisation measures involve a progressive transfer of ownership from foreign interests into the hands of local shareholders. They were undertaken in many African and Asian countries after independence to ensure that the termination of political control also meant the termination of economic control and the passing of such control into the hands of local entrepreneurs.[62] One factor that sets indigenisation measures apart from outright takings is that there is no vesting of any property in the hands of the state or a state organ. There is no

---

[62] For a description of these measures, see T. Biersteker, *The Political Economy of Indigenisation: Multinational Capital in Nigeria* (1987).

direct or even indirect enrichment of the government as a result of such measures. Unlike the classic situation of nationalisation where the state takes over a foreign-owned venture and runs it itself or through a state entity, indigenisation measures contemplate the transfer of ownership and control of such ventures into the hands of the local citizenry. There is, however, some authority for the view that there could be a taking by the state even where the state or state entity is not vested with the property that is taken. A second factor is that there may be no change in management control effected by the measures.

The foreign investor may remain in control of his venture and his control may even be desired as the local entrepreneurs may lack the skill to run the business as efficiently at least in the initial stages. When, eventually, the local shareholders displace the foreign managers, the displacement will take place in accordance with the corporate laws of the host state and not through any government fiat. Unless the state itself had bought the majority of the shares, which is unlikely as a purpose of the measures is to diversify the shareholdings among as many locals as possible and build up a local entrepreneurial group, the state seldom exercises control over the internal rearrangements in the control structure of any previously foreign-controlled company.

Yet, the transfer of the ownership is involuntary and the timing of the transfer of the shares in the venture owned by the foreigner is not left to him. As a result, he may not be able to secure the optimum price for his shares. There is no doubt that there is a resemblance to forced sales in indigenisation measures. However, few disputes have arisen from such indigenisation measures, because, in the context of the political developments that were taking place in the countries which adopted these measures, the relinquishing of controlling interests in foreign investment ventures was unavoidable. Foreign investors were content to accept it rather than face a protracted dispute with the host state. They reckoned that they would come out losers in the dispute and prejudice their continued business prospects in the host state. The maintenance of links with the host state was a much prized asset which multinational corporations did not want to lose. There were other strategies and realignments which the foreign investors adopted to maintain their position in the host state.[63] It may also be that home states of foreign investors were reluctant to take issue with host states as the phenomenon was widespread among newly independent states. There was little to be gained in diplomatic terms in making a stand against such a widespread practice that was brought about by changes which were taking place as a result of the ending of colonialism. The policy behind indigenisation measures may also have some merit in terms of the goals it seeks to achieve, and is sanctioned by the wider idea of economic self-determination. As such, it falls within the regulatory controls a state establishes in pursuance of its sovereign rights over economic matters rather than into the category of takings for which the state had to pay compensation. From the state's point of view, the sales took place openly on its stock market and that was the best way of assessing and paying for the value of the shares. Such a view was not based on reality, as a fair price could not be raised for the shares on the local stock exchange.

---

[63] Some sought to defeat these measures by buying and holding shares through local nominees or nominee companies. Such practices are obviously illegal. Others sought to maintain influence by entering into management and similar types of relationships with the venture.

Both in the *Barcelona Traction Case* and in the *ELSI Case*, there were allegations that the interference in the corporate affairs of the foreign investor was intended to effect a transfer of shares into local hands. Judge Tanaka referred to the allegation of 'hispanicisation' of the company in *Barcelona Traction* but had little to say on whether the technique was contrary to international law. In the *ELSI Case*, there was an effective transfer of the shares of the US-controlled company into Italian hands as a result of the sale in bankruptcy that ended the long conflict between the US shareholders and the Italian authorities. The United States objected to the process by which the transfer took place.[64] Again, the Court avoided pronouncing on the question of whether the requisitioning of the company, which, according to the United States, led to the bankruptcy of the company and its subsequent sale, amounted to indirect expropriation on the basis that the company was failing in any event.

Ethnicity has a role to play in government measures which seek to restructure companies on the basis of their racial compositions so as to achieve a measure of economic equity. In Malaysia, the *bumiputra* policy was intended to ensure this, and companies had to restructure in accordance with specified ethnic quotas as to shareholdings by each of the races in Malaysia, and foreigners were restricted to a percentage of the shareholdings. In South Africa, a similar policy is to be implemented to ensure that the economic cake is shared by the majority native community, whereas foreign investment has traditionally flowed into companies that were owned by the minority groups.[65] Where restructuring is done in order to avoid political conflicts based on past economic inequities, the resultant divestment that takes place could not be regarded as compensable takings. These are general policy measures that apply across-the-board in order to achieve certain political and economic objectives. Such measures must be considered a part of ordinary business risk. In the case of the Malaysian divestment programme, no argument was made that expropriation was involved.

In *Lauder* v. *Czech Republic*,[66] there was a suggestion that the expropriation should benefit the state or an entity associated with the state. This certainly does not seem to have been a requirement in past expropriations, many of which involved land-reform and other reform programmes which did not benefit the state but rather the people of the state. If the requirement is accepted, measures such as divestment measures do not benefit the state directly and will not amount to an expropriation.

1.3.2 Interference with property rights

There has been a general tendency in the international protection of alien property to transfer domestic norms of property protection onto the international sphere. The European capital-exporting states found it necessary to promote ideas of individual ownership of property in

---

[64] Para. 119.

[65] The Black Empowerment Act, and changes to the mining laws giving greater participation in the resources sector to black people, have resulted in one arbitration, *Piero Foresti, Laura de Carli and Others* v. *South Africa*, ICSID Case No. ARB(AF)/07/01. The new mining charter requires the transfer of 26 per cent of the shares in mining companies to black people. *Piero Foresti, Laura de Carli and Others* v. *South Africa*, ICSID Case No. ARB(AF)/07/01 was a claim brought before ICSID in 2007. European investors have agreed to suspend such claims.

[66] *Lauder* v. *Czech Republic*, UNCITRAL Arbitration Proceedings (Final Award, 3 September 2001), para. 57. The decision is available on the website of the Department of Finance of the Czech government.

their colonies and other states into which they exported investments, as the security of such investments were achieved by the spread of a uniform notion of property built on notions of sanctity of individual property. But, notions of property do not remain static. Whereas the protection of physical assets was emphasised in earlier times, both the function of property as well as the function of the state have undergone a radical transformation in the European legal systems to require a concept of property that extends beyond the protection of the physical assets.

The view that only an outright takeover of physical assets amounts to expropriation by a state no longer holds. Whereas stress on the physical nature of property was sufficient to protect ownership in times when there was a *laissez-faire* philosophy, the coming of the welfare state meant an increase in the nature and frequency of state interference with the ownership of property by individuals. Interference with the exercise of property or ownership rights by the host state could amount to takings which require compensation. Once the jurisprudential fact that ownership itself involves a bundle of intangible rights in relation to property is acknowledged,[67] then it follows that it is not only the outright taking of the whole bundle of rights but also the restriction of the use of any part of the bundle that amounts to a taking under the law. It is necessary to understand the course of developments relating to the concept of property in the municipal systems, in particular of the United States, as the leading capital-exporting states will contend for the transference of the system of property protection in their domestic sphere into the international sphere. There is evidence of such transference in the past.[68] There is evidence that the ideas that are generated in the domestic sphere shape the arguments on the international sphere. The pervasive influence of US jurisprudence on the taking of property is evident in modern discussions on taking in international law. The dominance they will come to have on the jurisprudence generated by arbitral tribunals considering takings under Chapter 11 of the North American Free Trade Agreement (NAFTA) is already evident. For this reason, a digression into US and European developments concerning the concept of property is necessary.

1.4 Evolving US and European notions of property

Property is constitutionally protected in the United States.[69] This is not so in all countries. In Europe, the European Convention on Human Rights did not initially recognise a right to property, but the First Protocol to the Convention now recognises such a right. These provisions do not prevent takings by the state, but subject them to the payment of compensation. There has been considerable case law in the United States in particular, discussing the

---

[67] There are, of course, different explanations of the right to property in municipal systems. There is no indication of a theory of property in international law itself. International law does not create property in an individual. It relies on municipal law for the recognition of property rights.

[68] See G. Lipson, *Standing Guard: Protecting Foreign Capital in the Nineteenth and Twentieth Centuries* (1985), pp. 16–18.

[69] The Fifth Amendment states: '[N]or shall private property be taken for public use, without just compensation.' It is generally suggested that the drafting of the clause was influenced by natural law theories on property rights. Natural law views and positivist views of property clashed in the early cases which dealt with the ownership of slaves. R. M. Cover, *Justice Accused: Antislavery and the Judicial Process* (1975).

issue as to the circumstances in which a taking will attract constitutional protection, thus requiring the payment of compensation. The general pattern has been that the US courts showed greater latitude towards state takings when the country was young and needed to create infrastructure through taking private property. There was a greater tendency to hold such takings to be exercises of police powers which did not require the payment of compensation. But, as the country progressed, there was a shift towards a greater constitutional protection of property rights, as a result of which payment of compensation for taking of property came to be increasingly accepted. Though the distinction between taking in the exercise of police powers and taking which required compensation is not clearly drawn, there is a swing towards the greater protection of property rights in US law. The tendency towards neo-liberal notions in modern times makes the swing even more pronounced. The great emphasis placed on individualistic notions of private property are born of the particular experiences of the United States and its espousal of a constitutional philosophy which elevates the protection of individual property rights as a centrepiece of its constitutionalism. This experience may not be repeated in other states.

European notions of property sought to balance the public interest in property use with those of private rights of ownership. They sought to recognise the idea that the interests of the individual in his property may have to be subordinated to those of society at large. The cases on the right to property under the European Convention on Human Rights reflect this difference in attitude. In the Canadian Bill of Rights, a statement of the right of property does not appear at all. In Commonwealth constitutions, the right to property is stated as being subject to the public interest and not in absolute terms. In Asia and Africa, the traditional systems generally favoured communal ownership of property and played down the idea of individual rights of ownership of property. The concept of the right to property that is sought to be universalised in foreign investment documents and in arbitral awards seems, however, to be an absolute right. To that extent, the universalisation of the idea of the right to property will meet with resistance. Yet, the capital-exporting states found the imposition of an absolute right to property through foreign investment instruments to their advantage and have persisted in that approach.[70]

Disputes relating to the taking of property have attracted greater and more consistent attention in US law than in any other system. In these decisions, the US courts have dissected property rights into fine categories. Many of these decisions were made in the context of regulatory legislation involving infringements of property rights. The unbundling of property rights and abstract notions of property came to displace physical notions of property.[71] These tendencies sought to entrench ideas that favoured the absolute protection of property through the payment of compensation if interference with the right was necessary. Yet, there were balancing notions that had been developed to ensure that a state's

---

[70] This unity might fail when instruments like NAFTA bring about disputes between the rich states. The schisms in attitudes are beginning to appear between the United States and Canada as to approaches to this area of the law. The changes are also evident in the newer investment treaties which incorporate wide exceptions to liability such as regulatory expropriation and measures taken to promote public welfare and health. Absolute notions of property protection in investment treaties have become things of the past.

[71] See T. Honoré, 'Ownership', in A. G. Guest (ed.), *Oxford Essays in Jurisprudence* (1961), p. 107.

regulatory interest was preserved in the circumstances where the public interest in the interference with the property outweighed the individual interest. The US courts had evolved a balancing test to resolve such conflicts which took into account the economic impact of the regulation, its interference with reasonable investment-backed expectations, and the character of the government action.[72]

But, there were competing tendencies that were evident as well. Populist notions which saw property as bringing with it power were also reflected in the law.[73] In addition, there are laws which increasingly affect the enjoyment of property rights in the interests of not only the immediate community but also the international community generally which have been mandated by different conventions on the environment.

These developments favoured the nature of property as involving a series of intangible rights in relation to property and its use.[74] Infringements of these rights could amount to a taking justifying compensation in some circumstances, but not in others. The making of the distinction becomes problematic once more.[75] The existing literature on the subject is unhelpful, as it merely seeks to study the situation from a US perspective and foist the US solution onto the international scene. It has already been demonstrated that, given the differences in attitudes to property, this solution is hardly one that would meet with general approval. Obviously, infringements of property rights in controlling hazardous or environmentally unsound use of property, in the course of planning decisions and in effecting consumer protection measures or restoring market forces in a situation of imperfect markets are regulatory takings which require no compensation.[76] The experience of the European Court of Human Rights has also provided a basis for discussion. A balancing test is applied by the Court to analyse the social function of property and its use by the state for a public purpose and the effect of the state interference on the individual owner.[77] But, the difficulty is in the formulation of a theory that could be used as a predictive device so that there could be guidance as to whether the taking is compensable or not. Here, though various efforts have been made at devising a theory capable of making the distinction, none has been successful.[78]

---

[72] The rules that are to be applied were worked out in a series of Supreme Court cases like *Penn Central Transportation Co v. New York City*, 438 US 104 (1978); *Tahoe-Sierra Preservation Council Inc.* v. *Tahoe Regional Planning Agency* (2002) 535 US 302.

[73] Until replaced by market-dominated theories, antitrust laws had a populist basis of interfering with large monopolies and price-fixing cartels. The rationale was that large conglomerations of economic power affected political decisions and were harmful to democracy. Market theories have tended to divert attention from this rationale and look at antitrust laws through the prism of price theory.

[74] The analysis was accelerated by the work of Hohfeld. His positivist analysis of rights ensured that US law viewed property as intangible rights held against others in the community. Rights had correlatives which resided in others. W. Hohfeld, 'Some Fundamental Legal Conceptions as Applied in Judicial Reasoning' (1913) 23 *Yale LJ* 16.

[75] There is an abundant literature analysing the case law. The leading works are: J. L. Sax, 'Takings and the Police Power' (1964) 74 *Yale LJ* 36; F. I. Michelman, 'Property, Utility and Fairness' (1967) 80 *Harvard LR* 1165; R. Epstein, *Takings: Private Property and the Power of Eminent Domain* (1985); and S. R. Munzer, *A Theory of Property* (1990), pp. 442–69.

[76] Sax's theory, that a taking is non-compensable when the state acts as an arbiter in deciding between the public interest and the rights of the owner (for example, in the making of a planning decision) and that it is compensable where it acts in an enterprise function (for example, where it takes over land to build roads), is popular. J. L. Sax, 'Takings and the Police Power' (1964) 74 *Yale LJ* 36. But, it too has limitations. S. R. Munzer, *A Theory of Property* (1990), p. 459.

[77] *James* v. *United Kingdom* (1986) 8 *EHRR* 123; *Sporrong and Lönnroth* v. *Sweden* (1982) 5 *EHRR* 85; *Holy Monasteries* v. *Greece* (1995) 20 *EHRR* 1; D. Anderson, 'Compensation for Interference with Property' (1999) 6 *European Human Rights Law Review* 543.

[78] The transference from domestic law is itself contestable. A Japanese court in *Tokyo Suikosha* v. *Tokyo Masonic Lodge Association* (1966) 53 *ILR* 1, resisted such a transference, noting that there is no principle relating to property among nations to justify its elevation to a principle of international law.

1.5 The impact on international law

There have been efforts to transfer the changing notions of domestic property law onto the international scene. Such transference is undesirable. The fact is that hegemonic powers have always sought to transfer their domestic law onto the international sphere. They have had a measure of success in their efforts. In the present situation, the need for such a transference is felt, due to the increase in administrative controls instituted in developing countries over the process of foreign investment. These administrative interferences are usually regarded as regulatory in character and thus as not requiring the payment of compensation. It is to counter this development that the arguments relating to absolute rights of property and the dissection of the different rights to property are made.

From the point of view of property protection, the abstract notion of property as a series of intangible rights has a positive effect in that it makes it easier to protect contractual rights and intellectual property rights. It can be used to accommodate new rights created in connection with ownership such as licences, planning permissions and administrative permissions necessary to operate businesses. The reinterpretation of these rights as constituting property is again a feature of the law both in the United States and in other developed countries.[79] In addition, protection could be extended to all manner of infringements of the rights of ownership of the foreign investor. The influence of the shift can be seen in US bilateral investment treaties. Thus, the United States–Argentina treaty states that 'neither party shall in any way impair by arbitrary or discriminatory measures the management, operation, maintenance, use, enjoyment, acquisition, expansion or disposal of investments'. The formula is repeated in other bilateral treaties made by the United States.[80] A complete range of possible uses of property is covered through an unbundling and spelling out of the package of rights that previously constituted a single bundle. The practice is followed in other investment treaties. This description of the whole process of foreign investment as being covered by the treatment standards in the investment treaties has become a standard feature of such treaties. One could argue that a series of property rights is spelt out and that impairment of any of those property rights could amount to a taking.

The effort to promote such unbundling of property rights is also evident in the awards of the Iran–US Claims Tribunal.[81] There were some early arbitral awards where taking was

---

[79] The concept of new property is created on the basis of trends in administrative law. These convert licences, permits and other administrative instruments into property rights, and seek to protect their withdrawal through due process safeguards. C. Reich, 'The New Property' (1964) 73 *Yale LJ* 733. Administrative law theories owe much to the idea that due process principles now protect interests akin to property from the abusive exercise of discretionary power. The seeping of the ideas of legitimate expectations into arbitration awards is a visible fact. Administrative law notions have been used to give protection to the administrative rights that arise in foreign investment. Such rights are treated as property rights and are included within the definition of foreign investment.

[80] The practice is not confined to the United States. The ASEAN Investment Treaty (1987) uses a similar formulation.

[81] This was established early in the jurisprudence of the Iran–US Claims Tribunal. See *Starret Housing Corp.* v. *Iran* (1987) 16 *Iran–US CTR* 112; and *Sedco Inc.* v. *NIOC* (1987) 23 *Iran–US CTR* 23. Whereas US arbitrators took a liberal view on what amounted to a taking, the Iranian arbitrators sought to justify the takings as necessary under the circumstances and hence not compensable. In some situations, the latter viewpoint prevailed. For example, *United Painting Company Inc.* v. *Iran* (1989) 23 *Iran–US CTR* 351 at 366–70, liability was found not on the basis of a taking but on the basis of a violation of a contractual duty to take care of the property.

found on the basis of an interference with specific rights of ownership.[82] But, the negative aspect of the development in US law is that it still recognises a category of non-compensable takings.[83] The application of such a notion of non-compensability will have adverse consequences on property protection. Many of the developing countries, after decolonisation, preferred mixed economic systems which provided for state regulation of industry and business. A complete transference of the US notions of property will mean that the notion of non-compensable regulatory takings will have to be transferred to the international plane. But, this is not an idea that has been taken over into the international arena until recently. There has been a selectivity that has generally favoured the interests of transnational corporations. The dilemma, simply, is that, whereas the abstract notion of property rights will afford greater property protection, its counterpart, the notion of non-compensable regulatory takings, will have disastrous effects for property protection. The argument that the notion that exists in US law as at present, including the notion of non-compensable regulatory takings, should be transferred will not be accepted by many arbitrators.[84] If it is necessary that guidance must be sought from US law, then the preference of the developing states would be to select an earlier stage of the development of US law at a time when the United States was in its developmental stage. At that time, it is evident that the United States did recognise a wider category of regulatory taking which was not compensated.

The issue as to regulatory taking will be fought out among the developed states themselves. If, each time there is an antitrust measure used against a foreign investor, he could allege a taking under some treaty such as NAFTA which needs to be compensated, regulatory measures against foreign investors could become impossible.[85] It is unlikely that there would be such measures taken against developing-country investors, as they are not of sufficient size to attract antitrust attention. The Exon–Florio Amendment to the Omnibus Trade Act, whereby the US President has been vested with powers to interfere with the inflow of large foreign investments into the US market on national security grounds, will also result in takings and compensation issues between the United States and states with which it makes treaties. It is possible to argue that the exercise of these powers violates the

---

[82] In *Sapphire* v. *NIOC* (1963) 35 *ILR* 136, one of the alleged acts of taking was the insistence by NIOC on a right of veto over all aspects of the operation. The Indonesian control measures involved indirect takings and were considered in the literature. Editorial, 'The Measures Taken by the Indonesian Government Against Netherlands Enterprises' (1958) 5 *NILR* 227. For other instances, see Whiteman, *Digest*, vol. 8, pp. 980–1016.

[83] The Harvard Draft Convention on International Responsibility, (1961) 55 *AJIL* 554 at 562, recognised the existence of a category of non-compensable takings. Article 10(5) reads: 'An uncompensated taking of an alien or a deprivation of the use or enjoyment of property of an alien which results from the execution of tax laws; from a general change in the value of currency; from the action of the competent authorities of the State in the maintenance of public order, health or morality; or from the valid exercise of belligerent rights; or otherwise incidental to the normal operation of the laws of the State shall not be considered wrongful.'

[84] This may account for the award in *Santa Elena* v. *Costa Rica* (2000) 39 *ILM* 317; (2002) 5 *ICSID Reports* 153, which asserted that all environmental takings have to be compensated. Such a *per se* rule on regulatory takings cannot be found in any domestic system of law. It can be explained only on the basis of the preference for pro-business norms. But, it could well be that awards such as *Methanex* presage a change. In *Marvin Feldman* v. *Mexico* (2002) 7 *ICSID Reports* 318; (2003) 42 *ILM* 625, environmental takings were considered an example of regulatory takings.

[85] An instance of the recognition of this by an arbitral tribunal is to be found in the award of the Iran–US Claims Tribunal in *Iran* v. *United States* (1988) 13 *Iran–US CTR* 173, where, in a dispute relating to the failure to return property belonging to Iran, the Tribunal said that the presidential determination preventing the export of the property involved 'the exercise of a sovereign right which is not subject to review by an international tribunal'. But, the Tribunal ordered that the property be compensated. The award will not mean that each time the power of preventing exports is exercised there should be compensation paid for interference with contract rights. If it does, there would be interesting consequences in the situations of extraterritorial exercise of the powers under export-control regulations.

pre-entry rights of establishment which may be regarded as property rights as well as rights relating to national treatment. The European Community has already protested against the legislation on the ground that 'such action is not subject to judicial review and no compensation is foreseen'.[86] The US view will be that the exercise of the Presidential power under the legislation is regulatory and leads to non-compensable takings.

Features of issues relating to regulatory taking are evident in NAFTA litigation. In *S. D. Myers* v. *Canada*,[87] regulations relating to the processing of hazardous waste were involved. In *Pope and Talbot* v. *Canada*,[88] Canadian timber regulations were involved. In *Methanex* v. *United States*,[89] as in *Ethyl* v. *Canada*,[90] the litigation related to the regulation of substances that were regarded as environmentally unsafe. The issue of regulatory taking will plague the developed states more and more, and will have to be settled in the context of litigation among them.[91]

In *Santa Elena* v. *Costa Rica*,[92] the tribunal addressed the issue of environmental regulation. It held that, where the taking is on environmental grounds, it must still be compensated. The tribunal stated that such expropriatory measures are 'similar to any other expropriatory measures that a state may take in order to implement its policies'. It is unlikely that arbitrators are going to deviate very much from this position. The *Santa Elena Case* itself was forced on Costa Rica through use of the Helms Amendment which threatens withdrawal of aid unless compensation is paid for expropriated property.[93] The principal position of arbitrators will remain that there will be little scope for regulatory taking to be pleaded in order to justify non-payment of compensation. *Dicta* to the effect that environmental takings are subject to compensation was followed in *Tecmed* v. *Mexico*.[94] But, as environmental exceptions come to be stated in the investment treaties, this line of awards will lose its force.

Regulatory functions are a sovereign right of the host state, and there could be no right in international law to compensation or diplomatic protection in respect of such interference. There is already a recognition of such a category of non-compensable taking. The identification of when there is a compensable taking as a result of interference with property rights and when there is non-compensable regulatory taking is fraught with the same difficulties that exist in domestic law. There is, in theory, no reason why a state restructuring its economy cannot argue that there were non-compensable regulatory takings involved in circumstances where property rights were infringed by such restructuring. But, given the present state of the authority, such an argument is not likely to succeed. The authorities seem to divide equally on this issue. The change will occur only when, in the context of disputes

---

[86] European Community, 'Statement on US Policy on Foreign Direct Investment' (1992) 31 *ILM* 467. See also US Treasury Regulations Pertaining to Mergers, Acquisitions and Takeovers by Foreign Persons, effective 21 November 1991, (1991) 31 *ILM* 424.

[87] NAFTA/UNCITRAL Tribunal, 21 October 2002.   [88] NAFTA/UNCITRAL Tribunal, 26 January 2000.

[89] NAFTA/UNCITRAL Tribunal, 7 August 2002.   [90] (1999) 38 *ILM* 708.

[91] Some US commentators have expressed the view that the NAFTA tribunals' 'nascent interpretations of Chapter 11 broaden the definition of compensable property interests in several significant ways, extend compensation requirements not only to legislative and administrative changes to the law but also to judicial decisions, and bypass ripeness and exhaustion requirement of the US domestic takings law'.

[92] (2000) 15 *ICSID Rev* 169 at 192.   [93] The tribunal itself provided this information in para. 24.

[94] *Tecmed* v. *Mexico* (2006) 10 *ICSID Reports* 54, para. 21.

between developed states, the absurdity of compensating regulatory taking comes to be recognised and clearer rules are stated to identify what constitutes a regulatory taking. Clearly, every taking motivated by an economic reason cannot qualify as non-compensable. But, where there is a preponderant public interest in the taking, particularly in a situation in which treaty commitments relating to the environment justify the interference with private property interests, tribunals must pause to give adequate consideration to whether the taking is a regulatory taking.

1.6 Survey of authorities

Older arbitral awards[95] that are quoted in this context are of little value, for they belong to a period when governments did not play an interventionist role in their economies. They were decided long before the dawn of the welfare state and its assumption of an interventionist role in the marketplace as well as in many spheres of economic and other activity.

The formulation of the rule that, from the foreign investor's point of view, there is no distinction between such takings and that therefore international law should not make a distinction between the two types of taking, is most consistent with investor protection.[96] But, from the point of view of the host state, it could be argued that the foreign investor entered the state voluntarily, knowing the risk of such regulatory laws being applied against him, and that he should bear the risk of such adverse changes as any citizen of the state would. It was implicit in the process of securing admission as a foreign investor that there would be regulation of the foreign investment. Developing states have such legislation in order to ensure that their objectives of economic development are achieved. International law does not question the wisdom of such legislation, as each state has the sovereign power to make such legislation and to ensure that it is obeyed. The issue is simply whether there is an obligation under international law to ensure that there is payment of compensation where there is a taking that is justified on the basis of the regulation.

As long as the regulation was non-discriminatory and not accomplished through abusive processes, there should be an acceptance of the legitimacy of the regulation. It should not be the function of international law to insulate the foreign investor from the regulatory regime of the host state's laws. The removal of the regulatory space for the state to control events which may pose dangers for its economic and political structure of the state should never be the function of international law. The safety and security of its people must constitute the main function of a state. It would be difficult for a law that does not reconcile this interest with those of the foreign investor to gain acceptance. To insist otherwise would be to create a regime akin to the regime created by the capitulation treaties of bygone times.[97] Domestic courts, in deciding issues of taking, balance the social benefits behind the taking against the

---

[95] *De Sabla v. Panama* (1934) 28 *AJIL* 602. The takings were in pursuance of land reform. There were internal procedures for securing relief by affected persons. The applicant had not resorted to them. The takings were held compensable. The *Santa Elena* award shows that things have not changed much. *Santa Elena* v. *Costa Rica* (2000) 39 *ILM* 317; (2002) 5 *ICSID Reports* 153.

[96] Higgins seems to prefer such a view: R. Higgins, 'The Taking of Property by the State' (1982) 176 *Hague Recueil* 331.

[97] Capitulation treaties ensured that the law of the home state of the alien applied to him while he was in the host state. The treaties were imposed by force and later repudiated as unequal treaties.

public objectives that are furthered. Arbitral tribunals are incapable of such an exercise simply because they have not experienced the situation and the context as a domestic court would have. Quite apart from that, many of the issues in the environmental area concern the international community as a whole and are incapable of being settled by an arbitral tribunal that draws its competence from the consent of the two immediate parties to the dispute.[98] The democratic legitimacy of a tribunal that is called upon to deal with such issues is suspect. In any event, developed countries, being themselves practitioners of such interference with foreign investment and increasingly being recipients of foreign investment, will not desire such an insulation of foreign investment from the scope of their regulatory laws. The arguments presented by the United States in *Methanex* v. *United States* indicate that there is no desire on the part of developed states to relinquish regulatory control or to have such control restricted by any norm that requires the payment of compensation. The fact that protection against expropriation is contained in a widely drafted formula in a treaty should not make any difference to these considerations. Many treaties now avoid the problem of regulatory expropriation by defining the investment that is protected in qualified terms so that only those investments that conform to the regulatory laws are given the protection of the treaty.[99] In the recently concluded United States–Singapore Foreign Trade Agreement, an exchange of letters provides that regulatory takings are not to be treated as expropriations.

There is little guidance to be had from the existing authorities on the making of the distinction between compensable takings and regulatory, non-compensable takings in international law. The writings of scholars recognise the existence of the distinction but do not shed much light on the criteria for making the distinction.[100] The older arbitral awards offer little guidance on the more complex regulatory structures that have been devised. In the *Sapphire* v. *NIOC* arbitration, which involved contracts in the petroleum industry, the state oil corporation was constantly interfering with the operations of the foreign investor. It insisted on the right of veto over many decisions that had to be made. This was held to amount to a taking. The arbitrator, Judge Cavin, observed that this 'was a typical case of a squeeze being placed by a state through a state-owned agency against a foreign company'. But, in the changed structure of the petroleum industry in modern times, control of operations by state oil corporations has become so commonplace that such interference can hardly be said to be a taking if the foreign oil company packs up and leaves as the oil company in the *Sapphire* arbitration did. The contractual regime to which the foreign investor agreed would itself usually provide for the exercise of control by a state agency. The complex production-sharing agreements that are drawn up in the petroleum industry contemplate the continuous supervision and control by the state agency of the process of

---

[98] In *Santa Elena* v. *Costa Rica* (2000) 39 *ILM* 317; (2002) 5 *ICSID Reports* 153, the dispute involved the conservation of an area which was the habitat of a protected species. In *SPP* v. *Egypt*, 3 *ICSID Reports* 101; (1983) 22 *ILM* 752, the dispute concerned the excavation of a site that was protected by the World Heritage Convention. It is true that a dispute could be dressed up so as to include such interests (as seems to have been the case in *Metalclad*, where the protection of rare cacti was stated to be the reason for the cancellation of the project, as an afterthought).

[99] *Fraport* v. *Philippines* (ICSID, 2007). The law and the cases on it are discussed in Chapter 9 above.

[100] Higgins, who discusses the issue thoroughly, neatly avoids the need for identifying the criteria for the distinction by suggesting that the distinction is not viable and that compensation is due for both types of taking. R. Higgins, 'The Taking of Property by the State' (1982) 176 *Hague Recueil* 331.

exploitation. There have been many changes in the different industries and in the attitudes to permissible state interference. It is unlikely that the mere giving of directions by a state agency that controls an industrial sector can amount to a taking. Such expansive notions of taking must be resisted, as regulatory control over economic and industrial sectors by states will otherwise become meaningless. The right of a state to so control sectors must remain a primary rule flowing from its sovereignty.

The more recent awards do not throw much light on the issue. An award of a US tribunal in *Revere Copper* v. *Overseas Private Investment Corporation*[101] is relevant in this context. The value of the award is diminished by the fact that the tribunal was a domestic tribunal considering the question as to whether the state insurance company ought to pay the claim of a foreign investor who had been subjected to an expropriatory measure.[102] The primary issue before the tribunal was whether the taking satisfied the requirements for the payment of the claim made by the injured investor against the insurance organisation. Yet, the problems involved in the area are illustrated by the facts. The case arose from a concession agreement for the mining of bauxite made by a subsidiary of the Revere Copper Company with the government of Jamaica. The agreement, which was to last for twenty-five years, contained a stabilisation clause to the effect that taxes and other financial liabilities imposed on the foreign company would remain as agreed for the duration of the concession. But, after a few years of operation, the government claimed additional sums as royalties on the ground of changed circumstances. The company found it difficult to continue operations under the new scheme, and therefore closed its operations. It then claimed on the insurance agreement, which protected it against 'expropriatory action' taken by the foreign government, and the issue before the tribunal was whether the conduct of the Jamaican government in increasing the royalties by legislation in violation of the stabilisation clause in the agreement amounted to an expropriatory action. There was no direct taking by the government. The claimant had shut the plant down as its continued operation was deemed uneconomic. The tribunal found that there had been a taking by the government. The tribunal observed:

In our view the effects of the Jamaican Government's actions in repudiating its long-term commitments to RJA [the subsidiary of Revere Copper] have substantially the same impact on effective control over use and operation as if the properties were themselves conceded by a concession contract that was repudiated ... OPIC argues that it still has all the rights and property that it had before the events of 1974: it is in possession of the plants and other facilities; it has its mining lease; it can operate as it did before. This may be true in a normal sense but for the reasons stated below we do not regard RJA's control of the use and operation of its properties as any longer effective in view of the destruction by government actions of its contract rights.

The tribunal held that the loss of effective control over the operations amounted to expropriation. Effective control of the operations of the company was taken to mean secure planning on the basis of the stabilisation clause which promised that there will be no change

---

[101] (1978) 17 *ILM* 1321, discussed by R. Higgins, 'The Taking of Property by the State' (1982) 176 *Hague Recueil* 331–7.

[102] The award was used by the United States in its memorial in the *ELSI Case* to support the view that a state's interference with 'the freedom to make rational management decisions' amounted to a compensable taking. Memorial submitted by the United States (15 May 1987) in the *ELSI Case* [1989] *ICJ Reports* 15 at 111.

in the operating conditions of the company for twenty-five years. Higgins commented on the award as follows:

Essentially, the tribunal took the view that – in this particular industry at least – effective control was inseparably linked with a stabilisation agreement. The explanation was offered that without it the risks could not be calculated, because 'what the government did yesterday it can undo tomorrow or next week or next month'. That comes very close to saying that all international contracts for the exploitation of resources are inherently immutable, and that any alteration of them (because it warns that further alteration *could* in principle occur again) takes away effective control; because effective control equals rational decision-making based on an ability to calculate the risks.

The tribunal was formulating too wide a rule. Neither its proposition that any interference with the external operating conditions of the contract nor the proposition that the stabilisation clause immunises the contract from the regulatory regimes of the host state can be accepted as a proposition of international law. It is unlikely that international law will admit that fetters can be imposed through contractual arrangements on the sovereign rights of a state to act in its economic interest. As the dissenting opinion pointed out, 'by any reasonable standard what Revere treats as expropriatory is within the proper taxing power of the Jamaican nation'. Attitudes to stabilisation clauses have also undergone significant changes since the opinion in the award was expressed, and the notions of immutability conjured up by the tribunal belong to a different period.[103] The power to increase taxation, which is akin to the power to increase royalties, is a regulatory power, and the generally accepted view is that the exercise of this power cannot be regarded as a taking in violation of property rights, unless there has been such excessive taxation as would indicate a disguised expropriation.[104]

In *Amco v. Indonesia*,[105] there was a withdrawal of licences, without which the foreign investor could not operate in the host state. The withdrawal was due to the alleged failure on the part of the foreign investor to capitalise the venture in accordance with the commitments he had given prior to entry. The tribunal did not pronounce on the question of whether the cancellation of the licences amounted to a taking. Instead, the award was based on the procedure followed prior to the cancellation of the licences. The failure on the part of the government organ to follow minimum standards of procedure was held to be a denial of justice, and damages were awarded on that basis. The inference that is to be drawn is that there could be an interference with the property rights of the foreign investor in accordance with the law of the host state, particularly in circumstances in which the foreign investor had undertaken obligations as a condition of his entry and does not satisfy those conditions. Minimum procedural safeguards must be followed prior to a finding of non-satisfaction of the conditions. The measures that were contemplated were in the nature of sanctions against

---

[103] For example, *Aminoil v. Kuwait* (1982) 22 *ILM* 976.

[104] *Gudmundson v. Iceland* (1960) 30 *ILR* 253. The European Court of Human Rights was not prepared to accept a 25 per cent tax as confiscatory. Though taxation is included in the lists of indirect expropriation, it will be difficult to maintain that taxation involves expropriation. Many investment treaties provide specifically for situations of excessive taxation. They would require parties to consult in order to settle any dispute, but would not treat such taxation as amounting to a taking. Yet, there could be efforts to cloak a taking through the exercise of taxation powers. But, this would be unusual.

[105] (1988) 27 *ILM* 1281.

breaking commitments and can be rationalised on the ground that the foreign investor had committed a transgression which he could have avoided by honouring his commitments. The cancellation of the licences was a sanctioning measure which could have been avoided by the foreign investor.[106] But, *Amco* v. *Indonesia* does not provide any guidance as to measures taken without any prior indication as to expected conduct.

There have been many awards involving the cancellation of licences since *Amco* v. *Indonesia*. In all of them, it is not the cancellation that is the focus of attention and the basis for the finding of an obligation to pay compensation but the faulty procedure that preceded the cancellation. Thus, in *Metalclad*, the finding was that there was a lack of transparency in the manner in which the licensing system was administered.[107] The finding was later overturned by a Canadian court. In *Middle East Cement Shipping Ltd* v. *Egypt*,[108] again, the absence of notice prior to the cancellation of the licence and the sale of the property of the foreign investor was the basis for liability. It would appear that the inference that, had proper administrative procedure been followed, there would be no liability is a safe one to draw.[109] Licences are often subjected to conditions. Their withdrawal through proper procedure based on a failure to abide by the conditions should not be subject to compensation. Such a situation rewards fault.

One further problem is that decisions in the regulatory field are administrative decisions taken not by the courts of the host state but by executive bodies. Even in advanced administrative law systems, it is recognised that the types of procedural safeguard which should be followed, prior to the taking of these decisions, will depend on the circumstances of each situation. The violation of the property rights of individuals is generally expected to be preceded by hearings. But, the situation may well be different where there is a rescission of a licence for non-satisfaction of a condition for in these circumstances no right could have arisen without the satisfaction of the condition. Could a lesser type of procedural protection be sufficient in these circumstances? Could procedural protection be dispensed with where it is clear that there had been no satisfaction of the condition? A state should act safely in such circumstances and provide procedural safeguards. Such procedural safeguards are now stated in investment treaties. It must be an assumption that, where these procedural safeguards are satisfied, the taking will be considered a regulatory taking. It cannot be expected that a foreign company, which was permitted conditional entry and was subjected to

---

[106] See further *Emanuel Too* v. *United States* (1989) 23 *Iran–US CTR* 378, where a cancellation of a licence for liquor was revoked for tax reasons. The Tribunal held that 'a state is not responsible for loss of property or for other economic disadvantage resulting from *bona fide* general taxation or any other action that is commonly accepted as within the police power, provided it is not discriminatory and is not designed to cause the alien to abandon the property to the state or sell it at a distress price'.

[107] The case cited with approval another award involving licensing, *Biloune* v. *Ghana Investment Board* (1993) 95 *ILR* 184. Withdrawals of permits and similar administrative measures are involved in several awards. *Lauder* v. *Czech Republic*, UNCITRAL Arbitration Proceedings (Final Award, 3 September 2001); and *CME* v. *Czech Republic*, UNCITRAL Arbitration Proceedings (Award, 14 March 2003) (both decisions are available on the website of the Department of Finance of the Czech government); *Middle East Cement Shipping and Handling Co.* v. *Egypt*, ICSID Case No. ARB/99/6 (12 April 2002); *Goetz* v. *Burundi* (1999) 15 *ICSID Rev* 457; (2001) 26 *YCA* 24.

[108] ICSID Case No. ARB/99/6 (12 April 2002).

[109] But, in *Goetz* v. *Burundi* (1999) 15 *ICSID Rev* 457; (2001) 26 *YCA* 24, the withdrawal of a 'certificate of free zone' which conferred tax and customs exemptions was withdrawn after independently commissioned studies without compensation. This was held to violate the treaty provision on expropriation. The only logical explanation is that it is an award which was prior to the recognition of the exception for regulatory expropriation. See further, on the case, C. Dugan, D. Wallace, N. Rubins and B. Sabahi, *Investor–State Arbitration* (2008), pp. 446–9.

interference because of the non-satisfaction of those conditions, could claim compensation for the revocation of any licence upon which entry was made.

The *Amco v. Indonesia* award seems to envelop the whole area in the formula of denial of justice, which is unsatisfactory.[110] The notion of denial of justice was formulated prior to the growth of administrative decision-making and catered for the judicial settlement of disputes. The fact that it has been attempted more frequently in investment cases in recent times does not mean that the fundamental criteria that applied to it have changed.[111] The rule on denial of justice has met with much opposition. The salutary reminder of Judge Tanaka in the *Barcelona Traction Case*, that it is 'an extremely serious matter to make a charge of denial of justice *vis-à-vis* a state', must be kept in mind. Whether the notion of denial of justice could be satisfactorily extended to the sphere of administrative decision-making is doubtful. Administrative systems permit decisions to be made without normal procedural safeguards in certain circumstances. What these circumstances are varies over time within each system, and the variance between different administrative systems of different states must be enormous.

Within the common law systems, the general tendency has been to ensure that there must be procedural safeguards when the legitimate expectations of individuals are affected by administrative decisions. But, there is no uniform rule on the point. Public interest in the taking of effective and quick decisions may override the need for any procedural safeguards. Whether an international court or tribunal should have the power to second-guess the existence of circumstances that would enable the administrative decision to be made without the procedural safeguards will remain a moot question.

In certain circumstances, the sanctions that are imposed for non-satisfaction of conditions attached to foreign investments are punitive in nature, and it is well established that the imposition of punitive sanctions does not amount to a taking by a state. The cancellation of a licence for non-satisfaction of a condition does, arguably, have the necessary punitive element. There are many unresolved questions that arise as a result of the transfer of the distinction between regulatory, non-compensable takings and compensable takings to the international sphere. As in the municipal sphere, the fashioning of any meaningful theory to distinguish between the two categories will be a difficult task. Developing states will institute more administrative controls over foreign investment. The need for the making of the distinction will become more apparent. As yet, no conclusive criteria exist in either the domestic or the international systems, apart from the identification of certain obvious regulatory acts as non-compensable. The literature on the subject also does not give much guidance on the issue.

In such a controversy, the nuance in the approach adopted in *Marvin Feldman v. Mexico*[112] affords some possibility of accommodating the conflicting interests of the host state and the foreign investor. The case concerned taxation, which, *prima facie*, would be

---

[110] There is also the further question as to whether an arbitral tribunal which derives its jurisdiction from an investment contract can pronounce on the issue of a denial of justice resulting from an administrative act which is a public law act falling outside the scope of the contract. Certainly, an international court could do so when asked to pronounce on an issue of state responsibility, but such competence cannot usually exist in an arbitral tribunal constituted at the behest of an individual party to an arbitration agreement.

[111] For references to it in modern cases, see *Azinian v. Mexico* (1998) 5 *ICSID Reports* 269; *Loewen v. United States* (2003) 42 *ILM* 811; and *Yaung Chi Oo Ltd v. Myanmar* (2003) 42 *ILM* 540; (2003) 8 *ICSID Reports* 463.

[112] (2002) 7 *ICSID Reports* 318; (2003) 42 *ILM* 625.

regarded as an instance of non-compensable taking. But, the allegation was that rebates that would ordinarily be granted to an exporter of cigarettes were not granted to the claimant, a foreign company operating an export business in Mexico. Mexico's case rested on the requirement that invoices should be produced for claiming rebates and that the claimant had not produced such invoices.

Faced with this issue, the tribunal admitted that the state had a considerable leeway in regulating its economy and the discomfort caused to the foreign investor should not be dressed up as expropriation. The tribunal observed that 'not all government regulatory activity that makes it difficult or impossible for an investor to carry out a particular business, change in the law or change in the application of existing laws that make it uneconomical to continue a particular business is an expropriation'. So, too, the reduction of profits as a consequence of regulation cannot be characterised as expropriation.[113]

The tribunal consistently spoke of a balance. The conflicting interests in respect of which the balance must be maintained are identified by the tribunal in the following passage:[114]

> The Tribunal notes that the ways in which governmental authorities may force a company out of business, or significantly reduce the economic benefits of its business, are many. In the past, confiscatory taxation, denial of access to infrastructure or necessary raw materials, imposition of unreasonable regulatory regimes, among others, have been considered to be expropriatory actions. At the same time, governments must be free to act in the broader public interest through protection of the environment, new or modified tax regimes, the granting or withdrawal of government subsidies, reductions or increases in tariff levels, imposition of zoning restrictions and the like. Reasonable governmental regulation of this type cannot be achieved if any business that is adversely affected may seek compensation, and it is safe to say that customary international law recognises this.

It is in identifying when the balance is tilted towards the interests of the foreign investor that problems arise. As the tribunal put it, 'it is much less clear when a governmental decree that interferes with broadly defined property rights crosses the line from valid regulation to a compensable taking, and it is fair to say that no one has come up with a fully satisfactory means of drawing this line'.[115] Apart from discrimination and arbitrariness in procedure and the idea that the circumstances should 'rise to a level of violation',[116] there is no further guidance given.

It is possible to construct a picture of when regulation crosses the line to become expropriation. It is clear that any depreciation in the value of the property will not be sufficient. That expansive notion, to be found in the litigation strategy in cases like *Ethyl* v. *Canada*, will no

---

[113] Para. 112. The *Ethyl* theory of depreciation of the value of shares and the *Methanex* theory of loss of earnings and profits as expropriation are diminished by the *dictum*. The tribunal stated: 'Governments, in their exercise of regulatory power, frequently change their laws and regulations in response to changing economic circumstances or changing political, economic or social considerations. Those changes may well make certain activities less profitable or even uneconomic to continue.' The *dictum* will also require environmental regulation to be reconsidered in *Santa Elena* v. *Costa Rica* (2000) 39 *ILM* 317; (2002) 5 *ICSID Reports* 153.

[114] Para. 103.

[115] Para. 100. The tribunal relied to a large extent on the analysis in the American Law Institute, *Restatement (Third) on Foreign Relations Law of the United States* (1987), section 712, comment (g). But, this analysis predates the problems relating to environmental regulations that have been the focus of the more recent awards and discussions.

[116] Para. 113.

longer find favour. With the phrase, 'tantamount to expropriation', in investment treaties coming to be treated as a mere surplusage,[117] the scope for such an argument has diminished considerably. Discriminatory treatment is a criterion for expropriation. But, absence of discrimination was stated to be a requirement for expropriation at all times. In any event, where discrimination in regulatory mechanisms is based on legitimate grounds, the discrimination is regarded as legitimate.[118] The stronger the public purpose behind the regulation, the less is the scope for the regulation being treated as expropriation. A general measure such as an exchange control that uniformly affects all business cannot amount to a compensable taking.[119] This is consistent with the position in most domestic law systems.

The only clear situation where the line between regulation and expropriation is crossed that is disclosed in the existing authorities is where there is an absence of procedural safeguards against the exercise of regulatory powers. In these circumstances, a situation akin to denial of justice prevails. Denial of justice normally applies to the exercise of judicial functions. But, it would appear that, where a discretionary power in a regulatory authority is exercised without procedural safeguards and the absence of such safeguards so transgresses the ordinary sense of justice, liability will arise. It is not every transgression that has this result. The transgression must be of such a kind as to justify international concern.

The starting-point must always be that the regulatory interference is presumptively non-compensable. The *per se* rule in the *Santa Elena* v. *Costa Rica* award has no place in the law, as it is not supported by any authority, either in domestic legal systems or in international law. That presumption against compensation is strengthened in circumstances where the regulation is in areas of environmental protection or cultural preservation which are of significance to the international community.[120] It is strengthened where the public interests are so dominant as to overwhelm individual interests. It is weakened where there is discrimination that cannot be explained in a legitimate manner. It is weakened also where the exercise is not accompanied by due process and other procedural safe guards that amount to a denial of justice in terms of international law. The construction of a model of decision-making in the area along these lines is a vital need. The case law that has been developed is in no way inconsistent with such a model.[121] The contrary decisions can be explained on factual and other grounds.[122]

---

[117] *Pope and Talbot* v. *Canada* (2002) 41 *ILM* 1347; *Marvin Feldman* v. *Mexico* (2002) 7 *ICSID Reports* 318; (2003) 42 *ILM* 625, para. 100. Sloane and Reisman build a thesis in their article, R. D. Sloane and W. M. Reisman, 'Indirect Expropriation and Its Valuation in the BIT Generation' (2003) 74 *BYIL* 115, that the future course of developments will concentrate on this phrase. But, it is most unlikely. The phrase has been removed in the newer investment treaties, and is unlikely to be given effect to in other treaties in which it appears.

[118] *Marvin Feldman* v. *Mexico* (2002) 7 *ICSID Reports* 318; (2003) 42 *ILM* 625.

[119] *CMS Gas Transmission Co* v. *Argentina* (2003) 30 *ILM* 788; (2005) 44 *ILM* 1205, para. 23. The dispute cannot be said to arise from an investment if this happens (see para. 27 of the award). The tribunal said that a state is entitled to follow its own policy choices (para. 29). See also *CME* v. *Czech Republic*, UNCITRAL Arbitration Proceedings (Award, 14 March 2003), para. 589, to the effect that a general measure cannot be a taking. Where the general measure is applied in a discriminatory manner to a specific investment, this could amount to a taking. The same case supports this view. The decision is available on the website of the Department of Finance of the Czech government.

[120] The presence of an international convention supporting the regulation would be an indication of this.

[121] Cases like *Amco* v. *Indonesia* support this model.

[122] *Santa Elena* may seem to conflict. The *per se* rule in this case is clearly in error. *Tecmed* was wrong in accepting the rule. It is not supported by awards such as *Feldman* or *Pope and Talbot*. But, in *Santa Elena*, as in *Metalclad* and *SPP* v. *Egypt*, the environmental and other motives adduced by the state were afterthoughts. So, too, in *S. D. Myers* v. *Canada*, the Basel Convention obligations were *ex post facto* rationalisations of the regulation, thought up at the time of the proceedings.

The above analysis is consistent with the side letter on expropriation accompanying the Singapore–United States Free Trade Agreement concluded in 2003. Explaining the provision on expropriation, the letter contains the following paragraph on regulatory takings:

Except in rare circumstances, non-discriminatory regulatory actions, designed and applied to protect public welfare objectives, such as public health, safety and the environment do not constitute direct expropriation.

This formulation has now found its way into the US model investment treaty (2004) and its Canadian counterpart. It or similar formulations have passed into other model treaties.[123] The annex to the model treaties in effect spell out the balancing tests in accordance with the statement of these tests by the US Supreme Court. The annex states:[124]

The determination of whether an action or series of actions by a Party, in a specific fact situation, constitutes an indirect expropriation, requires a case-by case, fact-based inquiry that considers, among other factors:
(i) the economic impact of the government action, although the fact that an action or series of actions by a Party has an adverse effect on the economic value of an investment, standing alone, does not establish that an indirect expropriation has occurred;
(ii) the extent to which the government action interferes with distinct, reasonable investment-backed expectations; and
(iii) the character of the government action.

Though Canada does not have any significant jurisprudence on takings, its annex contains an almost identical formulation.

Many newer treaties deal with regulatory takings as an exception to the rule on expropriation. Thus, Article 20(8) of the Investment Agreement for the COMESA Common Investment Area (2007) provides that:

Consistent with the right of states to regulate and the customary international law principles on police powers, *bona fide* regulatory measures taken by a Member State that are designed and applied to protect or enhance legitimate public welfare objectives, such as public health, safety and the environment, shall not constitute an indirect expropriation under this Article.

Likewise, Article 6(2)(c) of the Colombian model treaty provides:

Except in rare circumstances, such as when a measure or series of measures are so severe in light of their purpose that they cannot be reasonably viewed as having been adopted and applied in good faith, non-discriminatory measures of a Party that are designed and applied for public purposes or social interest or with objectives such as public health, safety and environment protection, do not constitute indirect expropriation.

Such provisions neatly dispose of the possibility of the *per se* rule in *Santa Elena* v. *Costa Rica* ever being applied to expropriation under the treaty. The formulation merely states the

---

[123] For example, the Colombian model treaty of 2007.   [124] US Model Bilateral Investment Treaty (2004), Annex B 4(a).

obvious, and seeks to restore the balance between expropriation and regulation.[125] But, striking an exact balance will prove to be elusive.[126] As the *Saluka*[127] tribunal pointed out, international law 'has yet to draw a bright and easily distinguishable line between non-compensable regulations on the one hand and, on the other, measures that have the effect of depriving foreign investors of their investment and are thus unlawful and compensable in international law'. Apart from the observation that each case must be separately considered in the context of proportionality and reasonableness and the factors involved balanced, little guidance has been forthcoming.[128]

It is instructive to compare the situation in international trade law. GATT provisions acknowledge that deviations from market access rules may be made if they are 'necessary' to achieve regulatory objectives.[129] But, the least trade-restrictive alternative reasonably possible should be used. There cannot be arbitrary application of the regulation, nor should it be a disguise for a trade restriction. The final test is one of balancing the values protected by the regulation against the impact of the regulation on trade.

Though such balancing tests may be useful in providing guidance, the starting-point of analysis, as indicated, must always be that the state has a right to protect its interests. A tribunal must show reluctance to review the state's assessment of its own needs for the regulation. Unless there is some strong *prima facie* evidence of abuse, there should be no interference. The fact that the protection of similar values in other states is achieved through similar regulation will add weight to the legitimacy of the regulation of a respondent state. Where clear discrimination exists, the regulation is unlawful. It would also cross the boundary into a taking where the regulation is a disguise for a taking. Here, the issue is as to the primary motive for the interference. As the tribunal in *Feldman* noted,[130] there can be no satisfactory solution proffered to the thorny issue as to when regulation transforms itself into expropriation. Each case has to be considered separately.

There is an emergence of trends relating to areas of activity. There is an obvious inference that the nature of some activity is so sovereign that one must start with a presumption that the measure involved is regulatory. The presumption would of course shift in accordance with

---

[125] The notion of balancing is implicit in the *dicta* of the award in *Tecmed* v. *Mexico* (2006) 10 *ICSID Reports* 54, para. 122, which refers to the proportionality between the public interest and the regulatory measure.

[126] The draft Norwegian model treaty of 2007 indicates the impossibility of a written text that would provide guidelines. It states the rule against expropriation in the first provision: 'A party shall not expropriate an investment of an investor of the other party except in the public interest and subject to conditions provided for by law and by the general principles of international law.' The statement itself presupposes that there could be agreement on what the general principles of international law are. The treaty then states the exception provision: 'The preceding provision shall not, however, in any way impair the right of a Party to enforce such laws as it deems necessary to control the use of the property in accordance with the general interest or to secure the payment of taxes or other contributions or penalties.' The effort seeks to capture the regulatory taking exception and is laudable. But, the complexity of the application of the two provisions is obvious. The breadth of the exception eats away the principal rule in the first provision. This wording is an indication of the difficulties that will confront the tribunals in this area. The problem can be defined but the search as to the criteria identification of the intersection of regulatory expropriation and compensatory expropriation is illusive. For attempts at this, see the papers published in a symposium in (2003) 11 *New York University Environmental Law Journal*; and A. Newcombe, 'The Boundaries of Regulatory Expropriation in International Law' (2005) 20 *ICSID Rev* 1.

[127] *Saluka Investments* v. *Czech Republic* (Award, 17 March 2006). The tribunal held that measures taken by the central bank in the context of the financial situation in the country were regulatory though they affected the claimant adversely.

[128] See further A. Newcombe, 'Boundaries of Regulatory Expropriation in International Law' (2005) 20 *ICSID Rev* 1; U. Kriebaum, 'Regulatory Takings: Balancing the Interests of the Investor and the State' (2007) 8 *Journal of World Investment and Trade* 717.

[129] Article XX(b) and (d).   [130] (2002) 7 *ICSID Reports* 318; (2003) 42 *ILM* 625.

circumstances. But, the existing awards as well as the formulation in some of the newer treaties seem to suggest that there is a recognition of such categories which are moved out of the expropriation law and subjected to other criteria. Some of these may be identified.

(i) *Taxation*. It is clear that taxation is emerging as the most obvious instance of a regulatory taking. Many recent treaties call for separate procedures to be invoked where taxation is involved. These involve some consultative procedure between the state parties. Recourse to arbitration is permitted only if there is disagreement between the parties. There is now a build-up of awards which justify the differential treatment of tax measures. Unless the tax measure is exorbitant and is clearly a disguise for an expropriation or it is discriminatory, it would be difficult to characterise a tax measure as a compensable taking. In *EnCana*, the tribunal stated that taxation 'in itself is not a taking of property; if it were, a universal state prerogative would be denied by a guarantee against expropriation which cannot be the case'.[131] Taxation of excess profits in the petroleum sector has been common. The usual pattern has been to accept such taxation as regulatory.

(ii) *Environmental interferences*. It is unlikely that the view taken in *Santa Elena* v. *Costa Rica*, that the interest of investment protection stated in the treaty trumps environmental considerations, however weighty, is likely to be followed in the future. More recent investment treaties state the environmental exception in stronger terms. Trends in the literature also suggest that there will be different attitudes taken to environmental interferences in the future. Environmental interests constitute essential interests of the state and may give rise to states of necessity.[132]

(iii) *Human rights and labour rights*. Treaties now provide expressly for labour rights. Foreign investment companies are prone to violate labour rights. They seek cheap labour and may economise by not providing adequate standards to their employees. Where the state interferes to ensure such standards, the interference should be considered regulatory and non-compensable. This would be particularly so where the interference is based on international conventions defining the standards. Likewise, where there are human rights violations, the interference would be justified. The issue was discussed in Chapter 9 above. There is much evidence of transgressions of human rights by foreign investors, sometimes in association with governments. Where policy changes take place redressing these violations, they must be regarded as non-compensable regulatory interventions.

(iv) *Interference supported by ius cogens norms*. Treaties cannot give protection to conduct that violates *ius cogens* norms. Treaties inconsistent with *ius cogens* obligations have no validity. In *Phoenix* v. *Czech Republic*,[133] the tribunal gave as obvious examples situations where the investment promotes genocide or racial discrimination. These are uncontroversial instances of violations of *ius cogens*. But, there are other candidates which may qualify as *ius cogens* principles. These arise usually in the human rights and environmental law areas, and may also fall within the categories identified above. But, where there is a norm emerging as a candidate for elevation to the *ius cogens* rule or as an *erga omnes* obligation, weight must be given to it when considering whether its place in the hierarchy of norms is so elevated as to displace an obligation owed to

---

[131] *EnCana Corporation* v. *Ecuador*, London Court of International Arbitration Case No. UN3481 (UNCITRAL) (27 February 2004); but, in *Link-Trading Joint Stock Company* v. *Moldova*, UNCITRAL Arbitration Proceedings (Award, 18 April 2002), taxation was found to be abusive and hence not regulatory. See further T. W. Walde and A. Kolo, 'Coverage of Taxation under Modern Investment Treaties', in P. Muchlinski, F. Fortino and C. Schreuer, *Handbook of International Investment Law* (2008).

[132] D. Gantz, 'Reconciling Environmental Protection and Investor Rights' (2001) 31 *Environmental Law Review* 106; *Gabcikovo–Nagymaros Case* [1997] *ICJ Reports* 7.

[133] ICSID Case No. ARB/06/5 (Decision on Jurisdiction, 15 April, 2009).

individual foreign investors.[134] An example may be obligations that are owed to indigenous peoples, violations of which usually take place in the context of mining concessions in tribal lands.[135] The position of permanent sovereignty over natural resources is in the eyes of some scholars a candidate for elevation as an *ius cogens* norm, though this is resisted by others. This would undermine many concession agreements. In the context of water disputes, Mexico has successfully argued that water was a natural resource that could not be transferred indefinitely out of the control of the state.[136] The right to secession creates similar difficulties. Where natural resources are involved and a previous government had transferred them in a manner deleterious to the interests of a colonised state, it is clear that the previous obligation is not binding on the new state formed on the basis of self-determination.[137]

2. The exercise of management control over the investment

Interference by the state to take over management and control of the foreign investor's affairs is *prima facie* a taking by the state which should be compensated.[138] The foreign shareholder is entitled to such control and management of his investment or property as he pleases, subject of course to the general laws of the host state. The extent of this exception that the regulatory laws of the host state have a role to play in the determination of the rights of the foreign investor generates considerable problems. The exception may be wide enough, if some views are accepted, to undermine the general rule altogether.

The exception flows from the fact that the host state has interests to safeguard as far as the operation of the investment is concerned. The *ELSI Case* illustrates the nature of the interests of the host state that could be involved. The foreign investor has to operate within the confines of the company and securities legislation of the host state. Interference based on such legislation is fully justified, provided procedures indicated in them satisfy due process standards. There may also be an interest of the host state in ensuring that the workforce of the foreign-owned company is not left without employment as a result of the decisions of the foreign investor. The state has an interest in ensuring that the economy of the area in which the foreign investor operates is not affected by the decisions he makes. The need for the protection of such interests entitles the host state to intervene in the management of the company. In the *ELSI Case*, as well as in some of the awards of the Iran–US Claims Tribunal, the conflicts in the interests of the foreign investor and the host state were graphically illustrated. The statement that an interference with management and control of

---

[134] See further M. Sornarajah, *The Settlement of Investment Disputes* (2000).

[135] *Grand River Enterprises Six Nations* v. *United States*, UNCITRAL Arbitration Proceedings (Decision on Objections to Jurisdiction, 20 July 2006).

[136] *Baywater Irrigation District* v. *Mexico*, ICSID Case No. ARB(AF)/05/1 (NAFTA Arbitration before ICSID) (Award, 19 June 2007).

[137] This would appear to be so from the *Urenco Case* (unreported), an incident relating to uranium transfers made by South Africa when it was the mandatory power over South West Africa. Clearly, these arrangements were not binding on the state after the termination of the mandate. The contractual obligations made for East Pakistan prior to the creation of Bangladesh were held not to be binding.

[138] An editorial comment in the *Netherlands International Law Journal* suggested that the assumption of management control over the Indonesian tobacco plantations amounted to nationalisation.

a foreign-controlled company is a taking is only a generalisation that provides a starting-point for discussion and no more.

In the *ELSI Case*, the US-controlled company in Italy which was the subject of the dispute between the United States and Italy, was failing. The fact that the company was failing had important consequences under Italian law. Quite apart from issues of bankruptcy, there were requirements in Italian law applying to all companies relating to minimum levels of capitalisation. In modern company law systems, such measures are usually taken by states in order to protect the integrity of stock markets. The state will also have an interest in the effect the failure of a company will have on local employment, particularly if the company was a large one. Such an interest in companies formed by foreign investors is logical, as they usually involve the employment of a large workforce. In the *ELSI Case*, when the foreign company contemplated the dismissal of a part of its workforce, there was widespread industrial action. The state had an obvious interest in ensuring that the dismissals did not lead to unemployment in an already economically depressed part of the country. Bankruptcy proceedings that were later instituted prevented the management from conducting an orderly liquidation of the company, which may have enabled the foreign company to realise a greater value for its assets. Interference in these circumstances in the management and control of the company by the host state was held to be justifiable. The state had a compelling interest in ensuring that the impact on its economy of the failure of the company was reduced or eliminated. The steps it takes to achieve this objective cannot be considered to be such an interference with the foreign investor's management rights as to amount to a compensable taking. Again, a regulatory interference was involved, and the approach of the International Court of Justice was not to second-guess whether the interference was necessary.

The analysis which was made of similar problems by the Iran–US Claims Tribunal is in agreement with the view taken that interference with management and control will not *per se* amount to a taking by the state. Though there are absolute statements of the rule in some of the awards that were made, there are qualifications of the rule in some of the later awards. The disputes, which involved the taking over of the management of US-controlled companies by the Iranian government, concerned companies whose management had fled the country as a result of the anti-American hostility that had been unleashed by the Iranian revolution. The government had then enacted legislation to deal with companies that were left without effective management. The legislation permitted the appointment of managers to companies whose managerial staff had left the country. The legislation could be justified on the basis that the government had to get the economic life of the country back into gear and that one of the ways of doing this was to assume control over the companies that were abandoned by their management. But, if such an assumption of control was permanent, then it destroys the rights of the shareholders in the company to appoint a new management, and it may be regarded as a taking. The awards of the tribunals could be reconciled on the basis of this distinction. The awards of the Iran–US Claims Tribunal must, however, be used cautiously, as the Tribunal had a wider mandate regarding what amounted to a taking.

2.1 Cancellation of permits and licences

The cancellation of permits and licences involves a regulatory taking, and has been dealt with above in that context. But, where such cancellations are made without due process, are discriminatory and violate commitments made regarding their issuance and validity, their subsequent withdrawal could amount to a compensable taking.[139] Where licences and permits are necessary to operate in certain sectors of the economy and these licences are withdrawn, the foreign investor's ability to conduct his business will be adversely affected. It could be argued that such measures involve a taking even if they do not affect the ability of the foreign investor to continue with the business or in any way affect the ownership of the property of the foreign investor. In modern investment treaties, such licences are protected, as they fall within the definition of investments.

Technically, the granting of a licence involves the conferment of a privilege in a Hohfeldian sense. There is no vesting of a right in the foreign investor. Where the privilege is revoked, the state is not benefited in any sense. Hence, it would be difficult to say that there had been a taking by the state in situations where there is a revocation of a licence. However, the foreign investor may have to relinquish his business as a result of such a termination and the assets of the business may then vest in some state entity. This will be so where the state entity is a partner in the venture with the foreign investor. In the alternative, it may have to be sold for a lower price than would otherwise have been the case.

In the administrative law systems in the common law world, there is generally no review permitted for the revocation of licences, as they are privileges the conferment of which is entirely at the discretion of the state.[140] There are many awards of arbitral tribunals and claims commissions which have asserted that the withdrawal of licences or the imposition of controls do not amount to the taking of property.[141] Such regulatory takings will fall within the category of lawful takings for which no compensation needs to be paid. It has always been the case that the taking of alien property as a means for the exaction of a criminal penalty is lawful and that such taking need not be compensated as compensation will negate the whole purpose behind the imposition of the criminal sanction.[142]

But, the law stated in these older cases must be reviewed in light of new developments. In most administrative systems, it is now recognised that cancellations of licences have a significance beyond the withdrawal of a privilege conferred by the state. It withdraws a right that is essential to the earning of a livelihood or the carrying on of business. In these circumstances, the licence gives rise to a legitimate expectation that is protected by due process requirements. The law is increasingly coming to accept that such a withdrawal must not be lightly done without warnings to the licensee to desist from the offending behaviour

---

[139] *Goetz* v. *Burundi* (1999) 15 *ICSID Rev* 457; (2001) 26 *YCA* 24 involved withdrawal of a certificate to operate in a free zone. This followed an economic review as to whether operators in gold and other natural resources sectors should be granted such certificates. The tribunal went through the exercise of finding whether the cancellation was lawful under the treaty formulation. It required payment of compensation as a condition to be satisfied. Notions of regulatory taking had not taken hold for it to be discussed.

[140] *Murphyores Ltd* v. *The Commonwealth* (1976) 136 CLR 1.

[141] *Kugele* v. *Polish State* [1931–2] *AD* 69; *Claim of Erna Spielberg* (1958) Whiteman, *Digest*, vol. 8, p. 988; and other awards mentioned at pp. 988–9 in the same volume of Whiteman's *Digest*.

[142] A. Freeman, *The International Responsibility of States* (1938), p. 518.

or to fulfil conditions attached to the licence. It must be preceded by an opportunity for the licensee to explain why the licence should not be withdrawn. In *Amco* v. *Indonesia*,[143] the several tribunals which dealt with the dispute were unanimous in holding that the due process requirement will be recognised in international law and that withdrawal of foreign investment licences are subject to the rule. The withdrawal of a licence may be considered a regulatory act, particularly where the conditions attached to the licence have not been satisfied. But, the substantive right is subject to procedural regularity. The proper exercise of the substantive right of revocation for non-satisfaction of the condition is not compensable, as it is a regulatory act. But, if it is done without procedural regularity, that irregularity gives rise to the duty to pay compensation.

Cancellation of licences on environmental grounds will become more frequent with the increasing concern for the protection of the environment. Such cancellations will often put an end to the foreign investment. They will usually not amount to compensable takings. In *Murphyores Ltd* v. *The Commonwealth*, a concession had been given to two US companies for sand-mining on Fraser Island, close to the Great Barrier Reef. The minerals did not have a local market. They had to be exported. An environmental study found that the sand-mining was harmful to the Great Barrier Reef. The Australian government refused to grant export licences for the export of the minerals. This effectively terminated the operations of the companies. The Australian High Court rejected the claims of the two companies for compensation on the basis that no compensable taking was involved. The Australian government also resisted efforts on the part of the home state of the foreign investor to ensure that compensation be paid to the foreign investor.

The awards in cases like *Amco* v. *Indonesia* and *Middle Eastern Cement Shipping Ltd* v. *Egypt* have found liability not for the cancellation of the permits but for the lack of due process prior to such cancellation. In *Metalclad*, again, it was not the cancellation that triggered liability, but the absence of transparency attending the process. A court of review found the tribunal's view on transparency to be improper. The withdrawal of a licence following proper procedure is an instance of a non-compensable regulatory taking. The foreign investor would be aware of the circumstances in which the licence is to operate. The cancellation is usually a punitive measure for not abiding by the purpose behind the regulation or the conditions to which the licence is subject. As such, the need for compensation does not arise from this situation, provided procedural safeguards had not been violated. Recent awards have emphasised the need for due process safeguards prior to the cancellation of licences and have deemed cancellations without due process as violations of treatment standards as well as of the expropriation provisions.[144]

---

[143] I *ICSID Reports* 509.

[144] In addition to *Biloune* v. *Ghana Investment Board* (1993) 95 *ILR* 184; and *Metalclad* v. *Mexico* (2000) 5 *ICSID Reports* 209; (2001) 40 *ILM* 55, see *Middle East Cement Shipping and Handling Co.* v. *Egypt*, ICSID Case No. ARB/99/6 (12 April 2002), para. 143; *Lauder* v. *Czech Republic*, UNCITRAL Arbitration Proceedings (Final Award, 3 September 2001); *CME* v. *Czech Republic*, UNCITRAL Arbitration Proceedings (Award, 14 March 2003) (both decisions are available on the website of the Department of Finance of the Czech government); and *Goetz* v. *Burundi* (1999) 15 *ICSID Rev* 457; (2001) 26 *YCA* 24. The creeping of administrative law theory into the area is evidenced by these awards. From such awards, it is possible to launch into the whole array of administrative law notions such as legitimate expectations, which has been done in cases like *ADF* v. *United*

2.2 *Takings by agents and mobs*

This is an area for the application of the rules on state responsibility for injuries to aliens. It has more features in common with confiscatory takings than the type of economic takings which have been considered so far. But, having made the point that they are different, it is convenient to consider them here. The rule is that, where there is destruction of property during civil strife or an insurgency, the state is liable for the destruction if it failed in its duty to protect the property of the foreign investor. It follows that, if there is active participation or instigation of the persons causing the damage by the state or its agents, then responsibility for the damage will arise. It is also clear that there must be a definite link between the perpetrators of the damage and the state or some attributability of the damage to the state through a theory of negligence. These rules have been established through many arbitral awards. They have also been stated in the Draft Code of the International Law Commission on State Responsibility.

The Iran–US Claims Tribunal dealt on several occasions with the situation where property was taken or destroyed by mobs. In all these situations, the essential element was the establishment of the link between the revolutionary gangs and the new government which emerged. In the early stages of the revolution, there were several gangs with which the emerging government did not have any links whatever. The Tribunal refused to hold Iran liable for the activities of these gangs. But, when the revolution took hold, groups emerged with links to and authority from the state. Iran was held liable for the acts of these groups.[145]

In the *ELSI Case*, one of the factors focused on by the United States in making its case against Italy was that the occupation of the factory by the workers was promoted by the mayor of the city in which the plant was situated, and that he had a sufficient connection with the state to make the state liable for the failure of the company. The court found that the occupation of the factory by the workers was peaceful and that there was no indication that production was affected by the occupation.[146] The inference is that there may be responsibility in the state for the omission, if there had been damage caused by the occupation and it had been condoned by the authorities. In such a situation, the omission to act could have consequences that are akin to a taking. For such a consequence to follow, it must be shown that the disturbance was not an ordinary consequence of the actions taken by the foreign investor himself and that there was a link between the state and the persons whose acts caused the disturbance. Though the existence of a bilateral treaty will enhance the inference of liability arising from the omission to give protection, liability in such circumstances flows from a rule of customary international law on state responsibility. Where an investment treaty exists, the requirement that the foreign investor should be given full protection and security will ensure that the situation is covered.[147] In this case, the matter will be dealt with as a failure to provide the requisite treatment rather than as a taking of property.

States, ICSID Case No. ARB(AF)/00/1 (NAFTA) (Award, 9 January 2003) and *Tecmed* v. *Mexico* (2006) 10 *ICSID Reports* 54. The present phase of extension of this area of the law is based on domestic administrative law notions, borrowed largely from common law states.

[145] On attributability, see *Yeager* v. *Iran* (1987) 17 *Iran–US CTR* 92.

[146] Para. 105. At para. 108, the Court said that the dismissal of 800 workers 'could not reasonably be expected to pass without some protest'.

[147] *American Machine Tools* v. *Zaire* (1997) 36 *ILM* 1531.

Where the armed forces of a state are involved in a taking of property, the attribution of the act to the state is clear. In *Amco* v. *Indonesia*, the taking was effected by the army, but the tribunal held that there was no attributability, as the army was acting in order to further the interests of its own pension fund. In *AAPL* v. *Sri Lanka*, there was destruction of property by the army during hostilities. Liability was based on the state's failure to protect the property. In *Wena Hotels* v. *Egypt*, there was interference by the army. Where the army is involved, the attributability of the act of taking to the state is easier to establish.[148]

2.3 Excessive taxation

As indicated earlier, taxation is within the sovereign power of a state. There is no rule in international law limiting the power of a state to impose taxes within its territory.[149] But, 'excessive and repetitive tax' measures have a confiscatory effect and could amount to indirect expropriation.[150] A uniform increase in taxation cannot by itself have such an effect. But, where a foreign investment is singled out and subjected to heavy taxation, a clear situation of expropriation can be made out. Such a result may not follow where sufficient justification for such taxation exists. The taxing of windfall profits (i.e. profits which arise without any act on the part of the investor) cannot amount to a taking.[151] Thus, taxation of the oil industry for windfall profits due to price hikes cannot amount to a taking.[152] Where the situation of excessive taxation is dealt with in investment treaties, the mechanism used is joint consultation between the parties to determine whether the excessive tax should be imposed.[153] *Marvin Feldman* v. *Mexico*[154] supports the use of a balancing test to deal with the situation where a complainant alleges unfair taxation. This would take into account the objects of the tax measures, the requirements that have to be satisfied if rebates are to be allowed and the need to prevent evasion, and balance these against the interests of the foreign investor to ensure non-discrimination and fairness. Except in certain obvious circumstances, it is unlikely that a charge of unfair taxation would succeed. Many investment treaties deal with taxation separately, requiring that allegations of unfair taxation be dealt with through consultation between the two treaty partners.[155] This removes the area from the scope of the taking provision in the treaty.

2.4 Expulsion of the foreign investor

The expulsion of the foreign investor will amount to a taking if the purpose of the expulsion is the taking of his property.[156] But, where national security or other sufficient grounds exist for the expulsion, this will be different. Objectively reasonable factors for the expulsion

---

[148] But, see *Yaung Chi Oo Ltd* v. *Myanmar* (2003) 42 *ILM* 540; (2003) 8 *ICSID Reports* 463.
[149] S. Picciotto, *International Business Taxation* (1992). [150] World Bank, 'Report and Guidelines' (1992) 31 *ILM* 1375.
[151] *Aminoil* v. *Kuwait* (1982) 21 *ILM* 976.
[152] See, for the US, *Crude Oil Windfall Tax* (United States Crude Oil Profit Windfall Tax Act, 1980, PL 96–223), upheld in *United States* v. *Ptasynki*, 462 US 74 (1983).
[153] Canadian investment treaties use this technique. [154] (2002) 7 *ICSID Reports* 318; (2003) 42 *ILM* 625.
[155] Canadian investment treaties adopt this mechanism. [156] *Biloune* v. *Ghana Investment Board* (1993) 95 *ILR* 184.

must exist if it were to be justifiable on national security grounds. A tribunal which has jurisdiction over the taking on the basis that it is a violation of a foreign investment agreement does not have jurisdiction to pronounce on the human rights issues involved in the taking.[157] This is a sensible idea, for a tribunal which deals with commercial matters is not justified in pronouncing upon disputes that are not commercial in nature.

2.5 Freezing of bank accounts

The freezing of the bank accounts of a foreign investor could amount to a taking of property in certain circumstances. Where bank accounts are frozen on the ground that it is necessary to do so in order to investigate a crime or a violation of banking regulations, the interference would be justified. But, where it is done in the process of an expropriation of the property of the foreign investor and as a part of a plan to deny him all his property rights, there is a strong case for the view that the freezing of the accounts amounts to a taking.[158]

2.6 Exchange controls

Exchange controls are imposed in order to meet economic crises and prevent the flight of capital from the state. These measures affect the whole economy uniformly and cannot be considered expropriation despite the fact that it affects foreign business along with local business. Though there may be a violation of the right to repatriation involved in the imposition of exchange controls, it is now accepted that such controls do not violate the treaty provisions on expropriation. The matter was considered in *CMS Gas Transmission Co.* v. *Argentina.*[159] The tribunal rightly held that a distinction should be drawn 'between measures of a general economic nature, particularly in the context of the economic and financial emergency and measures specifically directed to the investment's operation'. The making of economic choices cannot be prevented by treaties in these circumstances.

3. Illegal takings

The taking of foreign property by a state is *prima facie* lawful. Such legality is, however, subject to conditions. The taking of foreign property will be lawful only if such taking was for a public purpose and is not discriminatory. There is a duty in international law to pay compensation for the taking of alien property. Non-payment affects legality. But, the standard of compensation which must be paid is a matter of controversy. The controversy relating to the standard of compensation is dealt with in Chapter 11 below. There is a controversial view that a taking in breach of contractual commitments is also unlawful. This view also needs more exhaustive treatment, and is dealt with in Chapter 7 above. There is general agreement that a taking which lacks a public purpose and a discriminatory taking are

---

[157] *Ibid.*   [158] F. A. Mann, *Legal Aspects of Money* (5th edn, 1992).   [159] ICSID Case No. ARB/01/8 (2003), para. 25.

illegal in international law. Where a taking is done in violation of a treaty, the taking will be considered illegal.

The requirement of a public purpose and the requirement that the taking is not discriminatory are dealt with in this section. The illegality which is attached to a taking in violation of a treaty is also considered. The final section considers the consequences in international law of an illegal taking.

3.1 The taking must be for a public purpose

It is generally conceded that the requirement of public purpose for a taking to be lawful is not much of a limitation in modern times. The origin of the doctrine is probably to be found in the statement of public purpose as a limitation on the powers of eminent domain by Grotius. *Dicta* in later arbitral awards which are used to support the existence of the limitation are equivocal at best.[160] *Dicta* in some arbitral awards questioned the need for the requirement of public purpose.[161] Writers are divided on the need for the requirement.[162] But, the requirement continues to be stated in all bilateral investment treaties. This may be due to the compulsion to follow a time-tested formula rather than to any conviction that the requirement continues to have any force.[163]

The public purpose limitation may have had some significance in the period when the distinction between confiscation and nationalisation had an importance in the law, for the motive behind the taking was the basis of the distinction. The distinction itself originated at a time when state interference occurred only in exceptional circumstances. Writing in 1941 on the distinction made between types of taking of alien property, a commentator referred to the increasing difficulty of making such distinctions 'especially since states have more and more abandoned the *laissez-faire* conception of their functions and become welfare states interfering daily in all imaginable realms of private activities by all imaginable measures and procedures'.[164] State regulation of private property five decades later is so commonplace that it will be difficult for tribunals sitting outside the state to question the motives behind the taking. Yet, the strength of public purpose may serve to identify whether a taking is regulatory or not.

---

[160] *Walter Fletcher Smith Case* (1930) 24 *AJIL* 384 is a leading authority on the point. But, the arbitrator was there referring to an internal requirement of Cuban law. In addition, the taking was found to be for 'amusement and private profit'. As such, it was a confiscation more than an expropriation. *David Goldberg Case* (1930) 2 *UNRIAA* 901 concerned a military requisition. In *Sabbatino v. Banco Nacional de Cuba*, 193 F Supp 375 at 384 (1961), Judge Dimock found the Cuban nationalisation invalid for the want of a public purpose.

[161] *Schufeldt Claim* (1930) 2 *UNRIAA* 1079 at 1095: '[I]t is perfectly competent for the Government of Guatemala to enact any decree they like and for any reasons they see fit, and such reasons are no concern of the Tribunal.' The PCIJ in the *Oscar Chinn Case* (1934) PCIJ Series A/B No. 63 at 79, said that the Belgian state 'was the sole judge' of the situation.

[162] G. White, *Nationalisation of Foreign Property* (1961), p. 150; S. Friedman, *Expropriation in International Law* (1977), p. 142; and C. F. Amerasinghe, *State Responsibility for Injuries to Aliens* (1967), p. 138, oppose the need for the requirement. However, the older authors favoured it. B. A. Wortley, *Expropriation in Public International Law* (1959), pp. 24–5; Lord McNair, 'The Seizure of Property and Enterprises in Indonesia' (1959) 6 *Netherlands International Law Review* 218 at 243; J. L. Kunz, 'The Mexican Appropriations' (1940) 34 *AJIL* 48 at 54.

[163] Interestingly, the Abs–Shawcross Convention, an effort at a multilateral treaty on investment protection, left out the requirement. S. D. Metzger, 'Multilateral Convention for the Protection of Private Foreign Investment' (1960) 9 *JPL* 40, supported the leaving out of the requirement, but not Schwarzenberger in an article in the same volume of the journal.

[164] J. H. Herz, 'Expropriation of Foreign Property' (1941) 35 *AJIL* 243 at 251–2.

The requirement is kept alive in the practice of states. Thus, the notes of both the United States and the United Kingdom protesting against the Libyan oil nationalisations refer to the belief of these states that the nationalisations were not motivated by reasons of public utility.[165] These reasons were also pressed before the arbitral tribunals which later came to deal with the disputes arising from the Libyan nationalisations. There is little doubt that the requirement will be used as necessary for lawful nationalisations in the future, but it is unlikely that it will constitute more than a subsidiary, throwaway argument for illegality.

The requirement of public purpose is stated in the American Law Institute's *Restatement on Foreign Relations Law*.[166] But, in the commentary thereto, the significance of the requirement is played down. The commentary reads:[167]

The requirement that a taking be for a public purpose is reiterated in most formulations of the rules of international law on expropriations of foreign property. That limitation, however, has not figured prominently in international claims practice, perhaps because the concept of public purpose is broad and not subject to effective re-examination by other states. Presumably, a seizure by a dictator or oligarchy for private use could be challenged under this rule.

In the course of the disputes arising from the Libyan nationalisations, the public purpose requirement was given a new lease of life, with the argument that, where a nationalisation is motivated by way of reprisal, it would lack public purpose and should therefore be considered unlawful. In the *BP* award, which arose from these nationalisations, Judge Lagergren found the nationalisation to be illegal on the ground that the taking 'clearly violates principles of international law as it was made for purely extraneous political reasons and was arbitrary and discriminatory in character'.[168] But, in the *Liamco* award,[169] Arbitrator Mahmassani dismissed the argument based on the requirement of a public purpose in the following terms:

As to the contention that the said measures were politically motivated and not in pursuance of a legitimate public purpose, it is the general opinion in international theory that the public utility principle is not a necessary requisite for the legality of nationalisation. This principle was mentioned by Grotius and other publicists, but now there is no international authority, from a judicial or other source, to support its application to nationalisation. Motives are indifferent to international law, each state being free to judge for itself what it considers useful or necessary for the public good ... The object pursued by it is of no concern to third parties.

These trends accord with the view taken by the European Court of Human Rights in deciding whether the taking had a public purpose. The Court has held that it will not, as a general principle, question the state's view that the taking was in the public interest. The Court said:[170]

The Court, finding it natural that the margin of appreciation available to the legislature in implementing social and economic policies should be a wide one, will respect the legislature's judgment as to what is 'in the public interest' unless the judgment be manifestly without reasonable foundation.

---

[165] For the US statement, see (1974) 13 *ILM* 767 at 771.   [166] Article 712(1)(a).   [167] Vol. 2, p. 200.
[168] (1977) 53 *ILR* 296 at 317.   [169] (1981) 20 *ILM* 1.   [170] *James v. United Kingdom* (1986) 8 *EHRR* 123.

3.2 *Discriminatory taking*

A racially discriminatory taking is unlawful in international law. The principle against racial discrimination is an *ius cogens* principle of international law. It is odious to international law that nationalisation or any act of state should be based on considerations of race. But, a post-colonial nationalisation which is designed to end the economic domination of the nationals of the former colonial power is exempt from this general rule. Here, nationalisation would be directed at the citizens of a distinct state identifiable by race for the obvious reason that they alone are in control of the economic sectors of the nationalising state. A German court accepted the existence of this exception when considering the legality of the Indonesian nationalisations. It rejected the argument that the nationalisation measures were illegal as they were directed only against Dutch nationals. The court emphasised the fact that the Dutch were the colonial rulers of Indonesia and that they had control over the Indonesian economy.

The equality concept requires only that equals must be treated equally and that the different treatment of 'unequals' is admissible. For the statement to be objective, it is sufficient that the attitude of the former colonial people to its former colonial master is, of course, different from that towards other foreigners. Not only were production facilities in the hands of the Dutch for most colonial companies, but these companies dominated the worldwide distribution, beyond the production process, through the Dutch markets.

In the situation dealt with by the German court, there was a justification other than motives of racial hatred involved in the taking. Where racial motives alone are present, the taking cannot amount to a nationalisation. *Siderman de Blake* v. *Argentina*, a case heard in the United States, provides an illustration of a purely racially motivated taking.[171] Here, the ruling coterie in Argentina persecuted a family because of their Jewish origin and took over their property after ensuring that the family left Argentina as a result of the torture of the head of the family and threats of further violence. The racially motivated taking in this situation amounted to expropriation and had no economic purpose at all. In these circumstances, the taking becomes illegal and full compensation must be paid for the taking.

In clear cases of racially motivated takings, the illegality will be evident. Thus, in the case of the takings of Jewish property in Nazi Germany[172] or in the case of the takings of the property of Indians in Uganda during the regime of Idi Amin,[173] the racially motivated nature of the takings was clear. The governments themselves did not seek to hide the motives for the takings. But, difficulty will arise where both motives of racial hatred and economic objectives together inspire a taking. It is no easy task to assess which motive is the dominant one, for, when economic nationalism is the reason for the taking, both motives are present in equal strength. The better view in such circumstances may be to treat the taking itself as a

---

[171] In *Siderman de Blake* v. *Argentina*, 965 F 2d 699 (1992), only one member of the family was a US national, the others being Argentinian. As far as international law was concerned, only the taking of the share of the one member of the family involved state responsibility.

[172] *Oppenheimer* v. *Inland Revenue Commissioner* [1975] 1 All ER 538.

[173] F. Woolridge and V. Sharma, 'The Expropriation of the Property of the Ugandan Asians' (1974) 14 *Indian Journal of International Law* 61.

valid taking but to use the taking as the basis of a separate cause of action based on racial discrimination. As a result of movements within international law, it can now be claimed that the violation of the principle against racial discrimination gives rise to a separate cause of action, and it is on this basis that the responsibility of the host state should be pegged in cases where the motives for the taking are not clear.

3.3 *Takings in violation of treaties*

The *Chorzow Factory Case* concerned a taking in violation of a treaty. The view of the Permanent Court of International Justice was that, in circumstances of takings in violation of treaties, restitution was the proper remedy for the international wrong. The general proposition that is drawn from this case, that restitutionary damages is the proper remedy for all nationalisations, is wide of the mark, for the Court was only concerned with a nationalisation in violation of a treaty.

An interesting question that could arise is whether the nationalisation of an investment that is protected by a bilateral investment treaty will be illegal under this rule. Such treaties do not interfere with the right of the state to take foreign property but only seek to specify the manner in which such a taking should be made. Since the treaty itself will provide for the compensation for a taking that is protected by the treaty, the logical answer would be to apply the standard of compensation that is indicated in the treaty itself.

4. Conclusion

Though the law recognised that there could be takings of alien property other than through direct means, the indirect methods of taking have not been identified with any certainty either in arbitral decisions or in the literature. It is unlikely that this deficiency of the law will be cured. The law on alien takings, especially the law on state responsibility arising from such takings, was developed at a time when the state rarely interfered with the marketplace, and interference was effected for rather crude purposes such as the self-aggrandisement of ruling elites. It was easy to identify and stigmatise such takings as unlawful. Investment protection was facilitated by the uniform application of this rule to all types of taking. But, with increasing state intervention in the economy, the maintenance of this rule became unacceptable.

Regulatory takings have brought the tensions in this area to the fore. The interests of property protection favour a *per se* rule that was accepted in the *Santa Elena* v. *Costa Rica* award. But, it is not a rule that can be sustained, not only because of the fact that it is not based on any authority but also because it does not reflect developments in domestic or international legal systems. Domestic legal systems have recognised the need for balancing the competing areas in the situation of every taking. This rule of prudence is transferred into the international sphere by requiring that every situation of indirect taking should be examined as a distinct situation having its own circumstances which must be considered in determining whether it should be regarded as compensable or not. In the international sphere, rules on the environment and human rights have ensured that matters which were domestic are now of universal concern so that a state acting to promote environmental or human rights interests does so to advance universal objectives. In that light, it would be difficult to characterise such regulatory takings as compensable. The increasing tendency among both developed and developing countries to control foreign investments, albeit through different types of regulatory structures, will keep this issue in the forefront of the law in this area. As indicated, this issue has replaced the theory of internationalisation of foreign investment contracts and the debate on compensation – which are dealt with in the following chapters – as the central issue in the area of expropriation of foreign investments. But, it is an issue that involves interests that are so inconsistent that the challenge of reconciling them would prove difficult. When regulatory taking goes beyond the intersection to become a compensatory taking is a task that will tax the abilities of the best of tribunals.

11

Compensation for nationalisation of foreign investments

Compensation for nationalisation of foreign investment is a topic steeped in controversy. Opinions expressed as to the need for compensation have ranged from the payment of full compensation, a concept which includes consideration of future profits the investment would have made, to the payment of no compensation at all. The acuteness of the conflict was evidenced by the division that occurred within the academic and official quarters as to the statement of the rule on the standard of compensation in the American Law Institute's *Restatement (Second) of the Foreign Relations Law of the United States* and in the various awards of the Iran–US Claims Tribunal. The issue has remained dormant in more recent times, attention being shifted to issues such as the scope of taking and the meaning and extent of regulatory taking. Another feature is the attempt to shift the focus of the controversy by articulating standards of valuation. The topic will remain of great interest, despite the fact that there have been few spectacular nationalisations in recent times. The need for foreign investment and the inadequacy of foreign capital to supply this need keeps such activity dormant. Given this context, states will not seek to spoil their record of stability by engaging in any spectacular nationalisations. But, bouts of nationalism will occur in cyclical patterns in the history of nations. When the present philosophy of investment-led growth gives way to some other philosophy inimical to continued dependence on foreign investment, there will once more be hostility to foreign investment. Such hostility is all the more likely because many of the fund- and aid-giving organisations have imposed conditions which require the liberalisation of the entry of foreign investment as a requirement for the granting of such aid. When hostility to these measures gathers momentum, foreign investment may suffer and nationalisation may once more come into vogue. For these reasons, the issue of compensation for nationalisation, though dormant now, could become, once more, a hotly debated issue in the future. The relevance of the issue will continue as the notion of taking expands. Where expanded notions of taking become accepted, the compensation issue will again become significant.

Because of the controversial nature of the subject, the method of treatment of the subject which is adopted in this chapter is different. The discussion is based on the acceptance of the fact that there is no clear principle as to compensation for nationalisation in international law at the present time. Though most investment treaties require the payment of full market value as compensation, there is as yet no sufficient uniformity of practice to indicate a set pattern on this matter. For this reason, the different claims that have been made as to what the law is are stated and the support for them in the authorities is assessed. The strength of the different claims will appear as a result of the adoption of this technique. Some of the claims can then be discarded. The final process of elimination will be to examine the extent to which the remaining claims accord with or further the objectives of the international community. It must be stressed that the discussion relates to *lawful* nationalisation. Where nationalisations are unlawful, for example, where they are motivated by racial discrimination or are by way of reprisals, different considerations would apply, as international wrongs are involved. The rectification of these international wrongs, as was pointed out in the last chapter, justifies the assessment of damages on other considerations.

It is necessary to point out at the outset that the sources on which the competing claims to the standard of compensation are based are weak sources of international law. It is often pointed out that the claims to the new standards of compensation are based on weak norms or on 'soft law'. The sources on which the claims to the traditional standard of full or adequate compensation are based are by no means capable of producing hard law. The traditional claims are based on arbitral awards, which are often uncontested, and on the writings of jurists. They are weak, subsidiary sources of law. It has already been pointed out that the view that investment treaties bring about customary international law in the area on any point including that of compensation is a fallacy. The competing and relatively new claims are also based on a few arbitral awards, resolutions of the General Assembly of the United Nations as to whose law-making competence there have been doubts and an increasing body of writings of jurists. It is a facet of this area of the law that it is based on weak norms, and it does not help in the clarification of the law that supporters of the different claims refer to the weakness of the sources on which other claims are made, for all the claims are based on the weakest of the sources known to international law.

1. The competing norms: the views of the capital-exporting states[1]

The area of compensation for nationalisation is acknowledged to be one of the most controversial areas of international law. In an earlier period, there was a certain concordance in views so that it could be asserted that a head count of scholars showed a preponderant support for the view that full compensation should be paid upon nationalisation of foreign property. This was largely because the writers on the subject were European or American. The views of Latin American and other writers who opposed this view seldom came to light or were given prominence. But, since then, there has been a diversity of views expressed even within Europe and the United States. It cannot be asserted with any confidence that preponderant opinion favours one particular norm. This is evident simply by looking at the position in the United

---

[1] This is an old-fashioned distinction. The erstwhile capital-exporters are now massive recipients of capital, the United States being the obvious example. Yet, the distinction is useful in explaining the division of views, which are still largely on the basis of a divide between developed and developing countries.

States, where the official position has consistently been that full compensation must be paid on nationalisation of foreign investment, but where academic opinion has been keenly divided. The authorities supporting the different claims are examined first, before deciding on the position which best reflects contemporary international law.

1.1 The claim that 'prompt, adequate and effective' compensation must be paid

The claim to full or adequate compensation is supported by the majority of capital-exporting states, for the obvious reason that it affords the best protection for the capital which leaves these states as foreign investment. If the full value of the property which is subject to the expropriation and the anticipated earnings of the foreign investment are immediately replaced in currency which is convertible, the foreign investor will not have suffered in any material sense and the capital can be reinvested elsewhere or brought back home. The interest in the capital as well as in the national who takes it abroad makes it sensible from the point of view of the home state to hold out for what is the best possible solution from its point of view as the norm of international law. The formula of 'prompt, adequate and effective compensation' was first used by Secretary of State Cordell Hull during the Mexican expropriations and is generally referred to in the literature as the 'Hull formula'. The Mexican expropriations themselves were intended to achieve land reform in that state. One important factor was that the communication by Hull did not characterise the expropriations as illegal.[2] To this extent, the communication amounts to the relinquishing of older views relating to the illegality of takings and an acceptance of the emerging view that takings by the state in pursuance of economic objectives are lawful.[3] But, he insisted that even such lawful expropriation must be accompanied by the payment of full compensation. The communication did not refer to payment of compensation as being a condition precedent to the legality of the expropriation. Whereas previously, there was a view that expropriation may be unlawful in the absence of compensation, the change of opinion was that the socially utilitarian motive made the expropriation lawful in itself but that there should be payment of compensation following such an expropriation. It is this change of opinion as to the legality of expropriation measures which makes the use of precedents as to the standard of compensation from an earlier period suspect.

The view has been stated that it makes no difference to the standard of compensation whether the expropriation is lawful or unlawful. Such a view cannot rest on logical foundations, for every legal system must necessarily make a distinction between damages

---

[2] For the Mexican expropriations and the exchanges between the governments on the nature of the compensation that should be paid, see Whiteman, *Digest*, vol. 8, p. 1020; and Hackworth, *Digest*, vol. 3, p. 657. The Foreign Minister of Mexico had written to Hull: 'My Government maintains that there is in international law no rule universally accepted in theory nor carried out in practice, which makes obligatory the payment of immediate compensation nor even deferred compensation for expropriations of a general and impersonal character like those which Mexico has carried out for the redistribution of land.' Hull replied: 'Under every rule of law and equity, no government is entitled to expropriate private property, for whatever purposes, without provision for prompt, adequate and effective compensation.'

[3] In his note to the Mexican ambassador on 3 April 1940, Secretary Hull stated: '[T]he Government of the United States readily recognises the right of a sovereign state to expropriate property for public purpose.' Whiteman, *Digest*, vol. 8, p. 1020. What is done in pursuance of a right cannot be unlawful.

arising from lawful and unlawful acts. There must be a distinction between a wrong or injury which requires compensation by way of remedy and a justifiable act which requires that any person who has been adversely affected as a result is recompensed through the payment of money. Admittedly, the distinction between lawful and unlawful takings is difficult to make except in the cases where there had been a clear lack of a public purpose or the taking was racially discriminatory. However, if the law makes it lawful for a state to nationalise and makes certain types of taking unlawful, that law must also ensure that there is a distinction to be drawn in the awarding of damages.

Christine Gray points out in her study on judicial remedies that, though the distinction between legal and illegal acts causing harm exists, the nature of the distinction as to the award of damages in respect of the two categories of act has not been stated with clarity anywhere.[4] This is a matter which requires attention and will be examined in the course of the discussion of the different claims. The types of authority which support the norm of full or adequate compensation may now be looked at. The sources of law as stated in the Statute of the International Court of Justice will be looked at to determine the nature of the support they provide to each claim. Another problem in relation to full compensation is that full compensation has not been defined.[5] It is not confined to the market value of the property. There are loose formulations that full compensation means the awarding of *damnum emergens* and *lucrum cessans*, meaning that the value of the property as well as future profits must be paid. The formulation itself is imprecise. The absence of a firm definition of full compensation enables writers to project authorities to fit their own theories as to what is full compensation. The calculation of damages is an area that needs to be examined separately.

1.1.1 Treaties

There are no multinational treaties on the question of investment protection.[6] Of the several failed efforts to draft a multilateral agreement, the last was in 1998, when the OECD attempted a multilateral agreement on investment. In considering whether treaties give rise to any customary international law in this area, the tribunal in *United Parcel Services v. Canada* stated that 'the failure of efforts to establish a multilateral agreement on investment provides further evidence of the lack of a sense of obligation' in the various types of investment treaty to create customary international law in this area.[7] The payment of compensation for takings would have been the most central factor if any multilateral treaty had come into being.

The failure of the attempts at the formulation of such conventions indicates the absence of any consensus among states on many issues of foreign investment protection, including

---

[4] C. Gray, *Judicial Remedies in International Law* (1990), pp. 179–80.

[5] Gray, *ibid.*, p. 19, pointed out that full compensation 'has no single, locally determined, fixed meaning. This rather obvious point needs to be made only because there is a temptation facing writers in this area to choose between cases on the basis of their preconceptions as to what is meant by full compensation.'

[6] There are several guidelines and draft conventions. The World Bank Group in its survey of these documents found that the Hull formula 'is contained in only one of the multilateral documents reviewed'. World Bank Group, *Legal Framework for the Treatment of Foreign Investment* (1992), vol. 1, p. 88.

[7] Award on Jurisdiction, 22 November 2002. The award is available on various websites.

the standard on which compensation must be paid for nationalised property. The Economic Agreement of Bogota (1948) contained a clause requiring full compensation upon nationalisation. But, eight signatories entered reservations to it. The Draft OECD Convention (1967) contained the traditional limitations on nationalisation and required the payment of full compensation. The later 1998 draft also contained a provision that included the formula of prompt, adequate and effective compensation. But, this draft was made by developed states which would generally have subscribed to the formula reflecting full compensation. The failure of the multilateral efforts demonstrates that there is no identity of interests between the capital-exporting states and the capital-importing states on the issue.

There are several bilateral investment treaties which contain references to adequate compensation. The older friendship, commerce and navigation (FCN) treaties as well as the newer bilateral investment treaties contain references to the standard, but the terminology used is not uniform.[8] Consistent acceptance of a norm in bilateral treaties could convert that norm into a principle of international law. But, it is unlikely that such a view can be taken of bilateral investment treaty provisions on compensation. It has already been pointed out that the divergence in the standards used and the fact that many of them provide for valuation of compensation to be made by national authorities make the possibility of such treaties creating a norm as to the standard of compensation remote. One reason for the rapid accumulation of bilateral investment treaties is that, as the norms relating to compensation became diffused due to different formulations of the standard of compensation, parties to the investment treaties seek to formulate a binding standard as between themselves. The formulation that is finally included in the treaties on such matters as compensation reflects the compromise the parties had arrived at after negotiations. If this view is correct, then the chances of the standards stipulated in these treaties ripening into propositions of customary law are remote. Besides, many bilateral treaties heavily qualify the types of investment that are protected. In these circumstances, it is clear that, even where the provision on full compensation appears in a treaty, it does not protect all investments but only those of the type that qualifies for protection under the treaty. In the 1990s, there was a sudden growth in the number of these treaties. But, the mere increase in numbers affords no solution as to whether customary international law was created. Expediency and the need to attract foreign investment rather than a clear conviction seem to have been the reason for stating the rule on full compensation rather

---

[8] The US FCN treaties containing references to the standard of full compensation are listed in Whiteman, *Digest*, vol. 8, p. 1018. For the bilateral investment treaties and their treatment of the standard of compensation, see Chapter 7 above. UK practice is not uniform. The treaty with Tunisia simply refers to the payment of 'compensation' without a qualifying adjective. Treaties with Antigua and Barbuda (1987), Poland (1988), Guyana (1989) and Hungary (1988) use the Hull formula. The treaty with Bolivia refers to 'just and effective' compensation. But, these formulations are usually followed by a reference to the requirement to pay 'the market value of the property expropriated immediately before the expropriation became public knowledge'. Dutch treaties usually refer to 'just' compensation and are followed by references to the requirement to pay the 'genuine value' of the investment. The practice of China diverges markedly. The market value formula is used in the treaty with Australia (1988), but in the treaty with New Zealand concluded the same year there is merely a reference to compensation without a qualifying adjective. The later treaties made in the 1990s contain more references to the Hull standard, but no rule can be extracted as a general principle. Some of these treaties confine the types of investment that are protected by qualifying the investment. Thus, many of the Southeast Asian treaties protect only approved investments or investments made in accordance with laws and regulations. To extract rules by finding common denominators in them is an impossible task.

than any conviction that it represents a rule of law. As a result, the conclusion that there is no treaty law supporting a general norm of full compensation is inevitable.

1.1.2 Customary practice

Customary practice is not uniform as to the payment of full compensation on nationalisation. The Hull standard was resisted by Mexico when it was formulated.[9] The former communist states objected to the formula on ideological grounds. The Latin American states have consistently objected to the standard, though there are signs that many states are willing to subscribe to the standard in bilateral investment treaties. There has been ambivalence within developing states as to the standard which they would support. Individually, some of them have subscribed to the standard of full compensation in bilateral investment treaties, though collectively they have promoted different standards at the multilateral level.

There is no indication in modern practice of full compensation ever having been paid as compensation for nationalisation. States which have firmly held on to the standard of full compensation have accepted less than full compensation.[10] Nowhere is this more evident than in the settlement of compensation disputes through lump-sum payments. Though there are strenuous efforts made by some scholars to argue in support of the extreme view that the lump-sum settlement agreements did not deviate from the standards of full compensation, it is difficult to demonstrate that these agreements were not based on the acceptance of only partial compensation. The general tendency of those who seek to support the payment of full compensation is to underplay the relevance of these treaties.[11] The preponderant view is that they have nothing to contribute to the formation of any international law. Thus, the Iran–US Claims Tribunal stated in *Amoco Finance*:

As a rule, state practice as reflected in settlement agreements cannot be considered as giving birth to customary rules of international law, unless it presents specific features which demonstrate the conviction of the state parties that they were acting in application of what they considered to be settled law. The provisions of such an agreement, indeed, are the outcome of negotiations in which many motivations other than legal ones may have prevailed.

Lump-sum settlement agreements are an embarrassment to those who argue that there is a customary law which requires full compensation for nationalisation. These agreements

---

[9] Mexico, the state whose expropriations led to the formulation of the Hull standard, participates in NAFTA, which uses words that are similar to the Hull standard. Sensitivities perhaps necessitated the avoidance of the use of the formula itself, but the result arrived at is the same.

[10] The United States, for example, accepted less than full compensation in the Marcona nationalisation. G. Gantz, 'The Marcona Settlement: New Forms of Negotiation Compensation for Nationalized Property' (1977) 71 *AJIL* 474.

[11] Lillich and Weston are in a minority when they support the contrary view. R. B. Lillich and B. Weston, *International Claims: Their Settlement by Lump Sum Agreements* (1975), p. 35. There is a 'truly extraordinary consistency in these agreements', in favour of full compensation. See also R. B. Lillich and B. Weston, 'Lump Sum Agreements: Their Continuing Contribution to the Law of International Claims' (1988) 82 *AJIL* 69. The only consistent theme in these agreements is that they involved the acceptance of partial compensation. M. Sornarajah, *Pursuit of Nationalized Property* (1986), pp. 214–17. The overwhelming majority of writers support the view that partial compensation was the basis of these agreements. V. Pechota, 'The 1981 United States-Czechoslovakia Claims Settlement Agreement: An Epilogue to Post War Nationalisation and Expropriation Disputes' (1982) 76 *AJIL* 639; C. F. Amerasinghe, 'Issues of Compensation in the Taking of Alien Property in the Light of Recent Cases and Practice' (1992) 41 *ICLQ* 22 at 28; R. Dolzer, 'New Foundations of the Law of Expropriation of Alien Property' (1981) 75 *AJIL* 553 at 560; I. Seidl-Hohenveldern, Book Review (1991) 38 *German Yearbook of International Law* 592, who takes the view that lump sum agreements are not based on full compensation and that the home state should top up the balance.

demonstrate that states have settled claims arising from expropriation otherwise than on the standard of full compensation. To the extent that many of them were concluded with the former communist states of Eastern Europe, they constitute a rejection of the communist position that no compensation needs to be paid on nationalisation. They also support the claim that some compensation must be paid on expropriation, though they leave open the issue of the exact standard on which the compensation is to be paid. It is safe to conclude that there is no customary practice supporting the norm of full compensation for expropriation. The capital-exporting countries have articulated such a norm as a negotiating stance, and have been consistent in supporting it. But, it has not received such a generality of acceptance as to be regarded as an international practice that has matured into a rule of international law. The efforts to argue that bilateral investment treaties create custom have already been examined and found to be wanting. They do not create any custom on the question of the standard of compensation for expropriation.[12]

1.1.3 General principles of law

The strongest sources of international law, treaty and custom, have contributed nothing to the formation of any definite principle on the issue of compensation for expropriation of property. The claims as to the existence of a law have had to rely entirely on weak sources of international law, such as general principles of law, decisions of arbitral tribunals and the writings of publicists. The first of these are manipulable according to subjective preferences and the latter two are themselves expressions of the subjective preferences of arbitrators and writers.

General principles of law are a weak source of international law. Their weakness is accentuated by the common tendency to select a proposition from a few national systems and argue that they constitute a general principle, which should be treated as international law. Thereafter, like-minded scholars seek to achieve this conversion through constant repetition. This is a phenomenon which frequently occurs in international investment law. The selectivity involved in the technique is illustrated by the fact that often the choice of the principle is restricted to a particular period in the history of the legal system or the principle is chosen and the exceptions to it in the legal systems are jettisoned. The general principles which are used in this area consist of equitable principles of unjust enrichment and acquired rights and the principle of the right to property the violation which requires the payment of full compensation. Another, more recent, source in which general principles supporting the payment of full compensation is sought are the foreign investment codes of different states.

1.1.4 Unjust enrichment

The two principles which are frequently chosen to support the norm of full compensation are unjust enrichment and acquired rights. In the case of unjust enrichment, which as an equitable principle receives wide acceptance in legal systems, the argument is that, since a

---

[12] In a study of 154 cases of expropriation, Sunshine found that the general practice was to apply the net book value concept. The Hull formula and alternative formulas were used as bargaining counters but never adhered to. R. B. Sunshine, *Terms of Settlement in Developing Countries' Nationalization Settlements* (UNCTC, 1981).

state is enriched as a result of its taking of foreign property, it must repay to the alien owner as compensation a sum which reflects the extent of the enrichment. This sum, it is suggested, is the full value of the property which had been taken. The focus is to be on the act of expropriation alone. There is a discarding of the prior relationship between the parties or of the nature of the profits which accrued from the investment to the foreign investor. What is made solely relevant is the value of the property at the time of the taking. The argument is that it is this value which has to be paid as compensation.

The principle of unjust enrichment may not work in this manner. It is an equitable principle, and, where it is applied, many legal systems require that the whole course of the relationship between the parties must be taken into account in the determination of the equitable relief which is to be accorded to the party that suffered damage. In contract law and property law where the principle is recognised, it is not recognised as being applicable only by reference to the single act causing injury but as applying only after a nice analysis of the benefits and costs attending the whole course of the relationship had been made.[13] Unjust enrichment cannot uniformly support full compensation when applied to a situation of expropriation. It will support less than full compensation when the past benefits of the investment had weighed heavily in favour of the investor. It may support more than full compensation in situations in which the foreign investment is relatively new, had been enticed into the host country and had involved the transfer of assets and technology which would not otherwise have been obtained by the host state.[14] An equitable principle like unjust enrichment lends only equivocal support to full compensation. While there could be full compensation in appropriate circumstances, in other circumstances it could produce results varying from no compensation to less than full compensation.

1.1.5 Acquired rights

There is doubt as to whether the doctrine of acquired rights forms a part of international law at all. Rights are acquired under domestic law. The significance of international law to such rights, except when there is a treaty protecting them, is theoretically a difficult concept to fit into the scheme of international law. If it can be fitted in, the doctrine of acquired rights also does not provide any firm support for full compensation. The rights have to be vested under the municipal law of the host state, and one problem is that the municipal law which vests those rights should also be able to destroy them without reference to other legal systems.[15]

---

[13] F. Francioni, 'Compensation for Nationalisation of Foreign Property: The Borderland of Law and Equity' (1975) 24 *ICLQ* 255. W. Friedmann, *Changing Structure of International Law* (1962), p. 207, argued that the 'history of the economic-political relations between the parties' should be taken into account in considering unjust enrichment. See D. Dicke, 'Taking of Foreign Property and Compensation', in T. Oppermann and E. Petersmann (eds.), *Reforming the International Economic Order* (1987), p. 62 at pp. 73–9, for a comparative study of legal systems on the issue of unjust enrichment and the conclusion that 'unjust enrichment as an argument points both ways'.

[14] See *Sola Tiles* v. *Iran* (1987) 14 *Iran–US CTR* 223 at 237.

[15] D. P. O'Connell, *International Law* (1970), vol. 1, p. 305, stated that acquired rights 'cannot be cancelled without full satisfaction of the equities attaching to them'. On acquired rights, see G. White, *Nationalization of Foreign Property* (1961), pp. 13–16; N. Kaeckenbeck, 'The Protection of Vested Rights in International Law' (1936) 17 *BYIL* 1; Lord McNair, 'The General Principles of Law Recognised by Civilised Nations' (1957) 33 *BYIL* 1 at 16; and J.-F. Lalive, 'The Doctrine of Acquired Rights', in South Western Legal Foundation, *Selected Readings on the Protection of Foreign Investments* (1964). The argument relating to acquired rights continues to be used in modern arbitral awards, for example, *Amco* v. *Indonesia* (1983–90) 1 *ICSID Reports* 189.

The doctrine of acquired rights is also an equitable doctrine. To the extent that it is relevant to the assessment of compensation, it will, like other equitable doctrines, require that the equities involved in the whole course of the relationship between the parties be looked at in the determination of the compensation that is to be paid.[16]

Unjust enrichment and other equitable doctrines operate in the context of private law in domestic legal systems. They cannot be readily transported into an area in which public law features dominate. Rights, which are acquired through the exercise of public law, are generally recognised to be defeasible in the public law systems of major states.[17] So too, the principle of unjust enrichment is seldom the basis of compensation for property acquired under legislation permitting such acquisition for the purpose of development in the public interest. The relevance of these doctrines to the debate on expropriation is contestable. Even if relevant, they do not uniformly support a norm of full compensation. Equitable considerations can be used to support less than full compensation. There have been attempts on the part of some arbitral tribunals to do so.[18] Equity is a double-edged sword and its use can have undesired results for those who invoke it.

1.1.6 Right to property

The argument is sometimes made that the investment codes and constitutional provisions of a large number of states provide support for the existence of a right to property and for the payment of full compensation in the event of nationalisation in violation of such a right.[19] There is little evidence that there is such a widespread and unqualified recognition of the right to property in the constitutional systems of even the capital-exporting states on which any certain principle of international law can be based. At the international and regional levels, the various human rights documents do not accept a right to property without qualifications which justify interference in the public interest. Likewise, where references are made to property rights in the constitutions of states, they are usually defeasible in the public interest. In many instances, it would be uncertain whether these constitutional safeguards give protection to the property of foreigners as they are contained in statements of the rights of citizens.

In jurisprudential terms, it will be difficult to establish the right to property as a fundamental right even in Western systems. An examination of the philosophical basis of the right to property made by a US scholar contains the following conclusion:[20]

---

[16] F. Francioni, 'Compensation for Nationalisation of Foreign Property: The Borderland between Law and Equity' (1975) 24 *ICLQ* 255.

[17] It can never be seriously argued that the right of permanent residence granted to an alien cannot be taken away by the state, though it is also an acquired right. Thus, I. Brownlie, *Principles of Public International Law* (6th edn, 2003), p. 533, in rejecting arguments based on acquired rights, observed:

The argument based upon acquired rights could be applied to a number of reliance situations created by the host state by the grant of public rights such as citizenship or permission to reside or to work. The distinction drawn by partisans of responsibility in contract situations between loan agreements, concessions and other contracts is unsatisfactory. Why do they prefer their reasoning only in certain contract or reliance situations?

[18] For example, the Iran–US Claims Tribunal in *Phillips Petroleum* v. *Iran* (1989) 21 *Iran–US CTR* 79, citing in support the *Aminoil* award (1982) 66 *ILR* 518.

[19] B. M. Clagett, 'The Expropriation Issue Before the Iran–United States. Claims Tribunal' in R. B. Lillich, *Valuation of Nationalized Property* (1987), vol. 4.

[20] J. Waldron, *The Right to Private Property* (1988), p. 3.

Under serious scrutiny, there is no right-based argument to be found which provides an adequate justification for a society in which some people have lots of property and many have next to none. The slogan that property is a human right can be deployed only disingenuously to legitimise the massive inequality that we find in modern capitalist countries.

It is doubtful that there is any greater respect for the right to property in the non-capitalist systems.[21] But, taking Europe alone, it will be difficult to demonstrate that there is such an absolute recognition of the right to property that its violation must be followed by the payment of full compensation. The European Court of Human Rights has produced some case law on the right to property in the First Protocol to the European Convention on Human Rights.

The non-inclusion of the right to property in the main text of the Convention itself is significant. The Convention was drafted immediately after the Second World War, and many European states felt that the economic reorganisation that had to take place after the ravages of the war would be impeded by the recognition of a right to property in the Convention.[22] This explains the absence of a provision on the right to property in the Convention. A right to property was included later in the First Protocol to the Convention. In the drafting committee of the Protocol, there was considerable dispute as to whether there was a duty to pay compensation when property was expropriated in the public interest. Some of the European governments did not relish the prospect of their economic programmes being subjected to the scrutiny of a supranational court. It is a feeling which developing countries would share. The present statement of the right to property in the First Protocol is qualified in many ways. It reads:

Every natural or legal person is entitled to the peaceful enjoyment of his possessions. No one shall be deprived of his possessions except in the public interest and subject to the conditions provided for by law and by general principles of international law.

The interpretation of this provision by the European Court does not indicate a belief that the right to property is absolute in any sense. European states have had many socialist governments which embarked on programmes of nationalisation of the property of their citizens or have encroached on the property rights of citizens in the social interest. Since the Protocol refers to international law standards, the Court has had to take international law standards, particularly those relating to compensation, into account in applying the law in the cases generated by challenges to the takings effected by European governments. The case law of the Court indicates that the right to property 'has lost its inviolability' in European law. It will be sufficient to indicate this erosion by referring only to the manner in which the issue of compensation has been dealt with in European law.

---

[21] Communist systems are based on the rejection of the right to property. Philosophical attitudes to property in states influenced by non-materialistic religions are bound to be different. For an interesting account of Maori views on property, see A. Frame, 'Property: Some Pacific Reflections' (1992) 22 *New Zealand Law Journal* 21.

[22] For the drafting history, see W. Peukert, 'Protection of Ownership under Article 1 of the First Protocol of the European Convention on Human Rights' (1981) 1 *Human Rights Journal* 36 at 38–42; E. Schwelb, 'The Protection of the Right to Property of Nationals under the First Protocol to the European Convention on Human Rights' (1964) 13 *American Journal of Comparative Law* 518 at 533–40.

In *Lithgow* v. *United Kingdom*, which involved the taking of an aircraft industry belonging to a British subject by the UK government, the issue of the standard of compensation in international law arose. Since there was a reference to international law standards in the Protocol, the applicant argued that international law required the payment of full compensation. In presenting arguments to the Court, counsel for the European Commission denied the existence of such a standard in international law. He stated his view on the public international law position as to the standard of compensation as follows:[23]

[T]he European states would seem to have a more or less coherent view, according to which public international law requires the payment of at least appropriate compensation where foreign property is being taken. As to the practice it is extremely divergent. I am not aware of one single case where, for nationalisation of whole industries, full compensation was paid by the nationalising state to the foreign owners, without special investment treaties being applicable. In most cases of nationalisation, lump-sum agreements were reached clearly below the value of the assets taken. At least for large scale nationalisation, the notion of sovereignty over natural resources and freedom of decision over the economic order may easily come into conflict with a claim of full compensation.

The Court did not go into great detail on this issue. But, it did indicate that it will not interfere with the decision of the state as to the question of compensation, unless the state's decision as to the amount of compensation that was payable was 'manifestly without reasonable foundation'.[24]

On the issue of compensation, the general view taken by the Court is that, where the taking by the state is for a public purpose, the extent of the public purpose will affect the amount of compensation. Compensation becomes relevant to the Court in considering whether a fair balance was struck between the public interest in the taking of the property and the protection of the individual owner's right to the property. There is a utilitarian notion at play. The individual interest in securing compensation will diminish according to the strength of the justification for the taking provided by the public purpose. Compensation on this theory represents a balance struck between the individual interest and the public benefit which results from the taking. Payment of less than full compensation is justifiable where economic reform is the aim of the taking. The Court explained its position in the following terms:[25]

Clearly, compensation terms are material to the assessment whether a fair balance has been struck between the various interests at stake, and notably, whether or not a disproportionate burden has been imposed on the person who has been deprived of his possessions. The Court further accepts the Commission's conclusion as to the standard of compensation: The taking of property without payment of an amount reasonably related to its value would normally constitute a disproportionate interference which could not be considered justifiable under Article 1 [of the First Protocol]. Article 1 does not, however, guarantee a right to full compensation in all circumstances. Legitimate objectives of 'public interest', such as pursued in measures of economic reform or measures designed to achieve greater

---

[23] *Lithgow* v. *United Kingdom* (1986) 8 *EHRR* 329.   [24] *Ibid.*, p. 373.
[25] *James* v. *United Kingdom* (1986) 5 *EHRR* 35 at 147; *Lithgow* v. *United Kingdom* (1986) 8 *EHRR* 329; see also *Sporrong and Lönnroth* v. *Sweden* (1983) 5 *EHRR* 35 (paras. 69 and 73); G. Cohen-Jonathan, *La Convention Européenne de Droits de l'Homme* (1989), pp. 526–7.

social justice, may call for less than reimbursement of full market value. Furthermore, the Court's power of review is limited to ascertaining whether the choice of compensation terms falls outside the State's wide margin of appreciation in this domain.

In the United States, where one would expect property protection to be stronger because of its history and traditions, the picture is no different. Though there is constitutional protection for the right to property, the formulations are in less than absolute terms. The amount of compensation which is to be considered 'just' in the circumstances of state taking has been considered to be a factor in balancing individual rights and the public interest. The views taken in the United States on the issue closely parallel the balancing of factors adopted by the European Court.[26]

It could be that the US view has undergone several changes, with the public interest being dominant when the United States was in a stage of development. In this phase, infrastructure upgrading would have required that there be interference with private property, and the courts justified such interference as necessary in the public interest and as requiring no or lesser compensation. But, progressively as development was achieved, there may have come about a greater stress on individual property rights. This course of development indicates that in any given society a balance has to be struck between individual rights in property and the public interest and that balance can only be struck by each state having regard to its own developmental needs.

The regional documents on human rights in Latin America and Africa do not state the right to property in absolute terms. They have regard to the social function of property and state the right as subject to the public interest. Article 21 of the American Convention on Human Rights, after referring to the right to property, states that 'the law may subordinate such use and enjoyment to the interest of society'. It refers to the payment of 'just compensation' for the taking of property. Article 14 of the African Charter on Human and Peoples' Rights guarantees the right to property, but permits encroachment in the public interest. It makes no reference to the payment of compensation for the taking of property. The European Convention also makes no express reference to the payment of compensation, but the European Court has inferred the requirement.

The developments in the national and regional systems should be reflected in international law. If the notion of general principles must be applied in the area, it should not be selectively applied so as to support the norm of full compensation. Conclusions should not be drawn from abstract and unexamined claims that there is a universally recognised right to property. There is no case for an absolute right to property in any municipal, regional or international system. Taking only the Western legal systems into account, the notion of property always had a social content in these systems. The notion of *res communes* was taken from the Roman law into international law by Vattel and other institutional writers. In modern European law, the social function of property has made deep inroads into the individual's right to property. European legal systems do not provide a source from which

---

[26] See further B. Ackerman, *Private Property and the Constitution* (1977); and *Hawaii Housing Authority* v. *Midkiff*, 467 US 229 (1984), cited with approval by the European Court of Human Rights in *James* v. *United Kingdom* (1986) 5 *EHRR* 35, para. 40.

an absolute right to property can be imported into international law through general principles of law. In any event, there is no unanimity of treatment in national systems. Following Roman law, the European systems recognised that it was necessary to hold property for the common good and that private property was a man-made institution to serve individual needs. The Canadian Bill of Rights avoids stating a right to property. Constitutional systems within the Commonwealth state the right in a highly circumscribed fashion. As such, it would be difficult to argue that the right to property is a general principle recognised in law.

In international law, the growth of the law of development will introduce a concept which stipulates that the collective interests of peoples should take precedence over individual rights of ownership. The principle of permanent sovereignty over natural resources is conducive to the evolution of such an attitude to property in international law. The idea that the right to property could be used to support a claim to full compensation is based on insecure foundations.

1.1.7 Foreign investment codes

Investment codes are designed to attract foreign investors as well as to state the conditions on which foreign investment will be permitted entry into the host state. In such codes, a statement of the norm of full compensation could be expected, as this would be most attractive to foreign investors. Even in these codes, there is an absence of uniformity on the standard of compensation. While some investment codes contain the promise of payment of full compensation in the event of expropriation, there are others which do not contain such promises. In some, the promises relating to compensation are ambivalent at best. Thus, the Indonesian code recognises the state's right to nationalise alien property and promises to pay compensation 'in accordance with the rules of international law'. Much is going to depend on the state's appreciation of what international law on the point is. The Thai Investment Promotion Act contains a blanket undertaking not to expropriate a foreign investment which has been promoted by the government under the legislation. The Chinese Joint Venture Law accords the foreign party to the joint venture protection 'in accordance with the law'. There is much disparity in the promises which are made as to the compensation which is payable in the event of expropriation. Such disparity can hardly be the basis of general principles. The nature of these promises also deprives them of much legal significance. They are unilateral promises which are not binding on the state. There is little internal machinery provided for the enforcement of the rights which are provided in the investment codes. They are merely expressions of how the state hopes to act towards the foreign investor in the event of expropriation, and cannot form the basis of building up any norm of international law. These unilateral guarantees are akin to invitations to treat in the common law of contract and cannot be converted into obligations in law or the basis of the creation of principles of law.

The weakness of general principles of law as a source of international law has been frequently commented upon by scholars. It is futile to build any firm norm of international law in an area as controversial as compensation for expropriation of foreign property on the basis of general principles of law alone. The exercise is bound to attract charges of partiality simply because the approach to property protection in the different legal systems is so diverse that it would be difficult to extract principles that are common to all legal systems. With the crumbling of ideologically oriented legal systems and the building of market economies, common principles of property protection may evolve in the future, but at present it would be difficult to say that there is such commonality among legal systems that the payment of full compensation is a general principle of law.

The vigour of neo-liberal tendencies in the last decade has given rise to the impression that the absolute right to property has triumphed over other, competing notions of property. But, this is an illusory notion. Despite the fact that there are treaties which seek to act on such a premise and arbitral decisions which are based on the acceptance of such an ideology, there is no clear trend which has indicated the victory of one vision of property over another.[27]

1.1.8 Decisions of courts and tribunals

Decisions of courts, both international and domestic, as well as awards of tribunals may be evidence of the existence of international law principles. The subsidiary nature of the role of such sources is obvious. There is no system of precedent in international law. The statement of the principle by a court will provide evidence of the existence of a principle of international law and the strength of the evidence will depend on the prestige of the court. In many of the instances in which arbitral tribunals have pronounced on the issue of compensation, the arbitration proceeded with no participation by the state and the award was made by a single arbitrator.[28] In such circumstances, the award can hardly be regarded as anything more than the opinion of a single person on the dispute, formed without the state's case being presented before him. It is best therefore to approach the subject hierarchically, with the international courts being given precedence over arbitral tribunals and national tribunals.

1.1.9 International courts

The only occasion on which an international court had to pronounce on a taking by a state arose in the *Chorzow Factory Case* before the Permanent Court of International Justice.[29] The case is the source of all manner of wisdom in this area of law. The case is taken as supporting the claim of full compensation as including the market value of the property as well as future profits that could have been earned from the investment. In several awards of the Iran–US Claims Tribunal, the case is used as support for the norm of full compensation.

But, the use of the *Chorzow Factory Case* in this manner is unjustified. The case itself was concerned with a taking which was held by the Court to be illegal as it was a taking in breach of a treaty. The propositions in that case are concerned with illegal takings and not with

[27] See further M. Sornarajah, 'The Clash of Globalisations and the International Law on Foreign Investment' (2003) 10 *Canadian Foreign Policy* 1.
[28] On the possibility of bias by arbitrators in disputes arising from state contracts in favour of the views of capital-exporting states, see S. J. Toope, *International Mixed Arbitration* (1990), p. 346.
[29] (1928) PCIJ Series A No. 17.

expropriations which are considered lawful in modern international law. This will appear from the examination of the facts of the case.

A German company established a nitrate factory at Chorzow in Upper Silesia in pursuance of an agreement it made with the German government in 1915. In 1919, the land and the factory were sold by the German government to another German company. The first company still managed the factory. Upper Silesia passed into Polish hands after the Treaty of Versailles. In 1922, a Polish court declared the registration of the second company to be void and that the land on which the factory stood was to be transferred to the Polish treasury. A Polish ministerial decree vested management of the factory in a Polish official.

The issue which was presented to the Permanent Court of International Justice in 1926 was whether the taking over of the factory contravened the provisions of the Geneva Convention of 1922 between Germany and Poland. Article 6 of the Convention stated that Poland may expropriate major industries in Polish Upper Silesia but that it should not liquidate the rights of individual German nationals or companies in this region. The Court held that the taking of the factory was a violation of this treaty. The Court said that the Convention itself made certain expropriations lawful and others unlawful and that the expropriation of the factory fell within the category of unlawful expropriations under the treaty. It is clear that the case concerned expropriations which were considered unlawful because they constituted violations of a treaty.

After the judgment of the Court in 1926, negotiations took place between Germany and Poland for the restitution of the factory or, if this was not possible, for indemnity. It is clear that at this stage of the negotiations, the parties to the dispute themselves contemplated the possibility of restitution. When the negotiations proved unsuccessful, Germany claimed damages for the expropriation in a fresh claim before the Court. The German claim itemised the manner in which damages were calculated and did not include a claim for lost profits. The only claim relating to the future was the claim for an order preventing exports from the factory to certain countries. This aspect of the claim was refused by the Court. The Polish objection to the jurisdiction of the Court was overruled in 1927, and the Court pronounced on the merits of the case in 1928.

The Court reiterated the fact that it was not dealing with a lawful expropriation when it observed:

The action of Poland which the Court has judged to be contrary to the Geneva Convention is not an expropriation – to render which lawful only the payment of fair compensation would have been wanting; it is a seizure of property rights and interests which could not be expropriated even against compensation ... It follows that the compensation due to the German government is not necessarily limited to the value of the undertaking at the moment of dispossession, plus interest to the day of payment. This limitation would only be admissible if the Polish government had the right to
s wrongful act consisted merely in not having paid to the two companies the
as expropriated; in the present case such a limitation might result in placing
ts protected by the Geneva Convention, on behalf of which interests the German
, in a situation more unfavourable than that in which Germany and these interests
oland had respected the said Convention.

It should be clear to any reader of this passage that the Court was dealing with unlawful takings in violation of a treaty and not with takings which could have been rendered lawful by the payment of fair compensation. The passage indicates the Court's view that at the time of the decision the law considered the payment of compensation as an element of a lawful expropriation. The use of the case to support a blanket proposition that full compensation is due for all takings is clearly based on a misreading of the case.

The Court addressed the principles relating to damages for unlawful taking in a separate passage. The passage leaves no room for doubt that the Court was setting out the principles for damages for unlawful takings. The passage reads:

> The essential principle contained in the actual notion of an illegal act – a principle which seems to be established by international practice and in particular by the decisions of arbitral tribunals – is that reparation must as far as possible wipe out all the consequences of the illegal act and re-establish the situation which would, in all probability, have existed if that act had not been committed. Restitution, in kind, or, if this is not possible, payment of a sum corresponding to the value which a restitution in kind would bear; the award, if need be, of damages for loss sustained which would not be covered by restitution in kind or payment in place of it – such are the principles which should serve to determine the amount of compensation due for an act contrary to international law.

The Court also relied on the policy reason that the whole purpose of the treaty was to retain the *status quo* which existed as to property ownership. This was a matter protected by treaty, and the only way that the object of the treaty could have been ensured was through restitution of the property. Since that was not possible, the Court ordered damages which could have put the previous owner in a situation akin to his position prior to the taking. The case also illustrated the fact that, even in a clear situation of a treaty violation, the Court did not consider specific performance, despite the fact that the object of the treaty could have been best achieved by such an order.

It would be unnecessary to go on reiterating the point that the Court was not at all stating the principles applicable to the lawful taking of alien property if not for the fact that the case has, despite the clear language of the Court, mysteriously been construed to apply to all types of taking by states, despite the clarity with which the propositions were formulated by the Court. Another broad inference that is made is that the case contains *dicta* permitting the claiming of future loss. Germany did not make any claims for future loss. The only forward-looking claim that Germany made related to a request that the Court make an order prohibiting exports to certain countries. The basis of this claim was that there could be persons in the factory acquainted with the secret processes of the German owners which would enable the company to compete more effectively on the foreign markets with the German owners. The Court refused to make such an order, characterising the claim as insufficiently proven and as 'falling within the head of possible but contingent and inde-terminate damage which, in accordance with the jurisprudence of arbitral tribunals, cannot be taken into account'. After having stated the bases on which damages were to be assessed, the Court appointed a group of experts to assess the value of the property. The significance of this procedure, for claims that are later made on the basis of principles of valuation, should not be overlooked. Legal principles must first be laid down and damages assessed on the basis of such principles. It should not be the case that accountancy principles of valuation dictate which legal principles are relevant. In the event, in the *Chorzow Factory Case*, no valuation was made, as the parties settled the dispute.

The manner in which the case has been utilised in subsequent times is a sad commentary on international law academia. Faced with a paucity of authority that supports full compensation, the case has been utilised improperly by the proponents of full compensation to support their claim. It should be obvious to anyone reading the judgment of the Court that the Court sought to apply full compensation not to all instances of expropriation but only to those unlawful expropriations, such as those in breach of a treaty, to which restitutionary principles will apply.

Unfortunately, the *Chorzow Factory Case* has become the authority for a multitude of claims ranging from full compensation to fair and just compensation, which are terms used in the judgment. It illustrates that terminology has been a problem that has befuddled the law in this area. There are many difficult features in the judgment. But, despite these difficulties, it is difficult not to agree with the assessment of the case made by Judge Baxter who observed that the *Chorzow Factory Case*, 'so often resorted to as the source of wisdom on legal remedies for the taking of property', spoke of restitution only in the case of expropriations in violation of treaty commitments.[30]

Support for full compensation is to be found in the individual opinions of judges of the International Court of Justice in some later cases. For example, unequivocal support for full compensation is to be found in the dissenting judgment of Judge Carneiro in the *Anglo-American Oil Company Case*.[31] Judge Carneiro argued that full compensation for expropriated property must be made, as such a rule is a 'prerequisite of international cooperation in the economic and financial fields'. His view is based on the policy grounds that the flow of much-needed capital would be reduced if the norm of full compensation were not recognised, and not based on any examination of precedents.[32]

In the *Barcelona Traction Case*,[33] Judge Gros, in a separate opinion, made the statement that 'any nationalisations of a regular kind would have been accompanied by compensation'. But, the *dictum* must be limited to the situation that was being discussed. The judge had earlier pointed out that the 'opponents in the present case are two states whose economic and legal conceptions are the same'. Clearly, the statement was intended to be restricted to a regional standard that was to be applied to two European states with similar legal cultures.

---

[30] Foreword to R. B. Lillich (ed.), *The Valuation of Nationalized Property* (1987), vol. 1, p. vii; compare F. Francioni, 'Compensation for Nationalisation of Foreign Property: The Borderland of Law and Equity' (1975) 24 *ICLQ* 255 at 260, who observed: 'The case, often referred to as a decision which sanctioned the illegality of legislation having the effect of terminating foreign acquired rights, was strictly confined to a fact situation characterised by an *ad hoc* treaty that in itself imposed an obligation on Poland not to expropriate German assets and activities.'

[31] *Anglo-American Oil Company Case* [1952] *ICJ Reports* 93 at 151.

[32] Judge Carneiro observed (para. 15): 'When there are so many countries in need of foreign investment for their economy, it could be a mistake to expose such capital, without restriction or guarantee, to the hazards of the legislation of countries in which such capital has been invested.' The *dictum* of Judge Carneiro is incorrectly passed off as a *dictum* of the International Court of Justice in R. B. Lillich (ed.), *The Valuation of Nationalized Property* (1987), vol. 4, p. 174.

[33] *Barcelona Traction Case* [1970] *ICJ Reports* 3 at 274.

1.1.10 Awards of arbitral tribunals

The awards of arbitral tribunals stand in an even more inferior position to decisions of the International Court of Justice as sources of international law. Arbitral tribunals are constituted by the agreement of the parties to the foreign investment contract one of whom is not a state, and often the awards that they make are unilateral in that the state party does not appear before them or recognise their jurisdiction. More recently, the International Centre for the Settlement of Investment Disputes has been set up as a specialised body which deals with investment arbitration. The scope for awards made by this body as well as by *ad hoc* arbitral tribunals has increased ever since the possibility of tribunals exercising jurisdiction on the basis of treaty provisions has come to be accepted.[34] As a result, an increasing number of awards have been made. Despite this, the precedential value of these awards is not great. The awards that are so made reflect only the opinion of the arbitrators as to what the law is, and the weight these opinions carry depends on the eminence of the persons making them. It may be argued that the opinions of these tribunals have less weight than the views of publicists, as publicists take independent views as to what the law is whereas arbitrators on tribunals are motivated by other considerations such as the settlement of the dispute before them in an amicable or pragmatic fashion. The views that are expressed by these tribunals must therefore be approached with caution.

Full compensation was awarded by several tribunals established before the Second World War. These awards have continued to influence modern practice and deserve consideration. In the *Delgoa Bay Case*,[35] the tribunal awarded full compensation for the breach of a contract to build and operate a railway in a Portuguese-controlled area in southern Africa. A company formed in Portugal had raised capital for the purpose of constructing the railway. Many foreigners had contributed to the capital. The Portuguese took over the completed railway line without paying any compensation. The home states of the foreign investors and Portugal decided to submit the dispute as to compensation for the taking to an arbitral tribunal. The tribunal, in settling the dispute, applied Portuguese law, which, according to the tribunal, did 'not contain any particular provision on the decisive points that would depart from the general principles of the common law of modern nations'. The damages awarded included not only the value of the rights that were affected but also future profits.[36] The outcome is supportable simply because of the fact that the state party responsible for the breach obtained valuable property in a part of the world that was just opening up to commerce. The state itself did not have the capital or the expertise to build the railway. The foreign party had raised the capital and constructed the railway through difficult terrain. If the state was to put an end to the venture on some frivolous ground, then it should pay for what it takes. Here, payment of more than the immediate value of the property is fully justified for otherwise states may entice foreign investors into their countries, allow them to

---

[34] For an excellent work surveying the practice of arbitral tribunals, see S. Ripinsky and K. Williams, *Damages in International Law* (2009).

[35] Whiteman, *Damages* (1900), vol. 3, p. 1694.

[36] The tribunal stated that it was awarding damages according to 'the universally accepted rules of law, the *damnum emergens* and the *lucrum cessans*: the damage that has been sustained and the profit that has been missed.' The tribunal considered as an extenuating circumstance the failure of the company to indicate the time required to complete the railway.

build a project and then throw them out without any adequate recompense. There are punitive and sanctioning factors involved in the assessment of compensation, and one would have to accept the view both on policy as well as on legal grounds that the payment of more than full value as damages would be justified in these circumstances. The immorality involved in the conduct of the state may justify the treatment of cases such as this as akin to illegal takings. The types of situation like those that arose in the *Delgoa Bay Case* must be distinguished from other takings and they justify the payment of full compensation.

Full compensation was awarded in the *Schufeldt Claim*[37] on the basis of *damnum emergens* and *lucrum cessans*, a formula that has been taken to mean full compensation. The law which was applied was Guatemalan law, the law of the host state, which was held to be similar to all systems of law. In the *Lena Goldfields* arbitration,[38] the foreign concessionaire had been invited into the country by the state to prospect and mine gold. Here, again, full compensation was granted. In all these awards, there were contracts involved. Both in *Schufeldt* and in *Lena Goldfields*, there was a clear suggestion that a taking in violation of the concession agreement was an illegality. If such illegality had been the basis of the awards, their relevance in modern law is limited, as modern international law does not regard takings in violation of contracts as unlawful. Another factor which causes disquiet about these early awards is the use of arbitration in these cases to be a means of settling disputes between clearly unequal parties in a diplomatic manner and the arbitrators seemed to have approached their task with this purpose in view.

In the post-Second World War arbitrations, there continued to be an espousal of full compensation in the awards of several arbitral tribunals. But, some of the awards given in the 1970s show a movement away from the standard of full compensation. In the *Texaco* and *BP* awards, which involved Libyan nationalisations effected after the Arab–Israeli war and were said to be retaliatory measures against the United States for supporting Israel, there was reference to full value, but in both instances the arbitrators had found that there was illegality in the takings by the state. In *Texaco*, the remedy sought and awarded was restitution of the property, presumably to facilitate a strategy of pursuing Libyan oil through domestic courts into whose jurisdiction the oil is taken. *Texaco* is a heavily criticised award in which the arbitrator espoused theories which were totally beneficial to the claimant and bent the law in order to provide the remedy sought by the claimant. In *BP*, after finding illegality on the grounds of reprisal and want of public benefit, the arbitrator held that the 'claimant is entitled to damages arising from the wrongful act of the respondent'.[39] In the other arbitration arising from the same series of nationalisations, *Liamco*, the arbitrator held the nationalisations to be valid and did not accept full compensation as the standard. He referred to the earlier arbitral awards, which had favoured the standard of full compensation, and held that these awards were not good precedents in modern law as they were decided at a time when

---

[37] Whiteman, *Damages* (1930), vol. 3, p. 1652.

[38] *Ibid.*, p. 1737; A. Nussbaum, 'The Arbitration Between the Lena Goldfields Ltd and the Soviet Government' (1950) 36 *Cornell Law Quarterly* 31. Another case of relevance is *Goldenberg & Sons v. Germany* (1927–8) *AD* 542. It concerned a requisition of tin that was in transit to Romanian buyers prior to Romania's entry into the war. The claim was based on the Treaty of Versailles. The tribunal held that full compensation must be paid.

[39] (1977) 53 *ILR* 296 at 355.

expropriations were considered illegal. He then observed that, though the Hull formula may have been valid at an earlier time, it had now been replaced by the requirement to pay 'convenient and equitable compensation'. The arbitrator identified the factors which had brought about these changes, and held that under the new criteria the inclusion of future profits in the compensation payable would not be justified.

In the *Aminoil* arbitration, too, the tribunal did not hold that full value must be paid as compensation. The tribunal made an interesting distinction between states which want to break out of the hold of foreign investors entirely and those which welcome foreign investment. The purpose of the distinction was to hold the latter group of states to a higher standard of compensation. Kuwait was held to belong to the latter group of states. The parties had agreed that if compensation was to be awarded the legitimate expectations of the parties should be taken into account. The tribunal also took into account 'the reasonable rate of return' from the investment. It may be difficult to conclude that the standard of compensation which was used by the tribunal was full compensation.

It is clear that the *ad hoc* arbitral tribunals which have decided issues of compensation have not adhered to a single standard of compensation. In more recent times, there is a clear indication that expropriations are normally lawful and that full compensation may not be the general proposition with which to start the analysis of the compensation payable to the foreign investor.

ICSID tribunals ICSID tribunals are set up under the Convention for the Settlement of Investment Disputes. Unlike *ad hoc* tribunals, they function within the context of an international treaty. The Convention requires the tribunal to apply the law of the host state and international law to the dispute in the absence of an express choice of law by the parties. Though the interpretation of Article 42(2) which deals with the applicable law in the absence of express choice is a difficult issue, it is generally agreed that it gives primacy to the law of the host state. For this reason, ICSID tribunals do not apply international law but apply the domestic law of the host state in assessing damages owed to the foreign investor. Thus in *AGIP* v. *Congo*,[40] the tribunal purported to apply Congolese law in holding that Congo had to indemnify the loss suffered as well as the future profits lost as a result of the taking. The same standard was used in *Benvenuti et Bonfant* v. *Congo*[41] Since the tribunals have not indicated clearly whether they were applying domestic law or the law of the host state, the practice of these tribunals is of limited assistance.

Since the possibility of assuming jurisdiction on the basis of the dispute resolution provisions of investment treaties came to be recognised, the case load of ICSID has increased significantly. In these awards, the tribunals have applied the treaty provisions on compensation. These treaty provisions, consistent with the philosophy in treaties that provide for high standards of protection of investments, specify that full compensation must be awarded in the event of an expropriation. The tribunals have complied with these treaty prescriptions. To that extent, the rule applied was treaty-based and the extent to which they would contribute to the formation of any customary principle remains a matter of

---

[40] (1982) 21 *ILM* 726.   [41] (1982) 21 *ILM* 740.

conjecture. It can be argued that the treaties contribute to customary law, but it has been pointed out that such an argument is flawed.

Iran–US Claims Tribunals There is a rich body of awards generated by the Iran–US Claims Tribunal. The Tribunal was set up after the Iranian crisis which led to the overthrow of the Shah and the consequent exodus of US business from Iran. The Tribunal was set up under the Algiers Accord and was to hear the claims which US businessmen had against Iran. Many of these businessmen had been forced out of Iran as a result of the anti-American hostility that had been generated by the revolution. The exact nature of the contribution of a tribunal created by two states, which had prescribed the manner in which it was to act, given it a wide mandate and provided the means of enforcement of the award through the funds that had been frozen by the United States, has been a subject of debate. Some argue that the relevance of the work of the Tribunal to international law is limited because of the special circumstances in which it was created and because of the wide nature of the powers given to it. Others, however, point to the diverse nature of the problems that the Tribunal confronted and regard it as a rich storehouse from which principles on international business trans-actions could be quarried. The relevance of the decisions of the Tribunal to the general problem of nationalisations is limited by the circumstances in which they took place. They were motivated by hostility to US nationals, took place in the context of a revolutionary change and involved takings that were not associated with any economic programme. The takings took place in circumstances in which the continuation of US business in the country would have ended in any event, as such a continuation was fraught with dangers and difficulties. The value of the awards as precedents for large-scale expropriations in pursu-ance of economic programmes may be limited. The treaty setting up the Tribunal also gave it a wide remit to deal with all 'measures affecting property rights'.[42]

In any event, the jurisprudence of the Tribunal on compensation for nationalisations is ambivalent. The debate on the issue surfaced among the arbitrators on the Tribunal. The US arbitrators uniformly supported the norm of full compensation. The European arbitrators, who were the neutral arbitrators on the panel, also gave some qualified support to this norm. Though they supported the norm of full compensation, they regarded it only as a principle with which to start the inquiry and took several factors into consideration in reducing the compensation which was finally awarded so that on inspection it would appear that full compensation was never awarded by any of the individual tribunals. The Iranian arbitrators articulated norms which were favoured by the developing countries. They generally took the view that compensation was always due on expropriations or the taking of foreign property but that this requirement was satisfied if the net value of the property was paid as compen-sation. The response of the arbitrators to each other's views, sometimes in acrimonious terms, served only to highlight the divisions in the field. The US arbitrators asserted the Hull formula and the Iranian arbitrators rejected it.

---

[42] For an assessment, see M. Brunetti, 'The Iran–US Claims Tribunal, NAFTA Chapter 11 and the Doctrine of Indirect Expropriation' (2001) 2 *Chicago JIL* 203, who argues for the continuing significance of the jurisprudence of the Iran–US Claims Tribunal under later treaties.

There does not seem to be unqualified support for any definite standard of compensation, though there was acceptance that compensation was payable upon the taking of alien property. The leading awards involving the question of compensation for nationalisations should be examined. They are interesting for the reason that they indicate the range of views that could be taken on the issue of compensation for nationalisation as well as for the progressive evolution within the Tribunal of attitudes to the issue. Amusingly perhaps to an outside observer, they also show that the same authorities could be used by different jurists to support different propositions and arrive at different conclusions. This conclusion will also apply to the awards of the individual tribunals. Some have already begun viewing the awards as a victory for the standard of full compensation. Others are more circumspect in their analysis of the views of the tribunals on the issue of compensation.[43]

The first case in which the issue of compensation for the taking of alien property was considered by the Tribunal was *American International Group Inc.* v. *Iran.*[44] The case involved the taking of the equity interest of the US claimant in an Iranian insurance company. The taking was consequent upon the expropriation of the whole of the insurance industry in Iran. The claimant asked for full compensation and required that the business be valued as a going concern. On this basis, compensation would have included a sum for lost profits as well as the book value of the assets. Iran, however, maintained that compensation must be the book value of the assets which were taken. The Iranian view was rejected. But, in calculating the compensation, the Tribunal took into account factors such as the effect of the economic and political changes that had taken place in Iran that would have affected the future profitability of the business. The compensation which was awarded was almost one-quarter of the amount claimed by the foreign party. In view of the factors that the Tribunal took into account in calculating compensation, it may be possible to argue that what was awarded by the Tribunal was less than full compensation. In any event, the Tribunal's approach to the determination of the law seems flawed. Its view that the standard of damages for both legal and illegal takings is the same is not an accurate statement of the law, and it is contestable whether account should be taken of the future profitability of the company in assessing compensation for what was found to be a lawful act of expropriation. The Tribunal cited no authority for its view that market value was the correct basis of compensation for the lawful expropriation of foreign property. There are later awards of the Tribunal which state that future loss is not an element in compensation for the lawful taking of foreign property by a state. Arbitrator Mosk, who would have probably liked to see the claim awarded in full, characterised the award as a 'compromise solution' in his separate opinion. He indicated a preference for basing the award on the Treaty of Amity rather than on the customary international law which the Tribunal said it was applying.[45]

[43] There is now a substantial body of literature on the subject. R. Khan, *The Iran–US Claims Tribunal* (1990); J. Westberg, *International Transactions and Claims Involving Government Parties – Case Law of the Iran–United States Claims Tribunal* (1991); M. Pellonpaa and M. Fitzmaurice, 'Taking of Property in the Practice of the Iran–United States Claims Tribunal' (1988) 19 *Netherlands Yearbook of International Law* 53.

[44] (1983) 4 *Iran–US CTR* 96.

[45] Arbitrator Mosk pointed out that full compensation was justified, as the investment was made with the encouragement of the Iranian government and was not made in a quasi-colonial context and did not have an adverse effect on Iran (p. 117). He provided authority for the view of the tribunal by citing the *Chorzow Factory Case* and the *Norwegian Ship Owners' Claims*.

INA Corporation v. *Iran*[46] also involved the expropriation of an insurance company. The Tribunal characterised the expropriation as 'a classic example of a formal and systematic expropriation by decree of an entire category of commercial enterprises considered of fundamental importance to the nation's economy' and clearly regarded such expropriation as falling within a special category.[47] It pointed out that the law on this category of expropriation had undergone a change. It observed:

> In the event of such large-scale nationalisation of a lawful character, international law has undergone a gradual reappraisal, the effect of which may be to undermine the doctrinal value of any 'full' or 'adequate' (when used as identical to 'full') compensation standard as proposed in this case. However, the tribunal is of the opinion that in a case such as the present, involving an investment of a rather small amount shortly before the nationalisations, international law admits compensation in an amount equal to the fair market value of the investment.

The Tribunal was here concerned with customary international law and made the interesting distinction between large and small investments and investments made shortly before the nationalisations and those that had existed for a long time previously. However, it did not have to apply these distinctions, as it found an alternative basis on which to peg the standard of compensation in the Treaty of Amity between the United States and Iran. The Treaty required the prompt payment of 'just compensation' and defined such compensation as representing the 'full value' of the property taken. The Tribunal read such value as involving the 'fair market value of the shares'.[48]

In a separate opinion, Judge Lagergren had more to say on the issue of compensation. It is clear that the award already reflected his thinking but his own views were made clear in a separate opinion. As an experienced arbitrator who had made earlier awards on the issue of foreign investment contracts,[49] his views are entitled to respect. He confined full compensation to expropriations which were unlawful. He then referred to the Hull standard and its rejection by Sir Hersch Lauterpacht in his 1955 edition of *Oppenheim's International Law* on the ground that, where a state nationalises in order to effect far-reaching economic reforms, the payment of partial compensation may be sufficient. He then referred to Resolution 1803 (XVII) of the United Nations General Assembly on Permanent Sovereignty over Natural Resources which referred to 'appropriate compensation' as the standard of compensation, and said that this standard is one of 'inherent elasticity'. He observed:

Whether this standard is more correctly characterised as an exception to a still subsisting–though admittedly shrinking–Hull doctrine, or as evidence of a more general tendency towards the wholesale displacement of that doctrine as the repository of the opinio iuris, is still the subject of debate. But, the latter view appears by now to have achieved a rather solid bias in arbitral decisions and in writings.

---

[46] (1985) 8 *Iran–US CTR* 373.

[47] *Ibid.*, p. 378; it also regarded such a measure as 'among [the] risks which investors must be prepared to encounter'.

[48] Fair market value was defined as 'the amount which a willing buyer would have paid a willing seller for the shares of a going concern, disregarding any diminution of value due to the nationalisation itself or the anticipation thereof, and excluding consideration of events thereafter that might have increased or decreased the value of the shares': *ibid.*, p. 380.

[49] He was arbitrator in *BP* v. *Libya* (1977) 53 *ILR* 296 and in the *Argentine Bribery Case*, ICC Case No. 1110 (1963).

He concluded his opinion with the following passage:

[A]n application of current principles of international law, as encapsulated in the 'appropriate compensation' formula, would in a case of lawful large-scale nationalisations in a state undergoing a process of radical economic restructuring normally require the 'fair market value' standard to be discounted in taking account of 'all circumstances'. However, such discounting may, of course, never be such as to bring the compensation below a point which would lead to 'unjust enrichment' of the expropriating state. It might also be added that the discounting often will be greater in a situation where the investor has enjoyed the profits of his capital outlay over a long period of time, but less, or none, in the case of a recent investor such as INA.

The principles which were thus explained in the separate opinion of Judge Lagergren undoubtedly shaped the view in the award in the case that large-scale nationalisations intended to effect an economic restructuring may not be accompanied by full compensation. This was making a departure from the Hull formula. The US arbitrator, Judge Holtzmann, quickly responded by characterising this statement as an *obiter dictum*, as indeed it was, for the award rested on the standard of compensation referred to in the Treaty of Amity. He then pointed out that the passage was the 'hook' on which Judge Lagergren had hung his separate opinion that 'international law no longer favours full compensation'. He then made efforts to stabilise the official US position that 'appropriate compensation' meant 'full compensation'.[50] The dissenting opinion of the Iranian arbitrator, Judge Ameli, tends to favour the view of Judge Lagergren that the norm of full compensation no longer represents an absolute standard.

In *Sedco Inc.* v. *NIOC*,[51] the issue of the standard of compensation was addressed again. The claimant relied on the Treaty of Amity and alternatively on customary international law to claim full compensation as represented by the full market value of the property. The Tribunal started with the proposition that, prior to the Second World War, the payment of full compensation was the norm. One could take issue with this premise, as the Hull formula was not accepted by Mexico as representing the customary international law and there was no confirmed practice to show that there was any customary principle that had matured into law prior to the War. The Tribunal then stated that the issue was whether practice has changed this norm. It found the evidence provided by the lump-sum settlements inconclusive as these were diplomatic settlements induced by external constraints such as the need to restore trade relations and do not necessarily involve *opinio iuris*. Bilateral investment treaties also carry 'the same evidentiary limitations as lump sum agreements'. The tribunal was prepared to treat Resolution 1803 as reflecting the current international law. It took the view that the resolution applied to 'formal systemic large-scale nationalisations' but not to a 'discrete expropriation of alien property'. In the latter case, full compensation should be awarded.

---

[50] Judge Holtzmann used the *Chorzow Factory Case* to support full compensation, and pointed out that, in *Texaco v. Libya* (1977) 53 *ILR* 389, restitution was awarded, without mentioning that both involved prior findings of illegal takings. There is extensive reference to arbitral awards and to writings, though the writings are selective. Lauterpacht's view is regarded as *lex ferenda*.

[51] (1986) 10 *Iran–US CTR* 181.

Judge Brower's separate opinion, following the practice adopted by the US arbitrators on the Tribunal, sought to reiterate the norm of full compensation.[52] The award in *Sedco* establishes the view formulated in earlier awards that individual expropriations of smaller projects should carry full compensation, though the norm of full compensation for large-scale nationalisations has undergone a change.[53] Again, the award does not hold out authority for an unchanged, general principle that there is a duty to pay full compensation upon expropriation. The value of the distinction drawn in the award must be doubted. The award seeks to preserve full compensation for small-scale, single-industry nationalisations, while recognising that in light of modern authority full compensation for large-scale nationalisations is not maintainable. There are several problems with such a formulation. First, it does not specify how small the industry would have to be to qualify. Second, the era of full-scale nationalisations was the period following decolonisation. The effort is to contain the developments in the field to a specific period and continue as if nothing has happened in the area to change the norms outside this category which has now become largely redundant. The norms that were formulated in the period after decolonisation were not restricted in this manner.

There then followed a series of awards which involved smaller claims. In these awards, the individual tribunals regarded the standard applicable as full compensation, but, in calculating the compensation, the tribunals took into account factors such as the changes that had taken place in the Iranian economy as a result of the revolution and the effects it would have on the value of the shares and the property involved. In *Tams* v. *Tams-AFFA*,[54] full compensation was regarded as the standard of compensation on the basis of the Treaty of Amity as well as customary international law for the taking over of an engineering and consultancy firm. The takeover was found to have been effected through interference with management control. The situation was different from a nationalisation effecting economic reform. In *Phelps Dodge Corporation* v. *Iran*,[55] the claimant had controlling shares in a company for the manufacture and distribution of wire and cable products which was taken over. Full compensation was held to be the standard, but in calculating it the Tribunal 'could not properly ignore the obvious and significant negative effects of the Iranian Revolution' on the business prospects of the company. The sum that was awarded as compensation was the sum that was shown to have been invested originally in the company. In *Sola Tiles Inc* v. *Iran*,[56] where the taking was through interference with management control of a corporation in which the claimant had shares, the claimant based his case on general principles of law, but the Tribunal pointed out that the Treaty of Amity forms the background against which the tribunal would decide the case. This demonstrates a difficulty with the awards of the individual tribunals in general as it is difficult to determine when a tribunal was basing its

---

[52] In a well-crafted award, Judge Brower effectively states the US case for full compensation.

[53] No criteria have been devised for large-scale nationalisations. The distinction between the two has not been adequately explained. An across-the-board nationalisation of foreign property will obviously qualify, as presumably would an industry-wide nationalisation. There will be problems with selective nationalisation. Where a dominant foreign firm within an industry is taken over, it does not necessarily follow that full compensation must be paid.

[54] (1984) 6 *Iran–US CTR* 219.   [55] (1986) 10 *Iran–US CTR* 157.   [56] (1987) 14 *Iran–US CTR* 223.

award on customary law and when it was basing its award on the principles of the Treaty of Amity which it regarded as *lex specialis* as between the parties. The Tribunal took the view that, though there was an increasing reference to 'appropriate compensation' as the standard of compensation, this change of terminology did not indicate a change from the standard of full compensation and going concern value as representing the method of valuation. In assessing the value of the property, the Tribunal took into account the fact that the market for the type of high-quality tiles that the company manufactured had vanished after the revolution. The compensation awarded was almost one-sixth of what was claimed. The explanation of the change from adequate compensation to appropriate compensation – that was a mere terminological convenience in the award – is too facile. It is, once more, a technique to preserve the claims of the capital-exporting states in the face of the contrary claims which have been made by the capital-importing states.

Thomas Earl Payne v. *Iran*[57] involved the taking of a small business providing high-technology services and sales of electronic equipment. The takeover was effected through interference in the management of the company. The standard of compensation was held to be the one stated in the Treaty of Amity. Though the claim was for US $3 million, the Tribunal took into account the fact that the company would have lost much of its government-related business after the revolution and other relevant circumstances. It awarded a sum of US $90,000 as the 'fair value' of the claimant's share in the business. Though the tribunals did not themselves make the distinction, *Phelps*, *Payne* and *Sola Tiles* represent takings of smaller one-man businesses by indirect means such as interferences with management control. The tribunal was inclined to be more liberal towards such claimants and grant them somewhat close to the standard of full value though never close to full compensation. Where small, one-man operations are concerned, an atavistic view that makes the law come closer to its historical roots in protecting individual businessmen who ventured overseas to invest is permissible. As much as the law makes a distinction between large-scale and small-scale nationalisations, it is also permissible to make a distinction between investments made by one-man operations and multinational corporations. The views of the Tribunal may be taken as indicating that giving greater protection to the former is justifiable.

In some later awards, there were takings which could have been regarded as efforts on the part of the government to make economic reforms in industrial sectors. The awards in these cases do not show the same certitude as to the standard of compensation applicable. They show a reversion to the old view that the requirement to pay full compensation becomes considerably diluted and even substituted altogether by a different standard where the taking was for the purpose of effecting economic reform. *Amoco International Finance Corporation* v. *Iran*[58] involved the breach of an agreement between the claimant

---

[57] (1987) 12 *Iran–US CTR* 3.

[58] *Amoco International Finance Corporation* v. *Iran* (1982) 1 *Iran–US CTR* 493, Chamber Three: Virally (Chairman), Brower and Ansari (Members). Brower filed a concurring opinion and Ansari dissented in part. For comments on the case, see D. W. Bowett, 'State Contracts with Aliens: Contemporary Developments on Compensation for Termination or Breach' (1988) 59 *BYIL* 49. Judge Virally has been associated with several arbitrations involving state contracts. See A. S. El-Kosheri, 'Quelques Réflexions à Propos d'un Texte Inedit de Michel Virally', in *Mélanges Michel Virally* (1991), p. 297.

and the National Iranian Oil Company that was to last for thirty-five years and provided for the organisation of a joint stock company to extract petroleum-related products. There were several ancillary agreements concluded at the same time. The agreements were terminated by the Single Article Act Concerning the Nationalisations of the Oil Industry of Iran. The legislation sought to effect an industry-wide nationalisation. The claimant argued that the nationalisation was illegal on several grounds. The Tribunal rejected all the alleged grounds of illegality. In the process, it pointed out that there had been 'a very important evolution in the law … with the progressive recognition of the right of states to nationalise foreign property for a public purpose'. The *Chorzow Factory Case* was used by both parties to support different contentions as to the standard of compensation. The Tribunal therefore had to embark on determining the exact meaning of the decision in that case. The Tribunal held that the case dealt with unlawful expropriations and used restitution as the basis of damages for such takings. Since the Court had said that restitution in the case of unlawful takings is 'not necessarily limited to the value of the undertaking at the moment of dispossession', the Tribunal drew from this a consequence of 'paramount importance' that 'the compensation to be paid in the case of a lawful expropriation (or of a taking which lacks only the payment of a fair compensation to be lawful) is limited to the value of the taking at the moment of the dispossession'. It is not possible to award loss of future profits *(lucrum cessans)* in respect of lawful expropriations. This finding undermines the existence of a uniform requirement of full compensation for all expropriations and subverts the conventional wisdom that the *Chorzow Factory Case* provides the remedy of restitution equally to all types of nationalisation. The Tribunal stated this proposition in the following terms:[59]

> The difference is that if the taking is lawful the value of the undertaking at the time of the dispossession is the measure and the limit of the compensation, while if it is unlawful, this value is, or may be, only a part of the reparation to be paid. In any event, even in case of unlawful expropriation the damage actually sustained is the measure of the reparation, and there is no indication that 'punitive damages' could be considered.

The Tribunal pointed out that all the awards that have been cited to support full compensation had involved unlawful takings. The award punches a large hole in the case of those who support the Hull standard.

The jurisprudence of the Iran–US Claims Tribunal does not support the standard of full compensation in any meaningful sense. Though some commentators have drawn the conclusion that it does, a deeper examination of the awards do not lead one to such a conclusion. The US arbitrators strenuously tried to maintain the Hull standard, and equally the Iranian arbitrators held that the modern standard is one of appropriate compensation and generally favoured the payment of book value as compensation. The neutral arbitrators did not favour full compensation in all circumstances. While indirect takings, particularly of ongoing small businesses run by individuals by the ousting of management, resulted in awards of full compensation including sums for lost future profits, direct

---

[59] (1982) 1 *Iran–US CTR* 493.

nationalisations of whole industries in pursuance of what was considered economic reform did not result in awards of full compensation. Where future profits were awarded, it was recognised that such profits will be negligible in the context of the regime change and the hostile climate towards foreign investment which had been generated. One difficulty that analysts of the awards will have is to determine when the tribunals were making awards which were based on the Treaty of Amity, which was uniformly considered to be *lex specialis* between the parties by all the tribunals, and when it was making an award based on customary international law. The tribunals often recognised the interplay of the standards in their thinking. This failure to indicate a clear basis of the awards will diminish the utility of the awards as sources of customary law. The awards, which have generally reflected the views of the neutral arbitrators, have shattered many myths that have surrounded the issue of compensation. The *Chorzow Factory Case*, as the fountain of wisdom on matters of compensation for all expropriations, has been turned off and spurts only at half-strength as it has rightly been confined to unlawful takings. The view that illegality could arise from a mere breach of contract was also scotched. But, the tribunals were ambivalent on many issues. They reached decisions largely on the basis of compromise, particularly in the area of compensation for nationalisations and in the assessment of compensation. When the dust settles and the precise impact of these awards comes to be assessed, it will become apparent that one can cull from them statements in the awards as authority to support a diversity of views.

The general conclusion that has to be drawn from a study of arbitral awards dealing with the issue of compensation for nationalisations is that they do not support the norm of full compensation except in circumstances in which there had been a prior finding of illegality in the taking of the property.[60] Writers in the field have indiscriminately used the awards on unlawful expropriations to apply to the whole field of state takings. One merit of some of the awards made by the tribunals is to set the law straight by making a meaningful distinction between the two types of taking and also by rationalising the calculation of compensation in respect of the two types of taking. The awards also illustrate how men of obvious eminence could use the same authorities to arrive at different decisions. The explanation for this phenomenon may lie in the fact that the issue of compensation for nationalisations is approached with certain predispositions towards solutions. In the case of the US and Iranian arbitrators, these predispositions were obvious. In the case of the neutral arbitrators, some of whom had written extensively in related areas, the opportunity to sit on the Tribunal enabled an airing for their academic views. Apart from demonstrating the absence of any conclusive law on the question, the awards of the tribunals may have achieved little towards the clarification of the legal position on compensation for nationalisations.

---

[60] Abi-Saab rejects the awards which support full compensation in strong terms. He observed: '[A]part from the fact that these awards were not handed down by international tribunals properly so called, they do not sufficiently converge in language, in reasoning or in actual results to be really relevant as evidence of a consolidating trend.' G. Abi-Saab, 'Permanent Sovereignty over Natural Resources and Economic Activities', in M. Bedjaoui (ed.), *International Law: Achievements and Prospects* (1991), p. 597 at p. 613.

1.1.11 National courts

Domestic courts which have considered the question of the validity of foreign nationalisations without sufficient compensation did not regard the inadequacy of compensation as a ground for holding that the nationalisations were invalid. The only exception is *dicta* in a decision of a West German court which held that the nationalisation of the copper mines in Chile without payment of any compensation at all was invalid.[61] The latter case involved no payment of compensation and cannot be regarded as a pronouncement on the adequacy of compensation.

Two of the highest courts of common law, the English House of Lords and the US Supreme Court, have both held that there was no international law position on the standard of compensation. The House of Lords in *Williams and Humbert* v. *W. & H. Trademarks*[62] held that a Spanish decree on nationalisation of the property holdings of a family could not be questioned before the English courts on the ground that adequate compensation was not paid. Lord Templeman's speech indicated that, in modern law, attitudes to property have changed significantly, and that the state's right to nationalise has received general recognition. The issue of compensation had to be assessed in light of these changes. The US Supreme Court in the *Sabbatino Case*[63] reached a similar conclusion.

The US Court of Appeals (Second Circuit) made a survey of developments in the field in *Banco Nacional de Cuba* v. *Chase Manhattan Bank*.[64] The court held that the failure to pay any compensation at all would be a violation of international law, but that it was unclear as to what the standard of compensation prescribed by international law is. The court said:

It may well be the consensus of nations that full compensation need not be paid 'in all circumstances', and that requiring an expropriating state to pay 'appropriate compensation' – even considering the lack of precise definition of that term – would come closest to reflecting what international law requires. But, the adoption of an 'appropriate compensation' requirement would not exclude the possibility that in some cases full compensation would be appropriate.

The European Court of Human Rights is a regional court and as such enjoys more respect than national courts. In *Lithgow* v. *United Kingdom*,[65] it had to decide the interesting question of whether the taking of property without payment of full compensation was a violation of the right to property protected by Article 1 of the First Protocol to the European Convention on Human Rights. Article 1 makes reference to standards of international law, and the views of the Court have relevance to the standards of compensation in international law. The Court took the view that the decision of the state to nationalise and the amount of compensation it decides to pay are intertwined and that the Court will not question the amount of compensation which is eventually paid unless it is manifestly unreasonable. The Court said:

A decision to enact legislation will commonly involve consideration of various issues in which opinions within a democratic society may reasonably differ widely. Because of their direct knowledge

---

[61] *Sociedad Minera el Teniente SA* v. *Aktiengesellschaft Nordeutsche Affinerie* (1973) 12 *ILM* 251.
[62] [1986] AC 368.   [63] 376 US 378 (1964).   [64] 658 F 2d 875 (1981).   [65] (1986) 8 *EHRR* 329 at 373.

of their society and its needs and resources, the national authorities are in principle better placed than the international judge to appreciate what measures are appropriate in this area and consequently the margin of appreciation available to them should be a wide one. It would, in the Court's view, be artificial in this respect to divorce the decision as to compensation terms from the actual decision to nationalise, since the factors influencing the latter will of necessity influence the former. Accordingly, the Court's power of review in the present case is limited to ascertaining whether the decisions regarding compensation fell outside the United Kingdom's wide margin of appreciation; it will respect the legislature's judgment in this connection unless that judgment was manifestly without reasonable foundation.

With the exception of *dicta* in the West German case, which was concerned with a situation in which no compensation at all was paid and is therefore distinguishable, there are no decisions of national courts which support the view that full compensation is required in international law. These courts have reached that conclusion, despite the fact that the executive branches of these states have traditionally supported full compensation.[66] The judicial branches which have had to make an impartial assessment of the legal position have, however, pronounced that the norm of full compensation does not represent modern international law.

1.1.12 Writings of publicists

The writings of highly qualified publicists are regarded as subsidiary sources of law. Who a highly qualified publicist is, is nowhere defined. In an area of controversy, there will be much subjectivity in the choice of such persons. In the course of the life of the Iran–US Claims Tribunal, many counsel who represented clients on both sides as well as arbitrators have written on the issue of compensation for nationalisations as well as on other matters arising from the disputes before the tribunals. Those involved have also written books from different perspectives on the record of the work of the Tribunal. It would be a pity if their views are given independent weight even though they appeared in journals of diverse quality. If such weight were to be given, there would be great difficulty in distinguishing between the highly qualified publicist and the hired gun. It is an unfortunate facet of the whole law on foreign investment that writers have had the inclination by training or by preference to pursue certain interests.[67]

In the past, there was a practice of head-counting to show that the majority of the scholars favoured full compensation for nationalised property. There was hardly any meaningful writing emerging from the developing countries in the period before and after the Second World War. The debate took place in this period largely among Western scholars among whom a significant and increasing number began to move away from the norm of full compensation.

---

[66] One recent feature of case law is the increase in litigation against a state which settles investment disputes otherwise than in accordance with the norm of full compensation. But, so far, no claims against the state have been allowed. For a survey, see M. Leigh and J. A. Swindler, 'Constitutional Restraints of Foreign Economic Sanctions', in R. J. Ellings (ed.), *Private Property and National Security* (1991), p. 31. In England, the issue has been raised as to whether there is a duty on the part of the state to espouse the claims of its nationals who had suffered expropriation abroad. The issue was left open in *R. v. Secretary of State for Foreign Affairs, ex parte Pirbhai* (1984) 129 SJ 56. See also *Mutasa* v. *Attorney-General* [1979] 3 All ER 257.

[67] The present writer does not claim to be an exception.

When the New International Economic Order (NIEO) came to be articulated, the division among Western international lawyers became clearer. The General Assembly resolutions on NIEO make reference to appropriate compensation as the standard of compensation. These resolutions focused attention on the controversy, and writers began to take stances on the issue. There was also an emerging body of writing from developing country international lawyers supporting norms other than full compensation.

In the United States, the division of opinion between the supporters of full compensation and those who argue that the standard does not reflect modern international law became polarised when the American Law Institute sought to recognise that there has been a movement away from full compensation in its *Restatement of the Foreign Relations Law*. Professor Oscar Schachter, who was on the panel drafting the *Restatement*, has stated in his Hague lectures his understanding of the position as follows:

> Advocates of the Hull formula often characterise it as a traditional rule of international law. The record does not support this. No international judicial or arbitral tribunal, before or after 1938, has declared the 'prompt, adequate and effective' payment formula to be generally accepted international law. The leading European scholars, De Visscher, Lauterpacht,[68] Rousseau, have concluded that state practice does not support that standard. The Institut de Droit International reflected these views in a resolution adopted in 1950 and numerous studies in Europe and the United States have confirmed these conclusions with detailed evidence. I draw attention to the European and American studies to show that the opposition to treating the Hull formula as customary law does not come only from the 'third world'. Even in the United States, where the executive and legislative branches have sought to affirm the Hull formula as accepted law, the courts – including the Supreme Court – have noted the disagreement among states and have declined to find the prompt, adequate and effective standard to be customary law. The Restatement of Foreign Relations Law adopted in 1965 by the American Law Institute considered that the formula was qualified by 'what is reasonable in the circumstances' and it noted that 'less than full value' or 'fair market value' was acceptable in certain cases (for example, land reform). The revised Restatement of 1987 does not consider the Hull formula as internationally accepted law.

There is an increasing tendency among text writers to move away from the standard of full compensation as a uniform standard of compensation for nationalised property. The current edition of Oppenheim's text recognises the existence of the conflict as to the standard of compensation and is not partial to any view on the issue.[69]

---

[68] Sir Hersch Lauterpacht was the most significant of the writers to move away from the standard of full compensation. In a passage which appeared in his edition of *Oppenheim's International Law* (8th edn, 1952), p. 352, he suggested that the standard of full compensation was not applicable to nationalisations that took place in the course of economic reorganisation. The passage is missing from the ninth edition of *Oppenheim* edited by Sir Robert Jennings and Sir Arnold Watts: R. Jennings and A. Watts (eds.), *Oppenheim's International Law* (9th edn, 1992). In the ninth edition, it is conceded that the issue of compensation is an unsettled area of the law.

[69] R. Jennings and A. Watts (eds.), *Oppenheim's International Law* (9th edn, 1992), p. 921. At *ibid.*, p. 922, referring to the Hull standard, the editors state: 'There is … a question whether those elements constitute a separate and necessary part of the standard of compensation required by international law, or whether they are just considerations to be taken into account (perhaps along with others) in assessing whether compensation satisfies some much broader standard such as that it be "just", "equitable" or "appropriate".' Papers in a German symposium also note the deviations from the Hull standard: T. Opperman and E. Petersmann (eds.), *Reforming the International Economic Order* (1987), p. 40 (Weber); *ibid.*, p. 78 (Dicke); and *ibid.*, p. 115 (Hailbronner). For a Dutch rejection of the Hull standard, see W. D. Verwey and N. J. Schrijver, 'The Taking of Foreign Property under International Law: A New Legal Perspective?' (1984) 15 *Netherlands Yearbook of International Law* 3 at 20.

The survey of the traditional sources of international law that has been made shows that there is no support in them for the standard of full compensation for nationalisation. One has to be a committed advocate to a cause that is furthered by the claim to full compensation to believe that it does represent the norm of international law. Even then, support for the norm of full compensation can only be found in the weakest sources of law – the decisions of some tribunals and the writings of some publicists. The decisions of tribunals do not always provide clear evidence and have to be interpreted as favouring full compensation. Some are old and were made in an age in which nationalisations were uncommon. The writings of publicists do not provide unequivocal support for a standard of compensation. Even as a proposition of law formed at a time when state intervention in economic life was non-existent, it would be difficult to establish that there was evidence to regard full compensation as a norm of international law. In modern times, where such intervention is generally recognised as valid, there is no evidence that can be found limiting the right of a state to nationalise except on the payment of full compensation. Given the absolute weakness of the sources supporting the norm of full compensation, it is safe to conclude that, if there is a stronger norm based on even a slightly firmer base in the sources of international law, it would displace the norm of full compensation. It is necessary to examine whether there are any such norms.

2. The competing norms

Newly independent capital-importing states and other states whose economies were dominated by foreign corporations have refused to accept the norm of full compensation. The erstwhile Communist states of Eastern Europe held on to the consistent Marxist philosophy that nationalisation did not require the payment of any compensation. Leaving aside these ideologically inspired stances, which also contributed to the undermining of the norm of full compensation as they evidence the fact that a significant group of states for a long period of time did not accept the norm of full compensation, there were other stances taken by developing states which amount to state practice and constitute rejection of the norm of full compensation. The claim that has been advanced by these states, which has the greatest acceptance, is that only appropriate compensation need be paid upon nationalisation. Before discussing this claim, which now commands the widest support, some of the other claims inconsistent with the norm of full compensation are examined briefly.

2.1 The claim that it is permissible to deduct past excess profits from compensation

This claim was made by Chile during its copper nationalisation in 1971. The Chilean statute nationalising the interests of US copper companies, Kennecott and Anaconda, enabled past excess profits made by the two companies to be taken into account in calculating the compensation due to the companies. The tribunal that made the valuation decided that the corporations had made excess profits greater than the present value of the assets of the companies and that no compensation was therefore due them. No indication was given as to the valuation procedures adopted by the Chilean authorities.[70]

Before the controversy could be pressed any further, the Chilean government of President Allende was replaced in a coup which was alleged to have been inspired by the United States. The claim, nevertheless, remains an interesting proposition. It is a claim that is supportable as a matter of strict equity: if a foreign corporation had exploited a situation to its maximum advantage and reaped inordinate profits, the termination of the situation should not result in additions to that profit in the form of compensation. The idea that windfall profits should be shared with the state in the case of mineral resource exploitation receives support from the *Aminoil* award. Where *quantum meruit principles* are applied in fashioning a remedy, the past inordinate profits made by one of the parties is always relevant. But, the problem is to ensure that the state making such a claim is making an honest calculation. One problem with the Chilean claim was that the basis on which the state made the claim for the deduction of excess profits was never disclosed for objective scrutiny. Another is that the state or its authorities should not have had some complicity in permitting the foreign company to make the excess profits, as it may not be equitable for the company to have to pay what had previously been condoned by the state. Where the local elite collaborated in the exploitation, it would be difficult to assess how much of the profits were repatriated and how much were retained at home. In addition, condonation and ratification of the situation by the former government may prevent the situation being used by a later government.[71] But, as long as the claim to compensation is based on equitable notions such as unjust enrichment, fairness will require that the state also be permitted to take into account the past excessive profits made by the foreign company. In appropriate circumstances, the claim that excess profits should be deducted from the compensation payable does remain a valid proposition.

2.2 The claim that the taking is a 'revindication' for which no compensation is necessary

Such claims were made by Peru during the *La Brea y Parinas* dispute and the nationalisation of Gulf Oil in Bolivia.[72] The latter dispute was settled in a remarkably amicable fashion, the emphasis being largely on the agreement that normal commercialisation of hydrocarbons destined for export will continue through the agency of Gulf Oil. Both incidents involved the

---

[70] For discussions of the Chilean copper nationalisations, see R. B. Lillich, 'The Valuation of Copper Companies in the Chilean Nationalisation' (1972) 66 *ASIL Proceedings* 213; J. Rohwer, 'Nationalisation – Chilean Excess Profits Deduction' (1973) 14 *Harvard ILJ* 378; A. N. Heibein, 'The Chilean Copper Nationalisation: The Foundation for the Standard of Appropriate Compensation' (1974) 23 *Buffalo LR* 765; and F. Orrego Vicuña, 'Some International Law Problems Posed by the Nationalisation of the Copper Industry by Chile' (1973) 67 *AJIL* 711. D. Dicke, 'The Taking of Foreign Property and the Question of Compensation', in T. Oppermann and E. Petersmann (eds.), *Reforming the International Economic Order* (1987), p. 63 at p. 78, gives qualified support to the Allende principle on the basis of unjust enrichment.

[71] In many instances, Latin American dictators and ruling cliques worked together with foreign investors in making huge profits out of resource exploitation. G. Coronel, *The Nationalization of the Venezuelan Oil Industry* (1984), p. 8.

[72] D. B. Furnish, 'Peruvian Domestic Law Aspects of the La Brea y Parinas Controversy' (1970) 89 *Kentucky LJ* 351; D. B. Furnish, 'Days of Revindication and Dignity: The Petroleum Expropriations in Peru and Bolivia', in R. B. Lillich (ed.) *The Valuation of Nationalized Property* (1975), vol. 2, p. 55.

claim that the land subject to the concession could be taken over without compensation and that the investor should be entitled only to the value of the machinery and other assets. Bolivia insisted on deducting from the net value of the investment the taxes that were owed and the value of the minerals extracted from the land.[73] Revindication is a claim that is couched in emotive language. Its only legal significance may be to ensure that past malpractices which the foreign corporation adopted in exploiting resources could be taken into account in calculating compensation. There could be a punitive measure included in the assessment of compensation. In the *Aminoil* dispute, Kuwait argued that the exploitation practices of the claimant were harmful and that the damage thereby caused should be set off against the compensation that was due. The tribunal avoided pronouncing on the validity of this claim by its finding on the facts that the exploitation practices were not improper. But, future claims along these lines will continue to be made. Where the taking is based on the state's belief on objective grounds that the practices adopted in the exploitation of natural resources were harmful to the environment or depleted the resources unnecessarily, there is room for argument that this factor should be taken into account in assessing compensation.

2.3 The claim that appropriate compensation should be paid

This claim received unanimous support in Resolution 1803 of the General Assembly. There has been some effort to explain the use of 'appropriate' as meaning 'full' compensation. Short of rewriting English (and American) dictionaries, such an effort to give unnatural meanings to words must be dismissed as a feeble effort motivated only by an interest in keeping the norm of full compensation alive.[74] There was a clear effort made in the resolution to change the existing norms of international law relating to compensation for nationalisation and the usage of the word was intended to signal that change. The resolution referred to 'appropriate compensation in accordance with international law', thereby indicating that international law provided the standard as to what was appropriate. The resolution did not deny the relevance of international law as a controlling factor in determining the appropriate compensation.

Later resolutions in the General Assembly do not reflect such a compromise. Resolution 3171 (XXVII) seeks to give each state the sole right to determine the 'amount of possible compensation'. The resolution on the New International Economic Order seeks to assert national competence in determining the amount of compensation. The resolution on the Charter of Economic Rights and Duties of States requires that 'appropriate compensation be paid ... taking into account the relevant laws and regulations and all circumstances that the state considers pertinent'. There were similar resolutions enacted in other United Nations agencies.[75] These resolutions were passed without the support of the capital-exporting

---

73 (1968) 7 *ILM* 1201; (1969) 8 *ILM* 264.
74 The drafting history of the resolution indicates that the formulation was a compromise, the capital-exporting nations agreeing to the use of 'appropriate' provided there was a reference to international law as providing the standard. But, see S. Schwebel, 'The Story of the UN's Declaration of Permanent Sovereignty over Natural Resources' (1963) 49 *ABAJ* 463; and Ambassador Stevenson's letter in (1963) 57 *AJIL* 406.
75 See, for example, UNCTAD Res. 88 (11), which states that it is 'for each state to fix its compensation'.

states. Leaving aside the debate as to whether resolutions of the General Assembly have a law-creating effect, these resolutions, at the least, indicate a desire on the part of the states to reject full compensation as the standard of compensation. The draft Code of Conduct on Transnational Corporations also contains a similar formula.

In this context, the resolution that has received the most support will provide a basis upon which the law can be formulated as it represents a will that is common to all members of the international community. The view that General Assembly resolutions are generally not law-creating and that they are at best expressions of *lex ferenda* may be swept aside for in a field that is occupied largely by the inconsistent practice of a few states and the opinions of tribunals and writers – weak sources of law to say the least – it will be possible to postulate a norm built on the collective view of nations as best representing the law.

 Appropriate compensation is a reference to a flexible standard which could range from the payment of full compensation, the amount of future profits lost, to the payment of no compensation at all in circumstances where the foreign investor had visibly earned inordinate profits from his investment and the host state had no benefits at all from it. The relevance of international law to the assessment of compensation continues. The resolutions associated with the New International Economic Order are founded on appeals to justice and equity which are supranational concepts and are rooted in international law. It must therefore be conceded that any compensation must meet with supranational standards of appropriateness and be justifiable in terms of objective justice and equity.

The scope for full compensation in the earlier sense has considerably diminished in modern times. If full compensation did not have a basis in the past practice of states, recent practice indicates a total rejection of such a standard. Partial compensation seems to be the generally preferred solution. The Indian nationalisation of the oil installations of Burmah Shell in 1976 resulted in the payment of partial compensation.[76] Ceylon, which took over oil companies in 1964 and tea estates in 1976, paid only partial compensation. African nationalisations have also involved the payment of only partial compensation. Thus, Rood, after a survey of the compensation practices of African states, concluded:[77]

> The compensation promised or paid for the take-overs of foreign property in British Africa falls far short of what the former owner thinks is due. Fair market value, valuation based on capitalised earnings and effective compensation are distant ideals; reality is likely to be partial payment, a vague promise of something in the future or a statement of good intentions by the government.

Latin American practice seems uniform in the payment of some compensation but not full compensation. The settlement of the Marcona nationalisation dispute between Peru and the United States is a case in point. The dispute was settled by the conclusion of a lump-sum settlement agreement. Though the United States interpreted the agreement as involving adequate compensation, the agreement does not provide for monetary compensation equalling the value of the property taken. The emphasis was on the continuation of the

---

[76] Burmah Shell Act 1976.
[77] L. Rood, 'Compensation for Takeovers in Africa' (1977) 11 *Journal of International Law and Economics* 521; D. Ijalye, 'Multinational Corporations in Africa' (1981) 171 *Hague Recueil* 1.

relationship between the foreign investor and the host state.[78] Though partial compensation has been the normal practice, the notion of appropriate compensation is flexible enough to provide that full compensation should be paid in certain circumstances.

It is possible in the context of the acceptance of appropriate compensation to account for the case law that has been generated so far as to compensation for takings of foreign property by states. In the analysis that follows, all takings of foreign property and not only nationalisations are included. It is possible to identify five major categories.

2.3.1 Categories of takings for which damages rather than compensation must be paid

In the case of an illegal taking, the state must pay damages calculated on the basis of effecting a *restitutio in integrum*. The obvious instances of this would be where the taking is in violation of a treaty obligation owed to the home state of the foreign investor or where there had been a taking motivated by racial discrimination. The limitation of public purpose is of diminishing significance but the absence of a public purpose will help to establish racial discrimination as a ground of illegality. Where there has been an illegal taking, the classical position that the claimant must be paid both *damnum emergens* and *lucrum cessans* remains unaffected.

Christine Gray referred to the difficulty in distinguishing between the consequences of an illegal and a legal nationalisation in the present state of the law. The meaningful distinction is to ensure damages in the case of an illegal nationalisation which will include both present and future loss, whereas in the case of a legal nationalisation there is compensation which is payable by the state. Future loss has no role to play in the assessment of the compensation, as the state has a present right to terminate the venture.[79] The legality of the nationalisation depends on the recognition of that present right. Future loss which flows from the termination of the venture as a result of the exercise of the right is legally insignificant. In assessing present loss, there is a need to take into account a whole range of factors such as the nature of the past relationship between the parties, the extent of the profits made by the foreign investor, the duration of the investment, the legitimate expectations of the foreign investor and other like factors.

2.3.2 Categories of lawful takings for which full compensation must be paid

Full compensation must be paid in circumstances in which the foreign investor was invited by the host state to undertake a project which could not have been completed without his investment in resources and technology and the investment is taken over before the investor could receive any profit by his investment. Here, there is an element of fraud in the conduct

---

[78] D. Gantz, 'Marcona Settlement' (1977) 71 *AJIL* 474.

[79] D. W. Bowett, 'State Contracts with Aliens: Contemporary Developments on Compensation for Termination or Breach' (1988) 59 *BYIL* 49 at 63: '[T]he correct principle is believed to be that loss of future profits, whilst a legitimate head of general damages for an unlawful act, is not an appropriate head of compensation for a lawful taking.' See also M. Pellonpää and M. Fitzmaurice, 'Taking of Property in the Practice of the Iran–United States Claims Tribunal' (1988) 19 *Netherlands Yearbook of International Law* 53 at 123–7.

of the host state which apart from the equities of the situation justifies the payment of full compensation, which could include some element of future profits as a punitive measure. But, ordinarily, the taking of such punitive measures is not the function of an international arbitration. Where legitimate expectations had been created in the foreign investor by the conferment of guarantees and the inclusion of stabilisation clauses, the case for awarding full compensation will be strengthened. Cases which approach this paradigm situation will justify the payment of full compensation or near full compensation. The nature of the invitation held out to the investor and the period for which the investor was permitted to function prior to the taking are important factors. The greater the enticing efforts on the part of the host state and the shorter the period after the investment was beginning to bear profits before the taking, the greater is the justification for the payment of full compensation. The nature of the guarantees given against nationalisation and the absence of alternative sources from which the host state could have obtained the same type of skills or investments for the project concerned will also add to the case for full compensation.

2.3.3 Full compensation must be paid where there is a one-off taking of a small business

Here, the principle of allocation of risk will require the state which benefits by the takeover and can better absorb the risk should pay. The public benefits accruing from the takeover of a small business are unlikely to be high, and the motives for the taking cannot be clearly justified on an economic basis. This type of taking shares features with the confiscatory takings of the past. There is also justification for the payment of full compensation where a state had held out incentives to a foreign investor and had taken over the investment at the stage in which it was about to yield profits.[80] Where the state had created legitimate expectations of settled profits for a course of time, this factor too will indicate full compensation. The nature of the guarantees given and the absence of alternative sources from which the foreign investment could have been drawn are factors to be taken into account in considering whether full compensation should be permitted.[81]

2.3.4 Full compensation need not be paid as part of a full-scale nationalisation of a whole industry

Full compensation need not be paid where there is a full-scale nationalisation of an industry as a part of economic reform. There is overwhelming authority supporting a norm of partial compensation in situations in which there is a full-scale nationalisation

---

[80] *Aminoil* (1982) 21 *ILM* 976, which makes the distinction between states which actively seek foreign investment and states which do not. In the case of the former, there is an expectation that they will favour strong norms of foreign investment protection and hence compensation must be calculated on a basis which 'warrants the upkeep of a flow of investment in the future'. E. Jimenez de Arechaga, 'State Responsibility for Nationalisation of Foreign Owned Property' (1979) 11 *New York University Journal of International Law and Politics* 179, regarded the stabilisation clause as relevant for the assessment of compensation, as did the tribunal in *Aminoil*.

[81] The classic instance of this is the situation in the *Delgoa Bay Case*, where capital and technology for the building of a railway was procured from abroad with the promise that the profits of the railway could be enjoyed by the foreign investor. Also, *Starrett Housing Corporation* v. *Iran* (1987) 16 *Iran–US CTR* 112, where a housing project nearing completion was taken over.

programme as a part of economic reform.[82] Much of the post-Second World War nation-alisations were effected in pursuance of such programmes which were designed to end the dominance of the erstwhile imperial powers of the economies of newly independent countries. The notion of appropriate compensation was articulated in the context of such programmes. Some believe that the need for the norm has ended now that such dominance has ended. Others believe that such dominance continues to be exercised through the network of multinational companies.

The relevance of this norm will continue. Nationalisations will be a cyclical phenomenon. For various reasons, the climate at present is favourable to foreign investment. The shortage of foreign investment, the belief that foreign investment will lead to economic growth and the fact that trade, lending and aid are tied to developing countries maintaining a favourable stance towards foreign investment, are all responsible for this climate. The picture may change after a period when foreign investors have become stabilised in the host states. Nationalistic feelings will be aroused when the dominance of foreign corporations becomes evident. Ideological or economic attitudes to foreign investment may change. When that happens, we may expect a fresh bout of nationalisations. In these circumstances, the claim that such nationalisations could be effected through the payment of appropriate compensa-tion will become relevant. States could then assimilate the nationalisations they effect to the post-war or post-colonial nationalisations.

2.3.5 Partial compensation

Partial compensation is justified where the past practices of the foreign investor were harmful to the host state or where there had been inordinate profits made from the invest-ment. The duration of the foreign investor's stay in the host state is always relevant. If his profits had recompensed the investment initially made, the relevance of full compensation to him diminishes correspondingly to the extent of the profits. This will be particularly so where the ending of the investment is for reasons that the investor had adopted bad industry practices in the past or where he had made inordinate profits. In these circumstances, there must be objective evidence of the allegations made by the state. It would be improper to argue that no compensation need be paid on this ground. There is immediate benefit to the host state as a result of the taking of the assets of the foreigner which is a circumstance that usually justifies the payment of some compensation.

The five categories discussed above are merely guidelines as to how the notion of appropriate compensation is to be applied consistently with the past practice of states. It also helps to show that the past practice of states is consistent with the norm of appropriate compensation and that it is this norm which incorporates within it the notions of full

---

[82] Authority for this category comes largely from the General Assembly resolutions associated with the New International Economic Order and the writings of scholars like Sir Hersch Lauterpacht. The strategy adopted in the World Bank Guidelines is to accept the norm but confine it to the past nationalisations which effected wholesale economic reforms, and to state that these circumstances will 'rarely occur and may be expected to become uncommon in the future'. World Bank, *Legal Framework for the Treatment of Foreign Investment* (1992), vol. 2, para. 48. This overlooks the fact that the claims to the New International Economic Order were made long after the post-colonial and post-war nationalisations.

compensation for certain types of takings and partial compensation for others which best represents modern international law.

3. Valuation of nationalised property

The method of valuation of property has been considered in some recent arbitral awards. No consistent pattern has emerged as to methods of valuation. Valuation is a secondary issue. The primary issue is the standard according to which the law requires compensation to be made. Methods of valuation should not be the means by which the tail is made to wag the dog. In the *Chorzow Factory Case*, the Permanent Court of International Justice appointed a committee of experts to value the property after itemising the heads upon which damages could be awarded for the illegal nationalisation that was involved in the dispute. The identification of the legal basis on which damages or compensation should be awarded was the first step adopted by early tribunals.

The method of valuation was also discussed in the awards of the Iran–US Claims Tribunal and in some of the more recent awards of ICSID tribunals. In many of the awards of the Iran–US Claims Tribunal, the standard of compensation was held to be as stated in the Treaty of Amity between Iran and the United States. Valuation was often based on the standard in the Treaty. No conclusion of general relevance can be drawn from the valuation practice of the Tribunal.

There is now an accumulation of literature on the subject.[83] Much of the literature is aimed at projecting theories into methods of valuation used by arbitral tribunals, often despite the fact that the arbitral tribunals did not themselves disclose the method they used. There has emerged an unnecessary conflict on the subject. Valuation is an objective process. It should not be permissible for standards or theories of compensation to be built in through valuation principles. If there are technical problems of valuation, a tribunal can always obtain expert help in making the valuation. Valuation is not the main issue of controversy. Once a tribunal arrives at the standard of compensation, the value of the compensation payable according to that standard can be assessed with the help of experts, if need be. After reiterating the cautionary statement that these principles should not be the means of reintroducing standards of compensation through the back-door and that they are secondary to the finding of the compensation standard applicable to the dispute, some of the standards which have been used may be stated. There are three principal methods, which are discussed below.

The first method is book value. According to a study initiated by the United Nations Commission on Transnational Corporations, book value is the method of valuation most

[83] E. Penrose, 'Nationalisation of Foreign-Owned Property for a Public Purpose: An Economic Perspective on Appropriate Compensation' (1992) 55 *MLR* 351; W. C. Lieblich, 'Determining the Economic Value of Expropriated Income Producing Property in International Arbitrations' (1991) 8 *JIA* 59; S. K. Khalilian, 'The Place of Discounted Cash Flow in International Commercial Arbitrations' (1991) 8 *JIA* 31; P. D. Friedland and E. Wong, 'Measuring Damages for Deprivation of Income Producing Assets: ICSID Case Studies' (1991) 6 *ICSID Rev* 400; and E. Lauterpacht, *Aspects of Administration of International Justice* (1992), pp. 130–6.

used in assessing the value of property.[84] The book value of assets represents the difference between the corporation's assets and liabilities as stated in the accounts books. This method of valuation was widely used in the petroleum nationalisations that took place in the 1970s, though the companies which were taken over were going concerns. Where the expropriation is lawful and therefore where the award of *lucrum cessans* is not permissible, book value should be the method of valuation used.

The second method of valuation is market value. This method of valuation was favoured by those who argued for the Hull standard of compensation. All writers who have rejected the Hull standard have rejected the market value as the applicable method of valuation. Market value takes future profitability into account. Such a valuation is permissible only if an award can be made on the basis of both *damnum emergens* and *lucrum cessans*. The overwhelming view is that such a standard of compensation is possible only where there is an illegal taking of foreign property.

The third method of valuation is the discounted cash flow method. This is a new basis introduced to stem the tide running strongly against the market value method. This method requires the projection of the future receipts expected by the enterprise after deducting the costs associated with the making of the receipts. The World Bank Guidelines state that this is the method which should be applied where the company that is taken is a going concern. This introduces standards of compensation through the back-door and makes the distinction between lawful and unlawful takings meaningless. To the extent that the method requires future factors to be taken into account, those who seek its application must show that the taking involved was an unlawful taking.

4. Conclusion

The issue of compensation for the nationalisation of foreign property provides fascinating insights into how international legal principles are shaped. The principle that nationalisation was illegal was formulated at a time when takings by the state of the property of individual aliens for the self-aggrandisement of the ruling cliques was the normal situation of state takings. The issue of compensation was discussed in the context of this situation. But, when the normal situation of state takings became one of takings with the aim of restructuring the economy, the law underwent a change. This change was brought about by the challenges made to the existing claims relating to compensation by developing states which were in the process of restructuring their economies after the ending of colonialism. That challenge enfeebled the claim relating to full compensation considerably. The manner in which it was displaced by a new formula of appropriate compensation provides an illustration of international lawmaking. Given the existence of two conflicting norms, decision-making authorities within the international community had to quickly refashion the law on newer lines.

---

[84] A study of 174 nationalisations effected in the 1970s showed that the general practice was to apply the book value concept, though companies asserted fair market value, going concern value and replacement costs as the standards on which valuation should be made. R. B. Sunshine, *Terms of Compensation in Developing Countries' Nationalization Settlements* (UNCTC, 1981).

The solution adopted preserves the norm of full compensation but also accommodates the view that such full compensation need not always be paid and that each situation must be approached on a case-by-case basis.

In light of the controversy relating to the standard of compensation, the best solution that could be hoped for in the present state of international law is for states to settle the issue of compensation through bilateral investment treaties and agree upon the standard of compensation between themselves. This strategy is being increasingly resorted to. Where such a treaty exists, the standard referred to in the treaty is conclusive. Since nationalisation presents the greatest risk to foreign investment and the most controversial issue in the law of foreign investment relates to the standard of compensation, it is sensible to resort to this solution to the problem.

12

Defences to responsibility

As the number of arbitrations under the investment treaties increases and the perception of their legitimacy decreases with conflicting decisions, states have responded in three principal ways. The first has been one of withdrawal from the system of investment arbitration. Some states have announced that they will consider not extending the life of their investment treaties after they expire. Others have sought to withdraw from the ICSID Convention.[1] This response is a calculated decision based on the belief that the costs of arbitration and disputes outweigh the benefits that investment treaties bring to a state. Withdrawal and termination are matters of sovereign prerogative, but such a withdrawal has to be effected through the manner prescribed in the treaty. The effectiveness of withdrawal depends on its timing. Such withdrawal is not possible as to existing disputes or disputes that arose while the treaties were pending. The termination provisions in the treaties are relevant in determining such issues.

The second response is to change at lease future investment treaties so that there is an exclusion of certain sectors such as taxation from arbitration[2] and the inclusion of exceptions to responsibility in the treaty itself. The third has been to argue new types of defences to liability. It is the third response that this chapter will focus on.

It is a relatively new phenomenon that there should be such defences to responsibility in a system which was thought of as providing a virtually unchangeable system of secure protection to foreign investors. This has changed as a result of states invoking defences based on customary international law and ensuring that defences preserving regulatory space are stated in the more recent treaties. The increasing number of defences that are being explored as well as the broad manner in which they are stated in the investment treaties does have consequences for investment protection. Coupled with the tenacity with which jurisdiction has been resisted by states, the exploration of defences to liability may have the effect of undermining the system of investment protection that has been built up by investment treaties. It was pointed out that the object of investment treaties was to bring about secure rules of investment through their statement in investment treaties. That original aim

---

[1] Ecuador has withdrawn from the ICSID Convention. Withdrawal of a class of disputes is permissible under Article 25(4) of the Convention.

[2] Venezuela has withdrawn petroleum disputes from ICSID arbitration. The effect of these withdrawals on existing disputes is yet to be determined.

may have been undermined as a result of the increasing scope of defences to liability under the treaties. It could well be argued that the law has returned to the state of conflict and anarchical normlessness that existed prior to the advent of investment treaties. It is a point worth exploring at the end of this chapter, after dealing with the nature of the defences that have been constructed through arbitration as well as through treaty statements.

The transformation of investment treaties from those intended to provide protection alone to balanced treaties that consider the regulatory interest of the state in certain areas such as the environment, labour rights and the health and welfare of citizens has led to the statement of exceptions to liability in the investment treaties themselves. There are elaborations made of the scope of these exceptions in awards so that a body of exceptions to jurisdiction and responsibility are coming to be drawn more clearly. In some instances, the scope of the exceptions is potentially wide, such that the scope of the principle of responsibility itself is eaten up by the exception. The exception of regulatory expropriation that has emerged seems to have such an impact on the law relating to expropriation. The emergence of these defences has the consequence that there may be other avenues yet to be opened up in order to avoid responsibility. But, a reaction to this would also be to explore means of ensuring liability by asserting alternative bases of liability. The promotion of the hitherto little explored fair and equitable standard as a basis of liability can be seen as a consequence of the circumscribing of expropriation, the traditional basis of liability in this area.

Most of the defences that are pleaded are drawn from existing international law, demonstrating that responsibility under the investment treaties is not a self-contained notion but has to operate within the context of the principles of public international law. As the creative imagination of lawyers acting for foreign investors innovates new bases of jurisdiction and liability, there is a response to this by states in seeking methods of denying jurisdiction and responsibility. In the jurisdictional area, this has been witnessed in arguments relating to the definition of foreign investment, the nature of corporate responsibility necessary for standing and a reliance on non-satisfaction of national laws. Likewise, in the area of responsibility, hitherto unused notions such as regulatory expropriations as an exception to responsibility for taking and the plea of necessity are used.

As some awards expanded the meaning and scope of the provisions of the investment treaties, stabilising the neo-liberal aims of absolute investment protection through the fashioning of expansionist doctrines, states reacted by restricting the scope of investment treaties not only by creating exceptions in the newer treaties but also by arguing for defences to responsibility on the basis of customary norms of international law and on the basis of the aims behind the treaty. In the process, there was a retreat from neo-liberalism evident in the development of the law which coincided with the general retreat that was taking place in the world consequent upon a succession of economic crises following neo-liberal policies. This retreat from the old neo-liberal objectives is evident in the schisms that have developed within the system reflected in the conflicting arbitral awards involving the same propositions of the law. Many writers facilely explain the conflicting views on the different treaty formulations. The better explanation is that the schisms were a result of a fundamental clash in the policies that influenced the various arbitral tribunals. The schisms are best reflected in the response of the tribunals to the defences to liability attempted by respondent states. The creation and recognition of these defences are by themselves significant. Their significance is enhanced by the fact that they reflect a deep-seated conflict as to the policies behind the law adopted by the different arbitral tribunals rather than by variations in the text of treaties.

The widening clamour for representation of interested groups before arbitral tribunals dealing with investment disputes will entrench the public interest element of such arbitration. Whenever water disputes, as in *Biwater Gauff* v. *Tanzania*[3] and *Aguas del Tunari* v. *Bolivia*,[4] or issues involving corruption, as in *World Duty Free* v. *Kenya*,[5] come before investment tribunals, they attract world attention, indicating that the dispute does not affect only the foreign investors and the states involved but implicates global interests. As investment treaty arbitration becomes subject to greater scrutiny, the system will require greater transparency. A system that seems to insist that such transparency forms a part of the fair and equitable standard cannot remain closed to interested parties. Such global scrutiny will question the fairness of the results that are arrived at and foreign investors may themselves perceive that winning the arbitration through clever arguments may be counter-productive. It will also lead to the fuller consideration of defences to responsibility, particularly those reflecting global concerns.

There is no theme that emerges to the defences that permits categorisation. If a categorisation is possible, one could create one category of defences provided in the treaties and a second category of defences that arise from customary principles of international law. But, the two categories shade into each other. The statement of some of the defences, such as necessity, clearly has roots in customary international law. This chapter is necessarily short, not only because of the lack of material on a yet-to-be-developed area, but also because much of the material that needs to be explored has already been explored in earlier chapters. However, it brings together an area of potential future development that will acquire greater significance as time goes on.

1. Treaty-based defences

As the utility of investment treaties came to be challenged by various interest groups and experience relating to their operation grew, states began to respond by introducing defences to responsibility to address the concerns that were being raised by various interested groups. The contest prior to the OECD's effort to draft a multilateral agreement on investments brought the nature of the concerns of various non-state actors into the open. Thereafter, the same intensity of concern has been expressed in connection with types of disputes that have arisen such as those concerning water or bribery. The old view, that the only purpose of the treaty was to provide for an inflexible framework of investment protection, has given way to

---

[3] ICSID Case No. ARB/05/22 (Award, 24 July 2008).
[4] ICSID Case No. ARB/02/3 (Decision on Jurisdiction, 21 October 2005).
[5] ICSID Case No. ARB /00/7 (Award, 4 October 2006).

the need for a balance between that purpose and the regulatory interests that a host state may have over foreign investment as well as the interests of other concerned sections of the public. Perhaps, the Multilateral Agreement on Investment marked a watershed, in that the inflexible model of investment protection it sought was opposed with such vigour that such a model became a thing of the past. In the area of international trade, exceptions to rules based on the regulatory concerns of states had always existed and became a model for investment. The vigour of neo-liberalism was also spent.

Changes were taking place in the global picture on investments. The developed states themselves became targets of investment arbitration and quickly backtracked from the inflexible propositions they had helped to create. They argued for the need to preserve regulatory space in cases like *Methanex* and *S. D. Myers*. Neo-liberal tenets on which the system of inflexible norms had been formulated were shown not to be the panacea that it was touted to be. In the field of human rights litigation, particularly the cases under the Alien Tort Claims Act, the misdeeds of foreign investors were continually revealed so that it was difficult to justify another branch of the law clinging on to a system of inflexible protection of investment on the basis of the justification that foreign investments are uniformly beneficial. Besides, the persistence of NGOs highlighting human rights, labour and environmental standards made it difficult to maintain a system devoted to absolute protection of foreign investment. Thus, for example, environmental groups had consistently argued against investment protection being extended to multinational corporations which were seen in certain circumstances as massive polluters disregarding environmental concerns in search of profits. Likewise, there were labour rights and human rights concerns which did not sit easily with the conferment of absolute protection. The successive economic crises in Asia and Latin America raised concerns about the impediments investment treaties placed in controlling the economy during such crises. The arbitral awards resulting from the Argentine crisis display insensitivity to the law and, possibly, an erroneous application of the law that favoured foreign investment to the detriment of a state undergoing a crisis.[6] The long line of cases provides demonstration of the manner in which a system that cannot be controlled exercises such a hold on a state that is seeking to emerge from an economic and political crisis. The response of the states to these events was either to state new defences relating to these concerns or to refine the existing statements of the defences in light of experience.[7] Outright withdrawal from the system may be an extreme response. Some states withdrew from the system of investment arbitration and were prepared to terminate investment treaties.[8] Others withdrew specific sectors from arbitration. Modern investment treaties

---

[6] At least if the annulment committee in *CMS* is to be believed, then there was a gross misapplication of the law followed by other tribunals. The internal inconsistencies in the various awards and their divergence from each other did not help. For an analysis, see W. W. Burke-White and A. von Staden, 'Investment Protection in Extraordinary Times: The Interpretation and Application of Non-Precluded Measures Provisions in Bilateral Investment Treaties' (2008) 48 *Virginia JIL* 307.

[7] The 2004 model treaty of the United States itself signifies the change. Vandevelde explained that an objective of the model treaty was 'to preserve greater regulatory discretion for the BIT parties. This was to be achieved by increasing the number of general exceptions to BIT obligations, by allowing the parties greater latitude to maintain or adopt measures that do not conform to certain BIT obligations; and by limiting the remedies that investor-state tribunals may impose for a breach of a BIT obligation.' K. Vandevelde, 'A Comparison of the 2004 and 1994 US Model BITs: Rebalancing Investor and Host Country Interests' (2008) 1 *Yearbook of Investment Law* 257 at 283.

[8] Ecuador being an example.

also provide separate methods of dealing with issues of taxation and other areas, thereby restricting the scope of investment arbitration.[9] Continuance within the system would require statements of defences that exclude liability in circumstances where there is an overwhelming public interest that needs protection. But, the danger of this course is that the original purpose of investment protection could be severely undermined as a result. One negative feature of the developments is that the arbitrators who have consistently expanded the provisions of the treaty in favour of the foreign investor have also striven to constrict the scope of the possible defences to responsibility.[10] The fact that the two groups of arbitrators with these different visions can be identified does not bode well for the system. The treaty-based defences can be considered in turn.

1.1 National security

National security has been a concern largely of developed states, and found early expression in treaties. The FCN treaties of the United States contained statements of the exception, and the investment treaties continued the practice.[11] National security concerns will increase with the current global economic crisis and the penetration of the American and European markets by sovereign wealth funds from hitherto developing states, principally China.[12] Resentment felt on nationalistic terms may be articulated in the form of national security concerns. There could also be legitimate grounds for the belief that penetration of the economy by potentially hostile states would undermine security. Existing or new domestic laws already control the entry of such investments.[13] But, these laws deal largely with the inflows of new direct investments. Since the entry of sovereign wealth funds is made through the acquisition of shares, the foreign investment laws will usually not deal with such means of entry. But, existing laws, such as those on mergers or antitrust, could be manipulated to ensure that no entry is made by hostile states, though these laws have not been made in contemplation of the precise situation. More direct legislation may be needed to deal with the situation. The issue is whether such legislation and the exercise of powers under it may violate treaty provisions. Clearly, if there are provisions on pre-entry national treatment, this standard would be violated if a foreign sovereign wealth fund is not permitted entry through acquisition or merger.[14] The means of justifying refusal of entry is through an argument based on national security.

---

[9] Taxation is dealt with through consultation mechanisms. There is greater use of the local remedies rule.

[10] This is most evident in the manner in which the defence of necessity was disposed of in *CMS*, *Enron* and *Sempra*. The tribunals, which had the same president, read the defence of necessity very narrowly.

[11] FCN treaties were involved in the *Nicaragua Case* [1986] *ICJ Reports* 14 and the *Oil Platforms Case* [2003] *ICJ Reports* 161.

[12] Canada has enacted new amendments to the Investment Canada Act in 2009, increasing its screening powers on the basis of national security. See S. Bhattacharjee, 'National Security with a Canadian Twist: The Investment Canada Act and the New National Security Review Test' (Columbia Vale Centre on International Investment, No. 10, 30 July 2009).

[13] In the United States, the Exon–Florio Amendment to the Omnibus Trade and Competitiveness Act of 1988 gave the President the power to exclude foreign investments subjectively deemed to be threats to national security. An attempt by the Chinese National Oil Company (CNOC) to buy shares in Unocal was opposed. So, too, was the attempt of the Gulf states' investment arms to buy shares in companies running American ports. The purchase of shares by a Chinese state oil company in the Australian company, Rio Tinto, was similarly opposed.

[14] Negotiations between the United States and China towards an investment treaty have not made much progress, but it will be interesting to see whether pre-entry rights are permitted in the treaty. Whether indirect entry could be made by these funds by incorporating in a state with which the United States has an investment treaty remains unexamined.

Investment treaties provide for national security exceptions. These have significance particularly in those treaties which provide pre-entry national treatment,[15] as refusal to permit entry could be justified on national security grounds. After entry, an investment that becomes a threat to national security could be denied the protection of the treaty. The United States has maintained a statement based on the subjective appreciation of national security consistent with its internal legislation, the Exon–Florio Amendment, which enables the President to keep out foreign investment seen as a threat to national security through a subjective determination of such a threat posed by the entry of foreign investment. With the possibility of foreign sovereign wealth funds entering sensitive sectors of investment in the United States, the maintenance of such a reservation will be seen to be desirable. The national security exception would justify the exclusion of the foreign investment if it is argued that the treaty provision is violated.

National security has hitherto been looked at from the point of view of threats to the developed state. The obvious concern addressed is the prevention of foreign investment in sensitive sectors such as the armaments industries or technology-based industries which have technology that could be put to military use. The investment treaty between the United States and the former Soviet Union was an early treaty using the subjective appreciation of national security for these obvious reasons. Since that treaty, US treaties have uniformly contained national security provisions which use subjective appreciation of the threat.

The concern will continue with the larger industrialising states like China, Russia, Brazil and India which are rapidly becoming exporters of foreign investment into developed states. The smaller developing countries, like Singapore or Dubai, do not pose security threats, but their investments in certain sectors may raise nationalistic opposition.[16] In the case of developing countries, the concerns with the possible defence of national security are different. The defence is relevant to measures which are taken during times of economic and political crises. They would regard an economic crisis as being as severe as a military threat because of the fact that it affects the living conditions of its people. The tribunal in *LG&E*[17] conceded this by observing that, when economic foundations are 'under siege, the severity of the problem can equal that of any military invasion'.[18]

1.2 Economic crises and national security

Developed states are concerned with strategic security considerations. One would think that the presence of the national security defence in the investment treaty was to address such concerns in the developed country partner rather than to address the concerns of the developing state partner. But, the potential for use of the defence by developing countries has been shown in the Argentine cases. Some investment treaties tie public emergencies

---

[15] Pre-entry national treatment provides a foreign investor with a right of entry and establishment, treating such an investor as a national prior to his entry and giving him the same right of establishment as the national.
[16] In the past, Japanese activity in the United States raised such concerns.
[17] *LG&E Energy Corporation* v. *Argentina* (2007) 46 *ILM* 36.   [18] *Ibid.*, para. 238.

with national security. Economic crises do create public emergencies, in that the conditions of poverty and hunger that they bring about are bound to result in violent disturbances. They raise the possibility of equating economic crisis with military threats.

The Asian economic crisis raised such concerns.[19] Malaysia dealt with the crisis otherwise than in accordance with IMF prescriptions. Rather than get injections of capital through IMF loans with conditions relating to fiscal prudence and liberalisation of the economy,[20] Malaysia instituted currency controls and closed its economy. The measures affected foreign investment, but foreign investors were unable to invoke the protection of investment treaties as their investments had not been approved. The Malaysian treaties protect only 'approved' investments.[21]

The Argentine economic crisis raised such concerns afresh. The economic crisis sparked off rioting and political instability caused by rapid changes of government. A spate of arbitrations was brought against Argentina alleging that the measures it had taken to deal with the crisis were in violation of the investment treaties it had made. Argentina, the home of the Calvo doctrine, had given the doctrine up and taken to neo-liberalism in the 1990s, along with many other Latin American states.[22] It had made several investment treaties. The arbitrations were brought on the basis of these investment treaties. The issue was whether the provision on national security in the treaties, particularly the treaty with the United States, could be used in defence of the measures. The reasoning was that the violence on the streets and the frequency of changes of government within a short time amounted to a situation of urgency that required the measures. Argentina argued that the situation was a threat to national security and the measures taken were in response to the threat.

One issue was whether national security was a matter for subjective determination. The United States–Argentina treaty did not contain express words to indicate that a subjective determination was conclusive.[23] In that context, the position has been taken that, in the absence of express words necessary to make the subjective determination of the existence of national security conclusive, the tribunal should hold that there must be objective factors justifying the invocation of the national security defence. If there are such express words, then, clearly, the subjective determination by the state would suffice. But, the United States–Argentina treaty was held by the tribunals not to contain the necessary formula regarding subjective determination of national security. The new model treaty of the United States contains express words spelling out that a subjective determination of national security is conclusive. It states that 'nothing in the treaty shall be construed to preclude a party from applying measures *that it considers necessary* for the fulfillment of its obligations with

---

[19] It resulted in the overthrow of the Suharto regime, followed by intense political activity on the streets.

[20] Indonesia had recourse to IMF loans with conditions attached. Later, the IMF conceded that the Malaysian measures were as successful as the prescriptions it had imposed on Malaysia in dealing with the crisis.

[21] *Grueslin* v. *Malaysia* (2000) 5 *ICSID Reports* 483.

[22] Brazil did not make these treaties, and industrialised successfully without them. Constitutional problems deterred Colombia from making the treaties.

[23] The argument made was that the power to self-judge national security should be implied. There was discussion as to whether the United States had always understood national security issues as involving subjective determination. But, there was no clear evidence of this.

respect to the maintenance or restoration of international peace or security or the protection of its own essential security interests'.[24] Modern treaties increasingly contain the subjective formulation but many of them confine national security to situations of military threats, and spell out the circumstances for its invocation.

The India–Singapore Comprehensive Economic Cooperation Agreement (2005), though containing a subjective determination formula, spells out the instances of national security that are relevant, but does not include circumstances brought about by economic crisis. This type of treaty confines national security to military threats.[25] These circumstances include protection of fissionable materials, actions in times of war or emergency in international relations, action relating to the production of arms, and action in protection of essential infrastructure. The treaty provides that an understanding of the security exceptions is to be spelt out in an exchange of letters. The exchange of letters provides that the determination by a party is 'non-justiciable' and 'it shall not be open to any arbitral tribunal to review the merits of any such decision'. This is absolute, but confines the national security exception to limited circumstances which involve a military threat or activity involving violence against the state.[26] Clearly, there is no basis in the treaties which identifies the circumstances in which the national security exception can be invoked to extend the exception to economic crises unless the crisis sparks off threats to infrastructure or interferes with armaments manufacture or affects any of the activities mentioned in the provision.

The awards in *CMS*,[27] *Enron*[28] and *Sempra*[29] did not accept that the circumstances of national security were self-judging. They affirmed their competence to judge whether the situation justified the invocation of the national security exception. They held that the measures taken were not justified. It was evident that the awards were greatly influenced by the tying of the customary law on necessity with the statement of the justification contained in the treaty.[30] The annulment committee in *CMS* pointed out that this was an error. The treaty provision had to be considered as it stood. There was no need for its interpretation in light of the customary standard on necessity.

Where there is a provision containing an express subjective determination, there is a suggestion that the determination has to be made in good faith.[31] The good faith limitation may indicate that there must be objective circumstances which justify the subjective determination. Such a requirement may defeat the intention of the parties in including an express provision that a subjective determination of national security should be conclusive.

---

[24] The 1992 US model treaty did not contain the words in italics indicating subjective determination.
[25] See Article 10 of the Canadian model treaty of 2004, which also spells out the threats justifying the use of the exception.
[26] The formulation is derived from Article XXI of GATT, which refers to security in nuclear fission, armaments, etc., and contains a subjective determination formula.
[27] *CMS Gas Transmission Co* v. *Argentina* (2003) 30 *ILM* 788; (2005) 44 *ILM* 1205.
[28] *Enron Corporation* v. *Argentina*, ICSID Case No. ARB/01/03 (Award, 22 May 2007).
[29] *Sempra Energy International* v. *Argentina*, ICSID Case No. ARB/02/16 (Award, 28 September 2007). All three awards had the same presiding arbitrator. One arbitrator sat in both *CMS* and *Sempra*.
[30] In *Enron*, the tribunal specifically held that the treaty provisions on security are 'inseparable from the customary law standard'. *Enron Corporation* v. *Argentina*, ICSID Case No. ARB/01/03 (Award, 22 May 2007), para. 333.
[31] *LG&E Energy Corporation* v. *Argentina* (2007) 46 *ILM* 36. But, the tribunal found that a situation of necessity existed.

1.3 Necessity

The early Argentine awards analysed the national security exception contained in the United States–Argentina treaty in terms of the customary law principles on necessity. This, as the annulment committee in *CMS* pointed out, was improper. Yet, the error would mean that the two ideas of national security or public emergency and the customary law of necessity will be considered together, so that the views of the three awards in the Argentina situation may be elucidated.

The experience in the making of this plea largely focuses on the United States–Argentina investment treaty which does not contain a subjective formulation. Its provision refers to both public emergencies and national security situations. The relevant provision reads:

> This Treaty shall not preclude the application by either Party of measures necessary for the main-tenance of public order, the fulfillment of its obligations with respect to the maintenance or restoration of international peace or security, or the protection of its own national security interests.

There is no express reference to the defence of necessity in terms of customary international law in the provision. The tribunals took it upon themselves to analyse the exception in terms of the customary law on necessity.[32] Hence, when it is pleaded, the respondent would normally explore whether the treaty formulation is narrower than the customary law and argue as well for the consideration of the position in customary law on the basis that the treaty provision must be interpreted in the context of the customary law if there was room for the view that the treaty formulation was narrower than customary law.

The Argentine cases, as stated, arose from the economic crisis in 2001.[33] The crisis caused the fall of seven governments, widespread rioting on the streets and general turmoil. There was a situation of public emergency even if there was no threat to national security. The Argentine government then took some economic measures that impacted adversely on existing foreign investment. This included the removal of the peg between the Argentine peso and the US dollar. Foreign investors had been led to believe that the peg would not be removed, and a promise to that effect was written into many of the investment contracts. There was also a significant devaluation of the peso. The US investors argued that these measures violated the provisions of the United States–Argentina investment treaty. Argentina argued the exception provided for in Article XI of the treaty, and also argued the customary international law defence of necessity on the ground that the treaty had to be read in light of customary law principles.

Some time after the United States–Argentina treaty was signed, the United States declared that it would read the provision subjectively, so that measures it thought necessary would be exempted from liability under the provision. There is debate as to whether there was a

---

[32] *Enron Corporation* v. *Argentina*, ICSID Case No. ARB/01/03 (Award, 22 May 2007), para. 339; *CMS Gas Transmission Co* v. *Argentina* (2003) 30 *ILM* 788; (2005) 44 *ILM* 1205, para. 373.

[33] For a survey of the cases from the point of view of the necessity plea, see W. W. Burke-White and A. von Staden, 'Investment Protection in Extraordinary Times: The Interpretation and Application of Non-Precluded Measures Provisions in Bilateral Investment Treaties' (2008) 48 *Virginia JIL* 307; S. W. Schill, 'International Investment Law and the Host State's Power to Handle Economic Crises' (2007) 24 *JIA* 265; A. Bjorklund, 'Emergency Exceptions: State of Necessity and Force Majeure', in P. Muchlinski, F. Fortino and C. Schreuer, *Handbook of International Investment Law* (2008), p. 459.

consistent practice of the United States to read the circumstances constituting necessity to be a matter for self-judgment.

The ICSID awards have not been uniform in their approach to the necessity plea taken by Argentina. Except in the two awards which shared personnel, there was considerable disagreement on many points. The early awards refused both the defence under Article XI and the defence of necessity. *LG&E* however, allowed necessity. The awards constitute yet another instance of glaring disagreement between awards, which calls into question the legitimacy of the ICSID system. In *CMS*, *Enron* and *Sempra*, the necessity was not allowed.[34] The annulment committee in *CMS* subjected the award on the point of necessity to severe criticism, despite not annulling the award. The tribunal in *LG&E* upheld the plea as applying to the period of the crisis. In the first three awards, there was doubt as to whether the circumstances in Argentina in 2001 amounted to economic necessity. The *LG&E* tribunal had no such doubt, holding that Argentina was faced with an 'extremely serious threat to its existence, its political and economic survival, to the possibility of maintaining its essential services in operation, and to the preservation of its internal peace'. The factual findings are not significant in the disagreements on the legal issues.

The view taken in *CMS*, *Enron* and *Sempra* was that the tribunals had the power to review whether the methods adopted by Argentina to deal with the economic crisis were the only ones available, in which case the customary law standard would have been satisfied, or whether there were other methods, such as raising loans, which would not have resulted in the violation of the obligations under the investment treaty to foreign investors. The customary law rule that the availability of other means less onerous to a party would defeat the plea, according to the tribunals, even under the treaty formulation of the exception regarding necessity. The less onerous means that was suggested was the method of raising loans from the IMF, a solution that Malaysia rejected. In other words, what the tribunals were saying was that there was no way that a state could choose the solution it preferred. This view has been subjected to severe criticism. It is a view that advocates a neo-liberal solution to an economic crisis. It mandates the bitter pill administered by the IMF containing conditionalities to be swallowed.

In the three early awards, the tribunals claimed the power to review whether the method adopted by the state was the appropriate one under the circumstances. The reasoning was that the national security exception was self-judging and that the customary rules on necessity excluded necessity if there were less onerous ways of dealing with the situation. The three tribunals were inclined to the view that Argentina had contributed to the crisis and that this also meant that necessity could not be successfully pleaded.[35] Under the circumstances, there was little possibility of necessity being upheld by the three tribunals. The plea

---

[34] The constitution of the personnel of the tribunals was also unfortunate. The three awards had the same president. *Sempra* consisted of two arbitrators who sat on *CMS*. The awards contain variations. One arbitrator, rather inconsistently, sat on both *Enron* and *LG&E* and agreed with both awards. Despite this, there was no reference to *LG&E* in *Enron*, which was decided later. Such are the vagaries of investment arbitration that the legitimacy of the system came to be shaken by the awards.

[35] The rules on necessity were derived from the Draft Articles on State Responsibility. The manner of the statement of the rules on necessity in the Draft Articles has been queried. There was reference to the judgment of the International Court of Justice in the *Gabcikovo–Nagymaros Project Case* [1997] *ICJ Reports* 7.

was defined by the tribunals so restrictively that it would have been impossible to evoke the plea of necessity. In instances of economic crisis, there would always be alternative methods of approach. Economists debate the most appropriate method. The state which faces a crisis has to decide on the method for itself. It cannot afford detached reflection at the point of an uplifted knife,[36] while chaos reigns in the country. It would be invidious if a subsequent tribunal were to sit in judgment and take decisions removed from the pressure of the situation that confronted the state. It has been argued that a state should have a margin of appreciation in such circumstances and that, if there is to be a second-guessing of the state's decision by a tribunal that is distant from the circumstances both in place and in time, then some leeway should be given to the state. Criticisms of the awards doubt the legitimacy of a tribunal consisting of an appointee of the foreign investor and two other individuals deciding an issue that was of vital importance to the state.[37] Also, the rule that a state should not have contributed to the situation of necessity is difficult to apply in the situation of an economic crisis. No state deliberately adopts policies with the intention of bringing about an economic crisis. It may be the case that the choices made by the state would have contributed to the economic crisis. In the case of Argentina, it was the adoption of the much lauded neo-liberal policies – which arbitral tribunals have consistently lauded – which brought about the crisis. Holding that Argentina or any state under the circumstances contributed to the economic crisis would be difficult when it had carefully followed neo-liberal prescriptions advocated by the World Bank and the IMF. The threshold stated for the successful invocation of the pleas was so high that it could not have been satisfied in any economic crisis situation.

The report of the annulment committee in *CMS* criticised the manner in which the *CMS* tribunal had dealt with necessity. It found that the method employed by the *CMS* tribunal – of collapsing the treaty formulation on necessity and the customary international law on necessity into the same test for necessity – was erroneous. It felt that the two were distinct and should have been dealt with as separate issues. The annulment committee held that the tribunal had not even bothered to determine whether the basic criteria of the defence provided in the treaty formulation was, *prima facie*, satisfied. It explained that, if a situation of national security existed, no liability could arise. Necessity, on the other hand, did not preclude liability, but provided an excuse. The two were distinct propositions and had to be considered separately, and not conflated as the tribunal had done. The committee could not interfere with the award, as they had no power to do so. But, the annulment committee's ruling leaves the approach in the three awards, two of them presided over by the same arbitrator and adopting similar reasoning, subject to serious doubt.

The tribunal in *LG&E*, on the other hand, accepted that it was not equipped to decide whether the policy adopted was appropriate under the circumstances. It gave greater weight

---

[36] Adapting a sentence in a case involving self-defence that 'detached reflection cannot be had at the point of an uplifted knife', Justice Holmes suggested that a later court should not judge the situation too finely. Self-defence is a situation of necessity having similar rules as necessity such as the need for an absence of an alternative means of escape from the attacker, the use of appropriate force and not using a self-created situation.

[37] G. van Harten, *Investment Treaty Arbitration and Public Law* (2007); W. W. Burke-White and A. von Staden, 'Investment Protection in Extraordinary Times: The Interpretation and Application of Non-Precluded Measures Provisions in Bilateral Investment Treaties' (2008) 48 *Virginia JIL* 307.

to the treaty formulation which it found had lower criteria to satisfy than the customary principles on necessity. The *LG&E* tribunal upheld the plea of necessity under the treaty, and found support for the conclusion in customary law. It found that the plea excused Argentina from responsibility during the pendency of the economic crisis, thus confining the exception to the precise period in which the circumstances of necessity existed.

The customary law on necessity is unclear. The International Law Commission's Draft Articles on State Responsibility states an idiosyncratic view.[38] It does not accord with the statements in the earlier drafts made by the ILC. The Draft Articles place too much emphasis on the requirement that the measure taken by the state pleading necessity does not seriously impair an essential interest of the state towards which an obligation exists. The manner of its statement considerably circumscribes the defence of necessity. What should initially matter is how the defence is stated in the investment treaty, which is *lex specialis* and states the defence in the context of the obligation owed to the foreign investor rather than to his home state. The context in which the situation arises contrasts the public interest of the state and its people against the interest of the individual foreign investor who had taken the risk of the investment and of subsequent adverse changes. In that context, the application of a rule of preclusion in the investment treaty must be applied taking account of the fact that the initial decision has to be made by the state in the context of an ongoing situation.

The *LG&E* tribunal was correct in finding, first, whether the respondent state was entitled to the plea under the treaty, and then confirming its finding by looking at customary law to buttress its conclusion. In a later award, *Continental Casualty Company* v. *Argentina*,[39] the tribunal made a survey of the national security plea and necessity and upheld Argentina's defences to liability. The tribunal in *Continental Casualty* ruled that the national security preclusion extended to economic crises, and gave the state considerable leeway as to the timing as well as the measures that should be taken. It thus accepted the notion of a margin of appreciation which human rights courts had used in determining measures that a state could take in cases of terrorism.[40] The later award in *National Grid* v. *Argentina* acknowledged the possibility of necessity providing a defence, but found the circumstances did not require the application of the defence. It is difficult to reconcile these awards. The course of these arbitrations indicates that the unrestrained neo-liberalism that failed to accommodate the interests of the state by interpreting the law to favour foreign investment protection was not tenable. As criticisms mounted, there was a response, and an effort was made by the later tribunals to accommodate the defence in the context of the situation that faced Argentina. The law may be unclear, but it is evident that there are ideological predispositions towards outcomes that have been reached by differently constituted arbitral tribunals.

Whether the plea of necessity in customary international law must be applied without modification to the foreign investor must be queried. It is a plea designed in the context of inter-state liability, not in the context of an individual or a corporation operating within a

---

[38] Article 25 of the ILC Draft Articles on State Responsibility. The successive drafts by the different rapporteurs placed the emphasis on the requirements in different proportions.

[39] ICSID Case No. ARB/03/9.

[40] Again, creating a conflict of opinions, as *Siemens* v. *Argentina* ICSID Case No. ARB/02/8 had rejected the doctrine.

state. In the latter case, the issue arises as to why the foreign investor should not suffer the circumstances of the necessity in the same way as the citizens of the state. The risk in the situation was voluntarily assumed by the foreign investor. Necessity in customary international law was designed to apply to an entirely different situation of an obligation directly owed to another sovereign state.

The episode relating to the Argentine crisis has resulted in the exposure of several defects in investment arbitration. The selection of arbitrators presents a problem, as it is clear that arbitrators have ideological predispositions towards particular solutions. It does seem that some arbitrators do not take kindly to the existence of preclusionary rules, and take strict positions on them. Though there are efforts made to deny arbitral bias towards particular solutions, it is inevitable that, after the Argentine cases, a strong belief of there being such a bias will remain. The conflation of national security exceptions stated in the treaty with the defence of necessity was an error which persisted in affecting the validity of the three early awards. Though annulment is not possible, the possibility of enforcement of the awards in light of what the annulment committee in *CMS* stated becomes remote. The idea that only sovereign immunity stands in the way of enforcement has to be rethought when the legal reasoning in the award has been so powerfully challenged. The existence of defences to liability both under treaty and under customary international law opens a Pandora's Box. The effects of it will be felt as more cases are decided.

1.4 Force majeure

The situation of *force majeure* is distinct from necessity, in that, in the case of necessity, a state is said deliberately to take measures to deal with a situation. In the case of *force majeure*, a state is faced with circumstances where it has no alternative but to take a course of action to avert harm to itself. *Force majeure*, however, is used in civilian legal systems to avoid responsibility for breaches of contracts, and hence would be regarded as appropriate in the investment situation. One could argue that, if the circumstances were such that *force majeure* avoided contractual obligations, it may be argued that the same circumstances must permit the avoidance of responsibility under the investment treaty as well. But, given that a distinction is made between treaty claims and contract claims, it must be shown that the circumstances affected liability under the treaty as well.[41]

Force majeure has been pleaded in many foreign investment disputes. They arise from contractual disputes. The most recent were the series of awards resulting from the Indonesian economic and political crisis that followed the overthrow of the Suharto regime in Indonesia in 1998. The Indonesian government, on the advice of the IMF, suspended several project contracts it had made with foreign investors. Disputes resulted.[42] Indonesia

---

[41] In *SGS* v. *Philippines*, ICSID Case No. ARB/02/6 (Award, 29 January 2004), the tribunal suggested that an investment tribunal may have jurisdiction even if the claimant failed under a contract claim due to reasons such as *force majeure*.

[42] *Himpurna* v. *Indonesia* (2000) 25 *YCA* 13; and *Karaha Bodas Co.* v. *Perusahaan Pertambangan Minyak Dan Gas Bumi Negara*, 465 F Supp 2d 283 (SDNY, 2006). The third case, *Phaiton Energy* v. *Pertamina*, was settled before award. There are references to *force majeure* in the dissenting award in *AAPL* v. *Sri Lanka* (1992) 17 *YCA* 106; (1991) 30 *ILM* 577 and in *RSM Production Corporation* v. *Grenada*, ICSID Case No. ARB/05/14 (Award, 13 March 2009).

pleaded *force majeure*. But, the plea was rejected. In *Karaha Bodas*,[43] it was rejected on the ground that there was a clause in the contract anticipating such events and the requirement that the risk be carried by the state. In *Himpurna*,[44] it was rejected on the ground that the essential factors for the defence under the Indonesian civil code were not satisfied. Both awards accept that the plea existed in domestic law, as it indeed does in most continental systems, the Indonesian code being based on the old Dutch Civil Code.[45] It credibly forms a general principle.[46]

If there had been *force majeure* circumstances rescinding the contract, it would be difficult to think of measures taken in view of those circumstances as not affecting liability under the investment treaty. The only issue would be that there should have been no discrimination in the measures that were taken. As only large projects are affected by these measures, it is unlikely that the measures would affect nationals, but the discrimination between nationals and foreign investors in such a situation would be based on rational circumstances. There are no 'like' circumstances to support discrimination.

The general rules of *force majeure* have been worked out in arbitral awards. The events that constitute *force majeure* should not be foreseeable, and should not have been engineered by the state party. For *force majeure* to be pleaded by a state entity, the state entity must be independent of the state. The relevance of *force majeure* to treaty-based arbitration seems remote.[47]

2. Violation of the fair and equitable standard by the foreign investor

The trend in investment arbitration is to emphasise liability on the fair and equitable standard. This results from the fact that expropriation has become difficult to establish where there is no direct taking of property. Besides, the uncertain scope of regulatory expropriation makes it difficult for expropriation to be the peg for liability. The international minimum standard is too reified. As a result, there has been a shift towards the fair and equitable standard. There has been an effort to build rules into the fair and equitable standards. To a large extent, this standard has been fleshed out as a result of arbitral awards introducing into the standard ideas regarding transparency and violation of legitimate expectations. As these expansionary trends take place, arguments are made which reverse these trends. One of the main arguments is that, if fairness and equity are to be the standards on which blame is to be attached, then the tribunal finding a violation of the standard must also assess liability having regard to the conduct of the foreign investor and any causes that contributed to the action of the state.[48] Equity is a double-edged sword, and, in ascribing

---

[43] *Karaha Bodas Co.* v. *Perusahaan Pertambangan Minyak Dan Gas Bumi Negara*, 465 F Supp 2d 283 (SDNY, 2006).
[44] *Himpurna* v. *Indonesia* (2000) 25 *YCA* 13.   [45] That Code is in turn based on the French Civil Code.
[46] Though, in common law systems, some may argue that the doctrine of frustration is stricter.
[47] In *AAPL* v. *Sri Lanka* (1992) 17 *YCA* 106; (1991) 30 *ILM* 577, the dissent referred to the situation of the civil war as constituting *force majeure*.
[48] The pioneering statement in this field is P. Muchlinski, 'Caveat Investor? The Relevance of the Conduct of the Investor under the Fair and Equitable Treatment Standard' (2006) 55 *ICLQ* 527. The view that fairness has to be considered in light of the conduct of the foreign investor was accepted in *Biwater Gauff* v. *Tanzania*, ICSID Case No. ARB/05/22 (Award, 24 July 2008).

blame on the basis of equity, it is necessary to look into whether the claimant also was at fault and whether the respondent's conduct was a reaction to that fault. In this sense, a defence is created in respect of a standard that is becoming increasingly important as the basis of liability in modern investment arbitration.

The question has also been raised as to the extent of the margin of appreciation that is to be given to the decision that a state makes in the context of a situation. It is an idea borrowed from human rights law, where the European cases, dealing with the treatment of terrorists by states, has referred to a 'margin of appreciation' to be given to the state in the assessment of the propriety of the measures the state wishes to take to combat terrorism. In investment law, it has been discussed in the context of expropriation, necessity and the fair and equitable standard. There is an increasing acceptance that the examination of the measures taken by the state should not be assessed too finely.[49] Yet, these are at this stage genuflections in the direction of some consciousness that the rule that is applied is weighted against the exercise of regulatory powers by the state.

Adventurism in building up the fair and equitable standard through arbitral awards will be brought to a halt by the states themselves, for the newer treaties either dispense with the standard or tie it to the customary international minimum standard of treatment. Yet, there are treaties which still state the fair and equitable standard as a free-standing notion enabling it to be regarded as an autonomous concept. It is where the standard is treated as autonomous that there is scope for defences to emerge. These defences are considerably bolstered by the development of notions of corporate responsibility in international law and the emergence of rules, particularly in the human rights and environmental areas, which prescribe the manner in which a multinational corporation should conduct its affairs within a host state. Some of the notions of corporate responsibility, particularly with respect to taxation, human rights, the environment and labour, have found their way into modern investment treaties, but, even in the absence of their statement, their general recognition in terms of international law requires them to be balanced against claims of the investor as to violations of the fair and equitable standards. The acceptability of the prior conduct of the multinational corporation thus becomes relevant to any assessment of the fairness involved in the reaction of the state to such conduct.

Besides corporate responsibility, there is also the fact that the objectives of the foreign investment received into the state had been articulated by the state in its foreign investment laws. These objectives of economic development also constitute the reasons why developing states make investment treaties. The preamble to the typical investment treaty sets out economic development as the objective of the treaty. Fairness demands that the foreign investor abide by not only the objectives of the laws of the state but also the objectives of the treaty under which he claims relief. Hence, the violation of the objective of economic development would be a context for the assessment of the fairness standard which has to be weighed against the alleged violation of the fair and equitable standard.

---

[49] In *Goetz* v. *Burundi* (1999) 15 *ICSID Rev* 457; (2001) 26 *YCA* 24, the tribunal stated that 'it is not for this tribunal to substitute its own judgment for the discretionary analysis' of the state (as cited in C. Duggan, D. Wallace, N. Rubins and B. Sabahi, *Investor–State Arbitration* (2008), p. 448).

Developments in the two ideas of corporate responsibility and economic development are reflected in international law. Corporate responsibility has been developed through many international instruments. These have been surveyed in an earlier chapter. The underlying objectives of economic development in the foreign investment laws of the developing countries were also indicated in an earlier chapter. The growth of an international law on development which impacts on investment transactions is also relevant. The exercise of looking at fairness cannot be a one-sided exercise as has hitherto been the case in the awards of arbitral tribunals. The neo-liberal exercise in the creation of rules of protection on foreign investment on the basis of the fair and equitable standard cannot be continued meaningfully unless it is balanced against other considerations which have entered the field.

As much as there are expansive notions of the fair and equitable standard in some awards, there are also awards which require that fairness be assessed in the context of the whole dispute and its antecedent circumstances. *Genin* v. *Estonia*[50] signals a more balanced approach to fairness. It concerned revocation of a banking licence. The tribunal took into consideration that the regulation took place in a nascent economy unused to these controls in a vital sector. The tribunal stated:[51]

The Tribunal considers it imperative to recall the particular context in which the dispute arose, namely, that of a renascent independent state.

Genin illustrates that, as much as some tribunals are adventurist, others are more cautious and would look at the issues regarding fairness in the context of the situation in which they arose. It is interesting to note that the *Genin* tribunal considered subjective bad faith as a requirement for the finding of the violation of the standard, a criterion difficult to find in the present case. *Olguin* v. *Paraguay* contained views that the regulatory system should not be blamed for the failure of an investor to secure profits. *Generation Ukraine* v. *Ukraine* has *dicta* to the like effect. The tribunal there suggested that the vicissitudes of the host state economy were relevant in determining the investor's legitimate expectations. The fair and equitable standard should not be the basis on which rules favourable to the foreign investor can be made and his expectations protected without looking at competing factors of relevance to the state and its economy at the time of the regulation. *Thunderbird* v. *Mexico*[52] strikes a position that requires a return to orthodoxy by asserting the old *Neer* standard that requires substantial denial of justice. In that case decided after the NAFTA interpretative statement, the NAFTA tribunal said:

Notwithstanding the evolution of customary law since decisions such as *Neer Claim* in 1926, the threshold for finding a violation of the minimum standard of treatment still remains high, as illustrated by recent international jurisprudence. For the purposes of the present case, the Tribunal views acts that would give rise to a breach of the minimum standard of treatment prescribed by the NAFTA and customary international law as those that, weighed against the given factual context, amount to a gross denial of justice or manifest arbitrariness falling below acceptable international standards.

---

[50] (2002) 17 *ICSID Rev* 395.   [51] Para. 31.
[52] *International Thunderbird Gaming Corporation* v. *Mexico*, UNCITRAL (NAFTA) Arbitration Proceedings (Award, 26 January 2006).

These awards clearly illustrate the possibility of defences emerging to the claim of violation of the fair and equitable standard in that the context may be used to justify the course of action that was taken by the state.

Academic writings also reflect this position. Muchlinski stated this position in a recent article.[53] Commenting on *CMS* v. *Argentina*, Muchlinski pointed out:

The crisis had in itself a severe impact upon the claimant's business, but this aspect must to some extent be attributed to the business risk the claimant took on when investing in Argentina, this being particularly the case as it related to decrease in demand. Such effects cannot be ignored as if business had continued as usual. Otherwise both parties would not be sharing some of the costs of the crisis in a reasonable manner and the decision could eventually amount to an insurance policy against business risk, an outcome that, as the Respondent has rightly argued, would not be justified.

The reasoning is simply that there must be a consideration of the overall picture and not the effects of the measures taken by the state on the foreign investor. The approach signifies that expansionary trends also open up possibilities of new defences, as more cautious arbitrators would seek to determine liability in the context of the whole situation rather than look only at the violation of a particular standard.

3. Ius cogens, competing obligations and liability

Treaties cannot create obligations which require a party to violate an *ius cogens* obligation or to take measures which would violate such obligations. The Vienna Convention on the Law of Treaties stipulates that obligations under a treaty inconsistent with *ius cogens* standards must be regarded as invalid. This principle clearly applies to investment treaties.[54] In *Phoenix* v. *Czech Republic*,[55] an ICSID tribunal articulated the proposition that an investment transaction which involved the violation of an *ius cogens* norm such as one prohibiting genocide or racial discrimination would be void. The tribunal said that protection 'should not be granted to investments made in violation of the most fundamental rules of protection of human rights, like investments made in pursuance of torture or genocide or in support of slavery or trafficking of human organs'. The proposition is clearly sound. The issue is whether the notion of *ius cogens*, or obligations *erga omnes* to which it bears similarity, are based on closed lists. While it is certain that some rules form *ius cogens* norms, there are several candidates being considered for elevation to *ius cogens* norms. Among them are rules that have direct bearings on foreign investment, particularly in the human rights and environmental fields.

Apart from genocide and racial discrimination, candidates for elevation to the status of *ius cogens* norms include self-determination and its corollary, the permanent sovereignty over

---

[53] P. Muchlinski, 'Caveat Investor? The Relevance of the Conduct of the Investor under the Fair and Equitable Standard' (2006) 55 *ICLQ* 527.

[54] M. Sornarajah, *The Settlement of Foreign Investment Disputes* (2000), pp. 186–94; M. Hirsch, 'Conflicting Obligations in International Investment Law: Investment Tribunals' Perspective', in Y. Shany and T. Broude (eds.), *The Shifting Allocation of Authority in International Law: Considering Sovereignty, Supremacy and Subsidiarity* (2008), pp. 323–43.

[55] *Phoenix* v. *Czech Republic*, ICSID Case No. ARB/06/5 (Award, 19 April 2009), para. 78.

natural resources, the prohibition of torture and possibly the causing of such massive pollution as would affect the lives of a large number of people, their means of livelihood and their habitats. Another area would be the destruction of the rights of indigenous people. In the parallel area of litigation under the Alien Tort Claims Act, the effort to establish violation of these norms as creating tort liability has made progress. Even if they are not to be accorded the status of *ius cogens* norms, they are principles of international law and have to be taken into account when assessing liability for violation of treaty standards, as treaties can only operate in the context of international law.

In the mining sector, the conflict between the norm of permanent sovereignty over natural resources and the obligations under the investment treaty are bound to occur. The notion of permanent sovereignty has found its way into many constitutions of developing states. The conflict between the norm and the treaty obligations would have to be considered, though no doubt, unless a tribunal is willing to elevate the permanent sovereignty doctrine into an *ius cogens* norm, it would dismiss the argument.[56] Yet, the argument has to be seriously considered. It has to be more seriously considered where it involves aboriginal lands. In this case, there is added support to be had for the norm of permanent sovereignty from the law that has developed giving protection to the rights of aboriginal people over their lands.[57]

3.1 Transactions with undemocratic governments

More troublesome would be where the original transaction was made with an undemocratic government and a claim is made that the investment is protected by an investment treaty. It is claimed that a norm of democratic governance has emerged in modern international law.[58] The norm is supported by the principle of self-determination, which has credible status to being considered an *ius cogens* norm. Where a foreign investment is made with an unrepresentative government and a new, democratic government seeks to terminate it or rewrite its terms, the issue could arise as to whether the investment is protected by treaty. Rules on succession to responsibility may favour application of the treaty, but it would be in conflict with the norms relating to democratic governance.[59] The *Urenco Case*,[60] which is not a case proper and did not involve an investment treaty, provides a basis for analogy. South Africa, then continuing its mandate over Namibia, had illegally contracted for the mining of uranium. The validity of the contract was put in issue. There was no final outcome to the case, as the case was withdrawn. However, one may conclude that an investment

---

[56] In *Texaco v. Libya* (1977) 53 *ILR* 389, which was not a case involving an investment treaty, the arbitrator, Professor Dupuy regarded the permanent sovereignty doctrine as *lex ferenda*. But, in the *East Timor Case* [1995] *ICJ Reports* 139, Judge Weeramantry, in his separate opinion, regarded permanent sovereignty as a basic component of self-determination, which was an *ius cogens* principle.

[57] J. Anaya, *Indigenous People in International Law* (1996).

[58] G. Fox and B. Roth (eds.), *Democratic Governance and International Law* (2000).

[59] Such problems have arisen in the different context of bribery in Pakistan, where previous governments were treated as corrupt and their contracts invalid. The potential for its arising in Myanmar (Burma) or states with similar regimes is great. Investments in Myanmar are protected by the ASEAN Investment Treaty.

[60] The case was brought before Dutch courts to test the validity of contracts made by Dutch companies. It was withdrawn after Namibia became independent. It is described in C. Pilgrim, 'Some Legal Aspects of Trade in the Natural Resources of Namibia' (1994) 61 *BYIL* 249.

agreement made with a regime that is universally condemned cannot be binding on a legitimate government which succeeds it. The foreign investor fishes in troubled waters in concluding agreements with such states. There will be problems of the validity of the agreement in domestic law. In these circumstances, the issue of treaty protection should be decided in a manner that conforms with international objectives.

3.2 Investments in areas of secessionist claims

This issue also will cause problems in the future. Where an investment is made in an area subject to secessionist agitation, the issue would arise as to whether a foreign investment agreement made with the earlier government should be protected by the treaty. Such questions could arise in the context of southern Sudan or the oil-rich regions of Nigeria. Even if the secessionist claim is not wholly successful, a power-sharing agreement could result. The situation in Aceh in Indonesia provides an example. In these circumstances, the issue arises whether the internal shifts relating to power sharing and the resultant rearranging of any foreign investment contract are subject to investment treaty norms. The power sharing itself is supported by international norms, and it can be argued that the changes to foreign investment agreements that ensue are in conformity with international law and hence should not result in liability. Again, this is an area that will gain importance in the future.

3.3 Cultural property and foreign investment

Norms protecting cultural property could come into conflict with foreign investment principles in treaties. The *Malaysian Salvors Case* concerned cultural property, but the issue was not raised as to whether it was appropriate for a dispute involving cultural property of significance not only to the people of the respondent state but also to the region and perhaps to the entire world (as the ship salvaged was European and the porcelain recovered was Chinese), to be dealt with by an arbitral tribunal invoked by the two parties having an immediate interest in a contractual relationship. This interesting question was not raised. Issues relating to cultural significance was raised in *SPP* v. *Egypt*,[61] though not in the context of a treaty. One issue was whether a tourist complex under construction adversely affected the pyramids of Giza, a site protected by the World Heritage Convention. The issue was dismissed on the technical ground that the listing of the site was done after the contract had been made. The tribunal made a purely contractual analysis of a difficult issue. Clearly, if the excavation of the site for the building of the tourist complex would have destroyed material of archaeological significance listed under the World Heritage Convention, that would have been a matter to be taken into consideration. The possibility of a contract-based tribunal adequately considering such issues is remote.

---

[61] *SPP* v. *Egypt*, 3 *ICSID Reports* 101 at 255.

3.4 Environmental obligations

This is another issue which will gain in importance in the future. The blanket denial of its significance to investment arbitration in *Santa Elena* v. *Costa Rica* must be regarded as an outdated attitude. *Methanex* demonstrated that measures taken in order to protect against harm arising from environmental situations would be considered regulatory expropriations. Clearly, environmental degradation caused by a foreign investor would justify measures taken by the state. In terms of the treaty, the measures will not amount to compensable expropriation and will not violate standards such as the fair and equitable standard, if fairness is understood in the context of the situation. The burgeoning law on environmental standards and human rights will affect the consideration of liability under investment treaties. Though these considerations are not part of the treaties, they could be read into the treaties, as exceptions relating to health and welfare are increasingly coming to be part of the treaties. In the alternative, they constitute obligations in general international law, and investment treaties have to be read in the context of these obligations. Where a conflict between these general obligations and the investment treaty obligations arises, a tribunal will have to reconcile the conflict in an appropriate manner.

3.5 Human rights considerations

Again, the vast body of human rights principles will be a rich quarry for arguments that will come to be made in justification of state measures against foreign investors.[62] As with environmental concerns, tribunals were initially reluctant to deviate from the objective of investment protection by taking into account human rights concerns. The early awards on the Argentine economic crisis were not concerned with arguments as to the impact of the crisis on the people of Argentina, thus giving rise to the criticism that the interests of the foreign investor trumped all other considerations. Later awards do at least pay lip-service to the plight of the people consequent upon the economic crisis, though they are still inclined to favour the objective of investment protection.

Cases disclosing facts like those being litigated under the Alien Tort Claims Act have not yet come before investment tribunals. The full import of the conflict between human rights and foreign investment is yet to be explored. In a sense, the investment treaty itself protects a human right to the extent that it is concerned with the property rights of the foreign investor. But, it would appear that the standards of property protection go well beyond that which are given in the most advanced constitutional systems of the world.[63] In constitutional systems, private property rights are subject to the public interest.[64] It is this public interest that human rights law represents. When there is a clash between the rights of a foreign investor under the treaty and the human rights protected both by the constitutional system of the host state as

---

[62] L. E. Peterson, 'Selected Recent Developments in IIA Arbitration and Human Rights' (2009) *IIA Monitor*, No. 2. The issues relating to human rights and investment were discussed in Chapter 4 above.

[63] For the argument that it is above the standards of most systems, see D. Schneiderman, *Constitutionalising Economic Globalisation: Investment Rules and Democracy's Promise* (2008).

[64] T. Allen, *The Right to Property in Commonwealth Constitutions* (2000).

well as by the body of international law on human rights, a tribunal must consider the nature of the conflict and decide in an appropriate fashion. In most instance, that body of international human rights will also represent international public policy which may have over-riding effects.

4. Conclusion

The search for defences to liability will increase as claims against states increase.[65] The more the defences that are accommodated within the law, the weaker and more uncertain will be the system of investment protection. There is a search for a balanced investment treaty evident in the literature on the subject. The search is initiated not so much by the developing states but by the developed states which suddenly find themselves respondents in investment arbitration. The trend will grow as the erstwhile capital-exporting states which fashioned the law, including the standards in investment treaties, are now massive importers of capital. In fact, they are dependent on foreign investment and capital to lead them out of the global economic crisis which commenced in 2008. The law on protection will have to be rethought. Hence, the search is on for balance. The search for balance is also accentuated by the fact that the area had witnessed an ideological drive towards the establishment of norms preferred by neo-liberal models. The expansionist trends that were initiated during the period have resulted in responses that leave the law in a state of normlessness and anarchy, which is according to some the characteristic of international society.

Investment treaties were originally a response to normlessness. They were born in the context of a schism in the law brought about by contending sets of norms, those of the capital-exporting states and those of the new developing states which had articulated a set of norms in the form of a New International Economic Order. Clearly, the trend of events as shown in inconsistent awards involving the same set of facts or the interpretation of the same provision in a treaty, the withdrawal from the treaty system by some states, the increasing number of defences being created and the uncertainty that attends their scope will result in a return to normlessness, so that the law will once more reflect its true state as a continuing battle for different positions reflecting the inconsistent interests that operate in the field. Another round of consensus-seeking will, no doubt, be made, but the wisdom of the past dictates that the law will not stand for ever, whatever pundits with a certainty of the effects of globalisation may have to say. International law on foreign investment will continue to be a law that is in constant flux, reflecting the clashes of the various interests at play. The increasing presence of non-state actors having the power to act on both sides of the conflict will help to clarify the issues. The fluidity of the law, particularly international law, is a reality in its other branches. It is futile to expect that the international law on foreign investment would be different. It will remain a process to be studied in light of the rich conflicts that occur in the field.

---

[65] See, for example, the use of countermeasures as a defence in *Corn Products International* v. *Mexico*, ICSID Case No. ARB(AF)/04/1 (NAFTA) (Award, 15 January 2008).

Bibliography

Books

Ackerman, B., *Private Property and the Constitution* (1977)
Addo, M. K. (ed.), *Human Rights Standard and the Responsibility of Transnational Corporations* (1999)
Aldrich, G., *The Jurisprudence of the Iran–US Claims Tribunal* (1996)
Allen, T., *The Right to Property in Commonwealth Constitutions* (2000)
Amerasinghe, C. F., *State Responsibility for Injuries to Aliens* (1967)
   Local Remedies in International Law (1990)
   Jurisdiction of International Tribunals (2003)
   Local Remedies in International Law (2nd edn, 2004)
   Diplomatic Protection (2008)
American Law Institute, *Restatement (Third) on Foreign Relations Law of the United States* (1987)
Amin, S., *Unequal Development: An Essay on the Social Formation of Peripheral Capitalism* (1976)
   Obsolescent Capitalism: Contemporary Politics and Global Disorder (2003)
Anand, R. P., *The Afro-Asian States and International Law* (1978)
   International Law and Developing Countries (1987)
Anaya, J., *Indigenous People in International Law* (1996)
Anghie, A., *Imperialism, Sovereignty and the Making of International Law* (2005)
Arangio-Ruiz, G., *The United Nations Declaration on Friendly Relations and the System of Sources of International Law* (1979)
Arup, C., *World Trade Organization Knowledge Agreements* (2008)
Asouzu, A., *International Commercial Arbitration and African States* (2001)
Atiyah, P., *The Rise and Fall of the Freedom of Contract* (1979)
Audit, B., *Transnational Arbitration and State Contracts* (1988)
Bedjaoui, M. (ed.), *International Law: Achievements and Prospects* (1991)
Bennet, D., and K. Sharpe, *Transnational Corporations Versus the State* (1985)
Bergsten, F., *American Multinationals and American Interests* (1978)
Biersteker, T., *Multinationals, the State and the Control of the Nigerian Economy* (1987)
Birnie, P., and A. Boyle, *International Law and the Environment* (2002)
Borchard, E. M., *The Diplomatic Protection of Nationals* (1904)
   The Diplomatic Protection of Citizens Abroad (Kraus Reprint Co., New York, 1970; original edition, 1915)
Bradlow, D. D., and A. Escher (eds.), *Legal Aspects of Foreign Investment* (1999)
Brewer, T. (ed.), *Political Risks in International Business* (1985)
Brian, W. V. (ed.), *New States in International Law and Diplomacy* (1965)
Brierly, J., *Law of Nations* (5th edn, 1963)

Brower, C., *The Iran–US Claims Tribunal* (1998)

Brown-Weiss, E., *In Fairness to Future Generations* (1989)

Brownlie, I., *The System of the Law of Nations: State Responsibility* (1986)
  Principles of Public International Law (6th edn, 2003)

Bulajic, M., *Principles of International Development Law* (1992)

Calvo, C., *Le Droit International* (5th edn, 1885)

Cameron, P. D., *Property Rights and Sovereign Rights: The Case of North Sea Oil* (1983)

Cartwright, J. J., *Unequal Bargaining: A Study of Vitiating Factors in the Formation of Contract* (1991)

Castermans-Holleman, M., F. van Hoof and J. Smith (eds.), *The Role of the Nation State in the 21st Century: Essays in Honour of Peter Baehr* (1998)

Cattan, H., *The Law of Oil Concessions in the Middle East and North Africa* (1967)

Chang, Ha-Joon, *Kicking Away the Ladder: Development Strategy in Historical Perspective* (2005)
  Bad Samaritans: Rich Nations, Poor Policies and the Threat to the Developing World (2007)

Chayes, A., T. Ehrlich and A. F. Lowenfeld, *International Legal Process* (1969)

Cherian, J., *Investment Contracts and Arbitration* (1975)

Choate, P., *Agents of Influence* (1990)

Chua, A., *World on Fire: How Exporting Free Market Democracy Breeds Ethnic Hatred and Global Instability* (2003)

Clapham, A., *Human Rights Obligations of Non-State Actors* (2006)

Cohen-Jonathan, G., *La Convention Européenne de Droits de l'Homme* (1989)

Coronel, G., *The Nationalization of the Venezuelan Oil Industry* (1984)

Cover, R. M., *Justice Accused: Antislavery and the Judicial Process* (1975)

Coyle, D., *Governing the World Economy* (2000)

Craig, P., *Administrative Law* (5th edn, 2005)
  European Union Administrative Law (2006)

Crawford, J. (ed.), *The Rights of Peoples* (1988)
  (ed.), *The Rights of Peoples* (2001)
  The International Law Commission's Articles on State Responsibility (2002)

Cutler, C. (ed.), *Private Authority and International Affairs* (1999)
  Private Power and Global Authority: Transnational Global Law in the Political Economy (2003)

Daintith, T., *The Legal Character of Petroleum Licences: A Comparative Study* (1981)

Damrosch, L., and D. Scheffer (ed.), *Law and Force in the New International Order* (1991)

Davis, J., *Justice Across Borders: The Struggle for Human Rights in the US Courts* (2008)

Dawson, F. G., and I. L. Head, *International Law, National Tribunals and the Rights of Aliens* (1971)

Dawson, L. (ed.), *Whose Rights? The NAFTA Chapter 11 Debate* (2002)

Delupis, I., *Finance and Protection of Foreign Investment in Developing Countries* (1987)

Dezalay, Y., and G. Bryant, *Dealing in Virtue: International Commercial Arbitration and the Construction of a Transnational Legal Order* (1996)

Dine, J., *Companies, International Trade and Human Rights* (2005)

Dinstein, Y. (ed.), *International Law at a Time of Perplexity: Essays in Honour of Shabtai Rosenne* (1989)

Dixon, C., D. Drakakis-Smith and H. Wads (eds.), *Multinational Corporations and the Third World* (1986)

Dolzer, R., and C. Schreuer, *International Investment Law* (2008)

Dolzer, R., and M. Stevens, *Bilateral Investment Treaties* (1996)

Domke, M., *Trading with the Enemy in World War II* (1943)

Duggan, C., D. Wallace, N. Rubins and B. Sabahi, *Investor–State Arbitration* (2008)

Dunn, F. S., *The Protection of Foreign Nationals* (1932)

Eagleton, C., *The Responsibility of States in International Law* (1928)

El-Kosheri, A., *The Law Governing a New Generation of Petroleum Contracts* (1986)

Ellings, R. J. (ed.), *Private Property and National Security* (1991)

Epstein, R., *Takings: Private Property and the Power of Eminent Domain* (1985)

Evans, P., *Dependent Development: The Alliance of Multinational, State and Local Capital in Brazil* (1979)

Fatouros, A. A., *Government Guarantees to Foreign Investors* (1962)

Feller, A. H., *The Mexican Claims Commission 1923–1934* (1935)

Fitzgerald, A., *Mining Contracts* (2000)
  Australian Mining Law (2002)

Fletcher, G., *Tort Liability for Human Rights Abuses* (2008)

Flint, D., *Foreign Investment Law in Australia* (1986)

Ford, A. W., *The Anglo-Iranian Oil Dispute* (1954)

Fordham, M., *Tax Incentive for Investment and Expansion in Singapore* (1992)

Fox, G., and B. Roth (eds.), *Democratic Governance and International Law* (2000)

Fox, H. (ed.), *International Economic Law and Developing States* (1992)

Francioni, F., and T. Scovazzi (eds.), *International Responsibility for Environmental Harm* (1991)

Fredman, S. (ed.), *Discrimination and Human Rights* (2001)

Freeman, A., *The International Responsibility of States for Denial of Justice* (1938)

Friedman, S., *Expropriation in International Law* (1977)

Friedmann, W., *The Changing Structure of International Law* (1962)

Fukuyama, F., *The End of History and the Last Man* (1992)

Gaillard, E. (ed.), *Antisuit Injunctions in International Arbitration* (2005)

Galeano, E., *Open Veins of Latin America: Five Centuries of Pillage of a Continent* (originally published in Mexico in 1971)

Gallagher, K. P., and D. Chudnovsky, *Rethinking Foreign Investment for Sustainable Development: Lessons from Latin America* (2009)

Gallagher, N., and Wenhua Shan, *Chinese Investment Treaties: Policy and Practice* (2009)

Garcia-Amador, F. V., *Changing Law of International Claims* (1984)
  The Emerging International Law of Development (1990)

Garcia-Amador, F. V., L. Sohn and R. R. Baxter, *Recent Codification of the Law of State Responsibility for Injuries to Aliens* (1974)

Gilpin, R., *The Political Economy of International Relations* (1987)

Goodwin-Gill, G. S., *International Law and the Movement of Persons Between States* (1978)

Goodwin-Gill, G. S., and S. Talmon, *The Reality in International Law: Essays in Honour of Ian Brownlie* (1999)

Gordon, M. W., *The Cuban Nationalisations* (1973)

Gowlland-Debbas, V., *Multilateral Treaty Making* (2000)

Graham, E., and P. Krugman, *Foreign Direct Investment in the United States* (1991)

Gray, C., *Judicial Remedies in International Law* (1990)

Gregory, F., and B. Roth (eds.), *Democratic Governance and International Law* (2000)

Hahn, H. J., G. Kegel and K. R. Simmond (eds.), *International Law and Economic Order: Essays in Honour of F. A. Mann* (1997)

Hall, R., and T. Biersteker (eds.), *The Emergence of Private Authority in Global Governance* (2002)

Handl, G., and R. E. Lutz, *Transferring Hazardous Technologies and Substances* (1989)

Harrison, J., *Human Rights Implications of the WTO Organization* (2007)

Hart, M., *Decision at Midnight* (2001)

Heere, W. P. (ed.), *International Law and Its Sources: Liber Amicorum Maarten Bos* (1989)

Hettne, B., *Development Theory and the Three Worlds* (1988)

Himawan, C., *The Foreign Investment Process in Indonesia* (1980)

Hirschl, R., *Towards Juristocracy: The Origins and Consequences of the New Constitutionalism* (2004)

Hoekman, B., and M. Kostecki, *The Political Economy of the World Trading System* (2001)

Hossain, K., *Law and Policy in Petroleum Development* (1979)

(ed.), *Legal Aspects of the New International Economic Order* (1980)

Ijalye, D., *The Extension of Corporate Personality in International Law* (1978)

Indian Law Institute, *The Bhopal Litigation* (1989)

International Centre for the Settlement of Investment Disputes, *Investment Promotion and Protection Treaties* (1983)

International Monetary Fund, *Balance of Payments Manual* (1980)

Jackson, J. H., *Sovereignty, the WTO and the Changing Fundamentals of International Law* (2006)

Jägers, N., *Corporate Human Rights Obligations: In Search of Accountability* (2002)

Jennings, R., and A. Watts (eds.), *Oppenheim's International Law* (9th edn, 1992)

Jessup, P., *The Use of International Law* (1959)

Joseph, S., *Corporations and Transnational Human Rights Litigation* (2004)

Kay, C., *Development and Underdevelopment in Latin America* (1988)

Khan, R., *The Iran–US Claims Tribunal* (1990)

Kinley, David, *Human Rights and Corporations* (2009)

Krasner, S., *Structural Conflict: Third World Against Global Liberalism* (1985)

Kronfol, Z. A., *Protection of Foreign Investment: A Study in International Law* (1972)

Kronman, A., *The Lost Lawyer: Failing Ideals of the Legal Profession* (1993)

Kummer, K., *International Management of Hazardous Wastes: The Basel Convention and Related Legal Rules* (1995)

Kurshid, H., *Equality of Treatment and Trade Discrimination in International Law* (1968)

Kwiatkowska, B., and A. H. A. Soons (eds.), *Transboundary Movement and Disposal of Hazardous Waste in International Law* (1993)

Lang, W., H. Neuhold and K. Zemanek (eds.), *Environmental Protection and International Law* (1991)

Lauterpacht, E., *Aspects of Administration of International Justice* (1992)

Lauterpacht, H. (ed.), *Oppenheim's International Law* (8th edn, 1952)

Collected Papers (1978)

Laviec, P., *Protection et Promotion des Investissements: Etude de Droit International Economique* (1985)

Lee, L. T., *Consular Law and Practice* (1991)

Lefeber, R., *Transboundary Environmental Interference and the Origin of State Liability* (1996)

Lerner, N., *The United Nations Convention on the Elimination of All Forms of Racial Discrimination* (1980)

Lew, J. D. M., *The Applicable Law in International Commercial Arbitration* (1978)

Lillich, R. B., *International Law of State Responsibility for Injuries to Aliens* (1983)

The Human Rights of Aliens in Contemporary International Law (1984)
  (ed.), *The Valuation of Nationalized Property* (1987)
Lipson, C., *Standing Guard: Protecting Capital in the Nineteenth and Twentieth Centuries* (1985)
MacDonald, R. St J., and D. M. Johnston, *The Structure and Process of International Law* (1986)
Mann, F. A., *Further Studies in International Law* (1990)
  Legal Aspects of Money (5th edn, 1992)
Mann, H., *Private Rights, Public Problems: A Guide to NAFTA's Controversial Chapter on Investor Rights* (2001)
Mann, H., and K. von Moltke, *NAFTA's Chapter 11 and the Environment* (1999)
Maskus, K., *Intellectual Property Rights in the Global Economy* (2000)
Mathews, D., *Globalising Intellectual Property Rights* (2003)
Mayall, J., *Nationalism and International Society* (1994)
McDougall, M. S., H. D. Lasswell and Lung Chu Chen, *Human Rights and the World Political Order* (1980)
McLachlan, C., L. Shore and M. Weiniger, *International Investment Arbitration: Substantive Principles* (2007)
Mehmet, O., *Westernising the Third World: The Eurocentricity of Economic Development Theories* (1999)
Muchlinski, P., *Multinational Corporations and the Law* (2nd edn, 2008)
Muchlinksi, P., F. Fortino and C. Schreuer, *Handbook of International Investment Law* (2008)
Munzer, S. R., *A Theory of Property* (1990)
Nassar, N., *Sanctity of Contracts Revisited* (1995)
Neff, S., *Economic Liberalism and the Law of Nations* (1991)
Neufeld, H., *The International Protection of Private Creditors from the Treaty of Westphalia to the Congress of Vienna* (1971)
Newcombe, A., and L. Pradell, *Law and Practice of Investment Treaties* (2009)
Nussbaum, A., *A Concise History of the Law of Nations* (1954)
Nygh, P. E., *Party Autonomy in Private International Law* (1998)
O'Brien, R. (ed.), *Contesting Global Governance: Multilateral Economic Institutions and Global Social Movements* (2000)
  Contesting Global Governance: Multilateral Economic Institutions and Global Governance (2001)
O'Brien, W. V. (ed.), *The New States in International Law and Diplomacy* (1965)
O'Connell, D. P., *International Law* (1970)
Oppermann, T., and E. Petersmann (eds.), *Reforming the International Economic Order* (1987)
Paasivirta, E., *Participation of States in International Contracts* (1990)
Pauwelyn, J., *Conflict of Norms in Public International Law: How WTO Law Relates to Other Rules of International Law* (2003)
Pearson, M. M., *Joint Ventures in the People's Republic of China: The Control of Foreign Direct Investment under Socialism* (1991)
Peet, R., *Global Capitalism: Theories of Social Development* (1991)
Picciotto, S., *International Business Taxation* (1992)
Picciotto, S., and R. Mayne (eds.), *Regulating International Business: Beyond Liberalisation* (1999)
Pritchard, R. (ed.), *Economic Development, Foreign Investment, and the Law. Issues of Private Sector Involvement, Foreign Investment and the Rule of Law in a New Era* (1996)
Raggazi, M., *The Concept of International Obligations Erga Omnes* (1997)

Rajan, M. S., *The Doctrine of Permanent Sovereignty over Natural Resources* (1982)

Ralston, J., *The Law and Procedure of International Tribunals* (1926)

Randelzhofer, A., and C. Tomuschat (eds.), *State Responsibility and the Individual* (1999)

Reinisch, A. (ed.), *Standards of Investment Protection* (2008)

Reisman, M., *The Breakdown of Control Mechanism in ICSID Arbitration* (1989)

Remec, P., *The Position of the Individual in International Law According to Grotius and Vattel* (1960)

Ripinsky, S., and K. Williams, *Damages in International Law* (2009)

Rochmat, R., *Contractual Arrangements in Oil and Gas Mining Enterprises in Indonesia* (1981)

Rosenne, S., *Developments in the Law of Treaties* (1989)

Roth, A., *The Minimum Standard of International Law Applied to Aliens* (1949)

Rubin, S. J., and M. L. Jones (eds.), *Conflict and Resolution in the US–EC Trade Relations* (1989)

Rubin, S. J., and R. W. Nelson, *International Investment Disputes: Avoidance and Settlement* (1985)

Ryngaert, C., *Jurisdiction in International Law* (2008)

Schachter, O., *International Law in Theory and Practice* (1990)

Schneiderman, D., *Constitutionalising Economic Globalisation: Investment Rules and Democracy's Promise* (2008)

Schreuer, C., *The ICSID Convention: A Commentary* (2001)
  The ICSID Convention: A Commentary (2nd edn, 2009)

Schrijver, N., *Permanent Sovereignty over Natural Resources: Balancing Rights and Duties* (1997)

Schulsz, J., and J. A. van den Berg (eds.), *The Art of Arbitration: Liber Amicorum Pieter Sanders* (1982)

Schutter, O. de (ed.), *Transnational Corporations and Human Rights* (2006)

Schwarzenberger, G., *Foreign Investment and International Law* (1969)

Schwebel, S., *International Arbitration: Three Salient Problems* (1986)

Scott, C. (ed.), *Torture as Tort* (2000)

Seidl-Hohenveldern, I., *The Corporation in and under International Law* (1987)

Sell, S., *Private Power, Public Law: Globalization of Intellectual Property Rights* (2003)

Sen, A., *The Idea of Justice* (2009)

Sen, B., *A Diplomat's Handbook of International Law and Practice* (1988)

Serra, N., and J. Stiglitz (eds.), *The Washington Consensus Reconsidered* (2008)

Servan-Schreiber, J. J., *The American Challenge* (1969)

Shaw, M. N., *Title to Territory in Africa* (1986)
  International Law (5th edn, 2008)

Shea, D., *Calvo Clause* (1955)

Shepaher, G. W., and V. Nanda (eds.), *Human Rights and Third World Development* (1985)

Shihata, I., *The MIGA and Foreign Investment* (1988)

Sigmund, P. E., *Multinationals in Latin America: The Politics of Nationalisation* (1990)

Simmonds, K. R., and B. H. W. Hill, *Law and Practice under the GATT* (1989)

Sklair, L., *The Transnational Capitalist Class* (2001)

Smith, B. D., *State Responsibility and the Marine Environment* (1988)

Smith, D., and L. Wells, *Negotiating Third World Mineral Agreements* (1975)

Sornarajah, M., *The Pursuit of Nationalized Property* (1986)
  International Commercial Arbitration (1990)
  The Law of International Joint Ventures (1992)

The Taking of Property (UNCTAD Series on International Investment Treaties, 2000)

The Settlement of Investment Disputes (2000)

Stiglitz, J., *Globalization and Its Discontents* (2002)

Making Globalization Work (2006)

The Roaring Nineties (2006)

Strange, S., *Retreat of the State: The Diffusion of Power in the World Economy* (1996)

Sunshine, R. B., *Terms of Compensation in Developing Countries' Nationalization Settlements* (UNCTC, 1981)

Toope, S. J., *International Mixed Arbitration* (1990)

Tudor, I., *Fair and Equitable Standard in the International Law of Foreign Investment* (2008)

United Nations Commission on Transnational Corporations, *Bilateral Investment Treaties* (1988)

United Nations Conference on Trade and Development, *Bilateral Investment Treaties in the Mid-1990s* (1998)

Fair and Equitable Treatment (1999)

Bilateral Investment Treaties 1995–2006: Trends in Investment Rule Making (2007)

van Harten, G., *Investment Treaty Arbitration and Public Law* (2007)

Vandevelde, K. J., *United States Investment Treaties: Policy and Practice* (1992)

Vattel, E. de, *Les Droit de Gens* (1758)

The Law of Nations (1758)

Classics of International Law: The Law of Nations or the Principles of International Law (C. Fenwick trans., 1916)

Vernon, R., *Sovereignty at Bay* (1971)

Vitoria, F. de, *De Indis et de Jure Belli Reflectiones* (1557)

Walde, T. W. (ed.), *The Energy Charter Treaty* (1998)

Waldron, J., *The Right to Private Property* (1988)

Wallace, C. D. (ed.), *Foreign Direct Investment in the 1990s* (1990)

The Multinational Enterprise and Legal Control: Host State Sovereignty in an Era of Economic Globalization (2002)

Watson, P. S., J. Flynn and C. Convell, *Completing the World Trading System* (1999)

Wattal, J., *Intellectual Property Rights in the World Trade Organization: The Way Forward for Developing Countries* (2000)

Westberg, J., *International Transactions and Claims Involving Government Parties: Case Law of the Iran–United States Claims Tribunal* (1991)

White, G., *Nationalisation of Foreign Property* (1961)

Whiteman, H., *Damages in International Law* (1976)

Wilcox, C., *A Charter for World Trade* (1948)

Wilson, R., *United States Commercial Treaties and International Law* (1960)

World Bank, *Legal Framework for the Treatment of Foreign Investment: Survey of Existing Instruments* (1992)

Wortley, B. A., *Expropriation in Public International Law* (1959)

Yergin, D., *The Prize: The Epic Quest for Oil, Money, and Power* (1991)

Zerk, J., *Multinationals and Corporate Social Responsibility* (2006)

Articles

Abi-Saab, G., 'Permanent Sovereignty over Natural Resources and Economic Activities', in M. Bedjaoui (ed.), *International Law: Achievements and Prospects* (1991)

Adede, A. O., 'The Minimum Standards in a World of Disparities', in R. St J. Macdonald and D. M. Johnston (eds.), *The Structure and Process of International Law* (1983)

Adler, M., 'The Exhaustion of Local Remedies Rule after the ICJ's Decision in ELSI' (1990) **39** *International and Comparative Law Quarterly* 641

Akpan, G. S., 'Transnational Environmental Litigation and Multinational Corporations: A Study of the Ok Tedi Case' (paper published by the Centre for Energy, Petroleum and Mineral Law, University of Dundee, Scotland, CP 11/98, 1998)

'Multinational Corporations and the Impact of Natural Resource Exploitation in the Host State: The Inadequacy of Legal Protection for Host Populations and Implications for Foreign Investment' (PhD Thesis, Faculty of Law, National University of Singapore, 2002)

Alexandrowicz, C. H., 'The Afro-Asian Nations and the Law of Nations' (1968) **123** *Hague Recueil* 117

Alvarez, J. E., 'Political Protectionism and United States International Investment Obligations in Conflict: The Hazards of Exon–Florio' (1989) **30** *Virginia Journal of International Law* 1

'The Development and Expansion of Bilateral Investment Treaties: Remarks' (1992) **86** *ASIL Proceedings* 532

Amarasinha, S., and J. Kokott, 'Multilateral Investment Rules Revisited', in P. Muchlinski, F. Fortino and C. Schreuer, *Handbook of International Investment Law* (2008)

Amerasinghe, C. F., 'Issues of Compensation in the Taking of Alien Property in the Light of Recent Cases and Practice' (1992) **41** *International and Comparative Law Quarterly* 22

Anderson, D., 'Compensation for Interference with Property' (1999) **6** *European Human Rights Law Review* 543

Anderson, J. N. D., and N. J. Goulson, 'The Moslem Ruler and Contractual Obligations' (1958) **33** *New York University Law Review* 917

Anderson, M., 'Transnational Corporations and Environmental Damage: Is Tort Law the Answer?' (2002) **41** *Washburn Law Journal* 399

Anghie, A., 'Francisco Vitoria and the Colonial Origins of International Law' (1996) **5** *Social and Legal Studies* 256

Asante, S., 'International Codes of Conduct and NIEO', in *Proceedings of the First Yugoslav International Seminar on Legal Aspects of the New International Economic Order* (1986), p. 245

'International Law and Investments', in M. Bedjaoui (ed.), *International Law: Achievements and Prospects* (1991)

Asken, A., 'The Case for Bilateral Investment Treaties', in South West Foundation, *Private Investors Abroad* (1981)

Baily, D., G. Harte and R. Sugden, 'US Policy Debate Towards Inward Investment' (1992) **26** *JWTL* 65

Baker, M., 'Promises and Platitudes: Towards a New 21st Century Paradigm for Corporate Codes of Conduct' (2007) **23** *Connecticut Journal of International Law* 123

Bann, A., 'Using National Security to Undermine Corporate Accountability Litigation' (2003) **12** *University of Miami International and Comparative Law Review* 39

Bean, V., and J. Beauvais, 'Global Fifth Amendment? NAFTA's Investment Protection and the Misguided Quest for an International "Regulatory Takings" Doctrine' (2003) **78** *New York University Law Review* 30

Behrens, P., 'International Company Law in View of the Centros Decision of the ECJ' (2000) **1** *European Business Organization Law Review* 125

Bentham, R. W., 'The International Legal Structure of Petroleum Exploration', in J. Rees and P. Odell (eds.), *The International Oil Industry* (1987)

Bergman, M. S., 'Bilateral Investment Treaties: An Examination of the Evolution and Significance of the US Prototype Treaty' (1983) **16** *New York University Journal of International Law and Politics* 1

Betlem, G., 'Transnational Litigation Against Multinational Corporations in Dutch Courts', in M. Kaminga and S. Zia Zarifi (eds.), *Liability of Multinational Corporations under International Law* (2000), p. 283

Beveridge, F., 'Taking Control of Foreign Investment: A Case Study of Indigenisation in Nigeria' (1991) **40** *International and Comparative Law Quarterly* 302

Bianchi, A., 'Immunity Versus Human Rights: The Pinochet Case' (1999) **10** *EJIL* 237

Bjorkland, A., 'Emergency Exceptions: State of Necessity and Force Majeure', in P. Muchlinski, F. Fortino and C. Schreuer, *Handbook of International Investment Law* (2008), p. 459

Blakesley, C., 'United States Jurisdiction over Extraterritorial Crime' (1982) **73** *Journal of Criminal Law and Criminology* 1109

Book Review (1991) **38** *German Yearbook of International Law* 592

Borchard, E. M., 'The Minimum Standard of Treatment of Aliens' (1940) **38** *Michigan Law Review* 445

Bowett, D. W., 'Estoppel Before International Tribunals and Its Relation to Acquiescence' (1957) **33** *British Yearbook of International Law* 176

   'State Contracts with Aliens: Contemporary Developments on Compensation for Termination or Breach' (1988) **59** *BYIL* 49

Brewer, T., and S. Young, 'Investment Issues at the WTO: The Architecture of Rules and the Settlement of Disputes' (1998) **1** *Journal of International Economic Law* 457

Broches, A., 'Bilateral Investment Treaties and Arbitration of Investment Disputes', in J. Schulsz and J. A. van den Berg (eds.), *The Art of Arbitration: Liber Amicorum Pieter Sanders* (1982)

Bronckers, M., 'Private Participation in the Enforcement of WTO Law: The New EC Trade Barriers Regulation' (1996) **33** *CMLR* 299

Brower, C. N,. and S. W. Schill, 'Is Arbitration a Threat or a Boon to the Legitimacy of International Investment Law?' (2009) **9** *Chicago Journal of International Law* 471

Brownlie, I., 'Legal Status of Natural Resources in International Law' (1979) **162** *Hague Recueil* 245

   'Treatment of Aliens: Assumption of Risk and International Law', in W. Flume, H. J. Hain, G. Kegel and K. R. Simmond (eds.), *International Law and Economic Order: Essays in Honour of F. A. Mann* (1997)

Brunetti, M., 'The Iran–US Claims Tribunal, NAFTA Chapter 11 and the Doctrine of Indirect Expropriation' (2001) **2** *Chicago Journal of International Law* 203

Burke-White, W. W., and A. von Staden, 'Investment Protection in Extraordinary Times: The Interpretation and Application of Non-Precluded Measures Provisions in Bilateral Investment Treaties' (2008) **48** *Virginia JIL* 307

Burt, E., 'Developing Countries and the Framework for Negotiations on Foreign Direct Investment in the World Trade Organization' (1997) **12** *American University Journal of International Law and Policy* 1015

Campbell, E., 'Legal Problems Involved in Government Participation in Resource Projects' (1984) *Yearbook of the Australian Mining and Petroleum Law Association* 126

Canner, S., 'The Multilateral Agreement on Investment' (1998) **31** *Cornell JIL* 657

Carrasco, E., and Thomas, R., 'Encouraging Relational Investment and Controlling Portfolio Investment in Developing Countries in the Aftermath of the Mexican Financial Crisis' (1996) **34** *Columbia Journal of Transnational Law* 531

Carty, A., 'Critical International Law: Recent Trends in the Theory of International Law' (1991) **2** *EJIL* 66

Castenada, J., 'La Charte des Droits et Devoirs Economiques des Etats' (1970) **16** *Annuaire Francais de Droit International* 31

Cheng, B., 'United Nations Resolutions on Outer Space: Instant International Customary Law' (1965) **5** *Indian Journal of International Law* 23

Christie, G. C., 'What Constitutes Taking of Property in International Law' (1962) **38** *British Yearbook of International Law* 307

Chua, A., 'The Privatisation–Nationalisation Cycle: The Link Between Markets and Ethnicity in Developing Countries' (1995) **95** *Columbia Law Review* 223

'Markets, Democracy and Ethnicity: Toward a New Paradigm for Law and Development' (1998) **108** *Yale Law Journal* 1

'The Paradox of Free Market Democracy: Rethinking Development Policy' (2000) **41** *Harvard International Law Journal* 287

Civello, P., 'The TRIMS Agreement: A Failed Attempt at Investment Liberalisation' (1999) **8** *Minnesota Journal of Global Trade* 97

Clagett, B. M., 'The Expropriation Issue Before the Iran–United States Claims Tribunal' in R. B. Lillich, *Valuation of Nationalized Property* (1987)

Clapham, A., 'The Question of Jurisdiction under International Criminal Law over Legal Persons', in M. Kaminga and S. Zia Zarifi (eds.), *Liability of Multinational Corporations under International Law* (2000), p. 139

Clark, R., 'Public International Law and Private Enterprise: Damages for a Killing in East Timor' (1996) **3** *Australian Journal of Human Rights* 21

Cody, D. A., 'United States Bilateral Investment Treaties: Egypt and Panama' (1983) **13** *Georgia Journal of International and Comparative Law* 491

Compa, L., 'The Multilateral Agreement on Investment and International Labor Rights: A Failed Connection' (1998) **31** *Cornell International Law Journal* 683

Congyan, C., 'China–US BIT Negotiations and the Future of Investment Treaty Regime: A Grand Bilateral Bargain with Multilateral Implications' (2009) **10** *Journal of International Economic Law* 1

Cunningham, H., 'Multinationals and Restructuring in Latin America', in C. Dixon, D. Drakakis-Smith and H. Wads (eds.), *Multinational Corporations and the Third World* (1986)

Curtis, G. T., 'The Legal Security of Economic Development Agreements' (1988) **29** *Harvard International Law Journal* 317

Davidow, J., and L. Chiles, 'The United States and the Issue of the Binding or Voluntary Nature of International Codes of Conduct Regarding Restrictive Business Practices' (1978) **72** *AJIL* 247

Denza, E., and S. Brooks, 'Investment Protection Treaties: The United Kingdom Experience' (1987) **36** *International and Comparative Law Quarterly* 908

Detter, I., 'The Problem of Unequal Treaties' (1966) **14** *International and Comparative Law Quarterly* 1069

Dicke, D., 'Taking of Foreign Property and Compensation', in T. Oppermann and E. Petersmann (eds.), *Reforming the International Economic Order* (1987)

Dolzer, R., 'New Foundations of the Law of Expropriation of Alien Property' (1981) **75** *AJIL* 553

'Indirect Expropriation of Alien Property' (1986) **1** *ICSID Rev* 41

'Fair and Equitable Standard: Key Standard in Investment Treaties' (2005) **39** *International Lawyer* 87

Douglas, Z., 'The Hybrid Foundations of Investment Treaty Arbitration' (2003) **74** *BYIL* 151

Drahos, P., 'BITs and BIPs: Bilateralism in Intellectual Property' (2002) **4** *Journal of World Intellectual Property* 792

Eckes, A., 'US Trade History', in W. Lovett, A. Eckes and R. Brinkman (eds.), *US Trade Policy, History, Theory and the WTO* (1999)

Editorial, 'The Measures Taken by the Indonesian Government Against Netherlands Enterprises' (1958) **5** *Netherlands International Law Review* 227

El-Chiati, A. Z., 'The Protection of Investments in the Context of Petroleum Agreements' (1987) **204** *Hague Recueil* 1

El-Kosheri, A., 'Quelques Réflexions à Propos d'un Texte Inedit de Michel Virally', in *Mélanges Michel Virally* (1991)

El-Kosheri, A. S., and T. Riad, 'The Law Governing a New Generation of Petroleum Agreements' (1986) **1** *ICSID Rev* 259

Elkins, Z., A. T. Guzman and B. Simmons, 'Competing for Capital: The Diffusion of Bilateral Investment Treaties' (2008) *University of Illinois Law Review* 265

Ellis, C. N., 'Trade-Related Investment Measures in the Uruguay Round: The United States Viewpoint', in S. J. Rubin and M. L. Jones (eds.), *Conflict and Resolution in the US–EC Trade Relations* (1989)

European Community, 'Statement on US Policy on Foreign Direct Investment' (1992) **31** *ILM* 467

Fachiri, A. P., 'Expropriation and International Law' (1925) **6** *British Yearbook of International Law* 159

Fatouros, A. A., 'The Administrative Contract in Transnational Transactions: Reflections on the Uses of Comparison', in *Ius in Privatum: Festschrift fur Max Rheinstein* (1969)

Fawcett, J. E. S., 'The Havana Charter' (1949) **5** *Yearbook of World Affairs* 320

Foster, D., 'Some Aspects of the Commercial Treaty Program of the United States – Past and Present' (1946) **11** *Law and Contemporary Problems* 647

Frame, A., 'Property: Some Pacific Reflections' (1992) **22** *New Zealand Law Journal* 21

Francioni, F., 'Compensation for Nationalisation of Foreign Property: The Borderland of Law and Equity' (1975) **24** *International and Comparative Law Quarterly* 255

Franck, S. D., 'Empirically Evaluating Claims about Investment Arbitration' (2007) **86** *North Carolina Law Review* 1

Freeman, A. V., 'Recent Aspects of the Calvo Doctrine and the Challenge to International Law' (1946) **40** *AJIL* 131

Frey, B. A., 'The Legal and Ethical Responsibilities of Transnational Corporations in the Protection of International Human Rights' (1997) **6** *Minnesota Journal of Global Trade* 105

Friedland, P. D., and E. Wong, 'Measuring Damages for Deprivation of Income-Producing Assets: ICSID Case Studies' (1991) **6** *ICSID Rev* 400

Furnish, D. B., 'Peruvian Domestic Law Aspects of the La Brea y Parinas Controversy' (1970) **89** *Kentucky Law Journal* 351

'Days of Revindication and Dignity: The Petroleum Expropriations in Peru and Bolivia', in R. B. Lillich (ed.) *The Valuation of Nationalized Property* (1975)

Gaillard, E., 'Commentary' (2002) **18** *International Arbitration* 247

Ganesan, A., 'Development Friendliness Criteria for a Multilateral Investment Agreement' (1997) **6** *Transnational Corporations* 139

Gantz, D., 'Reconciling Environmental Protection and Investor Rights' (2001) **31** *Environmental Law Review* 106

Gantz, G., 'The Marcona Settlement: New Forms of Negotiation and Compensation for Nationalized Property' (1977) **71** *AJIL* 474

Gathii, J. T., 'International Law and Eurocentricity' (1998) **9** *EJIL* 184

Geer, M. A., 'Foreigners in Their Own Land: Cultural Land and Transnational Corporations – Emergent International Rights and Wrongs' (1998) **38** *Virginia Journal of International Law* 331

Geiger, R., 'Towards a Multilateral Agreement on Investment' (1998) **31** *Cornell JIL* 467

Goodwin-Gill, G. S., 'Crime in International Law: Obligations Erga Omnes and the Duty to Prosecute', in G. S. Goodwin-Gill and S. Talmon (eds.), *The Reality in International Law: Essays in Honour of Ian Brownlie* (1999)

Graham, D., 'The Calvo Clause: Its Current Status as a Contractual Renunciation of Diplomatic Protection' (1971) **6** *Texas International Law Journal* 289

Gross, S., 'BITs, Non-NAFTA MITs and Host-State Regulatory Freedom – An Indonesian Case Study' (2003) **24** *Michigan JIL* 893

Guha-Roy, S., 'Is the Law of State Responsibility for Injuries to Aliens a Part of Universal International Law?' (1969) **55** *AJIL* 562

Guzman, A., 'Why LDCs Sign Treaties That Hurt Them: Explaining the Popularity of Bilateral Investment Treaties' (1998) **38** *Virginia Journal of International Law* 639

Hailbronner, K., 'Foreign Investment Protection in Developing Countries in Public International Law', in T. Oppermann and E. Petersmann (eds.), *Reforming the International Economic Order* (1987)

Hallward-Driemeier, H., 'Do Bilateral Treaties Attract FDI? Only a Bit … And They Could Bite' (World Bank Development Research Group, Working Paper No. 3121, 2003)

Hamrock, K. J., 'The ELSI Case: Towards an International Definition of Arbitrary Conduct' (1992) **27** *Texas International Law Journal* 837

Heibein, A. N., 'The Chilean Copper Nationalisation: The Foundation for the Standard of Appropriate Compensation' (1974) **23** *Buffalo Law Review* 765

Hertz, A. Z., 'Shaping the Trident: Intellectual Property under NAFTA, Investment Protection Agreements and the World Trade Organization' (1997) **23** *Canada–United States Law Journal* 261

Herz, J. H., 'Expropriation of Foreign Property' (1941) **35** *AJIL* 243

Higgins, R., 'The Taking of Property by the State' (1982) **176** *Hague Recueil* 259

Hirsch, M., 'Conflicting Obligations in International Investment Law: Investment Tribunals' Perspective', in Y. Shany and T. Broude (eds.), *The Shifting Allocation of Authority in International Law: Considering Sovereignty, Supremacy and Subsidiarity* (2008), p. 323

Hohfeld, W., 'Some Fundamental Legal Conceptions as Applied in Judicial Reasoning' (1913) **23** *Yale Law Journal* 16

Honoré, T., 'Ownership', in A. G. Guest (ed.), *Oxford Essays in Jurisprudence* (1961)

Hoof, F. van, 'International Human Rights Obligations for Companies and Domestic Courts: An Unlikely Combination?', in M. Castermans-Holleman, F. van Hoof and J. Smith (eds.), *The Role of the Nation State in the 21st Century: Essays in Honour of Peter Baehr* (1998)

Hopkins, A. G., 'Property Rights and Empire Building' (1980) **40** *Journal of Economic History* 787

Hornick, H., 'The Mihaly Arbitration: Pre-Investment Expenditure as a Basis for ICSID Jurisdiction' (2003) **20** *Journal of International Arbitration* 189

Huiping, C., 'Comments on the MAI's General Principles for the Treatment of Foreign Investors and Their Investments: A Chinese Scholar's Perspective', in E. Niewenhuys and M. Brus (eds.), *Multilateral Regulation of Investment* (2001), p. 67

Human Rights Watch, *The Price of Oil: Corporate Responsibility and Human Rights Violations in Nigeria's Oil Producing Communities* (1999)

Huner, J., 'Lessons from the MAI: A View from the Negotiating Table', in H. Ward and D. Brack (eds.), *Trade, Investment and the Environment* (2001), p. 242

Hyde, J. N., 'Economic Development Agreements' (1962) **105** *Hague Recueil* 271

Ijalye, D., 'Multinational Corporations in Africa' (1981) **171** *Hague Recueil* 1

Ittersum, M. van, 'Profit and Principle: Hugo Grotius, Natural Rights Theories and the Rise of Dutch Power in the East Indies' (PhD thesis, Department of History, Harvard University, Cambridge, MA, 2002)

Jennings, R., 'State Contracts in International Law' (1961) **37** *BYIL* 156

Jimenez de Arechaga, E., 'International Responsibility', in M. Sorensen (ed.), *Manual of Public International Law* (1968)

'State Responsibility for Nationalisation of Foreign Owned Property' (1979) **11** *New York University Journal of International Law and Politics* 179

Jimenez de Arechaga, E., and A. Tanzi, 'International State Responsibility', in M. Bedjaoui (ed.), *International Law: Achievements and Prospects* (1991)

Jones, J. M., 'Claims on Behalf of Nationals Who Are Shareholders in Foreign Companies' (1949) **26** *British Yearbook of International Law* 225

Kaeckenbeck, N., 'The Protection of Vested Rights in International Law' (1936) **17** *British Yearbook of International Law* 1

Kaldermis, D., 'IMF Conditionality as Investment Regulation' (2004) **13** Social and Legal Studies 103

Katzarov, N., 'The Validity of the Act of Nationalisation in International Law' (1959) **22** *MLR* 639

Khalilian, S. K., 'The Place of Discounted Cash Flow in International Commercial Arbitrations' (1991) **8** *Journal of International Arbitration* 31

Koulen, M., 'Foreign Investment in the WTO', in E. Niewenhuys and M. Brus (eds.), *Multilateral Regulation of Investment* (2001), p. 181

Kriebaum, U., 'Regulatory Takings: Balancing the Interests of the Investor and the State' (2007) **8** *Journal of World Investment and Trade* 717

Krishnan, D., 'Indian and International Investment Laws', in B. Patel (ed.), *India and International Law* (2008)

Kunz, J. L., 'The Mexican Appropriations' (1940) **34** *AJIL* 48

Kunzer, K., 'Developing a Model Bilateral Investment Treaty' (1983) **15** *Law and Policy in International Business* 273

Lalive, J.-F., 'Contracts Between a State or a State Agency and a Foreign Company' (1964) **18** *ICLQ* 987

'The Doctrine of Acquired Rights', in South Western Legal Foundation, *Selected Readings on the Protection of Foreign Investments* (1964)

Lauterpacht, E., 'Issues of Compensation and Nationality in the Taking of Energy Investments' (1990) **6** *Journal of Energy and Natural Resources Law* 241

Lawson, R., 'Out of Control, State Responsibility and Human Rights: Will the ILC's Definitions of the Act of State Meet the Challenges of the 21st Century?', in M. Castermans-Holleman, F. van Hoof and J. Smith (eds.), *The Role of the Nation State in the 21st Century: Essays in Honour of Peter Baehr* (1998), p. 91

Leader, S., 'Human Rights, Risks and New Strategies for Global Investment' (2006)
    9 *Journal of International Economic Law* 657

Leboulanger, P., 'Some Issues in ICC Awards Relating to State Contracts' (2004) **15**(2)
    ICC International Court of Arbitration Bulletin 93

Leigh, M., and J. A. Swindler, 'Constitutional Restraints of Foreign Economic Sanctions',
    in R. J. Ellings (ed.), *Private Property and National Security* (1991)

Lieblich, W. C., 'Determining the Economic Value of Expropriated Income Producing
    Property in International Arbitrations' (1991) **8** *Journal of International Arbitration* 59

Lillich, R. B., 'The Valuation of Copper Companies in the Chilean Nationalisation' (1972)
    66 *ASIL Proceedings* 213

  'Duties of States Regarding Civil Rights of Aliens' (1978) **161** *Hague Recueil* 329

Lillich, R. B., and B. Weston, 'Lump Sum Agreements: Their Continuing Contribution to
    the Law of International Claims' (1988) **82** *AJIL* 69

Lippmann, M., 'Multinational Corporations and Human Rights', in G. W. Shepaher and
    V. Nanda (eds.), *Human Rights and Third World Development* (1985)

Lipstein, K., 'The Place of the Calvo Clause in International Law' (1945) **24** *British
    Yearbook of International Law* 1

Lissitzyn, O. J., 'International Law in a Divided World' (1963) **532** *International
    Conciliation* 58

Lowe, V., 'International Law Issues Arising from the Pipeline Dispute: The British Position'
    (1984) **27** *German Yearbook of International Law* 54

Malanczuk, P., 'Multinational Enterprises and Treaty-Making: A Contribution to the
    Discussion on Non-State Actors and the "Subjects" of International Law', in
    V. Gowlland-Debbas (ed.), *Multilateral Treaty Making* (2000)

Mann, F. A., 'British Treaties for the Promotion and Protection of Investment' (1981)
    52 *British Yearbook of International Law* 241

  'British Treaties for the Promotion and Protection of Foreign Investments' (1982)
    52 *BYIL* 241

  'Foreign Investment in the International Court of Justice: The ELSI Case' (1992)
    86 *AJIL* 92

McCorquodale, R., and P. Simons, 'Responsibility Beyond Borders: State Responsibility
    for Extraterritorial Violations by Corporations of International Human Rights Law'
    (2007) **70** *MLR* 598

McGovney, D. O., 'The Anti-Japanese Land Laws' (1943) **35** *California Law Review* 61

McNair, Lord, 'The General Principles of Law Recognised by Civilised Nations' (1957)
    33 *British Yearbook of International Law* 1

  'The Seizure of Property and Enterprises in Indonesia' (1959) **6** *Netherlands
    International Law Review* 218

Metzger, S. D., 'Multilateral Convention for the Protection of Private Foreign Investment'
    (1960) **9** *JPL* 40

Meyer, W. H., 'Human Rights and MNCs: Theory Versus Quantitative Analysis' (1996)
    18 *Human Rights Quarterly* 368

Michelman, F. I., 'Property, Utility and Fairness' (1967) **80** *Harvard Law Review* 1165

Mozarsky, S., 'Defining Discrimination on the Basis of National Origin under Article VII(1)
    of the Friendship Treaty Between United States and Japan' (1992) **15** *Fordham
    International Law Journal* 1099

Muchlinski, P., 'Caveat Investor? The Relevance of the Conduct of the Investor under
    the Fair and Equitable Standard' (2006) **55** *International and Comparative Law
    Quarterly* 527

Neal, A., 'Corporate Social Responsibility: Governance Gain or Laissez-Faire Figleaf' (2008) **28** *Comparative Labour Law and Policy Journal* 459

Neumayer, E., and Spess, L., 'Do Bilateral Investment Treaties Increase Foreign Direct Investment to Developing Countries' (2005) **33** *World Development* 1567

Nichols, P. M., 'Regulating Transnational Bribery in Times of Globalisation and Fragmentation' (1999) **24** *Yale Journal of International Law* 257

Nocker, T., and G. French, 'Estoppel: What's the Government's Word Worth?' (1990) **24** *International Lawyer* 409

Nussbaum, A., 'The Arbitration Between the Lena Goldfields Ltd and the Soviet Government' (1950) **36** *Cornell Law Quarterly* 31

O'Connell, D. P., 'Independence and State Succession', in W. V. Brian (ed.), *New States in International Law and Diplomacy* (1965)

O'Neal, J. R., and F. H. O'Neal, 'Hegemony, Imperialism and Profitability of Foreign Investment' (1988) **42** *International Organization* 347

Ohnesorge, J., 'Developing Development Theory: Law and Development Orthodoxies and the Northeast Asian Experience' (2007) **28** *University of Pennsylvania Journal of International Economic Law* 219

Olmstead, C. J., 'Economic Development Agreements' (1961) **49** *California Law Review* 621

Organization of Economic Co-operation and Development, 'Council Resolution on the Draft Convention for the Protection of Foreign Property' (1967) 7 *ILM* 117

Orrego Vicuña, F., 'Some International Law Problems Posed by the Nationalisation of the Copper Industry by Chile' (1973) **67** *AJIL* 711
   'Changing Approaches to the Nationality of Claims in the Context of Diplomatic Protection and International Dispute Settlement' (2000) **15** *ICSID Rev* 340
   'Foreign Investment Law: How Customary Is Custom?' (2005) **99** *ASIL Proceedings* 98

Osofsky, H. M., 'Environmental Human Rights under the Alien Tort Statute: Redress for Indigenous Victims of Multinational Corporations' (1997) **20** *Suffolk Transnational Law Review* 335

Osunbor, O., 'Nigeria's Investment Laws and the State's Control of Multinationals' (1988) **3** *ICSID Rev* 38

Paasivirta, E., 'Internationalisation and Stabilisation of Contracts Versus State Sovereignty' (1989) **50** *British Yearbook of International Law* 315

Palmer, G., 'Settlement of International Disputes: The Rainbow Warrior Affair' (1989) **15** *Commonwealth Law Bulletin* 585

Pattison, J. E., 'The United States–Egypt Bilateral Investment Treaty: A Prototype for Future Negotiation' (1983) **16** *Cornell International Law Journal* 305

Paulsson, J., 'Arbitration Without Privity', in T. W. Walde (ed.), *The Energy Charter Treaty* (1998)

Pauwelyn, J., and N. Di Mascio, 'Non-Discrimination in Trade and Investment Treaties: Worlds Apart or Two Sides of the Same Coin' (2008) **102** *AJIL* 48

Pechota, V., 'The 1981 US–Czechoslovakia Claims Settlement Agreement: An Epilogue to Post-War Nationalisation and Expropriation Disputes' (1982) **76** *AJIL* 639

Pellonpää, M., and M. Fitzmaurice, 'Taking of Property in the Practice of the Iran–United States Claims Tribunal' (1988) **19** *Netherlands Yearbook of International Law* 53

Penrose, E., 'Nationalisation of Foreign-Owned Property for a Public Purpose: An Economic Perspective on Appropriate Compensation' (1992) **55** *MLR* 351

Peters, P., 'Dispute Settlement Arrangements in Investment Treaties' (1991) **22** *Netherlands Yearbook of International Law* 91

Peterson, L. E., 'Selected Recent Developments in IIA Arbitration and Human Rights' (2009) *IIA Monitor*, No. 2

Peukert, W., 'Protection of Ownership under Article 1 of the First Protocol of the European Convention on Human Rights' (1981) **1** *Human Rights Journal* 36

Pilgrim, C. M., 'Some Legal Aspects of Trade in Natural Resources in Namibia' (1990) **61** *British Yearbook of International Law* 248

'Some Legal Aspects of Trade in the Natural Resources of Namibia' (1994) **61** *British Yearbook of International Law* 249

Pisillo-Mazzeshchi, R., 'Forms of International Responsibility for Environmental Harm', in F. Francioni and T. Scovazzi (eds.), *International Responsibility for Environmental Harm* (1991)

'The Due Diligence Rule and the Nature of the International Responsibility of States' (1992) **35** *German Yearbook of International Law* 46

'International Obligations to Provide for Reparation Claims?', in A. Randelzhofer and C. Tomuschat (eds.), *State Responsibility and the Individual* (1999), p. 149

Pogany, I., 'Economic Development Agreements' (1992) **7** *ICSID Rev* 1

Price, D., 'Investor–State Dispute Settlement: Frankenstein or Safety Valve?' (2000) **26** *Canada–US Law Journal* 107

Propp, K. R., 'Bilateral Investment Treaties: The US Experience in Eastern Europe' (1992) **86** *ASIL Proceedings* 540

Raby, J., 'The Investment Provisions of the Canada–United States Free Trade Agreement: A Canadian Perspective' (1990) **84** *AJIL* 344

Ramasastry, A., 'Secrets and Lies: Swiss Banks and International Human Rights' (1998) **31** *Vanderbilt Journal of Transnational Law* 325

Ratner, S., 'Corporations and Human Rights: A Theory of Legal Responsibility' (2001) **111** *Yale Law Journal* 443

Redfern, A., 'The Arbitration Between the Government of Kuwait and Aminoil' (1984) **55** *British Yearbook of International Law* 65

Reed, B., 'Sovereign Wealth Funds: The New Barbarians at the Gate? An Analysis of the Legal and Business Implications of Their Ascendancy' (2009) **3** *Virginia Law and Business Review* 97

Reich, C., 'The New Property' (1964) **73** *Yale LJ* 733

Reich, S., 'Roads to Follow: Regulating Direct Foreign Investment' (1989) **43** *International Organization* 543

Reisman, M., 'The Breakdown of Control Mechanism in ICSID Arbitration' (1989) **39** *Duke Law Journal* 739

Robinson, D., 'Expropriation in the Restatement (Revised)' (1984) **78** *AJIL Proceedings* 176

Rohwer, J., 'Nationalisation: Chilean Excess Profits Deduction' (1973) **14** *Harvard International Law Journal* 378

Rood, L., 'Compensation for Takeovers in Africa' (1977) **11** *Journal of International Law and Economics* 521

Root, E., 'The Basis of Protection of Citizens Residing Abroad' (1910) **4** *ASIL Proceedings* 16

Rose, P., 'Sovereigns as Shareholders' (2008) **86** *North Carolina Law Review* 83

Rosenne, S., 'State Responsibility and International Crimes: Further Reflections on Article 19 of the Draft Articles on State Responsibility' (1997) **30** *New York University Journal of International Law and Politics* 145

Rothger, J. M., 'Investment Dependence and Political Conflict' (1990) **27** *Journal of Peace Research* 255

Rowat, M. D., 'Multilateral Approaches to Improving the Investment Climate of Developing Countries: The Cases of ICSID and MIGA' (1992) **33** *Harvard International Law Journal* 103

Rugman, A., 'New Rules for International Investment: The Case for a Multilateral Agreement on Investment (MAI) at the WTO', in C. Milner and R. Read (eds.), *Trade Liberalization, Competition and the WTO* (2002), p. 176

Sacerdoti, G., 'Barcelona Traction Revisited: Foreign-Owned and Controlled Companies in International Law', in Y. Dinstein (ed.), *International Law at a Time of Perplexity: Essays in Honour of Shabtai Rosenne* (1989)

Salacuse, J. W., 'BIT by BIT: The Growth of Bilateral Investment Treaties and Their Impact on Foreign Investment in Developing Countries' (1990) **24** *International Lawyer* 655

'The Treatification of International Investment Law' (2007) **13** *Law and Business Review of the Americas* 155

Salacuse, J. W., and N. P. Sullivan, 'Do BITs Really Work? An Evaluation of Bilateral Investment Treaties and Their Grand Bargain' (2005) **46** *Harvard ILJ* 67

Sax, J. L., 'Takings and the Police Power' (1964) **74** *Yale Law Journal* 36

Schill, S. W., 'International Investment Law and the Host State's Power to Handle Economic Crises' (2007) **24** *Journal of International Arbitration* 26

Schneiderman, D., 'Investment Rules and the New Constitutionalism' (2000) **25** *Law and Social Inquiry* 757

Schreuer, C., 'Diplomatic Protection of Private Business Companies' (1990) **51** *British Yearbook of International Law* 155

'Fair and Equitable Treatment in Arbitral Practice' (2005) **6** *Journal of World Investment and Trade* 357

Schwebel, S. M., 'The Story of the UN's Declaration of Permanent Sovereignty over Natural Resources' (1963) **49** *American Bar Association Journal* 463

'The US 2004 Model Bilateral Investment Treaty: An Exercise in the Regressive Development of International Law', in *Liber Amicorum Robert Briner* (2005)

Schwebel, S. M., and G. Wetter, 'Arbitration and Exhaustion of Local Remedies' (1966) **60** *AJIL* 484

'Arbitration and the Exhaustion of Local Remedies Revisited', in *Festschrift for Joseph Gould* (1989)

Schwelb, E., 'The Protection of the Right to Property of Nationals under the First Protocol to the European Convention on Human Rights' (1964) **13** *American Journal of Comparative Law* 518

Seck, S., 'Home State Responsibility and Local Communities: The Case of Global Mining' (2008) **11** *Yale Human Rights and Development Law Journal* 177

Seidl-Hohenveldern, I., 'Hierarchy of Norms Applicable to International Investments', in W. P. Heere (ed.), *International Law and Its Sources: Liber Amicorum Maarten Bos* (1989)

Shawcross, Lord, 'The Problems of Foreign Investment in International Law' (1961) **102** *Hague Recueil* 334

Shihata, I., 'Towards a Depoliticisation of Foreign Investment Disputes: The Roles of ICSID and MIGA' (1986) **1** *ICSID Rev* 1

Sinclair, A., 'Nationality of Individual Investors in ICSID Arbitration' (2004) **6** *International Arbitration Law Review* 191

Sloane, R. D., and W. M. Reisman, 'Indirect Expropriation and Its Valuation in the BIT Generation' (2003) **74** *BYIL* 115

Sornarajah, M., 'The Extraterritorial Enforcement of US Antitrust Law: Conflict and Compromise' (1982) **31** *International and Comparative Law Quarterly* 127

'Towards an International Antitrust Law' (1982) **22** *Indian Journal of International Law* 1

'State Responsibility and Bilateral Investment Treaties' (1986) **20** *JWTL* 79

'The Supremacy of Renegotiation Clauses in International Contracts' (1988) **6** *JIA* 97

'Power and Justice in International Investment Arbitration' (1997) **14** *Journal of International Arbitration* 103

'Power and Justice in International Law' (1997) **1** *Singapore Journal of International and Comparative Law* 28

'South East Asia and International Law – State Responsibility and Sex Tours in Asia' (1997) **1** *Singapore Journal of International and Comparative Law* 414

'The Impact of Globalisation on the International Law of Foreign Investment', Simon Reisman Lecture, 2002, Ottawa, published in (2002) **12** *Canadian Foreign Policy* 1

'Neo-liberalism and International Law on Foreign Investment', in T. Anghie and B. Chimni (eds.), *Third World in International Law* (2003)

'The Clash of Globalisations and the International Law on Foreign Investment' (2003) **10** *Canadian Foreign Policy* 1

Staker, C., 'Diplomatic Protection of Private Business Companies: Determination of Corporate Personality for International Law Purposes' (1990) **51** *British Yearbook of International Law* 155

Stephens, B., 'The Amorality of Profit: Transnational Corporations and Human Rights' (2002) **20** *Berkeley Journal of International Law* 45

Sumner, A., 'Foreign Investment in Developing Countries: Have We Reached a Policy "Tipping Point"' (2008) **29** *Third World Quarterly* 239

Thomas, C., 'Where Is the Third World Now?', in P. Wilkins and C. Thomas (eds.), *Globalisation and the South* (1997)

'Developing Inequality: A Global Fault-Line', in S. Lawson (ed.), *The New Agenda in International Relations* (2001)

Thomas, J. C., 'Reflections on Article 1105 of NAFTA' (2002) **17** *ICSID Rev* 21

Tiewul, S., 'Transnational Corporations and Emerging International Legal Standards', in P. de Waart, P. Peters and E. Denters (eds.), *International Law and Development* (1988), p. 105

Tobi, N., 'Legal Aspects of Foreign Investment and Financing Energy Products in Nigeria' (1991) **14** *Dalhousie Law Journal* 5

Tobin, J., and S. Rose-Ackerman, 'Foreign Direct Investment and the Business Environment in Developing Countries: The Impact of Bilateral Investment Treaties' (Yale Law and Economics Research Paper No. 293, 2005)

Trimble, P., 'International Law, World Order' (1990) **42** *Stanford Law Review* 811

Tshuma, L., 'The Political Economy of the World Bank's Legal Framework for Development' (1999) **8** *Social and Legal Studies* 75

Turrell, R. V., 'Conquest and Concession: The Case of the Burma Ruby Mines' (1988) **22** *Modern Asian Studies* 141

Vagts, D., 'Protecting Foreign Investment: An International Law Perspective', in C. Wallace (ed.), *Foreign Investment in the 1990s* (1990), p. 102

van Aaken, A., 'Fragmentation in International Law: The Case of International Investment Law' (2008) **19** *Finnish Yearbook of International Law* 128

Vandevelde, K. J., 'The Bilateral Investment Treaty Program of the United States' (1988) **21** *Cornell International Law Journal* 201

'Investment Liberalisation and Economic Development: The Role of Bilateral Investment Treaties' (1998) **36** *Columbia Journal of Transnational Law* 501

Bibliography

'Sustainable Liberalism and International Investment Regimes' (1998) **19** *Michigan Journal of International Law* 373

'The Economics of Bilateral Investment Treaties' (2000) **41** *Harvard ILJ* 469

'A Comparison of the 2004 and 1994 US Model BITs: Rebalancing Investor and Host Country Interests' (2008) **1** *Yearbook of International Investment Law* 257

Vasciannie, S., 'The Fair and Equitable Standard in International Investment Law and Practice' (1999) **70** *British Yearbook of International Law* 99

Veeder, V. V., 'The Lena Goldfields Arbitration: The Historical Roots of Three Ideas' (1998) **47** *International and Comparative Law Quarterly* 747

Verdross, A., 'Les Règles Internationales Concernant le Traitement des Etrangers' (1931) **37** *Hague Recueil* 364

'Quasi-International Agreements and International Economic Transactions' (1964) **18** *Yearbook of World Affairs* 230

Verhoosel, G., 'Foreign Direct Investment and Legal Constraints on Domestic Environmental Policies: Striking a Reasonable Balance Between Stability and Change' (1998) **29** *Law and Policy in International Business* 451

Vernon, R., 'International Investment and International Trade' (1966) **2** *Quarterly Journal of Economics* 80

Verwey, W. D., and N. J. Schrijver, 'The Taking of Foreign Property under International Law: A New Legal Perspective?' (1984) **15** *Netherlands Yearbook of International Law* 60

Voss, J., 'The Protection and Promotion of European Private Investment in Developing Countries' (1981) **18** *CMLR* 363

Wagner, J. M., 'International Investment, Expropriation and Environmental Protection' (1999) **29** *Golden Gate University Law Review* 465

Waite, F. P., and M. R. Goldberg, 'National Security Review of Foreign Investment in the United States' (1991) **6** *Florida Journal of International Law* 191

Walde, T. W., and A. Kolo, 'Coverage of Taxation under Modern Investment Treaties', in P. Muchlinski, F. Fortino and C. Schreuer, *Handbook of International Investment Law* (2008)

Walde, T. W., and G. Ndi, 'Stabilising International Investment Commitments: International Law Versus Contract Interpretation' (1996) **31** *Texas International Law Journal* 215

Walden, J., 'International Petroleum Cartel: Private Power and the Public Interest' (1962) **11** *Journal of Public Law* 64

Walker, H., 'Modern Treaties of Freedom, Commerce and Navigation' (1958) **42** *Minnesota Law Review* 805

Ward, H., 'Legal Issues in Corporate Citizenship' (report prepared for the Swedish Partnership for Global Responsibility, 2003)

Weber, A., 'Investments Risks and International Law', in T. Oppermann and E. Petersmann (eds.), *Reforming the International Economic Order* (1987)

Weil, P., 'Problèmes Relatifs aux Contrats Passés Entre un Etat et un Particulier' (1969) **128** *Hague Recueil* 95

Weissbrodt, D., and M. Hoffmann, 'The Global Economy and Human Rights: A Selective Bibliography' (1997) **6** *Minnesota Journal of Global Trade* 189

Weston, B., 'Constructive Takings under International Law: A Modest Foray into the Problem of Creeping Expropriation' (1975) **16** *Virginia Journal of International Law* 103

Wilkie, C., 'Origins of NAFTA Investment Provisions: Economic and Policy Considerations', in L. Ritchie (ed.), *Whose Rights? The NAFTA Chapter 11 Debate* (2002), p. 7

Williams, J. Fischer, 'International Law and the Property of Aliens' (1928) **9** *British Yearbook of International Law* 20

Wimmer, M., 'The Impact of the General Agreement on Trade in Services on the OECD Multilateral Agreement on Investment' (1996) **19** *World Competition* 109

'Foreign Investment in the WTO', in E. Niewenhuys and M. Brus (eds.), *Multilateral Regulation of Investment* (2001), p. 288

Woolridge, F., and V. Sharma, 'The Expropriation of the Property of the Ugandan Asians' (1974) **14** *Indian Journal of International Law* 61

World Bank, 'Report and Guidelines' (1992) **31** *ILM* 1375

Zemanek, K., 'State Responsibility and Liability', in W. Lang, H. Neuhold and K. Zemanek (eds.), *Environmental Protection and International Law* (1991)

Index